D0113800

Salem
Is My
Dwelling
Place

Salem Is My Dwelling Place

A
Life of
Nathaniel
Hawthorne
By Edwin
Haviland
Miller

University of
Iowa Press
Iowa City

University of Iowa Press, Iowa City 52242
Copyright © 1991 by the University of Iowa
All rights reserved
Printed in the United States of America

Design by Richard Hendel

Printed on acid-free paper

Library of Congress Cataloging-in-
Publication Data
Miller, Edwin Haviland.
    Salem is my dwelling place: a life of
Nathaniel Hawthorne/by Edwin Haviland
Miller.—1st ed.
        p.   cm.
    Includes bibliographical references and
index.
    ISBN 0-87745-332-2
    1. Hawthorne, Nathaniel, 1804–1864—
Biography.   2. Novelists, American—19th
century—Biography.   3. Salem (Mass.)—
Biography.   I. Title.
PS1881.M48   1991
813′.3—dc20   91-14543
[B]   CIP

10 9 8 7 6 5 4 3 C 96 95 94 93 92

10 9 8 7 6 5 4 3 2 1 P 96 95 94 93 92

In Memory of My Mother

Lucinda Haviland Miller

August 8, 1889–March 8, 1980

Contents

Acknowledgments

During the decade I have spent in the exciting, sometimes frustrating engagement with the life and writings of a secretive author, I have accumulated many debts which I am delighted to acknowledge.

My gratitude to the following individuals is indeed great: Claire Badaracco, who edited Sophia Hawthorne's "Cuban Journals"; John C. Broderick, Library of Congress; Francis B. Dedmond; Gloria Erlich; Joseph Flibbert; Diane M. Gutscher, Bowdoin College; Walter Harding; the late Manning Hawthorne; Nancy A. Heywood, Essex Institute; Raymona E. Hull; John L. Idol, Jr.; Gregory A. Johnson, University of Virginia Library; John H. Lamont; William T. La Moy, Essex Institute; Luther S. Luedtke; Arthur Monke; Leslie A. Morris, Rosenbach Museum and Library; Joel Myerson; Irene Norton, Essex Institute; the late Norman Holmes Pearson; L. Neal Smith, associate textual editor of Hawthorne's letters; the late Lola L. Szladits, curator of the Berg Collection; the late Alvin Turner; Thelma Turner; Thomas Woodson, whose editing of Hawthorne's letters is exemplary; and Philip Young.

I have had access to the resources of the following: Robert Lincoln Straker Collection, Olive Kettering Library, Antioch College; Berkshire Athenaeum, Pittsfield, Massachusetts; Boston Athenaeum, Boston Public Library; Hawthorne-Longfellow Library, Bowdoin College; Bancroft Library, University of California at Berkeley; Trinity College Library, Cambridge; Butler Library, Columbia University; Concord Free Public Library; Detroit Institute of Art; Manuscript Department, William R. Perkins Library, Duke University; Essex Institute, Salem, Massachusetts; Folger Shakespeare Library; Harvard University Portrait Collection; House of the Seven Gables, Salem, Massachusetts; Henry E. Huntington Library and Art Gallery; Manuscript Division, Library of Congress; Massachusetts Historical Society; Metropolitan Museum of Art, New York; Pierpont Morgan Library; New Hampshire Historical Society; New-York Historical Society; Henry W. and Albert A. Berg Collection, New York Public Library; Bobst Library, New York University; Ohio State University Library; Historical Society of Pennsylvania; Herbert H. Lamson Library, Plymouth State College, University System of New Hampshire; Arthur and Elizabeth Schlesinger Library on the History of Women in America, Radcliffe College; Rhode Island Historical Society; Rosenbach Museum and Library; Owen D. Young Library, St. Lawrence Library; Sophia Smith Collection, Women's History Archive, Smith College; Humanities Research Center, University of Texas at Austin; Vermont Historical Society; Clifton Waller Barrett Library, University of Virginia; and Beinecke Rare Book and Manuscript Library, Yale University.

My obligations to predecessors and contemporaries who have for 150 years discussed and analyzed Hawthorne's writings and life story are acknowledged in the notes and the selected bibliography, which is only a partial listing of the sources I have consulted.

I am deeply indebted to the John Simon Guggenheim Memorial Foundation, which awarded me a fellowship at the beginning of my research for this biography.

I also want to express publicly my gratitude to the University of Iowa Press and its cooperative and supportive staff, particularly Holly Carver, Robert Burchfield, and Amy Roberts-Vanskike.

Finally, my greatest debt of all is my forty-five-year bond to Rosalind.

Preface

Shortly after the death of Nathaniel Hawthorne's father in 1808 the son composed tales which always concluded, "I'm never coming home again." The inevitable truth, however, was that despite Thomas Wolfe's claim that "you can't go home again" and Hawthorne's understandable ambivalence to Salem, he never left his dwelling place except physically, even though he returned there only rarely after incurring the wrath of the townspeople whom he savaged in the prologue to *The Scarlet Letter*.

Hawthorne's first published work, *Fanshawe*, draws upon the story of a young man memorialized on a gravestone in the Charter Street Burying Point, only a few blocks from his birthplace. There the child played among the markers, including a row of his Hathorne ancestors, among whom John Hathorne, the infamous judge at the Salem witch trials, rests perhaps uneasily. John and his father, William Hathorne, were the founders of the family in the New World and awesome Puritan patriarchs of Salem with whom Hawthorne conversed for a lifetime in an attempt to prove himself worthy of their praise.

His last work, "The Dolliver Romance," which became part of the burial rites at his death in 1864, is set in the Salem cemetery, and Dr. Dolliver himself occupies the house at the corner of the grounds, where years earlier the Peabody family lived and where Nathaniel courted

Sophia in a strange, hesitant romance which only she could have understood.

The hated-loved Salem was indeed Hawthorne's dwelling place, the source of his life, his family history, and his creativity.

In his fiction appear beautiful youths created in his own image, beginning with Fanshawe and including Robin Molineux, Cyrus Bourne, Owen Warland, Giovanni, and Donatello. Even men in their twenties and thirties—Arthur Dimmesdale and Septimius Felton—have not lost the glow of their youthful beauty. Dr. Dolliver, an eighty-five-year-old great-great-grandfather, in the light of the flickering flames from a fireplace is magically endowed with the beauty of his youth, while the author of "The Artist of the Beautiful" indulges in a fantasy as he watches in his ever-present mirror the deterioration of his own beauty.[1]

These youths—orphaned early and everlastingly wounded, vulnerable, and frightened—bear the burdens of painful memories of childhood. In youth and adulthood they are puzzlingly magnetic presences, like Hawthorne himself, and share his weaknesses, shyness, hesitancies, and daytime and nighttime fears. Dimmesdale has "a startled, a half-frightened look," and though he is a dynamic preacher, the greatest in the Massachusetts Colony, his mouth is "apt to be tremulous, expressing both nervous sensibility and a vast power of self-restraint."

As I perceive Hawthorne, he is not a historian of puritanism, an artist-intellectual employing romance to depict history. A tale like "The Gentle Boy" reverberates in our hearts not because of the depiction of the inhuman dogmatism of puritanism and quakerism but because of the plight of a youth shamefully abused by members of both sects. Nor is Hawthorne a kind of theologian unfolding in his fiction Manichaeism or the Calvinistic conception of original sin. The "No, in thunder!" that Herman Melville heard in Hawthorne's writings was the projection of the sound of the paralyzing despair of his own works and his tortured vision. With more than a little of Montaigne's skepticism but with qualified faith, at least some of the time, in amelioration Hawthorne, as observer always rather than participant, huddled in the middle way, saying neither yea nor nay.

I try to present Hawthorne as a sculpture that one observes from every angle, never descending into reductionistic debunking or ascending into hagiography which excludes the warts and flaws as well as mutes the egomania and narcissism. I seek to lift the veils with which Hawthorne guarded self and art but only partly succeed—mysteries inevitably elude biographical sleuthing—and to delineate the external and inner life of a man who hid himself in his fiction and was known to leave by the back door when someone stood waiting at the front door. In his art Hawthorne is shyly fascinating as he calculatingly holds and withholds, seductively arousing interest but keeping people at arm's length: he wants to touch but not be touched.

What he said at the end of his life in his unsuccessful attempts to narrate the story of Septimius Felton applies to all of his writings: "Our story is an internal one, dealing as little as possible with outward events, and taking hold of them, only when it cannot be helped, in order by means of them to delineate the history of a mind bewildered in certain errors." The inner landscape which was his subject was his own: when he looked into the ever-present mirrors, the hell fires he found behind the bland exterior were his objectifications of his self-analysis. In one of his public disavowals of autobiography he informs readers that external traits "hide the man, instead of displaying him" and directs them to "make quite another kind of inquest and look through the whole range of his fictitious characters, good and evil, in order to detect any of his essential traits." As usual, on the one hand Hawthorne invites and even directs scrutiny but on the other hand makes it extremely difficult, which no doubt was his intention. I have, however, accepted the invitation or the challenge, whichever it may be, in the knowledge that such exploration is as fraught with perils as was Christian's journey to the Celestial City. When Hawthorne abandoned the manuscript of "Septimius Felton" he commented that "Septimius was one of the most unapproachable persons, so far as his inner life was concerned, that ever lived." He of course described himself: he was far more complex intellectually and emotionally than any of the characters he created in his own image.[2]

In life and art Hawthorne assumed many poses and delighted in the masquerades provided by his veils. On graduation from Bowdoin College he concocted the tale of a man imprisoned in an attic study, "castle dismal" in his borrowing from Bunyan, where he was an isolate surveying the world from a protective, fastidious distance. Yet he was the intimate and drinking companion of the political hacks of Salem, men of the lower social class, of the Democratic rather than the fashionably Whiggish persuasion. We shall never know how often this self-styled "spiritualized Paul Pry" went slumming in Salem, Boston, Liverpool, and elsewhere. He liked a pretty leg, flirted with waitresses, observed the wiles of prostitutes and their pimps, and enjoyed the disorderly life of taverns—all of which, of course, imposed no entangling commitments and allowed him to keep his gentility while providing, temporarily, a needed freedom from that gentility. His peregrinations were not always spiritual.

While Hawthorne's fictional characters are usually adrift in a hostile environment, he himself established deep and lasting friendships. He understood the nature of friendship, the reciprocity, the need to substitute for lost relationships, and the support provided by such bonds of mutual trust. I have developed this neglected aspect of his life at length because of its importance in understanding his personal needs and insecurities, as well as to illustrate how people reacted to the aura of his silent presence and androgynous beauty which kept some at a distance but magnetically attracted others who found in him some kind of model or ideal which in turn answered their needs.

There were always in Hawthorne's life the alternations or rhythms of depressed periods of deep, sometimes suicidal intensity and periods of playfulness, evidenced in a fondness for masquerades, processionals, and veils. He wore a homemade New England approximation of a royal robe while he wrote *The House of the Seven Gables*. Thoreau recognized the childlike qualities which are not a part of the conventional portrait, and his own children remembered him climbing trees or sliding on the ice in front of St. Paul's in Rome, totally unconcerned with appearances or dignity. And then there is *The House of the Seven Gables*, an exquisite, playful work, filled with illogicalities which lead many critics to indict it as a failure, not willing to enjoy the comedy of observing the victory of soap bubbles over Judge Pyncheon and biological determinism. Even at the end of his life Hawthorne was still, despite the pain, weariness, and depression, making merry in the creation of Dr. Dolliver, but only briefly, neither the Doctor's elixir nor the flames from the fireplace being any more lasting than Clifford's soap bubbles.

The family is at the center of Hawthorne's fiction. The tragical disruption of his life when his father died at sea taught the four-year-old the painful meaning of loss and absence. A tapestry like *The Scarlet Letter* invites and survives interpretations from various viewpoints, but first of all it is a family romance, the tale of an unwed mother and her child. The A signifies many things but perhaps chiefly Absence, despite the presence of the father/husband. Donald Hall sums up my purpose perfectly: "Domesticity precedes ideology, for all men and women. The feelings between parents and children, siblings, men and women as lovers or as spouses—these relationships penetrate the life of genius as much as they penetrate the lives of the rest of humanity."[3]

Finally, this is the story of America's first great artist who never saw himself in the romantic role of an unacknowledged legislator of the world: even in art he could not abandon the middle course. Nor was he able to put to rest the inherited suspicions and contempt of his Puritan ancestors for the triflings of the artistic Tower of Babel. Despite his doubts he triumphed, but the tensions and feelings of guilt took a toll. He was one of the first writers to make the material and problems of art his subject. Owen Warland, "the artist of the beautiful," may war with the land: Hawthorne warred with himself, including his childhood fear which he never outgrew that he like other artists would end his life in the almshouse.

Though Sophia Hawthorne and her sister-in-law Elizabeth rarely agreed, they were in dogmatic agreement on one subject. "He had a horror," Sophia declared with finality, "that his life would be written," and Elizabeth asserted with her customary firmness, "It was my brother's especial injunction that no biography should be written." When Rose Hawthorne's husband, George Parsons Lathrop, came into print with the first full-length biography in 1876, Elizabeth was genuinely angry. Lathrop, she charged, could "at least have invented something better, and less impossible, if he had not facts to fill up his pages," which led her to concur with Thomas Carlyle that "the only good biography is one that ought not to have been written." This pronouncement was not the end of the subject. "I believe all biographies are false," she asserted, "just in proportion as they pretend to be true, and to deal with facts. Fiction is the proper sphere for the representation of character; there a portrait of any body may be drawn, avoiding name and dates, and if it is, or is not, a likeness, no harm is done."[4]

In defending her brother from detractors, Elizabeth Hawthorne hit upon a truth which she probably did not fully appreciate. Biography, like autobiography, is of necessity a fiction, that is, a construct arranged by an interpreter following examination and analysis of available evidence, published and unpublished writings, the works of critics and biographers, as well as the social, political, and artistic history of the age. The collected materials are shaped on the basis of the biographer's insights, empathy, and assumptions; the materials are inevitably incomplete, particularly for the formative years; the opinions of contemporaries are distorted by prejudices and limited knowledge; and the subject's carefully fabricated veils block insight and render judgments problematical. For these and other reasons no biography can be definitive or wholly truthful: it is only fitting that all individuals should have an inalienable right to their mysteries. The biographer, in the words of Reynolds Price, can aspire to compose "a book about a life, the map of a heart."[5]

Salem Is My Dwelling Place

Prolog
The Contemporary Portrait

Physically Nathaniel Hawthorne was the very model of the ideal artist, that Byronic figment of our romantic imaginations. But unlike Byron, Hawthorne ogled at a distance, a voyeur rather than a seducer, yet in his own way seductive. He was also, in Herman Melville's singularly apt phrase, "the shyest grape," although his withdrawals and hesitancies attracted, even commanded attention. He rarely looked a person in the eye, lowering his eyes bashfully and modestly as though in fear of a world with which he wanted to deal as little as possible. He was known to dart from the road into a nearby field when he spotted villagers in the distance. An Englishman who met Hawthorne in the 1850s, when the author was almost fifty years old, noted how at "our approach, he concealed himself, like a frightened school-boy." People, particularly his wife, apologized for his acts, offering explanations which were usually beside the point since his seeming weaknesses were sources of power, depending upon one's point of view and especially upon his expectations, and provided him with attention, which may have been his secret intention.[1]

Although Hawthorne would have failed as a dramatist in the theater, preoccupied as he was with the internal rather than the external landscape, he had a sense of theater and sometimes seemed to view the world as theater. Almost five feet ten inches in height, weighing between 160 and 170 pounds (information which he meticulously recorded in his notebooks), he dressed in black and often wore a large mantle which on occasion he drew about himself, veiling his face and elongating his lithe body with black drapery, like a mysterious stranger out of a gothic romance (a posture that the timid, tormented Arthur Dimmesdale in *The Scarlet Letter* affects briefly) or a ravaged, furtive-eyed Hamlet out of nineteenth-century romanticism. In Hawthorne's writing characters take the veil, sometimes quite literally as in the instance of the Reverend Mr. Hooper in "The Minister's Black Veil," at other times by living two kinds of existence, public and private, as in the case of Arthur Dimmesdale.

Hawthorne went to social gatherings usually reluctantly, then remained aloofly in a corner and often said nothing. Spectators recalled his silences long after they forgot what others had said. Almost everything he did in his diffident, unflamboyant manner created an air of mystery and made him a subject of conversation and recollection. The result is that we know more about Hawthorne than we do about most of his peers. If he did not establish himself with his world on a first-name basis like Walt Whitman—only D. H. Lawrence has attempted such a relationship with Hawthorne—his effect upon observers was magnetic and enduring. Descriptions, anecdotes, and gossip appeared in journals, diaries, letters, books, and magazines, for almost immediately upon the appearance of *The Scarlet Letter* in 1850 he became, in the eyes of many, the greatest of America's nineteenth-century writers, a position which he has more or less maintained for almost a century and a half. Other reputations have risen and fallen, but Hawthorne's has remained steady.

Some fell in love with Hawthorne—there was something (perhaps not quite unknowingly) seductive about his presence and gestures—and waxed poetic in icons that elevated him to the spheres. Others were puzzled, sometimes annoyed, by his acts and artifices which were perhaps more calculated than spontaneous, but spontaneity is rarely free of calculation. Perceptions of his contemporaries were accurate, perhaps even true, but generally limited and suggestive rather than developed, and it is difficult to evaluate the judgments of those who had only a peripheral acquaintance with a deliberately elusive author. Lifelong friends like Horatio Bridge and Franklin Pierce respected his injunctions of silence. Hawthorne commanded incredible loyalty—and returned it.

No one in the nineteenth century had access to the contemporary portrait that follows, since it has taken over a century to assemble a record which will be added to in the future but probably not substantially. The portrait like this biography will not remove the veil behind which Hawthorne like many other artists lived. What John Marin, the painter, observed—"There is a veil in front of the artist / he's got to pierce that veil"—is profoundly true of the creative act, but the creator rarely makes access easy for the intruder.[2]

Existing paintings, idealized as some of them may be, confirm Hawthorne's beauty, particularly the one executed by Charles Osgood in 1840 when Hawthorne was thirty-six. Yet acquaintances and family were agreed that none of the portraits did him justice. According to his sister, strangers stopped to comment that the young Hawthorne was "the finest boy . . . whom they had ever seen." At Bowdoin College a gypsy woman was said to have asked, "Is that an angel? for a man was never so beautiful." Anthony Trollope, as reported by James T. Fields, "fell in love . . . at first sight" with Hawthorne and swore that he was "the handsomest Yankee that ever walked the planet." William Ellery Channing, an eccentric poet of some renown in his day, spoke of "such grace as in Apollo's figure lay." Others noted the classic features, which some termed Byronic. To George W. Curtis, editor and essayist, Hawthorne was "a kind of poetic Webster." Moncure D. Conway, a clergyman as well as an early biographer of Hawthorne, recalled a half century after their first meeting that "he appeared to me the noblest human figure I had ever seen."[3]

Hawthorne's eyes had a hypnotic effect upon many viewers, although people disagreed about their color and about other characteristics. D. H. Lawrence wrote with flippant affection of the "blue-eyed Nathaniel," but he was mistaken as was Osgood in the famous portrait in which Hawthorne's eyes are powder blue. Because he had gray eyes, like his mother, observers were frequently confused. In the first months of their marriage, Sophia Hawthorne wrote to her mother about her Adam-Apollo-Ariel:

> I think you may search all the earth & not find two such eyes as my husband's are particularly beneath the skies as he lies on the ground. The deepest, clearest lakes, with swaying bamboos on their margins, & a mysterious light raying up from their inner fountains, can only faintly represent them—for who can describe soul?

Frederika Bremer, who came to America in search of famous men, was no less extravagant: "The fine, deep-set eyes glance from beneath well-arched eyebrows like the dark but clear lakes of the neighborhood, lying in the sombre bosom of mountain and forest." (She was referring to his temporary home in the Berkshires.) J. T. Headley, a nineteenth-century biographer, described Hawthorne's "dreamy face and dark eye" which made him look "as if life itself were a glen filled with nought but strange shadows and weird scenes," a description not uninfluenced by the tales and *The Scarlet Letter*. Richard Henry Stoddard, a poet of sorts and at the end of the century a literary arbiter, pronounced them "the most wonderful eyes in the world, searching as lightning and unfathomable as night." James T. Fields, Hawthorne's publisher, was reminded of Henry Vaughan's line, "Feed on the vocal silence of his eye." To Julia Ward Howe, the author of "The Battle Hymn of the Republic," the eyes were like "tremulous sapphires," and Conway referred to "soft-flashing unsearchable eyes, that *beauté du diable* at middle age."[4]

George Hillard, Hawthorne's friend and lawyer, observed that his "eyes would darken visibly under the touch of passing emotion, like the waters of a fountain ruffled by the breeze of summer." Many years after the collapse of the Brook Farm experiment and the death of Hawthorne, Catharine Sedgwick recalled her reactions at age sixteen: "Wonderful eyes they were, and when anything witty was said I always looked quickly at Mr. Hawthorne; for his dark eyes lighted up as if flames were suddenly kindled behind them, and then the smile came down to his lips and over his grave face." On the other hand, an unidentified citizen of North Adams, Massachusetts, found "something of the hawk-eye" about Hawthorne, and a young Englishman insisted that Hawthorne had "an eye so black and piercing you shrink away as he fixes it steadily upon you." With magnificent insight Bremer exclaimed: "Wonderful, wonderful eyes! They give, but receive not."[5]

Only rarely, despite the words of the young Englishman, did Hawthorne establish eye contact. Sedgwick remembered "a sidelong glance from his very shy eyes." A Bowdoin professor recalled Hawthorne's "reluctant step and averted look." A citizen of North Adams said that Hawthorne walked streets "with his eyes down," and Oliver Wendell Holmes referred in "At the Saturday Club" to "the maiden shyness of his downcast eyes."[6]

The head was massive, like Daniel Webster's, although only the portraits and photographs from the late years confirm this impression. Bremer observed that "the forehead is capacious and severe as the arch of heaven, and a thick mass of soft dark brown hair beautifully clustered around it." Yet in the eyes of a youthful English admirer he was "an odd looking person with a fine massive head," and a sympathetic contemporary with whom Hawthorne had difficult relations found "his brow thick, his mouth sarcastic, . . . his whole aspect cold, moody, distrustful." Dr. Loring noted that the "massive head sat upon a strong and muscular neck, and his chest was broad and capacious."[7]

Hawthorne walked with his head "a little to the left, with a decided swing of his right arm." In 1860 William Dean Howells commented that he carried "his head with a heavy forward droop." F. P. Sanborn, teacher, journalist, and biographer, spoke of his "distinguished" appearance "in spite of his singular flexibility, or dereliction of the spinal column, which forbade him usually to hold himself erect, and inspired Tom Appleton to say that he 'looked like a *boned pirate.*'" Apparently in the final years Hawthorne was no longer the "splendid specimen of manhood" Fields described in the early 1850s and bore even less resemblance to that romantic figure which to a great extent Channing created out of deep affection to commemorate an idyllic friendship, at least from Channing's viewpoint.

> His tall compacted figure, ably strung
> To urge the Indian chase or guide the way,
> Softly reclining 'neath the aged elm,
> Like some still rock looked out upon the scene,
> As much a part of Nature as itself.[8]

Julian Hawthorne believed that his father read aloud as powerfully as Dickens and with more refinement and that even Edwin Booth, the Shakespearean actor, did not approach the "simon-pure nature" of Hawthorne's voice. Sophia Hawthorne worshiped everything about her husband, including his majestic voice which she never tired of listening to and associating with the music of the spheres. Others were less extravagant but no less charmed by what one characterized as a "low musical voice," a second as "that soft melodious tone." Donald Grant Mitchell, better known as Ik Marvel, was awed by "his voice deep, with a weighty resounding quality, as if bearing echoes of things unspoken," but "there hung about his manner and his speech a cloud of self-distrust, or *mal-*

aise, as if he were on the defensive in respect of his own quietudes, and determined to rest there." One of Hawthorne's Salem acquaintances, Horace Conolly, noted a labored, uneasy speech pattern even in conversations with friends: "There was oftentimes a constraint, or hesitation, as if it required some extra exertion of the organs of the throat to bring out the voice."[9]

A. Bronson Alcott, the eccentric philosopher and father of Louisa May, recorded in his journal his impression of "a voice that a woman might own, the hesitancy is so taking, and the tones so remote from what you expected," and recognized the unconscious seductiveness of this "coy genius, and to be won as a maid is." Hawthorne's "hesitating manner and a peculiar half-timid smile" reminded George Duyckinck of a "Miss Codington." One of his Bowdoin professors recalled that Hawthorne came to his study "and with girlish diffidence submitted a composition which no man in his class could equal." Emerson reportedly observed that because of Hawthorne's gentleness he felt as if he were "speaking to a girl." G. P. A. Healy, who painted one of the famous portraits of Hawthorne, recalled, "I never had a young lady sit to me who was half so timid," while Fields was "charmed" that Hawthorne "blushes like a girl." Hillard was puzzled but not judgmental: "He looked like a man who might have held the stroke-oar in a university boat. . . . No man comprehended woman more perfectly. . . . And his face as mobile and rapid in its changes of expressions as is the face of a young girl." James Russell Lowell recognized in Hawthorne a strange blend of "strength and timidity" ("genius so shrinking and rare") as well as a combination of classical grace and John Bunyan and then went on to describe him after the hermaphroditic fashion of Shakespeare's well-known sonnet:

> When Nature was shaping him, clay was not granted
> For making so full-sized a man as she wanted,
> So, to fill out her model, a little she spared
> From some finer-grained stuff for a woman prepared,
> And she could not have hit a more excellent plan
> For making him fully and perfectly man.[10]

Hillard noted that at breakfast Hawthorne "could not lay a piece of butter upon a lady's plate without a little trembling of the hand." Charles King Newcomb, a member of the Brook Farm group, was spiteful in a journal entry: "He was unmasculine and unpositive. . . . He was a sort of humanitarian monk, so to speak, at least before his marriage. . . . I doubt if he would have married unless he had been encouraged by the special interest shown in him by her." Healy's wife wondered how Hawthorne mustered courage to propose, and her husband replied, "Depend upon it, Darling, he had encouragement!" (It was Lawrence's irreverent suggestion that Hester Prynne seduces Dimmesdale.) Henry James, Sr., who thought Hawthorne was not "a handsome man," remembered a social gathering at which Hawthorne looked like "a rogue who suddenly finds himself in a company of detectives," and then added, "How he buried his eyes in his plate, and ate with voracity! that no one would dare to ask him a question."[11]

Some of Hawthorne's friends felt compelled to justify the feminine components of his temperament and artistry and in the process sometimes drew unnecessarily rigid and sexist distinctions. In his effusive review of *Twice-told Tales* in 1837, Henry Wadsworth Longfellow, a classmate at Bowdoin College, maintained that Hawthorne's "genius, too, is characterized by a large proportion of feminine elements, depth and tenderness of feeling, exceeding purity of mind, and a certain airy grace and arch vivacity in narrating incidents and delineating character." In a letter sent to Sophia Hawthorne shortly before the marriage in 1842, Margaret Fuller commented, "If ever I saw a man who combined delicate tenderness to understand the heart of woman, with quiet depth and manliness enough to satisfy her, it is Mr. Hawthorne." In a review of *Twice-told Tales*, Evert A. Duyckinck, who as an editor played an important role in the careers of both Hawthorne and Melville, went considerably beyond Longfellow and Fuller in order to account for the union of genders in Hawthorne's fiction and person:

Imagine a man of rugged frame of body and a delicate mind, of a physical hardihood to tempt all extremes of weather and suffer no annoyance as a ploughman in the heat of midsummer, or an amateur traveller breasting the storm for mere pleasurable excitement, with a fancy within airy, fragile and sensitive as a maiden's; the rough hairy rind of the cocoa-nut enclosing its sweet whiteness; fancy all this as a type of Nathaniel Hawthorne. The perfectness of his style, the completeness of form, the unity of his subject and of all his subjects, are masculine; the light play of fancy, the sentiment, are feminine. There is a deeper vein which no woman could ever reach, an intimacy with the sterner powers of life which we should wish no woman to attain.[12]

Hillard contrasted the man and his writings: "I should fancy from your books that you were burdened with some secret sorrow, that you had some blue chamber in your soul, into which you hardly dared to enter yourself; but when I see you, you give me the impression of a man as healthy as Adam in Paradise." Alcott looked deeply and asked in a memorable sentence, "Was he some damsel imprisoned in that manly form pleading always for release?" On the festive occasion of Melville's first visit to Hawthorne's home in the Berkshires, Evert Duyckinck noted that Hawthorne popped champagne "in his nervous way" and characterized him as "a fine ghost in a case of iron"—like Alcott's, an extraordinary summation of the fissure in Hawthorne's personality.[13]

An anonymous reviewer in the *North American Review* in 1853 was apparently the first to state in print that Hawthorne's works "are, in the truest sense of the word, autobiographical":

We have learned from his books immeasurably more of his mental history, tastes, tendencies, sympathies, and opinions, than we should have known had we enjoyed his daily converse for a lifetime. Diffident and reserved as to the habitudes of the outer man, yet singularly communicative and social in disposition and desire, he takes his public for his confidant, and betrays to thousands of eyes likes and dislikes, whims and reveries, veins of mirthful and of serious reflection, moods of feelings both healthful and morbid, which it would be beyond his power to disclose through the ear, even to the most intimate friends or the dearest of kindred.

The source of these comments was Hawthorne himself, who in 1850 offered Lewis W. Mansfield, a businessman turned poet, advice as to the nature of a poet's audience: "To whom should you speak of matters near your heart, if not to these invisible friends? You need not dread being overheard, however loudly you may speak. . . . my theory is, that there is less indelicacy in speaking out your highest, deepest, tenderest emotions to the world at large, than to almost any individual. You may be mistaken in the individual; but you cannot be mistaken in thinking that, somewhere among your fellow-creatures, there is a heart that will receive yours into itself." Hawthorne admitted that he did not always put his theory into practice: "If I were a less sophisticated man, I suppose I should act upon it more perfectly than I ever yet have."[14]

Mary Peabody Mann, Hawthorne's sister-in-law, believed that whatever happened to him appeared "bye and bye in books, for he always put himself into his books; he cannot help it." Holmes came to the same conclusion and years after Hawthorne's death wrote, without divulging what with his psychological acumen he saw behind the veil:

> Count it no marvel that he broods alone
> Over the heart he studies,—'tis his own;
> So in his page, whatever shape it wear,
> The Essex wizard's shadowed self is there,—
> The great ROMANCER, hid beneath his veil
> Like the stern preacher of his sombre tale. . . .[15]

In the preface to *Mosses from an Old Manse* (1846), Hawthorne denied the autobiographical nature of his tales: "I veil my face; nor am I, nor have ever been, one of those supremely hospitable people, who serve up their own hearts delicately fried, with brain-sauce, as a tidbit for their beloved public." But this was an authorial fib, like Huck Finn's. Beneath the lovely surface of Hawthorne's writings—his stylistic veil—lies the subterranean, dreamlike stuff (still another veil) of inner conflicts and lifelong fears.

After his death Sophia insisted that Hawthorne veiled himself from others, "since he veiled himself from himself." "I never dared gaze at him," she confessed, "unless his lids were down. It seemed an invasion into a holy place—To the last he was in a measure to me a divine Mystery, for he was so to himself." These comments reveal how little, despite her reverence for his genius and her abasement before it, she understood Hawthorne's acute knowledge of his personal mystery that at times proved more than he could bear. For her own fulfillment and security, personal and spiritual, she needed an icon such as Hawthorne provided, particularly with the assistance of her almost incredible powers of idealization. He was, she firmly believed, an ideal artist who wrote something more spiritual and uplifting than autobiography. Further, she accepted literally his denials that he did not serve up his heart "delicately fried" in his writings. She refused to recognize, or perhaps it never crossed consciousness, that the depiction of Arthur Dimmesdale is the self-portraiture of a deeply conflicted author. The Puritan minister, attired in black, was a person of very striking aspect, with a white lofty, and impending brow, large, brown, melancholy eyes, and a mouth which, unless when he forcibly compressed it, was apt to be tremulous, expressing both nervous sensibility and a vast power of self-restraint. . . . an apprehensive, a startled, a half-frightened look . . . thus kept himself simple and childlike. . . . his large dark eyes had a world of pain in their troubled and melancholy depth. . . . The young pastor's voice was tremulously sweet, rich, deep, and broken.[16]

Hawthorne described himself with frightening exactness, as he translated his hellfires and demons into art. He was powerless to deceive himself, although he hid behind the veils he created.

"Salem Is My Dwelling Place"

In one of those classes in which nineteenth-century young ladies learned the art of embroidery and adjustment to a Christian society, Amy Kittredge of Salem made what was to become a well-known sampler:

> Amy Kittredge is my name,
> Salem is my dwelling place,
> New England is my nashun,
> And Christ is my salvation.[1]

Salem was Nathaniel Hawthorne's "dwelling place" for most of his first forty-six years except for brief stays in Maine, Boston, and Concord. *The Scarlet Letter* was to immortalize Hawthorne and Salem, but it was his "hail and farewell" to the place of his birth: although he rarely returned after 1850, in his fiction he was never to leave his "dwelling place." Unlike Amy Kittredge's, his relationship to Salem was never quite satisfactory, or at least so he alleged not without contradictions, but then his ties to "nashun" and to God were also uneasy.

Called Naumberg by the Indians, Salem was the second town in New England purchased and settled by the Plymouth Company. In 1785, with a population of 6,665, it was the sixth largest city in the new nation created after the Revolutionary War. Census figures in 1785 reveal that almost half of the inhabitants (3,095) were under sixteen years of age. Males between sixteen and thirty numbered 694, between thirty and fifty 589. There were 419 widows, many of whose husbands died in the shipping trade that made Salem famous and wealthy. Sixty-six people—or 1 percent of the population—were public wards in the almshouse. Life expectancy was not great, although some surpassed the biblical allotment of three score and ten against the depressing odds and perils of birth, childhood diseases, periodic epidemics involving water pollution, the perils of sin and overindulgence, and the other usual obstacles to longevity.[2]

In the eighteenth century and for the first two or three decades of the next century, Salem prospered as the center of the East India trade. Duties in the last decade of the eighteenth century amounted to almost $3 million, rose to over $7 million in the first decade of the nineteenth century, fell to slightly under $4 million in the second decade, and by 1850 amounted to slightly more than $1.5 million. The decline was attributable to a simple fact: the harbor was not ideal for commerce since vessels drawing over twelve feet had to be unloaded at a considerable distance from the wharves. Slowly but inevitably ships transferred to other ports, particularly nearby Boston.[3]

While trade flourished in Salem, fortunes were made almost overnight but also lost overnight. Pirates, wrecks, and diseases exacted a high toll. Some families won and lost fortunes and then rose again to affluence through the initiative, energy, and (it must be added) luck of the children. Captain Nathaniel Silsbee, who was about the same age as Nathaniel Hathorne, Hawthorne's father, recouped the family fortune as a very young man and promptly abandoned the perils of the sea to pursue a career in business and politics for the rest of his long life. Captain Hathorne, who sailed on one of Silsbee's ships, was not so fortunate.

Successful captains and merchants built unostentatious but grand homes appropriate to their means, station, and taste, transforming Chestnut Street into one of the loveliest streets in New England. Their wealth enabled them to engage Samuel McIntire to decorate and design their mansions. He introduced, in the words of F. O. Matthiessen, "one of the great chapters of American architecture." Their sons attended Harvard College. In the period between 1811 and 1819, forty Salem youths constituted about 10 percent of Harvard's graduates.[4]

The Hathornes—the author changed the spelling after graduating from Bowdoin—and his mother's family, the Mannings, occupied modest frame houses of no architectural distinction and without amenities either inside or outside on congested narrow streets lacking in charm. They were not poor, nor would they ever enjoy great riches. For generations the fortunes of the Hathornes had changed little, except for a fortunate marriage or two of the Hathorne women, while the Mannings slowly improved their circumstances. Hawthorne had almost nothing to say in his writings about Chestnut Street and the Salem aristocrats. Apparently only rarely was he invited into the homes of the first families, except for his venture in his thirties into the world of Nathaniel Silsbee's daughter Mary.

Hawthorne sometimes attributed to Salem his personal dissatisfactions and feelings of inadequacy. Everyone needs a scapegoat, perhaps an artist more than others. In his perceptive but sometimes wrongheaded study of his greatest American predecessor, Henry James observed with more cosmopolitan foppery than sense: "A hundred years of Salem would perhaps be rather a dead-weight for any family to carry, and we venture to imagine that the Hathornes were dull and depressed. They did what they could, however, to improve their situation; they trod the Salem streets as little as possible."[5]

But the truth was that Hawthorne trod the streets of Salem for forty years. Despite his reservations and grievances, he responded to Salem variously depending in large part upon mood and context. In "Little Annie's Ramble," the narrator, who is Hawthorne but thinly veiled, entertains Annie with "recollections of my boyhood":

How delightful to let the fancy revel on the dainties of a confectioner; those pies, with such white and flaky paste, their contents being a mystery, whether rich mince with whole plums intermixed, or piquant apple, delicately rose-flavored; those cakes, heart-shaped or round, piled in a lofty pyramid; those sweet little circlets, sweetly named kisses; those dark majestic masses, fit to be bridal loaves at the wedding of an heiress, mountains in size, their summits deeply snow-covered with sugar! . . . Oh! my mouth waters, Little Annie, and so does yours.

Some critics censure Hawthorne's lifelong attraction to what they in their denial of the pleasure principle deplore as sentimental and banal, but artists do not put away childish things or impale themselves on banal cerebrations.[6]

In *The House of the Seven Gables*, Clifford Pyncheon, a carefully drawn self-indulgent effete who embodies Hawthorne's awareness of de-

bilitating aestheticism and the egomania of the artist, derives great pleasure from "his long-buried remembrance" of the street scenes of, obviously, Hawthorne's youth:

> The butcher's cart, with its snowy canopy, was an acceptable object;
> so was the fish-cart, heralded by its horn; so, likewise, was the coun-
> tryman's cart of vegetables, plodding from door to door, with long
> pauses of the patient horse, while his owner drove a trade in turnips,
> carrots, summer-squashes, string-beans, green peas, and new pota-
> toes, with half the housewives of the neighborhood. The baker's cart,
> with the harsh music of its bells, had a pleasant effect on Clif-
> ford. . . . One afternoon, a scissor-grinder chanced to set his wheels
> a-going, under the Pyncheon-elm, and just in front of the arched win-
> dow. . . . It was an ugly, little, venomous serpent of a noise, as ever
> did petty violence to human ears. But Clifford listened with raptur-
> ous delight.[7]

In his published writings Hawthorne rarely, if ever, depicted the
seamy aspects of Salem, but in his notebooks, where he partly freed himself from his sense of decorum and fear of censure, one discovers that in
his wanderings in Salem and elsewhere he sought out, perhaps surreptitiously, the haunts and neighborhoods of the lower social order and at a
distance observed and perhaps envied behavior which was free of the
restrictions of the code by which he lived. He even sometimes engaged
members of this society, male or female, as eagerly, in his sly way, as he
avoided members of his own class. One Fourth of July, on his birthday,
he wandered alone about Salem and noted "customers rather riotous, yet
funny, calling loudly and whimsically for what they want,—young sailors
&c; a young fellow and a girl coming arm in arm; perhaps two girls approaching the booth, and getting into conversation with the he-folks
thereabout, while old knowing codgers wink to one another thereby indicating their opinion that these ladies are of easy virtue." As he wrote
he recalled other incidents, "a knock-down between two half-stewed fellows in the crowd—a knock-down without a heavy blow, the receiver being scarcely able to keep his footing at any rate. Shouting and hallooings,
laughter,—oaths—generally a good-natured tumult."[8]

"Dearest," he wrote to Sophia Peabody during a four-year period in
which it sometimes seemed that he was in flight from rather than in pur-

suit of a bride, although paradoxically he called himself "husband," "I am intolerably weary of this old town."

> Dost thou not think it really the most hateful place in all the world? My mind becomes heavy and nerveless, the moment I set my foot within its precincts. Nothing makes me wonder more than that I found it possible to write all my tales in this same region of sleepy-head and stupidity. But I suppose the characteristics of the place are reproduced in the tales; and that accounts for the overpowering disposition to slumber which so many people experience in reading thy husband's productions.[9]

When *The Scarlet Letter* appeared in 1850, the town of about nineteen thousand inhabitants did not applaud the appearance of the first truly great work in American literature but instead took offense at "The Custom-House," the essay which prefaces the romance. There Hawthorne, who had lost his post at the Salem Custom-House following the Whig victory in the elections of 1848, pours forth his fury with gossipy fervor. The characterization of his anger as a "decapitated" state reveals graphically how he perceived the wound.

> Indeed, so far as its physical aspect is concerned, with its flat, unvaried surface, covered chiefly with wooden houses, few or none of which pretend to architectural beauty,—its irregularity, which is neither picturesque nor quaint, but only tame,—its long and lazy streets, lounging wearisomely through the whole extent of the peninsula, with Gallows Hill and New Guinea at one end, a view of the alms-house at the other,—such being the features of my native town, it would be quite as reasonable to form a sentimental attachment to a disarranged checkerboard.

His unruffled prose does not always support the seeming fury, and in a familiar pattern in his art and life, aggression slides into moderation—understandably, for he was tied to Salem emotionally and imaginatively, as Hester Prynne is to Boston. His roots, his past, his childhood were in Salem, and so he had to admit, "Though invariably happiest elsewhere [which was not true], there is within me a feeling for old Salem, which, in lack of a better phrase, I must be content to call affection."[10]

Probably he was four or five when he began to share a room with his uncles in the attic of the three-story frame house of the Mannings at 12 Herbert Street. It became his room after he graduated from college and was named in one of his appropriations from Bunyan his "castle dismal." "If ever I should have a biographer," he wrote to his future wife, "he ought to make great mention of this chamber in my memoirs, because so much of my lonely youth was wasted here, and here my mind and character were formed; and here I have been glad and hopeful, and here I have been despondent." No biographer has failed to quote the passage, although more than his lonely meditations and self-imposed isolation there impacted upon the formation of his "mind and character."

When Hawthorne climbed down the two flights of stairs to venture into the larger world, he followed a map of Salem which derived, as it were, from the map of his internal landscape and led him usually to five destinations: the harbor, the rocky coastline, Gallows Hill, the Charter Street Burying Point, and the Salem almshouse.

The docks were only a few blocks from the Herbert Street house. One would not know from Hawthorne's writings what a colorful scene it was, at least in the eyes of one of his contemporaries who had a Whitmanesque enthusiasm for particulars. From the wharves floated a "queer spicy indescribable Eastern smell" of the "spoils from every country: pepper from Sumatra,—coffee from Arabia,—cinnamon, cloves and nutmeg from the Spice Islands,—ivory and dates from Africa,—sugar and molasses from the West Indies,—wine from Madeira, and figs and raisins from Spain." The area was filled with sailors of various nationalities as well as with merchants, whores, and derelicts. The impressive federal Custom-House, built in 1809, towered serenely over the harbor, and from the roof a fierce gold-plated eagle oversaw the proceedings.[11]

At the docks Hawthorne mingled with sailors and watched his father's ships leave and return, with the uncertainties of separation and the joys of reunion—until his father's ship failed to return. From the harbor uncles from both sides of the family sailed, and one year John Manning, like Hawthorne's father earlier, disappeared. In 1846 Hawthorne returned to Salem after his three-year honeymoon at the Old Manse in Concord and presided at the Custom-House as surveyor of the port—and, more important, as surveyor of his father's world, which was also the world of his two renowned ancestors, William and John Hathorne.

In youth Hawthorne walked along the coast of Salem, "which extends its line of rude rocks and seldom-trodden sands, for leagues around our bay," and the pattern did not change in maturity. His most elaborate account of a walk along the Atlantic Ocean appeared in the *Democratic Review* in January 1838. Although he was then thirty-three, "Foot-prints on the Sea-shore" was written from the perspective of recollected youth.

On a September morning, "the yearning for seclusion" overcoming him, Hawthorne sets out "with a hermit's vow, to interchange no thoughts with man or woman, to share no social pleasure, but to derive all that day's enjoyment from shore, and sea, and sky,—from my soul's communion with these, and from fantasies, and recollections, or anticipated realities." He walks along the sea, his feet sinking into the sand. For a time he drags a piece of seaweed "by its long snake-like stalk," and then skips pebbles over the water. Next he draws on the sandy canvas "huge faces—huge as that of the Sphynx on Egyptian sands." Bodies and legs have the proportions of the faces; "child's play becomes magnificent on so grand a scale." Then comes the "most fascinating employment": writing his name in gigantic letters—like a child thinking big in order to be big and to assert his identity—but in sand.

He leaves the beach to climb the rocks which in his perception assume human characteristics, rising "in every variety of attitude," and the "Sphynx" and the "gigantic letters" of his name, his temporary self-image, must now bow before what he transforms into a patriarchal figure wielding unlimited power over life and death: "One huge rock ascends in monumental shape, with a face like a giant's tombstone, on which the veins resemble inscriptions, but in an unknown tongue." This figure in rock, with mysterious funereal "inscriptions," reappears in "Young Goodman Brown," "Roger Malvin's Burial," *The Blithedale Romance*, and elsewhere, and the association is always in the context of the eternal conflict of father and child which Hawthorne struggled with for a lifetime.

Later in a "nook" or "hermitage" among the rocks—the Hawthornian hero is always in search of protection against the outside world—he eats his lunch and listens to the "melancholy voice" of the sea. Then, protected, he dares to vent his philosophical convictions—now in imagination Demosthenes on the Salem shore—against his "antagonist," "yonder shaggy rock, mid-deep in the surf." His "maiden speech" silences his opponent: "Oh, what joy for a shy man to feel himself so solitary, that he may lift his voice to its highest pitch without hazard of a listener."[12]

At the edge of Salem at the foot of Broad Street is Gallows Hill, "where guilt and phrenzy consummated the most execrable scene that our history blushes to record," Hawthorne writes in "Alice Doane's Appeal." "For this was the field where superstition won her darkest triumph; the high place where our fathers set up their shame, to the mournful gaze of generations far remote. The dust of martyrs was beneath our feet." Every year on November 5 there were bonfires on Gallows Hill to commemorate the hysteria of 1692, when innocent women became witches and were hanged from what Hawthorne called the "death-tree." Gallows Hill provided the locale for one of Hawthorne's earliest and most perplexing tales, "Alice Doane's Appeal," and evoked John Hathorne, his great-great-grandfather who was a presiding judge during the witch trials. A familial and haunting bond to this judge who participated in one of the most shameful and insane periods in Puritan history colored and stained Hawthorne's imagination.[13]

From the windows of his "castle dismal" Hawthorne looked down on the oldest cemetery in Salem, the Charter Street Burying Point, established in 1637 a few years after the settlement of the village. In the row of Hathornes the judge is second from the right.

$$\text{Here lyes inter}^{d} \, \mathring{y}^{e} \text{ body of Co}^{lo} \text{ Ioh}^{n} \text{ Hathorne}$$
$$\text{Esq}^{r} \text{ Aged 76 years who died May } \mathring{y}^{e} \text{ 10}^{th} \text{ 1717}$$

His grandson John, the son of Captain Joseph Hathorne, was buried to his left in 1750 at age twenty-eight, and to his right at the end of the row lies Captain William Hathorne, another grandson who died at eighty in 1794. William's brother Captain Daniel died two years later at sixty-five. Daniel's daughter Judith Archer was buried there in 1801. With the interments of Hawthorne's grandmother and two aunts the row in 1829 included eight Hathornes, an imposing memorial to the family. None of the Hawthornes joined the Hathornes in the Charter Street cemetery.

The "inmates" of the burial ground appeared in Hawthorne's writings from his first novel, *Fanshawe*, to his last unfinished work, "The Dolliver Romance." The life and gravestone of Fanshawe recall the life and monument of Nathaniel Mather. Mather is buried not far from Dr. John Swinnerton, who is summoned to treat the founder of the Pyncheon dynasty in *The House of the Seven Gables*. Dr. Grimshawe is to be buried next to Swinnerton, and Dr. Dolliver is Swinnerton's pupil and successor. The tombstone of William Hollingworth no doubt suggested the name of the blacksmith-reformer Hollingsworth in *The Blithedale Romance*. The two wards of Grimshawe, Ned and Elsie, convert the burial ground into a playground. "When seen at all," we learn, "they were sporting together in the grave-yard, making playmates of the tall slate grave-stones." In "graver moods, they spelled out the names and learned by heart doleful verses on the headstones."[14] In act and appearance, Ned and Elsie are Nat and Ebe, as his sister Elizabeth was called, and of both youths it can be said that the cemetery "might almost be called [their] natal spot."[15]

At the corner of the Charter Street Burying Point stands a modest dwelling—"its characteristic was a decent respectability, not sinking below the boundary of the genteel"—which, fictionally, is inhabited by Grimshawe, Ned, and Elsie in one tale and by Dr. Dolliver and Pansie in another, both unfinished works of the last years. In 1837 Hawthorne entered this house, perhaps for the first time, and there met Sophia Peabody, the daughter of an eccentric apothecary-dentist, Dr. Nathaniel Peabody. In the parlor Hawthorne slowly and shyly courted Sophia. When he looked out the windows he gazed directly at the row of eight Hathornes.[16]

Hawthorne was twelve years old when Salem erected its fourth structure for the accommodation of its indigent citizens, who were never allowed to forget the stigma of their failure to become self-reliant members of the community. A large structure, measuring two hundred by fifty feet, was built in 1816 at the Neck, at the opposite end of the village from Gallows Hill, near land once owned by the Hathorne family.

In the closing months of his life Hawthorne dwelt, according to his wife, almost obsessively on the possibility of ending his days in the Concord almshouse and caused, as he must have been aware, his wife and three children much anguish. His own anxiety is confirmed fictionally, for Ned, whose extraordinary beauty is a mirror image of his creator, is said to have been born in an almshouse.[17]

Amy Kittredge's "dwelling place" in Salem is depicted in an embroidery of disarming charm and idealism, with untroubled faith in God, "nashun," and Salem. Hawthorne's "dwelling place" is only occasionally delineated idealistically, for even "Little Annie's Ramble" has undertones of reality: an alarm is sounded for a missing little girl, who may have been abducted by one Nathaniel Hawthorne.

The Heritage
The Hathornes and the Mannings

Hawthorne was destined after the publication of *The Scarlet Letter* in 1850 to become the unofficial historian of puritanism and to shape indelibly posterity's view of it. Yet his conception of the past, and of puritanism as well, was determined by the careers and tyrannies of two ancestors—William Hathorne (1607–1681) and his son John (1641–1717). In "Main-street" Hawthorne wittily observes: "Let us thank God for having given us such ancestors; and let each successive generation thank him, not less fervently, for being one step further from them in the march of the ages."[1]

In 1630 William Hathorne sailed to the New World aboard the *Arbella*, in the company of John Winthrop, and settled in Dorchester, Massachusetts. About six years later, now married to Anne, he moved to Salem. There he began a career that eventually made him the most distinguished member of the Massachusetts Bay colony after Winthrop and John Endecott, another Puritan of iron with whom Hawthorne in his tales had a mixed relationship. William Hathorne became a deputy to the General Court of Massachusetts and subsequently speaker of the house, as well as one of the commissioners from the colony on the board of the United Colonies of New England. Versatile, ambitious, and a natural leader, he held the rank of major in campaigns against the Indians.

As magistrate and judge he was a man of his times. When the Puritans came to New England to establish a new Eden, they brought with them all the evils humans are heir to, such as murder, theft, alcoholism, incest, and whoring. To combat the wickedness the authorities transported across the ocean many of the brutalities of English justice: ears were cut off, holes bored in women's tongues with red-hot irons, and prisoners starved. Hathorne pursued the wicked "like a bloodhound" and on one occasion directed a constable not only to remove a burglar's ear but also to brand him on the forehead with the letter B.[2]

On several occasions Hawthorne retold the story of a Quaker woman named Ann Coleman, who,

> naked from the waist upward, and bound to the tail of a cart, is dragged through the Main-street at the pace of a brisk walk, while the constable follows with a whip of knotted cords. A strong-armed fellow is that constable; and each time that he flourishes his lash in the air, you see a frown wrinkling and twisting his brow, and, at the same instant, a smile upon his lips. He loves his business, faithful officer that he is, and puts his soul into every stroke, zealous to fulfill the injunction of Major Hawthorne's warrant, in the spirit and to the letter. There came down a stroke that has drawn blood! Ten such stripes are to be given in Salem, ten in Boston, and ten in Dedham; and, with those thirty stripes of blood upon her, she is to be driven into the forest. . . . Heaven grant, that, as the rain of so many years has wept upon it, time after time, and washed it all away, so there may have been a dew of mercy, to cleanse this cruel blood-stain out of the record of the persecutor's life![3]

But "this cruel blood-stain" perhaps troubled only Major Hathorne's great-great-grandson. Hathorne seemingly enjoyed his powers and distinctions and, if guilt-ridden at all, was no doubt convinced that his deeds were performed in the service of his God, who, like Jonathan Edwards's, was a vengeful deity that placed obedience above mercy. With shrewd practicality the major provided for his bodily and economic needs through operation of a still for what contemporaries euphemistically called "strong waters." Hathorne lived to a good age and left a considerable estate amounting to eight hundred pounds. To his descendant he bequeathed a portrait of an overman and a haunting scene that epitomizes patricidal horror, the father brutalizing woman, a subject which the future author is to treat obsessively, ambivalently fascinated by the sadistic tactics of men of iron.[4]

The fifth of Major Hathorne's children, John, followed in his father's steps. At thirty-four John married Ruth Gardner, the fourteen-year-old daughter of Lieutenant George Gardner, but he clearly learned little about the operation of the minds of adolescent females as later actions demonstrated. Before assuming public roles he established himself as a practical man by purchasing a wharf and obtaining a license to sell strong waters. In 1683 he was a deputy to the General Court in Boston. He achieved lasting fame and obliquy during the hysteria associated with the witch trials of the 1690s when he served as a magistrate and dealt out harsh punishment to innocent women and frenzied girls on flimsy and often contrived evidence. Like his father he tyrannized over defenseless women. He also served briefly as a colonel in the militia. John Hathorne enjoyed status, means, and a long life and seemingly permitted his heirs and posterity to bear the guilt of the atrocities of the witch trials.

William and John were the achievers, and men of iron among the American Hathornes. They were reborn in the nineteenth century in the imagination and fantasies of the Hathorne who, though he changed the name to Hawthorne, would confer immortality upon them. He converted these two pillars of the patriarchal Puritan world into substitute father figures and experienced an imaginary but real rivalry both to excel them and to prove himself worthy of their approval. In one of Hawthorne's unfinished romances at the end of his life, the narrator observes quite accurately that people "might have detected in the manner and matter of his talk, a certain hereditary reverence and awe, the growth of ages, mixed up with a newer hatred that impelled him to deface and destroy what, at the same time, his deepest impulse was to bow before."[5]

Hawthorne loathed and loved them and gave them little peace in his writings because they gave him little peace. William and John became the grandfather and father of Goodman Brown in one of Hawthorne's greatest tales. In *Grandfather's Chair*, which records the fortunes of a chair as it is handed down from generation to generation, the story begins with its arrival in the 1630s aboard the *Arbella*. The most detailed account of the ancestors appears in the foreword to *The Scarlet Letter*, in which expulsion from the Salem Custom-House is perceived as decapitation and confirmation of the opinion of the two "stern and black-browed" ancestors of "an idler" or teller of tales:

No aim, that I have ever cherished, would they recognize as laudable; no success of mine—if my life, beyond its domestic scope, had ever been brightened by success—would they deem otherwise than worthless, if not positively disgraceful. "What is he?" murmurs one gray shadow of my forefathers to the other. "A writer of story-books! What kind of a business in life,—what mode of glorifying God, or being serviceable to mankind in his day and generation,—may that be? Why the degenerate fellow might as well have been a fiddler!"

Hawthorne concludes ironically: "Such are the compliments bandied between my great-grandsires and myself, across the gulf of time!"—the time in which he had internalized their views. Finally he unveils his fantasy that he has proved himself worthy of the virile fathers: "And yet, let them scorn me as they will, strong traits of their nature have intertwined with mine."[6]

Most of John Hathorne's sons chose the sea rather than business or public service and accepted the attendant risks of such a life. The most successful offspring was Joseph (1692–1762), who became a ship captain but then abandoned the sea to pursue the career of farmer. He bequeathed "to my wife Sarah my silver tankard with H. marked on it" as well as one-third of an estate of sixteen hundred pounds, but the fortunes of the Hathornes began to decline in this generation.[7]

Joseph's son Daniel (1731–1796) was married at 27 Union Street in the house in which the novelist was to be born. Built in 1686, it was a modest dwelling of two stories with a large central chimney. During the Revolutionary War Daniel Hathorne served as commander of the *True American* and was celebrated in a ballad entitled "Bold Hathorne," which was reprinted about the time of his grandson's marriage in 1842:

> Bold Hathorne was commander,
>   A man of real worth,
> Old England's cruel tyranny
>   Induced him to go forth;
> She, with relentless fury,
>   Was plundering our coast.

His death in 1796 as reported in the *Salem Gazette* was the occasion of an impressive procession to the Charter Street Burying Point: "The funeral was attended on Wednesday last with that respect which real worth insures. The corpse was preceded by the Marine Society, and the Fire Club, of which he was a member. The flags of the ships in port were half mast high—and the numerous procession which attended on this melancholy occasion, fully evinced the regret they felt at the departure of their worthy townsman."[8]

Daniel's son Nathaniel was born at 27 Union Street apparently on May 19, 1775, although there are no extant records, and was baptized on May 21, 1776. He went like many another Hathorne before the mast at an early age, perhaps at fourteen. From three logbooks which were passed down to his son, it is possible to follow in some detail his adventures at sea. In the late 1780s he was on the *America*, which made history of a kind after it delivered the first elephant to the United States. In December 1796 he sailed aboard the *Perseverance*, which belonged to his brother-in-law, Simon Forrester, who as a young man was brought from England by Daniel Hathorne and rapidly rose to riches. During what turned out to be a seventeen-month voyage, Nathaniel read extensively and wrote sentimental verse in his logbook such as the following:

> In Storms when clouds obscure the Sky
> And thunders roll and lightning fly
> In the Midst of all these dire allarms
> I'll think dear Betsy on thy charms.

Betsy was Elizabeth Manning, who lived on Herbert Street behind the Hathorne house.[9]

One surviving portrait of Captain Hathorne indicates that he bore a close resemblance to his father, a family resemblance that followed into the next generation. An often repeated story had it that some old sea captains recognized the novelist as the captain's son forty years after the father's death. In 1851 Hawthorne himself noted "a singular resemblance" between a wood engraving based on the oil portrait of Cephas G. Thompson and "a miniature of my father." Hathorne was five feet ten inches tall, of light complexion, with a scar over his left eye. According to a Captain Knight, "He was the sternest man that ever walked a deck!"—a statement which has led some biographers to conclude that he was a tyrannical nineteenth-century captain out of Melville.[10]

Between voyages, on August 2, 1801, Nathaniel married his neighbor and shortly went to sea. Elizabeth Hathorne learned to adjust to the rhythms of the mariner's life, the goings and comings with the attendant anxieties and reliefs. Their first child, Elizabeth, was born seven months later, on March 7, 1802, before the father's return to Salem.[11]

Nathaniel Hathorne was born on July 4, 1804, as once again the new nation was indulging in its annual patriotic and alcoholic orgy. For the Hathornes and the Mannings the day marked the birth of the first male in the new century. The boy's father was at sea, and the mother, although surrounded by mothers, her own father, sisters, brothers, and sisters-in-law, had to suffer the usual uncertainties of childbirth and at the same time repress anxieties about her absent husband's well-being.

In 1804 Nathaniel's Uncle Daniel Hathorne died at sea and became the first name on Hawthorne's necrology, a list that was to be unusually long even for a nineteenth-century family. Hawthorne's father returned from the voyage a captain and was admitted to membership in the East Indian Marine Society in November 1804. But within the month he again went to sea, sailing on the *Neptune*.

Extant records do not account for Captain Hathorne's movements in 1805 and 1806. On December 28, 1807, he left Salem on the *Nabby*, a brig of 154 tons, for Surinam, or Dutch Guiana. In a flourishing trade, dried fish, hake, and mackeral were carried to Surinam and molasses and sugar brought back. The voyage out and back lasted about fifty days, and it took a month or more to sell the cargo and to load the vessel at Paramaribo. A third child, Maria Louisa, was born two weeks after the father sailed, on January 9, 1808. When Captain Hathorne arrived in Surinam six of the seven members of his crew, including himself, were ill with yellow fever. He stayed at a boardinghouse kept by an Englishwoman named Hannah Birch and died sometime between the end of January and March 15, when the *Nabby* left Surinam with a new crew.[12]

Elizabeth later recalled that, early in April 1808, "one morning my mother called my brother into her room, next to the one where we slept, and told him that his father was dead." She was six and Nathaniel three months short of four. Perhaps Elizabeth was informed first, or she may have learned of the father's death from Nathaniel. She said nothing about her own reaction or her brother's or what they talked about then and in the following weeks as they tried to understand that the father who had sailed only four months earlier was never to return to Salem. It was a traumatic moment, the worst in their young lives, and because of its early occurrence it would be consciously and unconsciously reexperienced endlessly, coloring their memories of their childhood. Even in retelling the incident Elizabeth understated, perhaps because the memory was still painful or because as a Hawthorne she understood that she was not entitled to display emotion: she was not unlike her "iron" ancestors in this respect. The Mannings and Hathornes attended church on April 10, when Captain Hathorne's name was handed up for prayer to Dr. William Bentley, who had married the Hathornes seven years earlier.[13]

In old age Elizabeth remembered two seemingly minor but deeply significant events of her brother's childhood. The stories he began to concoct for the entertainment of the family were told in the first person and invariably ended at the Salem seashore with the narrator promising or threatening, "And I'm never coming home again." Here he would appear to be associating himself with the father but at the same time to be saying, "I'll make you suffer as I've suffered." When Nathaniel started to read and to memorize passages from Shakespeare, he was fond of proclaiming in as booming a voice as he could manage a well-known passage from *Richard III*: "Stand back, my Lord, and let the coffin pass." Surely the line had unconscious reverberations. No one from the family having witnessed the coffin or the burial, the father was in effect unburied.[14]

Apparently about 1820 Captain Hathorne's logbooks were given to the son. So far as we know, Hawthorne had nothing to say of the gift, but he wrote his name experimentally at many places in the books, spelling it Hathorne as well as Hawthorne, wavering indecisively, it would appear, as he sought to establish his own identity, which meant freeing himself from three Hathornes, who were predetermining his course, or so it seemed.

By example and no doubt by precept Nathaniel like his sister Elizabeth learned at an early age to veil his feelings. The Hathornes as well as the Mannings were not given to public confession: they bore their woes in silence. Hawthorne, however, was to unveil his feelings of loss in his fiction over a lifetime. In "The Journal of a Solitary Man" he wrote: "My footsteps were not imprinted on the earth, but lost in air; and I shall leave no son to inherit my share of life, . . . when his father should vanish like a bubble." In one of the romances which Hawthorne at the end of his life could not shape into an artistic entity, he intruded in his narrative to raise a troubling question as to the motivation of a character. "What is the crime?" he inquired of himself rather than of the reader. "Each son murders his father at a certain age; or does each father try to accomplish the impossibility of murdering his successor?" He did not, could not, answer the questions, nor could he render the situation artistically. "This is not the right track," he commented, as though talking to himself, which was perhaps the only course he had since the situation was simultaneously insoluble and anxiety-producing, even though his father had died over fifty years earlier.[15]

In 1856 Hawthorne wrote to Horatio Bridge: "I am disposed to thank God for the gloom and chill of my early life, in the hope that my share of adversity came then, when I bore it alone, and that therefore it need not come now." It seems unlikely that "the frozen purgatory of childhood" referred to wintry Sabbaths spent in the old wooden meetinghouse, but he may have been recalling once again, as in "A Select Party" (1844), the frightening dreams of nighttime that caused him to shudder "anew at the forgotten terrors of his childhood."[16]

On April 19, 1808, Samuel Bolton, the judge of the probate of wills, issued a document to "Mrs. Elizabeth C. Hathorne, of Salem . . . Widow: Whereas your husband, Capt. Nathaniel Hathorne, late of Salem aforesaid, Mariner, deceased, intestate, having while he lived, and at the time of his decease, goods, chattels, rights or credits in the County aforesaid, . . . I do hereby ordain, constitute and appoint you Administratrix of all and singular the goods, chattels, rights and credits aforesaid." After creditors were paid, the widow was left with $296.21. There was no financial crisis since Richard Manning took his daughter and her children into his house and Captain Hathorne's relatives became the charge of Forrester, the wealthy newcomer to the family. Hawthorne's sister Elizabeth declared late in life that Richard Manning was "in comfortable circumstances & they were abundantly cared for, & after his death, they had their share, & more, of his estate, which was not divided until after the death of his widow in 1826."[17]

However, Hawthorne's obsession with the almshouse may have begun in this period when he perhaps learned through a chance remark from an anxious mother or an annoyed relative that his father had failed as a provider and that he was dependent upon his mother's family. Only naive adults can believe that children, though unable to articulate complexly, are not fully aware of the emotional consequences of what happens in their lives. In relating in the 1860s the story of Ned, who was supposedly abandoned by his parents at the door of an English almshouse and was adopted as Dr. Grimshawe's ward, Hawthorne decided "to present him to the reader as seen through the observations and conjectures of an imaginative boy." The youth is "like a child, when his mother sits by his bed, and he fears that she will steal away if he falls quite asleep, and leave him in the dark solitude." Ned has "a mark where a bullet went in some time ago—4 or 5 years since, when he could have been little more than a boy." When he wrote these lines Hawthorne was almost sixty years old: he was still frightened, and his internal calendar unconsciously recalled what had happened when he was four, when his father died and he became the ward, as it were, of his mother's family.[18]

Hawthorne never referred directly to his father's death, but it is written large in the fatherless universe of his fiction, from his first published work, *Fanshawe*, to the last uncompleted manuscript, "The Dolliver Romance." If assembled in one of Hawthorne's processionals, these orphans would number thirty or more, all of whom are as burdened as John Bunyan's Christian.

Some time during the spring of 1808 Mrs. Hathorne and her three children moved from the house on Union Street to the one on Herbert Street. At the time, the Manning household consisted of the two parents and their three daughters and five sons, who ranged in ages from seventeen to thirty-one.

Richard Manning (1755–1812), an apparently benign patriarch, began his career as a blacksmith and later established the Boston and Salem Stagecoach Line, which eventually prospered and provided, as Elizabeth Hawthorne was given to say, free transportation for the three children to visit relatives of both families. All Richard Manning's children except one, John, participated in what was genuinely a family enterprise. The older Manning also acquired property over the years, but, proceeding conservatively, the family did not markedly alter their style of living as they acquired wealth. The modest house on Herbert Street was a case in point. The parents and children, perhaps with some parental pushing, practiced thrift, and they preached the customary virtues of protestantism, with more consistency than the future writer of romances approved of, at least when his requests for money were denied. At his death in 1812 Richard Manning left an estate of more than $50,000, with real estate holdings worth about $33,000. Mrs. Hathorne did not inherit until 1826 and remained even then a charge of her brothers since she received less than $200 annually. But the Mannings took care of their own carefully and in their frugal way generously.[19]

Of the three other Manning daughters (Mary, Maria, and Priscilla), only Priscilla married, at age twenty-seven. Of the five sons (William, Richard, Robert, John, and Samuel), only two were to marry, Richard at thirty-four and Robert at forty. Robert, who managed his father's business as well as the family, opened a broker's office as a young man and was unusually successful. In addition he became one of the first important American pomologists and was the only one of the nineteenth-century Mannings included in the *Dictionary of American Biography*: "To Manning, more than to any other man of his time, and perhaps more than to all others combined, the fruit growers were indebted for the introduction of new and choice fruits, for correcting the nomenclature of fruit . . . and for identifying varieties."[20]

Robert, with the assistance of Mary, took charge of Nathaniel after Richard Manning's death and was, it would appear, an essentially kind man who was constantly being tested by a recalcitrant nephew. For the most part Robert's letters were supportive but occasionally direct in regard to Nathaniel, no doubt because he alone managed to set controls for the moody youth. The Hathorne children were generally guarded in their remarks about their aunts and uncles in their letters, perhaps to keep a fragile peace, perhaps in reluctant recognition that the aunts and uncles acted in their best interests. Hawthorne evidenced little grief on his uncle's death in 1842 and found an excuse for not leaving Concord to attend funeral services in Salem. He may have been ungrateful or may have nursed legitimate grievances: there is on the basis of extant evidence no way of knowing. It seems reasonably certain, however, that in the eyes of the Hathorne children Robert never replaced Captain Hathorne.

The biographer faces difficult problems in dealing with the Mannings. Hawthorne grew up and lived with them, except for brief periods, from 1808 until he married in 1842. It would be a plausible assumption that the Manning influence was greater than any Hathorne influence because Hawthorne was never intimate with any of the Hathornes after his father's death. That he was first of all a Manning, then, is an attractive, even logical, proposition. However, logic in matters that involve feelings and real as well as imaginary deprivations does not necessarily lead to the truth, if indeed it can be reached. Hawthorne had almost nothing to say about the Mannings in letters or other writings. Silence, however, can also speak; what it says is not fact but speculation.

Hawthorne rarely referred to his father, but one contemporary attributed to him the son's "natural tendency . . . toward seclusion." (The same might be said of Hawthorne's mother.) But orphandom, particularly the loss through death of the father, became a recurrent theme in his writings. He did, as we have seen, allude frequently to the two ancestral fathers, William and John, with whom he appeared to act out the oedipal rivalry and ambivalence. In maturity he never corresponded with the Mannings or showed interest in their affairs. When he went to England in the 1850s he searched for his Hathorne origins and paid no attention to his Manning roots. As he repeatedly made clear, he had to prove himself to the Hathornes and be accepted by them. There was no room for the Mannings.[21]

If Hawthorne was unfair to the Mannings—through silence and omission—the situation is confused because in the manuscript entitled "Some Facts about Hawthorne" his sister Elizabeth described the Manning household as "a tavern" and "the place for happy visits," where large numbers of Mannings and perhaps Hathornes assembled in a convivial environment. Nobody was melancholy, not even Mrs. Hathorne; "serious she might be, but that was customary for the elders in those days." Elizabeth alleged that "all, from grandparents down to the youngest uncle, were entirely devoted to the happiness & welfare of these children, Nathaniel being . . . the especial pet of all."[22]

Elizabeth wrote to her niece that "through our childhood we were indulged in all convenient ways, and were under little control except that of circumstances. There were aunts and uncles, and they were all as fond of your father and as careful of his welfare as if he had been their own child." The "boyhood" of this "very handsome child," she advised James T. Fields, "was very happy, . . . and his feelings were in all things considered." She informed her niece that Hawthorne "was both beautiful and bright, and perhaps his training was as good as any other could have been." He was "particularly petted" because "his health was then delicate and he had frequent illnesses."[23]

We can assume, on the basis of the letters the Hathorne children wrote in their early years and their close attachment to each other, that the Hathornes always remained an entity within the Manning family, to a large extent self-contained and perhaps even somewhat exclusive. Economically they may have been dependent, but Mrs. Hathorne's almost precocious children were clearly superior to the Mannings in writing skills and intellectual development. None of the Mannings—and this included Mrs. Hathorne—had more than elementary command of grammar. Nathaniel helped his Uncle Robert write professional articles. Aunt Mary had a card from the Salem Athenaeum, but Elizabeth and Nathaniel, particularly the former, were the readers. At the same time the Mannings like most ambitious middle-class Americans were devoted to education and provided for Nathaniel's schooling despite his grumblings, and after some difference of opinion they undertook the expenses of his college education, even though he often taxed their patience. He was to be the first Hathorne or Manning to graduate from college. What the Manning aunts and uncles thought of the nephew's published sketches and tales is not known, but they probably took the usual middle-class pride in publication.

If it is difficult to delineate Mrs. Hathorne because by nature and temperament she was not assertive, the fact remains that despite her self-effacing, unemphatic ways she was in the eyes of her children a powerful presence or image, even if because of her passivity and her chilled emotional responses not a wholly satisfying one. Though Robert and Mary, after the death of their father, made most of the decisions in the Manning household, the loyalty of the three Hathorne children was to their mother. Ineffectual and perhaps indecisive as she may often have been, she was the court of appeal, and the children expected her to defend them against real or imaginary grievances they experienced at the hands of the Mannings. Perhaps the children could twist their mother to their will, but by whatever means—her seeming weaknesses may have caused the children to believe they had to protect her—she retained, probably without even consciously trying, such a hold that only Hawthorne dared to venture, after years of vacillation, into marriage and separate himself from this closely knit unit.

Hawthorne's children portrayed his mother as an eccentric, tremulous grandmother, but at her death Una was five, Julian three, and Rose was not yet born. Their knowledge came from their mother and her sister, Elizabeth Peabody, who had a dogmatic but essentially good-natured opinion on every subject. The Peabodys depicted Mrs. Hathorne as a recluse who took her meals alone in her room and allowed no one to enter her almost sacred chamber. She wore a white dress, presumably in appearance if not an angel then a phantom on the order of Emily Dickinson.

Hawthorne's sister Elizabeth challenged the fidelity of the Peabody portrait. With emphasis she declared that she had never seen her mother in white and in one sentence consigned the angel-phantom to limbo. She defended her mother's right to admit whom she pleased to her chamber and noted that many women in the nineteenth century were not active socially. She saw nothing unusual in her mother's behavior, which, it must at once be added, was a model for her own. Elizabeth also sought to justify her mother's actions on the basis of her delicate health, about which few details are known.

Since her defense of her mother was offered in answer to a published account, Elizabeth would not have acknowledged, if it were actually the situation, that her mother mourned the loss of her husband for the rest of her life and refused the children the love they should have expected. Elizabeth denied that her mother was either "gloomy or melancholy" in appearance, only "serious." There is the possibility that Mrs. Hathorne resigned herself to her lot and dependency upon the Mannings, settling into patterns which with the passage of years could be expected to become more rigid. She and her children drifted where others acted and allowed themselves to be taken care of, without surrendering their many eccentricities.[24]

The Peabodys' portrait of Mrs. Hathorne is based on the last eleven or twelve years of her life. The Peabodys knew nothing firsthand about her until 1837 when Hawthorne met Sophia Peabody. At that time his mother was fifty-seven, and, except for the presence of her three children, her world was contracting. Her mother died in 1826, Richard in 1830, Samuel in 1833, Mary in 1841, and Robert in 1842. After Robert's death, only three Mannings were left, two of whom, William and Priscilla, outlived their sister. As the years passed, Elizabeth Hathorne had few people to talk to, and there was little for her to do except to bide her time, more and more surrounded by stillness.

In protecting her mother's memory Elizabeth covered up what would appear to be depressed states, not unlike those experienced by her brother and perhaps herself. Mrs. Hathorne's isolation from the world was extreme, granting all mitigating circumstances. At various times Elizabeth and Nathaniel noted without drawing somewhat obvious conclusions that their mother could not cope with feelings and demonstrations of affection. In Elizabeth's words, both the Hathornes and Mannings "possessed deep, strong, passionate affections & natures, but were very undemonstrative, with a real inability to express their deeper emotions." It was not her intention, but Elizabeth could have been describing Hawthorne's writings with the recurrent emphasis upon repression, noncommunication, and the absence and fear of tactile contact and gratification. She perhaps did not perceive that the mother's failure was often her brother's subject matter.[25]

The bond of children to parent, then, was intense but somewhat chilled. The mother was unable to supply the affection and support as fully as the children expected or perhaps needed. But she set a model for their behavior. Hawthorne was in many ways his mother's son. As everybody testified and his behavior illustrated, he was reclusive and often melancholic and like his fictional characters a spectator with the coolness and distance provided by such a stance. It was one way of keeping hell-fired emotions under seeming control. The energy lacking in his life and in his characters may be traceable to his mother and the ambience she created for her children.[26]

If Nathaniel was, as Elizabeth contended, the pet of the Mannings, he was the darling of the Hathornes. They understood his moods and accommodated his wishes. In their quiet, undemonstrative ways, they gave him the idolatry he needed in order to overcome his ingrained inertia and to manage the long wait until he established intercourse with the world through his writings.

In his writings Hawthorne would empathize with women betrayed or sometimes brutalized in one way or another by men. For a male he had unusual insight into the plight of women, and he constantly delineated the passive, long-suffering wife or fiancée. At the same time he was the heir of the two great Hathorne heroes and brutalizers, as he himself recognized.[27]

Hawthorne's ties to his sisters were close, perhaps too close for the emotional well-being of all concerned. In the early years after the death of their father, while they waited for Louisa to catch up with them, Elizabeth and Nathaniel played together and shared the same books. When Hawthorne took on his first job at age thirty-two, Elizabeth became his assistant and was assigned the research work in the Athenaeum. She waited on him and in every way protected him and after his death sought to keep his memory pure and uncontaminated, as earlier she had sought to keep him from marriage because no woman was worthy of him.

In letters written in her adolescence, Elizabeth revealed herself as strong-willed, outspoken, and often dogmatic, yet with a sense of wit that occasionally became caustic. In that period of her life she gadded about in the Manning carriages. Writing in the third person, she later said: "Miss E. H. was not a recluse in her young days, but was very fond of society. She was fond of it to the last, when it came to her, but a certain inertia of her nature prevented her seeking it."[28]

Elizabeth did not have special tutors like her brother and was not able to attend college. Like many middle-class nineteenth-century women, she was self-educated and probably better educated than many college graduates of the age. Elizabeth read extensively in the classics and contemporary literature and had a clear and vigorous critical sense. She evidently taught herself Spanish and was engaged for a large part of her life in a translation of Cervantes which never came to fruition and is apparently lost. Two years before his death Hawthorne said, "She is the most sensible woman I ever knew in my life, much superior to me in general talent, and of fine cultivation." According to his son Julian, Hawthorne admitted that his sister "had more genius" than he had and declared, "The only thing I fear is the ridicule of Elizabeth."[29]

Except for teaching, which would probably have placed her in a more intimate relationship with people than she desired or perhaps could tolerate, there was no outlet for her talents in her society. And so she was not much more than twenty when she followed her mother into seclusion. Perhaps she was overcome with inertia as she alleged, or perhaps she was more comfortable and secure near her mother in familiar surroundings. Like her mother, Elizabeth rarely left Salem in her maturity until she was freed after her mother's death in 1849, and then she chose to live alone, surrounded by a few strangers. In the words of her niece Rose Hawthorne Lathrop, "Aunt Ebie seemed to love moss and leaves as much as some people love souls," and, she added, "I thought she had chosen them as the least dangerous objects of affection."[30]

According to Rose, Elizabeth in old age had a "magic resemblance to my father in many ways." She had "large, lustrous eyes" with "dark brown, long lashes and broadly sweeping eyebrows [which] were distinct against the pallor of her skin." Rose had difficulty believing that her formidable aunt "trembled beside a steam-engine." To the end Elizabeth was a peppery eccentric who freely acknowledged and delighted in her biases: "My way is to let all prejudices meet together and have a fair fight, and then to yield to the strongest." She felt little responsibility for offering advice since nobody took it, and she had no patience with follies except her own, "which I flatter myself have the negative merit of being only passive,—merely shortcomings in wisdom."[31]

Elizabeth was the first and the last of the Hathorne children, but she never lifted the veil or revealed any secrets. Confession would have been out of character.

Since the appearance of Julian Hawthorne's biography in 1885 there has been speculation about Melville's comment to Julian during the course of an interview that he knew Hawthorne's "secret." Eager to defend his father, Julian alleged that the "secret" was Melville's, not Hawthorne's, which is a plausible allegation although it confuses the situation further since there is no way to determine Melville's "secret." Because of the recurrence of incest in Hawthorne's tales and romances, between brothers and sisters, fathers and daughters, and sisters, a number of commentators have suspected that the "secret" is an incestuous relationship between Nathaniel and Elizabeth. In "Grimshawe," one of the unfinished romances of his last years, the bond between Ned and Elsie is intense, although they are not brother and sister but the wards of Dr. Grimshawe.

In the most recent attempt to unravel the "secret," Philip Young, drawing upon his predecessors and introducing new speculations, has argued that the incestuous bond of Nathaniel and Elizabeth is the veiled subject of *The Scarlet Letter*, Arthur Dimmesdale and Hester Prynne being brother and sister, the A substituting for I, or incest, and the situation in the romance replicating an incestuous episode in the Manning family in the late seventeenth century. Two sisters had carnal relations with their brother, Captain Nicholas Manning, and in the words of the court clerk had to sit in "the meeting house with a paper upon each of their heads, written in Capital Letters, 'This is for whorish carriage with my naturall Brother.'" Hawthorne, it is proposed, over a century later assumed the burden of guilt, this Manning stain.[32]

The theme of incest appears with some frequency in his fiction— clearly in "Alice Doane's Appeal" and "Rappaccini's Daughter" and by intimation in *The Marble Faun*, "Grimshawe," "Septimius Felton," and "The Dolliver Romance." The subject poses difficulties: as several critics have noted, Elizabeth is the name of his mother and older sister. As we shall see, he also deals with parricide, fratricide, and matricide, usually by displacement, which veils the fantasies except from prying biographers.

To the end of his life Hawthorne kept not a "secret," as Melville alleged, but rather secrets—for he was in quest of a father, a mother, and perhaps even a brother to find security in a cold universe. Such longings he would never have revealed to Melville or to anyone else, at least not directly, only behind veils.

Because of the attention accorded to the long-lived and agressive sister Elizabeth, the much less colorful younger sister Maria Louisa had been neglected. She left no reminiscences and because of her early death in 1852 was not involved in protecting the memory of her brother. In the family she was called Louisa, probably to avoid confusion with Aunt Maria Manning. Unlike Elizabeth, Louisa was placid and easygoing; she stirred no waves and was genially accommodating. Yet she was in her letters pleasantly witty, without any of her sister's bite. Perhaps she more closely resembled the passive mother, except that she apparently was outgoing and not afraid of socializing. In youth she took dancing lessons and visited the homes of her Manning and Hathorne relatives. Although eligible for marriage, something held her back. She too opted for life with mother, and as she aged she ventured less and less often from her mother's side.

As the years passed, not unexpectedly she like the other two eccentric and unworldly women became a recluse. At least she dared to visit her brother and his family, not without trepidation and last-minute changes of plans. She apparently had to steel herself whenever she left her environs. Since her mother and sister would have little to do with household chores, Louisa performed the necessary services to keep the family functioning and in contact with the rest of the world. Everybody seemingly loved this self-effacing, passive sister. Louisa's was to be a brief, quiet life, as fulfilled perhaps as she could tolerate.

"The Gentle Boy"

No biographer is able to re-create adequately the most important years of a subject's life, the formative period when the child is seeking tactilely, emotionally, and verbally to cope with the seemingly gigantic puzzles of existence. There is no way to recapture the almost overwhelming excitements and equally overwhelming despairs of the years that constitute the underpinnings of the subject's life. What little we learn rests upon screened recollections and perceptions influenced by later events, failed dreams, and disappointed desires. Or members of the family— Elizabeth Hawthorne is an instance—may shape their recollections in terms of what for a variety of reasons they want the public and posterity to believe.

In many respects fiction is a child's world—or childscape—in which the macrocosm is viewed from the perspective of the suffering, victimized child. Only rarely does fiction deal justly with the difficulties of parents viewed from their perspective. Dickens's fictional universe achieves much of its powerful sway and its truthfulness because it is peopled with menacing, oversized adults eager to do in defenseless children, and we as readers identify with their plight, which is our plight in our conscious and unconscious perceptions of our own youth.

Near the end of his life Hawthorne confirmed that "The Gentle Boy" was one of the earliest of his tales. It is his quintessential childscape, composed of his memories of loneliness, feelings of rejection and loss, and, to draw upon his description of Ilbrahim's life, "moments of deep depression." Ilbrahim's lot is Hawthorne's burden, his reinterpretation of Christian's burden. If his youth was not so melancholy as that depicted in his fiction—Elizabeth insisted that his was a happy childhood—the truth is, simply, that he viewed it and felt it in that way. The depiction never altered even as he found fame, established a family of his own, and grew in years. Time healed no losses, altered no perspectives. It rarely does.[1]

At the center of his childscape is a beautiful youth—with the name of Ilbrahim in "The Gentle Boy," Pearl in *The Scarlet Letter,* or Ned in "Etherege" and "Grimshawe," all of whom resemble Hawthorne himself. The adult world—symbolized by a steam engine in "The Artist of the Beautiful"—hurts these fragile youths of otherworldly beauty who from the beginning have known only suffering. "If you know anything of me," Ned comments at one point, "you know how I sprang out of mystery, akin to none, a thing concocted out of the elements, without visible agency—how, all through my boyhood, I was alone; how I grew up without a root, yet continually longing for one—longing to be connected with somebody—and never feeling myself so."[2]

Hawthorne's childscape is a universe of "wounded love," of orphans, of parents who betray their offspring through death or other forms of abandonment, of quests for roots and an ancestral home or Eden, of circular journeys which return the victim to the scene of the crime, the place of birth. In age Hawthorne still wondered: "Where the child got the tenderness which a child needs to live upon is a mystery to me." He had not found the answer to the personal mystery, his own survival.[3]

"The Gentle Boy" is the story of a beautiful youth called Ilbrahim, a Quaker with a Turkish name who at six years of age is orphaned by the Puritan theocracy because of the religious beliefs of his parents. On an autumn day about 1659, a "slender and light-clad little boy" leans "his face upon a hillock of fresh-turned and half-frozen earth." Half-starved because the jailers have denied him and his father food, he has witnessed his father's hanging from a scaffold beneath a fir tree and has watched his mother disappear into the wilderness, "to perish there by hunger or wild beasts." The authorities spare the child in what they consider an act of kindness but make no provision for his welfare.

The truth, however, is that the Puritans have made official and seemingly final an orphandom which began almost at birth, since Ilbrahim's parents have sacrificed him to their religious persuasion. For years their flights from country to country denied the youth the opportunity to establish roots in any society or to form relationships. As his mother later reveals in her wild harangue to the Puritan congregation, she has placed God's will, as intuited by her inner light, above the nurturing of Ilbrahim. If the lad wishes himself dead—three times he insists that "my home is here" on the grave of his father—it is not an instance of nineteenth-century sentimentality but an all-too-human response of a child who, denied the love needed to survive in an unloving environment, represses his rage and craves the release of death to escape terrors and losses too gigantic for his undeveloped body and his hungry heart to deal with.

Ilbrahim is found on his father's grave by Tobias Pearson, a Puritan who with difficulty has struggled into middle age, hounded earlier by financial failure in England and then, in the New World, robbed of his children who could not survive transplantation to the harsh climate of New England. According to the Puritan hierarchy, Tobias has been punished by the loss of children because of his materialistic motivations in coming to the new Eden. In an attempt to remake his life and at the same time to gain community approval, he becomes "a Representative to the General Court, and an approved Lieutenant in the train-bands." His semimilitary attire veils an underlying anxiety which evidences itself in tremulousness, pallor, and vacillation.

When Tobias discovers Ilbrahim and lays a hand on his shoulder, the boy trembles "under his hand," which becomes the central motif in the tale, expressive of a desperate emotional need. When the Puritan learns that Ilbrahim is a Quaker he withdraws his hand "as if he were touching a loathsome reptile." Then, with characteristic vacillation, his fear of censure by the community giving way to compassion, he takes up the boy "in his arms," wraps him in his cloak, and carries him: "'Look up, child,' said the Puritan to Ilbrahim, whose faint head had sunk upon his shoulder, 'there is our home.'"

Tobias's wife, Dorothy, "a matronly woman," sits before a fire. Dramatically but tenderly, Tobias thrusts aside the cloak and unveils Ilbrahim's face. "Be kind to him," he says to his wife, "even as if he were of those dear ones who have departed from us." Such advice is scarcely necessary to a woman with an infinite capacity to love. "Dry your tears," she says, "and be my child, as I will be your mother." When she puts the child to bed that evening he occupies "the little bed, from which her own children had successively been borne to another resting place."

The reaction of the townspeople to the "adoption" of the orphaned child is immediate and hostile, and Tobias is "both hissed and hooted." When the three go to Sabbath services, Ilbrahim, "clad in the new mourning suit," walks between Tobias and Dorothy, "each holding a hand." The Puritan adults gaze stonily at the trio, and Ilbrahim hears "the reviling voices of the little children." At this first confrontation Ilbrahim is betrayed, not by Dorothy, who draws him protectively "closer to her," but by Tobias, who wavers self-protectively, finding "it difficult to sustain their united and disapproving gaze." Trapped by the fears of his years, Tobias cannot know what his momentary hesitation means to an unusually sensitive youth. If the boy is "wanting in the stamina for self-support," Tobais is paralyzed by "self-suspicion" and "nervous agitation." The agony of the relationship between "father and son" is that both have deep dependency needs. Fearful of censure and unsure of himself, perhaps even uncomfortable in the role of father, Tobias cannot make the personal loving gesture to Ilbrahim, his affection growing "daily less productive of familiar caresses."

After the clergyman in "black velvet scull-cap" warns his audience not to thwart God's will by showing pity to Quakers, a "muffled female"—it is Ilbrahim's mother, Catharine—mounts the rostrum and divests herself of cloak and hood. Her Quaker diatribe is as unloving and inhuman as the sermon of the Puritan. "Muffled" in her faith, she appears almost to welcome the prospect of martyrdom and the release of death. At the conclusion of her self-justifying but self-indulgent sermon, Ilbrahim runs to her and throws his arms around her. "I am here, mother, it is I, and I will go with thee to prison." At the touch of the warm hand Catharine is no longer the would-be martyr but a mother "as in the first moment when I pressed thee to my bosom." "It would seem," the narrator comments at this point, "that the indulgence of natural love had given her mind a momentary sense of its errors, and made her know how far she had strayed from duty, in following the dictates of a wild fanaticism."

As Catharine, perhaps with a "momentary" awareness of what she has denied to her son, hides her face on his head, her raven hair covering him "like a veil," Tobias becomes "agitated and uneasy," oppressed with "guilt," but Dorothy, "taking Ilbrahim's hand," offers to become his mother and asks for the natural mother's blessing. The voice "within" tells Catharine, "Break the bonds of natural affection, martyr thy love, and know that in all these things eternal wisdom hath its ends." She whispers her decision to Ilbrahim, who at first sobs and clings to her but suddenly becomes "passive." "Having held her hands over his head in mental prayer, she was ready to depart." The blessing, a "mental prayer" rather than a caress, is a nonverbal communication that every child dreads, "I do not want thee."

That winter, nurtured "with the gentle care of one who handles a butterfly," Ilbrahim finds the Pearson house a home. Within its protective shelter he is filled with "airy gaiety," "a domesticated sunbeam," but there are also "moments of deep depression," "from wounded love" and his awareness that "his equals in age, partook of the enmity of their parents." Stigmatized by his religion and baptized with a foreign name that sets him apart in a Puritan society, Ilbrahim silently broods over "a residue of unappropriated love." As comforting and comfortable as it is, the Pearson house is a prison since he cannot venture beyond its doors.

One day a Puritan lad two years older than Ilbrahim falls from a nearby tree, and Dorothy, always the attentive mother, takes him in. In effect she presents Ilbrahim with a brother. The invalid is as ugly and grotesque, almost snakelike in appearance, as Ilbrahim is beautiful and ethereal. Ilbrahim caters to him "with a fond jealousy" and relates tales "of human tenderness" drawn from the romantic atmosphere of his "barbaric birthplace." After the boy leaves, Ilbrahim does not see him again until one summer day when he discovers him with a group of Puritan boys. When Ilbrahim approaches timidly, the "baby-fiends" attack him with sticks and stones, displaying "an instinct of destruction, far more loathsome than the blood-thirstiness of manhood." The invalid calls out, "Fear not, Ilbrahim, come hither and take my hand." When Ilbrahim offers his hand, the "foul-hearted little villain" lifts his crutch and strikes him on the mouth, the mouth which has related tales of "human tenderness."[4]

It is the last wound, the final rejection. The acts of the howling "unbreeched fanatics" foretell a dismal future, that Ilbrahim will never find a home in this community to appropriate his love. He begins "to pine and droop like a cankered rosebud." For the Pearsons it is the same story continued: their children "had left their native country blooming like roses, and like roses they had perished in foreign soil." Ilbrahim recovers from the physical wounds but not from "the injury done to his sensitive spirit." He is now moody, sometimes sullen, and when Dorothy attempts "to revive his former sportiveness," he runs and hides, refusing "even the hand of kindness." Punishing himself, as though undeserving of kindness, he rejects Dorothy's love as the invalid rejected his. In his dreams at night he cries, "Mother! Mother!"

Dorothy silently endures rejection, still continuing to give of herself as is her wont, but Tobias experiences a physical and emotional collapse similar to that of his adopted son. Because Ilbrahim is "dearer to me than all my buried ones," Tobias has attempted to play father, not by spontaneous and tactile expressions of affection but by imitation of the natural father. He has embraced the Quaker faith despite doubts he cannot put to rest and suffers imprisonment and economic harassment. His love, he feels, becomes "poison," for once more he is to be a father in a childless household. He finds himself guilty, "an accursed man."

Cut off from the community and even from the child and needing a father as much as Ilbrahim does, Tobias seeks solace and guidance from a Quaker patriarch on a stormy night as the youth lies dying on the deathbed of the earlier Pearson offspring. As Tobias leaned "his forehead on his hands, his teeth were firmly closed; and his frame was tremulous at intervals with a nervous agitation." The patriarch makes a confession which he intends as a lesson. Years ago he abandoned his daughter on her "dying bed" after wrestling with two "inner" voices, one telling him to go forth and the other upbraiding him as a "cruel parent." Now after the passage of time a "hale and weather-beaten old man," he has no doubts as to the rightness of his decision. If Ilbrahim fails to find in Tobias an adequate, loving paternal figure, the Quaker fails to fulfill Tobias's expectations, for he has gained neither in wisdom nor in feeling, only in years. The tale of the elder Quaker, then, is one more instance of the failure of the fathers, one more instance of the abandonment and rejection of children.

Suddenly Catharine comes in out of the storm to announce "glad tidings," that King Charles II has ordered the colonists to cease persecuting Quakers. The patriarch informs her of the burden of proselytizing her faith and "leading an infant by the hand": "his tottering footsteps shall impede thine own no more." Shuddering, appalled, she wails, "Hath He crushed my very heart in his hand?" Her shriek is answered by "the very faint voice of a child."

Moments before he hears his mother's voice Ilbrahim begins to shiver and takes Dorothy's hand "in both of his." Catharine draws the child to her breast, where he nestles "with no violence of joy." Looking into her face "and reading its agony," Ibrahim pronounces his own benediction: "Mourn not, dearest mother. I am happy now." At the breast which the mother has denied him he dies and goes home to his father.

"The Gentle Boy" resonates on the deepest affective levels—a child's need for father and mother, home, caressing hands, and peers, for love and security. After its anonymous appearance in the *Token* in 1832 it became Hawthorne's most popular tale. In 1837 Henry Wadsworth Longfellow pronounced it "on the whole, the finest thing he ever wrote," and nineteenth-century readers from all classes concurred in his judgment that this "exquisite story" celebrates "the strength and beauty of a mother's love."[5]

Modern literary critics who find themselves uncomfortable with the sentimentality of this tale treat it as a historical commentary on the religious bigotry of all sects in the seventeenth-century colonies, old hatreds staining the new Eden. It is perverse, however, to deny that at the center of the story is a gentle child unable to live without love. The affect of the tale originates not in history but in Hawthorne's recollections of his own experiences as a child of "wounded love" as well as his awareness in adulthood of his inability to communicate feelings verbally and, perhaps more important, by touch. According to his wife, he hated "to be touched more than any one I ever knew." "The Gentle Boy" is not the first self-portrait in Hawthorne's writings, but it is the most detailed account of his recollections of his perceptions and depressions during his earliest years.[6]

Although he had the gratification of his success—"a Happiness that alighted on his pen"—his despair was neither sublimated nor lifted: art is rarely therapeutic. And so it was that in 1855, thirty years after the first appearance of "The Gentle Boy," he wrote to Longfellow, "I feel quite homeless and astray, and as if I belonged nowhere." In 1857, now fifty-three, he informed a friend that "I do not take root anywhere and never shall," and later in the same year he characterized himself as "a poor, wayside vagabond," which is still another picture of Ilbrahim sobbing at the grave of his father.[7]

When commentators censure Hawthorne's failure to keep his material at an ironic distance, unwittingly they ask that the tale be controlled and dominated by the kind of intellect that denies Ilbrahim the love he needs in order to survive. Hawthorne has chosen another course—to treat "wounded love" with an art that is itself a caress.

"Living upon Uncle Robert"

Long after Hawthorne's death his sister Elizabeth remembered that her "beautiful and bright" brother constructed tunnels of books for the cats to run through but on one occasion tossed a kitten over the fence. When he was reprimanded and it was suggested that the kitten would not like him in the future, he said, "Oh, she'll think it was William!"—the boy next door. If there were other playmates (or perhaps scapegoats), Elizabeth never mentioned them. At six, she alleged, although perhaps her memory played tricks, Nathaniel's favorite book was *Pilgrim's Progress*, which he read for half an afternoon without moving from the chair.[1]

Elizabeth insisted that her brother had a happy childhood—she was, however, correcting the depiction of a morbid, brooding Nathaniel in the early biographies—but her evaluation is not confirmed in "The Gentle Boy" or elsewhere in his writings. She likened life in the Manning household to the gaiety of a tavern filled with people, but she herself at an early age avoided convivial gatherings and kept to her room, sometimes it was said for days. Since loyalty to her brother's memory was more important perhaps than accuracy, she had nothing to say of what it meant to grow up in a household with two grandparents, three aunts, five uncles, and an unassertive mother: authority lines could only have been most confusing to children who probably considered themselves wards of the Mannings.

When their father died the three Hathorne children evidently shared the same bedroom, but after the move to the Manning house, where fourteen people had to share bed and board, Nathaniel slept in a room with his five uncles. The five bachelors were all involved in the Manning business ventures except for John, who went before the mast probably a few years after the Hathornes moved in with the Mannings. When Nathaniel was four, William was thirty, Richard twenty-six, Robert twenty-four, John twenty, and Samuel seventeen. Nathaniel established a close relationship with the youngest Manning, who as a horse trader in the family business was a frequenter of New England taverns, where drunks, drifters, whores, pimps, and transvestites hung out and where Queen Victoria's decorum dampened no spirits. Apparently Nathaniel slept in the same bed with Robert, who was to be his father's successor, perhaps because he was afraid to sleep alone or because beds were in short supply in the crowded household. There is no evidence, however, as some have claimed, that Robert initiated the youth sexually.

Elizabeth could hardly know anything about the intimate details of her brother's reactions to the oversupply of uncles, but she shared his introduction to death, loss, and mourning. Both children must have been bewildered by the story of a cousin, the son of Simon Forrester, who late in 1807 "upon his return from the East Indies plunged into the Ocean & perished." Young Simon, according to the village minister and diarist William Bentley, "had long been in habits which could not promise much for his future years," apparently because of alcoholism, an addiction which was pervasive early in the new Eden. In the following year their grandfather's brother Thomas died. In 1812 Uncle John, now twenty-four, went to sea and was never heard from again. His death recalled the fate of Captain Hathorne four years earlier and was for that reason more traumatic than the death of Grandfather Manning of a stroke in April. Nathaniel was to recall John's death forty-two years later: "As long as his mother lived (as much as twenty years afterwards) she never gave up the hope of his return." Even more significant was his admission that "to this day, I never see his name (which is no very uncommon one) without thinking this may be the lost uncle." Grandmother Rachel Hathorne died on April 16, 1813, and was buried at the Charter Street Burying Point. Three members of Thomas Manning's family died in the same year—his son Thomas (age twenty-nine) on May 22, another son William (age twenty) on June 11, and his wife, Rebecca, on October 19.[2]

It is scarcely surprising, then, that death hovered over Hawthorne's imagination, that he later took an interest in elixirs and was still toying with the panacea in his last years, and that he depicts in *Fanshawe* the death of a youth only a few years younger than himself and in "The Gentle Boy" a lad who loses his father and his mother's love at age six.

On November 10, 1813, Nathaniel was hit on the leg while playing "bat and ball." According to Elizabeth, writing decades later, "no injury was discernible," yet he was incapacitated for two or three years. Apparently he refused to walk and favored the injured leg for months following the accident. Elizabeth, not the mother, wrote urgently to Uncle Robert: "I dont know Nathaniel's foot will ever get well if you don't come home. He wont walk on it & the Doctor says he must; so do come soon." Perhaps after direct orders from Uncle Robert, who apparently was the only one who could manage the youth, Nathaniel began to walk with the aid of crutches.[3]

In the autobiographical materials which he furnished Richard H. Stoddard in 1853, Hawthorne made no reference to the accident. He admitted, however, to "delicate health" which he used successfully in his "grievous disinclination to go to school" and "I never did go half as much as other boys." If Hawthorne was pampered before the accident, as Elizabeth suggested, he received more attention afterward. Even Hawthorne eventually admitted that he was spoiled, but his mother denied the accusation: "She knocked me into a cocked hat, by averring that it was impossible to spoil such children as Elizabeth and me, because she had never been able to do anything with us. This I believe to be very true. There was too much gentleness in her nature for such a task." Yet at times his mother was not gentle but behaved according to convention and perhaps Manning principles. She never carried any of her children about or permitted anyone else to do so even after she discovered that it was the only way to quiet Elizabeth. A prisoner of duty, not unlike the gentle boy's mother, she denied her children tactile comfort and the warmth of the maternal breast.[4]

During Nathaniel's convalescence, Elizabeth recalled, "a good, kindhearted woman used to come to see him, and wanted to carry him about, in her arms, as he was fond of being carried." It may be strange for a youth of nine or ten to be carried, but the servant gave the boy what his mother denied. Yet he did not reciprocate the loving service in kind, for, according to Elizabeth again, "he seemed to feel as if she was an Ogress, and hated to have her look at him, only because she was ugly, and fat, and had a loud voice." Nathaniel responded with characteristic fastidiousness, as he had earlier when he had refused to have his clothes made by an "extremely plain" woman.[5]

The patient remained stubborn and uncooperative, and recovery was slow. Many doctors from Salem and elsewhere, including his future father-in-law, Dr. Nathaniel Peabody, examined and prescribed but produced neither cure nor diagnosis of the injury. Soon one leg was growing more slowly than the other. Only by January 20, 1815, was his mother finally confident. "Nathaniel has," she wrote, "entirely recovered the use of his foot, and walks as well as he did before he was lame, his joy was great, when he found he could walk without his crutches." She attributed the cure to a Dr. Smith of Hanover, who advised pouring cold water on his foot every morning, a remedy that sounds like the homeopathic nonsense to which some in that age were addicted. The mother was premature, for the son had at least one serious relapse during which he went back on crutches.[6]

The disability appears to have had psychological as well as physical origins. It occurred within a year of two traumatic deaths, which reactivated Nathaniel's memory of the death of his father four years earlier. Nathaniel was moved by the almost uncontrollable grief of his Grandmother Manning, who had lost a husband and son in the same year. He may even have envied her expression of grief: he never learned how to mourn. Robert became the head of the household, even though he was younger than William and Richard, because he was able to manage the family business interests as well as the nephew who shared his bed. The accident enabled Nathaniel to stay at home and to confirm his place and importance in the new family structure. He may have used his disability to guide and control the responses of his elders. He also may have had reasons for withdrawing from his peers. His beauty and seeming effeminacy, as well as aloofness, may have made acceptance difficult and provoked ridicule. His understanding of the cruelties of children is made amply clear in the harsh rejections Ilbrahim and Pearl experience at the hands of playmates. Nathaniel may also have needed time to order his life, and so he withdrew from Salem society into the seeming security of 12 Herbert Street. Finally, his withdrawal would seem to imitate his mother's and to comment upon it.

During what was a kind of self-imprisonment the boy's education continued at home with no peers present and no competitors. Joseph Emerson Worcester, who later was to become a famous lexicographer and rival of Noah Webster, came daily to Herbert Street to hear his lessons. Perhaps Worcester's philological conservatism and devotion to English examples influenced the development of Hawthorne's elegantly conservative, fastidiously correct prose style, which had more than a few similarities to aspects of his personality.

While he was convalescing, according to Elizabeth, "he acquired the habit of constant reading." He read Shakespeare, Spenser, Rousseau, and, above all others, Bunyan. He observed toward the end of his life that "my native propensities were towards Fairy Land," and he entered "Fairy Land" by way of Bunyan more than through Shakespeare or Spenser. He never outgrew Christian or the Delectable Mountains, the Slough of Despond, and the other delightful charades of the allegorical drama which on one level are frighteningly real because they evoke subterranean fears and anxieties but on another level are protectively unreal and external—wavering in and out of reality and belief, in and out of time. Bronson Alcott could have been describing Hawthorne's response to *Pilgrim's Progress* when he wrote: "This book is one of the few that gave me to myself. . . . It is associated with reality. . . . [It] was incorporated into the very substance of my youthful being. I thought and spoke through it."[7]

Although there can be no question as to the abiding influence of Bunyan on Hawthorne and his picture-making processes, we should not overlook his claim to have "read and re-read Montaigne" in "early youth." If the influence cannot be demonstrated in quotations and certainly not in allegorical pictures, Montaigne's skeptical cast of mind was present but with a significant difference: like his fictional characters Hawthorne was adrift in doubts and ambiguities.[8]

And so in his retreat he had time to read at random, to fantasize, to create stories, to indulge in the self-analysis of one approaching puberty with its inevitable physical and emotional changes. Such withdrawals—for recuperation, renewal, rebirth, not always successfully effected—were to appear in his writings when characters find themselves unable to cope with the demands of reality. In "The Artist of the Beautiful," Owen Warland is secretly creating an artifact—a butterfly, as it turns out—and three times in anger or by accident it is destroyed. Three times he withdraws in a depressed state and then gradually recoups his emotional and artistic resources, which are in his case not separable, in a patterned rhythm of failure and renewal, death and rebirth. When time had come to pass and Nathaniel had accomplished his purpose, which was to remain one of his well-guarded secrets, he put aside his crutches and reentered the world.[9]

Over the years, probably beginning in the lifetime of Hawthorne's grandfather, the Mannings had purchased real estate in Raymond, Maine, a small village situated on the shores of Lake Sebago, the largest lake in the southern part of the state. Robert, who managed all the family ventures, evidently placed his brother Richard in charge of the holdings. From Raymond, Richard wrote to his nephew warm and affectionate letters, not without unappealing Manning moralisms: "Nat you want to learn to Swim, & so you shall when your uncle comes home, but you must study the hard lessons, learn all you can at school. Mind your mother, dont look cross, hold up your head like a man, & keep you[r] cloths clean, & when uncle comes home, we shall enjoy ourselves as we did in Good old times."[10]

In 1816 Richard decided to settle in Raymond after he married a local girl named Susan Dingley. It was Robert, however, not Richard, who invited the nephew to Raymond. "Send Nathaniel," Robert wrote to his mother, "he may bring his 2 Suits of Mixt Cloths, & no more." Nathaniel's first visit to Raymond marked the end of his convalescence.[11]

The Manning brothers decided to build a home for Mrs. Hathorne and her children next to Richard's, and in 1818 for the first time since the death of her husband she had her own house and eventually, but briefly, her three children to herself. Since her health was uncertain, she had the security of knowing that her sister-in-law and brother were next door. In Raymond she did not live up to the legend which was imposed upon her life years later: she involved herself in Bible classes at the local church, managed her household without much trouble, and occasionally journeyed as far as Portland.[12]

Although the Hathorne children were together there only for a short period, Raymond assumed in recollection the aura of a lost paradise. They were free of aunts and uncles—and moralisms. They roamed at will in the woods and boated on the lake. Five months before his death Nathaniel informed James T. Fields that his stay at Raymond was the happiest period of his life. Louisa shared his nostalgia, writing to him in 1841: "Do not you remember how you and I used to go fishing together in Raymond. . . . I want to wander about as I used to do in old times." Even Elizabeth recalled the Raymond period affectionately:

> The walks by the Sebago were delightful, especially in a dry season, when the pond was low, and we could follow, as we once did, the windings of the shore, climbing over the rocks until we reached a projecting point, from which there was no resisting the temptation to go on to another, and then still further, until we were stopped by a deep brook impossible to be crossed; though [Nathaniel] could swim, but I could not and he would not desert me.[13]

In that rural setting Nathaniel was again ready to accept playmates, and in the winter of 1818 he went off to boarding school at Stroudwater accompanied by Jacob Dingley, the brother of his Uncle Richard's wife. Understandably, he was soon homesick, and Robert reported without much sympathy "doleful complaints[,] no mamma to take care of him," and wondered, "What shall I do with him when he comes. I think of sending him to Salem." Perhaps Robert was momentarily out of sorts with a youth whose demands never ceased and who sometimes was given to whining. In the spring of 1819 Nathaniel complained in a letter to his uncle that "the snow is going off very fast, and I dont thinke we shall have much more Sleighing[.] I hope we shall not for I am tired of winter." However, when Robert ordered him to return to Salem, he was not happy. "I have shot a partridge and a henhawk," he informed his uncle, "and caught 18 large trout out of our brook. I am sorry you intend to send me to school again. Mother says she can hardly spare me."[14]

By May or June Nathaniel was again in Salem, without either of his sisters. He had "a solitary Independence and birth day this year," Aunt Mary informed his mother, but the family allowed him to begin school on July 5. "He sighs for the woods of Raymond, and yet he seems to be convinced of the necessity of prepairing to do something. I think after he gets engaged in buisness his views of things will be much altered. we all endeavour to make him as comfortable & happy as we can." Mary restated the family creed in her conclusion, "It is best for us all to be content in that situation in wich an allwise Providence sees best to place us."[15]

Nathaniel was not resigned to the plans of the Mannings or Providence for that matter. He had no taste for business, the Mannings' or anybody else's, and, above all, he wanted company in the house of adults. Occasionally he was brash, as in his reminder to Uncle Robert that his new school cost "only 5 dollars a quarter," which apparently made it a bargain in comparison with the boarding school in Maine. Then he frankly described his situation from his perspective:

> I am as well contented here as I expected to be, but sometimes I do have very bad fits of home sickness, but I know that it is best for me to be up here as I have no time to lose in getting my schooling. I wish when you come you would bring Ebe with you not for her sake, for I do not think she would be half so well contented here as in Raymond but for mine for I have nobody to talk to but Grandmother, Aunt Mary & Hannah and it seems very lonesome here.[16]

Elizabeth did not arrive as requested, school started, and his "health and spirits" improved, according to Aunt Mary. She noted that he got up before six o'clock "to study his lesson. . . . until he went to school, I do not know that a day passed without his saying, 'I wish I was at Raymond,' but I do not recollect to have heard him say it since he went." Nathaniel, as might be expected, had another version for his sister Louisa. "I do not know what to do with myself here," he wrote. "I shall never be contented here I am sure. . . . I wish I was but in Raymond and I should be happy." Apparently in a letter no longer extant he poured out his unhappiness and threatened to go before the mast in his father's path, for on January 25, 1820, his mother wrote to Robert, "I hope Nathaniel has given up the thought of going to sea for some time at least." Robert, whatever his intention, made the situation appear ominous in a letter to Louisa shortly before the conclusion of the first quarter of the school: "I have no employment ready for him[.] indeed at the present situation of Buisness a choice is not readily made[.] however as a last resort we can bind him for 7 years to turn a Cutters wheel & perhaps better."[17]

The remark, whether serious or in jest, need not have been made about a sensitive boy bungling toward sixteen, but perhaps the uncle in the fashion of fathers and surrogates was foolishly trying to shove the boy into manhood. By the end of the month the situation had changed. "We must not have our expectations too much raised about him," Mary wrote to her sister, "but his Master speaks very encourageingly respecting his talents &c. and is solicitous to have him go to Colleg." Although business at the time was "dull," she was willing "to put down for 100 Dollars" and expected other members of the family to contribute. "I think his buckett would be full," she declared, "but to be more sedate it appears to me the prospect for his makeing a worthy & usefull man is better in that way than in any other."[18]

In this instance Mary evidently decreed, and shortly Nathaniel was studying under a Salem lawyer, Benjamin L. Oliver, and reciting his lessons at seven in the morning. He planned to matriculate in the fall of 1821. He was still "extremely homesick. Aunt Mary is continually scolding at me. Grandmaam hardly every speaks a pleasant word to me. If I ever attempt to speak a word in my defense, they cry out against my impudence. However I guess I can live through a year and half more, and then I shall leave them." After arousing his mother's guilt and indulging melodramatically in self-pity, he demonstrated why adolescence and adulthood are eternally at odds. "One good effect results from their eternal finding-fault: It gives me some employment in retaliating, and that keeps up my spirits." Then he rambled on to ask, "Shall you want me to be a Minister, Doctor or Lawyer? A Minister I will not be." The disgruntled, unhappy youth ended his letter with a flourish out of the books he was reading, which perhaps overimpressed his semiliterate mother: "I remain / your affectionate / and dutiful son, / and / most respectful, / and / most / hearty / well-wisher / Nathaniel Hathorne."[19]

The parody may indicate that he was perhaps not quite so unhappy as he imagined or even sometimes pretended. He was experiencing the not unusual confusions and depressions of adolescence. A few weeks later he complained to Louisa: "How often do I long for my gun, and wish that I could again savagize with you. But I shall never again run wild in Raymond, and I shall never be so happy as when I did." If he sometimes seemed determined to be unhappy, his quirks in diction ("savagize") would indicate that he fused self-dramatization and humor.[20]

Although the Mannings were work-directed, duty-driven, and God-oriented and seemingly had little appreciation of the potential literary talents of a moody youth who took secret pleasure in upsetting the Manning universe, the aunts and uncles tried to please a boy who frequently chose not to be pleased. On March 11, 1820, he attended a benefit concert which consisted of "an Oratorio selected from the works of Handel, Haydn, and other celebrated composers." A few weeks later he was in Boston to see his Uncle Samuel. On May 3 he went to the theater. He was growing up, for he assured Robert that "I sleep very comfortably alone," which may indicate (he was now almost sixteen) that independence from nighttime terrors was a long time in coming. In a postscript he related how one day he stayed late in the reading room of the library, a statement (as the sly youth intended) which compelled the uncle to observe: "Am pleased to find you frequent the reading room[.] hope you will Improve all the advantages of such good society." About the end of May, Louisa arrived in Salem to attend school. Mary informed their mother that "they are both much pleased with being to gether." On his birthday he "delivered a most excellent Oration this morning to no other hearers but me," according to Louisa. She attended dancing school, and sometimes her brother accompanied her, much to her delight. Their Aunt Priscilla, who had recently married John Dike, supplied a source of diversion, giving them paddles for battledore, an early form of badminton.[21]

That summer Nathaniel "learned to swim," he observed to his mother, "which I suppose you will be glad of." He ended the letter with an attempt at manhood, not unmixed with pity for himself: "I am 16 years old. In five years I shall belong to myself." In another letter he signed himself "amans filius" and added in a postscript: "Cara Mater, / Non possum dicere, ne potes legere Latinam linguam. Sed scribam te nonnihil in eam et Ebe leget." He demonstrated that he was learning Latin and no doubt impressed his mother, but he was also condescending to her, which may have been his intention after he learned from his uncle, "Your mother declines visiting Salem this Season." Almost a year later he reminded his mother, "It is now going on two Years since I saw you. Do not you regret the time when I was a little boy. I do almost." What a revealing evasion! Whether the mother understood the plea we shall never know. In his hurt eyes she appeared as uncaring and rejecting as Ilbrahim's mother.[22]

Although he was more content after Louisa joined him in Salem, his letters were not free of complaints. "I do find this place most horribly 'dismal,'" he wrote to his sister Elizabeth, "and have taken to chewing tobacco with all my might, which I think raises my spirits." Nathaniel flouted his independence but then asked his sister not to mention his bravado in her letters. "I do not think I shall ever go to College. I can scarcely bear the thought of living upon Uncle Robert for 4 years longer. How happy I should feel, to be able to say, 'I am Lord of myself.'" As a precautionary tactic he advised Elizabeth, "You may cut off this part of my letter, and show the other to Uncle Richard." Increasingly the Hathorne children had secrets which they kept from the Mannings.[23]

Early in March 1821 Hawthorne saw Edmund Kean perform as Lear

in Boston. "It was enough to have drawn tears from millstones. I could
have cried myself, if I had been in a convenient place for such an exploit,"
which is additional evidence of the restraints his family and society placed
upon the display of emotions. Now he studied Greek in the mornings and
copied for Uncle William in the afternoons for a salary of one dollar a
week, which was "quite convenient for many purposes."[24]

Hawthorne began his literary experimentations at an early age. If his
sister Elizabeth's memory is reliable, he wrote one of his first poems as
an epitaph to commemorate the death of a cat that was carried to its
grave in the garden "with a long procession," like a pet monkey earlier:

> Then, oh Thomas, rest in glory!
> Hallowed be thy silent grave,—
> Long thy name in Salem's story
> Shall live, and honour o're it wave.

Elizabeth also recalled some amorous lines written when he was about
sixteen:

> Lady fair, will you not listen
> To my ardent vows of love?
> Love that in my eyes doth glisten,
> And is firm as Heaven above.

Secretive, enigmatic Elizabeth hoarded for at least fifty years "melodious" poems which in her opinion demonstrated "a familiarity with the
language of poetry."[25]

The earliest verses in his handwriting, in a letter addressed to Louisa,
reveal that he was reading and imitating Milton and James Thomson. He
was in his own words "full of scraps of poetry":

> Oh earthly pomp is but a dream
> And like a meteor's short lived gleam
> And all the sons of glory soon
> Will rest beneath the mould'ring stone
>
> And Genius is a star whose light
> Is soon to sink in endless night
> And heavenly Beauty's angel form
> Will bend like flower in winter's storm

He admitted that "though those are my rhymes, yet they are not exactly my thoughts." He bragged "I could vomit up a dozen pages more if I was a mind to so turn over," but his phrasing indicated his dissatisfaction.[26]

While he was studying classical languages in order to qualify for admission to college, he extended his reading beyond Shakespeare, Spenser, and Bunyan. At fifteen he read Scott's romances, Radcliffe's *The Mysteries of Udolpho*, Smollett's *The Adventures of Ferdinand Count Fathom* and *The Adventures of Roderick Random*, and the first volume of *The Arabian Nights' Entertainments*. A year later he added to the list Hogg's *Tales, Caleb Williams, St. Leon*, and Godwin's novels. He planned to read *The Abbott*: "I have read all Scott's novels except that. I wish I had not, that I might have the pleasure of reading them again." A year or two later he boasted to Elizabeth, "I have read allmost all the Books which have been published for the last hundred Years. Among them are. Melmoth by Maturin. Tom Jones and Amelia by Fielding. Rousseau's Eloisa which is admirable. Memoirs of R. L. Edgeworth . . . Romantick Tales by M. G. Lewis." Out of his earnings he sometimes purchased books such as Scott's *The Lord of the Isles*.[27]

Hawthorne's boast to his sister can hardly be treated seriously: he was much too skeptical to believe it himself. Unlike Thoreau and Melville, to cite only two of his contemporaries, he was not bookish, nor was he given to quoting lines from Milton, Shakespeare, and others in the customary fashion of the age. Although many modern commentators seek literary and intellectual influences in his writings, they choose not to heed his remarkably frank and accurate evaluation in a letter to Longfellow in 1837. "You give me more credit than I deserve," he wrote, "in supposing that I had led a studious life. I have, indeed, turned over a good many books, but in so desultory a way that it cannot be called study, nor has it left me the fruits of study." After Hawthorne's death his old friend and executor, George Hillard, made almost the same evaluation: "A great library had no charms for him. He rarely bought a book, and the larger part of his small collection had come to him by gift. His mind did not feed upon the printed page. It will be noticed that in his writings he very seldom introduces a quotation, or makes any allusion to the writings of others."[28]

His most extensive literary effort in adolescence was the publication of a newspaper called the *Spectator* which he distributed to members of the family. Edited by "N. Hathorne & Co.," the newspaper ran for seven issues in the months of August and September 1820. It was hand-lettered in two columns by Nathaniel with some assistance from Louisa. The *Spectator* was a miscellany consisting of essays, poems, news notes, and advertisements. At the same time the Salem newspapers of the day were burlesqued, sometimes with more than the usual adolescent cleverness.

Two things are immediately striking about the newspaper: the wit and style. Nathaniel revealed a sense of comedy, even an ability to poke fun at himself at the age of sixteen when most youths, including Nathaniel much of the time, view themselves with tiresome seriousness. Although his letters were often carelessly written and sometimes annoyingly pretentious in their use of Latin (a vice which he shed along with adolescence), in the *Spectator* he writes in the balanced rhythms and correctness of the Age of Enlightenment.

In his "Prospectus" he states his purpose with clarity and grammatical balance:

> To commence a periodical publication at a time in which the Press is already overflowing with them, may appear to many to be unnecessary, and to raise it to eminence among the crowd of its rivals, is certainly a work requiring both industry & talents. The personal inducements to such an attempt must be inconsiderable; for wealth does not lie in the path of literature; and the wreath of Genius is not bestowed upon efforts so humble as these. Although we would not insinuate that in commencing this Publication we are guided solely by disinterested motives, yet the consideration that we may reform the morals, and instruct and amuse the minds of our Readers, that we may advance the cause of Religion, and give to truth and justice a wider sway, has been of the greatest weight with us.[29]

In prose and especially in verse the editor reveals a preoccupation with death and the passage of time—the subject matter of the graveyard school of poets as well as of the popular sentimental writers of the early decades of the nineteenth century. The dead in their graves warn us "that, when a few more years have rolled away, we must sleep with them." His friends from childhood "are in the grave," and he "looks to the Grave, as his only resting place." A poem begins, "Go to the grave where friend's are laid, / And learn how quickly mortals fade." In another poem

heroes are "slumb'ring here, / Beneath these tombstones cold & drear."
In an essay "On Hope" he concludes with a quotation—"Dying is but
going Home"—which could serve as an epitaph for "The Gentle Boy."

Nathaniel dwells on "the pangs of a seperation," which he misspelled,
and declares that home "is no longer the same as in his youthful days."
In a melancholy poem he

> sigh'd for the lone cottage where
> The early hours of life flew by,
> On wings of youthful ecstacy.

Occasionally he reveals that the platitudinous verse veils the personal
significance of his preoccupations: "We feel confident that we have not
viewed this Subject in too melancholy a light. We ourselves, after an absence of a few years from our home and friends, have felt in some degree
all that we have described, although the space of our wandering was not
long enough to suffer the affections of our friends entirely to grow cold."
Nor is he writing abstractly when in another essay he asks: "What then
is Benevolence? It is to seek out the habitation of Distress, and to comfort
its afflicted inmates. It is to protect the fatherless, and to make the Widow's heart to sing for joy." Probably none of the Mannings noted the self-
reference and the pleas for sympathy. Did they recognize that Captain
Hathorne is the implicit subject of a poem in the final issue of the
Spectator?

> The billowy Ocean rolls its wave,
> Above the shipwreck'd Sailor's Grave,
> Around him ever roars the Deep,
> And lulls his wearied form to sleep,
> Low in the deep Sea's darkest dell,
> He hears no more the tempest swell.

In the trial issue of the *Spectator* Nathaniel announces under
"BIRTHS," "Mrs. Hathorne's Cat SEVEN KITTENS"; under "MAR-
RIAGES" he weds Uncle Robert to a "Miss Mary Hubbs of Portsmouth";
and under "WANTED":

A HUSBAND, not above seventy years of age. None need apply
unless they can produce GOOD RECOMMENDATIONS or are possessed of at least TEN thousand DOLLARS. The Applicant is

YOUNG, being under FIFTY years of age, and of GREAT BEAUTY.

MARY MANNING, Spinstress.

Since witticisms of this sort disappeared in subsequent issues, it is a reasonable assumption that Aunt Mary and the others were not amused. The nephew was not unaware of the hostility of his wit, for he warns that "if any of our Readers, displeased with our observations, should invite us to a Duel, We must inform them, that . . . we intend to take a few lessons in the art of Fencing" and that he plans "to produce a stout oaken cudgel," which in one of his finest short tales, "My Kinsman, Major Molineux," becomes the weapon of the eighteen-year-old Robin in his struggle to establish his place in a frightening society characterized by violence, sexuality, and castrating father figures.

In one issue Nathaniel proposes to publish "A NEW EDITION OF THE MISERIES OF AUTHORS." Under "DEATHS" he announces that "no deaths of any importance have taken place, except that of the Publisher of this Paper, who died of starvation, owing to the slenderness of his patronage." In an essay entitled "Identity" he writes: "It has been somewhere remarked, that an Author does not write the worse for knowing little or nothing of his Subject. We hope the truth of this saying will be made manifest in the present article."

In the last issue of the *Spectator*, dated September 25, 1820, the following appears:

WANTED.

A Person to take the whole charge of the SPECTATOR ESTABLISHMENT, the present Editor intending soon to retire from Business.

The mastery of style was present from the beginning; he would simply apply the file more skillfully in the future. In the prose of the Enlightenment he would write one of the classics of Romanticism. The preoccupation with loss and death would remain. Later he was to develop a subtle sense of authorial play to replace the childish games with his sisters and the forced wit of the newspaper. The subject of his narratives would be, though veiled, Nathaniel Hawthorne, and even in works placed in a historical setting the dramatic focus would be on the family, not on the milieu. In life and art he was to assume the role of a spectator; the title he chose for his first publication could not have been more apt. At sixteen his pattern of work was established. "No man," he declared, "can be a Poet & a Book-Keeper at the same time." When for material reasons he had to take on nonliterary activities—his uncle was again paying him for copying business accounts—he was impotent creatively.[30]

With the suspension of publication of the newspaper he devoted himself almost exclusively to cramming in order to pass his entrance examinations. In the year before he entered Bowdoin College relations with the Mannings deteriorated and to his letters he appended warnings: "Do not show this to Uncle Richard," or "You must say nothing about these things in your letters." One night he had a dream about Lake Sebago and Raymond and presumably a reunion with his mother, and when he awoke and found it "all a delusion" he gave Uncle Robert, with whom he was sleeping, "a most horrible kick." In his perceptions the Mannings separated him from his mother, and he had his not very courageous revenge. A few months later he wrote: "I hope, Dear Mother, that you will not be tempted by any entreaties to return to Salem to live. You can never have so much comfort here as you now enjoy. You are now undisputed mistress of your own House." His mother could not follow his advice, dependent as she was upon the Mannings.[31]

Nathaniel continued to speculate about his career. Again he rejected the ministry as too "dull a way of life. Oh no Mother, I was not born to vegetate forever in one place, and to live and die as calm and tranquil as—A Puddle of Water." At an early age he sensed the inner restlessness that would only increase with the passage of time. He refused "to live by the diseases and Infirmities of my fellow Creatures." Occasionally he struck self-conscious postures:

> Oh that I was rich enough to live without a profession. What do you think of my becoming an Author, and relying for support upon my pen. Indeed I think the illegibility of my handwriting is very author-like. How proud you would feel to see my works praised by the reviewers, as equal to proudest productions of the scribbling sons of John Bull. But Authors are always poor Devils, and therefore Satan may take them.[32]

When he stopped posing he had a single, understandable desire. He wanted his mother to remain in Raymond, which is not far from Bowdoin College, so that he could stay with her during vacations. "If you remain where you are, think how delightfully the time will pass, with all your children round you, shut out from the world, and nothing to disturb us. It will be a second Garden of Eden." He wrote this letter two weeks before his seventeenth birthday. In his happiest romance, *The House of the Seven Gables*, Phoebe, also seventeen, blithely guides members of two feuding families to another Eden. The unrealized dream of the loving mother surrounded by loving children faded only during the disenchantment and deep depressions of the last years of his life.[33]

Bowdoin College

Venturing into the World

Late in October 1821, almost four months after his seventeenth birthday, Hawthorne set out by stagecoach from Salem with his Uncle Robert. They were bound for the little town of Brunswick, Maine, where Bowdoin College was founded in 1802. Sons of upper-middle-class Salem families almost invariably went to Harvard College. Nathaniel's uncle chose Bowdoin because it was not far from Raymond, Maine, but also no doubt because fees were lower and there were few expensive diversions in the immediate vicinity. Yet Bowdoin was not a poor person's college—there were no provisions for education of the disadvantaged at the time—and its students came from prosperous families in Maine and New Hampshire.

Established along the banks of the lovely Androscoggin River, by 1820 Brunswick had a population of about two thousand. Bowdoin College is situated on the edge of town in a grove of what Hawthorne called "academic pines," not far from the oldest cemetery in Brunswick. Like many other New England colleges, Bowdoin was modeled in appearance and curriculum after Harvard College. When Hawthorne arrived there were only three buildings—Maine Hall, Massachusetts Hall, and the chapel—which resembled Harvard's structures, but on a modest scale. Bowdoin grew slowly. In 1820 the second president, the Reverend William Allen, established a medical college, the first one in the state of Maine. In 1821 enrollment at Bowdoin was 108, 38 of whom were freshmen.[1]

There were five members of the faculty, including the president. Allen, the son of a clergyman, had served as president of Dartmouth College before coming to Bowdoin in 1819. He had compiled *The American Biographical and Historical Dictionary* (1809), which was reprinted several times, and during Hawthorne's stay at the college was to publish another compilation entitled *Accounts of Shipwrecks and Other Disasters at Sea, Designed to Be Interesting and Useful to Mariners* (1823). Allen was a strict disciplinarian and a cantankerous personality often at odds with students as well as trustees. Hawthorne objected to attending Allen's "red-hot Calvinist Sermon" every Sunday. "Our President," he informed his sister Elizabeth with all the nastiness he could muster, "is a short, thick little lump of a man, with no talents, and, as I have been told, no extraordinary learning. He is quite an inoffensive little animal, and causes me no trouble except to put my hand to my hat when I meet him."[2]

The most celebrated instructor was Parker Cleaveland, "Professor Mathematics, Natural Philosophy, Chemistry, and Materia Medica." An eccentric and much loved figure, at one time or another he taught almost every subject offered at the college. He was mortally afraid of lightning and at the prospect of a storm promptly adjourned his class. Because he feared dogs he rarely ventured out of his house at night and was reported when he spied a dog in the distance to have abandoned two young ladies whom he was escorting "to the protection of a kind Providence (in whom he cherished the most implicit confidence)." The other beloved professor was Alpheus Spring Packard, who served the college as professor of Latin for over sixty years. Years later Hawthorne thanked Packard for "faithful instruction in by-gone days, (and with regrets that I profited so little by it).[3]

Samuel Phillips Newman, with whom Nathaniel was to board in his first year, was professor of ancient languages and later of rhetoric and oratory. His textbook on rhetoric was widely used in the era. Hawthorne was highly commended by Newman for his Latin and English exercises, the only subjects in which he excelled in the Bowdoin years, perhaps because they were the only subjects in which he was interested. Another professor of some distinction was Thomas C. Upham, who in 1824 became professor of metaphysics and moral philosophy. Before coming to Bowdoin, he published *American Sketches* (1819), a collection of poems in which he called for a national literature. Upham wrote voluminously; among his later works were *Elements of Moral Philosophy* (1831), *Principles of the Interior or Hidden Life* (1843), and *A Treatise on Divine Union* (1857).[4]

The "terms of admission" for Bowdoin students were spelled out carefully: "Candidates for admissions into the Freshman class are required to write Latin grammatically, and to be well versed in Geography, in Walsh's Arithmetic, Cicero's Select Orations, the Bucolics, Georgics, and Aeneid of Virgil, Sallust, the Greek Testament, and Collectanea Græca. An examination in Xenophon's Cyropaedia is received as a substitute for that, required in the Acts and Epistles of the New Testament." Such requirements, limited and specific, could hardly have been formidable after students like Hawthorne were tutored for a year or two to pass the examinations. There was one additional qualification for students: "They must produce certificates of their good moral character."[5]

As the entrance requirements illustrate, training at Bowdoin was classical and religious in orientation, reflecting the patriarchal and theological principles upon which American colleges were founded in the days when their primary purpose was to prepare ministers. Students followed, without question or consultation, a prescribed curriculum which underwent few changes from decade to decade and which rested on the faculty's dogmatic convictions as to what constituted a well-educated gentleman who at the end of four years would perform his Duty in the home, church, and society. Bowdoin's professors perpetuated the curriculum on the unexamined assumptions of which they were heirs. Conservators, not innovators, they had no intention of allowing doubts to ruffle their closed universe.

The academic program for the first year reveals that assignments were not onerous and that a great deal of time was provided for reviews preceding formal examinations:

> *First Term.* Græca Majora (extracts from Xenophon's Anabasis and Heroditus); Livy (2 books); Lacroix's Arithmetic and Euler's Algebra.
>
> *Second Term.* Græca Majora (extracts from Thucydides, Lysias, Isocrates, Polyaenus, and Theophrastas); Livy finished (5 books); Lacroix's Algebra.
>
> *Third Term.* Græca Majora (Demosthenes and Xenophon's Memo-

rabilia); Excerpta Latina (extracts from Paterculus and Pliny's Letters); Murray's English Grammar; Lacroix's Algebra finished.

Six weeks preceding the annual examination are spent in review of the studies of the year.

During the whole year. Weekly translations into Latin and Greek; private Declamations; Recitations from the Bible every Sunday evening.[6]

The college year was divided into three quarters, the first of which began near the end of October and ran to the Christmas vacation. Tuition was $24.00, room rent $10.00, and the cost of board between $1.50 and $2.00 a week, or about twenty-five cents a day. Room services such as sweeping and bed-making amounted to about $3.00 annually. Wood sold for $1.00 a cord, but such costs are quaint and virtually meaningless unless measured against wages and price levels prevailing in Brunswick and Maine in the 1820s, during which Commons Hall, a brick building, was erected at a cost of $1,750.00.[7]

Student life was as severely regimented as the curriculum of the college. Students were awakened at six o'clock by the ringing of the chapel bell. They attended morning prayers, conducted by the president of the college, and then went to their first recitation of the day. This was followed by breakfast, some time for recreation, and a study period beginning at nine o'clock. Two hours later students attended the midday recitation. At noon they could go to the library of a few thousand books which was open for one hour each day. A freshman was permitted to take out only one book at a time. Then came dinner, more time for exercise, and a second study hall starting at two o'clock, which lasted until the afternoon recitation at four. After the final class came evening prayers, dinner, and relaxation. At eight o'clock students were again expected to be studying in their rooms. The day, then, was divided into almost equal thirds, for recitations, study, and recreation.[8]

Publicly, at least, members of the faculty took their roles as substitute parents seriously, discipline being a preoccupation of the college community. The first president had devoted much of his inaugural address to the subject, which no doubt indicated the importance of discipline as well as a lack of faith in the student species. But the students at Bowdoin did not always inspire faith, and the compilations of the executive government of the college itemizing infractions of the rules and the resultant punishments were long. There was little wrist-slapping at Bowdoin. After a warning, fines were assessed, which sometimes ran as high as fifty cents, the sum needed to pay for meals for two days. When the violations were major, letters were sent to parents and suspension followed. Seventeenth-century Puritans were no more exacting than nineteenth-century academicians, as the following rules make clear:

> No student shall eat or drink in any tavern unless in company with his parent or guardian, nor attend any theatrical entertainment or any idle show in Brunswick or Topsham, nor frequent any tavern nor any house or shop after being forbidden by the President or other Instructor . . . nor play at cards, billiards, or any game of hazard nor at any game whatever for money or other things of value nor without permission keep a gun or pistol, nor discharge one nor go shooting or fishing.
>
> No student shall be concerned in loud and disorderly singing in College, in shouting or clapping of hands, nor in any Bacchanalian conduct disturbing the quietness and dishonorable to the character of a literary institution. . . .
>
> Students must be in their rooms Saturday and Sunday evenings and abstain from diversions of every kind. They who profane the Sabbath by unnecessary business, visiting or receiving visits, or by walking abroad, or by an amusement, or in other ways, may be admonished or suspended.[9]

One of the worst offenses, and apparently one of the most frequent, was drunkenness. A college apologist years later attributed the alcoholic indulgence to "the habits of society" in the first decades of the century and to the number of wealthy students at the college: "The temptation to drink to excess . . . was surely far greater than at the present day." The commentator evidently knew little about the students of his day and was unaware that drunkenness was one of the major misdeeds in Puritan times as well as a characteristic of all social groups.[10]

At Bowdoin the alcoholic orgies took place at Ward's Tavern, which was located at the corner of the college grounds closest to the village. In Hawthorne's day it was presided over by Ward's thirty-year-old daughter, who continued a long New England tradition that permitted women to run taverns. Much of the drinking, however, was done privately, for many Bowdoin students learned early another use for their lamp-fillers.

One suspects that, despite the injunctions of the presidents and the code of crimes and punishments as well as the long lists of infractions, enforcement was lax. At a small college of slightly over one hundred students in a rural village, it should have been difficult for the students to get away with very much if surveillance had been strict. Perhaps it was not only Professor Cleaveland who feared to venture out after dark, or perhaps despite what youths thought the faculty remembered their own adolescent years.[11]

According to Robert Manning, Hawthorne was "doubtful" all the way from Salem to Brunswick that he would pass the entrance examination. Wisely, if cautiously, Manning "encouraged him as much as possible." Hawthorne passed the examination seemingly with little difficulty, which in view of his eighteen months of preparation was scarcely surprising.[12]

His roommate for two years was Alfred Mason, son of Jeremiah Mason, a distinguished lawyer in Portsmouth, New Hampshire. Alfred Mason performed two valuable services. He introduced Hawthorne to Horatio Bridge and also provided a means for him to wring money out of a family which could at times be generous but could also be embarrassingly tight-fisted. Because of his association with Mason, it became, Hawthorne declared, "absolutely necessary that I should make as good an appearance as he does." It was an adroit tactic on his part since the Mannings were impressed with the Mason relationship but not, as the nephew soon found out, to the point of changing their life-style completely.[13]

Before Robert Manning left Brunswick, he supervised the purchase of some furniture and supplies but left his nephew "so small a sum as after Buying wood & candles will be sufficient to procure him those small articles which are absolutely necessary." The fact that William Manning secretly gave his nephew a gift before he left Salem confirms the parsimoniousness of Robert Manning. For the next four years Hawthorne was short of funds, or so he claimed in letters to his uncle, mother, and sisters. The shortage was almost his sole subject. He wrote rarely and then claimed either to be working diligently or to have nothing of interest to report. By omission and brevity he made the years more drab than they were, although possibly he failed to record diversions (until he got himself into trouble) because the family would have believed that he was squandering time and, worse, money, neglecting Duty and God.[14]

After settling his nephew into his room at the beginning of the first term, it was Robert's impression that the "Laws of the Institution . . .

were irksome at first to him but habit already began to have a very per-
ceptable influence." The uncle's judgment was premature. Within a week
or two Hawthorne himself concluded, pragmatically, "The laws of the
College are not at all too strict, and I do not have to study near so hard
as I did in Salem," a discovery which American students have made about
college since the beginning of the republic. Hawthorne may not have
bragged when he informed his sister Elizabeth that he studied only three
hours a day although the college decreed seven hours of preparation:
"The lessons are so short that I want employment the greatest part of
the time."[15]

It is difficult to assess the intellectual and artistic influence of a college
or of professors. Hawthorne was thoroughly trained and disciplined aca-
demically when he arrived at Bowdoin, wrote a clean and classical prose,
and had been for many years reading widely in romances from Spenser
to Scott. Although declamation was part of the Bowdoin curriculum,
Hawthorne somehow managed to make only one appearance before an
official college audience in his four years at college. He refused to participate in commencement and did not deliver another public speech until his
consular position made it unavoidable while he was in England in the
1850s.[16]

The most meaningful part of Hawthorne's Bowdoin experience was his
long-delayed socialization. For the first time he formed close relationships
with his peers and began friendships that lasted a lifetime, with Franklin
Pierce, who was a year ahead of him, with Horatio Bridge, and to a lesser
degree with Jonathan Cilley.

Pierce was the son of a distinguished soldier in the Revolutionary War
who was twice governor of New Hampshire. When thirty years later
Hawthorne wrote Pierce's campaign biography for the presidential race
of 1852, he described the young Pierce in a warm, affectionate passage
that could have come from one of his tales:

> He was then a youth, with the boy and man in him, vivacious, mirth-
> ful, slender, of a fair complexion, with light hair that had a curl in it:
> his bright and cheerful aspect made a kind of sunshine, both as re-
> garded its radiance and its warmth; insomuch that shyness of dispo-
> sition, in his associates, could well resist its influence.[17]

No doubt because of Pierce, Hawthorne joined the Athenean Society,
which gave him access to a library of about eight hundred volumes. The

two youths served on the standing committee, which until 1832 was Hawthorne's "first and last appearance in public life." Recalling the experience in the Pierce biography Hawthorne wrote, "His slender and youthful figure rises before my mind's eye, at this moment, with the air and step of a veteran . . . as well became the son of a revolutionary hero." Such was the impact of Pierce that Hawthorne performed "the only military service in my life" as "a private soldier" in a college company of which Pierce was an officer. Although for many years the two men were not to be intimate, one following a political career and the other seeking to establish intercourse with the world through writing, Pierce was a supportive older brother to the very last hours of Hawthorne's life.[18]

Hawthorne formed an even closer relationship with Horatio Bridge, the son of a judge and wealthy banker in Augusta, Maine. Years after graduation he confirmed the bond in the preface to *The Snow-Image* (1851):

> . . . we were lads together at a country college,—gathering blueberries, in study-hours, under those tall academic pines; or watching the great logs, as they tumbled along the current of the Androscoggin; or shooting pigeons and grey squirrels in the woods; or bat-fowling in the summer twilight; or catching trouts in that shadowy little stream which, I suppose, is still wandering riverward through the forest. . . .

They had been, he was now free to acknowledge, "two idle lads, . . . doing a hundred things the Faculty never heard of, or else it had been the worse for us."[19]

Even though, as he admitted, he occasionally in prefaces arranged "some of the ordinary facts of life in a slightly idealized and artistic guise," their friendship constituted an idyllic and memorable interlude in his life. Apparently Bridge believed Hawthorne "overvalued" him, but Sophia Hawthorne after her husband's death reassured him: "He had the utmost reliance upon you, and reposed upon it with infinite satisfaction. It seems to me not a small merit to have inspired in him such respect, love and trust as he invariably expressed for you. . . . he had no more thorough friend than you in the world, and I know he thought so."[20]

After the early biographers began to delineate Hawthorne's life almost invariably in grays and blacks and readers emphasized the "hell-fired" aspects of his genius, Bridge put together his reminiscences with the intention of revealing that there "was much more of fun and frolic in his disposition than his published writings indicate." He confirmed the observations Hawthorne made in *The Snow-Image*. They took long walks together, drank together, and made visits to a local fortune-teller who read their futures in a cracked teacup or "from a soiled pack of cards." When Hawthorne was joshed too much at a "convivial" meeting, he chose the biggest of his tormentors, who had a reputation as a pugilist, and quietly told him that he had had enough. "His bearing was so resolute," Bridge writes, "and there was so much of danger in his eye, that no one afterwards alluded to the offensive subject in his presence."[21]

On their walks in the woods along the Androscoggin River when they ignored the college rules, they sometimes stopped indulging in the usual undergraduate chatter and recited poetry. On one moonlit evening Bridge leaned over the railing of a bridge across the river and began to recite the dialog on another moonlit night between Lorenzo and Jessica in the fifth act of *The Merchant of Venice*. Hawthorne responded "in his deep, musical tones" with verses written before he came to college, expressing sincerely but banally feelings of loss and separation.

> We are beneath the dark blue sky,
>   And the moon is shining bright.
> Oh, what can lift the soul so high
>   As the glow of a summer night,
> When all the gay are hushed to sleep,
> And they who mourn forget to weep
>   Beneath the gentle light?
>
> Is there no holier, happier land
>   Among those distant spheres.
> Where we may meet that shadow band,
>   The dead of other years,
> Where all the day the moonbeams rest,
> And where at length the souls are blest
>   Of those who dwell in tears?[22]

Theirs was a warm, sometimes adolescently ardent, enduring relationship in which the quiet, seemingly passive Hawthorne, abetted by the aura about his person and manner, his seductive shyness, and his obvious need for a brother or strong male figure, assumed a dependent role. According to Bridge, Hawthorne had a "high appreciation of the sex," yet "while a collegian, rarely sought or accepted the acquaintance of the young ladies of the village," although it was rumored that he was interested in Professor Cleaveland's maid. In their senior year Jonathan Cilley and Hawthorne each pledged to pay the other "a barrel of best old Madeira wine" if he was not twelve years later "a married man or a widower." On the due date Cilley admitted that he had misjudged Hawthorne "in the line matrimonial," while he himself was the father of six children "more or less." Cilley was glad that Hawthorne was achieving a reputation as a writer, "but just now it would have pleased me more to have heard that you were about to become the author and father of a legitimate and well-begotten boy than book." In contrast Hawthorne and Bridge even after graduation discussed women and marriage like two hesitant adolescents. Both dallied, and marriage overtook Hawthorne at thirty-eight, Bridge four years later in 1846.[23]

When Hawthorne jauntily informed his mother that he would be an author, he was not sure of himself then or later. When the two students discussed their futures, Bridge "foretold his success if he should choose literature as a profession." "I know not whence your faith came," Hawthorne wrote in the preface to *The Snow-Image*, but during the college years "it was your prognostic of your friend's destiny, that he was to be a writer of fiction." When in the difficult decade after graduation Hawthorne was depressed, without confidence in himself, fumbling for direction, sometimes talking of suicide, his confidant was Bridge, who handled him firmly but kindly and then destroyed the letters as directed, like a true friend.[24]

With Bridge and the others, Hawthorne sowed at least some of the wild oats of adolescence. He began gambling at cards, drinking at Ward's Tavern and probably elsewhere, smoking, and cutting clases as well as mandatory study periods. In the second quarter of his first year at college he assured Louisa that "I have, in a great measure, dis-continued the practice of playing cards. One of the Students has been suspended lately for this Offence, and 2 of our Class have been fined. I narrowly escaped detection myself, and mean for the future to be more carefull." Here he referred to indiscretions committed in the first quarter, but he was not to escape punishment. By the end of the following month "my unfortunate self" had been fined fifty cents. One of the card players had been dismissed and two suspended.

If I am again detected I shall have the honour of being suspended. When the President asked what we played for, I thought proper to inform it was 50 cts. although it happened to be a Quart of Wine, but if I had told him of that he would probably have fined me for having a blow. There was no untruth in the case, as the wine cost 50 cts. I have not played at all this term. I have not drank any kind of spirit or wine this term, and shall not till the last week.

He directed his mother not to show his letter—Uncle Robert was not to learn of the affair—and then asked her for money, having only seventy-five cents left. Hawthorne was not contrite but played it safe. "The reason of my good conduct," he wrote, "is that I am very much afraid of being suspended if I continue any longer in my old courses."[25]

On May 29 President Allen wrote to Hawthorne's mother:

By vote of the Executive Government of this college it is my duty to request your co-operation with us in the attempt to induce your Son faithfully to observe the laws of this Institution. He was this day fined fifty cents for playing cards for money the last term. He played at different times. Perhaps he might not have gamed, were it not for the influence of a Student, whom we have dismissed from college. It does not appear, that your Son has very recently played cards; yet your advice may be beneficial to him.[26]

A few months later Hawthorne advised Elizabeth that he had "been as steady as a Sign post, and as sober as a Deacon" but "penniless, for I have had no money this six weeks." He denied President Allen's charge that his lapse was attributable to the entreaties of "wicked ones." With bravado he declared, "I was full as willing to play as the person he suspects of having enticed me, and would have been influenced by no one. I have a great mind to commence playing again, merely to show him that I scorn to be seduced by another into anything wrong."[27]

He did not alter his ways, and each year until he became a senior the fines increased: $1.40 as a freshman, $3.04 as a sophomore, and $5.91 as a junior. On the other hand, Henry Wadsworth Longfellow, who was one of his classmates, was fined only once in four years, for twenty cents, but neither in life nor in poetry was he destined to unsettle decorum. It was perhaps no mistake that Hawthorne and Longfellow were not college chums.[28]

Despite the close ties between the four Hathornes, they had a way of failing each other when it came to communication. Hawthorne complained that his mother had written only one letter during his first term in college. Louisa and Elizabeth accused him of not writing for periods of six weeks. He may have been homesick at times, and the women may have missed him, but, as he was to put it later, the family's inability to "affectionize" must have aroused anger as well as guilt: if the mother could not give, the children could neither give nor perhaps receive.[29]

In October 1824 Hawthorne with no enthusiasm returned for his final year at Bowdoin. With more than one glance in the mirror he assumed the role of a condescending and somewhat obnoxious senior. "I have put on my gold watch-chain," he bragged to his sister Elizabeth, "and purchased a cane; so that, with the aid of my new white gloves, I flatter myself that I make a most splendid appearance in the eyes of the pestilent little freshmen." After the play-acting he proceeded to "serious" business. His term bills for the past year remained unpaid, and, it turned out, he was

> very low-spirited, and I verily believe that all the blue devils in Hell, or wherever else they reside, have been let loose upon me. I am tired of college, and all its amusements and occupations. I am tired of my friends and acquaintances, and finally I am heartily tired of myself. I would not live over my college life again, "though 'twere to buy a world of happy days."

The sentiments were melodramatic and self-pitying but not wholly false. The weariness and the depressed periods began in youth and were shortly to be recorded in the pages of his first romance, *Fanshawe*.[30]

But the "blue devils" came and went, and there were the usual college diversions. Probably in their senior year, Hawthorne and five classmates drew up the "Constitution of Pot-8-O [Potato] Club." In this somewhat heavy-handed takeoff on the structures of student organizations, the six youths promised to meet once a week, "at which time an entertainment shall be provided consisting of roasted Potatoes, Salt and Cider or some other mild drink, but *ardent spirits shall never be introduced*. . . . Some one of the members at each meeting shall read an original dissertation or poem, and if he omit to perform the same, after recieving notice, he shall pay a fine of a peck of Potatoes."[31]

To his sisters Hawthorne passed himself off as a man of the world, a dandy, but his classmates painted a somewhat less glamorous portrait.

His friend Cilley wrote later: "I love Hawthorne, I admire him: but I do not know him. He lives in a mysterious world of thought and imagination which he never permits me to enter." Another student, writing sixty years after graduation, reported that Hawthorne during his college years was

> a peculiar and rather remarkable young man,—shy, retiring, fond of general reading, busy with his own thoughts, and usually alone or with one or two of his special friends, Pierce . . . and Horatio Bridge. . . . he never told a story nor sang a song. His voice was never heard in any shout of merriment; but the silent beaming smile would testify to his keen appreciation of the scene, and to his enjoyment of the wit. He would sit for a whole evening with head gently inclined to one side, hearing every word, seeing every gesture, and yet scarcely a word would pass his lips.

One of the legends at Bowdoin had it that Hawthorne sat in a dark corner of Ward's Tavern sipping wine, with his hat pulled over his eyes.[32]

As he entered the third and last term of his senior year and passed his twenty-first birthday, which a few years earlier he had believed would mark his freedom from dependency upon the Mannings, little had changed. As he had known from the beginning, his years at Bowdoin would provide neither a profession nor a livelihood. He had also been aware while he edited the *Spectator* that authorship and starvation were virtually synonymous. And so he would have to return to Salem and be an overaged ward of the Mannings.

As he faced this prospect as well as the loss of the companionship of Bridge, who seemingly spent much time in bolstering Hawthorne's confidence in his literary ability, his relations with the Mannings became more troubled. He may have been in large measure responsible since he was given to gloomy moods, and they may have been apprehensive as to how they were to manage a young man with talents not suited to the needs of the family business. They must also have found Hawthorne's silent withdrawals difficult to cope with.

After a visit to Raymond probably in July 1825, Hawthorne concluded that "Uncle Richard seemed to care nothing about us, and Mrs. Manning was as cold and freezing as a December morning." He had no "desire to return there again." In this unusually candid letter to his sister Elizabeth he took exception to a report to the family in which John Dike, who had married Priscilla Manning in 1817, offered a positive assessment of the young man and his prospects. The depressed state in which he wrote emerged in his self-evaluation. "I am not very well pleased with Mr. Dike's report of me," he said. "The family had before conceived much too high an opinion of my talents, and had probably formed expectations, which I shall never realise. I have thought much upon the subject, and have finally come to the conclusion, that I shall never make a distinguished figure in the world, and all I hope or wish is to plod along with the multitude." He may have only partly believed what he said, although something, perhaps the short, unsuccessful career of his father, apparently had convinced him that he too would be a failure. "I do not say this for the purpose of drawing any flattery from you," he declared, "but merely to set Mother and the rest of you right, upon a point where your partiality has led you astray." He knew perfectly well how his adoring family would respond.[33]

Toward the conclusion of the letter, for the first time, at least in extant documents, Hawthorne commented on his relationship with Robert Manning. "I did hope," he wrote, in irony and no doubt ambivalence, "that Uncle Robert's opinion of me was nearer to the truth, as his deportment towards me never expressed a very high estimation of my abilities." Although he never accepted Robert Manning as a substitute father and clung to the Hathornes, his diction would appear to indicate that half of him wanted approval while the other half accepted his uncle's devaluation. Given his family's economic lot and his own uncertain prospects, he may also have been concerned when on December 20, 1824, his forty-year-old uncle married Rebecca Dodge Burnham, his second cousin who was thirteen years younger than her husband and only seven years older than himself. His own and his family's security may have appeared threatened, but Manning may have delayed marriage until he was free of responsibility for his nephew's education.[34]

At the Bowdoin commencement on September 7, 1825, Hawthorne's Latin oration was read for him, and Longfellow delivered a salutatory oration on American literature. President Allen chose as his topic "Humility" and encouraged achievement with appropriate warnings: "It is the order of providence, that you should be distinguished above many others;—it cannot be necessary that you should shrink from that sphere, in which God has placed you, but it should be your most anxious care that in that sphere you may carry with you a deep sense of your unworthiness and guilt. . . ." This was the last "red-hot Calvinist Sermon" Hawthorne heard at Bowdoin. Whether he listened or not, he never shed feelings of "unworthiness and guilt" as to his role as author.[35]

The Class of 1825 was to become one of the greats in the annals of Bowdoin College. It produced one United States senator, three congressmen, the most popular poet of the age, a prolific historian and clergyman, and a writer of romance whose reputation continues to grow.

Evidently neither the Mannings nor the Hathornes attended commencement. Distances were great and traveling uncomfortable and expensive, but someone from the family should have welcomed the first college graduate. Hawthorne's family, however, celebrated no anniversaries and absented themselves from every important rite in his life, including his funeral.

After the public ceremonies, Bridge and Hawthorne held a private celebration during which they exchanged gifts. In eloquent testimony to their friendship and the role Bridge played, and was to continue to play, in his life, he presented to Bridge a "watch-seal" with a "carnelian stone" belonging to Captain Hathorne.[36]

When after the publication of *The Scarlet Letter* the college honored him in *Sketches of Bowdoin*, in a somewhat affected letter Hawthorne confessed, "I did not submit myself to her intellectual discipline, during my college-years, so faithfully as I ought, but endeavored rather to find out modes of culture for myself, and often went astray in search of them." He had suffered, he claimed, unspecified "penalties" for his "derelictions" and had "repented of them." Now "after so many years, I do not think that anything could give me greater pleasure than the hope (which your letter encourages me to entertain) of possessing a creditable place in the estimation of the younger sons of Bowdoin." Two years after he wrote this apologia, he provided Richard H. Stoddard, who wrote the sketch, with the following: "I was educated (as the phrase is) at Bowdoin College. I was an idle student, negligent of college rules and the Procrustean details of academic life, rather choosing to nurse my own fancies than to dig into Greek roots and be numbered among the learned Thebans."[37]

Intercourse with the World

Fanshawe

Hawthorne may have insisted that he was ready "to plod along with the multitude," but three years after his graduation from Bowdoin, in October 1828, Marsh and Capen of Boston published a romance entitled *Fanshawe* in an edition of one thousand copies. The title page cited no author. To publish anonymously was not unusual in the nineteenth century—Scott, Emerson, and Whitman, among many others, did not identify themselves in their earliest writings—but it was a protected way of seeking fame, of establishing intercourse with the world. Probably few people knew that Hawthorne had apparently arranged for publication and had agreed to pay $100 as a subvention.

Elizabeth alleged that her brother began the romance while he was at Bowdoin, but since the manuscript was not submitted until three years after his graduation it seems plausible that most of the writing and revision occurred after his return to his attic room at 12 Herbert Street in Salem. There he looked down not only on Salem but also on the Charter Street Burying Point, which influenced the delineation of the central character, Fanshawe, whose name, in turn, is not without resemblances to Hawthorne and anticipates the appearance years later of Grimshawe in one of the unfinished romances of the last years.[1]

Fanshawe reflects its author's reading, particularly of Cervantes, Scott, Irving, and the gothic romances. At twenty-four, as was to be expected, Hawthorne was unable to transcend his influences and chose to emphasize plot and melodrama rather than explore the inner landscape in depth. He had much artistic growing to do before he found his voice and subject matter. At the same time, while *Fanshawe* is romance, it is also autobiography: it provides, to borrow one of Whitman's phrases, "faint clews & indirections" into the nature of the man. The author no doubt recognized its artistic weaknesses as well as its confessional nature since a few years after publication he asked Elizabeth, Horatio Bridge, and apparently others to burn their copies. For the rest of his life he pretended that *Fanshawe* did not exist. His wife learned of its existence only after his death.

The Harley College of the romance is in a rural New England setting, near a river where trout fishing is particularly good, and not far from dense forests, precipices, and caves such as he knew as a stroller along the river in Brunswick and the shores of Lake Sebago at Raymond. Harley College is presided over by a Dr. Melmoth, an academic Don Quixote or Rip Van Winkle who has given to generations of students the love and compassion of a childless father while he himself is shepherded through the trivialities of life and shielded from its complexities by a wife uncharitably labeled, perhaps after Dame Van Winkle, "a sort of domestic hedgehog." Dr. Melmoth's home is surrounded by gardens with labyrinthine paths along which grow natural and exotic shrubs that owe more than a little to the ambiance of gothic romances and will reappear in "Rappaccini's Daughter." In this transformation of the Bowdoin environs one expects mysterious strangers, death scenes, furious pursuits (with intense adjectives to keep pace), sexual innuendo and threatened rape, and virtue triumphing in the nick of time, with the help of God and plot chicanery, over evil and the inevitable villain with Heathcliffian disorders.[2]

Fanshawe is an extraordinarily handsome youth, about twenty years old. He

> was possessed of a face and form, such as Nature bestows on none but her favorites. There was a nobleness on his high forehead, which time would have deepened into majesty; and all his features were formed with a strength and boldness, of which the paleness, produced by study and confinement, could not deprive them. The ex-

pression of his countenance was not a melancholy one;—on the contrary, it was proud and high—perhaps triumphant—like one who was a ruler in a world of his own, and independent of the beings that surrounded him.

Fanshawe emerges from his study one hour a day at sunset. One evening he comes upon two young lovers: Edward Walcott, a classmate, and Ellen Langton, the ward of Dr. Melmoth and the only child of a father whom she hasn't seen in years. Edward, we are told, "was tall, and the natural grace of his manners had been improved (an advantage which few of his associates could boast) by early intercourse with polished society. His features, also, were handsome, and promised to be manly and dignified, when they should cease to be youthful," which may be a description of either Franklin Pierce or Horatio Bridge.[3]

Soon Fanshawe regularly chances upon the lovers, falls in love with Ellen in a platonic and unassertive way, and is accepted by Walcott as a rival. One day the trio encounters an unattractive stranger fishing in the stream who boldly invites Ellen to fish. Seemingly powerless to resist, she complies, but when the stranger whispers something to her, she suddenly demands that Walcott and Fanshawe take her home. That evening in Melmoth's garden, Ellen has an extended conversation with the stranger, now identified as Butler, who informs her that her father's life depends upon her. As Butler hands Ellen a letter, Fanshawe appears and, with suddenly hypnotic eyes and commanding voice, orders Butler to leave. Meanwhile, Butler has confided to Hugh Crombie, the proprietor of the local tavern called the Hand and Bottle, that he plans to compromise Ellen into marrying him in order to obtain the fortune of her father who has reportedly drowned at sea on his way back to America.

The next evening Walcott, upset by Ellen's coldness, is drinking recklessly at the Hand and Bottle. Fanshawe enters looking for Butler, and at the same time Dr. Melmoth takes shelter in the inn from a violent rainstorm after a visit to a sick woman. He opens the wrong door and discovers Ellen. After Fanshawe defends her honor, Melmoth, thoroughly bewildered, leads her home. With no one to confide in and her reputation damaged, that night Ellen rides away with Butler. When she is discovered missing, Melmoth, Walcott, and Fanshawe set off in the mandatory pursuit of romance, to protect the virgin from the rapist. Suddenly out of nowhere appears John Langton, Ellen's father, who did not sail on the boat that sank and who after a separation of five or six years has returned to America to establish a home for his daughter.

Despite their head start, Butler and Ellen seem to have made slow progress, one reason (beyond exigencies of suspense) being their stop at a humble cottage where a dying woman (the one visited by Dr. Melmoth) cries out in her last breath for her son. The son turns out to be Butler, who has a deathbed reunion with the mother he has not seen for years, but he remains unrepentant, his goal wealth.

Butler continues his flight with Ellen and eventually forces her into a cave at the bottom of a precipice. Fortunately for Ellen, Butler talks too much. At the moment when rape seems imminent, Fanshawe appears at the top of the precipice and spots the pair below. Insanely angry, Butler starts to climb up the rocky mountainside, but as he nears the top he grasps a shrub for support only to uproot it and plunge to his death not far from where Ellen stands.

Later Ellen offers herself to Fanshawe in marriage, and Edward recognizes the validity of her action. Fanshawe refuses union with Ellen and soon dies. Four years later Ellen and Edward marry and enjoy "a long life of calm and quiet bliss;—and what matters it, that, except in these pages, they have left no names behind them?"

The gothic and collegiate trappings of this melodramatic romance veil, but only partly, the self-portrait. Fanshawe evokes Hawthorne, superficially, in name, appearance, and the black clothes which he perhaps prefers because of his obsessive fascination with early death. Hawthorne may have been aware that one of his classmates at Bowdoin died shortly after graduation of "dyspeptic consumption," which was attributed to an addiction to studying. He may also have been influenced by a book which he borrowed from the Salem library on June 4, 1828. In *Remarks on the Disorders of Literary Men, or, An Inquiry into the Means of Preventing the Evils Usually Incident to Sedentary and Studious Habits*, Chandler Robbins cites the case of a John Galliston of Boston, who died in 1820 at age thirty-one of a life characterized "by too great love of learning." [4]

From childhood when he played among the tombstones in the Charter Street Burying Point Hawthorne had known the grave of Nathaniel Mather, who died on October 17, 1688. After graduating from Harvard College at sixteen, Mather continued to study until, in his own words, *"He thought his Bones would all fall asunder."* Apparently he had a malignant tumor of the hip which he ignored as he pursued his studies, to the disgust of his brother Cotton, who believed that Nathaniel should have served as an example to young students. Within two weeks of Nathaniel's death Cotton completed a biography, *Early Piety Exemplified*, in which he related the tragic story of this "humble Self loathing Young-Man." At the conclusion of the romance Hawthorne informs us that Fanshawe dies on the eve of his twentieth birthday and that his classmates "borrowed" the inscription on the stone "from the grave of Nathaniel Mather": "THE ASHES OF A HARD STUDENT AND A GOOD SCHOLAR." Actually the inscription reads: "An Aged person / that had seen but / Nineteen Winters / in the World."[5]

Willing one's death was to become a recurrent theme in Hawthorne's writings, from *Fanshawe* to "Septimius Felton," one of the unfinished romances of the last years. Surely the ultimate if perhaps unconscious source of the wish was tied to the death of his father in 1808, the reverberations of which surfaced in those early tales of his youth which ended, boastfully but in pain, "I'm never coming home again."

Fanshawe's physical beauty is marred, we learn toward the conclusion of a characteristic icon, by "a blight, of which his thin, pale cheek and the brightness of his eye were alike proofs." The physical appearance reflects deep internal conflicts, as do the wide mood swings, from laughter bordering on hysteria to depressions as dark as his attire.

The first artist portrayed in Hawthorne's works, Fanshawe is deeply divided, even trapped, between his dream of "undying fame" as an artist and his longing for a simple, well-adjusted life in a society where one is not driven by the imperatives, self-denials, and feelings of guilt which burden artists. Hawthorne dramatized the conflict in the choices which Fanshawe and Walcott make. The latter as a student aspires vaguely to be a poet but without much reluctance or regret surrenders the dream for the creativity of the husband-father in the contented anonymity of family life. Walcott becomes acceptable to Hawthorne's practical, God-fearing forebears who had no time for the frivolities of art, or so he supposed. Like Thomas Mann, Hawthorne almost compulsively examined the role and nature of the artist, without any essential change in viewpoint, in "The Artist of the Beautiful," *The Scarlet Letter*, and *The Marble Faun*, in which Kenyon's choice is Walcott's.

The juxtaposition of Fanshawe and Walcott—the melancholic and life-denying isolate-artist and the life-affirming husband—does not complete the self-portrait of a divided man, which here as elsewhere, as Hawthorne was later to admit, reveals itself in a composite of all his fictional characters. Butler and Ellen Langton also play important roles in the plot and portrait. Fanshawe and Butler, neither of whom is dignified with a surname, represent two contrasting kinds of negation. While Fanshawe turns his anger against himself for causes not even hinted at in the text—we know nothing of his early life—Butler aggressively acts out his rage against "fathers" who have betrayed him. Kicked out of the house by his father, the young Butler goes to sea, comes under the pernicious influence of Hugh Crombie in his unreformed stage, and is later more or less adopted as a son by Ellen's father, only to be rejected capriciously for some trivial offense. In getting even with the cruel "fathers" he schemes to rape his symbolic "sister." By this devious route Hawthorne introduces the subject of incest which is to haunt his writing to the final years. Through Butler and a long succession of villains or immoralists, he is preoccupied with the subjects of violence, murder, sexual assault, and aggression.[6]

Like Butler, Ellen experiences early in life the lot of the abandoned or rejected child. Her father goes abroad to protect his business interests and abandons wife and daughter, as Captain Hathorne had done. Four years after his departure her mother dies, and in effect, though not in fact, Ellen becomes an orphan, entrusted first to an aunt, who dies shortly thereafter, and finally to Dr. Melmoth. Ellen's ties to her father have been weakened.

> Her affection for Mr. Langton was not, indeed—nor was it pos-sible—so strong, as that she would have felt for a parent who had watched over her from her infancy—. . . her gentle nature and lov-ing heart, which otherwise would have rejoiced in a new object of affection, now shrank with something like dread from the idea of meeting her father—stately, cold, and stern, as she could not but imagine him.

This could be an account of Hawthorne's reaction following the death of his own parent, as well as the portrait he had internalized of a man whom he had stereotyped as cold and stern not because of any specific acts he could recall but because of unassuaged grief mixed with anger.

Despite the deprivations she experiences in childhood, Ellen is not to be the victim of the past or of deterministic theory. She is the ideal woman-mother, the savior of the encumbered, tremulous male. She brings gaiety into the joyless, childless home of the Melmoths, as Phoebe is to do for the Pyncheons in *The House of the Seven Gables*. She is the answer to the cry of Hugh Crombie, whose mother like Ellen's dies in his youth: "Oh, if I had had a mother—a loving mother—if there had been one being in the world, that loved me or cared for me, I should not have become an utter cast away."

In proposing marriage to Fanshawe, Ellen voices Hawthorne's desire to believe in the regenerative effects of love through the agency of woman: "Can it be misery—will it not be happiness to form the tie that shall connect you to the world?—to be your guide—a humble one, it is true, but the one of your choice—to the quiet paths, from which your proud and lonely thoughts have estranged you?" For a moment Fanshawe experiences "a joy—a triumph—that rose almost to madness," but he is locked into the despair and negations of Hawthorne's depressions.

With all its obvious weaknesses and excesses in language and plot contrivances, *Fanshawe* anticipates Hawthorne's major themes, conflicts, and personal longings—his connections to the world and to his own feelings. When the narrator writes, "the most powerful minds are not always the best acquainted with their own feelings," he does not speak for Hawthorne: self-analysis was a fate from which for him there was to be no escape.

Fanshawe received at least three favorable notices in the month following its publication. The *Yankee and Boston Literary Gazette* on November 6 observed that "this book, although it bears marks of haste or inexperience in composition, has, nevertheless, considerable merit" and went on to say that "although the author has not as yet added greatly to his country's literature, he should be encouraged to persevering efforts by a fair prospect of future success." The review in the *Boston Weekly Messenger* on November 13 was lengthy, constructively critical, and on the whole favorable to "the first effort of a Collegian": "To the elegance of language which frequently occurs in this volume, we are pleased to bear testimony. There are some beauties of more than an ordinary kind, and they give promise of better things hereafter."[7]

In the *Ladies' Magazine* of November, Sarah J. Hale, who was to spend forty years as editor of *Godey's Lady's Book* dictating fashion, decorum, and tastes for a large audience, decreed: "Purchase it, readers. There is but one volume, and trust me that it is worth placing in your library." If the number of extant copies is any indication—there are not many known copies of the edition of one thousand—Hale's readers did not follow her advice.[8]

Fanshawe is not a neglected masterpiece, nor does its author reveal unusual promise. Yet it is important in understanding the evolution of Hawthorne's themes as well as his art and as a portrait of the artist in his early twenties, depressed, lacking in self-esteem, and more than a little romantically fascinated with death.

About the time of the appearance of his first book he restored the older spelling of the family name, from Hathorne to Hawthorne. He toyed with the idea as early as 1820 when he scribbled signatures in his father's logbook. The alteration must have had deep, almost magical significance for him. In establishing his relationship to the Hawthornes of the sixteenth century he may have felt himself free of the legacy of the three Hathornes who haunted him. But, as his writings testify almost everywhere, he recognized that the present was conditioned by the burden of the past and that few managed to free themselves of the burden. As might be expected, mother and sisters dutifully became Hawthornes—without any alteration in life-styles.

"Castle Dismal"

Shortly after graduation in 1825, Hawthorne left Brunswick for Salem and settled at 12 Herbert Street with his mother and two sisters and possibly with one or more of the Manning aunts. Since his mother had given up her home in Raymond, Maine, the family was once more together under the same roof, and except for a three-year period, from 1829 to 1832, when they occupied a house next to Robert Manning's on Dearborn Street, mother and daughters lived in the family homestead for the next twenty years. As Hawthorne explained years later, "Instead of immediately studying a profession, I sat myself down to consider what pursuit in life I was best fit for." Not surprisingly, the Mannings who had made his education possible expected him to do something for and with himself, according to his sister Elizabeth. He was in no hurry, but at intervals, no doubt when he needed funds or was momentarily embarrassed, he performed clerical tasks for the Manning firm, accompanied his Uncle Samuel on business travels which for him provided more diversion than business, and edited some of Robert Manning's articles for the *New-England Farmer*. About the latter activity he was snide: "He employs me to correct his contributions and to form them into pretty sentences."[1]

On seeing Hawthorne one day at a fire nonchalantly observing the conflagration, one of his neighbors voiced her indignation "at a strong young man's not going to work as other people did." She could have been related to that neighbor of James Fenimore Cooper who said, "James, why don't you stop wasting your time writing these silly novels, and try to make something of yourself?" Perhaps Hawthorne recalled the neighbor's remark years later in his adaptation of the myth of Bellerophon and Pegasus in *A Wonder-Book*. When Bellerophon haunted the fountain of Pierene in search of the winged horse, the villagers "told him that an able-bodied young man, like himself, ought to have better business than to be wasting his time in such an idle pursuit."[2]

The Salem neighbor and no doubt members of the Manning family never understood the energy and dedication of Hawthorne in those years in which he restlessly and stubbornly sought after fame. He was prolific—writing, revising, destroying. The little attic room which in childhood and adolescence he had shared with his uncles was now his domain, his universe, and, in depressed moods, his "castle dismal."

Late in life he recalled "the dark seclusion—the atmosphere without any oxygen of sympathy—in which I spent all the years of my youthful manhood." Yet in his well-known comment about the study, to which he directed the attention of future biographers, he spoke of his "lonely youth" and his despondency as he waited more or less "patiently for the world to know me," feeling "as if I were already in the grave, with only life enough to be chilled and benumbed." "But oftener," he admitted, "I was happy—at least, as happy as I then knew how to be, or was aware of the possibility of being."[3]

In the Salem attic he established lifelong patterns. He wrote only when he was free of other responsibilities, and he required an isolated room on an upper floor. At the Wayside in Concord, which was to be his last residence, he constructed a tower that elevated him above the roof level and commanded a panoramic view of the environs. The position enabled him to enjoy the role of voyeur-artist, "a spiritualized Paul Pry, hovering invisible round man and woman, witnessing their deeds, searching into their hearts. . . . But none of these things are possible; and if I would know the interior of brick walls, or the mystery of human bosom, I can but guess." Invariably he positioned fictional characters who closely resembled him in elevated, isolated positions. Dimmesdale, for instance, in the opening scene of *The Scarlet Letter* is on a balcony above the platform where Hester Prynne stands with Pearl at her breast, and he writes his sermons in an upstairs room which overlooks a cemetery.[4]

Hawthorne's later reputation as a recluse was largely attributable to his own self-dramatizations in which he overstated his withdrawal from society. "I have made a captive of myself," he wrote in 1837 to Longfellow, "and put me into a dungeon; and now I cannot find the key to let myself out—and if the door were open, I should be almost afraid to come out." As he wrote the letter, he allowed fancy to distort reality. "For the last ten years, I have not lived, but only dreamed about living. It may be true that there have been some unsubstantial pleasures here in the shade, which I should have missed in the sunshine; but you cannot conceive how utterly devoid of satisfaction all my retrospects are." By the end of the letter, however, in a characteristic fluctuation, his mood suddenly changed, and he looked forward to a trip "somewhere" in New England: "Whenever I get abroad, I feel just as young as I did ten years ago."[5]

Hawthorne insisted, "I seldom venture abroad till after dusk," but his sister Elizabeth recorded frequent strolls in the countryside about Salem in the afternoon. He had deep feelings for the landscape, the seasons, the ever-changing light and shadows of the sky, the reflections in bodies of water. His love of nature did not lead to the religious extrapolations and transcendental leaps of Emerson and Thoreau or of the luminist painters of the age, but he painted in words with quiet delicacy and impressionistic strokes, reality modulating into unreality.

> Last evening, from the opposite shore of the North River, a view of the town mirrored in the water, which was as smooth as glass. . . . The picture of the town perfect in the water,—towers of churches, houses, with here and there a light gleaming near the shore above, and more faintly glimmering under water,—all perfect, but somewhat more hazy and indistinct than the reality.

Only rarely did people intrude on his landscape, the warmth of the prose substituting for their presence. Like Thoreau, Emerson, and Whitman, he veiled the loneliness of the landscape by dwelling upon its loveliness.[6]

His evenings were not always spent in his drab attic room or on lonely walks. He played whist with Louisa and three others: Susan Ingersoll, a second cousin who lived in the House of the Seven Gables, Horace Conolly, and David Roberts. Conolly, a graduate of Yale, where he studied for the ministry, was adopted by Ingersoll. He was pompous, extroverted, alcoholically convivial, and unreliable. In a letter to Louisa, Haw-

thorne called him "a real blackguard—which I have no hesitation in saying to you, as I often said it to himself." Conolly received and apparently
accepted a great deal of witty abuse but after Hawthorne's death took his
revenge. He asserted that Hawthorne would have been a great actor had
his inclinations been in that direction and "if great in nothing else, was
transcendently great in profanity and swearing."[7]

David Roberts was a lawyer who later wrote books on admiralty law
and served as a state assemblyman and as mayor of Salem during 1866
and 1867. Sophia Hawthorne, who put up with unexpected visits from
Roberts early in her marriage, was uncharacteristically caustic in her
comments about "that intolerable heavy lump of stupidity & clownish-
ness" but noted that her husband respected Roberts's character and
sometimes even called him "his pillow." Hawthorne remained faithful to
Roberts, as was his habit, for he did not take friendship lightly.[8]

The whist evenings were filled with banter, jests, and horseplay, the
men amusing and playfully shocking the women. With the cards there
was another game. Hawthorne and Louisa presided as Emperor and Em-
press; Ingersoll was the Duchess, Roberts the Chancellor, and Conolly
the Cardinal. No mention was made of the whereabouts of Elizabeth, who
as the intellectual of the family may not have been willing to stoop to such
frivolities.

Most of Hawthorne's Salem friends belonged to the Democratic party,
which was also the party of Bridge and Pierce. He shunned the company
of the Salem elite who were usually Harvard graduates, Whigs, and affluent maintainers of decorum, preferring the company of middle-class
Democrats, alcoholics, party hacks, and even a boozy former clergyman,
all of whom he no doubt met in Salem's disreputable taverns. Yet he was
often priggishly fastidious about personal cleanliness and on one occasion
was worried enough about shaking the hand of "an underwitted old man
. . . lest his hand should not be clean" that he duly recorded his fear in a
notebook. He was often, as we shall see, secretly attracted to the rough-
and-ready of both sexes. In such company he lost the shyness and tied
tongue that consigned him to the role of silent observer in genteel
gatherings.[9]

One of his heroes was the greatest Democrat of the era, Andrew Jackson, who was scarcely tolerated or even mentioned in elite circles in Salem. Jackson, however, was in the tradition of the Hathornes: virile, energetic, and more than a little ruthless. When Jackson visited Salem in

1833 after his reelection Hawthorne walked to the outskirts of the town, in the words of his sister Elizabeth, "to meet him, not to speak to him, only to look at him; and found only a few men and boys collected, not enough, without the assistance that he rendered, to welcome the General with a good cheer." Forty years later Elizabeth was still surprised: "It is hard to fancy him doing such a thing as shouting." Hawthorne's opinion remained fixed. In 1858 he insisted that Jackson "was the greatest man we ever had; and his native strength, as well of intellect as character, compelled every man to be his tool that came within his reach; and the cunninger the individual might be, it served only to make him the sharper tool." He wished in a strange mismatching that "it had been possible for Raphael to paint General Jackson." [10]

Among the Manning uncles Hawthorne's favorite was the youngest, Samuel, who was only thirteen years older than Hawthorne. Sam's role in the family business was to travel in Maine and New Hampshire to acquire horses for the stagecoaches. He was evidently a first-class swapper of horses and a professional trickster. He and one of his chums had on hand a supply of "long gleaming tails" which they attached to horses so cleverly that even the other Mannings were sometimes taken in. Sam was a convivial bachelor and enjoyed operating out of local taverns which were often owned by old or recently acquired friends. At one tavern "it was like the seperation of soul and body to get him away," Hawthorne explained to his sister. "Your Uncle Sam complains that his lungs are seriously injured by the immense deal of talking he was forced to do." It was clear that he did an "immense deal" of drinking too, which his nephew somehow forgot to mention. The only thing that discouraged him was to "meet with two or three bad taverns in succession." [11]

When traveling together, uncle and nephew frequently overslept and missed "divine service, which was (of course) very grievous to us both." On one occasion they "got into the State Prison, and had the iron door to a cell barred upon us. However, you need say nothing about it, as we made our escape very speedily." Hawthorne was never censorious of Sam's tippling or trifling, probably because he appreciated such an indulgent, fun-loving companion. He also enjoyed the slice of rural society he discovered. "I make innumerable acquaintances," he informed Louisa, "and sit down, on the doorsteps in the midst of Squires, judges, generals, and all the potentates of the land, discussing about the Salem Murder, the cowskinning of Isaac Hill, the price of hay, and the value of horse flesh." If it is difficult to visualize Hawthorne discussing horseflesh like a character out of Faulkner, the difficulty originates in our preconceptions.[12]

Sam was not a roué so far as we know, although in the taverns which were necessary for his well-being he hobnobbed with the town drunks as well as the tarts and their pimps who frequented such places. Whether Hawthorne learned about the realities of sex under Sam's guidance, there is no way of determining. Despite his fascination with all varieties of sexual experience and his tendency like Robin Molineux to seek out the pleasures of the flesh, usually at a protective distance, he was generally as secretive and evasive as Arthur Dimmesdale, who with downcast eyes surreptitiously ogles the white bosoms of young parishioners.

The travels of the horse dealer and "the artist of the beautiful"— Sancho Panza and Don Quixote, as it were—took them all over New England, from New Haven perhaps to Canada. On one occasion, in Canterbury, New Hampshire, while Sam lingered over his cups, Hawthorne took himself to a Shaker service where he watched thirty or forty Shaker women sing and dance, many of whom "looked pretty much as if they had just stept out of their coffins." The men were remarkable only for "their stupidity, and it did look queer to see these great boobies cutting all sorts of ridiculous capers with the gravest countenances imaginable." Before he concluded this lengthy letter to Louisa his opinion of the group shifted. He noted their "good and comfortable life, and if it were not for their ridiculous ceremonies, a man could not do a wiser thing than to join them. Those whom I conversed with were intelligent and appeared happy. I spoke to them about becoming a member of the Society, but have come to no decision on that point."[13]

These adventures ended on November 17, 1833, when Sam at forty-two died of tuberculosis.

On September 7, 1835, Bridge and Hawthorne celebrated the tenth anniversary of their graduation from Bowdoin in Ipswich, about fifteen miles from Salem. Apparently they went directly to a tavern where "an old fat country Major and another old fellow [were] laughing and playing off jokes on each other; one tying a ribbon in the other's hat." Then they walked about Ipswich—in what condition Hawthorne did not say—and wove their way, as was Hawthorne's wont, to the cemetery. There they admired the tombstone of the Reverend Nathaniel Rogers, which is distinguished by the finest bas-relief portrait of early American sculpture. On the return trip to Salem they stopped to ask directions of a young woman feeding a pig. She guessed the obvious, that they were making harmless fun of her, and replied good-naturedly to the two handsome young men who in their thirties were still playing at being students.[14]

Hawthorne's amorous involvements during these years appear to be about as consequential as the conversation with the young woman. According to Elizabeth, who of course knew only what he chose to tell her, his heart was engaged every time he left Salem on an excursion, but only for a brief period. At twenty-seven he boasted to Louisa that a silver three-pence piece "was a gift to me from the loveliest lady in the land, and it would break my heart to part with it." Perhaps the story is true, but it rings with the reality of fiction rather than of life. He was about thirty when he returned to Salem after a stay of several weeks in Swampscott, Massachusetts. There he became enamored of a "mermaid" he named Susan, and shortly thereafter he wrote a sketch about her entitled "The Mermaid; a Reverie," which appeared in the *Token* in 1835.[15]

Susan kept a penny shop in Swampscott. Apparently Hawthorne saw her for the first time standing on a bridge over a brook that runs into the ocean. It is a vision like Stephen Dedalus's in *A Portrait of an Artist as a Young Man*—

> fluttering in the breeze like a sea bird that might skim away at your pleasure. . . . As I drew nearer, I fancied you akin to the race of mermaids, and thought how pleasant it would be to dwell with you among the quiet coves, in the shadow of the cliffs. . . . And yet it gladdened me, after all this nonsense, to find you nothing but a pretty young girl, sadly perplexed with the rude behavior of the wind above your petticoats. . . .

Reality and fancy twine and untwine, and in her shop Susan is transformed into an ethereal saleswoman out of the pages of *Godey's Lady's Book*, the true friend of the virtuous male.[16]

In notebooks and sketches based loosely on his experiences, Hawthorne at thirty wrote from shifting perspectives, sometimes chaste, sometimes almost prurient, his inclinations inhibited by his fears. He imagined himself as an Adam before the Fall, a Shaker abstaining from sex, a village patriarch beyond libidinal desires, or a Paul Pry spying from a "hermitage" in the attic. In some detail he reported how "pleasant" it was to observe a group of young women "as they walked about the island, to see the wind reveal their shapes; their petticoats being few and thin, and short withall, showing a good deal of the leg in a stocking, and the entire shape of both legs, with the mist of a flimsy gown floating about it. The belt about their waist has an excellent effect in contrast with the freedom and looseness of their lower dress." His "imaginative eye" also understood the consuming fetish of a "dealer in women's black worsted stocking [who] was so in love with the article, that when it was going out of fashion, he still continued to buy large quantities, and invested his whole property in them; so that, by the reduction of the price, he was totally ruined." Hawthorne was always attuned to "secret sin," including in this case its price.[17]

In other entries social constraints checked him even in the seeming freedom notebooks provided. One projected "hero" in search of "passionate love" settles for a bride whom he can at least "esteem," accommodating his romantic ideal to reality. Another calculated "without any serious intentions" the successful pursuit of a woman whom he will shortly desert, but "a spirit of mischief" (or fear of public censure) frustrates his schemes. Still another male in a moment of insight discovers that he can give his heart neither in love nor in politics because everything seems "like a theatre." A lover "immures" his beloved in a cavern and "feels a loathing delight in his cruelty." A virtuous young woman who attempts to play a trick on a man places herself in his power and is ruined—"all in jest," Hawthorne added.[18]

The underworld that Hawthorne lay bare in his miscellaneous jottings was filled with seemingly unrelievable sorrows, abrupt metamorphoses, fears of loss of reason and descent into non-sense, and visions of a holocaust followed by the appearance of Adam and Eve. The source of sorrow surfaced perhaps unwittingly when he proposed to "picture a child's (of four or five years old) reminiscence. . . . his little fits of passion and grief," for in notebook entries and in tales as well he insistently recalled the bereavement of his own childhood. On another occasion he wrote with incongruous alliteration of a troubling deterministic relationship: "The Frenzied Father," "The Maniac Mother," "The Crazy Child."[19]

In the public mirror Hawthorne apparently maintained that beautiful, placid facade, underneath which gyrated the shadowy phantoms such as those that haunt Goodman Brown in the forest, and despite his shy modesty and seeming self-effacement he had a powerful, narcissistic craving for fame and immortality. The publication of *Fanshawe* brought him some recognition, but addicted as he was to self-scrutiny as well as to self-portraiture, he himself recognized not long after its appearance that he had fumbled and had not realized his genius or found his voice. He set to work again, and shortly he had ready, according to Elizabeth, a volume called *Seven Tales of My Native Land,* the title of which came from Wordsworth's "We Are Seven." The manuscript included tales of witchcraft and of the sea, particularly of "pirates and privateers."[20]

When a publisher was reluctant to print the collection, Hawthorne burned the manuscript in a kind of temper tantrum, or so he suggested in "The Devil in Manuscript" (1835). By the end of 1829 he had prepared another collection entitled *Provincial Tales* that included "The Gentle Boy," "Alice Doane's Appeal," and "My Kinsman, Major Molineux." A few years later, about 1834, Hawthorne gathered a third group of tales and sketches which he planned to call *The Story Teller.* These grew out of his travels in New England and upper New York with Sam Manning. His model was Washington Irving, whose *Sketch Book* a decade earlier had made him the first international celebrity among American writers. When Hawthorne found no publisher for this collection, he issued the works piecemeal over a period of years.[21]

We shall never know how many works were burned at various times, whether Hawthorne overstated when he suggested that as many were consigned to the flames as survived, or how extensively he revised those that survived. But the record of publication reveals that between 1830 and 1834 he published from two to four works annually, that in 1835 seventeen tales and sketches were printed, five in the following year, and thirteen in 1837 and again in 1838.

Hawthorne published primarily in three places: the *Salem Gazette,* the *Token,* and the *New-England Magazine.* The *Gazette* did not pay ordinarily for contributions. Samuel G. Goodrich, founder of the *Token,* evidently offered $35 for the right to publish "The Gentle Boy," but he admitted to having paid Hawthorne only $108 for the eight contributions that appeared in the *Token* in 1837. The *New-England Magazine* usually paid at the rate of a dollar a page, although there may have been special arrangements with certain contributors. Hawthorne, who was an unknown at the time, his pieces unsigned, received only $140 for the fourteen pieces he contributed to the magazine.[22]

By 1836 it was clear that the meager income from publication, which, worse, was not even paid promptly and sometimes not at all, was inadequate to support Hawthorne's modest needs. Through his association with Goodrich, early in 1836 he obtained the post of editor of the *American Magazine of Useful and Entertaining Knowledge*. The monthly magazine printed miscellaneous articles on a large variety of subjects, with engravings, for the improvement of mind and morals. It was one of those how-to publications, filled with shortcuts to education and success, which have been best-sellers since the invention of the printing press. Hawthorne was to receive $500 for what without assistance would have been a formidable task of finding, digesting, and rewriting material and then fusing illustrations and printed matter in the necessary juggling act to guarantee instruction and amusement.

The salary would appear to be meager, but Hawthorne was at last on his own, or so it seemed to Bridge, who was delighted on two counts: the editorship would provide "introduction to other and better employment," and it would free Hawthorne from the "peculiar dulness" and "heavy atmosphere" of Salem in "which no literary man can breathe."[23]

About the middle of January Hawthorne left Salem for Boston, where he boarded in the home of Thomas G. Fessenden, a poet as well as the editor of the *Farmer*. What Hawthorne needed for his editorial work in addition to writing facility was access to reference books in history, geography, science, industry, and the arts. Since the publishing firm was unwilling to pay for a membership, he was not permitted to take books out of the Boston Athenaeum, the venerable cultural institution of Brahmin Boston. He enlisted, or rather commanded, the services of Elizabeth, who had access to the Salem Athenaeum and obediently made digests and prepared articles for him. "Concoct—concoct—concoct" was his often repeated order.

Anyone but his doting sisters would have resented his injunctions, but they understood their brother's needs as well as his cynicism about what he had to do in order to become a "useful" member of society. "I make nothing," he boasted, "of writing a history or biography before dinner. Do you the same." Later he confessed: "My way is to take some old magazine and make an abstract—you can't think how easy it is." He urged Elizabeth to be on the lookout for good material on any topic, "provided always it be not too good; and even if it should be, perhaps it will not quite ruin the Magazine; my own selections being bad enough to satisfy any body." Sometimes he dropped the banter and the pose to confess that if he had not been so busy churning out copy he would have "had the blues most damnably." [24]

Hawthorne was to have received $45 on his arrival in Boston in January. By the middle of the next month he had concluded that Goodrich "is a good-natured sort of man enough; but rather an unscrupulous one in money matters, and not particularly trustworthy in anything." This observation led him to draw an analogy with the favorite cat of the Hawthorne family, Beelzebub: "This world is as full of rogues as Beelzebub is of fleas." And so his letters to the faithful sisters consisted of three imperatives: concoct, send money, and take care of my laundry and clothing. In May, after two issues of the magazine had appeared, he received a payment of $20, four months late and less than half of the promised sum. [25]

He ranted about Goodrich, but within a week or so after the receipt of the money he had agreed, with the promised assistance of Elizabeth, to edit a two-volume work to be entitled *Peter Parley's Universal History on the Basis of Geography*, which was to be part of the series that Goodrich edited, or more accurately manufactured, with the aid of scissors and paste. The *Universal History* was still being reprinted two decades later, and no doubt thousands of copies were sold since it was adapted to school purposes. The pay was to be $100, all of which Hawthorne promised to Elizabeth. "It is a poor compensation," he wrote, "yet better than the Token; because the kind of writing is so much less difficult." Perhaps Hawthorne agreed because it was one way of insuring payment for his services as editor of the magazine and author of pieces in the *Token*. [26]

He was to be disappointed, and in August he resigned his editorship. The following month Goodrich informed Hawthorne that he had instructed the publisher to "make you the earliest possible remittance" for the *Universal History* and promised payment of $108 for his contribution to the *Token* in 1837. Apparently some payments were made, for Hawthorne had begun negotiations with Goodrich for the publication of his first collection of tales and sketches. Despite his need for money, Hawthorne refused to undertake another piece of hackwork, a volume of six hundred pages "on the manners, customs, and civilities of all countries" for $300. [27]

Not in triumph but defeat, Hawthorne returned to his attic room at 12 Herbert Street in late August 1836. Now in his thirty-second year, he was, despite an enormous expenditure of effort and dedication, without fame, money, or serenity of mind. A favorable notice had appeared in the *London Athenaeum* on November 7, 1835—"My worshipful self is a very famous man in London," he crowed to Elizabeth—but the works Henry F. Chorley praised had been published anonymously. Reputations were being established by Longfellow, Whittier, and others, but in the eleven years since graduating from Bowdoin he was little known or appreciated except among friends in Salem and Boston. He may even have feared, as he was to do for a lifetime, that he had written himself out, which is always the artist's nightmare.[28]

As always Bridge was there for him to lean on for support and guidance. After graduation, they adopted "new signatures" in their correspondence. Probably the game originated with Hawthorne, who needed both for the sake of secrecy and excitement to heighten relationships by surrounding them with an aura which permitted role-playing and distancing. Hawthorne chose the name of Oberon, the king of the fairies in *Midsummer Night's Dream*; Bridge selected what he called "the more prosaic name of 'Edward,'" which may evoke the name of the friend-rival of Fanshawe, Edward Walcott.[29]

Hawthorne became so enamored of the disguise that in two tales, "The Devil in Manuscript" (1835) and "Fragments from the Journal of a Solitary Man" (1837), Oberon appears as "an intimate friend" of the narrator: it is "a name of fancy and friendship between him and me." Hawthorne, as it were, assumes now the role of Bridge in order to comment on himself. Oberon, we are informed, has a horror of his manuscripts and plans to burn what the narrator calls "his delightful tales." Over champagne Oberon relates his dreary record of rejections by publishers. Depressed, somewhat the worse for the tumblersfull, he is sick of his writings but ambivalent, drawing "the tales towards him, with a mixture of natural affection and natural disgust, like a father taking a deformed infant into his arms," Hawthorne's imagery as usual deriving from childhood trauma. He tosses the manuscripts into the fire and believes he sees a fiend emerge in the flames. Then "in his gloomiest tone" he avers: "There, too, I sacrificed the unborn children of my mind. All that I had accomplished—all that I planned for future years—has perished by one common ruin. . . . And what remains? A weary and aimless life—a long repentance of this hour—and at last an obscure grave, where they will bury and forget me."[30]

In these excerpts from his journal, Hawthorne comments on his own emotional and intellectual state with some confusion, or perhaps conditional accuracy, since Oberon is a self-image, an imaginative figment, and a narcissistic mirror of the artist looking at himself as he depicts himself. After he becomes an orphan in his twelfth year, Oberon chooses not to follow the usual course, to accumulate gold and "build a house"—like the Mannings. Not for him "the settled, sober, careful gladness of a man by his own fireside," to which, however, he appears attracted. He claims to be proud that his footsteps have not been "imprinted on the earth, but lost in air; and I shall leave no son to inherit my share of life. . . . when his father should vanish like a bubble"—as Hawthorne's had in 1808. He will not inflict upon children his orphaned lot.[31]

At the same time Oberon admits that "I have never truly loved, and perhaps shall be doomed to loneliness" because "my soul has never married itself to the soul of woman." It is no mistake that in the self-portraiture of his fiction the males, most of whom are descendants of Narcissus, establish no enduring bonds. Like Oberon they fear the necessity of growing old and losing "youthful grace." Sometimes Oberon looks in the "glass" and sees himself a wrinkled, bald, gray-haired man, with "a grisly beard sprouting" on his chin. Suddenly he changes the picture "for the dead face of a young man, with dark locks clustering heavily round its pale beauty, which would decay, indeed, but not with years, nor in the sight of men." The same fears emerge in a dream, perhaps one of the recurring dreams Hawthorne hints at. As Oberon walks on Broadway he has the feeling that some "singularity of dress or aspect" makes him an object of "horror and affright." When he examines himself in "a looking-glass" he has "a horrible sensation of self-terror and self-loathing": "I had been promenading Broadway in my shroud!" At this point the narrator intrudes to declare that he will publish no further extracts "even nearer to insanity than this."[32]

After resigning from the *Token* in 1836, Hawthorne poured out his discontent to Bridge, who understood Hawthorne's melodramatic stances and never failed to talk sense to his friend. Now Hawthorne compared himself "to one drifting helplessly toward a cataract. . . . 'I'm a doomed man, and over I must go.'" In a series of letters to Bridge written during a period of approximately nine months beginning about

September 1836, Hawthorne tested the bond of their friendship. Apparently he shared his inner feelings with rare candor to the only man whom he trusted completely. No doubt the revelations which Bridge dutifully burned would confirm the evaluation of a sensitive reviewer of *Twice-told Tales*: Hawthorne in his writings, he observed, appears as "a stricken deer in the forest of life."[33]

Bridge cajoled, supported, and sympathized. On one occasion he cited Pierce as a model after his election to the United States Senate: "There is an instance of what a man can do by trying. With no very remarkable talents, he at the age of thirty-four fills one of the highest stations in the nation." At other times Bridge was firm and cut through Hawthorne's overstatements and self-flagellation, but he was always kind, seeking, not often successfully, to lead Hawthorne to a more positive evaluation of his own worth as person and author. "I hope to God," Bridge wrote, "you will put your name upon the title-page, and come before the world at once and on your own responsibility. You could not fail to make a noise and an honorable name, and something besides." On October 16 Bridge ordered: "You have the blues again. Don't give up to them for God's sake and your own, and mine, and everybody's." He promised "brighter days" within six months and included a notice that he intended to submit to the *Boston Post* to call attention to Hawthorne's unrecognized talent and potential.[34]

Without Hawthorne's knowledge, Bridge wrote directly to Goodrich to offer financial assistance for the publication of a collection of Hawthorne's tales, and Goodrich was ready to make the necessary arrangements if Bridge "guaranteed $250 as an ultimate resort against loss." Bridge complied at once, with the proviso that Hawthorne was to know nothing about the matter. At the same time he wrote urgently but wittily to his friend:

> I have just received your last, and do not like its tone at all. There is a kind of desperate coolness about it that seems dangerous. I fear that you are too good a subject for suicide, and that some day you will end your mortal woes on your own responsibility.
>
> However, I wish you to refrain till next Thursday, when I shall be in Boston, *Deo volente.*

Bridge instinctively found the right tone. He understood Hawthorne and his flair for gothic posturing.[35]

Hawthorne went about preparing a manuscript and made necessary revisions in a few instances to accommodate what he hoped would be a large audience for his book, but he was convinced that it would not sell. Bridge advised patience and tried to instill confidence. His letter to Hawthorne on Christmas day was exceptionally perceptive.

> The bane of your life has been self-distrust. This has kept you back for many years; which, if you had improved by publishing, would long ago have given you what you must now wait a short time for. It may be for the best, but I doubt it.
>
> I have been trying to think what you are so miserable for. Although you have not much property, you have good health and powers of writing, which have made, and can still make, you independent.
>
> Suppose you get "but $300 per annum" for your writings. You can, with economy, live upon that, though it would be a tight squeeze. You have no family dependent upon you, and why should you "borrow trouble?"
>
> This is taking the worst view of your case that it can possibly bear. It seems to me that you never look at the bright side with any hope or confidence. It is not the philosophy to make one happy.[36]

It was decided to call the collection *Twice-told Tales*, a title which may have referred to the fact that they were appearing for the second time, now in book form, as he admitted to Longfellow, but which may have been suggested by these lines from Shakespeare's *King John*—"Life is as tedious as a twice-told tale, / Vexing the dull ear of a drowsy man"—which would have reflected Hawthorne's depressed state at the time. Despite the excitement and anticipation of publication, he remained restless and discontented. "I wish to God," Bridge wrote, "that I could impart to you a little of my own brass. You would then dash into the contest of literary men, and do honor to yourself and to your country in short time. But you never will have confidence enough in yourself, though you will have fame."[37]

After the appearance of *Twice-told Tales* on March 6, 1837, Hawthorne was still "blue," and Bridge reprimanded, to little avail:

> It is no use for you to feel blue. I tell you that you will be in a good situation next winter instead of "under a sod." Pierce is interested for you, and can make some arrangement I know. An editorship or a

clerkship at Washington he can and will obtain. So courage, and *au diable* with your "sods!"

Although Hawthorne had opened intercourse with the world, he had no expectations of substantial financial returns, but publication increased his eligibility for a governmental post since authorship even in a materialistic society commanded respect and often received it.[38]

That summer Hawthorne spent his thirty-third birthday and the next five weeks in Maine with Bridge, who was supervising the construction of a dam across the Kennebec River. Hawthorne became one of "three characters" in a "bachelors-establishment." An itinerant Frenchman named Schaeffer, who taught French to American "blockheads," shared space in the house and instructed Hawthorne in French in the evenings. Schaeffer "frenchified" their names, "calling Bridge Monsieur du Pont, myself M. de l'Aubepine, and himself M. le Berger, and all knights of the round table; and we live in great harmony and brotherhood—as queer a life as any body leads, and as queer a set as may be found anywhere." Hawthorne was later to adopt the translation of his name in letters to Sophia Peabody and as a pen name in "Rappaccini's Daughter."[39]

According to Hawthorne, the three men lived together "somewhat like monks." "The only petticoat," he wrote, "that comes with our premises appertains to Nancy, the pretty, dark-eyed maid-servant," who duly became "La belle Nancy." Bridge, he believed, had made up his mind "never to be married." Hawthorne himself had apparently given some thought— how seriously in the absence of documentation it is impossible to say—to marriage to Eliza Gibbs of Edgartown. He seemed surprised that Schaeffer, despite his travels in "dissolute countries, . . . had never yet sinned with woman" and noted that the Frenchman's "animal desires are none of the strongest." But we can hardly conclude on the basis of these comments that Hawthorne himself had strong "animal desires" in view of his willingness, perhaps even eagerness, to delay marriage until he was thirty-eight and in the absence of evidence of anything more than voyeurism, except in his sometimes lurid fantasies.[40]

The stay with Bridge confirmed the high esteem he felt for his college friend: "Polished, yet natural, frank, open, and straightforward, yet with a delicate feeling for the sensitiveness of his companions; of excellent temper and warm heart; well-acquainted with the world, with a keen faculty of observation, . . . and never varying from a code of honor and principle." Bridge was more or less the embodiment of Hawthorne's ideal male, fusing masculine strength and feminine delicacy, even though one day Hawthorne found himself "somewhat shocked" when Bridge handled a swallow that had flown into the house "by squeezing its head and throwing it out of the window."[41]

Intercourse with the World
The Early Tales

Alexis de Tocqueville toured the United States for nine months from May 1831 to February 1832 in order to study American prisons and the institutions of the new democracy. After returning to France, he wrote a book destined to become a classic, *Democracy in America*. With remarkable acumen and intuition he foresaw not only the future problems of a democratic society but also the course of the development of a new literature. He was too emphatic, however, when he declared that the United States had "no literature" in 1830. He was apparently unaware that at the time he came to this country two American authors commanded international audiences. Although the United States continued to suffer for decades from a cultural inferiority complex and groups like the Young Americans in New York at midcentury would loudly proclaim their independence from England, the umbilical cord was severed, at least in the judgment of one English critic, in 1809 when Washington Irving gave birth to *A History of New York . . . by Diedrich Knickerbocker*, a highly sophisticated burlesque of history in general and New York City, or New Amsterdam, in particular. In the country's first literary masterpiece, Irving demonstrated a virtuoso mastery of his craft and the intricacies of comedy which impressed and delighted many, including Scott and Dickens.

In *The Sketch Book* (1818–1820), despite debts to Joseph Addison and Richard Steele as well as to Oliver Goldsmith, Irving transformed two stories of German origin, "Rip Van Winkle" and "The Legend of Sleepy Hollow," into American genre pieces that for almost two centuries have delighted millions of readers as well as critics and artists with their human and cultural insights. Rip Van Winkle and Ichabod Crane, the boy-man and the foolish intellectual, have become American icons, so much a part of our inheritance that we sometimes forget the genius of their creator.

James Fenimore Cooper had never written a tale, not even many letters according to his wife, when in his early thirties he took up her challenge and wrote a novel. He then proceeded in an extraordinary outpouring of imagination and energy to write prolifically for the next thirty years. In 1823 while he was writing *The Pioneers* he suddenly fell in love with a grotesque character with the unimpressive name of Nathaniel or Natty Bumppo, who toward the middle of the romance was suddenly transformed from a caricature into a hero. A myth was born. The world fell in love with his creation, and after the appearance of two sequels, *The Last of the Mohicans* (1826) and *The Prairie* (1827), Cooper had captured a large and diversified audience that included former president John Quincy Adams, women as different as Elizabeth Peabody and Frances Trollope, and European artists on the order of Goethe, Balzac, and Schubert.

Part saint, part Daniel Boone, an isolate and a firm ecumenical moralist, Natty Bumppo exemplifies self-reliance and rugged individualism as well as nostalgia for, by 1800, a long-lost Eden. Natty goes farther and farther west in search of the silence of nature and freedom from civilization and its discontents. His semiliterate but poetic speech rhythms are still in the American grain. As Edwin Fussell suggested years ago, it is not difficult to make a case that American literature until the Civil War consisted of a series of footnotes to Cooper.

A new generation of writers, all of whom were born in the nineteenth century, began to emerge in the 1830s about the time of de Tocqueville's tour. Almost at once after graduating from Bowdoin College, Henry Wadsworth Longfellow won a large, devoted public. His dulcet lines satisfied almost everybody's conception of poetry, his romantic tales did not tumble into troubling abysses, and the pervasive melancholy was undisturbing and perhaps even consoling. His patriotic pieces and genre works are, whether we like it or not, essential Americana. Always a graceful writer and a splendid translator, Longfellow remained within the English tradition and explored no new terrain. Edgar Allan Poe, however, was anything but conventional in prose, poetry, or criticism. With monomaniacal restrictiveness and intensity, with pulsating adjectives, he plunges into the horrors of the dreamscape. He is perhaps our supreme fantasist. He celebrates in metronomic poetic lines, which continue to resonate long after the poem has been put aside, the beauty of dead women and the self-destructiveness of the narrators. His is the first important body of literary criticism in America, yet for many decades he remained an outsider in American literature, until the French symbolists and the public compelled a reevaluation of his genius.

In 1836, at his own expense, Ralph Waldo Emerson, who had undergone traumatic personal and intellectual pain in the loss of a young wife and the abandonment of his career as a clergyman, published *Nature*, which is perhaps the seminal work of American literature and thought. Emerson's essays, couched in the loveliest prose of the era, offer an intellectual critique of American life and to some a guide to conduct. They resonated throughout the century, and their influence extended to a more powerful and persuasive voice, that of Friedrich Nietzsche. Emerson epitomizes what Melville termed the "Yes Gentry," those who dive deep without loss of confidence in humanity or faith in deity and the cosmic order.

In 1837, with the prodding of Bridge, Nathaniel Hawthorne identified himself for the first time on the title page of *Twice-told Tales* and formally opened intercourse with the world. Quietly and shyly, as one would expect, he joined the emerging giants of the new literary world. With characteristic modesty he confessed to Longfellow at the time of the publication of his tales: "I do not think much of them—neither is it worth while to be ashamed of them." At the same time he lamented the lack of public interest and asserted that "if my writings had made any decided impression, I should probably have been stimulated to greater exertions." There is perhaps something perverse in his excessive self-disparagement. He never mentioned the excitement and gratification he must have felt—the texts of "My Kinsman, Major Molineux" and "Young Goodman Brown" reverberate with his delight and authorial playfulness—when he was able to realize his vision and his artistic intention. Even if he destroyed more of his early efforts than he kept, the exhilaration of his successes should have provided some compensation.[1]

Whether Hawthorne recognized it or not—and it is difficult to believe that he was unaware, although that ambiguous smile of Hooper beneath his black veil may have been his own—by the time he was in his early thirties he had established himself as an artist of the first order and had presented to America some of its greatest tales: "My Kinsman, Major Molineux," "Robert Malvin's Burial," "Young Goodman Brown," "The Gentle Boy," "Wakefield," "The Minister's Black Veil," and "Alice Doane's Appeal."

It is possible, however, that he failed to appreciate fully his achievement, for in *Twice-told Tales* he did not reprint three of these stories. Book publication of "Young Goodman Brown" and "Roger Malvin's Burial" had to wait until 1846 and "My Kinsman, Major Molineux" until 1851; "Alice Doane's Appeal," the most complex and possibly the most important of his stories, was not republished in his lifetime. Cautiously and shrewdly he selected for his first collection tales and sketches which he believed the public would accept, "Little Annie's Ramble," for example, rather than "Young Goodman Brown." People then and later were unaware that beneath the ethereal appearance Hawthorne was a pragmatic artist attuned to popular taste. Potentially troubling or anxiety-producing tales of the "Wakefield" order were offset by innocuous descriptive sketches, semihistorical accounts of seventeenth-century New England, and sentimental tales. Some of these works were not quite so innocent as many early readers apparently believed: they did not perceive that Hooper's veil was an objectification of Hawthorne's and that for a lifetime he cloaked himself in secrets, a characteristic which reappeared in his hesitant, tremulous, often deeply depressed fictional characters.

Unlike Melville, Whitman, and Twain, Hawthorne did not depart radically from the English literary tradition. Like Irving before him, he drew stylistically upon Addison, Steele, and Goldsmith, as well as Benjamin Franklin, and established his voice within the tradition. Every commentator has noted his debts to Edmund Spenser and particularly to John Bunyan. *Pilgrim's Progress*, one of the first books he read, served his purposes to use the tactics of allegory for exploration of the inner landscape, which was a kind of adaptation of the old for new ends. The gentle Irving was perhaps his most influential American predecessor, but Irving's intimations received new twists of complexity in Hawthorne's hands. *The Sketch Book* hovers over his imagination, and Rip Van Winkle was to achieve reincarnation in the person of Wakefield, who, unlike his progenitor, is not lovable and is lost in a world more unstable than Irving was willing to enter. Rip Van Winkle is a quaint boy-man, Wakefield a borderline psychotic.

Some critics, particularly those with a strong historical orientation, emphasize the influence of the Puritans, who were theologians as well as historians, upon Hawthorne, but this influence has been overstated, Hawthorne being neither theologian nor historian. Hawthorne drew pictorially and psychologically upon the stark drama of the American heritage—the existence of witches, the infamous trials, and the fiendish punishment of social and religious deviants by the Puritan theocracy—but the doctrine did not engage his imagination. He was perhaps more of the school of Goethe than of Cotton Mather and viewed the world and its demonology with more wit than the Puritan heritage sanctioned.[2]

On this point as on many others there can be no agreement. Melville first placed Hawthorne categorically among what he called the "No Gentry," but he was, understandably, not quite so positive at another time: "Whether Hawthorne has simply availed himself of this mystical blackness as a means to the wondrous effects he makes it to produce in his lights and shades; or whether there really lurks in him, perhaps unknown to himself, a touch of Puritanic gloom,—this, I cannot altogether tell." Here Melville moved toward the position taken later by Henry James, in many ways the artistic son of Hawthorne. James sensed an inherent ambiguity in Hawthorne's conception of evil, which, of course, may correspond to his own: "Nothing is more curious and interesting than this almost exclusively *imported* character of the sense of sin in Hawthorne's mind; it seems to exist there merely for an artistic or literary purpose. . . . It was a necessary condition for a man of Hawthorne's stock that if his imagination should take license to amuse itself, it should at least select this grim precinct of the Puritan morality for its playground."[3]

Hawthorne was apparently about fifteen when he read for the first time *The Arabian Nights' Entertainments* in a translation from the French of Antoine Galland. The stories made a lasting impact upon his imagination, which perhaps Longfellow sensed when at Hawthorne's death he wrote, "The unfinished window in Aladdin's tower / Unfinished must remain." Hawthorne's interest in *The Arabian Nights' Entertainments* is confirmed by his borrowings from the Salem Athenaeum between 1827 and 1836: in that period ten books dealing with the Near East were charged out to him.[4]

Luxuriant tropical colors attracted him, as seen in Hester's embroidery of the A and the exotic clothes she fashions for Pearl. Ilbrahim seeks to entertain a fiendish Puritan boy with magical tales he has heard in the Near East. In "Foot-prints on the Sea-shore" the narrator draws faces in the sand "huge as that of the Sphinx on Egyptian sands." In "Fragments from the Journal of a Solitary Man" he writes: "I had a strange longing to see the Pyramids. To Persia and Arabia, and all the gorgeous East, I owed a pilgrimage for the sake of their magic tales." In "The Hall of Fantasy" he likens a building to "some enchanted edifice in the Arabian tales." He refers to Aladdin's palace and lamp in "A Virtuoso's Collection," and in *The Scarlet Letter* Governor Billingham's hall has a "brilliancy" that "might have befitted Aladdin's palace." Hawthorne was to compose *The House of the Seven Gables* in a gown that could have come from *The Arabian Nights' Entertainments* in a room in an ugly American farmhouse with a "Turkish carpet." He looked out at Monument Mountain, which was, he imagined, in the shadow of "a huge headless Sphinx, wrapped in a Persian shawl."[5]

The relevant point about Hawthorne's influences is that, without visible anxiety, he blended them into his own form and voice which by the mysterious magic of his genius incorporated some of the imaginative qualities of Shakespeare's romantic comedies; Montaigne's skeptical cast of thought; an eighteenth-century prose style; a Wordsworthian interest in childhood, although Hawthorne probed the depths and the abiding impact of early traumas more complexly; and romanticism's preoccupation with the nature of the self.

The romance, especially under the Bunyan influence, molded and harmonized with his own pictorial sense, and if he frequently in later years referred to his writings as tapestries, the analogy was more exact than most comparisons of this kind. Hawthorne's texts imprint pictures. The landscape may lack concreteness and parameters but not symbolic forms or suggestiveness. Forests, hollows, large rocks resembling tombstones, trees and hills often in patterns of three, and mirrorlike surfaces of streams and fountains have their way of appearing and disappearing, leaving vague pictures which readers then complete and unconsciously distort because depths of the psyche are secretly evoked. Tales occur in time and place but also out of time and place. Romance allows everything to be in and out of focus, the lenses at the service of the needs and whims of the magician-artist who builds illusion upon illusion and then abruptly destroys the illusion.

Characters appear and vanish, as though they too are in and out of focus, yet leave behind an image that is at the same time memorable and amorphous. We see, or think we see, Goodman Brown, Leonard Doane, Robin Molineux, the good Mr. Hooper, and the others and even form definite impressions on the basis of Hawthorne's suggestiveness, impressions which reflect our own perceptions and anxieties perhaps more than the author's. These characters are real and simultaneously unreal or allegorical. They have a visual and emotional impact because their unreal reality is confirmed in our dreamscapes. Neither personalities nor images remain fixed except in our memories. They are not photographs arrested in time and space but are, like life and dream, in constant flux.

Light, either in daytime or nighttime, changes without cause. Sounds rise and fall like crescendos and decrescendos of music or ocean waves. Laughter is heard, now in the distance, now close at hand: it is joyous, hysterical, life-affirming, and anxiety-ridden. The kinetic motion reflects the rhythms of nature, the heart, panic states, depressive swings, human ambiguities. It is unreal and all-too-real; it is romance and the reality of the inner landscape. Hawthorne paints in primary colors, red and black predominating, because he deals with the primary needs of people: family, sexual fulfillment, death and mourning, and human connections. Conclusions, as in dreams, are often inconclusive and mystifying.

The extensive commentary on Hawthorne's writings, now almost a bibliographical nightmare, demonstrates their continuing relevancy a century and a half later as well as the diversity of his appeal. Too often, however, interpretation is limited to the head-heart conflict, which in its either/or orientation washes out Hawthorne's complexity with a neat but finally unsatisfactory formula; or to the historical-social significance when clearly Hawthorne is more than a historical or social commentator; or to the treatment of evil or original sin, when skepticism and agnosticism characterize his perspective, including his guilt-free attraction to the flowers of evil. Some critics seek to resolve his inconclusive conclusions, when his obvious intention is to posit several possibilities, sometimes even contradictory. Critics must be careful, although invariably they will fail, not to impose their own simplifications upon Hawthorne's profound penetration into human depths.

Hawthorne had the insights of a Dostoyevsky but not the consolation of that artist's faith in orthodox religion, in the educative effects of sin and suffering, or in the restorative effects of the return to Mother Earth or Russia. In one of his last uncompleted romances Hawthorne was to epitomize the human dilemma in this way: "But in most hearts, there is an empty chamber waiting, for a guest"—an evocative expression of human loneliness and alienation, the terror and emptiness of life without relationships or familial roots, and the absence of stability in a world in which old truths and old faiths no longer stabilize the lives of doubters. Hawthorne had few illusions about his forebears' world or his own. He could at the same time play with the edenic concept or indulge himself in wish-fulfillment, particularly in *The House of the Seven Gables*, without giving it full credence. He saw human beings as unchanged and unchangeable but did not fully believe his disbelief or trust his lack of trust.[6]

Although Hawthorne lacked faith in the emergence of the savior of Promethean dimensions, he analyzed power, its nature, structure, and potential destructiveness, as regularly as Carlyle, Emerson, Melville, and others. Because his emphasis is upon the most important human unit, the family, patriarchal power in its positive and negative aspects is a recurrent subject in *Twice-told Tales*. The first tale, "The Gray Champion," introduces the patriarch as savior. "The May-pole of Merry Mount" laments the passing of the freedoms of a pagan society and the necessity of civilization and its repressions when Governor Endecott introduces discipline and duty as substitutes for libidinal delights. Hooper's black veil transforms a mediocre preacher into a dynamic figure but at the price of the abandonment of love and family; children rightly distrust a minister who finds the world filled with the negations of "secret sin," which originates in Hooper's projection of his malaise upon the world. The painter in "The Prophetic Pictures" claims for himself the gift "to see the inmost soul." A slip of speech when he visits a couple whose portraits he has painted unveils the horror of his inhuman and monomaniacal dedication to art.

"The Portraits! Are they within?" enquired he, of the domestic; then recollecting himself—"your master and mistress! Are they at home?"

"They are, Sir," said the servant, adding, as he noticed that picturesque aspect of which the painter could never divest himself,—"and the Portraits too!"

Hawthorne did not subscribe to the salvational claims and arrogance of the romantic artist: despite his dedication to art he respected his bourgeois inheritance.[7]

The tales not gathered in *Twice-told Tales* confirm the compelling power of the patriarchal figure on Hawthorne's imagination. The reenactment in "Alice Doane's Appeal" of the horrors perpetrated on Gallows Hill in 1692 includes a processional dominated by the most potent intellectual and religious figure of the age, who gave sanction to John Hathorne's misdirected zeal to hang witches.

In the rear of the procession road a figure on horseback, so darkly conspicuous, so sternly triumphant, that my hearers mistook him for the visible presence of the fiend himself; but it was only his good friend, Cotton Mather, proud of his well won dignity, as the representative of all the hateful features of his time; the one blood-thirsty man, in whom were concentrated those vices of spirit and errors of opinion, that sufficed to madden the whole surrounding multitude.

Mather is one of the first of the Bad Fathers who tower over Hawthorne's landscape as he restages the eternal divisions between parents and children. Often, like Mather, they are sadistic men disguised as ministers, scientists, and artists, secretly lusting to destroy innocent women. Hawthorne recognizes the sexual dimensions of power, influenced no doubt by the wanton acts of his forebears and by his intuitive awareness of his own lusts and the compelling attractiveness of incestuous and deviant sexual desires.[8]

At the center of "My Kinsman, Major Molineux" is one of civilization's most ancient rites, the deposition of the ruler, or the father, by the son. An American colony unseats the representative of the English throne, Major Molineux, while his young kinsman, eighteen-year-old Robin, seeks to cross the bridge to maturity and seeming independence by freeing himself from a surrogate father whose favor and position he has been willing to exploit for his own ends. In the darkness of the night the colonists seize the major and bind him to a wagon, or death-cart, where, defiled in tar and feathers, he is jeered and mocked, his pain ignored in the crowd's lust for violence and sensual gratification. When Robin sees his relative in his debasement, he laughs loudest of all, anxious delight mixed with hysteria, and aligns himself, at least momentarily, with the rebels who have acted out his secret desire.

In the dreamlike ambiance of this tale the procession is led by a "single horseman, clad in military dress, and bearing a drawn sword, . . . and by his fierce and variegated countenance, appeared like war personified; the red of one cheek was an emblem of fire and sword; the blackness of the other betokened the mourning which attends them." The allegorical description cannot conceal either the introduction of the split personality, which characterizes the human condition, or the destructive base upon which civilization uneasily rests. The sympathetic figure in the spectacle is neither the leader of the colonists nor Robin but the fallen major, who, in the agony of physical distress and public humiliation, sits "in tar-and-feathery dignity"—the noblest of all among cowards, hypocrites, and sadists about to replace one tyranny with another.[9]

Hawthorne's two ancestors make their first appearance in his fiction in Goodman Brown's dreamlike journey into the forest, where he keeps a previously arranged "covenant" with a demonic figure in conventional garb who has a "staff, which bore the likeness of a great black snake, so curiously wrought, that it might almost be seen to twist and wriggle itself, like a living serpent." When Brown wants to break his "covenant" and return to his wife, Faith, he argues that he would be "the first of the name of Brown" to associate himself with evil forces. The demon interrupts to set the historical and familial records straight: he helped, he avers, Brown's grandfather to lash a Quaker woman through the streets of Salem and his father to set fire to an Indian village, acts attributed to William and John Hathorne in family history.

In "Young Goodman Brown" the devil figure turns out to be a wily, witty diplomat out of Goethe rather than Puritan lore, Hawthorne indicating perhaps his rejection of Brown's belief in demons or in what Puritans called "spectral evidence." The demon, we discover, is on familiar terms with Goody Cloyse, who years earlier taught Brown his catechism. He touches "her withered neck with what seemed the serpent's tail" and indulges in phallic play with her consent. "Then Goody Cloyse knows her old friend?" the demon observes. She has lost her broomstick and obviously her virtue, as the use of the ambiguous "knows" suggests. In giving her his staff, the apparition satisfies her sexual need, and she leaves to participate that night in a rite at which a young man (presumably Brown) is to be initiated into the catechism and bloodstain of sexuality.

The apparition confers manhood upon Brown when he presents the youth with a "maple stick," or phallus, but the youth is destined to remain trapped in his terror of sexuality. Behind Hawthorne's witty presentation of the tale lies a blistering, unpleasant truth such as few writers unfold: people may journey into the heart of darkness and emerge from their experiences without either enlightenment or faith in themselves and the world. Brown confirms the validity of his fears and depressions as he converts natural order to his own perversions. Hawthorne in his customary duplicitous fashion allows the reader escape from pessimism and despair: "Young Goodman Brown" may be only a dream signifying nothing—which no sensitive reader believes and neither does Hawthorne.

In "Young Goodman Brown," one of the world's great stories, Hawthorne demonstrates his authority and virtuosity. The oscillating tensions of the story—between pun and terror, laughter and anxiety, faith and despair, with Brown's loss of faith in his wife, Faith—are subtly delineated while the author plays a dual role as the demon and Brown. Hawthorne's identity as the apparition is established by means of the allusions to his ancestors, ruthlessly manipulative in bending people to his will, like an immoralist artist. At the same time he is the young bridegroom of three months who in his sexual panic sees the world as an orgy of sexual desire and bloodstains, as though the universe itself has been deflowered—an outlook which Hawthorne simultaneously accepts and rejects, for unlike Brown he has faith in women and believes in their redemptive power, at least on occasions.

Power exerts a magnetic attraction over Hawthorne's fantasies of himself but, afflicted with feelings of failure and lack of self-confidence, he also empathizes deeply with failure—of father and son, as in "The Gentle Boy," where Ilbrahim and Pearson are sensitively delineated. A contemporary critic insisted that "Roger Malvin's Burial" was one of those tales that revealed "the unhealthiness" as well as "the nettles and mushrooms of Mr. Hawthorne's mind," but he failed, or feared, to recognize Hawthorne's profound insight into the behavior and sensibility of a youth overcome with guilt feelings after his betrayal of the father figure.[10]

On May 12, 1725, Roger Malvin and Reuben Bourne, wounded veterans of Indian warfare, one middle-aged and the other a youth of about twenty years, are on their way home. Roger fears imminent death and, assuming "a father's authority," orders Reuben to go to the settlement alone in order to save his own life and to take care of Roger's daughter Dorcas. Reuben is to send assistance to bear Roger back if he is still alive or to bury him in the forest at the foot of a granite rock formation with hieroglyphics resembling a tombstone. In conferring sonhood on a seemingly parentless youth, Roger places a burden on Reuben: as the "son," he is obligated to bury the "father" and complete the eternal cycle. In return Reuben is to receive Roger's daughter in marriage as well as his goods.[11]

Because Reuben is delirious when he stumbles into the village, no one learns immediately about Roger's condition or whereabouts. Dorcas assumes that Reuben has buried her father and pronounces him a hero, and out of secret greed and desire Reuben fails to correct her. But when he marries Dorcas, he is pale and trembling, aware of his cowardly deceit and selfishness, and he begins an eighteen-year imprisonment in gloom and depression. Reuben cannot mourn, for "a thought would occasionally recur. . . . it was a haunting and torturing fancy, that his father-in-law was yet sitting at the foot of the rock, on the withered forest-leaves, alive, and awaiting his pledged assistance." At times Reuben imagines himself "a murderer," as in his mind the abandonment of Roger Malvin becomes parricide.

His rich farm deteriorates while those of the other settlers are "annually more fruitful." As a "husbandman" he fails and unconsciously punishes himself: he can allow himself neither to be happy in marriage with the daughter of the man he continues to betray nor to prosper with her father's goods. He sinks into depression. In another of his evasions, he turns his seething inner rage against his neighbors by means of harassing lawsuits which invariably he loses, this being his secret wish.

The eighteen years of marriage are redeemed only by the birth of Cyrus, "beautiful in youth, and giving promise of a glorious manhood." But Reuben's love is selfish, narcissistic: "The boy was loved by his father, with a deep and silent strength, as if whatever was good and happy in his own nature had been transferred to his child, carrying his affections with it." Eventually Reuben decides to start over and sets out to establish a new home, but he loses his way and moves in an ever-closing circle, such being the logic and power of the unconscious, until on May 12, 1743, he unknowingly arrives at the site in the forest where exactly eighteen years earlier he abandoned Roger Malvin.

When he searches for a deer for the evening meal, he hears a movement "behind a thick veil of underbrush," fires, and discovers—the veil suddenly lifted—his dearly beloved son dead at the base of the granite formation which now serves as a tombstone for "father" and son. Reuben's "accident" constitutes his atonement to Roger. It is also his final aggression and the punishment his long-festering guilt exacts. For the first time in eighteen years Reuben weeps and prays as at last he buries and mourns the father, but forever after May 12 is to be the anniversary of his slaying of his only son, his mirror image.

This is an awesome story of parricide, filicide, symbolic suicide or self-punishment, and role reversals. Hawthorne universalizes the tale by evoking the myths of Narcissus, Oedipus, and Abraham and Isaac. At the same time he reveals once again his profound understanding of mourning and grief, depression and aggression, self-destructive tendencies, and the inevitable circular return to the beginning.

In a revised version of the much revised "Alice Doane's Appeal," Hawthorne intrudes at one point to establish the publishing history of the work: it "was one of a series written years ago, when my pen, now sluggish and perhaps feeble, because I have not much hope or fear, was driven by stronger external motives, and a more passionate impulse within, than I am fated to feel again." He did not clarify the nature of this "more passionate impulse within." [12]

After Leonard and his sister Alice are orphaned early in life, he serves as father and brother. They live together contentedly until the appearance of Walter Brome. Alice falls in love with Walter, who, it later turns out, is Leonard's "very counterpart" or twin. On a lonely road outside of Salem, Walter torments Leonard "with indubitable proofs of the shame of Alice," and the Cain-Abel murder is reenacted. As Leonard looks down at Walter's body a confused picture of a traumatic event from childhood is suddenly clarified, its meaning unfolded:

> But it seemed to me that the irrevocable years, since childhood had rolled back, and a scene, that had long been confused and broken in my memory, arrayed itself with all its first distinctness. Methought I stood a weeping infant by my father's hearth; by the cold and

blood-stained hearth where he lay dead. I heard the childish wail of Alice, and my own cry arose with hers, as we beheld the features of our parent, fierce with the strife and distorted with the pain, in which his spirit had passed away. As I gazed a cold wind whistled by, and waved my father's hair. Immediately, I stood again in the lonesome road, no more a sinless child, but a man of blood, whose tears were falling fast over the face of his dead enemy. But the delusion was not wholly gone; that face still wore a likeness of my father. . . .

Leonard learns at last what he has self-protectively blocked from awareness.[13]

Everything in this tale is displaced. When Leonard looks at Walter's body and sees the father, fratricide conceals parricide. The Indian killer of the father substitutes for the son in a scene of violence which expresses a universal filial wish. The Indian presumably wielded a tomahawk, and Leonard is about to cut the ice of the lake with a hatchet in order to get rid of Walter's body in "a chill and watery grave." When Walter lusts after Alice and then boasts that he has seduced her, he acts out the desire Leonard has repressed. Surely Alice herself substitutes for the dead mother, who because of the hidden incestuous longings of Leonard is not even referred to: desire for the mother and rivalry with the father must be kept from consciousness. Since, however, Leonard is his brother Walter as well as his father, Leonard's act confirms his oedipal desire and, in addition, his need to punish himself through destruction of his image. The narrator describes Leonard after his confession as "stung with remorse for the death of Walter Brome, and shuddering with a deeper sense of some unutterable crime, perpetrated, as he imagined, in madness or a dream."

In this tale, which is the most complex of the early works, as disjointed structurally as the psychological materials he presents and anticipatory of the Freudian exploration of dreams and symbolism, Hawthorne introduces most of the motifs upon which for the next thirty-five years he was to play variations. The pages of his writings are as stained as "the cold and blood-stained hearth" where the father lies scalped, a whistling wind waving his hair. When Hawthorne was ousted from the Salem Custom-House he perceived himself in a political oedipal situation, the son victimized by the father or fathers, and, before he unfolded the story of the scarlet letter on Hester Prynne's breast, he depicted himself, half seriously, half facetiously, as "THE DECAPITATED SURVEYOR."

Hawthorne was rarely censured on moral or religious grounds until the heroine of *The Scarlet Letter* turned out to be an adulteress. His veils for the most part successfully concealed the sexualized environment, the almost prurient interest in sadism, voyeurism, incest, and male terror of sexuality and marriage. In "The Minister's Black Veil," Hooper dons the veil when he is on the verge of marrying Elizabeth and preaches the first sermon in masquerade on the subject of an undefined "secret sin." As a lady in the congregation observes, his veil is like a woman's "bonnet": it preserves his virginity and renders him in effect neuter; it keeps him from eye contact with the world but in the pulpit transforms him into a compelling preacher, at least to those who share his fears and distortions. Hooper is also the first of Hawthorne's characters to circumvent marriage—others like Goodman Brown find ways to free themselves from the marriage bed, or deathbed, out of fear of sexuality and perhaps of women whom they secretly hold in contempt, although at the same time some secretly crave the warmth of the maternal breast.

Of all the strange occupants of Hawthorne's landscape Wakefield is perhaps the most enigmatic and memorable. After ten years of marriage Wakefield, a man in his middle years, occupation unknown, sets off on a journey without informing his wife of his destination or the length of his stay. His destination turns out to be a lodging house in London a block away from his home, and his stay of a week or two turns into twenty years. "This long whim-wham," in Hawthorne's words, recalls Rip Van Winkle and his twenty-year sleep. Both are stories of evasion and disruption of the family and marriage.

Whatever the construction of the tale—and there will doubtless never be a consensus—Wakefield haunts us, partly because we are unable to explain him satisfactorily and because his asocial, seemingly mad behavior has a counterpart in our night and day reveries: everyone has at some time or another wanted to walk out of family, marriage, and life itself, to be in effect dead but also able to spy without detection upon those who have been abandoned. It is not an unusual "whim-wham," although most mortals manage not to act it out.

"Wakefield" is Hawthorne's "whim-wham" to explain Wakefield's. He plays with speculations, tentatively suggestive but essentially inconclusive. Wakefield evidently married late and is perhaps at what is sometimes called the middle-age crisis: ". . . his matrimonial affections, never violent, were sobered into a calm, habitual sentiment; of all husbands, he was likely to be the most constant, because a certain sluggishness would keep his heart at rest, wherever it might be placed. He was intellectual, but not actively so. . . ." Only his wife knows that he has a quiet "vanity" and "a disposition to craft." As time passes she remembers only one thing remarkable about his disappearance: his "quiet and crafty smile" as she closed the door when he disappeared.

An influence beyond his "control . . . weaves its consequences into an iron tissue of necessity. Wakefield is spell-bound." He remains under the spell for ten years. The only change is that Wakefield ages, perhaps prematurely: "He is meagre; his low and narrow forehead is deeply wrinkled; his eyes, small and lustreless, sometimes wander apprehensively about him, but oftener seem to look inward. He bends his head, but moves with an indescribable obliquity of gait, as if unwilling to display his full front to the world." And twenty years pass. Then standing outside his home in the rain on "a gusty night of autumn," Wakefield sees the reflections of a comfortable fire in the second-floor parlor and on the ceiling "a grotesque shadow of good Mrs. Wakefield. The cap, the nose and chin, and the broad waist, form an admirable caricature, which dances, moreover, with the up-flickering and down-sinking blaze, almost too merrily for the shade of an elderly widow." Suddenly Wakefield feels chilled by the raw wind and, not being a "fool," at least not forever, climbs the stairs "heavily!—for twenty years have stiffened his legs, since he came down." As he passes through the door we "recognize the crafty smile, which was the precursor of the little joke."

After spending twenty years spying on his wife, this "Outcast of the Universe" returns home to share her passionless age—"a loving spouse till death." Large of frame and bosom, Mrs. Wakefield plays mother to this boy-man who, like Rip Van Winkle, refuses to grow up. At the conclusion Hawthorne, like Irving before him, adopts an evasive, bantering tone which seems to make light of a strange and Kafkaesque tale.

Wakefield may be a fool or worse, as Hawthorne alleges, but he is also deeply felt by Hawthorne as well as by readers. The physical description of the character and his behavior—furtiveness, languid energy, and recourse to a protective hermitage where he can watch the world go by without detection and, more important, without involvement—is not wholly a figment of Hawthorne's imagination. If Rip Van Winkle is Irving's alter-ego, Wakefield is part of the self-portrait Hawthorne unveils stealthily, "as if unwilling to display his full front to the world."

Nineteenth-century readers from all classes immediately fell in love with "Little Annie's Ramble," while twentieth-century readers have dismissed the brief tale as maudlin and banal, although it is as charmingly rendered as a work of folk art. If we look at the story autobiographically, another dimension surfaces: the narrator relates a fantasy in which he is simultaneously father and the five-year-old child Annie. It is a lovely example of wish-fulfillment.

"She feels," the narrator explains, "that impulse to go strolling away—that longing after the mystery of the great world—which many children feel, and which I felt in my childhood. . . . I do but hold out my hand, and, like some bright bird in the sunny air, with her blue silk frock fluttering upwards from her white pantalettes, she comes bounding on tiptoe across the street." They set out "hand in hand" for the circus. They walk through the streets of Salem with the enthusiasm of a Walt Whitman, observing the cargoes at the wharves, listening to the organ grinder, delighting in the brightly decorated sweets and dolls in the shops. At last they reach the circus where they observe the animals. Suddenly they hear the town crier.

"Strayed from her home, a LITTLE GIRL, of five years old, in a blue frock and white pantalettes, with brown curling hair and hazel eyes. Whoever will bring her back to her afflicted mother—"

They have forgotten to inform the mother of their ramble! Still hand in hand, for she "has not once let go my hand," he takes her homeward and then draws a conclusion which, if not to our taste, decorates the tale as naturally as the blue frock adorns Annie.

When our infancy is almost forgotten, and our boyhood long departed, though it seems but as yesterday; when life settles darkly down upon us, and we doubt whether to call ourselves young any more; then it is good to steal away from the society of bearded men, and even of gentler woman, and spend an hour or two with children. After drinking from those fountains of still fresh existence, we shall return into the crowd, as I do now, to struggle onward and do our part in life, perhaps as fervently as ever, but, for a time, with a kinder and purer heart, and a spirit more lightly wise. All this by thy sweet magic, dear little Annie!

Hawthorne does not veil the self-portrait. If the description of the narrator as "a gentleman of sober footsteps" who "walks in black attire, with a measured step, and a heavy brow, and his thoughtful eyes bent down" does not establish the identification, he has "father" and "child" pass a bookstore in which are displayed Peter Parley's tomes, one of which Hawthorne was editing at that time. The tale ends sentimentally—readers no doubt cried and perhaps so did Hawthorne—yet truth asserts itself even in fancy: the kidnapper returns the child to her mother and leaves her seemingly without a father.

Hooper, the clergyman who actually assumes the veil, is another self-portrait of the deeply troubled, fearful Hawthorne close to the abyss. A bachelor of thirty, "fastidious" and narcissistic, Hooper walks slowly, "stooping somewhat and looking at the ground, as is customary with abstracted men." Like Goodman Brown and Reuben Bourne, he is a "melancholy man," characterized "by so painful a degree of self-distrust, that even the mildest censure would lead him to consider an indifferent action a crime." Hooper is a forerunner of Arthur Dimmesdale; in both characterizations Hawthorne vicariously entered a profession which he refused to consider before he left for Bowdoin College. By strange coincidence the minister at Hooper's funeral is named Clark. Hawthorne was married and buried by the Reverend James Freeman Clarke.

Melville found "Young Goodman Brown" as "deep as Dante," and Henry James termed it a "magnificent little romance." But neither quite knew how to read, in Melville's words, "this same harmless Hawthorne" who could choose a title recalling "Goody Two Shoes." Despite his uncertainty as to Hawthorne's intention and design, Melville, tending as is the wont of genius to make over others in his own image, claimed that "this great power of blackness in him derives its force from its appeal to that Calvinistic sense of Innate Depravity and Original Sin, from whose visitations, in some shape or other, no deeply thinking mind is always and wholly free. . . ." James was too dogmatic in his assertion that the tale "evidently means nothing as regards Hawthorne's own state of mind, his conviction of human depravity and his consequent melancholy; for the simple reason that, if it meant anything, it would mean too much." As Mark Van Doren commented years ago, "Too much, that is, for Henry James." Melville and James were as eager, or anxious, as Hawthorne not to encourage autobiographical readings of their works.[14]

What Melville and James could not have recognized was that "Young

Goodman Brown" was in many respects to foretell the course of Hawthorne's own life: he was to be in his own eyes, in periods of depression, "an outcast of the universe." He projected his despair upon the universe and was to wrestle all his life with the failure of woman (meaning mother) to fulfill the childlike vision of the Madonna shielding her child.

It is possible to universalize "Roger Malvin's Burial," but the affect of this deeply moving tale surely originates in Hawthorne's abiding awareness of the uncompleted cycle, that no one in the family attended the burial or ever saw the grave of Captain Hathorne. If, as seems likely, Hawthorne wrote this story about 1828, it was at the time of the twentieth anniversary of Captain Hathorne's death. Like Reuben Bourne, Hawthorne never succeeded in burying the memory of his unburied father. Years later he wrote in his notebook: "If it is not known how and when a man dies, it seems to make a kind of ghost of him for many years thereafter—perhaps for centuries." [15]

In the week following the appearance of *Twice-told Tales* Hawthorne wrote for the first time to a classmate who had already achieved the fame for which he longed. From the beginning Longfellow found an audience which increased with the appearance of each book.

> We were not, it is true, so well acquainted at college, that I can plead an absolute right to inflict my "twice-told" tediousness upon you; but I have regretted that we were not better known to each other, and have been glad of your success in literature. . . . The present volume contains such articles as seemed best worth offering to the public a second time; and I should like to flatter myself that they would repay you some part of the pleasure which I have derived from your own Outre Mer.

Longfellow agreed at once to write a review of the book. In his reply Hawthorne depicted his life since the Bowdoin years in dark tonalities, denied that he had led a studious life, as Longfellow generously assumed, and disparaged his literary efforts—"another great difficulty, in the lack of materials; for I have seen so little of the world, that I have nothing but thin air to concoct my stories of, and it is not easy to give a lifelike semblance to such shadowy stuff." [16]

"Whether or no the public will agree to the praise which you bestow on me," he wrote on receipt of a copy of Longfellow's review, "there are at least five persons who think you the most sagacious critic on earth—viz. my mother and two sisters, my old maiden aunt, and finally, the sturdiest believer of the whole five, my own self." In the July issue of the *North American Review* Longfellow was truly generous, even extravagant in his praise. "To this little book," he observed, "we would say, 'Live ever, sweet, sweet book.' It comes from the hand of a man of genius." The first to insist that Hawthorne was a poet in prose, Longfellow dwelled repeatedly on the "exceeding beauty" of the style. (In later years Hawthorne tired of this emphasis and insisted that his prose was wedded to content.) Longfellow admired the historical and national characteristics of the tales and generally ignored those that probed the universal terrain of the psyche. The delightful volume, he maintained, aroused a reader's interest in the author: "A calm, thoughtful face seems to be looking at you from every page; with now a pleasant smile, and now a shade of sadness stealing over its features. Sometimes, though not often, it glares wildly at you, with a strange and painful expression."[17]

Hawthorne's principles of selection in *Twice-told Tales*, then, were justified. The reviewers were almost unanimous in singling out "Little Annie's Ramble," "Sights from a Steeple," "A Rill from the Town Pump," and "Sunday at Home," while Longfellow made more of "The Great Carbuncle" than later commentators. On the other hand, because Hawthorne decided not to reprint at this time "Young Goodman Brown," "My Kinsman, Major Molineux," "Alice Doane's Appeal," and "Roger Malvin's Burial," the totality of his achievement was hidden.

And so in 1837 Hawthorne identified his authorship and modestly announced himself. A great artist had arrived, but almost no one noticed.

The Peabodys

Saturday, November 11, 1837, is not a memorable day in the history of the United States, the Commonwealth of Massachusetts, or perhaps even Salem, although it was predestinated, in the words of Herman Melville, to be a fateful evening in the life of Salem's most distinguished son. On that Saturday evening, three people—two hooded women supported by a tall, athletic-looking man—made their way from 12 Herbert Street to a three-story frame house, unpretentious and unattractive, situated at one corner of the Charter Street Burying Point. The slate tombstones were (and are, for little has changed in the past century and more) "almost within arm's reach of the side windows of the parlor,—and there being a little gate from the back yard through which we step forth upon those old graves." The two or three apple trees in the cemetery were leafless, the "blighted fruit," according to Salem's romancer, having long since rotted.[1]

It was to the house of Dr. Nathaniel Peabody that the three Hawthornes had been summoned. Rarely did the Hawthornes go out together on walks, and even more rarely did they make visits to the homes of people they knew but casually. Ordinarily Hawthorne avoided self-conscious literary women like the three Peabody sisters, all of whom had more than a little of the transcendental overconfidence in humanity's goodness and the efficacy of books and education to return a wayward world to Eden and Paradise. He was more at ease with the culturally uninhibited members of both sexes. Perhaps he suspected that Elizabeth Peabody could promote his interests through her Boston friends, for earlier in the year he had sent her an inscribed copy of *Twice-told Tales*. Whatever his reasons, he agreed to accompany his sisters.

The visit and the inscribed book followed an unannounced call that Elizabeth Peabody made late in 1836 to see Elizabeth Hawthorne, who sent word through Louisa that she never received in the daytime, although she promised to receive at an appropriate evening hour. Elizabeth Peabody heard nothing more from the sisters. She discovered, however, that she had been mistaken in her assumption that the tales published anonymously in the *Token* and elsewhere had been written by Elizabeth. That Elizabeth Peabody, who frequented literary circles in Boston and Salem, both of which were small closed "universes," should have made the error is surprising unless she preferred to believe that only a woman could have written such a tender tale as "The Gentle Boy." After Louisa corrected her, the indomitable woman exclaimed, "But if your brother can write like that, he has no right to be idle," by which she probably meant that he should leave that "dismal chamber" at once and perform his Duty. She and her family were wedded to the three Ds—Duty, Discipline, and Decorum.[2]

The Hawthorne sisters intended no slight when they neglected to establish a new date. Though they had known the Peabodys at least distantly all their lives, such was their fear of personal involvement that, like Clifford and Hepzibah Pyncheon in *The House of the Seven Gables*, they were given to attacks of nerves.

Elizabeth Peabody's chance meeting with Louisa on the morning of November 11 led to the evening visit. By her own admission, Elizabeth Peabody devised "the pretext of asking Nathaniel Hawthorne about the terms of the Democratic Review," the journal edited by John Louis O'Sullivan for which Hawthorne was to write during the next half dozen years. What we know about the visit is based on the recollections of Elizabeth Peabody in her eighties. Usually she tidied up her remembrances of things past, but her account of this momentous meeting for the most part rings true.

When the Hawthornes, their diffidence and anxiety visible, climbed the steps and knocked, Elizabeth Peabody sat alone in the parlor examining an "edition of Flaxman's outlines." Mary Peabody was not at home, Sophia was upstairs in her bedroom, and the parents were either out for the evening or banished to another part of the house. Elizabeth Peabody recalled that when she opened the door, "there stood your father in all the splendor of his young beauty, and a hooded figure hanging on each arm."

In the Peabody parlor the three Hawthornes sat in a row, uneasy and flustered, until Elizabeth Peabody invited them to examine Flaxman's illustrations of Dante, Homer, and Aeschylus. She intuited rightly the power of culture and art to soothe hypersensitive mortals of the Hawthorne order, sparing them the necessity of social chitchat for which they had almost no aptitude, except possibly with familiars. Flaxman even provided Elizabeth Peabody with the opportunity to rush upstairs to Sophia's bedroom.

Breathlessly—or so we imagine—she exclaimed, "Oh, Sophia, Mr. Hawthorne and his sisters have come, and you never saw anything so splendid—he is handsomer than Lord Byron! You must get up and dress and come down." So charming is the story that no biographer wants to fault it, but we are asked to believe that the Peabody sisters who had lived much of their lives in Salem were not acquainted with the town's "Lord Byron," or that Sophia, who despite her illnesses was quite a social being, would choose to stay in her room, acting more like a Hawthorne than a Peabody. But stay she apparently did, though not without uttering a sentence worthy of a comedy of manners, "If he has come once he will come again."

At nine o'clock Mary Peabody made an appearance and, at once taking in the situation, talked Flaxman and literature to ease everyone of "embarrassment." The Peabody sisters perhaps wore their culture conspicuously, with the fervor of self-cultivated women who, denied the college education of Dr. Peabody and Hawthorne, felt obliged to demonstrate their literary propensities a bit too insistently at times.

And so the evening ended, and a comedy of manners commenced, with delicacies and subtleties, reticences and fears, emotional currents guarded and silent but no less fierce because of the obliquities decreed by social conventions and, above all, by the temperaments of the participants.

In 1800, or perhaps later in 1799, two young people arrived in Andover, Massachusetts, one the newly appointed preceptress of Franklin Academy and the other a recent graduate of Dartmouth College and the newly appointed preceptor of Phillips Andover Academy.

Elizabeth Palmer, twenty-three, and Nathaniel Peabody, twenty-seven, almost at once became friends, shortly warm friends. Gratefully she accepted "the tuition of *such an Instructor*," the underscoring emphasizing her enthusiasm. Her ardor sometimes barely under control, she prayed that he would "readily consent to Friendship, such as I hope exists in our bosoms, [which] is the most serious, most sublime of all affections, because it is founded on principle, and cemented by time, because it excites that tender confidence, which is one of the sweetest joys of life, and blends sincere respect, with perfect freedom." With disarming candor, or naïveté, but not without a touch of perhaps unknowing seductiveness, she admitted that at first sight she "beheld" him "as I should one of the planets in the canopy of heavens; as something which I ought to admire, but never hope to call mine."[3]

Elizabeth Palmer and Nathaniel Peabody were married in November 1802. Almost at once it became clear that they were not to prosper materially: she had married a man who was to be as unsuccessful as her father. The Peabodys taught in an academy in Billerica in 1804. To supplement their income he sold flour and found time somehow to begin an apprenticeship in dentistry and medicine. In 1806 they established a school in Cambridge and took in boarders. In the following year, in Salem, Nathaniel Peabody set up a practice as dentist, doctor, and pharmacist which never flourished. Perhaps his great moment came in 1824 when he published a pamphlet—*The Art of Preserving Teeth. By Nathaniel Peabody, Fellow of the Massachusetts Medical Society.* Years later the eldest daughter Elizabeth comically, but perhaps bitterly too, summed up her father's lot: "He seems destitute of all kinds of get-a-long-ity."[4]

Elizabeth Palmer Peabody managed to bear children almost punctually at two-year intervals, until by 1820 there were eight, the last of whom died within a few months of birth. In addition, she conducted a school in Salem, which must have taxed the limited energies of a woman who never enjoyed robust physical or emotional health. She published an edition of Spenser's poetry and supervised meticulously the education of her children, particularly of the three talented girls, Elizabeth, Mary, and Sophia. As important as training in academic subjects was the inculcation of religious and ethical values. There were in her universe God and obligations. "Amusements," she proclaimed as a fact, "however graceful and innocent, become criminal whenever they encroach on our hours of duty, of reflection, of prayer"; "it is madness in the extreme to waste hours which are bearing us on irresistibly to the awful retributions of Eternity"; "idleness is a crime, and God has made action absolutely necessary to happiness."[5]

Dr. Peabody, at least in the eyes of Hawthorne, was charming in his childlike ineffectuality and stubbornness, but Mrs. Peabody was left with the problems of providing for a large family. She watched as her daughters were sent off to teach in order to make up for the deficiencies of their father. "My mind has been anxious," she declared, "my spirit wounded and agonized. And at what? Not at sickness, poverty, or labour, but at blighted hopes, at the real or imagined alienation of those for whom I lived and delighted to labour." Letters to her grown children marked "Sub-rosa" reveal that her lot was not a happy one. "Destroy this when read," she ordered, and then accused Dr. Peabody of "raking up objections for argument's sake," of "constitutional timidity," of being unable to alter his opinions or habits, and of feeling inferior because of "deficiencies of his early education." What she had to say, she alleged, should not undermine their "love and veneration."[6]

To compensate for her husband's failures and her own disappointed great expectations, Mrs. Peabody loved her children to excess and at the same time dominated them by her overstrenuous inculcation of religious and moral principles. More talented than her husband, she epitomized the plight of similar women in a century in which many men were often so concerned about their masculinity that they demonstrated it by exploiting women. "I long for means and power to remedy this increasing misery," she wrote toward the end of a life of frustration, "but I wear petticoats and can never be Governor, Mayor, nor alderman, Judge or jury, senator or representative—so I may as well be quiet."[7]

Elizabeth, the first and longest-lived of the children, was born in the same year as Hawthorne, in 1804. She watched over the Peabodys, and later the Hawthornes, for ninety years, intruding with the best of intentions into their lives, sacrificing time and energy recklessly out of her love and her need to be loved. Energetic, dedicated, tireless, Elizabeth became renowned for her innovations in kindergarten training. For years New England intellectuals assembled in her bookshop at 13 West Street in Boston, which, in the words of Emerson, was "a private theatre for the exposition of every question of letters, of philosophy, of ethics, and of art." She was the publisher of the *Dial*, the journal of the transcendentalists, of which Margaret Fuller for a period was editor. A believer in principles, she was an abolitionist, an educational reformer, and a partisan of exploited Indians.[8]

A woman of Elizabeth's vitality and firm opinions aroused various and sometimes vigorous responses. Emerson's Aunt Mary, it was said, always referred to her as "Miss pea." Bronson Alcott, who was even more of a character than Aunt Mary or Elizabeth Peabody, had his reservations: "She may perhaps aim at being 'original' and fail in her attempt by becoming offensively assertive. On the whole there is, we think, too much of the man and too little of the woman in her familiarity and freedom, her affected indifference of manner."[9]

In old age Elizabeth Peabody was well known in Boston and Cambridge, not only because of her voluminous publications but because of her presence at every public lecture, which led William James to characterize her as "the most dissolute woman" in the city and his brother Henry to caricature her in Miss Birdseye in *The Bostonians*, although he denied the accusation, though not too convincingly.[10]

Even her admirers admitted that she could be "very rambling" in conversations or, in the words of a lifelong friend: "I have watched the rapids about Lake Erie, and the opening of the Gulf of the St. Lawrence, with precisely the same feeling. . . . I was obliged to hold the helm, with all my strength, to escape the Maelstrom of her affectionate mistakes." Elizabeth was aware of her loquacity—"If I do not resolutely say *no* to my pen, it goes on prosing interminably"—but she rarely said no either to tongue or to pen.[11]

She was so remarkably good-natured that everybody imposed on her. In the lovely words of Sophia, "I seem to realize with peculiar force that beautiful, fathomless heart of Elizabeth—forever disappointed but forever believing—sorely rebuffed yet never bitter—robbed day by day—yet giving again from an endless store—more sweet, more tender, more serene as the Hours pass over her. . . ." Elizabeth gave and gave, but who gave to her? She became the intellectual in the family, but surely she stuffed her stomach—her nephew, Julian Hawthorne, estimated her weight at "several tons"—because she ate out her heart. She looked like an old woman at too early an age. She had skipped childhood, which may have been one of the reasons why she was relentlessly earnest, and had been her mother's assistant as sisters and brothers arrived biannually. As soon as she was able, she took over their education. In a household where the relationship between parents was sometimes strained by economic and temperamental problems, she became her mother's confidant.[12]

All her life she took delight in intellectual, social, and artistic matters, but with a seriousness that was excessive and perhaps even oppressive. Before she returned to Salem for a brief stay at home she wrote: "I go to Concord next week to get *wound up* for the year." The winding up exacted a price. She herself admitted that she required "encouragement from every human eye"—she needed to be loved—and informed an older woman among her acquaintances that she required "the tenderness of the *ideal* Father Confessor—which makes me so often use my privilege of writing to you." Apparently Mrs. Richard Sullivan for a time served this function. To her Elizabeth confessed, "You know I hold my mind by so frail a tenure that the slightest disorganization reduces me below par."[13]

Though destined to remain unmarried, Elizabeth was always in love, but usually with the "intellectual soul" or with a "brother." When she studied Greek with Emerson in the 1820s, she promptly fell in love. At twenty-one she was more than enamored of William Ellery Channing, a happily married clergyman of forty-five. She was so much in love with Horace Mann, in a sisterly way, she was to aver, that she did not realize for years that her sister Mary was in love with him. Elizabeth had convinced herself that there was nothing sexual in what she characterized to Mary as *"torrent feelings"*: ". . . they are feminine. They are sentiments, not passions. . . . They do not come from the blood but from the intellectual soul and they are *pure*." She lived her life in conformity to ideals of femininity and fears of impurities. Without complaint she paid the price in loneliness and unfulfilled desire. At eighteen she had pronounced with a dogmatic emphasis that never changed, "The pleasures of life outweigh by an immense quantity the *pains* of life." One of her friends, Sarah Clarke, wrote with affectionate acumen: "Not always sane in her enthusiasms, or wise or prudent, but such sweet insanity, such generous imprudence won our hearts, though our heads did not always follow our hearts."[14]

Next to Elizabeth, Mary and Sophia cast fainter lights, as did anyone else in the presence of a woman whose eccentricities converted her into a memorable character, which was one more way in which she shielded herself. Mary was the beauty of the three sisters and also the wittiest according to Sophia, although the wit is not easy to discover in surviving documents. Mary was sensible, blunt, and concise, but she had been conditioned by the Peabody ideals which were simultaneously a comfort and a burden, a guide and a cross. As in the case of her sister, these ideals survived deep and protracted emotional and physical disturbances. Elizabeth remembered Mary's "change of character from extreme talkativeness to reserve" when she put away "childish things" on the death of a younger sister, Catherine.[15]

When she was in her twenties, Mary evidently suffered from extended periods of depression. "There was a time," Sophia wrote after Mary's marriage, "when I used to *try* to wish GOD would take you hence." Mary had "seemed to have an incommunicable sorrow, . . . gradually becoming paler & dimmer." Perhaps Sophia overstated—none of the Peabodys mastered the art of understatement—but the mother had also advised Mary not to "suffer those blue demons to get hold of you again. . . . I am puzzled to account for the feeling of apathy . . . but am inclined to think . . . that your only security against its attack is, to avoid wasting your energies, either by enjoying too much, indulging anxieties about the future, or by sympathizing too deeply with those who suffer."[16]

Like the other women in the Peabody household, Mary was given to self-sacrifice, which may have been one of the reasons why the bodies of these overly sensitive, anxious women often rebelled. When the family decided in 1833 to send Sophia to Cuba for the sake of her health, Mary accompanied her and in fact supported her by teaching the children of American officials. Mary did not want to go to Cuba, for she was silently in love with Horace Mann. "He was too much my God," she wrote, "but like God he pervades all space for me." She waited patiently, ready to make whatever sacrifices he demanded: "In those years when I loved him as one unapproachable by human affection . . . I could have seen him happy with another without ever *letting him* know my pain in it—so truly & disinterestedly did I love him." She even became the custodian of his first wife's letters. "I have always felt," she informed Mann, "that I hold communion with that blessed spirit, and that she understood my love for you better than you do yourself."[17]

When at last they were married on May 1, 1843, he was forty-seven and she ten years younger. They sailed on the same day to investigate educational institutions in England and on the Continent. In a memorial following his death she wrote: "Principles were more to him than even friends; which is no light praise of one who loved so tenderly. . . . He rarely unbosomed himself. . . . He was too earnest a man to be able to sustain superficial relations with other men. . . ." Although Mary wrote to praise, one wonders what it must have meant to be married to "principles" and "the demands of duty." But, as she never confessed publicly, she understood Mann's vulnerability and his need for a woman to support his almost monomaniacal dedication that led to great successes as an educator, theorist, and president of Antioch College.[18]

Of the three intense sisters, Sophia was the most frail and sickly. She was in fact a semi-invalid for most of her early years, but she was imbued with what Geroge Bernard Shaw was to call the "life force."

As a child when she suffered unduly from teething, she was, the story went, overdrugged. In puberty and later Sophia suffered from severe headaches, no doubt migraines, which were treated, probably over-treated, with morphine. When she was about twenty-five she described the "rooted pain of fifteen years or more" which included headaches, "terrific visions" at night, sleeplessness, "infinite fatigue," and extreme sensitivity to noise "like the perpetual stabbing of daggers into the very fountain of my nerves."[19]

As everyone in the family knew, Sophia enjoyed the security of an unusually close attachment to her mother. Near the end of her life, Mrs. Peabody wrote to her daughter, "Of you I think with more unalloyed delight than of others of my children." About the same time Sophia commented to Elizabeth: "You know there is very peculiar sympathy between mother & me. We seem wound up together in some inexplicable way, so that I even feel her bodily pains." When their mother was in the terminal phases of cancer, Elizabeth informed a friend that Sophia would not survive the blow—the "interlocking of heart fibres," in the friend's lovely words. But Elizabeth exaggerated, for Sophia in sickness and in health coped successfully in trying situations, even in her complex relationship with her mother, from whom she freed herself with less difficulty than perhaps anyone expected. Observers made the mistake of construing Sophia's somewhat wide-eyed femininity as indicative of weakness.[20]

As the invalid of the family Sophia received a great deal of attention and at the same time exerted a great deal of power. Mary in effect made this point: you "always had just what was convenient, & all the world to wait upon you, you know. I am used to discomforts, & have learnt to think lightly of them, & be content having hearts right." The favored position, supported by the mother, together with Sophia's high moral principles, made her seem the censor of her sisters. "I never considered myself better than you or Mary or whoever," she wrote to Elizabeth, "but in some things I am very *different*, in my habits of mind."[21]

Sophia loved her parents deeply but was in conflict. During the extended stay in Cuba she wrote of her profound attachment to her home: ". . . if there ever was heavenly love, it is the pure, earnest—& unalloyed filial sentiment, such as I feel now when words seems utterly powerless to express my devoted affection & respect. I thank GOD daily for what you are to me, & for what He allows me to be to you." On another occasion she reflected: "I think that next to Evil—*Separation* is the most dreadful thing in the world." Yet her mother's love was a prison as well as a comfort. The improvement in health which Sophia enjoyed during her eighteen-month stay in Cuba vanished almost at once upon her return to Salem. It was easy, too easy, to blame the New England weather, particularly the east wind which made breathing difficult for her. It would appear that Sophia's health improved when she was free of her mother. Yet she apparently needed her mother, as the mother in turn needed the child to care for even after she became a young woman.[22]

The Peabodys were agreed, no doubt on the mother's authority, that Sophia would never marry. Although Sophia did not publicly disagree, she had no intention of remaining unmarried. She was filled with love of beauty, which she tried to keep on a spiritual or intellectual plane, although she tended to eroticize the ideal. She revered Ralph Waldo Emerson—"the most complete man." At eighteeen she was deeply moved at a performance of Edwin Forrest as Othello: "His limbs are the most exquisitely beautiful created things I ever saw in a man." On the voyage to Cuba in 1833 she was introduced to James Burroughs, an American employee of a Cuban sugar plantation. Perhaps it was the intimacy of the voyage or the freedom of life in Cuba, but shortly the forty-year-old man proposed marriage. Mary, apparently unable to check the romance, informed Elizabeth of the state of affairs. Elizabeth pronounced Burroughs "ignorant, sensual, selfish," and "a perfect Cain"—and the romance ended in September 1834. But soon Sophia was involved with two Cubans who lived on an adjoining estate. When they became "attentive," one of Sophia's friends, Elizabeth Williams, warned, "Take care of your heart, dearest, those mellifluous tones you extol so much are *said to be* admirably calculated for the outpourings of the impassioned soul, & how easy it would be to turn *teacher* into *lover*."[23]

At eighteen Sophia articulated with finality a faith that never altered: "I *was* born under the most fortunate star that ever twinkled into being." As some people labor to inventory the world's evils, Sophia inventoried the good without labor: "We do not hear of all the good in the world; because the bad is the more noisy. Yet that good exists in a predominating degree, is, I think, blasphemy against the Holy Spirit, to doubt." Like Emerson, she declared Calvinistic concepts in conflict with the harmony of God's universe. She found diseased those who could not "give up that darling of their hearts, . . . the long loved aroma of the brimstone of the bottomless pit. . . . It seems as if nothing were so unacceptable to *mankind* as simple Love & Truth." On another occasion she expressed the pragmatism of Huck Finn, who had no truck with dead people: "It is not in my nature to gloom over what has happened apastime."[24]

Sophia's was a simple religion of the heart—"claims of the heart have great weight with me"—and her cosmogony was family-centered in a lovely, unintellectual way. God was the father-mother of the family. Although she would have found it sacrilegious to say, "God, Thy name is Mother," she subscribed to the feminine principle which had been excluded by Calvinists and other Protestants. In a sense her greatest praise of her future husband was that "his vigilance & care are comparable only to a mother's, & exceed all other possible carefulness & watching." "Every true and happy family," she emphasized, "is a solar system that outshines all the solar systems in space and time." Her faith in and love of the family as an approximation of the divine family led her to a comforting insight: "I am conscious of no hopeless misery or death except being deprived of the power of loving."[25]

At the urging of Elizabeth, Sophia took up drawing and painting and copied Flaxman's sketches and other works, with even some encouragement from Washington Allston. Except for a copy of Chester Harding's portrait of Allston (now in the Massachusetts Historical Society), her paintings and sketches reveal no exceptional talent, but as an illustrator of her letters and journal she had the skill and sometimes the charm of the amateur. In truth, Sophia's talent lay not in the paintbrush but in her quill pen. That she gradually gave up painting and drawing was no mistake.

It is easy to fault Sophia's prose, for she was wordy and unanalytic, with little sense of discrimination or proportion. The discursiveness was redeemed, however, by her ear for a well-turned phrase or sentence and by an enthusiasm unrelenting, perhaps, but captivating in its childlike way. Though the other sisters wrote pedestrian prose, Sophia poured herself unabashedly into her letters: "Today I have written myself into an ecstasy with gain and relief." Sometimes, as here, writing renewed spirits which had sagged momentarily, but letters were her medium—personal, digressive, and intended for a known audience of family and friends.[26]

Sophia's fifteen hundred extant letters and journals running to several thousand pages together constitute an autobiography of a middle-class nineteenth-century genteel woman with a vibrating sensibility and an enthusiasm and all-consuming love that appear almost unreal in our unidealistic age. "I cannot be despondent," she wrote, "for the universe, from all points, sends arrows of light into my heart & mind. I richly enjoy each thing. . . ." One day in Cuba she noted: "The sky looked exactly as if a spirit had passed along with his pencil dipped in ethereal rose colour, & had dashed it sportively about him in his rapid flight." At times it appeared as though she had just read Emerson's essays, but at this point none had appeared. "This is one of those mornings which seem just from the hand of GOD. . . . Grand clouds with sharp jagged outlines like rocks rent by a thunderbolt in the east, seem actually to *wound* the soft delicate hue of the sky." Like the luminous painters of the century, Martin Johnson Heade, Thomas Cole, and FitzHugh Lane, Sophia had a deep feeling for cloud architecture and the omnipresence of the deity.[27]

Many twentieth-century readers and critics tend to see her as the very model of Victorian prissiness and prudery because she had the audacity to cut out or to ink out suggestive or vulgar phrases, paragraphs, and situations in her husband's notebooks. Bowdlerizers are always roundly censured in an inevitably repetitive litany that assumes the absolute rights of posterity. Yet Sophia acted out of love, a deep, abiding love which gave her rights to present to the world the Hawthorne image in her mirror. In her excisions she was not flouting his will, she followed his example. Hawthorne loathed snooping biographers who sometimes act not out of love but out of self-interest. The letters he ordered Bridge to destroy were probably far more revealing of his inner turmoil and suicidal wishes than anything Sophia deleted, and in his published works Hawthorne himself avoided the vigorous, sometimes racy prose and occasional sexual innuendoes of the notebooks for the sake of a respectable public image.

In 1846 Mrs. Peabody accepted two dollars from Mary in order to purchase "a Bonnet, which I need much to make me appear respectable as the Mother of such distinguished Ladies as Miss Peabody, Mrs. Horace Mann, and Mrs. Nathaniel Hawthorne!" Her three daughters left marks on the "hours," to use one of Sophia's phrases—as their mother had intended.[28]

A mother so devoted to her daughters posed problems for sons, particularly in the absence of a strong male role model. Dr. Peabody was ineffectual, charmingly so only to those not in the family. The firstborn son and the only one to survive into maturity, Nathaniel Cranch, married early, fathered two children immediately, and struggled in his father's footsteps as a teacher, a grocer, and finally an apothecary. In a letter to Elizabeth he poured forth his envy and his animus toward the *"aesthetic culture"* which his sisters venerated:

> I have very little sympathy with those who admire and worship brilliant men, and the enthusiasm which many people feel for art, and the almost man-worship they practice rather disgusts me than otherwise; and this not because I cannot understand and appreciate as well as they whatever is beautiful or godlike in art or nature, but because they apply the term divine (and other attributes dreadfully misapplied) to individuals who are remarkable only for saying brilliant things, uttering striking thoughts or broaching profound views, but who are detestable in respect to personal character—and it seems to me that the aesthetic portion of our community indirectly support vice, by the countenance they give to individuals who ought to rank with stable boys in spite of all their genius.

In one brief paragraph Nathaniel managed to assault many of his sisters' most cherished beliefs. As extant correspondence indicates, relations between the brother and the sisters were not intimate. Nathaniel went his way, no more successfully, it would appear, than his father.[29]

Two Sisters in Love

According to Elizabeth Peabody's recollection, Hawthorne returned without his sisters to the Peabody house within a few days of his first visit. If her facts are not exactly accurate, there is nothing wrong with her sense of drama. Shortly after Hawthorne's arrival, Sophia, dressed in white, descended the stairs from her bedroom to the parlor.

> As I said "My sister Sophia—Mr Hawthorne," he rose and looked at her—he did not realise how intently, and afterwards, as we went on talking, she would interpose frequently a remark in her low sweet voice. Every time she did so, he looked at her with the same intentness of interest. I was struck with it, and painfully. I thought, what if he should fall in love with her; and I had heard her so often say, nothing would ever tempt her to marry, and inflict upon a husband the care of such a sufferer.[1]

Of course at the time of Hawthorne's visit Elizabeth had no such concerns—they came later—and Hawthorne probably did not know when he met Sophia for the first time that she was testing another cure in what had become a lifelong search for physical well-being. Under the ministrations of her father's assistant, Dr. Fiske, she was magnetized every day and "extremely soothed by it."[2]

Soon messages went back and forth between 12 Herbert Street and the house at the edge of the Charter Street Burying Point. Then there were visits and sometimes walks along the beach, which was only a short distance away. To everyone's surprise Hawthorne's sister Elizabeth began to be seen in the daylight. Soon the mothers were involved since their daughters needed permission as well as an appropriate escort if they ventured out by day or, worse, by night. That the participants were not exactly young was beside the point. In 1837 Sophia Peabody was twenty-eight, Louisa Hawthorne twenty-nine, Mary Peabody thirty-one, Elizabeth Peabody and Nathaniel Hawthorne thirty-three, and Elizabeth Hawthorne thirty-five. Because of her seniority Elizabeth Hawthorne became the chaperon. When she refused the role, the Peabody daughters were denied the pleasure of Hawthorne's company, which may have been Elizabeth's intention. She was at times as secretive and devious as her brother, particularly when his well-being was from her perspective in danger.

The villagers had to accustom themselves to the spectacle of a strange procession passing slowly through the streets. A handsome man attired in black was surrounded by four women who were more or less dowdy in appearance, at least not attired according to the standards of *Godey's Lady's Book*. Sophia's "delicate organization" kept her from these promenades except under ideal weather conditions. What they lacked in sartorial splendor, however, they made up in adoration of Salem's Apollo. The Hawthorne sisters, who idolized their brother but were too victimized by ingrained reticences to verbalize feelings, allowed their eyes to speak for them. The Peabody sisters, on the other hand, were addicted to demonstrating their love of beauty and the ideal in word and glance. In Elizabeth Peabody's judgment Hawthorne was not only Byron in more appropriate American attire but also Ariel, which for emphasis she wrote in capital letters. Even Mary Peabody, who for years remained patiently faithful to Horace Mann, extolled Hawthorne's "temple of a head (not a tower) and an eye full of sparkle, glisten, & intelligence."[3]

Hawthorne was spared, we can assume, the difficulty of concocting small talk for which he had almost no talent whatever. He was probably granted his silences since the Peabody sisters were rarely at a loss for words under any circumstances. They were no doubt unaware of Hawthorne's timidity in the presence of aggressive women, particularly on the order of Elizabeth Peabody, who rather wonderfully was unaware of her aggressiveness. Hawthorne found himself in a situation in which he had to adjust to two zealously genteel ladies for two reasons: he did not want to offend Elizabeth Peabody or to acknowledge his interest in Sophia, although, since he was not decisive in such matters, he probably had not as yet made up his mind about Sophia. Moreover, as we shall see shortly, he was enjoying adoration in another, more exciting quarter.

Without any hesitation but with her customary fumbling, Elizabeth Peabody took charge of the proceedings, her mission being to have Hawthorne realize his potential to the fullest. She was so in love with his prospects that she could not refrain from dogmatic pronouncements, as in this passage in a letter to Elizabeth Hawthorne:

> But the most perilous season is past for him. If, in the first ten years after leaving college, a man has followed his own fancies, without being driven by the iron whip of duty, and yet has not lost his moral or intellectual dignity, but rather consolidated them, there is good reason for believing that he is one of Nature's ordained priests, who is consecrated to her higher biddings. . . . I feel sure that this brother of yours has been gifted and kept so choice in her secret places by Nature thus far, that he may do a great thing for his country.

One of Elizabeth Peabody's problems was her willingness, even her eagerness, to succumb to her own hyperbole, which created "the ambrosial moral *aura*" about him.[4]

She watched over Hawthorne and protected him, although she sensed that he could only be nudged, not shoved. "We will not," she wrote to Louisa, "interrupt the bird in his song—*I wonder* what sort of preparation he found an evening of whist for the company of the Muses!" She tried to understand, but the "bird" had been naughty. Nor was Elizabeth always pleased with the company Hawthorne kept. "I have no idea that any such temptation has come to your brother yet," she observed, "but no being of a social nature can be entirely beyond the tendency to fall *to the level* of his associates." She was upset when he attended a "smoking party," for she had an infinite revulsion to smoking. When Horace Mann found Hawthorne smoking a cigar he observed: "I as a gentleman, Mr. Hawthorne, must tell you that I no longer respect you as I did."[5]

In age Elizabeth Peabody re-created (or more probably created) a conversation with Hawthorne about his mother and sisters which supposedly took place shortly after he began to visit the house on Charter Street.

> "They are out of the world so completely . . . that they do not know its customs. . . . My sister Elizabeth is very witty and individual, and knows the world marvellously, considering it is only through books. I wish you would come for my sake—for I want you to see her—I have not seen her for three months!" I made an exclamation of surprise, and he continued, "No—and we do not live at our home, we only vegetate. Elizabeth never leaves her den: I have mine in the upper story, to which they always bring my meals, setting them down in a waiter at my door, which is always locked. . . . My mother and Elizabeth each take their meals in their rooms. My mother has never sat down to table with anybody, since my father's death." I said, "Do you think it is healthy to live so separated?" "Certainly not—it is no life at all—it is the misfortune of my life. It has produced a morbid consciousness that paralyzes my powers."

It strains belief that Hawthorne would have bared such family matters to a woman whom he hardly knew. Furthermore, Elizabeth distorted the family situation grossly.[6]

Another of her anecdotes—once again reported years later—points up the strange and somewhat strained behavior of the participants in the romance. The two Elizabeths and Hawthorne were strolling one day when Elizabeth Hawthorne suddenly went off by herself, and then as she was returning she abruptly disappeared. Elizabeth Peabody had such a fright that she stopped coughing, for the first time in weeks. Apparently Elizabeth Hawthorne made her way home. Later in the day, her agitation much in evidence, Elizabeth Peabody wrote to warn Elizabeth Hawthorne, "I am afraid that [Mrs. Hawthorne] will never let us go again if she knows it." She decided also that "Nathaniel must idealize" the episode and provided the story line. Elizabeth Hawthorne "must be a coquettish girl—that torments some faithful swain—& gets punished by a fright—& the adventure must tame the wild Belphoebe into a true Amoretta—and Benedict must tell the story—I must figure in it as some old Aunt—I have not doubt he will make it up wisely."[7]

The relationship of the two families was odd from the outset. Suddenly Hawthorne, who generally avoided genteel circles of the Peabody sort, was a frequent, if shy, visitor at the Peabody house. Because Sophia rarely ventured out of the house, he accompanied Mary and Elizabeth on walks, enduring seemingly without too much difficulty their aesthetic and political chatter. He even took the unusual course of attending lectures with Mary, who duly informed Horace Mann that she found Hawthorne "deeply interested in such things as interest my mind—& you know what they are." Mary did not bother to enumerate, but something is wrong here since Hawthorne was ordinarily not interested in what preoccupied Mary. Perhaps his behavior was part of his secret design to keep the older sisters from recognizing his interest in Sophia.[8]

Another of his duties was to attend the Saturday night gatherings over which Susan Burley presided. These "Hurley-Burleys," as he labeled them, were held at the home of her sister, Mrs. Frederick Howes, on Federal Street. Although no detailed accounts of the meetings appear to be extant, there can be little doubt that discussions were Serious, Cultural, and Moral. Emerson praised Burley's "deep interest . . . in securing the highest culture for women. She was very well read, and, avoiding abstractions, knew how to help herself with examples and fact." If the "Hurley-Burleys" had little effect upon Hawthorne's life or his writings, Burley herself made a positive contribution to romance and art when in 1839 she subsidized the publication of "The Gentle Boy" with a Flaxman-like illustration by Sophia.[9]

On the night of January 3, 1838, before a lecture at the Salem Lyceum, Elizabeth Peabody introduced Hawthorne to another local celebrity, Jones Very, a poet, a sometime teacher at Harvard College, an unordained preacher, a mystic, and, in the eyes of townspeople understandably confused by his erratic behavior, an eccentric. Very was deeply burdened: he was one of six children born out of wedlock, his mother was in his eyes an infidel, and his beloved father died suddenly when he was eleven. In quiet moments he was a child, and Lidian Emerson remembered "how he sat there with a piece of gingerbread in each hand, so innocent, and unconscious! and how beautifully he was talking." Some of Ralph Waldo Emerson's detractors—and they were a virulent lot—attributed Very's religious delusions to the "Divinity School Address" which Emerson delivered in June 1838. Very was probably a manic-depressive who in delusional moments was given to assuming religious roles and to uncontrollable outbursts. Late in 1838 he was to be confined for a month in an institution near Boston.[10]

Elizabeth Peabody called Very's poetry to the attention of Emerson, who agreed to edit a selection for publication in 1839, but Very was averse to any alterations, believing his poetry to be "the utterance of the Holy Ghost." Emerson refused to yield, "we cannot permit the Holy Ghost to be careless (& in one instance) to talk bad grammar." [11]

One day Very decided several Salem preachers were in need of baptism and met with a vehemently unchristian response. He then went to the Peabody house, where Elizabeth admitted him.

> He looked much flushed and his eyes very brilliant, and unwink-ing—It struck me at once that there was something unnatural—and dangerous in his air—As soon as we were within the parlor door he laid his hand on my head,—and said "I come to baptize you with the Holy Ghost & with fire"—and then he prayed—I cannot remember his words but they were thrilling—and as I stood under his hand, I trembled to the centre—But it was my instinct—not to antagonize but to be perfectly quiet—I felt he was beside himself and I was alone in the lower story of the house.—. . . said he hurriedly—"I am the Second Coming—Give me a Bible". . . . I was silent but respect-ful even tenderly so. . . . [12]

Unlike some, Hawthorne was not impressed by Very's supposed illu-minations but treated the troubled man with tact and kindness. His re-ward was that soon Very began to come to 12 Herbert Street, always unannounced. Shortly after his one-month stay in the asylum, Very made what his biographer terms "his supreme gesture of love toward Haw-thorne." Elizabeth Peabody characterized the encounter at which she was present as the fulfillment of Very's "mission."

> Hawthorne received it [she wrote] in the loveliest manner—with the abandonment with which it was given . . . it was curious to see the respect of Very for *him*—and the reverence with which he treated his genius—There is a petulance about Hawthorne generally—when truth is taken out of the forms of nature. . . . But in this instance he repressed it & talked with him beautifully—[13]

According to Mary Peabody's construction, Very sought "a brother" and went to Hawthorne's home to "convert" him, that is, to accept and fulfill Very's need for a male figure, perhaps to replace his dead father. In his delusional state religion and personal loss were, it would appear, hopelessly confused. Very was too troubled to realize that his awesomely intense pursuit was an invasion of private space which Hawthorne guarded fearfully, as Melville was to discover years later.[14]

That winter Hawthorne in his usual fashion disclosed little of personal significance either in his journals or in his letters. On February 8, 1838, he observed to Horatio Bridge, "My life, till latterly, has gone on in the same dull . . ." but at this point Bridge, the ever-protective friend, deprived posterity of three and one-half lines which may have shed a great deal of light on what was taking place in the winter of 1838. In April he informed Lydia T. Fessenden, with whom he had boarded in Boston in 1836, "It has been a winter of much anxiety and of very little pleasure or profit." He could not leave Salem for at least three weeks because of "pressing" engagements, the nature of which he did not divulge. He included a bantering postscript to Fessenden's niece Catherine Ainsworth, whom he got to know when both stayed with the Fessendens two years earlier. Toward the conclusion of the note he reported some "nonsense": "I have heard recently the interesting intelligence that I am engaged to two ladies in this city. It was my first knowledge of the fact. I do trust that I shall not get married without my own privity and consent." The last sentence may confirm his amusement as well as his unawareness of the effect of his charades on the participants, especially on Elizabeth Peabody.[15]

Seemingly the least vulnerable, Elizabeth was no doubt the most hurt when the comedy of manners reached its denouement. During that winter she was in her customary role of the pursuer. In a letter in February 1838 to William Wordsworth, for whom she had "*filial* respect & gratitute," she praised Hawthorne with her usual extravagance:

While he breathes the spirit of humanity with a tenderness & depth of tone to which utilitarianism and empirical politics are strangers, he dares to write for Beauty's sake, not doubting but this will involve the highest use, & result in the purest truth. He is almost the only young American of any ability that I have known, who has hidden himself during his nonage and kept his own secret.—A fineness of stature and holiness of spirit—which have nothing in common with effeminacy, seem to have borne him quite above the career of vulgar ambition. . . .

How sad that such a confession of passion had to be intellectualized and her beloved transformed into an icon, but her prison was her protection.[16]

Years after Hawthorne's death Caroline H. Dall alleged that Elizabeth and Hawthorne were engaged and that he lived "in terror" that Elizabeth would inform Sophia, but there is no evidence that this was so. It is more likely that, recognizing Elizabeth's usefulness to his career, Hawthorne used her for his own ends, and she duly published a review of *Twice-told Tales* in the *New Yorker* on March 24, 1838, in which she reserved her highest praise for two sketches which most modern readers pass over as quickly as possible, "Sunday at Home" and "Little Annie's Ramble."[17]

When she left Salem in April 1838 to stay with her brother Nathaniel in West Newton, Elizabeth was still enamored of Hawthorne and extracted two promises. Hawthorne agreed to correspond but only on condition that she was not to show his letters to anyone. (She respected his wishes since none of the letters appear to have survived.) Elizabeth asked Sophia to keep a journal as she had done during her stay in Cuba and to forward it periodically to West Newton. Elizabeth kept her promise, but Hawthorne was careless. Elizabeth called on Sophia to intervene—at once. "I was quite disappointed not to find any letter from Hawthorne—I hope you sent mine in time enough.—When you see him tell him I was *very much disappointed*—knowing that he had one on hand,—I can only be consoled by having one *very soon*."[18]

Sophia dutifully began an epistolary diary in which she kept Elizabeth informed of happenings in Salem and at the same time, although her sister evidently did not recognize the symptoms, revealed that she was falling in love. On April 23 Sophia had such a headache that she could not see Hawthorne when he came to the Peabody house looking "very brilliant." She dreamed, she confessed, "about him all night, & he was Charles Emerson every other moment." Charles was Emerson's younger brother whose premature death in 1836 at twenty-eight Sophia had commemorated in a medallion relief which had pleased his fiancée, Elizabeth Hoar, and his brother.[19]

Later in the month Hawthorne's appearance at the Charter Street house clearly agitated Sophia.

After tea I laid down, & pulled all the combs out of my hair, & sent it streaming like a comet over my shoulders, untied all my dress, supposing I should have no occasion to appear. But I had scarcely touched my cheek to the pillow when the bell rang, & I was just as sure it was Mr Hawthorne as if I had seen him. Rebecca admitted him, & I told Mary I should go down if it proved to be he. She soon called to me, & I verily thought I never should become rearranged,—such was my haste—but finally I descended, armed with a blue odorous violet. Mr Hawthorne would not take off his coat or stay, because he had the headache & an engagement. . . . He looked very brilliant notwithstanding his headache. . . .

Sophia had "a delightful night" and remembered with amusement that Hawthorne expressed a desire to "have intercourse with some beautiful children—beautiful little girls—he did not care for boys."[20]

In May he came to see Elizabeth. When he discovered that she had not arrived in Salem, he put her letter into his pocket without breaking the seal. "He looked very handsome and full of smiles," Sophia reported.

I inquired, whether the story of the Picture [probably "Edward Randolph's Portrait"] were written yet, and he replied, "no" but this week he was going about it. I said that I should be very proud if I should be ever so indirect a means of causing a creation, and he replied "that he should make a great many stories from my *works*." That sounded very comical to me. . . . He said he believed he would go and take a walk in South Salem. "Won't you go?" he asked of me. The wind was east.

On June 1 he came "to see our ladyships, and I never saw him look so brilliant and *rayonnant*. . . . Only think what a progress, to come and *propose* a walk at mid day." Such were the measures one had to resort to in order to see change in a man who shyly (or slyly) proceeded in his own fashion. Perhaps Sophia's underscoring of "propose" told more than she realized.[21]

Whatever his intentions at the time—and his life was at the moment complicated—Sophia Peabody did not share his indecisiveness or complications. By May 2, 1838, she had reached a decision and had to remind herself, "Oh! I forgot, I never intended to have a husband. Rather I should say, I never intended any one shall have me for wife." She was ready to marry Hawthorne.[22]

When Sophia and Hawthorne were dead and Julian Hawthorne had published his two-volume biography, Elizabeth Peabody commented with touching candor,

It is *because* I believe marriage is a sacrament, and nothing *less*, that I am dying as an old Maid,—I have had too much respect for marriage to make a conventional one in my own case.—I am free to say that had Hawthorne wanted to marry me he would probably not have found much difficulty in getting my consent;—but it is very clear to me now, that I was not the person to make *him* happy, or to be made happy *by* him, and Sophia *was*.—If there was ever a "match made in Heaven" it was *that*. . . .

In youth as in age—fortunately in view of her fragilities—Elizabeth Peabody lived more or less securely inside the shelter provided by fantasies of innate goodness which reduced human complexities to a comforting symmetry.[23]

11

Mary Silsbee

"Star of Salem"

About the time Hawthorne began to call at the modest
house at the edge of the cemetery, he also entered the
stately parlors of a beautiful mansion at 94 Washington
Square East at Briggs Street, the home of one of Salem's
elite, Nathaniel Silsbee. At this time, two years after the
death of the mother, the home was presided over by a
beautiful daughter, Mary Crowninshield Silsbee, who
was called by some of her detractors, of whom there
seem to have been many, the "Star of Salem."

Although Elizabeth Peabody was not one of Mary
Silsbee's admirers—quite the opposite—both apparently
sought out Hawthorne after the publication of *Twice-told
Tales*. An amateur poet, Mary had a fondness for authors. Again her critics would have phrased the sentence
somewhat differently, no doubt adding "and handsome
men." How the shy Byronic-looking Hawthorne acted
when he entered the Silsbee parlor for the first time
he never said, but if he shrank as he went into the Peabody home, intimidated by the overly assertive presence
of Elizabeth, he must have hastily lowered his eyes,
blushed, and almost stammered in the presence of a
beautiful and seductive young woman who from considerable experience knew how to use a room and its appointments for her own purposes.

The same age as Sophia Peabody, Mary was a woman

of the world, having moved in the upper circles of Salem, Boston, and Washington. Every gesture, as the Peabody sisters suggested, may have been calculated, with the result that in their eyes she was a siren, or worse. Elizabeth Peabody pronounced her "a handsome girl, a great coquette, a mischief-maker, a fearful liar." Lydia Haven, who was a friend of the Peabodys, could hardly control her contempt (or her spitefulness) in referring to Mary's appearance, "her head caught in a snarl of laces . . . rigged out in a gown that had the appearance of just kindling into a blaze," or to her manners, a "torrent of affectation." In their fury, which could appear to be somewhat overdone, proper ladies were unkind to a young woman who may have been vain, even superficial, but who was not insensitive. Her worst flaw in the eyes of her critics may have been her ability to attract and charm men of considerable distinction, such as Jared Sparks, the celebrated historian, and Nathaniel Hawthorne. Yet it is perhaps strange, given her beauty, means, and eligibility, that a woman approaching thirty was unmarried.[1]

Mary Silsbee was not inhibited by the Peabody concept of Duty or the Hawthorne reserve, and it may be that her freedom from the sometimes precious intellectuality of the Peabody and Burley set and willingness to indulge in frivolous banter freed Hawthorne from his customary reticence. On the other hand, he may have sat tongue-tied in the elegant surroundings, in his own quiet way taxing Mary's resources. Hawthorne had long since intuited the powers of passivity. Even when the drama ended, when Mary for the last time had manipulated him, he as an artist had vast admiration for the performance: she was "a perfect work of art."[2]

A man of considerable inexperience, except perhaps among people from the lower social orders, Hawthorne had never before confronted anyone like Mary Silsbee. Apparently he fell in love with the "Star of Salem"—foolishly and clumsily. For a time she toyed with him, no doubt attracted to and amused by his tremulous, hesitant manner, and perhaps she used him and his connections for her own ends. Yet she may have been in love. This, however, was not the perception of Elizabeth Peabody, who loved generously and hated on the same uncritical scale. She waited fifty years for her revenge, when she manipulated Julian Hawthorne's account of the relationship in his biography of his parents.

Julian Hawthorne should not have accepted his aunt's recollections uncritically—at no time, certainly not in her eighties, did she worry unduly about accuracy when she had a point to make—but he was guided by the principles of hagiography, not of biography. Thus he treated Mary Silsbee as an enemy of his mother and aunt and attributed the "rash and regrettable episode" about to be related to his father's "impetuous youth," though Hawthorne was all of thirty-three.[3]

Perhaps fearing charges of libel, Julian referred to her only as Mary from the "'best circles' of Salem and Boston." He neglected to mention that she was still alive and could have been interviewed or that she was the widow of a former president of Harvard College. Julian attacked with a foolish fury that exposed more about him and his aunt's long-repressed rage than it did about Mary Silsbee.

He alleged that "as a child, she had been the victim of an abnormal and almost diseased sensitiveness, which often caused her to behave oddly and unaccountably." At dancing school she suffered from imaginary slights and withdrew. She then aspired to "the power of intellect" but with a mind "not of the calibre of De Staël or even of Margaret Fuller." After "hobbledehoyhood" she became "a social enchantress" with "the art of an actress"—a "marvellously skilful liar; she was coarse in thought and feeling, and at times seemed to be possessed by a sort of moral insanity."[4]

With the assistance of previously neglected materials, including a volume of poetry published many years after Hawthorne's death, the story can be retold without Julian's (or, more accurately, Elizabeth's) bias as a Salem comedy of manners in the winter of 1838. In addition to Hawthorne, Mary Silsbee, and Elizabeth Peabody, the other principals were Ann Storrow, Jared Sparks, John Louis O'Sullivan, and Jonathan Cilley.

Mary Silsbee and Hawthorne were children of sea captains, both of whom at very early ages struggled to revive declining family fortunes. Nathaniel Silsbee, who was two years older than Captain Nathaniel Hathorne, enjoyed a spectacular success and was able to retire from the sea in 1801. In 1800 Hathorne sailed to the Pacific under Captain Silsbee. Hathorne married in 1801, Silsbee in 1802. Nathaniel Silsbee, Jr., was born in 1804, the same year as Nathaniel Hawthorne, in whose life he was to play a role at a critical juncture in 1849. Captain Silsbee on his retirement pursued an active career in commerce in Boston and Salem before he went into politics. After serving as United States senator from Massachusetts, he retired in 1835 to Salem.

Mary Silsbee was named after her mother, Mary Crowninshield, a member of one of the first families of Salem. After her mother's death in

1835, Mary recorded in one of her poems her deep grief and exposed feelings of inadequacy which may not have been evident when Hawthorne was in her parlor. If Elizabeth Peabody had seen the poem, she would no doubt have accused Mary of insincerity, but it is equally plausible that the daughter genuinely mourned the loss of her mother, which may even have influenced her conduct two years later.

According to her own account, Mary Silsbee began to compose poems and translate poetry at age ten. Probably she never aspired to be a professional writer—women of her class and leisure at that time in America seldom did, few privileged women following the example of Madame de Staël. When Mary Silsbee came into print in 1883 the title page of *Hymns, Home, Harvard* was carefully worded, "Printed, not published," her nonmaterialistic motivation being of significance in the circles in which she moved.

On the basis of her collected poetry it is only fair to observe that she was not one of the neglected poets of the age, but—which is not to praise excessively—she was no worse than dozens of other poets of both sexes who had a talentless love affair with poetry, printed volumes at their own expense, and are no longer remembered. Probably intended only for the eyes of her children and perhaps the few friends of a woman almost seventy-five years of age, her volume unfolds the life not of the coquette who aroused the wrath and envy of her peers but of a young woman whose private life had little glitter and much sadness. The poems are melancholic in tone, perhaps fashionably so in what could be called the Age of Melancholy, although it would be kinder to assume that the expression of her sorrow is more than literary convention despite the clichés that dominate the lines.

In 1830 Mary, nineteen, was in Washington, where she was the reigning belle. A woman in her forties, Ann Storrow, wrote a long letter to the first important American historian, Jared Sparks, who eventually wrote and edited over a hundred volumes. He was a successful preacher at the beginning of his career, the editor and owner of the *North American Review*, biographer of Washington and others, and a social lion. Like Hawthorne a handsome man, he was painted by Rembrandt Peale, Gilbert Stuart, and Thomas Sully.

Ann Storrow set out to warn the thirty-nine-year-old Sparks of Mary Silsbee's notoriety. "The Star of Salem I think is Lord of the Ascendant everywhere, but I must say it gave me a sore feeling when I heard that you must be one of the worshippers of Miss S., of a woman to whom common report gives so very little that is intrinsically interesting and valuable, though so much that is glaring and attractive." Storrow itemized unsparingly the "Star's" failures:

I doubt not the lady has a great deal of talent, and *power* she must have. This I hear from every source. But her thirst for display and admiration is so utterly insatiable that it leads her I verily believe to sacrifice for the sake of it much that is lovely and beautiful in a woman's character—properties which you, my susceptible friend, love and admire as much as anybody when you have the clear possession of your faculties. A year of absence and change will do much to cure you of your fever of the brain. I do not speak of all this as any violation of propriety or good feeling, but I always dislike to see you whom I set so high, descend from your elevation, and I trust you will forgive me for supposing you superior to *common* weakness, or to the enticements of *common* vanity. . . . I cannot bear to have you let a reigning Belle lead you captive.

Storrow's bias led her to debase a young woman who had done her no harm except to attract the man whom she was to love secretly all her life.[5]

There were three important women in Spark's life, Ann Storrow, Frances Anne Allen, and Mary Silsbee. The first maintained a lifelong platonic relationship as his "sister." Four years after the warning, Sparks married Allen, a wealthy woman. Storrow was not pleased, although eventually she became the intimate of wife and daughter. In 1833 the Sparkses, along with Mary and Elizabeth Peabody and Horace Mann, boarded with Rebecca Clarke in Boston. Sophia was also acquainted with Frances Anne Sparks. The Peabodys were not admirers of Jared Sparks, despite his physical charms and intelligence. Mary Peabody called him "crusty Jared Sparks," and her future husband referred to him as "the Right Reverend Rude Rough." After his wife's death of consumption in 1835, Sparks became an endowed widower.[6]

In 1837 John Louis O'Sullivan founded the *United States Magazine and Democratic Review* and invited Hawthorne to contribute to a journal "designed," in his words, "to be of the highest rank of magazine literature, taking *ton* of the first class in England for model." Hawthorne's "The Toll-Gatherer's Day" appeared in the first issue of the magazine in October 1837.[7]

The son of an American consul, O'Sullivan had the distinction of being born aboard a British man-of-war in 1813 in the harbor at Gibraltar. The father was shipwrecked and died when his son was ten. O'Sullivan attended Columbia College and received degrees in arts and law; he occasionally practiced law, but the profession did not accommodate his personality and versatility. He had for a time a meteoric career in journalism, politics, speculation, and adventure. He coined the phrase "Manifest Destiny" and later stood trial after organizing an expedition to seize Cuba. The jury split and O'Sullivan was freed. Flamboyant, charismatic, energetic but with a restless attention span, he had great potential, but easy recourse to convenient expediencies and his eternal need of money transformed him slowly into a con-artist who usually remained within legal boundaries. As a friendly critic observed, "When he set out to picture the simple and easy methods whereby he proposed to make millions, it was next to impossible to resist him." Longfellow was one of those who resisted his charm and characterized him in 1839 as a "young man, with weak eyes, and green spectacles . . . [who] is a *Humbug*, nevertheless and notwithstanding."[8]

For almost twenty years O'Sullivan advised Hawthorne, zealously worked on his behalf for a political sinecure, and became the godfather of the Hawthornes' first child, Una. Hawthorne appreciated his friend's abilities as a con-artist, but when his wife began to succumb to O'Sullivan's charm, he presented her with a judicious but cautionary evaluation:

> It has sometimes seemed to me that the lustre of his angel-plumage has been a little dimmed—his heavenly garments a little soiled and bedraggled—by the foul ways through which it has been his fate to tread, and the foul companions with whom necessity and politics have brought him acquainted. But I had rather thou should take *him* for a friend than any other man I ever knew . . . because I think the Devil has a smaller share in O'Sullivan than in other bipeds who wear breeches. . . . I have a genuine affection for him, and a confidence in his honor. . . .[9]

Wandering between the Peabody and Silsbee houses, Hawthorne ingested in one cultural and spiritual eroticism, a diet usually not to his taste, and in the other a wily, sophisticated eroticism, fascinating but perhaps frightening to a man of great trepidations. Julian Hawthorne charged that Mary Silsbee "at once perceived how great [Hawthorne's] value would be to her, as a testimony to the potency of her enchantments, and set herself to ensnare him." She was, in short, Duessa loose in Salem. Julian, who turned out to be a man of the world himself and of adjustable principles (he was to serve a prison term for embezzlement), consistently chose to paint his father as Robin Molineux.[10]

Coincidentally, O'Sullivan's planned visit to Salem led Elizabeth Peabody, as we have seen, to seek out Elizabeth Hawthorne because she wanted to know "what were the steps to take to put an article into the Democratic Review," and this in turn led to the initial meeting of the Hawthornes and Peabodys on November 11. When O'Sullivan arrived in Salem, Hawthorne no doubt took him to the Peabody house where he was introduced to Elizabeth. One of her articles duly appeared in O'Sullivan's magazine.[11]

It seems plausible, admittedly in the absence of documentation, that after introducing O'Sullivan to the Peabodys, Hawthorne guided his friend into the Silsbee parlor, where O'Sullivan would have been completely at ease: after all, it was one artist meeting another, which is not a judgment, only an amused description. In fact, we can suppose that the nonverbal Hawthorne delighted in witnessing the exchanges of two cunning verbalists. Mary Silsbee would scarcely have tried to persuade O'Sullivan to publish one of her poems, but something occurred, for a few months later Mary would assume a new role which inevitably she would play with all the sincerity of her artifices.[12]

After O'Sullivan's departure, Hawthorne's oscillations between two worlds continued. In the elegant ambience of the Silsbee rooms Hawthorne listened to Mary read her poetry, no doubt with an appropriately melancholic sensuousness. In the volume published in 1883 she included a poem which she declared was "first published in a tale of Hawthorne, at his kind request, and printed, as a song of his ('Faith') in a Salem paper." Neither the tale nor the newspaper appearance of the poem can be traced. Perhaps she fabricated or memory failed her. Perhaps Hawthorne and she played a joke on Salem readers. No matter. The important thing is that years later she recalled Hawthorne's memory with pleasure. The poem is suffused with melancholy, perhaps because the mismatched lovers recognized that they would go separate ways.

Take back the flowers, 't will only fling
  A perfume round my way,
Like music from a worn-out string,
  Sooner to shrink away.

Take back the bud, 't is like my dream,
  Nurst in a sunny hour;
And, while its hopes the fairest seem,
  Broke—it will never flower!

Only a love-struck youth, not a man of Hawthorne's years, should have been impressed by these lines, but never before had he encountered a woman with Cleopatra's charms and wiles.[13]

In the confidences they exchanged, according to the account Julian received from Elizabeth Peabody, Mary Silsbee unfolded "the most private passages of her autobiography" and attempted to beguile Hawthorne into similar personal revelations. When she encountered Hawthorne reserve, she tried another "mode of attack." Hawthorne himself was to admit, after the "affair" was over, that he now "put a different interpretation on the 'secret spring,' which I was to discover 'soon, or never'"—evidently a secret Mary wanted to share and at the same time to conceal, in a cat-and-mouse game. The secret was not her "father's disapprobation," Hawthorne declared. "That 'spring' was within her own heart, and I was to discover it by reflecting on something she had formerly revealed to me. I have reflected, and think that I have penetrated the mystery." But he kept what he discovered to himself.[14]

Hawthorne declared that he "had reason to suppose" that Nathaniel Silsbee, Sr., "knew something of the affair, and sanctioned it." Surely Hawthorne deceived himself. The father knew that Captain Hathorne left his family penniless at death and that the widow had to move in with the Mannings. Everyone in Salem must have known that Hawthorne after graduating from Bowdoin had neither profession nor visible means of livelihood, not even in the Manning "counting house." At thirty-three Silsbee's son was a successful businessman and lawyer. At the same age Hawthorne was unable to support himself, let alone a wife with Mary Silsbee's tastes.[15]

If Elizabeth Peabody's report is correct—her source may even have been Hawthorne himself—Mary promised to marry Hawthorne "when he had an income of $3000." Either Mary was naive or, more probably, agreed with the family's evaluation of Hawthorne's potential resources and took the seemingly playful way of informing him of the material realities on which her charm reposed.[16]

Sometime that winter, probably toward the end of January or early in the following month, Mary Silsbee "summoned Hawthorne," in the words of Julian, who wrote as though he had witnessed the meeting,

> to a private and mysterious interview, at which, after much artful preface and well-contrived hesitation and agitated reluctance, she at length presented him with the startling information that his friend Louis [O'Sullivan], presuming upon her innocence and guilelessness, had been guilty of an attempt to practise the basest treachery upon her; and she passionately abjured Hawthorne, as her only confidential and trusted friend and protector, to champion her cause.[17]

It must have been quite a scene, to which neither Julian Hawthorne nor anyone else can do justice. After all, the only ones present were forever silent, no doubt aware, afterward at least, that the drama teetered on farce. Mary was the outraged virgin, O'Sullivan the compromiser of her virtue, and Hawthorne the knight errant who was to set out to confront O'Sullivan in Washington. The plot could have come from *Fanshawe*, which Mary, we are safe in adding, had never read, let alone heard of. Exactly what O'Sullivan had done, or perhaps not done, to arouse her wrath, there is no way to determine. There are possibilities. In person or in letter, O'Sullivan may have crossed a boundary of intimacy at which Mary drew a line. On the other hand, she may have been bored with Salem and Hawthorne too and craved excitement to recharge her life or to escape from a melancholic state by means of a not very imaginative scenario. There was no way, despite Hawthorne's unfounded fancies, that the relationship would lead to marriage.

Julian Hawthorne had it all wrong when he alleged that "without pausing to make proper investigations" his father issued a challenge to O'Sullivan. If Hawthorne couldn't say no to Mary, he also couldn't exactly say yes. No doubt he disappointed her as well as his son: in a fury he should have set off by stagecoach for Washington armed with a brace of pistols. Instead, as one would expect, he wrote a letter to O'Sullivan, in his decorous eighteenth-century prose mentioning the possibility of a duel—and then sat back to wait for an answer. He may not have loved wisely, but it is doubtful that, given his hesitancies and his fears, he was about to make a fool of himself. If Mary Silsbee knew how to whip up a rage, he knew how to stall.

On the basis of an excision in a letter Hawthorne wrote to Bridge on February 8, 1838, we can assume that the challenge to O'Sullivan may have been sent about this time. Following the deletion appeared the following: "It is my purpose to set out to Washington, in the course of a fortnight or thereabouts—but only to make a short visit." In a postscript Hawthorne warned, "Be mum." And Bridge was. Possibly the excised material would clarify the Silsbee-O'Sullivan-Hawthorne situation. In this "winter of much anxiety," as he characterized it to another correspondent, Hawthorne may have intended to go to Washington in order to challenge O'Sullivan in person, but it is also possible that he planned the trip in pursuit of a governmental post. He did neither: he went to Washington for the first time in 1853.[18]

The play-acting in Salem collided at last with reality and proved a bubble. After receiving Hawthorne's letter O'Sullivan in reply detailed, according to Julian, the "ins and outs of the deception which had been practiced upon him." Sadly, both letters remain unlocated. Hawthorne accepted O'Sullivan's explanation, renewed his friendship, and, in the words of Julian, "went to Mary and 'crushed her.'" The last statement is patently false. Hawthorne never summoned up courage to crush Mary, then or later. Confrontation was not his style, evasion was.

No doubt he entered the Silsbee house one day and timidly told Mary what O'Sullivan had said. No doubt she, after momentary surprise, emoted and explained—at considerable length but not without her usual charm. Quietly the relationship changed and visits became fewer. But when Mary summoned, Hawthorne returned, until, since she was not ultimately to be defeated, she rediscovered another suitor who this time was not to follow Ann Storrow's advice.

Seemingly like many other things in the story of Hawthorne's life, acts had unforeseen ramifications and strange reverberations. At this time Jonathan Cilley, who had lost the wager on Hawthorne's marital status, was serving in the House of Representatives in Washington. At the beginning of his second year as a congressman, Cilley became involved in an almost farcical situation that led to a duel which achieved a great deal of notoriety. Matthew L. Davis, a correspondent for the *New-York Courier and Enquirer* and, curiously, a biographer of

Burr, charged that an unnamed congressman had been guilty of what we would now term a conflict of interests. Davis's editor, James Watson Webb, supported his correspondent and demanded a congressional investigation. In opposing the resolution when it was brought before the Congress, Cilley criticized the editor from the floor. Webb took offense and challenged Cilley, who refused to recognize Webb's rights in the matter. Whereupon the congressman from Kentucky, William J. Graves, had Representative Henry A. Wise deliver a challenge to Cilley, who did everything possible to pacify the partisans. Finally Cilley agreed to a duel on the morning of February 24, 1838, which cost him his life. [19]

According to Julian Hawthorne, who was once more drawing upon Elizabeth Peabody, Cilley hesitated before accepting Graves's challenge until "at length, however, some one said, 'If Hawthorne was so ready to fight a duel without stopping to ask questions, you certainly need not hesitate.' . . . This argument . . . put an end to Cilley's doubts." When Hawthorne learned of Cilley's act, so his son declared, he felt "almost as much responsible for his friend's death as was the man who shot him. . . . He had touched hands with crime; and all the rest was but a question of degree." Here Julian wrote nonsense, and Bridge categorically repudiated Julian's version: "I never heard, at that time nor afterwards, that Cilley was in any way influenced by Hawthorne's example. Nor did Hawthorne himself ever intimate to me, by word or letter, that he considered himself at all responsible for Cilley's course in accepting Graves's challenge." [20]

When that fall at the request of O'Sullivan, Hawthorne agreed to write a eulogy of Cilley for the *Democratic Review*, he did so not out of a sense of guilt but out of respect for a classmate who at the time of his death was seeking a governmental sinecure for him. In the eulogy Hawthorne spoke, somewhat loosely, of knowing Cilley "since early youth, when he had been to me almost as an elder brother," and declared that Cilley "had an impending brow, deep-set eyes, and a thin and thoughtful countenance, which, in his abstracted moments, seemed almost stern; but, in the intercourse of society it was brightened with a kindly smile that will live in the recollection of all who knew him." An earlier description in his notebooks was less kind but probably more accurate: "His person in some degree accords with his character—thin, and a thin face, sharp features, sallow, a projecting brow, not very high, deep-set eyes; an insinuating smile and look, when he meets you, or is about to address you." [21]

Hawthorne's eulogy was one of the reasons why he was appointed to the Boston Custom-House in 1839: it proved him a loyal Democrat. Ten years later when he lost his post in the Salem Custom-House, one of the explanations the Whigs advanced was his partisan writings. The only article that could be called political was the eulogy of Cilley.

In 1839 an outraged Congress, goaded to action by the impassioned denunciation of former president John Quincy Adams, outlawed dueling. Representative Wise declaimed with fervor: "Let Puritans shutter as they may—I proclaim that I belong to the class of Cavaliers, not to the roundheads! . . . You have passed a penitentiary act." In another climate four years later, partisan outrage gave way to expediency. In the May 1842 issue, the *Democratic Review* acknowledged that "a great and serious injustice had been done to Mr. Wise." Eighteen months later, in November 1843, when O'Sullivan was seeking the Salem postmastership for Hawthorne, he wrote at length to Wise promising to "render full credit," presumably in the pages of the *Democratic Review*, in return for the congressman's support of the appointment.[22]

Several times in the spring of 1838 Elizabeth Peabody alluded to Hawthorne's "unhappiness" without offering an explanation, until she became quite explicit in a letter to his sister Elizabeth: "I came to suspect that M. C. S. was coquetting—I interpreted their hieroglyphics—by means of that—in some measure." Characteristically she placed the blame on Mary Silsbee. If Sophia knew as much as her sister Elizabeth about the relationship of Mary Silsbee and Hawthorne, it is surprising that on May 1, 1838, she and her sister Mary paid a visit to see a painting owned by the Silsbees. "We were put into the drawing-room," Sophia informed Elizabeth, "before Miss Mary appeared. She received us very simply and pleasantly, and I was very agreeably impressed with her." But when Sophia discovered striking parallels between Mary Silsbee and a portrait of a hunter or bandit, she began, in her words, to "kindle" to the point that she wanted "to put Miss Mary out the window," an unusually violent response of a gentle woman, unless she feared that Mary Silsbee had tried to steal Hawthorne from her, which, if true, she would probably never have admitted.[23]

It had been a winter in Hawthorne's judgment "of much anxiety and of very little pleasure or profit." He did not explain. The entries in his notebook in May and June, probably reflecting his response to the impact of

Mary Silsbee's potent gentility, focused on the power of one person to enslave another. One entry recorded the attempt of a "virtuous but giddy" woman to deceive a man only to find herself completely in "his power and . . . ruined." Another, anticipating the situation in *The Scarlet Letter*, was concerned with the "influence of a peculiar mind, in close communion with another, to drive the latter to insanity." A third notation dealt with the "situation of a man in the midst of a crowd, yet as completely in the power of another, life and all, as if they were in the deepest solitude."[24]

On July 4 Hawthorne celebrated his thirty-fourth birthday. Alone in the Salem Common, he observed the festivities of a group of young women who in the moonlight looked "beautiful and fairy-like" but, when they spoke, betrayed their "plebeianism by the tones of their voices." Evidently Hawthorne had to qualify his interest in plebeian women by objecting to the uncultivated tintinnabulation of their voices.[25]

Later in the month he returned to Sophia the three-volume manuscript of her "Cuban Journals," which Elizabeth Peabody had evidently entrusted to him, and pronounced her "Queen of Journalivres." "He looked," Sophia exclaimed, "like the sun shining through a silver mist when he turned to me & said that—It is a most wonderful face." Then he informed her that he was about to leave on a three-month journey without a forwarding address and that he planned to change his name "so that if he died no one could be able to find his grave-stone." Clearly Hawthorne enjoyed assuming the role of Fanshawe, including his preoccupation with dying, but Sophia, not taken in by the melodramatic posture, extracted from him a promise that instead of dying he would keep a journal.[26]

On July 23 Hawthorne left for Boston by stage and on the next day arrived in the "large village" of Pittsfield in the Berkshires. There is no way of determining what drew him to the mountains of western Massachusetts, although the locale was to provide him years later with the setting for the tale of another wanderer-isolate, Ethan Brand. Almost at once he visited the cemetery in Pittsfield and noted the tomb of the Reverend Thomas Allen, the father of Bowdoin's president. On the following day he went to North Adams which, either by design or by accident, was to be his primary place of "seclusion" in August and early September. At once he directed David Roberts, one of his Salem friends, to forward his mail. "Do not tell anybody that you have heard from me," he warned, "or that you know anything of my whereabouts. You will see me again (God willing) in the course of six months." If he visited the cemetery in North Adams, he made no notations in his journal, but on August 10 he attended a child's funeral, and on August 26 he saw "a coffin of a boy about ten years old, laid in a one horse wagon among some straw. . . . a few men formed a brief procession in front of the coffin, among whom was Orrin Smith and I."[27]

Smith was one of the local characters with whom Hawthorne struck up an acquaintance. A widower with three children, he was "a dissolute and mirth-making middle-aged man, who would not seem to have much domestic feeling," and "a dry jester" who "drinks sometimes more than enough and has pecadillos with the fair sex." Hawthorne found Smith engaging, perhaps because of his witty, off-color conversation and behavior. Yet at other times Hawthorne acted in his squeamish, overfastidious fashion. Sardonically he observed "people washing themselves at the common basin in the bar-room, and using the common hairbrush— perhaps with a consciousness of praiseworthy neatness." According to his careful compilation he bathed on July 27, 30, 31; August 8, 11, 14, 21, 29; and September 5, 7, and 9. If he itemized his amorous adventures as he did his ablutions, Sophia later took care of that indiscretion when she excised two pages, which, however, given his reticences and even fears as to the fate of the journals, probably contained few if any intimations. And it was in North Adams that a stranger said to him: "I do not know your name, but there is something of the hawk-eye about you too."[28]

After Hawthorne left North Adams on September 11, he made his way as far south as Litchfield, Connecticut. He apparently had no particular reason for going there except perhaps for its association with Dr. Samuel Johnson, whose life he was shortly to write in one of his children's books. He went almost at once to the lovely cemetery at the foot of the main street of the village, where he admired the splendid carved tombstone of a clergyman who died in 1796. After his return to Salem on September 24, he assured Longfellow that he had "had such a pleasant time as seldom happens to a man of my age and experience."[29]

The Comedy of Manners
Ends Happily

When Hawthorne returned from North Adams he had completed another of his periodic flights from gentility and duty. He had ogled a little, flirted a little, and enjoyed a pretty leg, but almost at once he resumed his visits to the Peabody house and again attended the meetings of Susan Burley and her group of idealists. In the fall Elizabeth Peabody came back to Salem and with her usual restless energy and unlimited enthusiasm created a great deal of intellectual excitement. No doubt she was still in love with Hawthorne but even more with the prospect of guiding him in the best interests of society. Since Sophia was artful in her quiet, determined way and Hawthorne as usual was secretive, we can assume that Elizabeth was unaware of his attraction to Sophia or her response, just as a few years earlier she had failed to recognize the developing bond between Horace Mann and her sister Mary until she had almost made a fool of herself.

In his usual indecisive manner, Hawthorne had not made a clean and definitive break with Mary Silsbee. That fall she summoned him to the Silsbee mansion. Fearful of the outcome, he consulted with O'Sullivan before he accepted the summons. His reluctance was understandable: he was no match for her, any more than

Miles Coverdale is for Zenobia in *The Blithedale Romance*. Taking the offensive—always a superb tactician—Mary Silsbee marshaled her enormous seductive resources and once more overwhelmed him, as he reported to O'Sullivan.

> . . . in accordance with your exhortations, I have seen our fair friend. Her manner of receiving me was incomparably good—perfectly adapted to the circumstances—altogether beyond criticism. It might seem that I should have had the vantage-ground in such an interview—having been virtually invited to it by herself, after expressing a desire and determination to break off all intercourse—and having expressly stated, moreover, that any future intercourse should not be on the ground of friendship. But it was no such thing. All the glory was on her side; and no small glory it is, to have made a wronged man feel like an offender—and that, too, without permitting any direct allusion to the matter in dispute—and to have put on just so much dignity as to keep me precisely at the distance she chose, tempered with just so much kindness that I could not possibly quarrel with her. She was dressed in better taste and looked more beautiful than ever I saw her before; and she, and her deportment and conversation, were all of a piece, and altogether constituted a perfect work of art—meaning the phrase in no bad sense.

Perhaps Mary outdid herself in enjoying her mastery of the situation and her former lover, for her imperious manner freed him of enchantment.

> Yet the interview had not produced the effect that she anticipated from it. I came with, I think, the most dismal and doleful feeling that I ever experienced—a sense that all had been a mistake—that I never really loved—that there was no real sympathy between us—and that a union could only insure the misery of both. . . .
>
> It is fit that I do her all manner of justice, as respects her treatment of me. Looking back at her conduct, with the light that her last letter has given me, I am convinced that she has meant honorably and kindly by me,—that I have nothing to complain of in her motives, though her actions have not been altogether so well-judged.[1]

At this meeting Hawthorne was introduced to a recently widowed professor from Harvard College who, as he probably did not know, was an old suitor now about to become a new and successful one—Jared Sparks. Mary Silsbee did not waste the hours. Curiously, one of Mary Peabody's friends used Ann Storrow's image to characterize the impending marriage: "So one of your stars is to wander our way and shine & I hope bless Mr. Sparks' solitude."[2]

Before her marriage on May 21, 1839, Mary Silsbee wrote for the last time to Hawthorne, requesting him to forward the only letter from O'Sullivan in her possession, the rest having been burned along with Hawthorne's letters. "I hardly expected," he wrote to O'Sullivan, "to be the medium of another communication between our fair friend and yourself, but now certainly the last knot of our entanglement is loosed. She is to be married, I believe, this week—an event which, I am almost sorry to think, will cause a throb in neither of our bosoms. . . . I have found no time to call on her these three months; but I understand that I am still in good odor with her."[3]

Later in the same letter Hawthorne declared, "I have neither resentment nor regrets, liking nor dislike"—a statement which was not quite true—"having fallen in love with somebody else." A year later, perhaps in another mood, he was hardly gentlemanly in his comment to O'Sullivan: "Did I tell you . . . that our friend, Mrs. S[parks] has had a miscarriage? Such seems to be her fate, in her life as a whole, and in all details." His prediction as to the course of Mary Sparks's life, however, proved inaccurate. She was to be the mother of five children. To celebrate their tenth wedding anniversary—it was the year in which Jared Sparks became president of Harvard College—she wrote one of her most delightful poems, the rhythms confirming the enduring joy.[4]

Since fictional characters are often composites of many people in an author's experiences, in addition to his or her own complexities and fantasies, it is not usually possible to make positive identifications, but Mary Silsbee Sparks, whose "secret spring" Hawthorne claimed to have discovered, may have influenced the delineations of Zenobia in *The Blithedale Romance* and Miriam Schaefer in *The Marble Faun*, both powerfully erotic and mysterious figures whose pasts are veiled in mysteries. These seemingly strong women, however, are held in bondage and denied fulfillment. In the role of brutalizer, like his Hathorne forebears, Hawthorne perhaps took secret revenge on those women who in his perception had exploited him. Or, human motivations rarely being reducible to such simplifications, in his art Hawthorne may have experienced simultaneously the gratifications of the exploiter and the exploited.

Hawthorne's involvements in 1838 produced diversion and gossip in Salem, but the real drama was being unfolded quietly, decorously, and unobtrusively. While Hawthorne escorted Mary and Elizabeth Peabody about to satisfy their intellectual thirst, he was entering the Peabody parlor frequently and, without any awareness on the part of the older sisters, was gradually falling in love with the fragilely feminine Sophia, who rarely left the house. Hawthorne was duplicitous, for apparently at one time he informed Elizabeth Peabody in a letter that Sophia "was a flower never destined to be worn in any man's bosom, but lent from Heaven for a *season* to mortals to show the possibilities of human purity and womanliness."[5]

In age Sophia wrote in one of her exquisite sentences, "I am all love and memory" and went on to recall her first meeting with Hawthorne: "Can I ever forget when I first looked into the abyss of suns which were his eyes! And how it all grew like a flower,—our love—so still, so inevitable, so consummate, and never, never to fade." Soon came the day— and it was not long in coming—when Mr. Hawthorne, as she referred to him, "rose upon my eyes and soul a King among men by divine right." Although she publicly seemed to accept the fact that her illnesses precluded marriage, she had secretly never renounced the possibility, as her conduct in Cuba demonstrated. What she said in the twilight years following Hawthorne's death aptly described her belief in and expectations of marital union: "What a divine economy and celestial gift to man is this of marriage—of course I mean the true marriage—which absolutely prevents the possibility of aloneness—of being alone. We are not one until we are two, and then we truly understand unity."[6]

They did not find the "unity" she sought without agonizing reticences, excessive modesty, and self-effacement, with vibrations such as only two supersensitive, hungrily repressed individuals could create. Hawthorne was too diffident to be assertive, she was too ladylike to dominate. If he lowered his eyes modestly, evading direct glances or confrontation, he also knew that when he dared eye contact he would find her bright, enthusiastic eyes fixed meltingly on him. Her eyes encouraged without arousing fears or producing flight. Her willingness to listen flattered, triumphing over his reserve. Intuitively she understood his hesitancies, his tremulousness, and waited. Yet she had to proceed with such care and tact that the meetings must have produced emotional strains and troubled nerves. As she confessed years after their marriage, "I never dared to gaze at him, even I, unless his lids were down—It seemed an invasion into a holy place."[7]

Sophia understood what eluded both her sister Elizabeth and Mary Silsbee. She was softly and gently feminine, physically unintimidating, and eager to subordinate herself to a male who embodied her ideals and fantasies. She also evoked his sympathy because, in his words, she lived "in the shadow of a seclusion as deep as my own had been." Not without her own quiet arts, Sophia took great pains with her appearance, "to look like a lady before my husband, & in my own eyes." If she etherealized her husband, she provided a lovely physical ambiance. "Ever since our marriage," she wrote twelve years afterward, "we have always eaten off the finest French china—& had all things pretty & tasteful—because, you know, I would never have *second best* services, considering my husband to be my most illustrious guest."[8]

Given their ages and inhibitions, the relationship had to evolve in slow, careful stages. Although neither recorded the process of the journey into love, it seems clear that at first they eased difficulties by dwelling upon artistic matters, which was Elizabeth Peabody's tactic at the first meeting. Early in the fall, when Sophia delivered one of Elizabeth's letters at the Herbert Street house, Louisa at her brother's suggestion showed Sophia miniatures of his father and uncle. Sophia found no resemblance. Hawthorne duly presented her with a copy of *Twice-told Tales*, with the following inscription: "Miss Sophie A. Peabody, with the affectionate regards of her friend, Nath. Hawthorne." Like everybody else Sophia admired "The Gentle Boy," and he—or perhaps she—suggested that it be illustrated. On December 22, 1838, Wiley and Putnam advertised *The Gentle Boy: A Thrice-told Tale*, which was dedicated to Sophia A. Peabody: "Whatever of beauty and of pathos he had conceived, but could not shadow forth in language, has been caught and embodied in the few and simple lines of this sketch." It was a gracious overstatement.[9]

Early in the same month Sophia added a dedication to the third and final volume of her "Cuban Journal":

To Nath[l] Hawthorne Esq[r]
Whose commendation & regard

> alone give value to the previous
> Journal, this closing record
> is inscribed by his true
> and affectionate friend
> "Sophie"

Now Sophia had no reason to look back longingly to that romantic island to which she had escaped. Eden lay ahead, although it was farther off than she supposed.[10]

In a lengthy letter in early December—nineteen pages measuring approximately eight by ten inches—he was still a friend, a close one indeed, but not apparently her betrothed. She felt confident enough to ramble as she pleased and to be personal within, of course, genteel parameters. She mentioned a pen portrait which has seemingly disappeared.

> When I was drawing you last evening, I was obliged first to observe your actual countenance & then see it in my mind before I could make it visible again. There is a certain still stream in our inside where we find every real form reflected in ideal perfection—& this *truer* than what passes before our careless glance when we think we see all. This is why I said I had never beheld your face before I tried to reproduce it. Now I shall recognize it, I am certain, through all eternity.

At the conclusion of the letter she wrote with a self-effacement that proved their intimacy: ". . . I will bid you good night, my dear friend—with many congratulations that you have arrived at the end of this document—& with the assurance that though I have put such an infliction upon you I am your truly affectionate / friend / Sophie."[11]

About the same time Hawthorne made an entry in a notebook under the heading "S. A. P.": "Taking my likeness, I said that such changes would come over my face, that she would not know me when we met again in Heaven. 'See if I don't!' said she, smiling. There was the most peculiar and beautiful humor in the point itself, and in her manner, that can be imagined."[12]

What a wonderfully adroit performance, perhaps better than Mary Silsbee's! Sophia knew the art of flattery and the art of love, if they are indeed separate. Surely in December 1838—a little more than a year after the visit on the evening of November 11, 1837—Sophia and Nathaniel arrived, timidly but inevitably, at a decision to become engaged—secretly. While most lovers are ready to shout from the rooftop, these two almost middle-aged lovers had to cloak their happiness. Sophia's mother could not part with her semi-invalid daughter, while Hawthorne's mother liked the security of having her son occupy his attic room, even if she saw him only at intervals.[13]

Perhaps most important, the lovers had to accustom themselves gradually to the prospect of marriage. The adjustment as it turned out took four years, by which time they were comfortably old hands at marriage, except physically.

By the end of 1838 Mary Silsbee had been reunited with Jared Sparks, Hawthorne and Sophia were clandestinely engaged, and once more Elizabeth Peabody was abandoned. But not quite. O'Sullivan had published her article on "Claims of the Beautiful Arts" in the *Democratic Review* of November 3, and Hawthorne had appointed her, or so she alleged, "his official biographer." But he withheld as he gave: she was not to come into print for fifty years, and in the meantime he instructed her to destroy all his letters to her, as she (almost) faithfully did.[14]

Port-Admiral at the Boston Custom-House

The publication of *Twice-told Tales* made Hawthorne's name known, but earnings from the book and from journals such as the *Democratic Review* were scarcely enough to support him. The economic situation was further complicated after his engagement to Sophia Peabody, although they had no plans as to when they would marry. No more did he have specific ideas as to what he should do to improve his lot. As was so often the case, he waited for others to come to his assistance, as they invariably did.[1]

Apparently early in 1838 Longfellow proposed that they collaborate on a "book of Fairy Tales" designed for the rapidly growing juvenile market. Hawthorne was enthusiastic. "I think it a good idea, and am well inclined to do my part towards the execution of it. . . . Possibly we may make a great hit, and entirely revolutionize the whole system of juvenile literature." Longfellow was to be the editor, Hawthorne a contributor.[2]

Nothing happened for months, and after his return from the Berkshires in 1838 Hawthorne wrote to "My dear Professor" in the joshing tone that often characterized the correspondence of two men who seemed most comfortable when they reverted to collegiate jocularity which concealed the superficiality of the relationship.

> It is a dreadful long while since we have colloqued together. . . . Meantime, how comes on the Boy's WONDER-HORN? Have you blown your blast?—or will it turn out a broken-winded concern? I have not any breath to spare, just at present—yet I think it a pity that the echoes should not be awakened, far and wide, by such an admirable instrument.

Shortly thereafter Longfellow informed Hawthorne that he had decided to devote his efforts to poetry and translation, and Hawthorne in turn claimed, almost jauntily, to "have abundance of literary labor in prospect. . . . Really I do mean to turn my attention to writing for children, either on my own hook, or for the series of works projected by the Board of Education—to which I have been requested to contribute."[3]

Soon there was another scheme. Through Jared Sparks, Hawthorne learned that Longfellow was planning "a literary paper." "Why not?" he wrote to his friend. "Your name would go a great way towards insuring its success; and it is intolerable that there should not be a single belles-lettres journal in New England." He offered his assistance and, facetiously, a name for the journal: "'The Inspector' would be as good a title for a paper as 'The Spectator.'" Soon there was no more talk of a literary magazine, which may have been needed but required more worldly editors than these two men.[4]

Their third scheme—we do not know who was the instigator—was as quixotic as the earlier ones: they decided to rescue Boston from its sloth by means of an evening newspaper. Hawthorne wrote for advice to Caleb Foote, an old friend as well as editor and owner of the *Salem Gazette*, and his queries exposed his ignorance of the most elementary problems of publication. What Hawthorne later said about a prospective position in the Custom-House—"I am going to accept it, with as much confidence in my suitableness for it, as Sancho Panza had in his gubernatorial qualifications"—was more applicable to this scheme, which, given the inexperience of the prospective editors, came to naught.[5]

There was another course open to him: the largess of government and the spoils system of American politics enabled wholly unqualified people to hold posts which provided guaranteed incomes and easy working hours, subject only to the whims of the voters every four years. Hawthorne's Bowdoin chums—Bridge, Cilley, and Pierce—were involved in politics in one way or another, and O'Sullivan, as editor of the *Democratic Review*, had many Washington connections. Hawthorne made his own contribution in 1837 with the publication of *Twice-told Tales*, which opened his "intercourse with the world" following years of anonymous publications.

On March 26, 1837, Bridge sent a copy of Hawthorne's collection of tales to Cilley, "telling him that his assistance would be needed." At that time Bridge had to inquire of Hawthorne, "What is the situation you want? I only wait to know this before procuring some letters for you." Not waiting for a reply, Bridge got in touch with Pierce, who a few days later recommended Hawthorne as historian for the South Seas expedition of Commodore Charles Wilkes. "He is," Pierce observed, "extremely modest, perhaps diffident,—a diffidence, in my judgment, having its origin in a high and honorable pride; but he is a man of decided genius, without any whims or caprices calculated to impair his efficiency or usefulness in any department of literature."[6]

Bridge, who was the only one of the friends aware of Hawthorne's inner turmoil, wondered whether rejection could "be borne." But he wrote to George Bancroft, sometimes called the father of American historians and an important figure in the Democratic party in Massachusetts: "I don't know whether he will comply, but I think I tickled him in the right place." The tickling produced no results immediately.[7]

Shortly after Hawthorne's return from the Berkshires in September 1838, Elizabeth Peabody, with characteristic energy, took matters in hand. She had known Bancroft for about ten years, but instead of writing to him she chose to approach Orestes A. Brownson, a minister of various persuasions and finally a convert to Catholicism, who had recently been appointed by Bancroft to the Custom-House in Boston. She laid it on the line. Brownson was to secure for Hawthorne "an office like his— requiring very little time & work—& having abundant leisure & liberty—& in or about Boston." Elizabeth had also decided that "it would be better for him to be in Boston" than in Salem. "I am afraid he never will be happy here." Brownson dutifully replied that Bancroft was willing to give Hawthorne a place immediately, "but he had supposed he was a sort of man who would by no means accept one." "So much for the Sovereign people," Elizabeth exclaimed, both amoral and undemocratic for the moment. "But for the life of me, whatever is the political autocracy of it, I cannot help being glad."[8]

Apparently in October Elizabeth Peabody called on Bancroft and his wife and assured Bancroft that Hawthorne would be an effective governmental employee and a loyal worker for the Democratic party. When Hawthorne received no word from Bancroft, Elizabeth wrote to Mrs. Bancroft, who was to inform her husband that even though Hawthorne "has little interest & takes no personal part in electioneering and local subjects of party division . . . yet were it a matter of duty—he would doubtless make these investigations and do his part." She did not know that a day earlier Hawthorne informed O'Sullivan: "Mr. Bancroft has offered me the post of Inspector in the Custom-House, with the salary of $1100. The office has many eligibilities, and I think I shall accept it." At the same time he urged O'Sullivan to be no "less zealous to get me the Post-Office; for the salary may purchase other comforts, as well as matrimonial ones. Do move heaven and earth."[9]

Eventually Hawthorne settled for the position of measurer of coal and salt rather than the post of inspector. The salary was $1,500 per year. According to Mary Peabody, "*He felt very bad* when he found he had actually got it," but on January 11, 1839, he sent his formal acceptance. On January 17 Bancroft informed Levi Woodbury, secretary of the treasury: "I have appointed Nathaniel Hawthorne, Esq., of Salem (biographer of Cilley) a measurer, in place of Paul L. George, dismissed, and request your approval of his appointment."[10]

Actually, Hawthorne earned considerably more than his official salary. "Throughout the summer and autumn," he explained to O'Sullivan, "I expect to be almost constantly employed from sunrise till sunset. The more business the better; for, by the omission of Congress to pass a certain regulation, I shall be entitled to the whole fees of my office, amounting possibly to $3000, instead of the paltry $1500." The fees for measuring cargoes of salt and coal made these posts lucrative, as long as Congress failed to curb the racket. With "customary levity" Hawthorne wrote to Longfellow: "I have no reason to doubt my capacity to fulfil the duties; for I don't know what they are; but, as nearly as I can understand, I shall be a sort of Port-Admiral."[11]

During his tenure at the Custom-House Hawthorne occupied a parlor and bedroom in the home of George Hillard at 54 Pinckney Street. A Boston lawyer in a firm with Charles Sumner, Hillard had taught school with George Bancroft, was a friend of the Peabody sisters, and for a period shared the editorship of the *Christian Record*. After Hillard delivered a "triumphant" Phi Beta Kappa address at Harvard in 1843, Hawthorne commented with the generosity he reserved for friends: "It gladdened me much to see this melancholy shadow of a man for once bathed and even pervaded with sunshine; and I must doubt whether any literary success of my own ever gave me so much pleasure."[12]

Since life as a measurer was often dull and chilling, Hawthorne's responses fluctuated like the New England weather. At times he depicted his lot after the style of Bunyan. He noted the "brawling slang-whangers . . . in that 'earthy cavern' of the Custom-House." "I am convinced," he declared to Sophia, "that Christian's burthen consisted of coal; and no wonder he felt so much relieved when it fell off and rolled into the sepulchre. His load, however, at the utmost, could not have been more than a few bushels; whereas mine was exactly one hundred and thirty-five chaldrons and seven tubs." He brawled "from morning till night" with "thick-pated, stubborn, contentious men." In his notebook he recorded sights and events without editorializing or allegorizing. On one occasion he watched an English ship unload "seventy or thereabout factory girls, imported to work in our factories. Some pale and delicate-looking; others rugged and coarse." He watched them "at the wharf-stairs, to the considerable display of their legs," a voyeur who had a leg fetish. He had nothing to say of their potential exploitation, although his knowledge of the American labor market may have been limited.[13]

At "this unblest Custom-House," he informed Sophia, he endured "a very grievous thraldom. I do detest all offices—all, at least, that are held on a political tenure. And I want nothing to do with politicians—they are not men; they cease to be men, in becoming politicians." Relations with Bancroft became strained, as he explained cryptically to William B. Pike, one of his political cronies in Salem: "What an astounding liar our venerated chief turns out to be! . . . There are some things that I should like to impart to you, but hardly feel myself at liberty—certainly not on paper." Apparently Pike was attempting to negotiate a position for Hawthorne in the Salem post office. At the same time, no doubt because of Hawthorne's complaints, O'Sullivan found a position for him in Washington. Hawthorne, however, was not interested in moving because at least in Boston he was "singularly independent of the general government of the Custom-House."[14]

What he did not acknowledge was that he himself made his job more time-consuming and tiring than it had to be because he wanted to wring as much as he could out of it. Although he failed to achieve the income of $3,000 which he had set for himself in the first year, he expected, he informed O'Sullivan, to earn at least $2,000 in the following year "and am resolved to save at least half of it. Then I will retire on my fortune—that is to say, I will throw myself on fortune, and get my bread as I can." When Hawthorne quit the Custom-House, he had not reached his financial goal. "If ever I come to be worth $5000, I will kick all business to the devil,—at least till that be spent." He perhaps did not miss his goal by much, since Congress failed to put "that accursed restriction" on the fee offices of the Custom-House. [15]

In October 1840 he submitted his resignation to Bancroft. "I have broken my chain and escaped from the Custom-House," he declared to Longfellow. Bancroft requested that he withdraw his resignation, but he refused. On January 8, 1841, he wrote to Bancroft: "I know not whether you will think it necessary for me again to express my wish to retire from the Custom House. But as I have not yet been informed of my removal, I would respectfully request that it may now take place." He was free before the end of the month. Although his plan had been from the beginning to remain in the Custom-House only two years, the Democrats were about to lose their slots following their defeats in the election of the previous year. [16]

Though he professed to despise the Custom-House, Hawthorne was driven by a powerful desire to get what he could out of this position, by any tactic at his disposal. In the process he proved to himself, his family, and, above all, to the Mannings that he could succeed in the world of commerce. For the first time he supported himself and even accumulated what for him was a substantial sum of money. The mirror at this time did not reflect the shy, withdrawing "artist of the beautiful" or "the gentle boy."

When Hawthorne went to the Custom-House in January 1839 he was in the midst of discussions with the Massachusetts Board of Education about the publication of a child's history of the United States by Marsh, Capen, and Lyon, publishers of textbooks. Hawthorne informed Sophia that Capen "torments me every now-and-then about a book which he wants me to manufacture." He had not been very long at the Custom-House when he complained to Longfellow, "If I write a preface, it will be to bid farewell to literature; for, as a literary man, my new occupations entirely break me up." However, he found time to continue negotiations with his publishers, who prematurely announced the publication of a book to be called *The New England Historical Sketches* on January 1, 1840, although it was but a working title and apparently nothing had been written.[17]

Early in the year a woman at the House of the Seven Gables suggested that Hawthorne write about "that old chair in the room; it is an old Puritan relict and you can make a biographical sketch of each old Puritan who became in succession the owner of the chair." Two months later he had "nearly completed" a manuscript, and on December 3, 1840, *Grandfather's Chair: A History for Youth* was officially published and bore the name of Boston's newest publisher, E. P. Peabody. Evidently Hawthorne had some misunderstanding with his original publisher, and Elizabeth Peabody, with no experience and no fear (and less money), took over. A plum-colored book of 140 pages measuring three by five inches, *Grandfather's Chair* was designed to be easily handled by a child but contained no illustrations, a mistake which was corrected in later printings.[18]

An old oak chair was brought to America in the early seventeenth century by a Lady Arbella, who upon her arrival died and was buried in what later became King's Chapel in Boston. After her husband within a few months also died, the chair began a journey from one important figure to another—including Roger Williams, Anne Hutchinson, and Sir William Phips—until it came into the possession of Samuel Adams, who died in 1803. It took two companion volumes of the same size for Hawthorne to complete his condensed history of the American colonies. *Famous Old People* was probably published on January 18, 1841, and two months later *Liberty Tree* completed the trilogy.[19]

On April 12, 1842, Hawthorne issued *Biographical Stories for Children*, an account of the lives of people such as Benjamin Franklin, Dr. Samuel Johnson, and Oliver Cromwell. This time a father relates stories to a son who has recently gone blind. Although the device is contrived and the blind boy too sentimentally conceived for modern taste, the sketches are better organized and written, for Hawthorne was beginning to learn the art of writing for juveniles.

He had difficulty both in establishing the tone of these little books and in keeping his youthful audience in mind. The preface of *Grandfather's*

Chair opens with an inappropriate jest—"In writing this ponderous tome"—and in *Famous Old People* Hawthorne may have amused himself but hardly his youthful audience: "Happy boys! Enjoy your play-time now, and come again to study, and to feel the birch-rod and the ferule, tomorrow. . . . and after that, another Morrow, with troubles of its own." It is doubtful that children would have agreed with Hawthorne that "the veil of mortality" was preferable to "the best happiness of childhood," which was the message of Sunday school pamphlets, popular literature, and samplers of the era.[20]

The public did not respond to his wit or his books: in June 1841 copies of *Grandfather's Chair*, which had been issued in a small edition, were still on hand. Elizabeth Peabody, however, had begun negotiations with James Munroe of Boston for a new printing of the children's books as well as of *Twice-told Tales*, apparently without Hawthorne's authorization. He wrote to her on June 23, 1841, in the third person and not without a barb: "Mr. Hawthorne particularly desires that the bargain with Mr. Munroe, in respect to the remaining copies of Grandfather's Chair &c. may be concluded on such terms as Miss Peabody thinks best, without further reference to himself. Being wholly ignorant of the value of the books, he could do no other than consent to any arrangement she might propose." Because her intentions were magnanimous and her big heart most vulnerable, no one evidently ever told Elizabeth bluntly to mind her own business. That there was a "temporary quarrel" Elizabeth confirmed later, because Hawthorne had refused royalties for *Grandfather's Chair*. She was hurt since she no doubt construed Hawthorne's refusal of royalties as an act of charity to ease her lot when her intention had been to assist him and Sophia. It was a senseless dispute, perhaps a matter of honor rather than of economics, since from a small edition of a book which must have sold for fifty cents or less royalties amounted to very little.[21]

Soon Hawthorne took over the negotiations with Munroe and discussed not only the reprinting of his books but also the position of editor of a series which the firm planned to issue. As he explained to Sophia: "Other persons have bought large estates and built splendid mansions with such little books as I mean to write; so perhaps it is not unreasonable to hope that mine may enable me to build a little cottage—or, at least, to buy or hire one." Hawthorne did not accept the editorship (if it was offered) and Munroe did not reprint the children's books, but a contract was signed for a new and enlarged edition of *Twice-told Tales*, not to exceed 1,500 copies and with a royalty rate of 10 percent.[22]

The publication of this second edition of his tales was marked by Hawthorne's customary vacillation. In 1838 he informed a publishing house that he had given no "serious consideration" to an augmented collection, which in the absence of sales of the first edition made sense. When in the following year Hawthorne changed his mind, Longfellow sounded out his publisher, Samuel Colman. Then Elizabeth Peabody asked Elizabeth Hawthorne about the existence of unpublished tales, for she planned to make a collection after Hawthorne refused. "I regret," Hawthorne's sister wrote, "as much as you do that he would not be prevailed upon to collect them himself."[23]

It seems safe, however, to assume that the tales in the new printing of *Twice-told Tales* were chosen by Hawthorne, not by either of the Elizabeths. Despite his indecisiveness he managed to run his affairs in his own way. In the 1842 printing he added twenty-one pieces but again passed over "My Kinsman, Major Molineux," "Roger Malvin's Burial," and "Young Goodman Brown." Munroe published *Twice-told Tales* in 1842, and the children's books were reissued in 1842 by the Boston firm of Tappan and Dennet, each with an unsigned illustration. Sophia was his unacknowledged collaborator. When the books were reprinted by Ticknor and Fields in the 1850s and finally found an audience of some size, Sophia's pedestrian illustrations were replaced by engravings by W. Roberts from designs by Hammatt Billings.[24]

Hawthorne turned again to children's books after he was a father and the author of *The Scarlet Letter*. These tales became nineteenth-century classics, their popularity continuing into this century.

14

"Thou Art My Type of Womanly Perfection"

"Nothing like our story was ever written," Hawthorne declared to Sophia, "or ever will be—for we shall not feel inclined to make the public our confidant; but if it could be told, methinks it would be such as the angels might delight to hear."[1]

Though lovers are rarely given to understatement, at least in their protestations of the uniqueness of their love, Hawthorne did not exaggerate. If he had known that posterity would peep and biographers would pry into the intimacies of their love, he would have been troubled, no doubt indignant. He tried to cheat posterity when he burned his wife's letters before the family left for England in 1853, leaving only two or three of Sophia's letters. But Sophia was more generous. Although out of love she overemployed her scissors, she preserved over one hundred letters unique in American literary annals, and we remain in her debt for a truly original love story which recorded the excesses and distortions of lovers, the verbal fictions in which they indulged as well as the truths they tenderly unfolded to each other. The destruction of his love letters would have deprived us of a work of art—what Mark Van Doren has called "the masterpiece" of this period of Hawthorne's life.

The correspondence had a strange beginning, that is,

strange for anyone except Hawthorne. On March 4, 1839, he went to the Peabody house on Charter Street in the forenoon to say good-bye to Sophia before leaving for Boston. For various reasons he worked it out in such a way that Sophia did not see him.

> I had a parting glimpse of you, Monday afternoon, at your window—and that image abides by me, looking pale, and not so quiet as is your wont. I have reproached myself many times since, because I did not show my face, and then we should both have smiled; and so our reminiscences would have been sunny instead of shadowy. But I believe I was so intent on seeing you, that I forgot all about the desirableness of being myself seen. Perhaps, after all, you did see me—at least you knew that I was there. I fear that you were not quite well that morning.

Such rationalizations could only have increased Sophia's disappointment, although she understood his timidity and perhaps intuited that her Apollo found separation difficult to handle.[2]

Most of the love letters were written in the little apartment of two rooms at 59 Pinckney Street in Boston, in the home of George Hillard. Unlike the drab attic at 12 Herbert Street, these rooms reflected the taste of Sophia, who provided him with prints as well as her own oil copies of masterworks.

> I am writing now at my new bureau, which stands between the windows; there are two lamps before me, which show the polished shadings of the mahogany panels to great advantage. A coal fire is burning in the grate—not a very fervid one, but flickering up fitfully, once in a while, so as to remind me that I am by my own fireside. I am sitting in the cane-bottomed rocking-chair (wherein my Dove once sate, but which did not meet her approbation;) and another hair-cloth arm-chair stands in front of the fire. . . . Sophie Hawthorne, what a beautiful carpet did you choose for me! I admire it so much that I can hardly bear to tread upon it.

In the first of the decors created by Sophia, he was, willingly, being domesticated, prepared for marriage.[3]

The letters tell the story of Romeo and Juliet not in their passionate adolescence but in their thirties, when verbalization sometimes substituted for passion. Yet occasionally he erupted with the hyperbole of youth—"I feel as if I could run a hundred miles at a stretch, and jump over all the houses that happen to be in my way"—or he felt irresponsible and blithe: "Thou makest me behave like a child, naughtiest. Why dost thou not frown at my nonsensical complaints, and utterly refuse thy sympathy?" This was the playfulness of a man of thirty-five, who combined with the play a command of language and art beyond the capacities of the verbally immature.[4]

As one letter followed another, he began to improvise, to create stories sometimes as allegorical as his published writings, to split personalities in order to discuss, sometimes humorously or evasively, human complexities as well as to conceal his own desire and to play like a virtuoso upon the theme of love. He was helpless: his was the gift of language.

Despite the improvisatory character of the letters and the sincerity of the sentiments, Hawthorne filed his prose and turned a delicate phrase. He enjoyed being in love and inventing amorous games and matched art to pleasure. Two years after the correspondence opened he wrote:

My breast is full of thee; thou art throbbing throughout all my veins. Never, it seems to me, did I know what love was, before. And yet I am not satisfied to let that sentence pass; for it would do wrong to the blissful and holy time that we have already enjoyed together. But our hearts are new-created for one another, daily; and they enter upon existence with such up-springing rapture as if nothing had ever existed before—as if, at this very *now*, physical and spiritual world were but first discovered, and by ourselves only.

Many a time he in effect did not "let that sentence pass," and, as we shall see, Sophia eventually was forced to assert the supremacy of the life-force which Hawthorne was content to release only in the verbal patterns of his sentences and paragraphs.[5]

To celebrate their love he evoked the original parents but with awareness of the imperatives of reality.

How happy were Adam and Eve! There was no third person to come between them, and all the infinity around them only served to press their hearts closer together. We love one another as well as they; but there is no silent and lovely garden of Eden for us. Mine own, wilt thou sail away with me to discover some summer island?—dost thou not think that God has reserved one for us, ever since the beginning of the world? . . . then we are the Adam and Eve of a virgin earth.

He recalled the prefallen state of humanity, and Sophia became his "sinless Eve." After their marriage the Manse at Concord became the Eden of Adam and Eve, which anticipated the departure of Phoebe and Holgrave from the House of the Seven Gables, where miraculously after generations of evil and misery "the flower of Eden has bloomed, likewise in this old, darksome house, to-day." Such had to be the setting for the woman he transformed into an archetype. "I knew Sophie Hawthorne of old," he wrote, "yea, of very old time do I know her; or rather, of very old eternity. There was an image of such a being deep within my soul, before we met in this dim world; and therefore nothing that she does, or says, or thinks, or feels, ever surprises me. Her naughtiness is as familiar to me as if it were my own."[6]

Shortly after the beginning of the correspondence Hawthorne tentatively, or perhaps the word should be tremulously, pronounced himself married:

> I am tired this evening, as usual, with my long day's toil; and my head wants its pillow—and my soul yearns for the friend whom God has given it—whose soul He has married to my soul. Oh, my dearest, how that thought thrills me! We *are* married! I felt it long ago; and sometimes, when I was seeking for some fondest word, it has been on my lips to call you—"Wife"! I hardly know what restrained me from speaking it—unless a dread (for *that* would have been an infinite pang to me) of feeling you shrink back from my bosom, and thereby discovering that there was yet a deep place in your soul which did not know me. Mine own Dove, need I fear it now? Are we not married. God knows we are.

Sophia lifted his fears and allowed him to take the initiative, although, if her letters were available, one would expect to find that she had led him with her exquisite tact to pose the question. "Oh, how happy you make me by calling me your husband," he exclaimed, "by subscribing yourself my wife. I kiss that word when I meet it in your letters; and I repeat over and over to myself, 'she is my Wife—I am her Husband!'"[7]

Almost from the beginning Sophia was his "Dove" and occupied an otherworldly habitation. "My beloved," he declared, "you make a Heaven roundabout you, and dwell in it continually; and as it is your Heaven, so is it mine. . . . My stock of sunshine is so infinitely increased by partaking of yours, that, even when a cloud flits by, I incomparably prefer its gloom to the sullen, leaden tinge, that used to overspread my sky." He was determined to adopt her diet of bread and milk and to provide "clean white apparel every day for mine unspotted Dove." The lovers did not use the "thou" form consistently until March 15, 1840, when he introduced it or followed her example. For the rest of their lives they employed the biblical form in letters to each other.[8]

After two years of correspondence, still as far from marriage as ever, he concluded a letter: "Now good bye, dearest, sweetest, loveliest, holiest, truest, suitablest little wife. I worship thee. Thou art my type of womanly perfection. Thou keepest my heart pure, and elevatest me above the world. Thou enablest me to interpret the riddle of life, and fillest me with faith in the unseen and better land, because thou leadest me thither continually." He never read the letters of his "sinless Eve" "without first washing his hands!"[9]

This exaltation of the Dove posed problems, for Hawthorne like Everyman, wanted an angel as well as a mortal. "Oh, how I do wish that my sweet wife and I could dwell upon a cloud, and follow the sunset round about the earth! Perhaps she might; but my nature is too earthy to permit me to dwell there with her—and I know well that she would not leave me here." And so he decided to have an ethereal being who was also a sexual being, which he accomplished by dividing her in unspecified proportions into a Dove and a human called quite simply Sophie Hawthorne. He apparently stumbled upon this dualism quite accidentally one day when he began a letter, "Belovedest little wife—sweetest Sophie Hawthorne." He was as happy as a child with his invention, for Sophie, unlike the Dove, could be naughty. "And now if my Dove were here," he wrote, "she and that naughty Sophie Hawthorne, how happy we all three— two—one—(how many are there of us?)—how happy might we be!" At once he elevated his invention into an ideal: "A woman, then, who should combine the characteristics of Sophie Hawthorne and my Dove would be the very perfection of her race."[10]

Soon he was sending a "kiss apiece to the Dove's eyes and mouth, and to Sophie Hawthorne's nose and foot," which was one way to take care of the anatomy of the soul and the body or of what at another time he described as "Strophe and Antistrophe" or "the two in one."

Have the Strophe and Antistrophe made up their quarrel yet? There is an unaccountable fascination about that Sophie Haw-

> thorne—whatever she chooses to do or say, whether reasonable or unreasonable, I am forced to love her the better for it. Not that I love her better than my Dove; but then it is right and natural that the Dove should awaken infinite tenderness, because she is a bird of Paradise, and has a perfect and angelic nature—so that love is her inalienable and unquestionable right. And yet my wayward heart will love the naughty Sophie Hawthorne;—yes, its affection for the Dove is doubled, because she is inseparably united with naughty Sophie. I have one love for them both, and it is infinitely intensified, because they share it together.

Then he shifted his allegory, the Dove now becoming the "heart" and Sophie "intellectual life," which hardly seems at one with Sophie as nose and foot. But only a pedant asks consistency of lovers.[11]

When he declared that "truly I have reason to apprehend more trouble with Sophie Hawthorne than with my Dove," surely he implied—on no evidence whatever—that she would surrender her soul and heart (Dove) more quickly than her body (Sophie). Yet it was Hawthorne who, as he perhaps forgot, created out of his own fantasies and sexual hesitations a split personality which had little to do with Sophia Peabody. She, like the lady of Shakespeare's sonnets, walked on earth, even if she sometimes idealized it beyond recognition. His assumptions were projections and his allegorical playthings his means of recharging emotions, of prolonging the courtship, or, bluntly, of postponing marriage and consummation.[12]

He himself made the admission, perhaps by accident, perhaps by design, in describing the actions of the naughty Sophie Hawthorne: "Mine own Dove, how unhappy art thou to be linked with such a mate!—to be *bound up in the same volume* with her!—and me unhappy, too, to be forced to keep such a turbulent little rebel in my inmost heart!" On another occasion he expressed their state with precision in a most unusual but apt grammatical analogy: "My Dove and I are no verbs—or if so, we are passive verbs, and therefore happy ones."[13]

Unless Sophia in her widowhood excised passages charged with sexuality—which seems doubtful, since Hawthorne obviously accepted the ground rules of decorum which he attributed to Sophia, although they were his own—the lovers (or, more accurately, Hawthorne) avoided references to passion, except of a nonphysical kind. Occasionally he slipped (although the slips may only be the imaginings of the Freudian age). "Oh, my dearest, I yearn for you," he declared in one of his early letters, "and my heart heaves when I think of you—(and that is always, but sometimes a thought makes me know and feel you more vividly than at others, and *that* I call 'thinking of you')—heaves and swells (my heart does) as sometimes you have felt it beneath you, when your head or bosom was resting on it." Here Hawthorne lost his usual precision probably because he perceived something beyond the surface meaning. Such earthy and anatomical passages were rare.[14]

Although Sophia did not publish the love letters, she went over them carefully during the years in which she sought to establish the author's image for posterity. The widow was apparently not troubled by two naughties, unless she never perceived them as such: "I would thou hadst my miniature to wear in thy bosom; and then I should feel sure that now and then thou wouldst think of me. . . ." One spring he searched for a violet "to which I should award the blissful fate of being treasured for a time in thy bosom; for I doubt not, dearest, that thou wouldst admit any flower of thy husband's gathering into that sweetest place."[15]

As he perceived it, both were recluses confined to dismal chambers which they would leave to form a perfect union. "[I] found nothing in the world that I thought preferable to my old solitude, till at length a certain Dove was revealed to me, in the shadow of a seclusion as deep as my own had been. . . . Oh what happiness when we shall be able to look forward to an illimitable time in each other's society. . . . Then a quiet will settle down upon us, a passionate quiet, which is the consummation of happiness." At another time he remarked: "I love not surprises, even joyful ones—or at least, I would rather that joy should come quietly, and as a matter of course, and warning us of its approach by casting a placid gleam before it."[16]

Only a solitary person would find quiet passionate, and only those who at all times needed to be in control of their emotions would find joy in "a placid gleam." Early in the correspondence he informed Sophia: "I never, till now, had a friend who could give me repose;—all have disturbed me; and whether for pleasure or pain, it was still disturbance. But peace overflows from your heart into mine." "Repose" was also one of Sophia's favorite words, although, as we shall see, it was a state which she but rarely experienced. "But perhaps," he wrote, "when thou hast my bosom to repose upon, thou wilt no longer feel such overwhelming weariness. I am given thee to repose upon, that so my little tender and sensitivest little Dove may be able to do great works." As usual, he explained more fully and beautifully than his biographer: ". . . nothing that I ever enjoyed before can come into the remotest comparison with my continual enjoyment of thy love—with the deep, satisfied repose which that consciousness brings to me; a repose subsisting, and ever to subsist, in the midst of all anxieties, troubles and agitations."[17]

If in these letters Sophia Peabody was both Dove and Sophie Hawthorne, there were at least two Hawthornes—the dependent male (the Arthur Dimmesdale and Holgrave of the fiction) and the self-reliant, self-contained artist (the Owen Warland of the tales).

Hawthorne likened his Dove to the "water-sprite Undine" and her soul to a fountain that healed and restored. "Write often to your husband, and let your letters gush from a cheerful heart; so shall they refresh and gladden me, like draughts from a sparkling fountain, which leaps from some spot of earth where no grave has ever been dug." At another time he described himself, unknowingly, as a mature Ilbrahim: "My spirit would droop and wither like a plant that lacked rain and dew, if it were not for the frequent shower of your gentle and holy thoughts."[18]

In one of the loveliest passages in his writings Hawthorne universalized his feeling: "Indeed, we are but shadows—we are not endowed with real life, and all that seems most real about us is but the thinnest substance of a dream—till the heart is touched. That touch creates us,— then we begin to be—thereby we are beings of reality, and inheritors of eternity."[19]

Gradually, perhaps, Hawthorne came to recognize Sophia's strengths, which he immediately exaggerated: "Thou art ten times as powerful as I, because thou art so much more ethereal." He even went so far as to swear that "I am insufficient for my own support." Here he overstated as he did in the following: "Thou art a mighty enchantress, my little Dove, and hast quite subdued a strong man, who deemed himself independent of all the world."[20]

Watching her care for her brother George, who came home and ended his short, unhappy life on November 25, 1839, Hawthorne observed: "My heart is weak in comparison with yours. . . . I have never been called to minister at the dying bed of a dear friend; but . . . I should need support from the dying, instead of being able to give it." He also planned to utilize her grace to rescue him in uncomfortable social situations, such as dining with Margaret Fuller, whose aggressive loquacity was too much for what he not immodestly called his "golden silence": "Would that Margaret Fuller might lose her tongue!" In the future, accompanied by his Dove and Sophie Hawthorne, "I shall not be afraid to accept invitations to meet literary lions and lionesses; because then I shall put the above-said redoubtable little personage in the front of the battle." Because the ritual of love mandated icons of ethereal dimensions and then abasement before the beloved, the other Hawthorne, the self-reliant artist with great inner resources, intruded infrequently in these letters. He acknowledged that he was "sometimes prone to the sin of exaggeration," and at times he was most explicit: "But I forewarn thee, sweetest Dove, that thy husband is a most unmalleable man;—thou art not to suppose because his spirit answers to every touch of thine, that therefore every breeze, or even every whirlwind, can upturn him from his depths." Yet when she trembled with self-doubt, he supported her with sensitivity. "You *are* beautiful, my own heart's Dove," he reassured her. "Never doubt it again. . . . My Dove is beautiful, and full of grace; she should not have an ugly mate." Perhaps only lovers approaching their middle years could so delicately voice awareness of human fragility and the deep need for mutual support.[21]

Hawthorne proclaimed his need, and she returned the tribute with praise that elevated him to a deity whose will was her pleasure. In one of her extant letters she exalted her subordination with a kind of pride.

Oh King by divine right! no one can love & reverence thee as does thy wife. In her heart centres the world's admiration, & from its depths sparkles up, beside, the starry foam of her own separate incomparable love. . . .

My best beloved, words cannot tell how immensely my spirit demands thee. Sometimes I almost lose my breath in a vast heaving towards thy heart. It is plain enough that for me there is no life without a response of life from thee. All my hope & peace & satisfaction lie in thy bosom. . . . Thou art literally my All-the-World, because where thou art not there is no world, but a vacuum. I cannot even look at a gilded cloud or a new-born-tree, or hear the gold robin triumph, that I do not instantly turn to thee, to thine express image every where pictured to thee in spirit. Thou art a necessity of my nature as well as its crown of perfection & voluntary grace.[22]

In the midst of their icon-making the lovers shared their dreams unselfconsciously. One time she reported that in a dream he wrote her a letter beginning, "My dear Sister." Although it was not his dream, he immediately insisted that he could not have sent such a letter since "we are, I trust, kindred spirits, but not brother and sister." Perhaps he felt it necessary to assert, tactfully, the physicality of their relationship. Perhaps Sophia in the dream revealed her sexual fears as well as incestuous confusion of Hawthorne with the two Nathaniels, father and brother, in the Peabody family.[23]

The dreams Hawthorne reported unveiled feelings of futility and desolation. On May 26, 1839 he wrote:

> Since writing the above, I have been asleep; and I dreamed that I had been sleeping a whole year in the open air; and that while I slept, the grass grew around me. It seems, in my dream, that the very bed-clothes which actually covered me were spread beneath me, and when I awoke (in my dream) I snatched them up, and the earth under them looked black, as if it had been burnt—one square place, exactly the size of the bed-clothes. Yet there was grass and herbage scattered over this burnt space, looking as fresh, and bright, and dewy, as if the summer rain and the summer sun had been cherishing them all the time.[24]

Another dream described a rescue fantasy. He "was engaged in assisting the escape of Louis XVI and Marie Antoinette from Paris during the French Revolution. And sometimes, by an unaccountable metamorphosis, it seemed as if my mother and sisters were in the place of the King and Queen." Without straining for an interpretation of what may be a censored report of the dream, Hawthorne replaced the father and assumed the role of savior-son, in an incestuous context. Or perhaps the dream disguised the desire to be rescued from marriage to Sophia. Whatever the meaning it meant more than he granted: "I think that fairies rule over our dreams—beings who have no true reason or true feelings, but mere fantasies instead of those endowments."[25]

In at least one other letter the unconscious broke through, and though Hawthorne reported the matter wittily, he perhaps intuited that the ink spot on the page of the letter was transformed into an account of the dark side of the Narcissus legend, the self-destructiveness of self-contemplation.

> . . . but, sweetest, there is, at this moment, a portrait of myself in the mirror of that ink-spot. Is not that queer to think of? When it

reaches thee, it will be nothing but a dull black spot; but now, when I bend over it, there I see myself, as at the bottom of a pool. Thou must not kiss the blot, for the sake of the image which it now reflects; though, if thou shouldst, it will be a talisman to call me back thither again.[26]

Sophia had "always been positively happy. Not so thy husband—he had only not been miserable." "My only hope of being a happy man," he declared, not without a dramatic flourish, "depends upon the permanence of our union." Yet he did not dare to inform his mother or sisters of the engagement, although apparently he had promised Sophia that he would broach the subject shortly. "It is very painful to me to disturb and derange anybody in the world"—except perhaps Sophia.[27]

On June 2, 1840, about eighteen months after their engagement, Sophia's patience was seemingly sorely taxed. His answer was to propose patience.

> Belovedest, I know not what counsel to give thee about calling on my sisters; and therefore must leave the matter to thine own exquisite sense of what is right and delicate. . . . I think I can partly understand why they appear cool towards thee; but it is for nothing in thyself personally, nor for any unkindness towards my Dove, whom everybody must feel to be the loveablest being in the world. But there are some untoward circumstances. Nevertheless, I have faith that all will be well, and that they will receive Sophie Hawthorne and the Dove into their hearts; so let us wait patiently on Providence, as we always have, and see what time will bring forth.[28]

More months passed, then years, and he had resigned from the Custom-House and then from Brook Farm, but he had not informed his family of his engagement. Probably at last Sophia delivered some kind of ultimatum, for he referred to her "injunction to tell my mother and sisters that thou art her daughter and their sister." "I do not think," he continued, "that thou canst estimate what a difficult task thou didst propose to me." Then he outlined the reserve of his family and their inability to display emotion, which he shared. He claimed that "it is hard to speak of thee—*really* of thee—to any body! I doubt whether I ever have *really* spoken of thee, to any person." Such evasions were answerable only at a price Sophia was wisely unwilling to pay—she would have had to remind him that while he protected himself he placed her in an awkward position. But he was not finished:

> Thou wilt not think that it is caprice or stubbornness that has made me hitherto resist thy wishes. Neither, I think, is it love of secrecy and darkness. I am glad to think that God sees through my heart; and if any angel has power to penetrate into it, he is welcome to know everything that is there. Yes; and so may any mortal, who is capable of full sympathy, and therefore worthy to come into my depths. But he must find his own way there. I can neither guide him nor enlighten him.[29]

His words were at once an invitation and a warning: while he was ready to surrender, he wanted to withhold; some things would be inviolable. At times he seemed eager for physical consummation, but then he seemed afraid of his own ardor, perhaps of the uncertainties and losses implicit in any union. As usual he articulated his conflict with exquisite but evasive candor.

> It is a bliss which I never wish to enjoy, when I can attain that of thy presence; but it is nevertheless a fact, that there is a bliss even in being absent from thee. This yearning that disturbs my very breath—this earnest stretching out of my soul towards thee—this voice of my heart, calling for thee out of its depths, and complaining that thou art not instantly given to it—all these are a joy; for they make me know how entirely our beings have blended into one another.[30]

Sophia was an astute woman. She listened, she supported, she aroused no unnecessary anxieties. She too shared his love of words and was often his equal in sublimation. "Thou lovest like a celestial being," he had written earlier, "and dost express thy love in heavenly language;—and it is like one angel writing to another angel."[31]

She was eager to be an angel to his angel, a Dove to his Apollo. She was even more eager to be Mrs. Nathaniel Hawthorne.

Brook Farm
"That Abominable Gold-Mine"

On April 12, 1841, Hawthorne arrived at Brook Farm during a snowstorm—"a polar Paradise," he informed Sophia. "I know not how to interpret this aspect of Nature—whether it be of good or evil omen to our enterprise. But I reflect that the Plymouth pilgrims arrived in the midst of storm and stept ashore upon mountain snowdrifts; and nevertheless they prospered, and became a great people—and doubtless it will be the same with us." The prediction proved wrong on two counts. Hawthorne stayed at Brook Farm less than a year, and the experiment in utopianism encountered enormous financial and ideological difficulties and lasted only until 1847.[1]

The Brook Farm pilgrims went with great expectations to a farm of about two hundred acres in West Roxbury, about eight miles from Boston. They planned a return to a simple agrarian life and to simple Christian principles, on the assumption that an agricultural society and plain religious virtues could be summoned at will. Imbued with nineteenth-century, and particularly American, faith in the wonders of education, they expected to inculcate among youth their ideals and their dissatisfaction with a money-oriented, industrialized society.

The Articles of Agreement of their association pronounced impressively unrealizable ends:

In order more effectually to promote the great purposes of human culture; to establish the external relations of life on a basis of wisdom and purity; to apply the principles of justice and love to our social organization in accordance with the laws of Divine Providence; to substitute a system of brotherly coöperation for one of selfish competition; to secure to our children, and to those who may be entrusted to our care, the benefits of the highest, physical, intellectual and moral education in the present state of human knowledge, the resources at our command will permit . . .[2]

The members of the community reflected the alienation of young and middle-aged intellectuals who found themselves on the periphery of a society that believed in material progress and the future of an industrialized, affluent America. The most important idealists and transcendentalists, whose views were reflected in the principles of Brook Farm, failed to become part of the experiment. Too poor to pay for a share, Elizabeth Peabody visited frequently, commented volubly, and staunchly defended the community in the pages of the *Dial*, the literary organ of Boston and Concord idealists. Margaret Fuller participated in discussion groups but would not make a personal commitment. Emerson refused to invest money and stated candidly that the community "has little to offer me, which, with resolution, I cannot procure for myself." These supporters of an individualism almost as extreme as that advocated for different reasons by industrialists, or so-called rugged individualists, had difficulty in subordinating themselves to any larger unit or, in Emerson's language, "prison" and had faith primarily in self-improvement or cultivation of one's own garden.[3]

The founder of Brook Farm was a Unitarian clergyman, George Ripley, who had not been particularly successful as a pastor in Cambridge, Massachusetts, because the profession had placed him in conflict with his solitary nature. He became convinced, however, that Christian doctrine and modern life could be harmonized and consented to undertake a role for which he was temperamentally unfit. His wife and other women were to take charge of the educational program which was to provide, in Ripley's words, "the most complete instruction . . . from the first rudiments to the highest culture." Again the goal was lofty but quixotic, since the group had neither personnel nor funds to support a program of such magnitude to reduce "the pressures of competitive institutions." It was the quixotism which Thomas Carlyle recognized when he termed Ripley "a Socinian minister who left his pulpit in order to reform the world by cultivating onions." Yet such wit is unfair to a man who, when the experiment was on the verge of financial collapse, sold his library, probably his most precious possession, in order to pay creditors.[4]

As one would expect, a strange collection of people took up residence at Brook Farm. There were disaffected clergymen like Ripley, young aesthetes like Charles King Newcomb, youthful members of the upper middle-class like George William Curtis and his brother or Margaret Fuller's brother Lloyd, and disenchanted women, some young, some along in years. It is perhaps not unfair, or even unkind, to note that many of these people were long in enthusiasm and verbal skills but short in common sense and that they went to Brook Farm with expectations which no organization could satisfy.

The most unlikely of these utopians was Nathaniel Hawthorne. He was too skeptical to place much confidence in Christian or utopian idealism, and ideology was not to his taste. Yet he purchased two shares, numbers fifteen and nineteen, at $500 each and made an additional investment of $500. This was a substantial sum on the part of a man who earned before the extras only $1,500 annually. He claimed that he wanted to purchase a home on the grounds of the colony, although such a location would have wedded him to the community. With a similar investment he could have purchased property elsewhere and obtained the privacy he needed. Perhaps he chose to be an observer of communal life, a voyeur as it were, but he generally avoided intellectuals and idealists. Perhaps—and this appears more plausible—sojourn at the farm was but another tactic to postpone marriage. Whitman flaunted his contradictions, Hawthorne hid furtively behind his.[5]

The members of the community worked long, tedious hours to make themselves independent of the larger society, but at the same time a spirit of fun prevailed: they were in a real sense adults playing house. Emerson characterized Brook Farm as "a perpetual picnic, a French Revolution in small, an Age of Reason in a patty pan." With wit he pointed out some of the absurdities.

Of course every visitor there found that there was a comic side to this Paradise of shepherds and shepherdesses. There was a stove in every chamber, and every one might burn as much wood as he or she would saw. The ladies took cold on washing-day; so it was ordained that the gentlemen-shepherds should wring and hang out clothes; which they punctually did. And it would sometimes occur that when they danced in the evening, clothespins dropped plentifully from their pockets.[6]

At work the women dressed in skirts with matching knickerbockers, but at leisure they had "long flowing coiffeurs, absurdly wide brimmed hats, and the adorning wreaths of vines, berries, and flowers." The men wore blue frocks or tunics with collars after Byron, sack trousers, and heavy boots. Some of the males allowed their hair and beards to grow "perhaps to demonstrate indifference to the demands of a relatively clean shaven and shorn age."[7]

Hawthorne assumed the blue frock but not the beard. (The moustache appeared during the Italian years in the late 1850s.) Perhaps because of his fame and his solid financial investment, he received favored treatment. "Thy husband," he wrote to Sophia, "has the best chamber in the house, I believe; and though not quite so good as the apartment I have left, it will do very well. I have hung up thy two pictures; and they give me a glimpse of summer and of thee."[8]

"I feel the original Adam reviving within me," he declared to Sophia, and proceeded wittily to attack a woman much admired by Sophia and her sisters. Hawthorne alleged that the eight cows at the farm were joined "by a transcendental heifer, belonging to Miss Margaret Fuller. She is very fractious, I believe, and apt to kick over the milk pail. Thou knowest best, whether, in these traits of character, she resembles her mistress." On the following day he informed Sophia that "Miss Fuller's cow hooks the other cows, and has made herself ruler of the herd, and behaves in a very tyrannical manner." Soon the cow was on such bad terms with her bovine companions that she clung for protection to Hawthorne, who was compelled to give "two or three gentle pats with a shovel. . . . She is not an amiable cow; but she has a very intelligent face, and seems to be of a reflective cast of character. I doubt not that she will soon perceive the expediency of being on good terms with the rest of her sisterhood." Probably Sophia laughed as she read this account, but Hawthorne had accomplished his purpose, to reduce Fuller to size.[9]

As long as he enjoyed the novelty of rural life, his reports of life at Brook Farm were entertaining.

Sweetest, I did not milk the cows last night, because Mr. Ripley was afraid to trust them to my hands, or me to their horns—I know not which. But this morning, I have done wonders. Before breakfast, I went out to the barn, and began to chop hay for the cattle; and with such "righteous vehemence" (as Mr. Ripley says) did I labor, that, in the space of ten minutes, I broke the machine. Then I brought wood and replenished the fires; and finally sat down to breakfast and ate up a huge amount of buckwheat cakes. After breakfast, Mr. Ripley put a four-pronged instrument into my hands, which he gave me to understand was called a pitch-fork; and he and Mr. Farley being armed with similar weapons, we all three commenced a gallant attack upon a heap of manure. [10]

Soon the revived Adam milked a cow, an event he emphasized with three exclamation points, but the self-styled "clod-compelling husband" sometimes lacked energy to write to Sophia and was, he maintained, the prisoner of the dung-heap.

That abominable gold-mine! Thank God, we anticipate getting rid of its treasures, in the course of two or three days. Of all hateful places, that is the worst; and I shall never comfort myself for having spent so many days of blessed sunshine there. It is my opinion, dearest, that a man's soul may be buried and perish under a dung-heap or in a furrow of the field, just as well as under a pile of money. [11]

Sophia visited Brook Farm in May and confirmed his recognition that despite his "exquisite courtesy & comfortableness & geniality," he was not leading an "ideal life." "Never upon the face of any mortal," she wrote rapturously but perceptively, "was there such a divine expression of sweetness & kindliness as I saw upon thine. . . . Yet it was also the expression of a witness & hearer rather than of comradeship." [12]

The Hawthornes in Salem were concerned, according to his sister Louisa, "because you stay away so long, and work so hard." Even Beelzebub, the family cat, wanted him home but "begs that you will leave your thick boots behind you, as her nerves are somewhat delicate, and she could not bear them." When Louisa wrote again she was prepared to spend the summer at Brook Farm because it conjured up memories of pleasant days at Raymond, Maine, which remained her Eden. She did not mention the fact that she would have her brother to herself. The Hawthorne women were worried about his clothes, which they took care of in the absence of a wife, and feared the effects of too much time and work in the sun. "What is the use," Louisa asked, "of burning your brains out in the sun when you can do something better with them?"[13]

Mrs. Ripley wrote exuberantly about Hawthorne's presence at Brook Farm: "Hawthorne is one to reverence, to admire with that deep admiration so refreshing to the soul. He is our prince—prince in everything—yet despising no labour and very athletic and able-bodied in the barnyard and field." This view was not shared by Georgiana Kirby, who wrote long after the appearance of *The Blithedale Romance*, which was resented, often bitterly, by the believers:

> No one could have been more out of place than he in a mixed company, no matter how cultivated, worthy, and individualized each member of it might be. He was morbidly shy and reserved, needing to be shielded from his fellows, and obtaining the fruits of observation at second-hand. He was therefore not amenable to the democratic influences of the Community which enriched the others, and made them declare, in after years, that the years or months spent there had been the most valuable ones in their lives.[14]

Not everyone recalled Hawthorne as a shy misfit. In a reminiscence entitled "A Girl at Sixteen at Brook Farm," Ora Gannett Sedgwick related an incident in which Hawthorne's boyishness, even at age thirty-seven, showed through.

> One evening he was alone in the hall, sitting on a chair at the farther end, when my roommate, Ellen Slade, and myself were going upstairs. She whispered to me, "Let's throw the sofa pillows at Mr. Hawthorne." Reaching over the banister, we each took a cushion and threw it. Quick as a flash he put out his hand, seized a broom that was hanging near him, warded off our cushions, and threw them back with sure aim. As fast as we could throw them at him he returned them with effect, hitting us every time, while we could hit only the broom. He must have been very quick in his movements. Through it all not a word was spoken.[15]

One of the first young people to arrive at Brook Farm was Charles King Newcomb of Providence, Rhode Island. A graduate of

Brown College, he briefly studied for the Episcopalian ministry and then for a period studied Catholicism, only to become a protégé or "votary" of Margaret Fuller and later a Swedenborgian. Fuller enthusiastically recommended the youth to Emerson. Perhaps because of his own doubts and turbulences beneath the somewhat impassive facade, Emerson empathized with troubled youths who were articulate, religious, even mystical, and usually aesthetic. He wanted to surround himself with their hidden, undeveloped talents, to make Concord truly an Athens. Newcomb, he declared, was "the subtlest observer and diviner of character I ever met," and in "Montaigne," Emerson addresses Newcomb as San Carlo, "one of the most penetrating of men," both of which judgments proved premature and finally erroneous.[16]

"A slight, dark young man, with a hesitant manner and a nervous laugh," as well as a stammer, Newcomb had "a heavy mass of tangled hair which was always slipping over his eyes and being flipped back with an impatient gesture." Newcomb's father died at sea when he was five years old, and at nine the son compiled a journal dealing with children taken from their families. He was the favorite but sickly child of a dominating mother who asserted with finality, "We are brother & sister, as well as parent and child." People sometimes construed Newcomb's verbal brilliance as mystical illumination instead of a veil to hide his intellectual, sexual, and emotional confusion. Emerson chose to characterize Newcomb as "the quiet, retreating, demoniacal youth," although at another time he was more insightful in recognizing that Newcomb's preoccupation with love expressed "only the wish to be cherished."[17]

Newcomb arrived at Brook Farm about a month after Hawthorne, in May 1841. He was twenty-one and Hawthorne thirty-seven. Apparently the youth was attracted to the handsome author whose *Twice-told Tales* he had already read. Shortly after his arrival Newcomb's mother wrote, "So you mean to wear gloves & a veil to bed," and then asked, "do you remember Parson Hooper, one of Mr. Hawthorne's heroes—who wore a black veil always & no one could see his face or divine the cause?" Apparently mother and son in their incestuous relationship, which no doubt involved only thinly disguised erotic charades, exchanged intimate confidences. Hence, she was not surprised by his bed attire which approximated, as she detected, the effeminacy of the "fastidious" Hooper, who by the assumption of the black veil publicizes his "secret sin" but, more important, saves himself from the marriage he secretly fears.[18]

Years later, after Hawthorne's death, Newcomb recalled "my own sympathy of sentiment with Hawthorne . . . , as I knew long since from a summer with him when I was a youth & we walked like two boys together, though he was much older. . . . Hawthorne would smile with me, in incessantly renewed wonder, on finding our senses reflected where we never thought of seeing them in any shape." In another jotting he commented without elaboration that Hawthorne "had something of childlike virtue, & something of childish vice." Apparently Hawthorne and Newcomb romped like boys as Hawthorne often did with his college chums, but in view of the age difference such behavior may have confused a youth who had more mother than he could handle and needed a stabilizing father figure in his life. As Emerson observed and Newcomb's journals confirmed, Newcomb formed his "closest friendships" with athletes and delighted "in the petulant heroism of boys."[19]

After Hawthorne left Brook Farm, Newcomb completed the first part of "The Two Dolons," which was printed in the *Dial* in July 1842 with the subtitle, "From the MS. Symphony of Dolon"; characteristically, he never completed the second part. This tale of a youth of idyllic beauty related what Henry James was to call a "vastation." After a three-day vigil Dolon, attired "in a surplice-like robe, gathered in at the waist by a white tasseled girdle, and a wreath of laurel and wild lilies of the valley on his left arm," hears the voice of an older man preparing for a rite. The man lays his hand on Dolon's head, transfers the wreath there, and plunges a "sacrificial knife" into the youth's breast. Then he throws "himself prostrate before the rock as before an altar."[20]

The tale restored Emerson's faith "in the repairs of the Universe" after the death of his six-year-old son Waldo, whom Newcomb mentions in the story. In "The Hall of Fantasy" Hawthorne refers to Newcomb's "deep mist of metaphysical fantasies." Fantasies, but not "metaphysical" ones, would appear to characterize this retelling of the Abraham and Isaac story, except that Newcomb's Isaac suffers Newcomb's fate and the transfer of the floral wreath from father to son before the knife plunges into the youth's breast suggests a sexual fantasy or longing.[21]

Late in 1842 or early in the following year Newcomb sent an inscribed copy of his translation of Elizabeth von Arnim's *Die Günderode*— "Nathaniel Hawthorne from his friend C. K. N." *Die Günderode* records in evasive nineteenth-century sentimental prose an unsatisfying friendship between two young women who fumble toward a satisfaction that society denied.

In 1843 Margaret Fuller suggested that Hawthorne and Sophia accept Newcomb as a boarder while he worked in Concord at the invitation of Emerson. Hawthorne refused, politely. There evidently is no record of Newcomb's reaction, but in view of his later comments about Hawthorne he may have been deeply wounded, feeling himself once again rejected by a male. Later that year Hawthorne heard from one of the members of Brook Farm that Newcomb was "passing through a new moral phasis; he is silent, inexpressive, talks little or none, and listens without response except a sardonic laugh; and some of his friends think he is passing into permanent eclipse."[22]

Newcomb's comments in his journals after Hawthorne's death revealed his abiding rancor yet predictable ambivalence. He termed Hawthorne "a hermaphroditical sort of thinker & artist," "a sort of humanitarian monk, so to speak, at least before he married," who was "unmasculine & unpositive." He doubted that Hawthorne would have married if it had not been for Sophia's encouragement. He canceled the passages containing these remarks but two days later resumed his commentary: "He was such an exclusively, introvertively, & isolately reflective person, that he reflected mostly himself, & was scarcely anything more than a self-centered, self-reproductive, & soliloquial person." But Newcomb told more about himself than about Hawthorne. He had failed while Hawthorne had become a world figure. Newcomb was lonely, aging, and, sadly, still in search of love.[23]

Later in life, a homeless aesthete, Newcomb wandered between Paris and Providence, kept a voluminous diary, and secretly wrote in "Songs of Love" 1,015 pornographic poems. Long before Newcomb's death Emerson lamented the "overcasting of my brightest star. . . . An arrested mind, a bud that is principled against flowering. . . ."[24]

As was to be expected, the novelty of communal life at Brook Farm soon wore off. Hawthorne complained to one correspondent that "the summer is passing with so little enjoyment of nature," although he also admitted that "my views in this respect vary somewhat with the state of my spirits." After four months with the cows, the milking, the furrowing, and the "gold-mine," Hawthorne in a letter to Sophia once more dramatized his life with the assistance of John Bunyan:

And—joyful thought!—in a little more than a fortnight, thy husband will be free from his bondage—. . . free to think and feel! I do think that a greater weight will then be removed from me, than when Christian's burthen fell off at the foot of the cross. Even my Custom House experience was not such a thraldom and weariness. . . . Dost thou think it a praiseworthy matter, that I have spent five golden months in providing food for cows and horses? Dearest, it is not so. Thank God, my soul is not utterly buried under a dung-heap.[25]

He now had little faith in the economic viability of Brook Farm. "I can see few or no signs that Providence purposes to give us a home here. I am weary, weary, thrice weary, of waiting so many ages." He admitted also to a lack of confidence in his ability "to gather gold" and concluded: "I am becoming more and more convinced, that we must not lean upon the community. What ever is to be done, must be done by thy husband's own individual strength." He would not remain through the winter, "unless with an absolute certainty that there will be a home ready for us in the spring." The conclusion, as usual, was inconclusive since he planned to remain "an associate of the community; so that we may take advantage of any more favorable aspect of affairs." By the end of the letter he had almost succeeded in writing himself out of his gloom by means of the Adamic tactic of depositing it upon Eve, although he was aware of his cowardice:

Dearest, I have written the above in not so good spirits as sometimes; but now that I have so ungenerously thrown my despondency on thee, my heart begins to throb more lightly. I doubt not that God has great good store for us; for He would not have given us so much, unless He were preparing to give a great deal more. I love thee! Thou lovest me! What present bliss! What sure and certain hope![26]

Hawthorne spent most of September in Salem with his mother and sisters and the family cat, Beelzebub. To Sophia he depicted himself as "a shadow of the night," perhaps a latter-day member of a coven of witches: "If it were not for my Dove, this present world would see no more of me forever. The sunshine would never fall on me, no more than on a ghost. Once in a while, people might discern my figure, gliding stealthily through the dim evening—that would be all." Hawthorne could not resist the role of Fanshawe, the Byronic youth stalking the streets, for no illicit purposes. Though he often had doubts about his dismal attic study and his solitary life in Salem, he was not given to self-deception about the "real Me."

But really I should judge it to be twenty years since I left Brook Farm; and I take this to be one proof that my life there was an unnatural and unsuitable, and therefore an unreal one. It already looks like a dream behind me. The real Me was never an associate of the community. . . .[27]

By September 22, however, he was back at the farm and "was most kindly received." This time he came to observe, to determine "whether thou and I have any call to cast in our lot among them." He felt "friendless . . . now that I am no longer obliged to toil in its stubborn furrows." He filled his letter to Sophia with complaints. He missed her. He needed her help to decide about their future at Brook Farm. He would not stay there, for "the time would be absolutely thrown away, so far as regards any literary labor to be performed." Yet four days later he became "a Trustee of the Brook Farm estate, and Chairman of the Committee of Finance!!!!" After the four exclamation points he had to reassure Sophia, who could have been slightly bewildered by his whim-whams: "Belovedest, my accession to these august offices does not at all decide the question of my remaining here permanently. I told Mr. Ripley, that I could not spend the winter at the farm, and that it was quite uncertain whether I returned in the spring." Of course, Hawthorne had a substantial investment to protect. Since during his stay at Salem he had not screwed up his courage to inform his family of his engagement to Sophia, he may even have returned to Brook Farm to gain time for himself. It is pointless to observe that the simple course was to act, for Hawthorne was anything but a simple man.[28]

His letters to Sophia at this time were short, grouchy, and choppy; he seemed restless and unhappy. When his entries in his notebook are juxtaposed with his letters, another picture emerges. On October 9 he complained to Sophia of "this dismal gloom! I positively cannot submit to have this precious month all darkened with cloud and sullied with drizzle." In the notebook entry of the same day the weather was "dismal," but the household was more cheerful after the arrival of a young woman.

For a week past, we have been especially gladdened with a little sempstress from Boston, about seventeen years old, but of such a petite figure that, at first view, one would take her to be hardly in her teens. She is very vivacious and smart, laughing, singing, and talking all the time. . . . On continued observation and acquaintance, you discover that she is not a little girl, but really a little woman, with all the prerogatives and liabilities of a woman. This gives a new aspect to her character; while her girlish impression still continues, and is strangely combined with the sense that this frolicksome little maiden has the material for that sober character, a wife.

Quite obviously Hawthorne was eyeing the nubile young woman closely. "Be it said, among all the rest, there is a perfect maiden modesty in her deportment; though I doubt whether the boys, in their rompings with her, do not feel that she has past out of childhood." He found her "well worth studying," even though "her intellect is very ordinary, and she never says anything worth hearing, or even laughing at, in itself."[29]

On October 21 he exclaimed to Sophia, "What atrocious weather! In all this month, we have not had a single truly October day; it has been a real November month, and of the most disagreeable kind"—which was an overstatement. "I came," he continued, "to this place in one snow-storm, and shall probably leave it in another; so that my reminiscences of Brook Farm are like to be the coldest and dreariest imaginable." According to jottings in his notebook, it was a lovely autumn. No "process of word-daubing," he declared, could recapture the "unsurpassable" colors of "Autumn's petticoat," and there is "a feeling of shelter and comfort, and consequently a heart-warmth, which cannot be experienced in summer."[30]

Sophia knew nothing of these inconsistencies, but even if she had, it would have made no difference. Hawthorne fulfilled her fantasy of the ideal male, and she silently endured his procrastinations, indecisiveness, and wayward moods. What would have been a sacrifice for another woman, subordination to the husband, was for her a desired state. Hawthorne understood Sophia's needs—and her willingness, as in her relationship with her mother, to give without limit or complaint—and exploited them. Sternly and decisively he reproved Sophia when he learned that she was under the spell of a magnetic lady, which was but one more attempt on her part to find an earthly paradise by means of supernatural trickery. "If I possessed such a power over thee," he wrote, "I should not dare to exercise it; nor can I consent to its being exercised by another. . . . there would be an intrusion into thy holy of holies—and the intruder would not be thy husband!" (Here he was without knowing it gathering material for *The House of the Seven Gables*.) "Keep thy imagination sane," he directed, "that is one of the truest conditions of communion with Heaven." A day later he added: "Love is the true magnetism. What carest thou for any other?"[31]

Early in November Hawthorne left utopia. He spent the winter and spring traveling between Salem and Boston. Sophia now lived with her parents and Elizabeth, who had opened a bookshop on West Street. Although Hawthorne never returned to Brook Farm, at least so far as we know, he carried on a flirtation with communal life in the spring of 1842. As late as May of that year, little more than a month before his marriage, he planned to visit David Mack, who had organized a cooperative farm near Northampton, Massachusetts. At the last moment he declined: "I confess to you, my dear sir, it is my present belief that I can best attain the higher ends of life by retaining the ordinary relation to society."[32]

On October 17, 1842, he formally resigned from Brook Farm:

I ought, some time ago, to have tendered my resignation as an associate of the Brook Farm Institute, but I have been unwilling to feel myself entirely disconnected with you. As I can see but little prospect, however, of returning to you, it becomes proper for me now to take the final step. But no longer a brother of your band, I shall always take the warmest interest in your progress, and shall heartily rejoice at your success—of which I can see no reasonable doubt.

This was not to be the last word. In 1845 he sued to recover his investment, which he sorely needed in the lean years following his marriage. In 1846 when he published *Mosses from an Old Manse*, a complimentary reference to Brook Farm in "The Hall of Fantasy," published in the *Pioneer* in February 1843, was excised. He reserved his last word for *The Blithedale Romance*, which despite the furor it provoked among partisans, conferred immortality upon a timid, unsuccessful experiment.[33]

"I Take This Dove in Bed and Board"

In love with their verbalizations of passion, welcoming (or so it sometimes seemed) separation in order to have opportunities to play variations upon their mutual adoration, Hawthorne and Sophia had dallied unduly, though rumors were evidently afloat. In the fall of 1841 Lucretia Hale related the latest gossip to Sarah J. Hale: "O! there's a new engagement—Miss Sophia Peabody!!!! to Mr Hawthorne!!! They have been attached for a long time, but Mr Hawthorne has been waiting till he should get something to live upon, and as his affairs have become more hopeful, the engagement has come out."[1]

This gossip was not quite accurate since neither the Salem Hawthornes nor Sophia's intimate friends knew of the engagement. It wasn't until 1842 that Sophia began in her gentle but firm way to free a tremulous bachelor of his bachelordom. In April she lifted the veil of secrecy about the romance when she informed one of her oldest friends that she was engaged to "the visual reality" of her "ideal." "I marvel," Sophia wrote to Mary Wilder Foote, "how I can be so blessed among mortals—how the very king & poet of the world should be my eternal companion . . . but I am not afraid." To deny fear was perhaps to admit it, but at least Sophia was not so paralyzed as Hawthorne, who for more than three years had kept his mother and his two sisters uninformed of the engagement. He did exert himself, however, to look out for their economic well-being when he went to New York and Albany with Colonel Joseph Hall, a former associate at the Boston Custom-House, in order to consult with O'Sullivan about contributions to the *Democratic Review*.[2]

At the urging of Elizabeth Hoar, who had commissioned Sophia to design a medallion after the sudden death of her betrothed, Charles Emerson, Hawthorne and Sophia journeyed to Concord in May to look at a house available for rent after the death of the Reverend Ezra Ripley, the eccentric and lovable step-grandfather of Ralph Waldo Emerson. In noting their presence on May 7, Emerson observed: "If they shall come to live here I shall be content . . . I like him well." If he was "content," Sophia was rapturous (although she had her customary spelling problem with *ei*) after "Emerson recieved us with such a welcoming, shining expression of face & figure that we were penetrated with joy. . . . He accompanied us to the ancient parsonage, & to Sleepy Hollow, over violets and anemones. . . . It was a fine afternoon & all things were new." Sophia was one of those rare and fortunate souls to whom the world is new every day.[3]

Early in May Sophia informed Margaret Fuller that the wedding was to take place in June, "the month of roses & of perfect bloom," but there was still unfinished business in both the Hawthorne and Peabody households. Sophia proceeded to handle both situations. It was perhaps life following art, for in Hawthorne's tales the women are generally more effective in problem-solving than the fearful, hesitant males to whom they are attracted. Sophia sent Elizabeth and Louisa Hawthorne a letter which was "sweet, gentle, and magnanimous; such as no angel save my Dove, could have written." Hawthorne assured Sophia, "They will love thee, all in good time, dearest; and we will be very happy."[4]

The assurance was necessary, for on May 23 Elizabeth Hawthorne replied to Sophia in a stilted letter that lay bare the hurts of the sisters in the loss of a brother who was almost their only tie to the world outside their Herbert Street house.

Your approaching union with my brother makes it incumbent upon me to offer you the assurances of my sincere desire for your mutual happiness. With regard to my sister and myself, I hope nothing will ever occur to render your future intercourse with us other than agreeable, particularly as it need not be so frequent or so close as to require more than reciprocal good will, if we do not happen to suit each other in our new relationship. I write thus plainly, because my brother has desired me to say only what was true. . . .

Before she concluded, she conveyed her "pleasure" but so stiffly that Sophia may have drawn another conclusion: "I anticipate with pleasure the renewal of our acquaintance, with the opportunity of becoming better known to each other."[5]

It took a week or two before the sisters, with nerves as fluttering as Hepzibah's or Clifford's in *The House of the Seven Gables*, steeled themselves to inform their mother that she was within weeks to lose a son. Their hesitations had some justification since, as Hawthorne informed Sophia, "I knew that almost every agitating circumstance of her life had hitherto cost her a fit of sickness." But the mother was wiser than her children, for she "had seen how things were, a long time ago. At first, her heart was troubled, because she knew that much of outward as well as inward fitness was required to secure thy foolish husband's peace; but, gradually and quietly, God has taught her that all is good; and so, thou dearest wife, we shall have her fullest blessings and concurrence." Following the mother's example, the sisters began, according to their brother in one of his half-truths, "to sympathize as they ought; and all is well." If it took the sisters, particularly Elizabeth, longer to reconcile themselves, they had more to lose than the mother, whose protracted mourning for her husband was almost over, while they, Elizabeth at forty and Louisa at thirty-four, had weary years ahead.[6]

According to Elizabeth Hawthorne, her mother wanted to see Sophia before the marriage took place on June 27, but Mrs. Hawthorne did not insist, long since having surrendered rights as well as pleasures perhaps because she considered herself worthy neither to order nor to enjoy. Sophia, however, had too much to cope with in her own home in Boston to take time for a trip to Salem. Aware that her clumsy letter had offended Sophia, Elizabeth wrote again, sorrowfully but candidly, wishing the couple well but at the same time revealing her own fears of middle age, celibacy, and the future.

I deeply regret that I said any thing in my note to give you pain; if we can all forget the past, and look forward to the future it will be better. The future seems to promise much happiness to you, for certainly I think your disposition and my brother's well suited to each other; but have you no dread of the cares and vexations inevitable in married life, and in *all* life, I allow, only in some situations we have in a great degree the power to withdraw from and forget them? I confess I should not have courage to incur any responsibility not forced upon me by circumstances beyond my control. I should not like to feel as if much depended upon me. In this, however, I am aware how much I differ from almost every one else, and how strange it must appear to you, especially just now.[7]

Elizabeth Hawthorne never altered her opinion about the marriage and stayed out of Sophia's way. When Sophia published *Passages from the American Note-Books* after Hawthorne's death, Elizabeth found it "melancholy reading . . . because it recalls the period of my Brother's marriage and residence in Concord, and other doings of like kind." It remained her conviction until death that the parties to a marriage "are the least fit to decide, because they cannot be calm enough for a rational determination, so they ought to be governed by the counsel of their friends." She did not have to explain which marriage she had in mind.[8]

Another aging unmarried woman, Margaret Fuller, unaware that in the Brook Farm period Hawthorne had conferred bovinity upon her, blessed the union: ". . . if ever I saw a man who combined delicate tenderness to understand the heart of a woman, with quiet depth and manliness enough to satisfy her, it is Mr Hawthorne. . . . to one who cannot think of love merely in the heart, or even in the common destiny of two souls, but as necessarily comprehending intellectual friendship too, it seems the happiest lot imaginable that lies before you."[9]

As the wedding day approached Hawthorne suddenly, but in a protective jesting tone, assumed an assertive role. "Ah, foolish virgin!" he declaimed. "It is too late; nothing can part us now; for God Himself hath ordained that we shall be one. So nothing remains but to reconcile thyself to thy destiny. Year by year, thou must come closer and closer to me; and a thousand ages hence, we shall be only in the honeymoon of our marriage. Poor little Dove!" It was ill timed and perhaps somewhat assaultive to dwell on loss of virginity to a woman of delicate sensibilities. Besides, the fear was probably his more than hers.[10]

Within a week Sophia suffered from one of the nervous attacks typical of her semi-invalid condition, and the wedding had to be postponed. Sophia was at once put to bed under the care of her mother who was also experiencing a grave crisis, hoping secretly that she would be spared the loss (or death) of her favorite daughter.

In a letter to her mother written a month after the wedding, Sophia laid bare what had taken place in the Peabody house in the months before the marriage.

> How I wish that in a letter I could come so near you that you would not miss me at all. I wish I could be wife & daughter at the same time, so that your dear heart might not feel desolated of me. While I was at home I never dared once to refer to our separation, for I knew that it was too tender & overcoming a subject for you & me to talk about. I knew that I could not bear your emotion without nearly being beside myself, because we are so closely bound together that you can never be glad or sorry, well or ill, without my feeling it most deeply.

Although Sophia had every right to be resentful that her joy had to be repressed, she praised her mother extravagantly but sincerely, for she recognized the depths of her love even when she was hurt by the demands of that love. Sophia wanted the letter burned, yet when she had the opportunity to destroy it following her mother's death she neither bowdlerized nor destroyed it.[11]

Hawthorne was not so forgiving of the mother, comprehending only the negative aspects of her love; perhaps he allowed his own hurts to intrude as he usually did in his perception of his own mother. Sophia was wiser about the complexities of love. Out of unending gratitude she handled her mother delicately, with a reassurance which, if not exactly true, was not false: "If my husband had not found me till I had gone to heaven, it would have been my dearest happiness to have endeavoured to remunerate you by the tenderest care, for your life of toil & care." She flattered as she acknowledged the lack of fulfillment in her mother's life. The future was hers; her mother had to make what she could of the past.[12]

Sometime after the marriage Mrs. Peabody made a painfully honest admission which confirmed Sophia's opinion of her love:

> When I gave you up, my sweetest confidant, my ever lovely and cheering companion, I set myself aside and thought only of the re-

pose, the fulness of bliss, that awaited you under the protection and in possession of the confiding love of so rare a being as Nathaniel Hawthorne. Still, my heart was at times rebellious, and sunk full low when I entered the rooms so long consecrated to you; and I had to reason with myself and say, "I have not lost her, but have gained a noble son, and we can meet often."[13]

Publicly Mrs. Peabody accepted her daughter's happiness, but privately she nursed a hurt which was not exposed until her death. Among her mother's papers Sophia discovered a curious manuscript which led her to write to her sister Mary: "You will see by the date it was begun the month after my marriage. Do you know of any one who died then, whom she loved with such a fervor & mourned with such hope & sorrow?" If Sophia did not immediately recognize that the death was her own, she probably came to that realization later since the manuscript has evidently disappeared.[14]

Because Sophia's health after her collapse remained uncertain, Hawthorne waited until July 8 before he asked James Freeman Clarke to perform the ceremony on the following day. Writing from his apartment in George Hillard's home on Pinckney Street, he informed the minister, "Unless it should be decidedly a rainy day, a carriage will call for you at half past eleven o'clock, in the forenoon." And so it came to pass that the prelude which began on the evening of November 11, 1837, culminated almost five years later in a simple ceremony on the morning of July 9, 1842, five days after Hawthorne celebrated his thirty-eighth birthday.[15]

The scene was the modestly furnished apartment at 13 West Street in Boston where years earlier Margaret Fuller had held her celebrated "conversations" and Elizabeth Peabody had published the *Dial*. Since Clarke had been editor of the *Western Messenger*, another transcendental publication, the not-so-transcendental Hawthorne took vows in a transcendental atmosphere. The witnesses of the rite included the Peabodys, the minister's sister Sarah Clarke, and Cornelia Park. The Hawthorne women did not attend.[16]

Immediately after the service the couple set out for Concord by carriage. Before the coming of the railroad, which within a few years was to disturb the quiet of Walden Pond, it was, although the distance was only twenty or so miles, a long journey from Boston to Concord, particularly for two impatient but timid lovers. There were two showers and a delay of about an hour, but Sophia minded not at all, as she informed her mother on the following day. Only her eager prose can do justice to her feelings on the greatest day of her life. She begged her mother not to show this letter to "a mortal out of the family," an injunction which was not respected either by Mrs. Peabody or by Sophia, who preserved the epistle for posterity.

> We arrived at about five o'clock. Never was any fairy palace more exquisite than the house. Spirit Elizabeth [Hoar] had filled all the vases with the loveliest of flowers . . . & fine grass half shrouding them in mist made them look more lovely still. . . . It seemed as if some angel had come down from Paradise with the flowers of life & adorned our temple for us. . . .
>
> Dear, dear mother, every step the horses took, I felt better, & not in the least tired. . . . My husband looked upon me as upon a mirage which would suddenly disappear. It seemed miraculous that I was so well. After dinner, which was after six, I heard a voice in the kitchen & knew it must be our messenger from Paradise [Elizabeth Hoar]. I went out & met her in the hall. She embraced me & looked so happy for me, that one would have thought she herself was the happiest bride since six thousand years. For has it not taken six thousand years for my bloom of Time to flower? . . .
>
> Mr Hawthorne was sure that to day I should feel fatigued—but to day I have been very well still & just now I have walked with him to the monument & home through the road. It is a perfect Eden round us. . . . We are Adam and Eve. . . . The birds saluted us this morning with such gushes of rapture, that I thought they must know us & our happiness. My appetite is excellent & I feel a clear, new life which I think must be like the Phoenix's when it rises from the old ashes.[17]

Truly she was "the happiest person in this earth," and if her imagery invoked Eden by way of Milton's epic, her very real joy justified the aggrandizement. Hawthorne's joy peeped through the bantering tone he adopted in his letter to his sister Louisa on July 10: "The execution took place yesterday. We made a christian end, and came straight to Paradise, where we abide at this present writing. We are as happy as people can be, without making themselves ridiculous, and might be even happier; but, as a matter of taste, we choose to stop short at this point."[18]

Even Emerson smiled on the union when he commented that the old Manse had become "all new & bright again as a toy." Nine days after the marriage Mary Peabody wrote to her sister, "You are so entirely satisfied that you do not feel inclined to have any communication with other portions of humanity." Then, with characteristic Peabody anxiety, she warned Sophia "not to lose all your hold upon the human family. . . . You do not care what any one thinks about it now, but later in your life you may possibly regret having neglected social duties." [19]

Sarah Clarke summed up the effect of the marriage on Sophia this way: "The same miracle was performed as in the case of Mrs. Browning, love conquered neuralgia." This was not quite true, but near enough. [20]

Eden in Concord

The Eden of the new Adam and Eve had been the parsonage of two clergymen, William Emerson and Ezra Ripley. Emerson had boarded with the widow of his predecessor and had fallen in love with her eldest daughter, Phebe. In 1769 Emerson built the Manse, in the words of his grandson, as "a nest for his phebe-bird." It was a lovely coincidence that Hawthorne took his Phoebe to this house. A few hundred yards from the Manse, at the corner of the meadow, Emerson's parishioners and neighbors from Concord and Lexington in 1775 fought the British at the celebrated bridge over the Concord River, and in 1837 a statue was erected to commemorate that glorious day, a dedication that included an ode composed by Ralph Waldo Emerson.[1]

Phebe Emerson and her five children remained in the "nest" after her husband's death in 1776. Four years later she married Ezra Ripley. During a pastorate that lasted sixty-three years, Ripley became a Unitarian and a sometimes stern paternal figure for generations of Concord citizens. He changed little in appearance or opinions over the years, wearing the costume of his early manhood and claiming the privilege of kissing all the women, young and old. The women, his step-grandson related, accepted his addiction even though, as one declared, it "seemed as if he was going to make a meal of you."[2]

Ralph Waldo lived briefly at the Manse as a child of ten and again in 1834 and 1835. There he wrote *Nature*, which on its publication in 1836 became one of the landmarks of American life and literature, comparable in significance to the appearances of *The Scarlet Letter* (1850), *Moby-Dick* (1851), *Walden* (1854), and *Leaves of Grass* (1855). After Ripley's death in 1841, his son Samuel was not ready to move back to Concord, and the Manse became available to the Hawthornes.

The exterior of the simple frame house was, to quote the new tenant, "a sober greyish hue," but "to re-paint its venerable face would be a real sacrilege; it would look like old Doctor Ripley in a brown wig." From the road there was "a noble avenue of Balm of Gilead trees" to the modest door. When Hawthorne composed "The Old Manse" to introduce the collection of tales called *Mosses from an Old Manse*, he noted with his usual interest in such matters that the former owner of the house had gone down the avenue to the road which led "towards the village burying-ground" less than a mile away. After this somber introduction he jested that the Manse had never "been prophaned by a lay occupant, until that memorable summer-afternoon when I entered it as my house. . . . I took shame to myself for having been so long a writer of idle stories, and ventured to hope the wisdom would descend upon me with the falling leaves of the avenue." He was to make much the same comment in his preface to *The Scarlet Letter*.[3]

From the rear door of the Manse a winding path leads to the Concord River, which gently twists through the meadows. Hawthorne compared the river to "one of the half torpid earthworms which I dig up for the purpose of bait. The worm is sluggish, and so is the river—the river is muddy, and so is the worm—you hardly know whether either of them is alive or dead; but still, in the course of time, they both manage to creep away." Hawthorne delighted in a comparison which he knew would amuse Sophia in the journal they kept jointly during the Concord years. On the following day he playfully inflated, no doubt for Sophia's benefit: this "most turbid mud-puddle can contain its own picture of Heaven. . . . This dull river has a deep religion of its own; so, let us trust, has the dullest human soul, perhaps unconsciously." Sophia may have had the last word about the stream when she commented, "It was too lazy to keep itself clean."[4]

Despite their jests about the sluggish river, which were more playful than truthful, they had a quiet love affair with its eccentricities, its lilies, and its charms. They walked beside it, boated, fished, and skated, and

Hawthorne bathed there with his usual frequency, sometimes twice a day in the summer, the water "being as soft as milk, and always warmer than the air. Its hue has a slight tinge of gold; and my limbs, when I behold them through its medium, look tawny."[5]

Between the house and the river was an orchard that supplied them with more apples, peaches, and pears than they could eat. They sometimes bartered fruit for meat. The large garden which Thoreau had planted for them before their arrival in Concord produced quantities of vegetables. Also on the grounds were a barn, sheds, a henhouse, a pigeon house, and "an old stone pig-stye . . . overgrown with tall weeds, indicating that no grunter has recently occupied it."[6]

Sophia redesigned the interior according to a taste under the influence of Flaxman's classical illustrations of Homer and the neoclassicism of the era. She decorated the furniture in the bedroom with pen and ink outlines of Flaxman's mythical scenes. On the washstand was "outlined Venus rising from the Sea." She replaced "the grim prints of Puritan ministers," to quote her husband, with reproductions of Michelangelo, and Caroline Sturgis assisted in the transformation when she presented the couple with a bust of Apollo, the god whom Hawthorne most resembled in the eyes of his admirers, especially his wife. "If the brindled cow is permitted to feed in the Battle field" near the Manse, Sturgis wrote, "I am sure Apollo may be allowed to look upon it. . . . Therefore I hope you will give him a place in your studio & find him a good companion here." The bust was to occupy a prominent position in this and every other house the Hawthornes occupied in America. Sophia's unimpressed maid observed, "I tell you what, Mrs. Hawthorne, when you get a little baby to lug about, you won't think so much of your Apollers." To these reproductions Sophia added her own copies of masterworks. A lonely stuffed owl, one of the few pieces of Americana in the house, rested, where it still rests, on the mantelpiece in the parlor.[7]

Sophia brightened the small study on the second floor with paint, gold-tinted wallpaper, a reproduction of Raphael's Madonna, and her own painting of the Lake of Como. Not for her Apollo the dreary surroundings of Calvinism. On April 3, 1843, they dedicated the room by inscribing glass panes with a diamond:

> Man's accidents are God's purposes
> Sophia A. Hawthorne   1843

Nathl Hawthorne
This is his study
1843 . . .
Inscribed by my
husband at sunset
April 3rd 1843
In the gold light.   SAH

But, as Hawthorne explained, it was *their* room: "It is not difficult to detect the hand and heart of woman in many of its arrangements. . . . In size, the room is just what it ought to be; for I never could compress my thoughts sufficiently to write, in a very spacious room."[8]

Three windows in the study look down on the Concord River, the bridge, the statue, and the grave of two unknown English lads who died on the memorable day. According to legend, the two soldiers were lying on the ground, one dead and the other barely alive, when a youth who had been working at the Manse came upon them and, startled at the sight, "uplifted his axe, and dealt the wounded soldier a fierce and fatal blow upon the head." Hawthorne sought to trace the youth in order to "observe how his soul was tortured by the blood-stain, contracted, as it had been, before the long custom of war had robbed human life of its sanctity, and while it still seemed murderous to slay a brother man." "This one circumstance," he added, "has borne more fruit for me, than all that history tells us of the fight."[9]

"How sweet it was," he wrote in his notebook in August 1842, "to draw near my own home, after having lived so long homeless in the world; for no man can know what home is, until, as he approaches it, he feels that a wife will meet him at the threshold." He seemed startled to find himself a husband, as he admitted to "a pleasant sensation . . . that I was regarded as a man with a wife and a household—a man having a tangible existence and locality in the world."[10]

During the summer of their honeymoon at the Manse they were visited by a ghost that heaved deep sighs in the parlor and sometimes rustled papers because, Hawthorne explained, "he wished me to edit and publish a selection from a chest full of manuscript discourses, that stood in the garret." In February 1843 the ghost pinched Sophia's shoulder at midnight while she lay in bed. Hawthorne got out of bed to search the chamber and, "finding nothing, concluded the touch was a fancied one." Sophia, however, "never varied in her belief that the incident was supernatural." When Louisa stayed at the Manse in the following year she informed her mother: "I have seen no ghost but we are overrun with mice, which are not so bad." [11]

"The perfect ease & freedom from haste and interruption," Sophia explained to her mother, "bring out all the frolic grace & beauty of this king of men." Hawthorne had another perception: "My life is more like that of a boy, externally, than it has been since I was really a boy. It is usually supposed that the cares of life come with matrimony; but I seem to have cast off all care, and live on with as much easy trust in Providence, as Adam could possibly have felt, before he had learned that there was a world beyond his Paradise." A few months later he made much the same point to Margaret Fuller: "The circle of my life seems to have come round, and brought back many of my school-day enjoyments. . . . I pause upon them, and taste them with a sort of epicurism, and am boy and man together." [12]

In the exhilaration of the early months of her marriage, Sophia considered herself transformed spiritually as well as physically. She declared, more ecstatically than accurately, that "I grow round apace" and that she no longer was "the shadowy spirit" of last month. She was, however, not strong enough to attend church in the weeks following their arrival, and in the middle of August she described herself as "in one of my states." On her good days she like Hawthorne traveled back in time and danced "before him to the music of the musical box" given to them by Thoreau. Hawthorne added another dimension to the dance when he said that she deserved "John the Baptist's head," which is a strange association, even if he passed it off as jest. They fell into and out of each other's arms, usually in the security of the second floor. But on one afternoon Sophia was in her "husband's embrace" when they heard "a gentle step" and discovered Margaret Fuller. In the evenings they entertained each other telling stories. "We shall have the thousand & one nights over again," Sophia declared. [13]

When winter came and there was no more boating on the river, they took daily cold baths in the kitchen according to the principles of homeopathy to which Sophia was fanatically devoted. Hawthorne skated before sunrise and at sunset in the meadow which was frozen over. He assured the women in his family, all of whom had spent their lives mothering him, that there was no danger. Sophia's descriptions of him on skates made him resemble that elegant skater in Gilbert Stuart's famous painting. "It was like a sea of gold," she wrote, "for the sun was just setting & threw a glorious hue over it. I took his arm & slid & ran as he skated, while I could, & then he darted away by himself, perpetually returning to me."[14]

In lengthy letters to her skeptical family Sophia praised Hawthorne's virtues tirelessly. She assured her mother in detail that she was not the prisoner of her husband's will. "Do not fear I shall be too subject to my Adam, my crown of Perfection," she explained. "He loves power as little [as] any mortal I ever knew." At the same time she admitted that it was her pleasure to subordinate herself: "He is such a simple transcript of the angelic nature—so transparent, so just, so tender, so magnanimous that even should he will me to do it, I should find my highest instinct corresponds with his will," which, despite its logical quirks, was perhaps a deeply sincere conviction or a deliberate misstatement designed to pacify her family. Yet on one occasion she admitted to her sister Mary: "He cannot bear to have a woman come out of the shade, far less his wife, & never has forgiven himself for dedicating his Gentle Boy to me." Eden, in short, was not always edenic.[15]

One month after his marriage Hawthorne told Margaret Fuller that "he should be much more willing to die than two months ago, for he had had some real possession in life, but still he never wished to leave this earth; it was beautiful enough." After sixteen months of connubial bliss he declared himself "preposterously happy," which, however, was a sincere overstatement.[16]

Concord is one of the most modestly beautiful towns in America. The Concord River meanders through the flat meadows. The streets, many of which were once horse-and-buggy paths, also meander, demonstrating that the shortest distance between two points is an ugly contrivance of human efficiency. The houses, frame and usually white, meander too, generations of owners having added and subtracted according to family needs. At the center of town the First Parish Meeting House, simple but majestic with lines chastely classical, towers serenely over the townscape. The interior of the building seems a tribute to an unpretentious deity of a people who made God over in their democratic image. The church faces the low hill where Concord's earliest citizens rest beneath gravestones carved by sculptors whose artistic intuitions sometimes exceeded their skill.

In the 1840s the population of the village was about 1,800. As Emerson recognized, "Without navigable waters, without mineral riches, without any considerable mill privileges, the natural increase of her population is drained by the constant emigration of the youth." A recent analysis reveals that the village in the 1840s was neither homogeneous nor stable, that a few people possessed most of the wealth, and that the appearance of homogeneity is attributable to the fact that 40 percent of those who lived there for generations were related. In the two decades after the arrival of the Hawthornes, 15 to 20 percent of the population consisted of migrant laborers, mostly Irish. Mobility was high: the census reports of 1850 and 1860 indicate that only 29 percent of the inhabitants remained in Concord from the beginning to the end of the decade.[17]

Culture in Concord, again according to Emerson, mixed intellectual content and hoopla: "We have had our share of Everett & Webster, who have both spoken here. So has Edward Taylor. . . . We have had our shows & processions, conjurors, & bear-gardens, and here too came Herr Driesbach with his cats & snakes, lying down on a lioness, & kissing a tiger, & rolling himself up not in leopard skins, but in live leopards. And his companion with his tippet of anacondas."[18]

It was Emerson's desire to transform Concord into a community of intellectuals and artists, including a group of young poets on the order of Charles King Newcomb. He welcomed the Hawthornes to Concord and looked forward to other additions to the community, to women such as Margaret Fuller, Elizabeth Peabody, and Caroline Sturgis. "These if added to our present kings & queens," Emerson wrote in his journal, "would make a rare, and unrivalled company. If these all had their hearth & home here, we might have a solid social satisfaction, instead of the disgust & depression of visitation. We might find that each of us was more completely isolated & sacred than before." Later in the year, in another mood or, in his words, during an "obstinate propensity," he wondered about the circle of "kings & queens" and found himself looking "with a sort of terror at my gate."[19]

After Hawthorne's arrival, Emerson sought him out and attempted to break through the barriers of his shyness. On September 27 and 28, 1842, the two men, probably because Hawthorne could find no easy way to extricate himself from the situation, set out on a walking expedition to Harvard, Massachusetts, to inspect a Shaker village, and left Sophia "widowed" for the first time. In his journal Hawthorne had little to say about the excursion except to note that he had missed his wife and that it was "the first time I ever came home in my life; for I never had a home before." Emerson and Hawthorne took walks, had dinners together, and skated on the Concord River, but no intimacy developed. Emerson talked too much, in his attempts to draw out Hawthorne; the latter listened too much, in his attempt to keep Emerson at a distance. Sophia declared that "Mr Emerson was always content to talk to those wells of light & recieve as whole response that smile only."[20]

Sophia overstated. There was little compatibility between the two men intellectually or imaginatively, although they had in common lucid prose styles and exquisite, perhaps too refined, sensibilities. Both valued privacy and feared violation of their space, and both epitomized self-reliance. Hawthorne stopped at the threshold of Emerson's cosmos, unconvinced of his idealistic premises, and Emerson sought vainly in Hawthorne's writings for what he called "a purer power." Hawthorne, it would appear, never read deeply in Emerson, and Julian Hawthorne alleged, probably correctly, that Emerson never finished one of his father's romances. Emerson sent copies of his books as they appeared, and Hawthorne reciprocated. They observed the amenities but went their own ways, respectful but distant, neighbors rather than friends.[21]

Emerson's inability to embrace Hawthorne's sensibility was foreshadowed in his complaint after reading "Foot-prints on the Sea-shore" that Bronson Alcott and Hawthorne "together would make a man." Early in their relationship Hawthorne appraised in his notebook the future sage of Concord as "the mystic, stretching his hand out of cloud-land, in vain search for something real. . . . Mr. Emerson is a great searcher for facts; but they seem to melt away and become unsubstantial in his grasp." At another time he characterized Emerson as "that everlasting rejecter of all that is, and seeker for he knows not what. . . ." His public statements were more generous. When in the prefatory essay to *Mosses from an Old Manse* he reviewed the years in Concord, he recognized in a wonderfully apt phrase Emerson's "austere tenderness." Hawthorne "sought nothing from him as a philosopher. It was good, nevertheless, to meet him in the wood-paths, or sometimes in our avenue, with that pure, intellectual gleam diffused about his presence, like the garment of a shining-one; and he so quiet, so simple, so without pretension, encountering each man alive as if expecting to receive more than he would impart." Here Hawthorne captured Emerson's childlike, eager questing which made him in the eyes of some detractors an "ineffable idiot."[22]

Sophia had to reconcile her earlier opinion of Emerson as "the most complete man" and her appreciation of his many kindnesses as a neighbor with her adoration of Hawthorne. Both were *"great,"* she italicized, "but Mr Emerson is not so whole sided as Mr Hawthorne. He towers straight up—from a deep [root?]—Mr Hawthorne spreads abroad many branches also." After living as his neighbor for about a year, Sophia concluded that "Waldo Emerson knows not much of love—He has never yet said anything to show that he does—He is an isolation—He has never yet known what union meant with any soul." Perhaps like others she knew of the strains in Emerson's second marriage.[23]

Shortly after the Hawthornes settled into Concord, Thoreau took Hawthorne sailing on the Concord River in the *Musketaquid* and at once demonstrated his skill as a pilot. Because Thoreau was "in want of money," Hawthorne soon found himself the owner of the boat for "only seven dollars." "I wish," he observed, "I could acquire the aquatic skill of its original owner at as reasonable a rate." He changed the name to *Pond Lily* because he planned to bring "home many a cargo of pond lilies from along the river's weedy shore." At once he was in Sophia's adoring eyes "a magical steersman" who ventured intrepidly with her over "the great deep."[24]

In a spontaneous portrait in his notebook Hawthorne may have captured the essence of the quirky genius of "a wild, irregular Indian-like sort of fellow," although he had trouble spelling Thoreau's name.

> He is a singular character—a young man with much of wild original nature still remaining in him; and so far as he is sophisticated, it is in a way and method of his own. He is as ugly as sin, long-nosed, queer-mouthed, and with uncouth and somewhat rustic, although courteous manners, corresponding very well with such an exterior. But his ugliness is of an honest and agreeable fashion, and becomes him much better than beauty. . . . Mr. Thorow is a keen and delicate observer of nature. . . . and Nature, in return for his love, seems to adopt him as her special child, and shows him secrets which few others are allowed to witness. . . .

In recommending Thoreau a few years later to Evert A. Duyckinck, who was editing a series of books which was to include *Mosses from an Old Manse* and Melville's *Typee*, Hawthorne pointed out the difficulties of dealing with Thoreau: "He is the most unmalleable fellow alive—the most tedious, tiresome, and intolerable—the narrowest and most notional," but he concluded in his usual fashion, "and yet, true as all this is, he has great qualities of intellect and character."[25]

Thoreau praised Hawthorne fondly, if somewhat romantically: "Hawthorne too I remember as one with whom I sauntered in old heroic times along the banks of the Seamander, amid the ruins of chariots and heroes." In *A Week on the Concord and Merrimack Rivers* he was somewhat coy in his characterization of Hawthorne as Ripley's successor at the Manse:

> Anon a youthful pastor came,
> Whose crook was not unknown to fame,
> His lambs he viewed with gentle glance,
> Spread o'er the country's wide expanse,
> And fed with "Mosses from the Manse."
> Here was our Hawthorne in the dale,
> And here the shepherd told his tale.[26]

In one of her lovely word portraits Sophia sought the essence of the three men. If she failed, she caught in few words more than most writers do in paragraphs.

> One afternoon, Mr. Emerson and Mr. Thoreau went with him down the river. Henry Thoreau is an experienced skater, and was figuring dithyrambic dances and Bacchic leaps on the ice—very remarkable, but very ugly, methought. Next him followed Mr. Hawthorne who, wrapped in his cloak, moved like a self-impelled Greek statue, stately, and grave. Mr. Emerson closed the line, evidently too weary to hold himself erect, pitching headforemost, half lying on the air. He came in to rest himself, and said to me that Hawthorne was a tiger, a bear, a lion,—in short, a satyr, and there was no tiring him out; and he might be the death of a man like himself.[27]

Hawthorne's closest relationship in Concord during the Manse years was with William Ellery Channing, one of the most eccentric of the Concord residents whom Thoreau termed "the moodiest person, perhaps, that I ever saw. As naturally whimsical as a cow is brindled, both in his tenderness and his roughness he belies himself. He can be incredibly selfish and unexpectedly generous."[28]

William Ellery Channing, the son of Walter Channing, a Harvard professor and physician who had treated Sophia years earlier, bore the name of his uncle, the most distinguished Unitarian clergyman of the age. To avoid confusion the youth was called Ellery, but his achievements, of which there were to be only a few, were inevitably measured against those whose name he bore. Another uncle, Edward T. Channing, was Boylston Professor of Rhetoric at Harvard College.

Ellery's was the kind of childhood that no child should have to endure. At five his mother died, and the children were almost at once distributed among relatives. Still another separation followed when at seven Ellery was sent off to a private boarding school in Northampton, Massachusetts. In an early poem he lamented the loss, "my mother died / Before I clasped her," and perceived himself as an orphan, rejected by mother, father, and even his brothers.

> That early life was bitter oft,
>> And like a flower whose roots are dry
> I withered; for my feelings soft
>> Were by my brothers passèd by.

He acted out his rage, which probably no one understood, in such tantrums and erratic behavior that relatives sometimes called him mad.[29]

At seventeen he published in one year nineteen poems in the *Boston Mercantile Journal* and seemed about to launch himself on a career that would separate him from a family of successful professionals. He may even have chosen the pen name of Hal Menge to escape the burden of the Channing identity. But he was too young to handle his conflicts, the desire for independence but also the eagerness for acceptance, and so, perhaps even willingly, he followed in the steps of his father and entered Harvard College. He dropped out within three or four months and began a long, endless drift.

Margaret Fuller, who shared Emerson's fascination with precociously talented but emotionally unstable young men, befriended Channing and noted that he was aware that "he disappointed every one, and most me, and there was no hope in its ever being otherwise." In periods of depression, which were apparently frequent, his self-devaluation was truly overwhelming:

Dull I came upon the planet, untalented, the one talent still in that tremendous napkin, out of which I have never been able to unwrap it and where it is still like to be for all I can discern thro its fold. . . . every animal makes tracks [in the snow], only some do not come into view. Why even I succeed in making tracks in the snow, and others in walking in them. Methinks, this is the greatest success I ever had in my life.[30]

Despite the mediocrity of Channing's poetry, Emerson praised it with kind but foolish extravagance in the *Dial* in 1840: "Here is poetry more purely intellectual than any American verses we have yet seen, distinguished from all competition by two merits—the fineness of perception and the poet's trust in his own genius." Thoreau admired the poetry too but characterized its style as "sublimo-slipshod." Poe, however, in reviewing Channing's first published volume of poems in 1843, was venomous: "His book contains about sixty-three things, which he calls poems. . . . They are not precisely English—nor will we insult a great nation by calling them Kickapoo; perhaps they are Channingese."[31]

After a brief stay at Brook Farm, where Channing apparently met Hawthorne for the first time, he went to Cincinnati and fell in love with and married Ellen Fuller, Margaret's younger sister. One of Ellen's friends commented that she suffered from "Emersonianism"—"she has felt a divine inspiration to marry, Ellery, and at once." For complex reasons, no doubt to satisfy complex needs, both erred. Margaret Fuller was understanding and deeply concerned, as she confided to Emerson, but her erotic and intellectual aggressiveness may have made her part of the problem both for her sister and Ellery. Earlier he had been, or so he thought, in love with Margaret Fuller and a woman with whom she had one of those passionate nineteenth-century relationships, Caroline Sturgis. Not inappropriately, the first child of the couple was named Margaret Fuller Channing, and the second, Caroline Sturgis Channing. After the birth of the first child, Channing fled to the mountains accompanied by Thoreau. With his wife's approval he went to Europe before the birth of their second child. He could not endure being in the same house with new children: the situation reactivated too many painful memories.[32]

Shortly after their marriage, Emerson invited Ellery and Ellen to Concord, and when Margaret Fuller arrived in the village that summer, she suggested to the Hawthornes that they receive the Channings as boarders. With tactful firmness Hawthorne replied that Adam and Eve had no intention of sharing Eden with the Channings. Hawthorne noted in a barb which he evidently could not resist that Channing "is one of those queer and clever young men whom Mr. Emerson . . . is continually picking up by way of genius." Hawthorne recognized "some originality and self-inspiration in his character, but none, or very little in his intellect." He concluded once again in an ambivalent summation: "I like him well enough, however; but after all, these originals in a small way, after one has seen a few of them, become more dull and common-place than even those who keep the ordinary pathway of life." [33]

The relationship changed quickly, no doubt on the initiative of Channing, who, thirteen years younger, like Newcomb earlier, was magnetically drawn to an older man who understood (and shared) his shyness, reclusiveness, and mood swings, including depressed periods. Soon they were fishing in the Concord River in the boat that once belonged to Thoreau and his brother John. "Strange and happy times were those," Hawthorne was to write in the idealized language of "The Old Manse," "when we cast aside all irksome forms and strait-laced habitudes, and delivered ourselves up to the free air, to live like Indians or any less conventional race, during one bright semi-circle of the sun." The boy in Hawthorne valued the freedom from constraints that Channing offered, but the man in the boy was aware of the youth's lack of control. "On the whole," he informed Sophia, "he is but little better than an idiot, He should have been whipt often and soundly in his boyhood; and as he escaped such wholesome discipline then, it might be well to bestow it now. But somebody else may take him in hand; it is none of my business." [34]

At first Sophia was more attracted to Channing than to Thoreau, whose ugly nose caused her quite a bit of trouble. As the tie between her husband and Channing deepened, she accused Channing, perhaps in jest, of stealing her husband. A similar situation occurred a few years later when Bridge arrived at the Manse only to find Sophia ill. He sent her a bantering note: "What queer expedients Mrs. H. resorts to for driving off her husband's bachelor friends! A suspicious man would think that the lady was shamming," to which, in deadly seriousness, she replied: "I am particularly anxious to banish from your mind the ignoble & narrow idea

that a wife must necessarily be jealous of her husband's best friends."
And the denial wandered on and on.[35]

When Hawthorne left Concord for Salem in 1845, he bequeathed his
boat to Channing as well as the blue frock coat from his days at Brook
Farm. In 1847 Channing spent a week in Salem with Hawthorne while
Sophia and the two children were in Boston. According to Hawthorne,
they had "a very pleasant time" taking "immense walks" and "talking till
midnight. He eats like an Anaconda." Every morning they took walks,
Channing recalled, sometimes to Gallows Hill and "often to the Point,
by the Almshouse," a tour which conformed to Hawthorne's map of
Salem.[36]

About 1852 or 1853 Channing wrote "Poems of the Heart," a series in
which he recalled his friendship with Hawthorne a decade earlier. Unlike
Newcomb, he was not embittered by the experience but nostalgic and
puzzled that the bond had not endured. Channing relates how in the role
of "The Gentle Boy" he is attracted to a substitute brother or father, then
as a poet writes, ". . . thou art the fire / That sparkles on the strings of
my dark lyre." Finally, as "a fallen creature" he abases himself before
"sole majesty":

> Remember him who sought thee in his youth,
> And with the old reliance of the boy,
> Asked for thy Treasures in the guise of truth . . .[37]

Later in the poem Hawthorne bears the name of Count Julian, with
its associations to the apostate, to Shelley's poetic account of his relationship with Byron, and perhaps most important of all to Hawthorne's son
Julian, who had, in Channing's hungry imagination, a father who understood him.

> His pure slight form had a true Grecian charm,
> Soft as the willow o'er the River swaying;
> Yet sinewy and capable of action;
> Such grace as in Apollo's figure lay,
> When he was moving the still world with light,
> So perfect balanced, and convinced with art.
> About his forehead clustered rich black curls,
> Medusa-like, they charmed the student's eye.
> Those soft, still hazel orbs Count Julian had,

Looked dream-like forth on the familiar day,
Yet eloquent, and full of luminous force,
Sweetly humane that had no harshness known,
Unbroken eyes where Love forever dwelt.
This art of Nature which surrounded him,
This made Count Julian what he was to me,
Which neither time, nor place, nor Poet's pen,
Nor Sculptor's chisel can e'er mould again.

As he wrote these lines Channing knew that "thy hand is closed" and that once more he was experiencing Ilbrahim's rejection.[38]

Channing's deeply felt poem illustrates again the power that Hawthorne exercised over younger men in search of physical and intellectual fulfillment. Such was their need, or expectation, that they transformed Hawthorne into Apollo, the most admired of the Greek deities in the nineteenth century, not knowing that their newly created man-god had from childhood, as Bridge recognized, little self-trust and greatly wanted to be loved. Hawthorne apparently never analyzed these flattering but perhaps at the same time frightening relationships—they satisfied, at least temporarily, a deep need—and he was unable (or unwilling) to prevent them. Channing's successor was to be another searching young man, Herman Melville.

Sophia's life in Concord was more constricted than her husband's. Her universe was the home, and at the center of this universe was Nathaniel Hawthorne. To a childhood friend she observed that he was

fresh as a young fountain, with childlike, transparent emotions; vivid as the flash of a sword in the sun with sharp wit and penetration; of such an unworn, unworldly observance of all that is enacted and thought under the sun; as free from prejuduce and party or sectarian bias as the birds, and therefore wise with a large wisdom that is as impartial as God's winds and sunbeams. . . . His magnanimity, strength, and sweetness alternately, and together, charm me. He fascinates, wins, and commands.

Her pen drew in gold leaf, for she was powerless to curb her exuberance, her love, or her fantasies.[39]

Sophia lived contentedly under the spell of his shy eyes. On returning to Concord after a visit with her mother she met "my kingly husband, with a sun of radiant welcome in his eyes," but they could not embrace until they were out of the sight of their one servant. "This love is Paradise," she murmured. On another afternoon a week later she stood beneath the windows of the second-floor study and with trepidation, her nerves fluttering, dared to break one of the inviolable laws of their household, that he was not to be interrupted while he wrote. "His noble head appeared at once & a new sun & dearer shone out of his eyes on me, but he could not come then because the Muse had him entrapped in a gold net."[40]

Sophia created an atmosphere worthy of her lord. Within their sometimes stringent means she prepared little delicacies because, she explained to her mother, "he cares more about the elegance of the board than for the substance." During her pregnancy, while she was cutting out and preparing a child's wardrobe, she decided, with the assistance of Louisa, to dress up her husband, her royal child as it were, in a purple robe which made him look "very imperial." "I wish," she wrote to Louisa, "you could see him. He does not need any garnishing to make him splendid, but splendid attire becomes him very much." He wore the robe when he went walking with Sophia—which must have been somewhat of a spectacle in staid Concord. He asked Louisa "to send those pearl buttons—they being all that is wanting to the perfection of the imperial robe." If he poked fun it was a face-saving tactic of "the artist of the beautiful" ridiculing his delight in masquerade and elegance.[41]

Unless she only toyed with the idea in her journal late in 1843, Sophia sometimes dressed herself in royal splendor, away from the "world's eye." "Not at balls & courts should I care to walk in silk attire," she confessed, "but in the profound shelter of the home, I would put on daily a velvet robe & pearls in my hair to gratify my husband's tastes & appear to him alone as beautiful as possible." Evidently to escape from the ordinary world and pinching poverty, they continued after marriage to play games, now through masquerades in which they acted out fantasies in the simulated exotic atmosphere of *The Arabian Nights' Entertainments*, forgetting at least for the moment the presence of all those divines in the Manse. After his marriage a number of exotically attired women of overwhelming erotic fascination emerge in his fiction—Beatrice Rappaccini, Hester Prynne, Zenobia, and Miriam Schaeffer.[42]

In the evening, particularly in the winter, Hawthorne read to Sophia. "You know," she informed Louisa, "his voice in reading is most musical thunder & I like to have great works set to such music." In the first year of their happiness, "the voice of voices" read Milton, Bacon's *Advancement of Learning*, and Cary's translation of Dante. In the second winter he read a dozen or more of Shakespeare's plays in what must have been lengthy sittings on cold winter nights, for it took but two evenings usually to listen to a play.[43]

Sophia learned to cover over Hawthorne's social lapses. One day Julia Ward Howe and her husband arrived at the Manse and were received, she reported, "very graciously" by Sophia. "Just then a male figure descended the stairs. 'My husband,' she cried, 'here are Dr. and Mrs. Howe.' What we did see was a broad hat pulled down over a hidden face, and a figure that quickly vanished through an opposite door." Why Hawthorne indulged in such childish and hostile behavior we can only guess, although it mirrored in life the melodramatic posturing of Fanshawe.[44]

More difficult was Sophia's continuing task of keeping the Hawthornes and the Peabodys content. She walked a tightrope, for the most part successfully. Sophia reassured the Hawthornes: "His loving me does not cast you out of his heart, but rather makes more room there, & he appreciates your worth & values your regard more & more. I could not love him so much, if this were not so." She concocted plans to have the three recluses visit the Manse and in her solicitude for his mother promised to stay out of her way: "Nobody shall disturb her. . . . & she shall not even see *me* except when she desires it." Such abasement seems almost unbelievable but, given her attitude toward her own mother, not out of character.[45]

Hawthorne, on the other hand, tried little to conceal his feelings about the Peabodys. He preferred the father to the women, perhaps in part because he knew he would annoy them. He accepted assistance from Elizabeth when it served his ends, but she talked herself into one crisis after another and serenely smiled her way out, without taking offense herself but sometimes unaware of the hurt feelings her candor left behind. Mrs. Peabody visited Concord periodically but with little enthusiasm on her son-in-law's part. In 1843 either Elizabeth herself or Mrs. Peabody on her behalf informed Sophia of Hawthorne's flaws. In an eight-page letter, which may not be complete, Sophia replied to the charges. Apparently Elizabeth, with little wisdom and less tact, stated categorically that her friends Anna and Samuel Ward embodied the ideal of Emersonian love better than did the Hawthornes because the Wards had metamorphosed into one unity. Although Sophia could have ignored what was beyond demonstration, she responded that Emerson "knows not much of love" and that, unlike the Wards, "no two minds were ever more completely independent & individual than Mr. Hawthorne's and mine. . . . It gives a constant raciness & spirit to our daily life, & preserves that fine damascus-blade keenness & shine to any expression of thought." After extolling at length her husband's virtues, with an extravagance that invited disagreement, Sophia at last got to the heart of the criticism, Hawthorne's absence of social graces. "Whatever he does, he does perfectly & like a man," she charged. "It is not his vocation to be a social visitor & chattering companion. . . . Are there not enough persons to pass their days . . . in social intercourse with men & women?" He is "a poet, of the highest grade. . . . With his extremely fine & harp-like organization."[46]

Out of love and loyalty Sophia presented what her son years later was to describe as an "unfailing History of Happiness." She had a wonderful way of making over reality to conform to her ecstatic fulfillment in her role as Mrs. Nathaniel Hawthorne. Yet she had a history of punishing her delicate body and straining her limited physical resources. Her ecstatic Eden and "unfailing History of Happiness" no doubt exacted a toll physically as well as emotionally. Hawthorne, on the other hand, lifted the veils frequently in his fiction and achieved some relief and escape, at least temporarily. Without his art, she lacked his outlet.

Margaret Fuller in Concord

During that first summer of marriage Hawthorne made no attempt to write. He always insisted, although circumstances in the following year compelled him to alter his plans, that he could not write during warm weather. With the coming of fall the couple settled into a routine. Until two o'clock he was alone in his study. After they dined, about three o'clock, he went into the village to the Athenaeum and the post office. He returned toward sunset, when Sophia usually joined him in a short stroll to the river. They had tea early, "to have," in her words, "a long evening—Then he reads aloud to me one or two hours or more."[1]

The rhythm of their life was not quite so inflexible as this description suggests, for not only were there meetings, casual and planned, with Concord residents—Sophia being especially drawn to Elizabeth Hoar and Lidian Emerson—but also there were house guests at frequent intervals in the milder months. Louisa was the first, to be followed by Mrs. Peabody, David Roberts, George Hillard, John Louis O'Sullivan, and others. Sophia had socialized a great deal before her marriage within, of course, the restrictions of her semi-invalid state, but gradually after marriage she seemed to lose contact with former friends. With the passage of years most of the visitors, except for members of the Peabody family, were his friends rather than hers. Increasingly she isolated herself as she subordinated herself first to her husband and later to her children. After her marriage Sophia was uncomfortable in large gatherings. "I am like a bewildered bee among choice flowers," she wrote, "when so many rare people are all present, attracting me."[2]

When in October or November she found herself pregnant, she was overjoyed at the prospect of complete fulfillment. The pregnancy proceeded normally until February 1843 when she fell while walking with Hawthorne on the frozen river. Mrs. Peabody hurried to Concord to be with her daughter but then left when it appeared that Sophia had not miscarried. However, on February 22 Sophia informed her mother that she had aborted and was recovering satisfactorily. A few days later Sophia had the bedroom cleaned and repainted and waited in her husband's study for his return from the village. She "sat decked up in a tight dress instead of flowing robes, it required a great deal of credence to believe that any thing at all had happened to us, so exactly the time seemed to join upon our last presence in the same place."[3]

In his notebook Hawthorne revealed a resilient attitude. "One grief we have had," he wrote, "all else has been happiness. Nor did the grief penetrate to the reality of our life. We do not feel as if our promised child were taken from us forever; but only as if his coming had been delayed for a season. . . ." When Sophia did not recuperate as expected, she went to Boston to consult the family physician, while Hawthorne made a brief visit to Salem. By March 25 Hawthorne could write, "My wife has entirely recovered her health, and seems even stronger than before—a result which is said sometimes to follow such an accident as she met with."[4]

Late in March Sophia learned that, after a courtship of over a dozen years, her sister Mary was to be married to Horace Mann. "I rushed up to Mr. Hawthorne's study," she wrote to her sister, "& with overflowing eyes, & covered face I sobbed out, 'good news'—& he, persuaded that some one was dead, caught me in his arms to administer comfort. I presently articulated the truth." Mary Peabody and Horace Mann were married on May 1, 1843, at 11:30 A.M. and sailed for England at 12:30. "Thus," Hawthorne wrote a little maliciously to Bridge, "there is only one old-maid in the family."[5]

As the first anniversary of their union approached, the Hawthornes found separations difficult. When Sophia was in Boston in April, probably to help her sister prepare for her wedding, he split wood because of "an inward inquietness, which demanded active exercise." A few days later he entered into their journal a passage designed to tease Sophia with a gentle eroticism that he dared to unveil for her (blushing) pleasure, although many, perhaps most, of such passages she was to expunge from the notebooks. "My greatest enjoyment in bed," he confided, "is to extend myself cross-wise, diagonally, semi-circularly, and in all other postures that would be incompatible with a bed-fellow. I believe, too, that, during my sleep, I seek thee throughout the empty vastitude of our couch; for I found myself, when I awoke, in quite a different region than I had occupied in the early part of the night."[6]

Early in June Sophia again feared a miscarriage, but this time it was a false alarm. Hawthorne delighted in watching the "little woman" round into motherhood. If he teased, he pleased. He was, Sophia joyously informed her mother, "quite persuaded that I am 'a saint' (as he renders '*enceinte*') & he is the most superb worshipper 'a saint' ever had—to say nothing of most tender & devoted. I have constantly thought that it was a sufficient end to have been born for to cause the daily happiness of such a being as he is."[7]

The Hawthornes were not given to observing birthdays, but he commemorated the first anniversary of their marriage in a lovely passage designed for Sophia's perusal:

> We were never so happy as now—never such wide capacity for happiness, yet overflowing with all that the day and every moment brings to us. Methinks this birth-day of our married life is like a cape, which we have now doubled, and find a more infinite ocean of love stretching out before us.[8]

Because they were "so poor in worldly goods," they were without domestic help that winter. When Hawthorne assumed some domestic duties, Sophia could contain neither enthusiasm nor hyperbole. "Apollo boiled some potatoes for breakfast. Imagine him with that magnificent head bent over a cooking stove & those star-eyes watching the pot! There never were such good potatoes in consequence." Sophia prepared a wardrobe for the infant and at the same time copied an engraving of Endymion which she had borrowed from Emerson. "You can imagine," she wrote to Louisa, "what satisfaction I feel to have done a little myself . . . towards filling our purse & restoring a little the beloved & miraculous brain, which seems so inexhaustible in riches & wonders as Aladdin's lamp."

As genteel as Sophia was, she was willing without self-pity to assume these tasks. Meanwhile, the Hawthorne women indicated their preference when at Christmas they sent one of their most precious possessions, "two linen cambric shirts" worn by Hawthorne's father in infancy.[9]

January 1844 was "the coldest for an hundred years," but they got through it with little trouble perhaps because "Nathaniel blasphemed superbly whenever he looked at the thermometer." Despite her pregnancy Sophia continued her homeopathic habit of taking cold baths in the morning in that wonderful copper basin which Mrs. Emerson had installed in the kitchen shortly after the Manse was built. A case of the sniffles early in February was dispatched at once by means of the cold ablutions. "We consider that we have proved homeopathy," Sophia declared.[10]

On Sunday March 3, 1844, "a little girl . . . came head-first into this world at 1/2 past 9 o clock," after taking "ten awful hours in getting across the threshold." "I can say nothing," Hawthorne wrote to his sister, "except that it already roars very lustily. It is averred by all to be in the finest possible condition." They named her Una.[11]

As the parents might have expected, not everybody was pleased with the literary name given to the child. Hawthorne offered an exquisite justification: "I like the name, not so much from any associations with Spenser's heroine, as for its simple self—it is as simple as a name can be—as simple as a breath—it is merely inhaling a breath into one's heart, and emitting it again, and the name is spoken."[12]

Una's godfather was O'Sullivan, who had begun to organize another campaign to secure a governmental post for the author. After his first visit in January 1843 to the Manse, which was Sophia's introduction to O'Sullivan, she observed of her husband's "perhaps most highly valued friend": "I was struck with his gentleness & earnestness, his humanity & fine inward honour, which I felt to be as pure as diamond & as hard to destroy." Thoreau had reservations about "a rather puny-looking man. . . . We had nothing to say to one another, and therefore we said a great deal!" Emerson considered O'Sullivan a "politico-literary [who] has too close an eye to immediate objects." Two months after Una's birth, O'Sullivan presented her with a Newfoundland dog named Leo.[13]

Hawthorne was always more attached to Una than to the two children who followed, partly because her birth altered his life in fundamental ways. At forty he assumed fatherhood for the first time, and his comments at this turning point in his life recalled the lot of the beautiful young couple in "The May-pole of Merry Mount" who surrender pagan delights for the sobrieties of Puritan maturity:

> I find it a very sober and serious kind of happiness that springs from the birth of a child. It ought not to come too early in a man's life—not till he has fully enjoyed his youth—for methinks the spirit never can be thoroughly gay and careless again, after this great event. We gain infinitely by the exchange; but we do give up something nevertheless. As for myself, who have been a trifler preposterously long, I find it necessary at last to come out of my cloud-region, and allow myself to be woven into the sombre texture of humanity. There is no escaping it any longer. I have business on earth now, and must look about me for the means of doing it.

A month after Una's birth Hawthorne was almost certain about one point. "I think I prefer a daughter to a son," he wrote to Bridge; "there is something so especially piquant in having helped to create a future woman."[14]

Una's arrival provided Sophia with a new subject for her icon-making, for which, as we have seen, she had almost inexhaustible resources. To her mother she inventoried Una's charms. Her eyelashes were like her father's, "a mile long & curled up at the end." A month after her birth Una was sending letters to aunts and friends of her mother. Una reported to Aunt Louisa that she liked her mother to brush her hair every day, for "I believe it magnetizes me a little." No doubt because of Sophia's lavish praise, the Hawthornes reminded her that Nathaniel had been "beautiful & radiant" at six months. Diplomatically Sophia admitted that the resemblance of Una to her father "may be a repetition of the beauty of his infancy." To make peace, she affirmed that "he looks like Uriel with the Dawn." In her own family Sophia vied with Mary Mann, whose son was born a month earlier. Mary set the pattern for the exchange of superlatives when she declared, "We can baby it to our heart's desire."[15]

Una did not grow up in encomia. Her father maintained his sense of humor. On the sixteenth morning of Una's life, according to her mother, the child smiled. "I was inclined," he recorded, "to attribute it to wind, which sometimes produces a sardonic grin." On another occasion he called her Arethusa, "because she is so much wet." By August Una wet neither day nor night except by accident and sat obediently on "a funny little chair" and was "exemplary in the proceedings thereon." [16]

In Sophia's eyes, Hawthorne was an ideal father. Because she nursed the child during the night and feared exposure to drafts, he occupied a separate bedroom for six or more months after Una's birth. Sophia decreed that her husband was not to tend the child "because I only want him to have the felicity of her & not a particle of trouble." [17]

On February 16, 1845—age eleven months—"UNA WALKS ALONE!" The father chose a nautical analogy: she was "putting out to sea." About the same time Una said, "Adam!" Sophia thought Una was "addressing her father, he being the first of men." It turned out that she was uttering with gusto a "naughty oath," Sophia informed her mother. "She will take a book I have given her for a plaything, in which she often reads aloud, & sit down & begin—Damn—damn—damn—often in dulcet tones, & then again as loudly & emphatically as if she were firing a cannon." No doubt the child had recourse to her father's expletive in order to frustrate a mother who, when the child was one, was "quite anxious to enlarge her vocabulary, that she may have some variety of language in which to express her mind." Like Sophia, Una was destined to carry a burden of love almost too heavy to bear. According to Sophia, she was only one year old when she discovered the bust of Apollo which she examined with care before exclaiming, "It is truly superb.—I have never seen any thing like it in my little life." [18]

Margaret Fuller presided over American intellectual life, at least in Boston and eventually in New York, in the late 1830s and early 1840s. If her writings were unimpressive, her personality was so magnetic, her manner so forceful and at the same time intellectually seductive, that men as well as women succumbed to her presence. The clergyman who married the Hawthornes, James Freeman Clarke, was in awe of "the power of so magnetizing others, when she wished, by the power of her mind, that they would lay open to her all the secrets of their nature." According to Hawthorne, Emerson apotheosized her as "the greatest woman, I believe, of ancient or modern times, and the one figure in the world worth considering." Bronson Alcott was no less extravagant: "She had the intellect of a man inspired by the heart of a woman, combining in harmonious marriage the masculine and feminine in her genius. We have no woman approaching so near our conception of the ideal woman as herself." Margaret Fuller concurred in the judgment: "I know all the people worth knowing in America, and I find no intellect comparable to my own." [19]

Crusty Carlyle recognized Fuller's Faustian grasp: "Such a predetermination to eat this big Universe as her oyster or her egg . . . I have not before seen in any human soul." Carlyle and the others did not perceive that a woman who deliberately dressed dowdily or, in Emerson's phrase, with "external plainness," long before chronologically she had reason to be dowdy, may have been in deep conflict as to her self-image and her role as a woman. She herself complained that she was "not born to the common womanly lot," but she writhed because, as she said, "I could not be my truest childlike self. But I might be my truest manlike self." Behind the facade was a complex, tragic woman. [20]

Margaret Fuller had a consuming hunger for gratifications denied her by the intellectual training which her father had imposed upon her, Fuller being as much a victim of seeming kindness as her English counterpart, John Stuart Mill. Perhaps after her father's death she realized that through his educational fixations she became "a youthful prodigy by day, and by night a victim of spectral illusions, nightmare, and somnambulism, which at the time prevented the harmonious development of my bodily powers and checked my growth, while, later, they included continual headache, weakness and nervous affections, of all kinds." In that "lonely childhood" she had endured migraines and psychosomatic disorders and in the absence of human connections had eroticized flowers. "I kissed them," she wrote, "I pressed them to my bosom with passionate emotions, such as I have never dared express to any human being." Her mother also had a passion for flowers, perhaps in part because she was married to a man who was, in her daughter's words, not a companion, "much less a lover." [21]

After a concert on November 25, 1843, she wrote to Ludwig van Beethoven, whom she addressed as "My only friend." She admitted that for months she had been depressed, overcome with feelings of inadequacy. She desired, she confessed, not intellectual eminence but "a son of my own." Before Beethoven she knelt and, her incestuous fantasies emerging, asked to be wife-mistress-daughter: "But thou, oh blessed master! dost answer all my questions, and make it my privilege to be. Like a humble wife to the sage or poet, it is my triumph that I can understand, can receive thee wholly, like a mistress I arm thee for the fight, like a young daughter, I tenderly bind thy wounds. Thou art to me beyond compare, for thou art all I want."[22]

In the summer of 1844, Margaret Fuller became an imposing presence in Concord. She arrived on July 9 to see the "noble" Una and her niece Greta, the newly born child of Ellen and Ellery Channing. Two days later Lidian Emerson gave birth to Edward. Fuller's first stop was to see "the happy pair," the Hawthornes. Una "lay in her basket-cradle outdoors, looking up and smiling to the whispering trees." Fuller was attracted to the child's "noble and harmonious beauty," her language taking on Sophia's verbal colorations. If her account is to be trusted, the four-month-old child was more drawn to her than to the parents. Una, she averred, "often kisses me in her way, or nestles her head in my bosom. But her prettiest and most marked way with me is to lean her forehead upon mine. As she does this she looks into my eyes, & I into hers."[23]

Fuller preferred Una to any other child she had known except the ill-fated Waldo Emerson, who had died in 1842. It was her feeling that Una was "a child of a holy and equal marriage. She will have a good chance for freedom and happiness in the quiet wisdom of her father, the obedient goodness of her mother." Fuller reserved superlatives for the child and the "mild, deep and large" father, although she was impressed when Sophia became wet nurse to her niece: "It was most touching to see the gratitude of Greta . . . looking up in Sophia's face and cooing."[24]

As much as Fuller doted on children, she spent more time with their fathers, especially with Emerson. She was, she confessed, "intoxicated with his mind. I am not in full possession of my own. I feel faint in the presence of too strong a fragrance," as in the presence of her flowers. On the day after the birth of Edward, Emerson read his essay "Life" to her. "How beautiful, and full and grand. But oh, how cold," she commented. "Nothing but Truth in the Universe, no love, and no various realities." On this occasion "he showed me a page from his journal which made me rather ashamed of ever exacting more. But lure me not again too near thee, fair 'Greek.' I must keep steadily in mind what you really are." A few weeks later she heard him lecture and confessed her attraction and frustration: "Yes: it is deeply tragic on the one side, my relation to him, but on the other, how noble, how dear!" Then she complained that "he is hard to know, the subtle Greek!"[25]

On many evenings, while Sophia nursed two children, Fuller and Hawthorne went sailing on the Concord River and stayed until after sunset. "We talked a great deal this time," she confided in her journal. "I love him much, & love to be with him in this sweet tender homely scene. But I should like too, to be with him on the bold ocean shore." What transpired on those shared evenings we do not know, but it is interesting, although not necessarily significant, that in recopying her journal at a later date she or someone else bowdlerized some of the accounts of her walks with Hawthorne. One such notation read: "H. walked home with me beneath the lovely trembling—" and five asterisks followed. Perhaps only the moon trembled, but Hawthorne himself usually quivered, in silence, in the presence of erotic, aggressive women.[26]

Toward the end of her stay in Concord, Fuller summarized her associations with the three fathers, Emerson, Channing, and Hawthorne, and concluded that Hawthorne "has not the deep polished intellect of the one or the pure and passionate beauty of the other. He has his own powers: I want them all." Her greed, as Carlyle noted, was insatiable, but she trifled with three married men. Her justification of her conduct had appeared two years earlier in her journal: "I should acquiesce in all these relations, since they needed them. I should expect the same feeling from my husband, & I should think it little in him not to have it." Such a cerebral response to the nuances of emotional commitments perhaps reflected the revered father.[27]

A few days after her evaluation of the three men she sailed on the river with Hawthorne and had an idyllic experience, although she "regretted afterward that I had been led to talk so much." Too moved to "write about it," she wanted to compose two poems to describe an elation which produced a fierce headache. A few days later she sailed again with Hawthorne, who, unlike her, made no entries in his journal; but then he had Sophia looking over his shoulder. Fuller had walked "with H. in the woods, long paths, dark and 'mystical'. . . . I feel more like a sister to H. or rather more that he might be a brother to me than ever with any man before. Yet with him it is though sweet, not deep kindred, at least, not deep yet." She was to learn, as Melville did a few years later, how Hawthorne reacted to those who wanted to be "deep kindred" or "brother."[28]

In September she returned to Concord, took tea at the Hawthornes', and walked with Hawthorne in the "very bright, cold moonlight." This was all she had to say, but perhaps the "moonlight" was made colder by a reserve that was truly chilling. There was no mention of "noble" Una or "obedient" Sophia.[29]

What the three wives thought of Fuller's behavior during these visits does not appear in surviving documents, but it may be significant that Sophia, whose idolatry of Fuller at one time was boundless, reacted negatively to *Woman in the Nineteenth Century*, which appeared in the following year:

> The impression it left was disagreeable. I did not like the tone of it—& did not agree with her at all about the change in woman's outward circumstances—But I do not think a single woman can possibly have any idea of the true position of woman. Neither do I believe in such a character of man as she gives. It is altogether too ignoble. I suspect a wife only can know how to speak with sufficient respect of man—I think Margaret speaks of many things that should not be spoken of.[30]

In search of new opportunities and perhaps a new audience as well as new heroes, Margaret Fuller soon left Boston and New England and began her association with Horace Greeley and the *New-York Tribune*. In 1846 she praised *Mosses from an Old Manse* but with a major qualification: "Hawthorne intimates and suggests, but he does not lay bare the mysteries of our being." No more than Emerson could she allow herself to grasp Hawthorne's insights.[31]

New York could not contain Margaret Fuller for long. She left for Europe to serve as a correspondent for Greeley's newspaper and finally went to Italy. There she dared to form a public liaison with Count Ossoli, who was many years younger. They married and had the child she longed for. Fate treated her shabbily. On her return to the United States in 1850 the sea swept up her and her family off Fire Island, not far from the New York harbor. Her unhappy and unfulfilled life ended at age forty.

As soon as *The Blithedale Romance* appeared in 1852, readers quickly concluded that the exotic Zenobia was the fictional counterpart of Margaret Fuller, although Hawthorne as well as Sophia steadily denied the similarity. Years later in Rome, Hawthorne recorded in his journal nasty gossip about Ossoli, who was alleged to be "entirely ignorant, even of his own language, scarcely able to read at all; destitute of manners,—in short, half an idiot." Hawthorne bore no responsibility for the gossip, except for accuracy in reporting it, although he accepted the report as fact and proceeded, on the basis of the new information and his first-hand experiences many years earlier, to draw such an acute but controversial portrait of a complex woman that Sophia (wisely perhaps) did not include the section in *Passages from the Italian Note-books*, which she published after his death:

> . . . at least, this is my own experience—Margaret has not left, in the hearts and minds of those who knew her, any deep witness for her integrity and purity. She was a great humbug; of course with much talent, and much moral reality, or else she could not have been so great a humbug. . . . Thus, there appears to have been a total collapse in poor Margaret, morally and intellectually; and tragic as her catastrophe was, Providence was, after all, kind in putting her, and her clownish husband, and their child, on board that fated ship. There never was such a tragedy as her whole story; the sadder and sterner, because so much of the ridiculous was mixed up with it, and because she could bear anything better than to be ridiculous. It was such an awful joke, that she should have resolved—in all sincerity no doubt—to make herself the greatest, wisest, best woman of the age; and, to that end, she set to work on her strong, heavy, unpliable, and, in many respects, defective and evil nature, and adorned it with a mosaic of admirable qualities, such as she chose to possess; putting in here a splendid talent, and there a moral excellence, and polishing each separate piece, and the whole together, till it seemed to shine afar, and dazzle all who saw it. She took credit to herself for having been her own Redeemer, if not her own Creator; and, indeed, she was far more a work of art than any of Mr. [Joseph] Mozier's statues. But she was not working on an inanimate substance, like marble or clay; there was something within her that she could not possibly come at, to re-create and refine it; and, by and by, this rude old potency bestirred itself, and undid all her labor in the twinkling of an eye. On the whole, I do not know but I like her the better for it;—the better, because she proved herself a very woman after all, and fell as the weakest of her sisters might.[32]

Hawthorne has often been censured for this vivid delineation of Margaret Fuller, the intellectual star of the age married to an oaf, the queen in ruins. The passage reflected his usual ambivalence as well as a harshness not unlike that of his Hathorne forebears in appraising moral lapses. At the same time, as in his treatment of Mary Silsbee Sparks, he admired Fuller's artistry, the "humbug" in her nature which cloaked the inner hurts, the vulnerabilities behind the arrogance and egomania. He may have come closer to understanding her than many of her contemporaries.

In myth and metaphor Edens transcend such terrestrial subjects as economics, but the Eden in Concord needed financial under-pinnings for survival in a nonedenic world. When Hawthorne resigned his post at the Boston Custom-House, his savings had been substantial enough for him to invest $1,500 in Brook Farm, to lend unspecified sums to O'Sullivan and two or more fellow employees at the Custom-House, as well as to give a note to the Salem editor Caleb Foote for at least $500. If interest had been received regularly or the loans had been paid off, the Hawthornes would have had few problems in maintaining their modest life-style. The largest expense was the annual rent of $100. The Haw-thornes had few expensive habits, traveled seldom, and purchased little clothing. They raised most of the vegetables and fruit they ate and bar-tered for fowl and meat. Wood was plentiful and inexpensive, and Haw-thorne chopped logs for the fireplaces daily. Besides, he had been assured of the postmastership in Salem or "something satisfactory in the course of six months or so," as he informed his sister Louisa late in 1842.[33]

Winter that year in Concord was long and hard, and by March 1843 the Hawthornes could not "very well afford to buy a surplus stock of paper." Hawthorne "dreamed the other night that our house was broken open, and all our silver stolen." A few weeks later he could not visit Bridge because he "was very short of cash," and he began to "sigh for the regular monthly payments at the Custom House." He vented his feelings in a sweeping indictment:

The system of slack payments in this country is most abominable, and ought of itself to bring upon us the destruction foretold by Fa-ther [William] Miller. It is impossible for any individual to be just and honest, and true to his engagements, when it is a settled prin-ciple of the community to be always behindhand. I find no difference in anybody, in this respect; all do wrong alike.

His anger was mostly rhetorical and by the end of the next paragraph had subsided: "We are very happy, and have nothing to wish for, except a better-filled purse; and not improbably gold would bring trouble with it—at least, my wife says so, and therefore exhorts me to be content with little."[34]

According to an entry in his notebook at this time, he was resigned to delay and admitted that he was not eager to leave the Manse to return to Boston or Salem "because an office would inevitably remove us from our present happy home—. . . we taste some of the inconveniences of poverty, and the mortification—only temporary, however—of owing money, with empty pockets. It is an annoyance; not a trouble." Even when Sophia was pregnant he did not appear overly concerned: "I have nothing to wish for—except, perhaps, that Providence would make it somewhat more plain to my apprehension how I am to earn my bread, after a year or two. But it will be time enough for that, when the necessity comes." Yet after the birth of Una he worried not only about the child who "would have to take refuge in the alms-house—which, here in Concord, is a most gloomy old mansion" but also about his family in Salem. "The moment I have more than enough for my own immediate use," he promised Louisa, "I shall send it to you. I must, within no long time, make some arrangements to establish a more regular income."[35]

Hawthorne spent more time in his second-floor study in the fall following his marriage as he resumed writing for magazines. O'Sullivan had evidently agreed to publish tales and sketches every other month in the *Democratic Review*, twelve appearing in the next two years. In addition Hawthorne published five pieces in 1843 and three in the following year. Magazines, however, paid little and too often only after long delays. Hawthorne was disappointed in the sales of the second edition of *Twice-told Tales*, which in the year following publication had not sold enough copies to pay printing costs. Two years after publication only four hundred copies had been purchased, and O'Sullivan suggested that Hawthorne buy up unsold copies and issue them as a new printing. Hawthorne reluctantly accepted the advice despite qualms about a shoddy tactic. "I wish Heaven would make me rich enough," he declaimed, "to buy the copies for the purpose of burning them. This humbug of a new edition is not pleasant to my feelings." *Twice-told Tales* appeared in 1845 with Munroe's imprint but without additions which would have increased costs, and Evert Duyckinck dutifully reviewed the volume in the *Democratic Review*. Probably O'Sullivan had no expectations of greatly increased sales, but during the negotiations for a governmental post, it was important to keep attention focused on Hawthorne.[36]

He published "Little Daffydowndilly" in the *Boys' and Girls' Magazine* but declined the invitation of the editor to write a series of tales to appear first in the magazine and then to be issued in book form: "If I saw a probability of deriving a reasonable profit from juvenile literature, I would willingly devote myself to it for a time. . . . But my experience hitherto has not made me very sanguine on this point. In fact, the business has long been overdone." Nor did anything come of plans to write "one or two mythological story books" to be published under O'Sullivan's auspices, and Hawthorne declined to follow Duyckinck's suggestion that he undertake a "History of Witchcraft" for a new series of books to be published by Wiley and Putnam.[37]

Early in 1843 Hawthorne undertook what he later called a "piece of book-manufacture" after he convinced Horatio Bridge to write a travel book about his visits to Africa. The book was to be issued without acknowledgment of Hawthorne's role as editor, and Bridge with his usual generosity was to waive all royalties in Hawthorne's favor. Hawthorne's advice to Bridge about the handling of fact confirmed his own fictional license. "I would advise you," he wrote, "not to stick too accurately to the bare fact. . . . Allow your fancy pretty free license, and omit no heightening touches merely because they did not chance to happen before your eyes. If they did not happen, they at least ought—which is all that concerns you. This is the secret of all entertaining travellers." *Journal of an African Cruise* appeared in June 1845, with Hawthorne's name on the title page, at the insistence of the publisher. Sophia wrote to the author: "Through your magnanimous desire to benefit my husband, you have caused your name to be entered upon 'Fame's eternal bead-roll,' as Spenser sings. Now my husband has returned your favor of the past with regard to his tales."[38]

When James K. Polk, a Democrat, was elected president in 1844, Hawthorne's prospects for a governmental post improved, but not at once, as it turned out. Hawthorne urged Bridge to use his "influence" to oust Benjamin F. Browne, who in August had been confirmed as postmaster of Salem. George Bancroft, the patronage distributor in Massachusetts, decided not to remove Browne, a decision that in the end worked to Hawthorne's advantage. The immediate result was that the family was hard-pressed economically. Hawthorne was irate when he discovered that Charles W. Upham, the clergyman who decades later was to write definitively about the Salem witch trials, had related "most pitiable stories about our poverty and misery; so as to make it appear that we were suffering for food. Everybody that speaks to me seems tacitly to take it for granted that we are in a very desperate condition, and that a government office is the only alternative to the alms-house." [39]

It was not until after the inauguration of Polk and the appointment of Bancroft as secretary of the navy, as well as the recognition on the part of his friends that Hawthorne was not about to be awarded a post without a major effort, that a full-scale campaign was undertaken. When the post-mastership in Salem did not materialize, O'Sullivan recommended him, haphazardly it would appear, for "consulships" in Marseilles, Genoa, and Gibraltar. He inquired whether Hawthorne would consider a position in China, where the trade "would give, I should suppose, excellent opportunity for doing a business which would soon result in fortune." O'Sullivan persuaded Duyckinck to write an article about Hawthorne for the April issue of the *Democratic Review*. "By manufacturing you into a Personage," O'Sullivan admitted, "I want to raise your mark higher in Polk's appreciation." [40]

Franklin Pierce had for a time not involved himself actively in Hawthorne's quest for an office, at least such was the author's perception, and in 1843 in an outburst of pique Hawthorne wrote off his old friend: he "has faded out of my affections." The rift was patched, probably through the intervention of Bridge, who accompanied Pierce on his first visit to the Manse in May 1845. Sophia, who was meeting Pierce for the first time, described the reunion of the three Bowdoin chums who, though in their forties, shed their years for the occasion.

> Mr Hawthorne was in the shed, hewing wood—Mr B caught a glympse of him, & began a sort of waltz towards him—Mr P. followed, & when they reappeared, Mr Pierce's arm was encircling my husband's old blue frock—How his friends do love him! Mr Bridge was perfectly wild with spirits. He danced & gesticulated & opened his round eyes like an owl. . . . All went to the hotel to spend the evening & talk of business. . . . [Pierce] called him "Nathaniel," & spoke to him & looked at him with peculiar tenderness.

Greatly impressed, Sophia "saw by a glance that [Pierce] was a person of delicacy & refinement." Pierce attempted to revive Hawthorne's candidacy for the Salem post office in a letter to Bancroft, who had received a "confidential" communication from a party member attacking Hawthorne's appointment on the grounds that in the two years he had lived in Concord he had not voted.[41]

On May 31, 1845, O'Sullivan peremptorily instructed Bancroft that Hawthorne wanted no clerkships in Boston. "Some place of independent position," he explained, "and no great amount of clerical drudgery, somewhere near Boston, is what he ought to have. It sounds badly that something fitting & worthy was asked for in vain for such a man as Hawthorne!" Hawthorne in turn declined positions on Santa Rosa Island and in the Charlestown Navy Yard in Boston because of low salaries. "Such is his character," O'Sullivan informed Bancroft, "he would rather live on a moldy crust than take a place below his dignity & conscious claims."[42]

The delay in securing a governmental post proved embarrassing. The Hawthornes failed to pay the rent for many months. The Ripleys wanted to return to the Manse, and Sophia was most upset. "Let us see you all," she wrote to her oldest friend, "before we are driven out of Paradise—not by Cherubim, but by the most antiangelic of men, Mr. Sam Ripley of Waltham." In May Hawthorne borrowed $100 from Bridge, and in September he instructed George Hillard to sue George Ripley, of Brook Farm, for nonpayment of interest on his investment.[43]

In order to conserve funds the Hawthornes decided to move into 12 Herbert Street with the Salem Hawthornes, gambling that he would eventually land a position there. Sophia supervised the planning with Louisa in order to spare her husband unnecessary distractions. Despite the changes and necessary accommodations, Sophia did not complain. "I assure you," she wrote to her mother, "it is neither heroism nor virtue of any kind for me to be beyond measure thankful and blest to find shelter anywhere with my husband. . . . He and Una are my perpetual Paradise." She had been "gradually weaned" from the Manse by "the perplexities that have vexed my husband the last year, & made the place painful to him."[44]

In September 1845 Hawthorne appealed to Bridge for $150 in order to defray moving expenses and promptly received the sum and a rebuke: "The habitual belief which you have in your own bad luck must have made you doubt of its success and I fear you may even have begun to distrust

one who can never fail to serve you and yours to the utmost of his power."
O'Sullivan unexpectedly sent $100, and the Hawthornes were able to
leave the Manse on October 2 "with flying colors," in Hawthorne's words,
"although I found only ten dollars in my pocket on reaching Salem."[45]

The move to Salem made the search for a post more urgent. Senator
John Fairfield of Maine wrote on Hawthorne's behalf to Bancroft and
Polk. Hawthorne was confident that he would secure a place in the Custom-House and was content, at least on November 10, to wait for "definite intelligence." By December, when Bancroft had still not acted,
O'Sullivan informed Fairfield that the two factions in the Democratic
party in Salem had now agreed that Hawthorne was an acceptable candidate for the post at the Custom-House and asked him to write to Bancroft: "I trust there may be as little delay as possible in making an appointment so clearly proper on local political grounds, and at the same
time so eminently calculated to reflect credit on the administration in
making it."[46]

The new year came and Hawthorne's appointment remained pending.
Short of funds, he again borrowed from Bridge on his expectations. To
complicate matters, Sophia was pregnant. "What a devil of a pickle I shall
be in," he complained, "if the baby should come, and the office should
not!" Yet he remained confident: "My mind will now settle itself, after the
long inquietude of expectation; and I mean to make this a profitable year,
in the literary way."[47]

On February 26, 1846, almost a year after Polk's inauguration, Ban-
croft was ready to ask for Hawthorne's confirmation as surveyor in the
Custom-House. On April 3 Polk signed Hawthorne's appointment as
"Surveyor for the District of Salem and Beverly and Inspector of the
Revenue for the Port of Salem," at an annual salary of $1,200.[48]

"I have grown considerable of a politician," Hawthorne declared, "by
the experience of the last few months." He made the claim after suggesting that Bridge leak some confidential information in the right places. He
discussed the situation candidly with Epes Sargent, a Boston editor and
journalist:

It is no great affair, but suits me well enough, as ensuring me a
comfortable living, with a little margin for luxuries, and occupying
only a moderate portion of time—so that I shall have as much freedom for literary employment as hitherto. . . .

I wish your fate had happened to cast you on the winning side in politics. It is exceedingly convenient for a literary man to be able to ensconce himself in an office, whenever his brain gets weary and his pen blunted. I have had good luck in this respect, and really do not know what so idle and inefficient a fellow could have done without it.[49]

Intercourse with the World

Mosses from an Old Manse

Before Sophia entered the Concord Eden, she knew a great deal about her Adam and perhaps intuited more, although her idealistic creed permitted her, even encouraged her, to be blind to what she chose not to see. She knew of his moods and the attendant gyrations. He himself in one of the love letters unfolded the truth in memorable phraseology:

> Lights and shadows are continually flitting across my inward sky, and I know neither whence they come nor whither they go; nor do inquire too closely into them. It is dangerous to look too minutely at such phenomena. It is apt to create a substance, where at first there was a mere shadow.

However, she transformed Concord into an idyllic setting worthy of her lord and of her devotion.[1]

In a rare revelation in her journal she indicated that her saint sometimes taxed her patience, which was saintly in its kind: ". . . he is so seldom satisfied with any thing—weather, things or people that I am always glad to find him pleased." His fastidiousness was such that he would "never have a cracked or broken dish on the table." Hawthorne could be stubbornly, if elegantly, negative.[2]

While Sophia strove to surround Hawthorne with an

Apollonian glow, which would fulfill her need for a heroic figure, Hawthorne himself continued after marriage to explore and to record the Dionysian depths or the underworld of the unconscious. In his journals he still recorded sadomasochistic and violent desires which would, if she had allowed herself to understand them, have terrified Sophia. One of his fantasy figures with "the malignancy of a witch" taught children unnamed vices, which was to take on new significance in *The Scarlet Letter* when Arthur Dimmesdale plays in fantasy the role of a corrupter of youth. A chemist shut himself up in his laboratory, along with "a singing girl," where "he drank spirits; smelled penetrating odors, sprinkled cologne-water round the room &c &c. Eight days thus passed, when he was seized with a fit of frenzy, which terminated in mania."[3]

One day while Hawthorne was lying on the ground at Sleepy Hollow, where he was to be buried, he observed a colony of ants which he labeled Fourierites, an amusing burlesque of the transformation of Brook Farm according to the principles of the French socialist. But abruptly Hawthorne assumed the role of a magician: "Like a malevolent genius, I drop a few grains of sand into the entrance of one of these dwellings, and thus quite obliterate it." This led on another occasion to ruminations on the complexity of the master-slave relationship. "Then show, that the person who appears to be the master, must inevitably be at least as much a slave, if not more, than the other. All slavery is reciprocal, on the supposition most favorable to the rulers."[4]

Occasionally he was overcome with the kind of suicidal despair which he confessed to years earlier in the letters that Bridge burned. "In moods of heavy despondency," he wrote in his notebook, "one feels as if it would be delightful to sink down in some quiet spot, and lie there forever, letting the soil gradually accumulate and form a little hillock over us, and the grass and perhaps flowers gather over it."[5]

After his death Sophia excised a comment written during the first year of their marriage in which he exposed feelings of sterility and inadequacy, which anticipated the crack-up of the final years: "But here I linger upon earth, very happy, it is true, at bottom, but a good deal troubled with the sense of imbecility—one of the dismallest sensations, methinks, that mortal can experience—the consciousness of a blunted pen, benumbed figures, and a mind no longer capable of a vigorous grasp. My torpidity of intellect makes me irritable. . . ." Perhaps the comment reflected a passing mood, one of the shadows so commonplace in his writings, but

246 Mosses from an Old Manse

stories circulated in Concord about this strange occupant of the Manse who stood in the pathway with folded arms for hours, eyes fixed on the ground: "Poor fellow, . . . he does look as if he might be daft."[6]

Although no one had Sophia's opportunities to observe Hawthorne in the throes of writing—however, we must remember that he kept her at a distance, his study being sacred ground—she proceeded to place an aura about the creative process which no artist would recognize, least of all Hawthorne.

> I can comprehend the delicacy & tricksiness of his mood when he is evolving a work of art. . . . He . . . waits upon the Light. . . . Of several sketches, first one & then another come up to be clothed upon with language after their own will & pleasure, & he follows the Muse. . . . He does not meddle with the clear, true picture that is painted on his mind.[7]

Not a word did Sophia have to say about his continuing fears of depletion and the attendant anxiety. A year before his marriage, while he was still at Brook Farm, he explained to Hillard that "stories grow like vegetables, and are not manufactured, like a pine table. My former stories all spring up of their own accord, out of a quiet life. Now, I have no quiet at all; for when my outward man is at rest—which is seldom, and for short intervals—my mind is bothered with a sort of dull excitement, which makes it impossible to think continuously of any subject."[8]

Less than a year after his marriage he commented, "I could be happy as a squash, and much in the same mode. But the necessity of keeping my brains at work eats into my comfort as the squash-bugs do into the heart of the vines. I keep myself uneasy, and produce little, and almost nothing that is worth producing." Hawthorne, as we know, was in periods of depression given to overstatement, which he frequently modified almost immediately, and the truth was that in the two years following his marriage he wrote twenty works, a few of which are memorable achievements. As his economic situation deteriorated and fears of poverty troubled him, he dried up creatively. In 1845 he came into print only in the April issue of the *Democratic Review*.[9]

At this time he was in the midst of negotiations with Duyckinck as representative of Wiley and Putnam to issue a new collection of tales which was eventually given the title *Mosses from an Old Manse*. It was to include stories written since the appearance of the second edition of

Twice-told Tales in 1842 as well as two of his greatest works from the 1830s, "Young Goodman Brown" and "Roger Malvin's Burial." Hawthorne planned an introductory sketch—a loose "frame-work," like those in his children's books—which would present, in his words, "an idealization of our old parsonage, and of the river close at hand, with glimmerings of my actual life—yet so transmogrified that the reader should not know what was reality and what fancy." [10]

He wrestled with the sketch for almost a year. At one moment he was "not in good trim for writing" and at another felt that he was capable of nothing better than "book-manufacture" in his role as supervisor of the publication of Bridge's book. After he left Concord for Salem and returned to the attic at 12 Herbert Street, he assured Bridge, and himself, that "the old chamber where I wasted so many years of my life" would again prove "rather favorable to my literary duties." A few days later he was less confident.

> However, my youth comes back to me here; and I find myself, sad to say, pretty much the same sort of fellow as of old—and already, though not a week established here, I take out my quire of paper and prepare to cover it with the accustomed nonsense. Doubtless, there will be a result of some kind or other, in the course of two or three weeks, so soon as my mind has deposited the sediment of recent anxieties and disturbances. [11]

At Christmas 1845, still without confirmation of his appointment to an official position, he had to confess, "Peradventure, I have reached that point in an author's life, when he ceases to effervesce; and whatever I do hereafter must be done with leaden reluctance, and therefore had better be left undone." Within a few months, when he had financial security, he woke up one "fine morning unbewitched" and completed the sketch now entitled "The Old Manse," which is a graceful farewell to Concord and a worthy predecessor of "The Custom-House," in which his farewell to Salem serves as a prelude to one of the world's great tales, *The Scarlet Letter.* [12]

The subtitle of "The Old Manse" is "The Author Makes the Reader Acquainted with his Abode." Hawthorne has much to say about Concord, his historical house, and his acquaintances, but from an acknowledged idealistic focus which, curiously, at places resembles Sophia's. At the same time he plays hide-and-seek with his reader as he admits while he denies that *Mosses from an Old Manse* is autobiographical. "How little have I told!" he exclaims, "and, of that little, how almost nothing is even tinctured with any quality that makes it exclusively my own!" The dodge is artful but hardly persuasive and only partly true. He denies that the reader has "gone wandering, hand and hand with me, through the inner passages of my being," but why suggest the possibility? Even his often-quoted disclaimer—"So far as I am a man of really individual attributes, I veil my face; nor am I, nor have ever been, one of those supremely hospitable people, who serve up their own hearts delicately fried, with brain-sauce, as a tidbit for their beloved public"—suggests, even confirms, the opposite construction.[13]

Writing in 1854 to his publisher, James T. Fields, who had reissued *Mosses from an Old Manse*, Hawthorne maintained on his "honor" that he no longer comprehended his own meaning "in some of these blasted allegories; but I remember that I always had a meaning—or, a least, thought I had." Then, unwittingly, he admitted that *Mosses from an Old Manse* unveils a self-portrait. "I am a good deal changed since those times" (which was palpably untrue), "and, to tell you the truth, my past self is not very much to my taste, as I see myself in this book."[14]

In 1850 Melville observed that "The Christmas Banquet" and "Egotism; or, The Bosom-Serpent," two of the tales which appeared in the first printing of *Mosses*, would be fine subjects "for a curious and elaborate analysis, touching the conjectural parts of the mind that produced them. For spite of all the Indian-summer sunlight on the hither side of Hawthorne's soul, the other side—like the dark half of the physical sphere—is shrouded in a blackness ten times black." What Melville intuited he kept to himself, but he insisted that Hawthorne shared his own "Calvinistic sense of Innate Depravity and Original Sin," which was only partly true.[15]

Melville termed "A Select Party" "the sweetest and sublimest thing that has been written since Spenser," an accolade which no one else has bestowed on Hawthorne's whimsy about the journey of two characters, the Master Genius and the Man of Fancy, into cloudland or nowhere, where guests meet nobody. Melville believed that the Master Genius was a self-portrait, and he asserted that "the American, who up to the present day has evinced, in literature, the largest brain with the largest heart, that man is Nathaniel Hawthorne." Melville did not deduce that the Man of Fancy, who has been "tormented" by moods of "morbid melancholy," mirrors Hawthorne's lifelong terrors:

> The walls of his castle in the air were not dense enough to keep them out; nor would the strongest of earthy architecture have availed to their exclusion. Here were those forms of dim terror, which had beset him at the entrance of life, waging warfare with his hopes. Here were strange uglinesses of earlier date, such as haunt children in the night time. He was particularly startled by the vision of a deformed old black woman, whom he imagined as lurking in the garret of his native home, and who, when he was an infant, had once come to his bedside and grinned at him, in the crisis of a scarlet fever. This same black shadow, with others almost as hideous, now glided among the pillars of the magnificent saloon, grinning recognition, until the man shuddered anew at the forgotten terrors of his childhood.[16]

While the Hawthornes became parents and seemingly enjoyed an edenic period, Hawthorne in the second-floor study overlooking the slow-moving Concord River was not confirming Sophia's lovely idealizations—or bubbles. "The Intelligence Office" examines wishes or, more accurately, fantasies, of people who go to an office in order to discover the meaning of life as well as their own identities. Echoing Ilbrahim, Brown, and others who find themselves "awry," one man cries: "I want my place!—my own place!—my true place in the world!—my proper sphere!—my thing to do, which nature intended me to perform when she fashioned me thus awry, and which I have vainly sought all my lifetime!"

In "Earth's Holocaust," which was probably written about the time of Una's birth, Hawthorne creates a universal fire in order to free the world of creeds, books, and art, only to declare with shattering negation that after the destruction "it will be the old world yet." We must go, he proposes, "deeper than the Intellect," but his meaning is obscure. He warns that after a man disposes of "the mouldy bones of his ancestors"—the Hathornes, for example?—he may face "worse nonsense." Again he checks his speculation, perhaps fearing the course it is taking, and at the conclusion admits that his fantasy may be "only a phosphoric radiance, and a parable of my brain!"

"The Birth-mark," which appeared in print a month after Sophia's miscarriage, unfolds the story of an alchemist named Aylmer—he truly *ails*, as we soon discover—who one day almost capriciously leaves his labora-tory and his faithful assistant Aminadab and takes a wife. Georgiana is distinguished by a birthmark on her left cheek which has the shape of a reddish hand and changes color according to her moods. The birthmark is of no significance to Aylmer until "after his marriage, for he thought little or nothing of the matter before." The motions of the birthmark— "now vaguely portrayed, now lost, now stealing forth again, and glim-mering to-and-fro with every pulse of emotion"—approximate the sexual rhythm, a natural, life-enhancing rhythm which terrifies Aylmer, but they also resemble the motions of the flames of his fires where he brews unnatural concoctions which, while invariably failing to fulfill his aspira-tions, confirm his intellectual and emotional inadequacies.

When the birthmark is described for the first time, it appears in low-ercase letters, but as Aylmer reveals his fixation it is capitalized: Aylmer like Ahab or Dimmesdale is consumed by his obsession. The hand is de-scribed as "bloody," "crimson," "spectral," "odious," "dreadful," "little," and, finally, "fatal." Years ago Simon O. Lesser observed that the hand is associated with Aylmer's sexual panic and arrestment which are estab-lished in the first paragraph. In referring to Aylmer's aspirations to "make new worlds for himself," Hawthorne likens the quest to a "conge-nial aliment," which places matters in an oral framework that is further elaborated a few lines later: Aylmer "had devoted himself, however, too unreservedly to scientific studies, ever to be *weaned* from them by any second passion." When he finds himself confronted with the power of Georgiana's natural desires, he projects his panic on the birthmark, thus creating an excuse to return to his laboratory, where he feels secure and in control, in order to prepare a concoction that will remove "the Crimson Hand." As Gaston Bachelard observes, "Alchemy is uniquely a science engaged in by men, by bachelors, by men without women, by initiates cut off from normal human relationships in favor of a strictly masculine society."[17]

In a dream Aylmer attempts to perform what appears to be an obstet-rical procedure displaced: "But the deeper went the knife, the deeper sank the Hand, until at length its tiny grasp appeared to have caught hold of Georgiana's heart; whence, however, her husband was inexorably resolved to cut or wrench it away." If at times Aylmer wants to destroy the mother figure, he at other times craves her attention and support. When he is depressed because his search for a potion is unsuccessful, he says, "Sing to me, dearest!" She then pours out "the liquid music of her voice to quench the thirst of his spirit." He leaves "with a boyish exuberance of gaiety," for the wife-now-mother has supplied the needs of the boy-man who in his laboratory seeks to imitate woman's fertility.

One day Georgiana drinks the potion Aylmer has concocted. As the birthmark begins to fade on her cheek, he exclaims: "My peerless bride, it is successful! You are perfect!" Aylmer's potion is successful, his panic alleviated. Georgiana is perfect—and dead—which is as the dream corroborates his secret wish.

A few months after Una's birth Hawthorne wrote "Rappaccini's Daughter," one of his most enigmatic and unsettling tales. Rappaccini, an eminent Italian botanist, creates in Padua on the grounds of a man immortalized in Dante's *Inferno* an "Eden of poisonous flowers." His greatest achievement takes place apparently shortly after the birth of his only child Beatrice, who evokes Dante's beloved as well as Beatrice Cenci, who allegedly was raped by her father. Rappaccini, in competition with Beatrice's dead mother, creates a shrub "set in a marble vase in the midst of the pool, that bore a profusion of purple blossoms, each of which had the lustre and richness of a gem."

The shrub dominates the setting and the story, functioning as a motif not unlike the scarlet letter or Georgiana's birthmark and in appearance resembling the floral vulvas in the paintings of Georgia O'Keeffe. The plant, poisonous to the touch and fatal to inhale, becomes Beatrice's "sister" in a kind of symbiotic relationship: "Yes, my sister, my splendor, it shall be Beatrice's task to nurse and serve thee; and thou shalt reward her with thy kisses and perfumed breath, which to her is as the breath of life!" In the role confusions of this tale, Beatrice is a substitute mother-sister of the shrub and Beatrice is denied a father—he can neither touch her nor approach her, a prohibition which frustrates his incestuous longings, in a garden which was once a "pleasure-place" for people with devious desires.

Rappaccini decides to lure a mate for Beatrice into the poisonous garden, a handsome youth with glistening gold ringlets named Giovanni. If Rappaccini appears to be motivated by a desire to bestow upon his daughter a human companion of her own age, he is at the same time aware that Beatrice will infect him with her poison. Like the father denied tactile contact and sexuality, Giovanni becomes her "brother"—which may have been Rappaccini's intention.

Baglioni, a rival scientist, is jealous of Rappaccini's scientific successes and of Beatrice's hold over Giovanni. An old friend of the youth's father, Baglioni wants to substitute for the dead parent despite Giovanni's resistance. That his interest may be more than paternal adds to the deviant aura of the tale. Baglioni concocts a potion supposedly to free Beatrice of her poisoned nature. Like Aylmer he is successful: she dies—which may also have been the unconscious desire of the father and of her lover.

This construction, however, is as problematic as the tale itself, for Hawthorne utilizes every possible means to frustrate a clear and simple reading of his story. He prefaces it with a commentary in which authorship is attributed to "Aubepine," a name given to him in 1837 by a French friend of Bridge during Hawthorne's retreat from Salem. Even the titles of his tales are rendered in French. This farcical tactic presumably hides the latent and autobiographical content of the story—Rappaccini's daughter and Hawthorne's daughter. Sophia is supposed to have asked Hawthorne before he completed the work whether Beatrice is to be "a demon or an angel." His answer, "I have no idea!"—at least not one that he would divulge to Sophia or to future commentators, who have not succeeded in lifting the veils surrounding this tale.[18]

Three months after the birth of Una he published his most exhaustive and playfully ironic portrait of an artist. "The Artist of the Beautiful" relates the story of Owen Warland, which, if not in every detail a self-portrait, unfolds Hawthorne's doubts about the makers of trifles and reluctant agreement with the Hathorne ancestors, the personal and sexual problems of the artist, and the emotional and physical ordeal of creativity.

"The Artist of the Beautiful" is another story of hands, on the Ilbrahim order, for Owen, a watchmaker by trade, fashions with his small hands not a sculpture of Michelangelo scale but a butterfly so small and realistic in all details that people are confused. Is it a toy or a real butterfly? Owen, somewhat effeminate in appearance, introverted, and secretive, is measured against his school chum, Robert Danforth, a virile village blacksmith almost out of Longfellow. Danforth lays "his vast hand beside the delicate one of Owen." "I put more main strength," he declares, "into one blow of my sledge-hammer, than all that you have expended since you were a 'prentice." Owen has a "diminutive frame," "little fingers," and a "slender voice." Adjectives such as "slight," "delicate," and "small" appear repetitively. If Owen's brain is "sensitive," it is also "microscopic," and Hawthorne even notes the "minuteness" of his "accomplishments." It is as though Hawthorne mocks, in a kind of self-laceration, those feminine aspects of his nature which some contemporaries referred to and which he himself acknowledged several times in his juxtapositions of himself and his forebears. Yet there is unwavering sympathy for Owen—how could it be otherwise?—but there is no doubt that Annie Hovenden, the daughter of Owen's employer and the object of rivalry with Danforth, will go to the blacksmith.

Two symbols hover over the story—a steam engine and the butterfly. The narrator traces Owen's timidity and isolation from his peers and society to an incident in his childhood: "Being once carried to see a steam-engine, in the expectation that his intuitive comprehension of mechanical principles would be gratified, he turned pale, and grew sick, as if something monstrous and unnatural had been presented to him. The horror was partly owing to the size and terrible energy of the Iron Laborer. . . ." Although Hawthorne provides no specific information about the Warland family, Owen's reaction to the engine, verbal as well as visceral, more than hints at deep, still unresolved difficulties in his relationship with his father. In the action described in the tale, Danforth's forge, beautiful as a source of brilliant light effects but awesome in its demonstration of power, replaces the steam engine. Danforth is a "Man of Iron," as is Hovenden, who symbolizes materialism and practicality. They are in the tradition of Governor Endecott and the Hathorne ancestors themselves.

At the beginning as at the end Owen is a boy, or child-man, in pursuit of a butterfly, which may represent the soul, immortality, death, or the winged phallus or indeed all of these. The end of Owen's artistic achievement—and the extent of his imagination—is the creation of a mechanical butterfly of uncanny fidelity to the original. The irony is clear: Owen's butterfly is a "mechanism" like the steam engine but smaller, less frightening, useless except as a plaything, and, worse, less imaginative than the monster.

Stealthily, behind closed doors and shelters, at night Owen labors to give birth to his butterfly. These recurrent imitations of the birth process must be pursued in secret, like fertility rites to which only males are admitted. In contrast, Danforth performs his function as a blacksmith in public, attended by the brilliant flames and light of his hearth. When Hovenden sees Owen's construction for the first time, he, like a Hathorne, exclaims: "Owen, Owen! there is witchcraft in these little chains, and wheels, and paddles!"

After a visit from Danforth, Owen, enraged by the self-created warfare between the Beautiful and the Brute, drops one of his minute instruments and destroys his creation. "I am ruined!" he exclaims like a violated virgin in a nineteenth-century melodrama. He now enters one of his infertile periods—he even speaks in a "depressed tone"—but during these phases he is an excellent restorer of clocks. Like Hawthorne, he is capable of only one activity at a time. Gradually he begins "accumulating fresh vigor" and is, as it were, reborn as an artist. The renewed creative state is shattered when Annie, who has come to the shop to have a thimble repaired (which, as William Bysshe Stein points out, is a genital joke), touches Owen's artistic creation with a needle and shatters it. "You have ruined me!" he declaims, again like an innocent violated by a stronger force.

This time in his depression he regresses to the bottle and oral pleasure but recovers his confidence and his creativity in the spring at the appearance of a butterfly. The recovery is short-lived, for when he learns that Annie is about to marry Danforth, by accident or unconscious design he destroys his artifact. He now realizes that the Annie he has loved is an "inward vision" which is "as much a creation of his own, as the mysterious piece of mechanism would be were it ever realized." He does not admit what is implicit, that out of his need for security he has sought a mother figure.

During the ensuing depression, the deepest and longest of all, he is seriously ill and physically regresses to childhood: "His thin cheeks became round; his delicate little hand, so spiritually fashioned to achieve fairy task-work, grew plumper than the hand of a thriving infant." This time he truly goes under to the beginnings of life, and of art, before he recovers. While Owen is in this physical and artistic stupor, Annie and Danforth marry and have a child. When Owen calls on them he discovers "a little personage who had come mysteriously out of the infinite." The phrasing suits, and mocks, Owen's childish conceptions of sexuality.

In the presence of the new child and the happy family Owen seeks to rival the natural process, but, since he is both father and mother, the attempt results in a parody which consists of familiar symbols of dreams. Owen opens a jewel box, "carved richly out of ebony by his own hand, and inlaid with a fanciful tracery of pearl, representing a boy in pursuit of a butterfly." From the box-womb-tomb an "ideal butterfly" emerges and flutters about the room until it rests upon the "plump hand" of the little boy, which evokes Owen's during his period of depression and regression. When the butterfly flies away in fear, "the little Child of Strength, with his grandsire's sharp and shrewd expression in his face, made a snatch at the marvellous insect, and compressed it in his hand," presumably after the fashion of the "Iron Laborer."

The seemingly inconclusive conclusion is actually as conclusive as humans can be about certain subjects. With fine critical intelligence and empathic insight, Hawthorne evaluates the artist as well as the nonartist and comments presumably on his personal dilemma. Life demands that there be Danforths and Hovendens for survival and progress. Annie admires "her own infant, and with good reason," we are informed, "far more than the artistic butterfly." If the Danforth child appears to be a carbon copy of the grandfather, the family seems content in its unity and its kind of creativity. Owen Warland has apparently achieved contentment in sublimation so that with nonchalance, real or assumed, he can witness the destruction of his butterfly, for "he had caught a far other butterfly than this," which he prefers not to specify. In what Owen construes as a moment of triumph, he remains a model of Emersonian self-reliance and of the Hawthornesque artist, free of connections and sexual desires, his fears evaded rather than dealt with: he is still in an anomalous state somewhere between childhood and adulthood, which may be the state of the artist.[19]

While Hawthorne was mining the inner landscapes of Aylmer, Rappaccini, and the others and exposing anxieties and sexual fears in fictional disguise, he wrote to Sophia with such ardor that she had to excise in order to protect posterity from the passionate, intemperate Hawthorne. She must have trembled when she read his protestation of passion. "Ah, dost thou think of me?" he wrote while she visited her family, "dost thou yearn for me?—does thy breath heave and thy heart quake with love for thy husband?—[excision] I can hardly breathe for loving thee so much."[20]

Mosses from an Old Manse was to be Hawthorne's last collection of tales and sketches. "I thank God," he wrote, "I have grace enough to be utterly dissatisfied with them, considered as the productions of a literary life—or in any point of view whatever; not but what I see the degree of merit they possess. If they were merely Spring blossoms, we might look for good fruit hereafter." "My health is not so good," he confessed, "as it always has been hitherto. I feel no physical vigor; and my inner man droops in sympathy," a state which he delineates in "The Artist of the Beautiful."[21]

Salem, Hail and Farewell

At the conclusion of "The Old Manse" Hawthorne sums up, according to his stated principle of idealization, the first three years of his marriage, referring not to "the terrors" but only to the "fairy-land," and likens the departure from Concord to the emergence of Adam and Eve from Eden: "Providence took me by the hand, and—an oddity of dispensation which, I trust, there is no irreverence in smiling at—has led me, as the newspapers announce while I am writing, from the Old Manse into a Custom-House! As a storyteller, I have often contrived strange vicissitudes for my imaginary personages, but none like this."[1]

On April 9, 1846, Hawthorne took the oath of office as surveyor of the port of Salem. Overlooking Derby's Wharf, the Custom-House is one of the impressive Federal-style structures of Salem, with its portico supported by white classical columns, an impressive wooden railing outlining the roof, a white lookout tower at the center of the roof, and a gilded eagle looking down over the railing at the granite steps leading to the main entrance. In Hawthorne's words, "With the customary infirmity of temper that characterizes this unhappy fowl, she appears, by the fierceness of her beak and eye and the general truculency of her attitude, to threaten mischief to the inoffensive community; and especially to warn all citizens, careful of their safety, against intruding on the premises which she overshadows with her wings." From his room on the first floor of "Uncle Sam's brick edifice," Hawthorne commanded a view known intimately by his father at the turn of the century.[2]

He acknowledged that although "Uncle Sam claimed as his share of my daily life" only three and one-half hours a day, it was a "numbing" experience. Yet the salary of $1,200 annually was substantial at the middle of the century. As at the Boston Custom-House, a much more substantial sum accrued from the fees paid by ships entering and leaving the harbor. Hawthorne had been at the Custom-House only a few days when he observed that the "fees were tolerably good, yesterday and to-day."[3]

During the next few months the Custom-House provided adequate income to relieve economic pressures and presumably to repay debts. In the summer he was pressed because fees fell off, but by October he was euphoric at least for the moment. "I am jogging onward in life," he informed Bridge, "with a moderate share of prosperity, and am contented and happy. My wife and children are well—my expenditures come within my income—and, all things considered, I have great reason to be thankful to Providence." Sophia had another perception, for two months later she reported to Bridge that "the Surveyorship is pleasant, but very far from profitable, I believe." To this Hawthorne added a postscript: "My wife knows no more about these matters than I do about baby-linen."[4]

Relations between Sophia and Hawthorne's family were, predictably, sometimes difficult. The Hawthorne women were accustomed to their rigid routines and hermitlike isolation, and although a bundle of light and gentleness, Sophia was in her own quiet fashion as rigid and dogmatic as Elizabeth Hawthorne, who skirted confrontation by staying out of Sophia's way. Sophia worried about the health of Mrs. Hawthorne and Louisa because of the effect their colds and other ailments might have on Una. The parents had not permitted Una to enter "the mysterious chamber" of the grandmother "since November, partly on this account, & partly because the room is much colder than the nursery or parlor, & has no carpet upon it." This was the kind of act Sophia was capable of in order to protect her child. She was also too impatient when Louisa insisted that she had to travel with her own pillow, which perhaps provided her with a little security in a universe that she found threatening.[5]

Sophia moved to 77 Carver Street in Boston in March 1846 to be near her own family and Dr. William Wesselhœft during her pregnancy. Hawthorne soon joined her and commuted daily to the Salem Custom-House. Sophia declared with finality that this time she was to have a boy. Her intuition proved correct. On June 22, 1846, Hawthorne announced to his sister:

> A small troglodyte made his appearance here at ten minutes to six o'clock, this morning, who claims to be your nephew, and the heir of all our wealth and honors. He has dark hair and is no great beauty at present, but is said to be a particularly fine little urchin by everybody who has seen him.[6]

Although the new child was of the correct sex, he was fated to remain nameless for about eight months—a fate which should befall no child, particularly not the son of a man who wrote with sensitivity about the earliest years of life. Apparently Sophia wanted to name the child George, but after Hawthorne for some reason objected, they were unable to agree upon a name. A month or more after the boy's birth, Mrs. Peabody urged her daughter to name *"Bouncing B"* and in October submitted a list of names: Arthur, Edward, Horace, Robert, and Lemuel. While the search went on, and even after the baptism, Julian remained "Bundlebreech" to his father.[7]

Meanwhile the baby grew with amazing speed. By November he weighed twenty-three pounds, and although she rarely had a critical word to say about either child, Sophia was concerned. "Would he were leaner however for beauty's & grace's sake." Soon she took pride in her giant and heralded him as the true son of his Apollo-father—"such Hyperion curls of thick chestnut brown—'locks of lovely splendor' as some German says of Apollo." She went even further and announced that Julian "is the son of a King—to be sure—of a King anointed by Heaven—if not by High Priests."[8]

Shortly before Julian's birth Sophia informed Louisa that her husband would *"never* go back to Herbert St. . . . under any circumstances." It was more than Herbert Street—it was Salem itself. "I hate the thought of Salem as well as my husband does," Sophia wrote to Louisa, who was never to leave the town. But despite their desire to remain in Boston, the Hawthornes finally rented a small house in Salem at 18 Chestnut Street, which they probably moved into in July, only to move two months later into a larger three-story house at 14 Mall Street for $200 annually. Hawthorne had his study on the upper floor. His mother had a separate suite of rooms, "so that we shall only meet when we choose to do so," an arrangement that proved satisfactory to everybody.[9]

After close acquaintance Sophia had only praise for Mrs. Hawthorne, "so perfectly ladylike—so uninterfering, & of so much delicacy. . . . I am so glad to win her out of that Castle Dismal & from the mysterious chamber, into which no mortal ever peeped till Una was born & Julian—for they alone have entered the penetralia." Of the two sisters she noted, "Elizabeth is an invisible entity—I have seen her but once for two years—& Louisa never intrudes." Sophia proudly compared herself to "some kind of india rubber. . . . I have sprung so elastic from all physical wrong—with all my vital functions so fresh & unimpaired."[10]

"The happiest of women," she protected her husband from "the wear and tear of the nursery. It is contrary to thy nature and to thy mood. Thou wast born to muse and to be silent and through undisturbed dreams, to enlighten the world." In return she expected and received control over the nurturing of the children. Julian slept with his mother for two years. At two Una had "never seen nor heard children play." She was willful and negative, but her mother considered the negatives positive, for they "will serve her a good turn in mature life, & so will her independent choice in action. She never will be made an automaton of while the breath of life is in her. . . . she chooses another way." Una chose "another way" within rather severe limitations. For example, she had to listen to Milton's poetry at age three, a decree questioned even by Mrs. Peabody, who had established an overzealous regimen for Sophia. Una was not taught to read until she was seven, "after the first cycle" of teeth. The children's mother remarked that "not a sweetmeat, not the simplest cake—not a particle of butter or any kind of fatness, nor any flesh of beast has defiled their little temples of spirit."[11]

Hawthorne's sisters had to put up with Una's moody disposition and her mother's strange combination of overregulation in some matters and excessive leniency in others. With pride Sophia described how Una was maturing, at Louisa's expense she might have added: "If Louisa comes down with her hair undressed & in a dishabille, she will cloud up & *formerly*, would say 'Go upstairs, Aunt Louisa—I do not wish to see you—' *Now*, she is convinced this is not polite nor kind, & so she only looks wretched & goes as far off as possible." Unlike Louisa, who suffered abuse too easily, Elizabeth Hawthorne set out to undermine Sophia's authority by giving Una candy. When Una insisted that her mother did not want her to have it, Aunt Ebe said, "Oh, never mind; your mother will never know!" Soon Una, a "noble child," informed her mother that "Aunt Ebe makes me naughty," and visits to the aunt's room ceased at once.[12]

Having abdicated a strong paternal role, Hawthorne himself had to submit to Una's "imperative mood. . . . She uses it to me, I think, more than to her mother, and, from what I observe of some of her collateral predecessors, I believe it to be an hereditary trait to assume the government of her father." (He referred to the burdens of Dr. Peabody with three daughters and a wife.)[13]

Despite strains in family harmony, which were to increase, Hawthorne asserted his love in his letters when Sophia and the children stayed with her sister Mary in West Newton, Massachusetts. "The children," he wrote, "are dear to me; but thou alone art essential. Thou art the only person in the world that ever was necessary to me. Other people have occasionally been more or less agreeable; but I think I was always more at ease alone than in any body's company, till I knew thee."[14]

Yet, about ten days later, on July 4, 1848, on his forty-fourth birthday, he went to Boston alone, enjoyed the fireworks, and weighed himself, at 178 pounds, but did not go to his family who were still with the Manns in West Newton, which was only a few miles away. On his return to Salem that evening, Elizabeth, who was almost never in sight when Sophia was in residence, was in the sitting room. She may have been making an oblique acknowledgment of her brother's birthday, the family not being given to celebrations of that sort, or she may have been desirous of having her brother to herself once more. A day or so later she walked with him in the rain, and on another evening they "confabulated till eleven o'clock." When Sophia returned to Salem, Elizabeth vanished. How she remained invisible in a relatively small house remains one of the mysteries of Hawthorne scholarship.[15]

At the Custom-House Hawthorne was once again associated with two Salemites, both Democratic officeholders, with whom he maintained lasting relationships—Zachariah Burchmore and William B. Pike. Burchmore, a simple man with a marked taste for alcoholic infusions, served in successive administrations at the Salem Custom-House because he was what Hawthorne termed the "rare instance" of "a person thoroughly adapted to the situation which he held." The high point of Burchmore's life was when he was lifted out of mediocrity in the introduction to *The Scarlet Letter:*

> His gifts were emphatically those of a man of business; prompt, acute, clear-minded; with an eye that saw through all perplexities, and a faculty of arrangement that made them vanish, as by the waving of an enchanter's wand. . . . He was, indeed, the Custom-House in himself; or, at all events, the main-spring that kept its variously revolving wheels in motion. . . .[16]

Burchmore was one of Hawthorne's favorite drinking companions, and in his letters Hawthorne joshed his friend and his addiction. After Burchmore lost his post at the Custom-House he became for a period a liquor dealer. Hawthorne "earnestly" hoped "that you may not be your own best customer." Later Hawthorne returned to the subject without banter: "I should hate to have you get to be a sot (plain speaking must be excused, in a friend,) and what is worse, a great many people in Salem would rejoice at it. At any rate, keep straight till after the next Presidential election; for it appears to me that you have considerable of a stake in it." After Pierce's election in 1852, Burchmore received, according to the *Salem Gazette*, the position "as some sort of Special Appraiser" in the Custom-House at the annual salary of $1,200.[17]

Unlike Burchmore, Pike was a self-educated man of high potential in Hawthorne's judgment. Burchmore may not have read Hawthorne's writings, but Pike's criticisms were perceptive and valued. Pike's weakness was that he went in too many directions. A Methodist, he contemplated the ministry and was recommended as a chaplain in the navy although he was not ordained. He was a pioneer member of the New Jerusalem Society in Salem and a leader of the Democratic party in Essex County. He was an assistant measurer in the Boston Custom-House when Hawthorne was employed there, an inspector in the Salem Custom-House during his friend's tenure, and in 1857 was appointed collector of the ports of Salem and Beverly. On at least three occasions in their warm correspondence over seventeen years Hawthorne wrote candidly of Pike's great expectations. "You will never, I fear (you see that I take a friend's privilege to speak plainly), make the impression on the world that, in years gone by, I used to hope you would. It will not be your fault, however, but the fault of circumstances. Your flower was not destined to bloom in this world. I hope to see its glory in the next." [18]

A short, stocky man, "ugly, but with a pleasant, kindly, as well as strong and thoughtful expression," Pike was subject to asthma and apoplectic fits, perhaps psychological in origin, and had watched as both parents and four sisters died of tuberculosis. He never married and lived with and took care of unmarried aunts all his life, yet he was lively, witty, and sensitive. Of the Salem friends Pike was the one to whom Hawthorne was most attached. "I do long to see you," Hawthorne wrote, "and to talk about a thousand things relating to this world and the next." He wanted to take Pike with him to England and place him in a consular post: "There is no man whom I should like so much to have for a companion; and I never see anything interesting without thinking of you." After his retirement Pike began a "Memoir of Hawthorne," which he evidently completed but then burned. Hawthorne would have slyly smiled his approval. [19]

Hawthorne understood Burchmore completely and praised him excessively, but in his famous indictment of the employees of the Custom-House he vents accumulated hostility against the town and its inhabitants.

> Oftentimes they were asleep, but occasionally might be heard talking together, in voices between speech and a snore, and with that lack of energy that distinguishes the occupants of alms-houses, and all other human beings who depend for subsistence on charity, on monopolized labor, or any thing else but their own independent exertions. These old gentlemen—seated, like Matthew at the receipt of custom, but not very liable to be summoned thence, like him, for apostolic errands—were Custom-House officers. [20]

In summarizing his tenure at the Custom-House in the preface to *The Scarlet Letter*, Hawthorne explains that a "strange, indolent, unjoyous attachment for my native town" had led him to the Custom-House. "My doom was on me. It was not the first time, nor the second, that I had gone away,—as it seemed, permanently,—but yet returned, like the bad half-penny; or as if Salem were for me the inevitable centre of the universe."

Here in Salem for centuries the Hathornes had lived and died, but like the town the family had degenerated from the two magistrates of Puritan days to, in Hawthorne's mocking words, "as its topmost bough, an idler like myself." Then he bandies "compliments" with those two ancestors whom he could not bury. "'What is he?' murmurs one gray shadow of my forefathers to the other. 'A writer of story-books! . . . Why, the degenerate fellow might as well as have been a fiddler!'" Secretly enjoying the exchange, Hawthorne at last makes a long-withheld admission: "Let them scorn me as they will, strong traits of their nature have intertwined themselves with mine."[21]

During his time at the Salem Custom-House Hawthorne's reputation grew, even though his books continued to have small sales. He was made an honorary member of the Kappa Epsilon Society at Bowdoin College. In his own way he promoted himself. Advance copies of *Mosses from an Old Manse*, usually lavishly bound, were sent to pay off his political obligations to such people as Mrs. Bancroft and senators George Gordon Atherton and John Fairfield. He also directed that copies be sent to Margaret Fuller, Poe, Henry T. Tuckerman, George W. Curtis, and Rufus Griswold, all of whom were either associated with or had access to important journals of the era. He agreed to review books in the *Literary World*, which was jointly edited by Evert Duyckinck and his brother George. He expected no remuneration for "what I may do for the Literary World, and shall be glad to do anything in my power," and he promised to review books "for better or worse, in the Democratic papers of this town," most of which were edited by political and personal friends.[22]

Hawthorne did not consider himself a professional critic and was not tied to any critical theory. When he wrote reviews or commented informally in letters, he sought to "enter into the spirit of a work and see it as the author sees it." He argued that a "reviewer of an unrecognized writer should be drunken with his spirit, like the immediate converts of a new prophet," and insisted that "the deepest and warmest sympathy" must "co-exist between two perfectly independent perceptions" of the artist and the critic.[23]

In 1848 Hawthorne became the corresponding secretary of the Salem Lyceum. The twentieth season opened with the appearance of Daniel Webster and included such men (there were no women on the list) as

Emerson, Louis Agassiz, and Theodore Parker. Presumably at Hawthorne's invitation, Thoreau, who was usually as reticent as his host, made two appearances during the season. His first lecture, which contained an excerpt from what would become six years later the first part of *Walden*, kept "the audience in almost constant mirth" because of its "exquisite humor, with a strong under current of delicate satire against the follies of the time," according to the *Salem Observer* of November 25, 1848. During this renewed friendship Sophia changed her tune: "Mr. Thoreau has risen above all his arrogance of manner, and is as gentle, simple, ruddy, and meek as all geniuses should be; and now his great blue eyes fairly outshine and put into shade a nose which I once thought must make him uncomely forever."[24]

For the most part these were sterile years creatively. Sophia was confident that after the move to Mall Street something magical would take place. Hawthorne, however, explained to Longfellow: "I am trying to resume my pen; but the influences of my situation and customary associates are so anti-literary, that I know not whether I shall succeed. Whenever I sit alone, or walk alone, I find myself dreaming about stories, as of old; but these forenoons in the Custom House undo all that the afternoons and evenings have done. I should be happier if I could write."[25]

In the winter of 1848–1849 Hawthorne completed the first tale he had written since 1844, "Ethan Brand—A Chapter from an Abortive Romance," which has always been one of his most popular and memorable stories. Brand pursues the unpardonable sin and in the process commits it, destroying connections between head and heart, severing the magnetic bonds of humanity. After eighteen years of fruitless journeying and the corruption of a villager named Esther, Brand returns to the limekiln near North Adams, Massachusetts, at the foot of Mount Greylock, where in his youth he tended the furnace. The circle of his life is about to close.

That evening, estranged from humanity, he sits alone before the kiln engaged in what is to be his final stocktaking. Having "lost his hold of the magnetic chain of humanity," he is "now a cold observer, looking on mankind as the subject of his experiment." He climbs to the top of the tower and looks down into a fire "sending up great spouts of blue flames, which quivered aloft and danced madly, as within a magic circle." Indicting himself as a "fiend," he cries out to "Mother Earth, . . . who art no more my Mother, and into whose bosom this frame shall never be resolved! . . .

Come, deadly element of Fire—henceforth my familiar friend! Embrace me as I do thee!" With this wrenching cry of total emptiness he plunges into the limekiln.

The next morning Bartram, Brand's successor, and his son Joe climb to the top of the kiln and look down into the snow-white lime: "In the midst of the circle—snow-white too, and thoroughly converted into lime—lay a human skeleton, in the attitude of a person who, after long toil, lies down to long repose. Within the ribs—strange to say—was the shape of a human heart." Delighted that his kiln "is half a bushel the richer for him," Bartram drops his pole into the kiln, and "the relics of Ethan Brand were crumbled into fragments."

"Ethan Brand," Hawthorne admits, did not experience an easy birth: "I have wrenched and torn an idea out of my miserable brain, or rather, the fragment of an idea, like a tooth ill-drawn and leaving the roots to torture me." The description anticipates Kafka's: "The story came out of me like a real birth, covered with slime and blood." Hawthorne never wrote another chapter to his "Abortive Romance"—rightly so. As a fragment it makes a frightening statement.[26]

About the same time Hawthorne wrote "Main-street," the most elaborate of his processionals, which recapitulates subjects and themes that had preoccupied him since graduation from Bowdoin. A showman has "contrived a certain pictorial exhibition, somewhat in the nature of a puppet-show, by means of which [he proposes] to call up the multiform and many-colored Past before the spectator, and show him the ghosts of his forefathers," who, not surprisingly, are primarily Hathornes. At first Salem is a lovely pastoral setting, edenic and peaceful. The ruler is "an Indian woman—a majestic and queenly woman," seemingly a great matriarch, although her second husband, Wappacowet, will infiltrate the dreams of the new English settlers with phantoms of terror. Soon the Indian is in retreat before the superior firepower and ruthlessness of the whites. "The pavements of the Main-street," the showman observes in one of his most memorable comments, "must be laid over the red man's grave."

Endecott arrives to rule as governor while the settlement grows with "Anglo-Saxon energy," "patriarchal edifices" replacing Indian wigwams. "Thirteen Men, grim rulers of a grim community," decree religious conformity, personal and social repressions, and growth, at the expense of the free play of minds and bodily pleasure. The showman sums up with devastating wit: "Let us thank God for having given us such ancestors; and let each successive generation thank him, not less fervently, for being one step further from them in the march of the ages."

Hawthorne was of two minds about many, perhaps most subjects. When in 1849 his tenure in the Salem Custom-House was threatened and the political position he held was claimed by the Whigs, who had elected Taylor to the presidency in 1848, he sometimes felt relieved that he would no longer have to continue in an office which provided income but little gratification. At the same time he was outraged that "the slang-whangers—the vote-distributors—the Jack Cades" connived to oust him unceremoniously, questioning not only his competency but also his stance that as an author he was above politics.[27]

As soon as Hawthorne learned of the campaign to unseat him, he set the wheels turning for a full-scale counteroffensive which in the next few months would involve political figures as influential as Daniel Webster and newspapers of both parties in Salem, Boston, Philadelphia, Baltimore, New York, and probably elsewhere. His cause became one of those much discussed scandals which temporarily arouse partisan outcries and extend language to its outer limits, only to be barely remembered within six months or a year. Hawthorne's case was an exception, for, his sensibilities wounded—"my head has been chopt off" was the way he characterized the indignity—he attacked those who in his perception had deprived him of livelihood as well as of masculinity: Hawthorne had a way of transforming situations into confirmations of lifelong fears.[28]

What rankled many people in Salem, particularly among the local Whigs, was the support Hawthorne received from outsiders. Salem Democrats were also annoyed by this outside support as well as by Hawthorne's well-publicized abstention from the usual party activities such as parades, conventions, and committees. As Hawthorne himself noted when he began to defend his position and his integrity, "A large portion of the local Democratic party look coldly on me, for not having used the influence of my position to obtain the removal of whigs." The truth apparently was, if it is possible to arrive at truth in emotionally charged situations where ideologies and self-interest inevitably produce distortions, that Hawthorne had lost the support of many Salem Democrats, merchants, and even friends like Horace Conolly and Caleb Foote.[29]

Hawthorne's first reference to the campaign to unseat him appeared in a letter on March 5, 1849, to Hillard, the Whig lawyer in Boston. "It seems to me," Hawthorne wrote, "that an inoffensive man of letters—having obtained a pitiful little office on no other plea than his pitiful little literature—ought not to be left to the mercy of these thick-skulled and no-hearted ruffians." This, of course, re-created in the real world the plight of Owen Warland, the artist, in his warfare with Hovenden.[30]

When Hawthorne wrote three months later to Longfellow after the Whigs had made more specific charges, he was exhilarated at the prospect of doing battle, his pen itching for victims.

> I must confess, it stirs up a little of the devil within me, to find myself hunted by these political bloodhounds. If they succeed in getting me out of office, I will surely immolate one or two of them. . . . I have often thought that there must be a good deal of enjoyment in writing personal satire; but, never having felt the slightest ill-will towards any human being, I have hitherto been debarred from this peculiar source of pleasure. I almost hope I shall be turned out, so as to have an opportunity of trying it.[31]

On June 8, 1849, the ax fell. "I am turned out of office!" he wrote to Hillard. Concerned at first about his immediate familial and economic problems, he was ready to accept any kind of "subordinate office": "I shall not stand upon my dignity: that must take care of itself." Later that day, if his son's account can be trusted, Hawthorne informed Sophia that "he had left his head behind him. 'Oh, then,' exclaimed Mrs. Hawthorne, buoyantly, 'you can write your book!'" When he mentioned the need of money for bread and butter, she informed him that she had set aside a small sum each week for the past three years.[32]

Sophia reported to her father that Hawthorne "never liked the office at all, & is rather relieved than otherwise that it is taken out of his hands. . . . As for me you know I am composed of Hope & Faith." As Sophia proceeded in her letter, she made over reality to accord to her "Hope & Faith": "I have not seen my husband happier than since this turning out. He has felt in chains for a long time & being a *man* [underscored three times], he is not alarmed at being set upon his own feet again—or on his *head*, I might say, for that contains the available gold—of a mine scarcely yet worked at all."[33]

Sophia shortly changed her euphoric tone when she learned that her husband was far from resigned about what he considered his "decapita-

tion." The charges which had been bandied about for months were for-
mulated in a communication to William Meredith, the secretary of the
treasury—that Hawthorne had written political articles for newspapers
and magazines and had, despite his denials, actively participated in party
affairs and that many irregularities had been uncovered in the Custom-
House during his surveyorship, although he may not personally have
been responsible. The first two charges were without substantiation, and
the third indicated at most incompetency rather than dereliction of duty.
Since the document was signed, the controversy now had specific villains
who were, in Sophia's words, "covering themselves & each other with the
hopeless mud of Dante's Inferno." [34]

The most influential signer, everybody judged, was Charles W. Upham, who, in Sophia's opinion, was "a liar & a most consumate hypocrite,"
a betrayer of the frock. What rankled the Hawthornes was that eleven
years earlier Upham had been more than a casual acquaintance. In
1838 they exchanged inscribed copies of recently published works, Hawthorne's being the reprint of "The Gentle Boy" illustrated by Sophia. [35]

Among the signers of the document, Sophia singled out for special censure Nathaniel Silsbee, Jr., the mayor of Salem and "a man of the smallest scope, narrow & stingy to the last degree," and she called George H.
Devereux, whose sister was Silsbee's wife, "a furious demagogue, & a
most rancorous spirit in all points . . . venomous against Mr Hawthorne
on account of an ancient feud between Hawthorne & Devereux!" Apparently she referred to Hawthorne's relationship with Mary Silsbee Sparks
eleven years earlier. [36]

Primarily through the efforts of Hillard, prominent Whigs such as Rufus Choate, W. H. Prescott, and Daniel Webster wrote to Meredith urging that the ouster be rescinded. Hillard also persuaded Edward Everett,
the master of florid oratory and at this time president of Harvard College, to write to Meredith. On June 25 Everett confessed that he could
not "personally feel much sympathy for gentlemen like Mr Hawthorne,
men of education and letters, who think proper to attach themselves to
the radical party" but considered his removal "an ill-considered step."
Two days later he reversed his position because he had learned, probably
from Upham, that Hawthorne had allowed himself to be used for party
purposes so "as to destroy all claim to neutrality." [37]

Shortly before the Whig group prepared a memorial to Meredith on
July 6, introducing new charges of mismanagement through neglect or

naïveté, Hawthorne began to have doubts as to the wisdom of a protracted controversy. Serious but politically motivated allegations appeared in the memorial, along with aspersions and innuendos about Hawthorne's conduct, but toward the conclusion of the document Upham drew back to assert that Hawthorne had been, "to a great extent, the abused instrument of others. . . . His entire ignorance, previous to his appointment, of matters of business, his inexperience of the stratagems of political managers, and the very slight interest which his thoughts could take in such things, have made him less conscious of the part he has performed, than almost any other man would have been." Upham's explanation, ingenious as it was, never salved Hawthorne's wounded ego.[38]

Although it was a fact of American political life that heads fell when administrations changed, the Salem incident attracted widespread attention and confirmed that Hawthorne's reputation had outpaced the sales of his books. Except for the local newspapers, the press treated Hawthorne sympathetically, as an Owen Warland battling against the philistines. The *Philadelphia Evening Bulletin* devoted little space to the political details of the controversy, which were of no great consequence to its readers, but emphasized the usefulness of governmental patronage to "a worthy man like Hawthorne": "It is not our politicians, not even our statesmen, who are forming the minds of the next generation: it is the men who write the books, which millions will read, and whose influence millions will follow." If the nineteenth century sometimes appeared to wax oratorical at the drop of the pen, or the voice, it managed to keep its values and priorities clear, and the media respected rather than exploited the nation's artists.[39]

Aggrieved and deeply wounded, Hawthorne did not bury his anger when he left office. In the preface to *The Scarlet Letter* he refers (in caps) to the "POSTHUMOUS PAPERS OF A DECAPITATED SURVEYOR."

   In July 1849, Mrs. Hawthorne, now sixty-nine years old and a widow of forty-one years, became ill. There were days of "excessive agony, relieved by intervals of unconsciousness." Sophia, Elizabeth, Louisa, and Priscilla Dike, Mrs. Hawthorne's sister, took turns caring for her. They kept off the flies and held her to provide what comfort they could. Hawthorne saw his mother infrequently; the pain was too great.

In this crisis as in others Sophia bore a heavy, unequal burden. The children were permitted to visit their grandmother only at intervals. They usually remained downstairs with a servant or their father, troubled in their own way as for the first time they encountered the ultimate separation, and they were eager, desperately eager, to assert continuity.

On July 29 Una complained, whined, and teased "about her hair, which had not been combed and put in order this morning—everybody being busy with grandmamma." Una needed the customary order and attention to clarify the situation, to reestablish her niche as well as her importance. When Sophia entered the room briefly that morning, Julian begged to visit his grandmother but was refused. He demanded and received a kiss while he again pleaded.

In this period of stocktaking, Hawthorne, perhaps the most troubled of the observers, put things in order in the only way he knew, in his notebook, and summed up the life of his three-year-old son:

> Julian has too much tenderness, love, and sensibility in his nature; he needs to be hardened and tempered. I would not take a particle of the love out of him; but methinks it is highly desirable that some sterner quality should be interfused throughout the softness of his heart; else, in course of time, the hard intercourse of the world, and the many knocks and bruises he will receive, will cause a morbid crust of callousness to grow over his heart; so that, for at least a portion of his life, he will have less sympathy and love for his fellow-beings than those who began life with a much smaller portion.

Unwittingly, Hawthorne wrote not about Julian but about a forty-five-year-old son who was about to become an orphan. He compared the death of a child, when "Nature . . . destroys her own prettiest plaything," with death in age, when "there is so much gloom and ambiguity about it, that it opens no vistas for us into Heaven." As his mother's beauty faded, he experienced at firsthand, when he could bring himself to enter her chamber, the transformation he feared all his life, the loss of beauty to disease and death. A year before he had observed to Longfellow, "Ten years more will go near to make us venerable men; and I doubt whether it will be so pleasant to meet, when each friend shall be a memento of decay to the other."[40]

Una was allowed in her grandmother's room on the 29th and fanned away the flies. Then she explained how sick grandmother was to Julian, who wanted to see her and "stroak her." Shortly, putting death in the back of their minds, or seeming to, they played with a "black, crested hen" (which reappeared in the description of Hepzibah in *The House of the Seven Gables*).

At about five o'clock Hawthorne went to see his mother for the first time in two days. The "alteration" shocked him. In act and then in his notebook he relived the despairs and inevitabilities of a lifetime and found what solace there is in releasing incarcerated feelings.

> I love my mother; but there has been, ever since my boyhood, a sort of coldness of intercourse between us, such as is apt to come between persons of strong feelings, if they are not managed rightly. I did not expect to be much moved at the time—that is to say, not to feel any overpowering emotion struggling, just then—though I knew that I should deeply remember and regret her. . . . I was moved to kneel down close by my mother, and take her hand. She knew me, but could only murmur a few indistinct words—among which I under- stood an injunction to take care of my sisters. . . . and then I found the tears slowly gathering in my eyes. I tried to keep them down; but it would not be—I kept filling up, till, for a few moments, I shook with sobs. For a long time, I knelt there, holding her hand; and surely it is the darkest hour I ever lived.

Shortly Hawthorne rose, stood at an open window, "and looked through the crevice of the curtain." Once again Paul Pry seeking per- spective through distance and disengagement, he heard what for a few moments in grief he had blocked out—the laughter and cries of his chil- dren below. He saw Una's "golden locks" and then turned to look again at his mother. "Oh what a mockery, if what I saw were all," he thought, as he re-created in words a balancing perspective. Soon he heard Una's voice "very clear and distinct. . . . 'Yes;—she is going to die!' I wish she had said 'going to God'—which is her idea and usual expression of death; it would have been so hopeful and comforting, uttered in that bright young voice."

On the following day Hawthorne's mother grew weaker and was con- scious only for brief periods. Julian was below playing in the yard. Una, Hawthorne observed, took "a strong and strange interest in poor moth- er's condition" and teased to be permitted into the chamber. He noted her "intense curiosity" and her "natural affection," which troubled him, though having experienced death at any early age himself he perhaps should have realized the effects upon the young. It was now Una's turn to be evaluated by her father.

> . . . there is something that almost frightens me about the child—I know not whether elfish or angelic, but, at all events, supernatural. She steps so boldly into the midst of everything, shrinks from nothing, . . . seems at times to have but little delicacy, and anon shows that she possesses the finest essence of it; now so hard, now so tender; now so perfectly unreasonable, soon again so wise. In short, I now and then catch an aspect of her, in which I cannot believe her to be my own human child, but a spirit strangely mingled with good and evil, haunting the house where I dwell.

In the afternoon the children, who were never permitted to leave the Mall Street house unless accompanied by an adult, acted out what was taking place in the bedroom above. Una and Julian played all the roles—grandmother, mother, and doctor, changing abruptly from one to another in accordance with whim and boredom. Soon there were two doctors present, one allopathic, the other homeopathic, as Una mirrored Sophia's convictions about the two medical fashions of the age. After a jest about "this instantaneous conversion from allopathy to homeopathy," Hawthorne, his defenses exhausted, wrote nothing more in his journal about "the darkest hour." That task now fell to Sophia.

There was no visible suffering as Mrs. Hawthorne hour by hour gradually faded. "I thought," Sophia confessed, "I could not stay through the final hours—but found myself courageous for Louisa's & Elizabeth's sakes." The mother sighed for the last time and journeyed into unconsciousness, the final destination at hand. On the following day she died.

Nathaniel had "a brain fever" and "Elizabeth & Louisa are desolate beyond all words," Sophia informed her mother. "We all have lost an angel of excellence & in mind & person an angel." Apparently alone, Sophia was left to perform "the saddest most terrible offices" after death. "But she looks so heavenly sweet, calm, happy, peaceful, that I cannot see Death in her now—I only *hear* Death as I stand over her, for what else can such silence be?"[41]

Elizabeth Manning Hawthorne was buried on August 2 at four o'clock, not with the Hathornes in the Charter Street Burying Point, but a short distance away in the Howard Street Cemetery, where eventually she would be joined by Louisa and Elizabeth.

Despite the pain and the ambivalence that he could not put to rest, life continued for the "decapitated surveyor" and newly created orphan. Upham's innuendos about his conduct in the Salem Custom-House irritated. Though he had "no expectation," he maintained to Horace Mann, of "regaining" the surveyorship, he sought an opportunity to defend himself. "Then, if Mr. Upham should give me occasion—or perhaps if he should not—I shall do my best to kill and scalp him in the public prints; and I think I shall succeed." (At this point Hawthorne was apparently so bloodthirsty that Sophia excised the rest of the passage.) This resolution he would fulfill at the end of the following year in the pages of *The House of the Seven Gables* in the character of Judge Pyncheon, a pompous politician whom death robs of the governorship of the state.[42]

His mother had been buried less than a week when Hawthorne declared himself ready to "bid farewell forever to this abominable city; for now that my mother is gone, I have no longer anything to keep me here." On August 22 he admitted to being "in a very unsettled condition, and am looking about me for a country or sea-shore residence, for the sake of economy and quiet." Putting down roots elsewhere proved no easy matter. Horatio Bridge wanted the Hawthornes near him, and they journeyed to Kittery, Maine. They also looked in Manchester, which is only a few miles away from Salem, and at different times Sophia and Hawthorne went to the Berkshires at the suggestion of Samuel G. Ward and Caroline Sturgis, who was now married to William A. Tappan. They negotiated for rentals in Lenox only to have plans collapse at the last moment. In February 1850 they still had no place to move to, although they planned to be rid of Salem by April or May. Toward the end of March they found a small red farmhouse near Lenox.[43]

While they searched for another home, there were the demands of daily existence which had to be met mostly from Sophia's small savings. In September 1849 O'Sullivan paid $100 of his long-standing debt, and Sophia informed her mother, "We have access to another hundred if we want it before we earn it. So do not be anxious for us in a pecuniary way." Although given in joy to hyperbole, in difficult times Sophia was careful not to arouse other people unnecessarily. She began to decorate lamp shades and screens with classical and literary scenes derived from her old master, Flaxman, and Elizabeth Peabody found orders for Sophia among Boston friends. While Sophia worked at least three hours a day in order to produce income and to free her husband from economic problems so that he could write, Louisa and Elizabeth grieved over the loss of their mother. Their only contribution was to agree not to move until the following summer. "This," Sophia explained, "would simplify our lives very much in the first struggle for bread; for they cannot help us possibly,—we only must help them. Louisa is not in strong health enough to do anything, and it would be a pain to me to see her making the efforts; and Elizabeth is not available for every-day purposes of pot-hooks and trammels, spits and flat-irons." Whatever the circumstances, Elizabeth went her own way, elusive and aloof, self-imprisoned in her chamber, where, perhaps in rivalry with her brother, she translated Cervantes' tales, a lifelong project that was never completed.[44]

On January 13, 1850, James Russell Lowell informed Evert Duyckinck that Hawthorne's friends in New England were raising money to assist him and suggested that a similar campaign be undertaken in New York. On January 17 Hillard provided Hawthorne with what he called "a little pecuniary care" and urged: "Let no shadow of despondency, my dear friend, steal over you. Your friends do not and will not forget you. You shall be protected against 'eating cares,' which, I take it, mean cares lest we should not have enough to eat." The euphemisms and pedantic jests were part of the tact of a century that appreciated and worked at friendships and understood the emotive powers of language.[45]

The letter, Hawthorne admitted, brought "the water to my eyes; so that I was glad of the sharply cold west wind that blew into them as I came homeward, and gave them an excuse for being red and bleared." The offer touched off emotions of gratitude, shame, and concern for his manhood. In attempting to explain his reaction to Hillard's gesture, Hawthorne revealed with unusual candor the exacting creed by which he lived—and punished himself.

There was much that was very sweet—and something too that was very bitter—mingled with that same moisture. It is sweet to be remembered and cared for by one's friends—some of whom know me for what I am, while others, perhaps, know me only through a generous faith—sweet to think that they deem me worth upholding in my poor walk through life. And it is bitter, nevertheless, to need their support. It is something else besides pride that teaches me that ill-success in life is really and justly a matter of shame. I am ashamed of it, and I ought to be. The fault of a failure is attributable—in a great degree, at least—to the man who fails. I should apply this truth in judging of other men; and it behooves me not to shun its point or edge in taking it home to my own heart. Nobody has a right to live in this world, unless he be strong and able, and applies his ability to good purposes.

The self-evaluation was worthy of an Arthur Dimmesdale, whose painful final hours he was recording in the manuscript of *The Scarlet Letter* as he wrote to Hillard.[46]

When Hawthorne repaid the loan on December 9, 1853, "with interest included," he expressed his gratitude that "anybody thought it worth while to keep me from sinking. And it did me even greater good than this, in making me sensible of the necessity of sterner efforts than my former ones, in order to establish a right for myself to live and be comfortable. For it is my creed . . . that a man has no claim upon his fellow creatures, beyond bread and water, and a grave, unless he can win it by his own strength or skill." Hawthorne never put to rest his fears of poverty.[47]

Almost a year after his official "decapitation" and the publication of *The Scarlet Letter,* his feelings toward Salem and its inhabitants had not changed. He delighted in his (imaginary) martyrdom: "I wish they *would* tar-and-feather me—it would be such an entirely novel kind of distinction for a literary man!" He fantasized himself in the role of Major Molineux, who, overthrown and humiliated in a public spectacle, triumphs over the townspeople in his "tar-and-feathery dignity" as he sacrifices himself and spares his craven kinsman. Perhaps Hawthorne came closest to the truth when he thanked Conolly, his "pet serpent," for helping to have him "kicked out": "I came forth as fresh as if I had been just made, and went to work as if the devil were in me, if it were only to put my enemies to the blush." He assured Conolly, a former minister: "Certainly I must say it for myself there is the least gall and animosity in my nature, and the greatest and sweetest quantity of the milk of human kindness, that ever existed in any son of Adam. I am a true Christian and the only one I ever met with. . . . There is one Christian in the world and I am he."[48]

"The people of Salem," he declaimed in another mood, "certainly do not deserve good usage at my hands, after permitting me—(their most distinguished citizen; for they have no other that was ever heard of beyond the limits of the Congressional district)—after permitting me to be deliberately lied down, not merely once, but at two separate attacks, on two false indictments, without hardly a voice being raised in my behalf." He never quite forgave Salem and its citizens, but he never forgot them either. Emotions are rarely uncomplicated, and in "The Custom-House" he freely expresses his ambivalence: "Though invariably happiest elsewhere, there is within me a feeling for old Salem, which, in lack of a better phrase, I must be content to call affection." It was, after all, the town of his ancestors, of Hathorne dust, as he explains: "In part, therefore, the attachment which I speak of is the mere sensuous sympathy of dust for dust."[49]

And so as he prepared to say "farewell forever to this abominable city," he wrote his greatest romance and became in fact Salem's "most distinguished citizen."

21

Intercourse with the World

The Scarlet Letter

One of Hawthorne's most fanciful tales is his account in the preface to *The Scarlet Letter* of how one day in an upper room of the Salem Custom-House he found a "mysterious package" with "a certain affair of fine red cloth, much worn and faded," which turned out to be the letter A, "precisely three inches and a quarter in length." He found himself hypnotized. "My eyes fastened themselves upon the old scarlet letter, and would not turn aside." With the letter he discovered a manuscript describing the lot and life of a Mistress Hester Prynne, whose adulterous transgression in Puritan Boston two centuries earlier had led to a twofold punishment—exposure on the town scaffold for three hours and the wearing of the red A on her bosom.

"The Custom-House" is as much a romance as the tale that follows. The truth, as revealed in his notebooks, is that for more than a decade Hawthorne had been haunted by a tale of a woman whose punishment for adultery was to wear an A on her breast as an advertisement of her sinfulness. There were also historical records that among his Manning ancestors of the seventeenth century two sisters had to sit in the Salem meetinghouse with bands about their foreheads identifying their incestuous misconduct, while their brother, Captain Nicholas Manning, hid in the Maine woods.

In the foreword Hawthorne claims, with a fib worthy of Huck Finn, that the manuscript he found was written by a predecessor at the Custom-House, surveyor Jonathan Pue, an amiable fellow with a name that no doubt tickled Hawthorne's somewhat ribald sense of humor. Delighting in his whim-wham, he adopts Pue as a "father" to whom he performs "my filial duty, and reverence towards him,—who might reasonably regard himself as my official ancestor." The playfulness conceals his seriousness. In the romance the absence of a father is a terrible void in Pearl's life, as it was in Hawthorne's own life. This solemn pronouncement of sonhood, then, provides him with a Good Father to replace his two ancestors, William and John Hathorne, who reappear in "The Custom-House" in their customary roles of Bad Fathers, as censorious of his frivolous dedication to romance and art as the Puritan community is of Hester Prynne.[1]

In his preface Hawthorne describes the creative process with affectionate mockery which at the same time accepts and questions the tenets of both romanticism and the romantic artist. He creates the aura of romance while he jests that what he is about to create is but "the semblance of a world out of airy matter, when, at every moment, the impalpable beauty of my soap-bubble was broken by the rude contact of some actual circumstance." In his witticism he manages simultaneously to disparage and to hint at the beauties of his art in the rainbow colors of soap bubbles. He claims that in his deep involvement in the story of Hester Prynne, he paced the floors of the Custom-House and interfered with naps of his fellow employees, who "used to say that the Surveyor was walking the quarter-deck"—a barb which disguises the association with the only important sea captain in his life, Captain Nathaniel Hathorne.

Repeatedly he admits, almost insists, that the book wears "a stern and sombre aspect," not unlike the faces and costumes of those dour Puritans dedicated to God, Discipline, and Duty. Their sobriety "is no indication, however, of a lack of cheerfulness in the writer's mind; for he was happier, while straying through the gloom of those sunless fantasies, than at any time since he quitted the Old Manse." Here Hawthorne varnishes reality somewhat and simplifies for public consumption the complexity of the creation of his masterpiece. In the period during which he wrote *The Scarlet Letter*, from after his mother's death until February 2, 1850, when he read the final pages to Sophia, his emotional-intellectual state vibrated as intensely as the scarlet letter on Hester's bosom. Despite the disguise of the wit, his reference to himself as "A DECAPITATED SUR-VEYOR" at the conclusion of "The Custom-House" indicates the depth of the hurt.

In addition, his mother's death had recalled old wounds and unsated hungers, and he would memorialize her by creating a woman worthy of America, of American literature, and, most important, of his fantasy of motherhood. In hate and in love he wrote, in Sophia's words, "immensely," for many hours each day, in a kind of frenzy. Sophia admitted to being "almost frightened about it. . . . he has written vehemently morning & afternoon & has not walked as much as he used to do. He has become tender from confinement & brain work." Sophia did not exaggerate. Written in the aftermath of two wrenching hurts, the book took a toll.[2]

Anxious that the tone was too unrelieved and bleak for public taste, he planned to make *The Scarlet Letter* the centerpiece in a new collection of tales in which he would include such recent works as "The Great Stone Face" and "Ethan Brand" as well as some uncollected pieces. He toyed with such titles as *Old-Time Legends, Together with Sketches, Experimental and Ideal.* When his new publisher, James T. Fields, insisted that the book include only *The Scarlet Letter*, Hawthorne, still not trustful either of his art or of his great romance, replied:

> Is it safe, then, to stake the fate of the book entirely on this one chance? A hunter loads his gun with a bullet and several buck-shot; and, following his sagacious example, it was my purpose to conjoin the one long story with half a dozen shorter ones; so that, failing to kill the public outright with my biggest and heaviest lump of lead, I might have other chances with the smaller bits, individually and in the aggregate.[3]

On a visit to Salem late in 1849, so the apocryphal story goes, Fields asked whether Hawthorne had any manuscripts he could examine. Hawthorne said no. As Fields was going down the steps, Hawthorne called him back and handed him, bashfully and almost secretively, a substantial manuscript which he had removed from a desk drawer. Fields began to read the manuscript on the train to Boston and could scarcely contain his excitement.

Probably Hawthorne met Fields at the Old Corner Bookstore while he was at the Boston Custom-House. A little man of substantial girth, Fields was one of the colorful figures of the era, an amateur poet given to undistinguished commemorative verse, a raconteur of great charm, an effective performer on the lyceum circuit, and eventually the host in the most distinguished literary salon in America, on Charles Street in Boston. Fields's geniality veiled the tragedies of his life. His father, like Hawthorne's a sea captain, died of fever when Fields was not quite three. As soon as Fields stepped aboard a ship, he became violently ill. At fourteen he left Portsmouth, New Hampshire, to work at the Old Corner Bookstore, where he began his long association with William D. Ticknor, who eventually made him a partner in Ticknor and Fields. For several decades the firm was perhaps the most celebrated in America, a house with such authors as Longfellow, Holmes, Whittier, Tennyson, and later Dickens, all of whom appeared in probably the most pedestrian bindings of the age. Fields, in addition to his other talents, was one of the most successful and shrewd book promoters at a time when bribes for reviews and other shoddy practices were a way of life among publishers and newspapers.[4]

Hawthorne enjoyed an unusually harmonious relationship with Fields. "I care more for your good opinion," he wrote, "than for that of a host of critics, and have excellent reason for so doing; inasmuch as my literary success, whatever it has been or may be, is the result of my connection with you."[5]

Although Hawthorne worked on his manuscript "immensely," there were delays and obstacles. There was the embarrassment of their economic lot—he was fiercely proud—and Sophia was ill during parts of December and January. Hawthorne needed an ideal environment, free of distractions and the usual clutter of living, but somehow he managed. About the middle of January 1850 he sent Fields all but the last few chapters, "one end being in the press in Boston," as he explained to Bridge, "while the other was in my head here in Salem—so that, as you see, the story is at least fourteen miles long."[6]

In one of the most gracious and extended commentaries written by one artist about the works of another, Henry James compared Hawthorne's artistry in *The Scarlet Letter* to that of a silversmith. James recognized, and perhaps envied as a great artist must in his rivalry with a literary father, the delicacy of Hawthorne's strokes in the evocation of characters and the Puritan ambience. But James's analogy may have limitations, for, in addition to exquisite visual and psychological details, *The Scarlet Letter* unfolds a narrative of an adulterous woman, her lover, her husband, and her child—Hester Prynne, the Reverend Arthur Dimmesdale, Roger Chillingworth, and Pearl—with the clarity and grandeur of a tapestry in which people are important both in their own right and as members of a community.

Hawthorne places the soul-wracking, emotionally debilitating deprivations of these four characters in a linear structure dominated by three scenes that take place at the town scaffold: the midday public censure and exposure of Hester and Pearl; the midnight scene seven years later when Arthur Dimmesdale goes there stealthily in the darkness to proclaim his guilt while everyone is sleeping; and the final tableau on Election Day when the clergyman confesses, or seems to, to the paternity of Pearl. Literally and visually the scaffold functions as a pole that asserts the power of society and a patriarchal religion to check emotional excess and natural drives and at the same time serves as an artistic curb upon exploding emotions. In *The Eight Poles*, Jackson Pollock achieves a similar visual and emotional effect when his eight verticals contain the restless squiggles of his paints and feelings and introduce a semblance of rational order in a churning, perhaps disintegrating, environment.

Hawthorne handles the colors, the crowds, and the movements with the skill of a tapestry artist or, among his literary forebears, of James Fenimore Cooper, whose genius in depicting public occasions and assemblies rarely receives its due. In compliance with her punishment but in defiance of the authorities, Hester embroiders an A of exotic form with red and gold threads that vibrates and gleams in sunlight, arouses various responses depending upon the fantasies of viewers, and shifts in its public meaning from Adultery, a word which is never used in the book, to Angel, in recognition of her self-sacrificing services to the community that ostracizes her. The letter on her bosom fluctuates endlessly and ambiguously like life itself, never achieving stasis or repose until the last line of the romance. Hawthorne's art frames Hester's in a larger embroidery. Visually, verbally, symbolically, and emotionally, Hawthorne relates a story as bewitching as the A on Hester's bosom about four people who suffer for seven years after a moment of passion presumably at the edge of the forest where Hester and Dimmesdale free their bodies to express irresistible needs.

In a peculiarly Hawthornesque fashion that unveils, but secretively, his conflicts and contradictions as well as his skeptical intelligence and defensive wit, *The Scarlet Letter* blends what formally and traditionally are not usually blended: satire, comedy, tragedy, psychology, and autobiography. Hawthorne intrudes at will in his work, careless of point of view and other technical concerns more important to critics than to artists, in order to shatter novelistic illusions for his own ends.

Blooming in front of the prison is a wild-rose bush, which surreptitiously juxtaposes nature's fertility and civilization's preoccupation with repression and anticipates in color and in function the embroidered letter Hester wears on her breast. Playfully Hawthorne chooses to "pluck one of its flowers and present it to the reader." The erotic nature of the gesture is confirmed later when Pearl is said to have been "plucked by her mother off the bush of wild roses, that grew by the prison-door." Authorial intrusions and puns—Hawthorne is in his art as duplicitous and seductive as Dimmesdale in his sermons—ordinarily belong to comedy rather than to tragedy, to *Don Quixote* rather than to *Hamlet*, but *The Scarlet Letter*, like the other great works of America's coming of literary age in the 1850s, refuses to bow to usual modes and asserts its uniqueness.

Artistically, as Hawthorne recognized, the fluidity achieved by mixing genres and modes matches the fluidity of the emotional ranges of characters who, despite superficial resemblances to gothic types, gyrate from exhilarated highs to suicidal despair. The changing perceptions of the characters also require freedom from formula. The verbal games were perhaps Hawthorne's defense against the affect of the materials he dealt with in the romance, as well as evidence of his delight in the dual maternal-paternal role of the artist. When he was fully engaged and completely in control, he indulged that sense of playfulness, as in "My Kinsman, Major Molineux" and "Young Goodman Brown," that asserts the pleasure and life principles against the tyrannies of society and iron-willed Puritan monomaniacs, thus placing his hell-fired subject matter in perspective. It was his way of establishing a balance, necessarily precarious, between contradictory moods, uncertain life attitudes, and irrelevant genres.

Hawthorne ventured farther than any of his predecessors or contemporaries in America into the labyrinths of the unconscious or the inner landscape. He understood and attempted to render nonverbal communication and the internal drama which are externalized in tics, compulsive gestures, and illnesses. His characters speak in glances or by means of averted eye contact. Hester walks upright, proud of her womanhood; Pearl flits about like a bird, joyful but frightened; Chillingworth moves haltingly, the left shoulder higher than the other; and Dimmesdale, glancing sideways, holds his hand tremulously to his breast. Their limitations as well as their futures are suggested in their physical motions. Their perceptions shift seemingly without reason or plan, influenced by unstated needs out of the past and its deprivations, by reactions to the present containment, and by fantasies and dreams which are understandable attempts to shape the future.

There is perhaps no more perfect work of the American imagination, as D. H. Lawrence suggests, than *The Scarlet Letter*. The portrait of Hester Prynne with the A on her breast has stamped itself on our consciousness indelibly, and the letter resonates socially, historically, aesthetically, and, above all, humanly. The romance transcends the puritanical time and space in which it is set to offer a universal commentary on human needs and the discontents of civilization.

The Scarlet Letter unfolds a tale in which the participants, having suffered grievous deprivations and rejections, search for roots, love and nurturing, and a society in which the patriarchal code is humanized by matriarchal values. Mistress Hibbins, the Evil Mother, wants us to believe that witches and demons hover over the land with mad, destructive purposes, but she embodies the nightmare of patriarchy and the debasement of women. Hawthorne's romance focuses not on such aberrations and perversions of human potential and love but on the breast, symbol of fertility, nurturing, and creativity.

When Hester, holding her child Pearl "closely to her breast," ascends the scaffold to endure three hours of humiliation for her violation of the moral code of Boston, she transforms the occasion into a moment of apotheosis.

On the breast of her gown, in fine red cloth, surrounded with an elaborate embroidery and fantastic flourishes of gold thread, appeared the letter A. It was so artistically done, and with so much fertility, and gorgeous luxuriance of fancy, that it had all the effect of a last and fitting decoration to the apparel which she wore; and which was of a splendor in accordance with the taste of the age, but greatly beyond what was allowed by the sumptuary regulations of the colony.

The five hundred spectators only dimly appreciate this woman "with a figure of perfect elegance, on a large scale," either not perceiving or being reluctant to recognize her mythic and epic grandeur. "The point which drew all eyes, and, as it were, transfigured the wearer, . . . was that SCARLET LETTER, so fantastically embroidered and illuminated upon her bosom. It had the effect of a spell taking her out of the ordinary relations with humanity, and inclosing her in a sphere by herself."

When the romance is felt as well as understood, when we open out our feelings, shedding our intellectual interpretations and defenses, it has the effect of the convex mirror in the mansion of Governor Bellingham, where "the scarlet letter was represented in exaggerated and gigantic proportions, so as to be greatly the most prominent feature of her appearance." The visual and emotional effect is similar to that of the gigantic breasts created by Gaston Lachaise, the sculptor whose art, like Hawthorne's, confirms the longing for the maternal bosom and the security of matriarchy.

The opening scene of the romance is brilliantly staged. There on a bare elevated platform is the pillory, in the words of Jean Normand, "a masochistic symbol of delight in misfortune. It is also a deformed cross, hideously seeking to embody human suffering." About the platform mill leering, sadistic townspeople and visitors and, in a biting touch, big-bosomed Puritan matrons who violate maternity in their verbal abuse of Hester and her child, deploring the leniency of the magistrates to the whore of Babylon. On the balcony above the pillory sit three men, Governor Bellingham, Pastor Wilson, and the Reverend Dimmesdale, the custodians of the political and religious patriarchy.[7]

Hester with her child at her breast endures "the heavy weight of a thousand unrelenting eyes, all fastened upon her, and concentred at her bosom. It was almost intolerable to be borne." The situation repeats Hawthorne's account of his discovery of the manuscript in the Custom-House: "My eyes fastened themselves upon the old scarlet letter, and would not be turned aside."

Suddenly, and with the wickedness of a Melville or a Whitman, Hawthorne, knowing that Raphael's Madonna was in his day revered above all other paintings, avers that Hester recalls "the image of Divine Maternity, which so many illustrious painters have vied with one another to represent." An adulteress is elevated to the role of Madonna in Puritanland! The three-month-old child—in appearance an extension of the letter and in emotions a mirror of the mother—clings to the breast. Since she is human in her needs though mythic in her presence, Hester, seeking to protect the cowardly father from exposure and her erotic fulfillment from public scrutiny, temporarily forgets Pearl and her needs, until the baby cries out for what she is denied: Hester "strove to hush it, mechanically, but seemed scarcely to sympathize with its trouble." If Pearl hungers for love, so too do Hester, Dimmesdale, and Chillingworth.[8]

Among the eyes fastened on Hester are those of her husband, who has assumed the name of Roger Chillingworth, a kind of itinerant doctor who is no more able now to love and to act except in his own self-interest than he was when he persuaded Hester's parents to consent to the marriage of their daughter to a man old enough to be her father. Not long after the family-arranged marriage, against Hester's desires, he fled the marital bed in search of medicinal potions in the American wilderness. Like Arthur Dimmesdale, who is to shelter himself in the pulpit and in a bachelor existence, and like all the other frightened males in Hawthorne's writings, Chillingworth is unable to cope with a woman's sexual drives. Chillingworth's eyes are "dim and bleared by the lamp-light" of the school, but they possess "a strange, penetrating power . . . to read the human soul," without empathy, however. In order to play, more than a little hypocritically, the betrayed husband or cuckold, he abandons Hester once again, this time to public violation: "A whole people, drawn forth as to a festival, staring at the features that should have been seen only in the quiet gleam of the fireside, in the happy shadow of a home, or beneath a matronly veil, at church."

At the urging of his superiors Dimmesdale rises and "with a startled, a half-frightened look" asks Hester to name the father of her child. "Even the poor baby, at Hester's bosom, . . . directed its hitherto vacant gaze towards Mr. Dimmesdale, and held up its little arms, with a half pleased, half plaintive murmur." Three times Dimmesdale, in his "tremulously sweet, rich, deep, and broken" voice, begs Hester to reveal the identity of the father "who, perchance, hath not the courage." Three times Hester refuses to betray him.

Later that evening the cuckolded husband, his identity still a secret, comes to quiet the agitated mother and child. After confessing that he has wronged Hester in marrying and then deserting her, he "laid his long forefinger on the scarlet letter, which forthwith seemed to scorch into Hester's breast, as if it had been red-hot." Again the romance repeats almost literally Hawthorne's account of his discovery of the letter in the attic of the Custom-House: "I happened to place it on my breast. It seemed to me,—the reader may smile, but must not doubt my word,—it seemed to me, then, that I experienced a sensation not altogether physical, yet almost so, as of burning heat; and as if the letter were not of red cloth, but red-hot iron. I shuddered, and involuntarily let it fall upon the floor." The A, real or imaginary, also burns on Dimmesdale's breast.

For the next seven years Hester and Pearl live alone in a small cottage at the edge of the settlement. The mother receives no visitors, and the child has no playmates. Mother and daughter are unusually close, but the closeness creates problems as the child eventually senses that the A is the cause of their banishment, and the mother, with no one to offer her solace or guidance, is sometimes evasive in handling her daughter's questions. One day Pearl flings "handfuls of wild-flowers" at her mother's breast, "dancing up and down like a little elf, whenever she hit the scarlet letter." While the child acts out her anger, which is not untinged with love, Hester at first seeks to shield herself but then sits passively, hands at her side, in "penance" to the child who is compelled to share her ostracism and her "sin." Suddenly she "half playfully" pretends to reject the child, who, however, perceives at once that her mother wants to tell her something, to unburden her heart. It is a scene of great sensitivity and insight.

"Thou art not my child! Thou art no Pearl of mine!" said the mother, half playfully; for it was often the case that a sportive impulse came over her, in the midst of her deepest suffering. "Tell me, then, what thou art, and who sent thee hither?"

"Tell me, mother!" said the child, seriously, coming up to Hester, and pressing herself close to her knees. "Do thou tell me!"

"Thy Heavenly Father sent thee!" answered Hester Prynne.

But she said it with a hesitation that did not escape the acuteness of the child. Whether moved only by her ordinary freakishness, or because an evil spirit prompted her, she put up her small forefinger, and touched the scarlet letter.

"He did not send me!" cried she, positively. "I have no Heavenly Father."

Because Hester's evasion is a deception, Pearl touches the emblem on the breast as coldly and skeptically as Chillingworth.

When the narrative shifts to Arthur Dimmesdale, the emphasis remains still on the breast, for the clergyman walks, eyes lowered, often in a Geneva cloak such as Hawthorne himself wore, with one hand held to his bosom. Because of Dimmesdale's mysterious maladies, Chillingworth, with the congregation's and the minister's approval, occupies an adjoining room in a house that overlooks the cemetery at King's Chapel in Boston. There, unknowingly, the cuckolder and the cuckolded live together in a seven-year relationship which, as Robert Penn Warren points out, is the only one in the romance that approximates, but at the same time parodies, marriage. Burdened with secrets, theirs is an uneasy relationship, as indicated in the wavering, sporadic use of the "thou" form, and they keep each other at a distance—Chillingworth retreating to his laboratory and Dimmesdale to his study. Themselves deceivers, both lack trust, but at the same time each needs the other. On the wall of Dimmesdale's study is a tapestry of David and Bathsheba, the old king comforted in age by a young wife, which comments on the relationship of a doctor old enough to be the preacher's father. Dimmesdale's health gradually declines although he suffers from no disease or physical symptoms, but Chillingworth intuits that there is some correlation between Dimmesdale's physical and emotional states.[9]

Then one day "it came to pass"—the cadence is biblical—that at "noonday," the time of Hester's exposure in the marketplace, Dimmesdale falls asleep in his chair. Chillingworth thrusts aside the vestment— "Mr. Dimmesdale shuddered, and slightly stirred"—and over the physician's face passes "a wild look of wonder, joy, and horror!" Incapable, like Milton's Satan, of abandoning his self-destructive course, Chillingworth decides to wait and to arouse further the anxiety of a man already given to self-flagellation. The decision may serve Chillingworth's desire for revenge, but his exploitation of Dimmesdale's vulnerability creates sympathy for and deflects attention from the minister's self-interested pursuit of his career at the expense of mother and child. While Hester and Pearl live in isolation, shunned by townspeople, Dimmesdale is venerated by his congregation.

At midnight on an "obscure night of early May," Dimmesdale, always preoccupied with his public image, dresses himself carefully as though he is about to deliver a sermon and goes "under the influence of a species of somnambulism" to the scaffold where seven years earlier Hester refused to divulge his identity. He shrieks from the pillory. "The town did not awake," the narrator observes, "or, if it did, the drowsy slumberers mistook the cry either for something frightful in a dream, or for the noise of witches; whose voices, at that period, were often heard to pass over the settlements or lonely cottages, as they rode with Satan through the air." Mistress Hibbins, who is in communication with spirits, hears the shriek, and "possibly, she went up among the clouds," as Hawthorne's wit links witch and preacher. When Father Wilson passes near the platform Dimmesdale wants to shout to attract his attention, but he sounds no words and experiences "a crisis of terrible anxiety." He seeks to relieve the tension "by a kind of lurid playfulness" which unveils his erotic fantasies and frustrations. With a "grisly sense of the humorous," he imagines himself still standing on the scaffold in the morning, when he will be discovered by partly clothed matrons and scantily clad virgins with heaving white bosoms. Apparently sensing that repressed sexual desires have emerged, he expresses horror and anger in "a great peal of laughter."

By chance Hester and her daughter pass by at this moment on their return from a vigil at the deathbed of Governor Winthrop, and Pearl responds to Dimmesdale's anxiety-ridden laughter with "a light, airy, childish laugh." When Hester and Pearl mount the platform, for the first time the family is united, but in the darkness. Dimmesdale answers Pearl's request that they stand there together on the following day at "noontide" with an evasive "another time." As Pearl laughs skeptically, suddenly a meteor—"a great red letter in the sky"—illuminates "the minister, with his hand over his heart; and Hester Prynne, with the embroidered letter glimmering on her bosom; and little Pearl, herself a symbol, and the connecting link between these two." The meteor reveals the presence of the family to Chillingworth, who has also been in attendance in Winthrop's mansion. He expresses concern for the frightened preacher who must deliver a sermon on the following day. At once Dimmesdale assumes the role of the child in accepting the father's authority, as he replies, "I will go home with you."

Hester is "shocked" by the physical deterioration of both men. Dimmesdale is wasting away, hand held desperately to his bosom. More hunched than before, "a glare of red light out of his eyes," Chillingworth has come to resemble a fiend. While the two men squander physical and intellectual resources and remain locked in their fixed worlds with fixed ideas, Hester has grown intellectually, her mind freed from the shackles of convention and religion to speculate, although thought perhaps substitutes for ungratified passion. While she envisions a new social order for women in the future, for the present she serves as an angel of mercy: "Her breast, with its badge of shame, was but the softer pillow for the head that needed one." The sick liken the A to "a cross on a nun's bosom." As the adulteress becomes a saint—Hawthorne's satire is relentless but covert, as Anthony Trollope was among the first to recognize—apocryphal stories about Hester begin to accumulate. An Indian's arrow is said to have struck the scarlet letter and fallen "harmless to the ground." Hawthorne intrudes to scoff, but affectionately. The reluctant acceptance and the veneration, however, fail to satisfy Hester's affectional needs, and she suffers depressed states and, we learn, has even contemplated suicide.

The A dominates Pearl's life as it does her parents', and hers is the formidable task—how formidable she is too young to conceive—of integrating it constructively into her growth from girlhood into womanhood. Shortly after the second scaffold scene, in an interlude deriving from Eve's mirror scene in *Paradise Lost*, Pearl observes her image in the water. Then, having "inherited her mother's gift for devising drapery and costume," she dresses herself as a mermaid (as Hawthorne perhaps remembers his first love, the subject of "The Village Uncle," later retitled "The Mermaid"). With the aid of "some eel-grass" Pearl makes an A for her bosom "but freshly green, instead of scarlet!" When Pearl becomes in fancy a woman, she substitutes for the restless, wavering ambiguities of red (fire and passion) the fertility and repose of green and for Hester's exotic embroidery commonplace eelgrass.

Eventually Pearl deduces that her mother wears the scarlet letter for the same reason the minister keeps his hand on his heart. Once again the mother cannot cope with her daughter's sexual awareness and in her embarrassment resorts to an unworthy, but conventional, threat: "Do not tease me; else I shall shut thee into the dark closet!" For the third time the mother fails her daughter when Pearl observes that the sunshine

". . . is afraid of something on your bosom. Now, see! There it is, playing, a good way off. Stand you here, and let me run and catch it.

I am but a child. It will not flee from me; for I wear nothing on my bosom yet!"

"Nor ever will, my child, I hope," said Hester.

"And why not, mother?" asked Pearl, stopping short. . . . "Will not it come of its own accord, when I am a woman grown?"

"Run away, child," answered her mother, "and catch the sunshine! It will soon be gone."

In the light of her own unfulfilled life Hester may mean: child, don't grow up.

While Pearl entertains herself, fertile in her inventions and tireless in her energy, Hester meets Dimmesdale at the edge of the forest where presumably they consummated their passion years earlier. Tentatively and sadly, aware of time lost, they inquire of each other's welfare. "Art thou in life?" he asks. After she confesses that she has concealed from him Chillingworth's identity, he is angered: his pity is mostly self-pity and his love self-love, and only occasionally is he aware of what his cowardice and silence have meant in the life of the family he is not ready to acknowledge. When Dimmesdale proves as stubborn as a child, Hester like a mother "threw her arms around him, and pressed his head against her bosom; little caring though his cheek rested on the scarlet letter." Then with the "energy" characteristic of Pearl, Hester outlines plans for their future in another land, with other names. Despite many reservations, some voiced, some unstated in his fear, Dimmesdale agrees to flee Boston after he delivers the Election Sermon three days later. The family reunion must wait while he experiences his greatest hour. Hester does not know that Dimmesdale sees himself as "irrevocably doomed," yet he hungers for the comfort of her presence and her breast: "Neither can I any longer live without her companionship; so powerful is she to sustain,—so tender to soothe!"

Joyful, eager after her seven-year deprivation, Hester removes the letter on her breast and, in the loveliest erotic moment in nineteenth-century American literature, reemerges as Aphrodite in Puritanland, while she replicates their hour of passion.

The stigma gone, Hester heaved a long, deep sigh, in which the burden of shame and anguish departed from her spirit. O exquisite relief! She had not known the weight, until she felt the freedom! By another impulse, she took off the formal cap that confined her hair;

and down it fell upon her shoulders, dark and rich, with at once a shadow and a light in its abundance, and imparting the charm of softness to her features. There played around her mouth, and beamed out of her eyes, a radiant and tender smile, that seemed gushing from the very heart of womanhood. A crimson flush was glowing on her cheek, that had been long so pale. Her sex, her youth, and the whole richness of her beauty, came back from what men call the irrevocable past, and clustered themselves, with her maiden hope, and a happiness before unknown, within the magic circle of this hour. And, as if the gloom of the earth and sky had been but the effluence of these two mortal hearts, it vanished with their sorrow. All at once, as with a sudden smile of heaven, forth burst sunshine. . . .

The tapestry is resplendent, the colors vibrant, as nature and Hawthorne rejoice and make love to the embodiment of love. Here we witness the freeing of American women, their coming-of-age in art.

But Hester's release into loveliness proves a soap bubble. Pearl insists her mother restore the A to her breast, for without the letter, Hawthorne informs us, the child "could not find her wonted place, and hardly knew where she was." In Pearl's eyes the loss of the letter is rejection. She is also "influenced by the jealousy that seems instinctual with every petted child towards a dangerous rival." What a lovely and acute insight! And so Hester stuffs her hair into her tight-fitting cap and restores the A to its proper place as she returns home with Pearl, but she still lives with expectation that the family will at last be united aboard a ship bound for Europe.

Hester is never to know that as Dimmesdale goes home that day in a "maze," he feels exhilarated as he releases pent-up negative fantasies such as appear recurrently in Hawthorne's notebooks. When he sees a deaconess he wants to confide a blasphemy about the communion supper. To the oldest woman in his congregation he is prepared to repudiate the immortality of the soul. When a virgin approaches he holds "his Geneva cloak before his face" and gives her a "wicked look." He is ready to teach children "wicked words" and to exchange with a drunken sailor "improper jests." Here Dimmesdale unveils his doubts, his rage at his society and perhaps at himself, and his arrestment in infantile sexual fantasies. He does not act out his fantasies but returns to his room, where he eats "with ravenous appetite" (again a brilliant insight into his arrestment) and—Eros surrendering to Logos—proceeds to write or rewrite the Election Sermon.

One great moment remains for Arthur Dimmesdale, the delivery of the sermon to commemorate a day of renewal and rebirth when "a new man is beginning to rule over them." Wearing her familiar emblem seemingly for the last time, Hester attends the festival, her demeanor marked by "unquiet," which Pearl also reflects. After the dignitaries enter the church, only the "indistinct, but varied, murmur and flow of the minister's very peculiar voice" is heard by those who remain in the square. Inside the church all eyes are on Dimmesdale. In the square the center of attention, as in the first scene of the romance, is Hester's scarlet letter. Some throng about her "with rude and boorish intrusiveness." Others fasten "their snake-like black eyes on Hester's bosom."

> . . . the inhabitants of the town . . . tormented Hester Prynne, perhaps more than all the rest, with their cool, well-acquainted gaze at her familiar shame. Hester saw and recognized the self-same faces of that group of matrons, who had awaited her forthcoming from the prison-door, seven years ago. . . . At the final hour, when she was so soon to fling aside the burning letter, it had strangely become the centre of more remark and excitement, and was thus made to sear her breast more painfully, than at any time since the first day she put it on.

After the sermon Dimmesdale, visibly spent, emerges from the church and refuses the arm of Father Wilson and the assistance of Governor Bellingham. He is beyond the help of the "fathers": "He still walked onward, if that movement could be so described, which rather resembled the wavering effort of an infant, with its mother's arms in view, outstretched to tempt him forward." Then "leaning on Hester's shoulder, and supported by her arm around him," and clasping his daughter's hand, Dimmesdale ascends the scaffold despite Chillingworth's angry protest. There he confesses himself "the one sinner of the world!"

> With a convulsive motion he tore away the ministerial band from before his breast. It was revealed! . . . For an instant the gaze of the horror-stricken multitude was concentred on the ghastly miracle; while the minister stood with a flush of triumph in his face, as one

who, in the crisis of acutest pain, had won a victory. Then, down he sank upon the scaffold! Hester partly raised him, and supported his head against her bosom.

The circle is closed and the family is at last publicly united. All eyes are again "concentred," now on Dimmesdale's bosom, and Hester is once more the Madonna, now with a dying child at her breast—the son joined to the Eternal Mother.

Within a year Chillingworth dies and bequeaths "a very considerable amount of property" to Pearl. Years later Pearl goes abroad with her mother, eventually marries, and has children. One day Hester returns to Boston, quietly reenters her cottage, and reappears wearing the A, which is no longer a "stigma." In his final sermon and greatest hour, Dimmesdale speaks vaguely of the future of the colony, of the America that is to emerge, although his words to those in the square, and to readers, are only the sounds of his peculiar, tremulous voice. In age Hester assures those who come to her for aid

of her firm belief, that, at some brighter period, when the world should have grown ripe for it, in Heaven's own time, a new truth would be revealed, in order to establish the whole relation between man and woman on a surer ground of mutual happiness. . . . The angel and apostle of the coming revelation must be a woman, indeed, but lofty, pure, and beautiful; and wise, moreover, not through dusky grief, but the ethereal medium of joy; and showing how sacred love should make us happy, by the truest test of life successful to such an end!

Then she glances "her sad eyes downward at the scarlet letter."

Hawthorne's tapestry is finished. In the first scene Dimmesdale looks down on Hester from the balcony "appended to the meeting-house." In the last scene of the canvas we discover that the opposite side of the church overlooks the burial ground in which among many monuments "carved with armorial bearings" is a "simple slab of slate" that serves as a tombstone for the new grave and "an old and sunken one." It bears the ambiguous words: "ON A FIELD SABLE, THE LETTER A, GULES."

On February 2, 1850, Sophia sat in the parlor of the house on Mall Street in Salem to hear the final chapters of *The Scarlet*

Letter. She listened with the intensity of all her years as Hawthorne, deeply moved himself, read the lovely prose with the "tremulous" intonations of Dimmesdale. "I really thought," Sophia wrote to her sister Elizabeth, "an ocean was trying to pour out of my heart & eyes—but I had the magnetic power upon me of Mr Hawthorne's voice also—swaying me like a mighty wind . . . tremulous with the pathos of GOD's Word speaking through him." That night Sophia went to bed, Hawthorne reported to Horatio Bridge, "with a grievous headache—which I look upon as a triumphant success!" In recalling the evening five years later Hawthorne observed, in phraseology remarkably similar to Sophia's as well as to his own in the romance, that "my voice swelled and heaved, as if I were tossed up and down on an ocean, as it subsided after a storm."[10]

Consciously or not, both drew upon the sea imagery which emerges quietly in the background toward the conclusion of the romance, as Hawthorne lifts the drama out of specific time and place into a universal and timeless context which in turn derives from his profound involvement in the story he tells. Pearl "seemed to be borne upward, like a floating seabird, on the long heaves and swells of sound." "The eloquent voice" of the preacher, "on which the souls of the listening audience had been borne aloft, as on the swelling waves of the sea, at length came to a pause." After Dimmesdale delivers the Election Sermon, the colonists unite in a spontaneous outburst of feeling and sound: "There were human beings enough, and enough of highly wrought and symphonious feeling, to produce that more impressive sound than the organ-tones of the blast, or the thunder, or the roar of the sea; even that mighty swell of many voices, blended into one great voice by the universal impulse which makes likewise one vast heart out of the many." As the pastor walks with death weariness from the church, the citizens observe "the state in which Mr. Dimmesdale was left by the retiring wave of intellect and sensibility."

Everything we know about the writing of the romance confirms that Hawthorne, like Arthur Dimmesdale, was physically and emotionally spent, and no doubt depressed, from his "immense" concentration and, more important, investment in his subject matter, which is another variation on the family romance. In the "Introductory" Hawthorne admits that he is giving way once again to the "autobiographical impulse" as he records his view of the employees at the Salem Custom-House. At the conclusion of the preface he says farewell to Salem or, perhaps more accurately, washes his hands of the village and its inhabitants. "I am a citizen of somewhere else," he declares, which is a not-so-veiled plea for sympathy as he departs from "this abode and burial-place of so many of my forefathers."

The romance itself is a veiled résumé of his life, which was his way of handling his grief and anger after the death of his mother in 1849. The story, as the diction repeatedly reminds us, is "concentred" on the A on Hester's breast, and the sea imagery evokes the cradle endlessly rocking, birth and death, Aphrodite and the Eternal Mother, and a gentle boy's loss of his father at sea in his youth and of a mother in age.

While the four characters have separate identities, collectively they constitute a subtle and complex self-portrait, Hawthorne being the sum total of all his characters. Each is an artist: Hester in embroidery, Dimmesdale in the outpourings of the tongue of flames, Chillingworth in his concoctions for body and soul, and Pearl in her fashionings of natural objects. Like artists they brood over and live in the "interior kingdom." Hester transcends a hostile world, first, by her quiet dedication to the public good and, second, by her speculation as to the nature of the patriarchal world and a future society which will "establish the whole relation between man and woman on a surer ground of mutual happiness." Dimmesdale's "constant introspection" stems not so much from guilt because of his "sin" as from his inability to establish loving connections because of the self-love and egomania which stem from insecurities and fright. Chillingworth is "a man chiefly accustomed to look inward, and to whom external matters are of little value and import, unless they bear relation to something within his mind." Pearl's "inner world" seethes with her repressed rage as an isolated child in a hostile environment: "The singularity lay in the hostile feelings with which the child regarded all these offsprings of her own heart and mind. She never created a friend, but seemed always to be sowing broadcast the dragon's teeth, whence sprung a harvest of armed enemies, against whom she rushed to battle." Because Pearl seems to originate in allegory or in the myth of Cadmus, we as readers forget that her deprivations are Hawthorne's: he too understood what it meant to be fatherless.

In delineating the characters, Hawthorne has drawn upon his own mirror image. Pearl may recall Una Hawthorne as many have suggested or his sister Elizabeth, as a recent commentator has proposed, but one suspects she is essentially a portrait of Hawthorne as a child, with "a beauty that shone with deep and vivid tints; a bright complexion, eyes possessing intensity both of depth and glow, and hair already of a deep, glossy brown." Dimmesdale mirrors Hawthorne's physical appearance and the indecisive, conflicted part of his nature.

> He was a person of very striking aspect, with a white lofty, and impending brow, large, brown, melancholy eyes, and a mouth which, unless when he forcibly compressed it, was apt to be tremulous, expressing both nervous sensibility and a vast power of self-restraint. [There was] a startled, a half-frightened look,—as of a being who felt himself quite astray and at a loss in the pathway of human existence, and could only be at ease in some seclusion of his own.

Roger Chillingworth, eyes spurting fire, like one of the Gorgons, would seem to originate in the gothic and the unconscious monsterland of dreams and nightmares. But he walks with one shoulder raised, like Hawthorne himself, and familially he is the descendant of those two Hathorne men of iron whom the heir feared and revered. Chillingworth also shares with the author the roles of Paul Pry or voyeur and analyst of psychosomatic disturbances. (Some claim that he is fiction's first psychoanalyst.) Although Chillingworth plays the role of cuckold and villain—and Hawthorne poses the question as to who is the greater sinner, the deceitful, hypocritical clergyman or the duplicitous doctor—it is perhaps closer to the truth, and reality, to observe that Chillingworth is the sadistic side of Dimmesdale's masochism. Hawthorne himself repudiates the seeming contrast of the two men in a passage that sums up the ambiguous nature of love and hate:

> It is a curious subject of observation and inquiry, whether hatred and love be not the same thing at bottom. Each, in its utmost development, supposes a high degree of intimacy and heart-knowledge; each renders one individual dependent for the food of affections and spiritual life upon another; each leaves the passionate lover, or the no less passionate hater, forlorn and desolate by the withdrawal of his object. Philosophically considered, therefore, the two passions seem essentially the same, except that one happens to be seen in a celestial radiance, and the other in a dusky and lurid glow.

At the center of the romance is Hester Prynne, mother figure and symbol, and the major theme running through it is not Dimmesdale's feelings of or wrestlings with guilt—he is no more penitent than Hester and less honest—but the assertion of the maternal principle and the redemption it promises personally and culturally. As we have seen, Hester appears first as the Madonna with child, later as Aphrodite in the American forest with a new "consecration" beyond Christian morality, then as mother with a child-man at her breast in an American pietà, and finally as angel in Puritan Boston—all of which leads to her apotheosis in the book and in the American imagination.

Pearl in her fear clings tenaciously to the only connection she has in a hostile environment, her mother. The mirror in which Dimmesdale examines himself constantly one day pictorializes his feelings of loss and rejection: "Now came the dead friends of his youth, and his white-bearded father, with a saint-like frown, and his mother, turning her face away as she passed by. Ghost of a mother,—thinnest fantasy of a mother,—methinks she might yet have thrown a pitying glance towards her son!" The passage turns into a wail for the "pitying" mother, a wish shared by the narrator. At that very moment Hester appears outside "leading along little Pearl, in her scarlet garb"—a nurturing mother with his unacknowledged child. Chillingworth makes no reference to his parents, but his final gesture in life atones for his abandonment of Hester and her child and his persecution of her lover and his rival: after Dimmesdale's death he assumes the role of father by making it possible for Pearl to become, in Harry Levin's happy suggestion, a Jamesian heiress and expatriate.

Hester Prynne, then, is at once Hawthorne's love object as well as the fulfillment of his deepest desire for an ideal mother of beauty and tender feelings. If he is in love with Hester, as every page of the romance testifies, he is in love, too, it must be acknowledged, with his own image as refracted in his artifact and with the woman within himself, which may explain in part why he probes the feminine psyche more successfully than most male authors. He achieves, as Nina Baym acutely observes, what perhaps every son craves: he gives birth to his mother. Maybe this confirms Phyllis Greenacre's speculation: "The creations of artists are often the rearranged responses to the primal object (mother's breast) expressed in aesthetic forms."[11]

Mother and son were unable in life to communicate their love either in word or in gesture, and in death his need had to be satisfied and communicated in his art as veiled autobiography.

The Berkshires, 1850
Enter Herman Melville

When he sent off the final pages of *The Scarlet Letter* to James T. Fields in February 1850, Hawthorne summed up his achievement to Horatio Bridge. He admitted that "some portions of the book are powerfully written" but doubted that the work would attain wide popularity. Because of the "imaginative" touches he thought that the sketch of the Custom-House might be "more widely attractive than the main narrative. The latter lacks sunshine. To tell you the truth it is—(I hope Mrs. Bridge is not present)—it is positively a h-ll-fired story, into which I found it almost impossible to throw any cheering light."[1]

Hawthorne wrote without the perspectives of time or distance and in a state of exhaustion and self-doubt. He informed Bridge confidentially that "my health, latterly, is not quite what it has been, for many years past. I should not long stand such a life of bodily inactivity and mental exertion as I have led for the last few months." He asked Bridge not to "allude to this matter in your letters to me; as my wife already sermonizes me quite sufficiently on my habits—and I never own up to not feeling perfectly well. Neither do I feel anywise ill, but only a lack of physical vigor and energy, which re-acts upon the mind."[2]

Since the farmhouse in Lenox for which they had contracted was not to be ready for occupancy until May, the Hawthornes had to remain in Salem. He was determined not to seek another political post, for he found it "very agreeable to get rid of politics and the rest of the damnable turmoil that has disturbed me for three or four years past." "I have no business," he declared emphatically, "nor mean to have any, but my pen," but he knew from the sales of his writings in the past the problems he faced. As always, friends came to his aid. Bridge tried to find employment for Hawthorne with *Blackwood's Magazine*, and Elizabeth Peabody sought a post for him on Horace Greeley's *New-York Tribune*.[3]

In March 1850 Sophia was seriously ill. Mrs. Peabody hurried to Salem, where friends and the Hawthorne children proved attentive nurses. The husband in his usual fashion fell apart. "Hawthorne," Mrs. Peabody reported to her family, "looks as if he had been the greatest sufferer, to day he looks some better." Shortly Sophia was out of danger. She "seems to have nothing to contend with now but weakness—She will require the greatest care to keep her from running risques—Her husband is very watchful and for his sake I think she will be easily kept in order." Although Mrs. Peabody carefully refrained from describing the illness, it would appear that Sophia had experienced another miscarriage. The events of the preceding year as well as their economic and emotional problems had been especially trying for a woman given too emphatically to denying her fragility in order to demonstrate her love and to maintain her "sphere" at the center of the family.[4]

As the day of publication of *The Scarlet Letter* approached, Hawthorne was gloomy again about the success of his romance. "I don't expect," he wrote to Fields, "even this small modicum of luck. It is not in my cards." Fields read the cards differently, and his faith proved justified. The first edition of 2,500 copies sold out within ten days. At once the book created a sensation in Salem. Within a few days of publication, on March 21, a review appeared in the *Salem Register*, a Whig publication. In the opening paragraph the unidentified reviewer carefully praised Hawthorne the romancer but devoted the rest of the lengthy notice to a denunciation of the preface and of Hawthorne the surveyor. He revealed himself as "a despicable lampooner," a "malignant Hawthorne" rather than the "reputed *'gentle'* Hawthorne, of former days." The reviewer reserved his final blow until the last sentence: "The *'Posthumous Papers of a Decapitated Surveyor'* amply vindicate the justice of this application of the political guillotine."[5]

Hawthorne's birthplace, 27 Union Street, Salem.
Courtesy Essex Institute, Salem, Massachusetts.

Salem Custom-House. Courtesy Essex Institute.

Gallows Hill, scene of the witch trials of 1694. Courtesy Essex Institute.

Almshouse, Salem Willows. Courtesy Essex Institute.

Charter Street Burying Point and the Nathaniel Peabody house.
Courtesy Essex Institute.

Captain Nathaniel Hathorne, a
miniature. Courtesy Essex Institute.

Robert Manning, a miniature.
Courtesy Essex Institute.

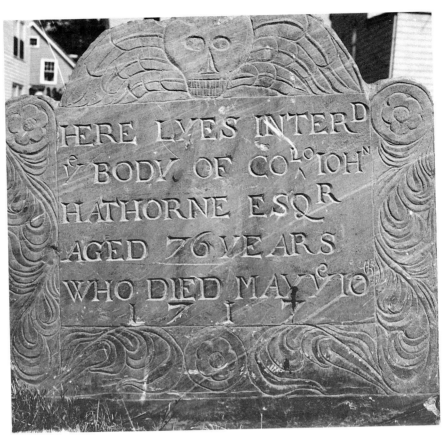

Gravestone of Colonel John Hathorne. Photograph by the author.

THE GENTLE BOY.

The boy had hushed his wailing at once and turned his face upward to the stranger.

*Drawing by Sophia Peabody for the second printing of "The Gentle Boy"
in 1839. Courtesy Essex Institute.*

Salem, Tuesday March 7th 1820

Dear Mother,

As we received no letter last week, we are in anxiety about your health. All of us are well. Mrs Forrester & Mrs Crowninshield are better. I have left school, and have begun to fit for College under Benjn. L. Oliver, Lawyer. So you are in great danger of having one learned man in your family. Mr. Oliver thought I could enter College next commencement, but Uncle Robert is afraid I should have to study too hard. I get my lessons at home, and recite them to him at 7 o'clock in the morning. I am extremely homesick. Aunt Mary is continually scolding at me. Grandmaam hardly ever speaks a pleasant word to me. If I ever attempt to speak a word in my defence, they cry out against my impudence. However I guess I can live through a year and a half more, and then I shall leave them. One good effect results from their eternal finding-fault. It gives me some employment in retaliating, and that keeps up my spirits. Mother I wish you would let Louisa board with Mrs Löthe if she comes up here to go to school. Then Aunt M. can't have her to domineer over. I hope, however, that I shall see none of you up here very soon. Shall you want me to be a Minister, Doctor or Lawyer? A Minister I will not be. I beleive M. Louisa has not written one letter to me, Well, I will not write to her till she does.

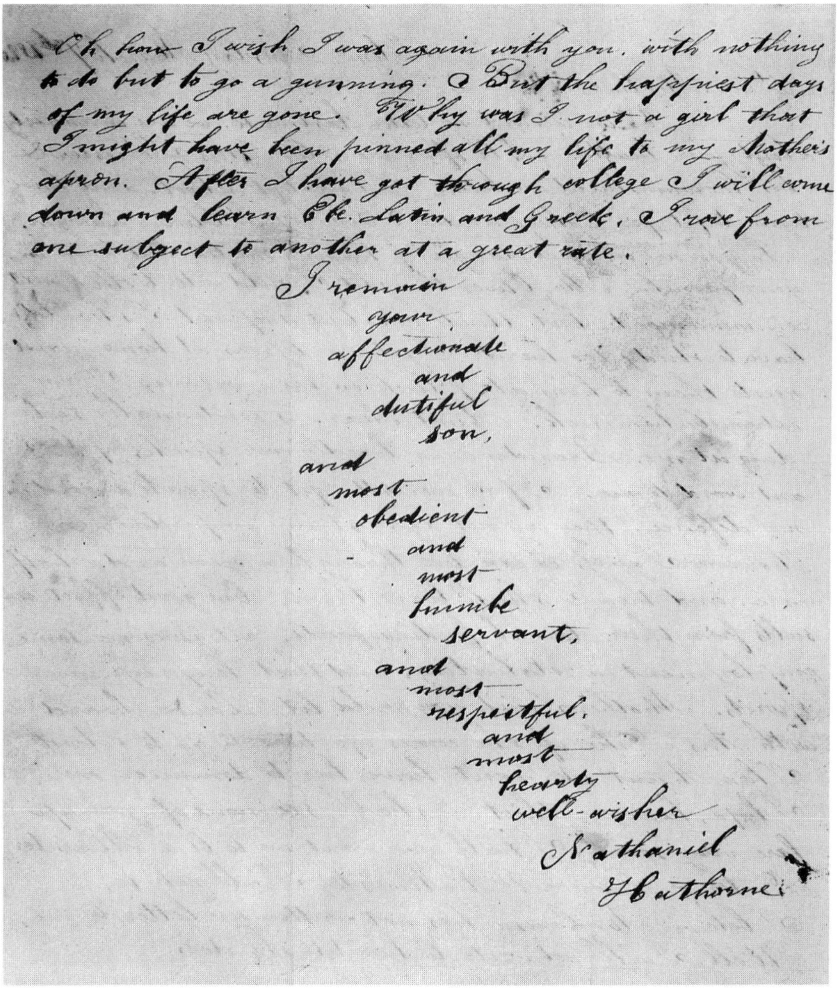

Oh how I wish I was again with you, with nothing to do but to go a gunning. But the happiest days of my life are gone. Why was I not a girl that I might have been pinned all my life to my Mother's apron. After I have got through college I will come down and learn Eke. Latin and Greek. I rove from one subject to another at a great rate.

I remain
your
affectionate
and
dutiful
son,

and
most
obedient
and
most
humble
servant,

and
most
respectful
and
most
hearty
well-wisher
Nathaniel
Hathorne

Letter from Nathaniel Hathorne at age sixteen to his mother, March 7, 1820.
Courtesy Essex Institute.

The campus at Bowdoin College, lithograph, 1821. Courtesy Bowdoin College.

Horatio Bridge, oil portrait by Eastman Johnson. Courtesy Bowdoin College Museum of Art, bequest of Marion Bridge Maurice.

Henry Wadsworth Longfellow, daguerreotype by Southworth and Hawes, before 1855. Courtesy Metropolitan Museum of Art, gift of I. N. Phelps Stokes, Edward S. Hawes, Alice Mary Hawes, and Marion Augusta Hawes, 1937.

Jonathan Cilley, lithograph. Courtesy Bowdoin College.

Gravestone of Nathaniel Mather, Charter Street Burying Point. Photograph by the author.

Second from left: 12 Herbert Street, Salem, Hawthorne's self-styled "castle dismal," actually the Manning house. Courtesy Essex Institute.

Silhouettes of the Peabody family, 1835. Above, left to right: Mrs. Elizabeth Peabody, Dr. Nathaniel Peabody, Elizabeth, and Nathaniel Cranch. Below, left to right: George, Sophia, Mary, and Wellington. Courtesy Essex Institute.

*Elizabeth Palmer Peabody,
oil portrait by Charles
Burleigh, 1878. Courtesy
Essex Institute.*

*Jones Very, portrait from a
carte de visite. Courtesy
Essex Institute.*

Sophia Peabody, oil portrait by Chester Harding, from Louise Hall Tharp's The Peabody Sisters of Salem, *1950.*

Nathaniel Hawthorne, oil portrait by Charles Osgood, 1840. Courtesy Essex Institute.

Mary Crowninshield Silsbee, oil portrait by Francis Alexander, 1830. Courtesy Harvard University Portrait Collection, bequest of Lizzie Sparks Pickering, wife of Edward C. Pickering.

Jared Sparks, oil portrait by Rembrandt Peale. Courtesy Harvard University Portrait Collection, bequest of Lizzie Sparks Pickering.

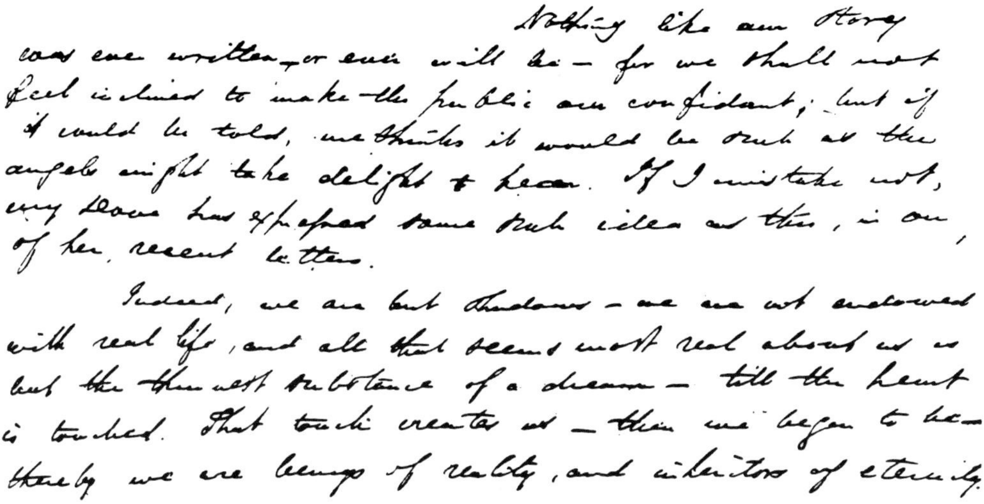

[handwritten letter excerpt]

... Nothing like our Story
was ever written—or ever will be— for we shall not
feel inclined to make the public our confidant; but if
it could be told, methinks it would be such as the
angels might take delight to hear. If I mistake not,
my Dove has expressed some such idea as this, in one
of her recent letters.

Indeed, we are but shadows—we are not endowed
with real life, and all that seems most real about us is
but the thinnest substance of a dream—till the heart
is touched. That touch creates us—then we begin to be—
thereby we are beings of reality, and inheritors of eternity.

*Excerpts from letters of Nathaniel Hawthorne to Sophia Peabody in 1840,
January 3 (above) and October 4. Courtesy Huntington Library.*

*Brook Farm, by M. G. Cutter, 1910, after a contemporary drawing.
Courtesy Concord Free Public Library.*

Charles King Newcomb, daguerreotype, from Ralph Waldo Emerson's Journals, *1912.*

CENTRAL PART OF CONCORD, MASS.

The above is a northern view in the central part of Concord village. Part of the Court-House is seen on the left. Burying-ground Hill (a post of observation to the British officers in the invasion of 1775) is seen a short distance beyond. The Unitarian Church and Middlesex Hotel are seen on the right.

Central part of Concord, drawing by J. W. Barber about 1840, engraved by James Downes. Courtesy Concord Free Public Library.

The Manse. Courtesy Essex Institute.

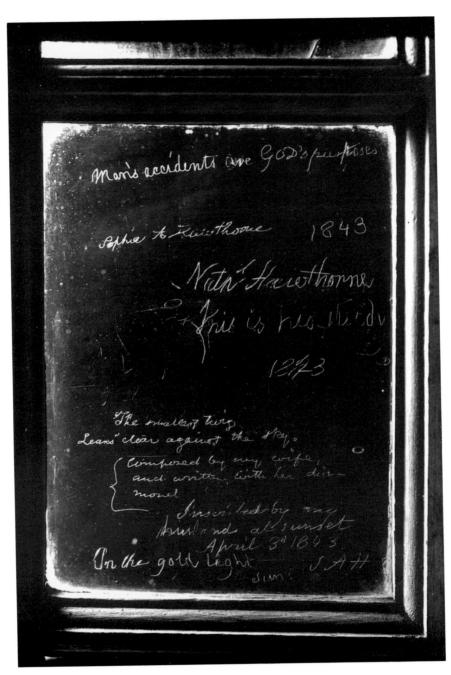

Window in the Manse incised by Sophia and Nathaniel Hawthorne on April 3, 1843. Courtesy Concord Free Public Library.

Above, left: Ralph Waldo Emerson,
photograph by Black. Courtesy
Concord Free Public Library.

Above, right: Henry David Thoreau,
daguerreotype by Maxham. Courtesy
Concord Free Public Library.

Right: William Ellery Channing, a
miniature. Courtesy Concord Free
Public Library.

Margaret Fuller, engraving from a portrait by Chappel. Courtesy Concord Free Public Library.

Una and Julian Hawthorne, daguerreotype, about 1850. Courtesy Boston Athenæum, gift of the estate of Mrs. James H. Beal.

William D. Ticknor, engraving by
S. A. Schoff. Courtesy Essex
Institute.

James T. Fields, cabinet card by
Warren of Boston, ca. 1870. Courtesy
Essex Institute.

The "little red house," Lenox, from R. DeWitt Mallory's Lenox and the
Berkshire Highlands, 1902. Courtesy New York Public Library.

*Herman Melville, oil portrait
by Rodney Dewey. Courtesy
Berkshire Athenæum,
Pittsfield, Massachusetts.*

Monument Mountain,
Berkshires, *oil on canvas
by Asher Brown Durand,
1855/60. Courtesy Detroit
Institute of Arts, Founders
Society Purchase, Dexter M.
Ferry, Jr., Fund.*

Gravestone of William Hollingworth and his mother, Elianor, Charter Street Burying Point. Photograph by the author.

Burning of Steamboat Henry Clay, *Riverdale, New York, July 28, 1852, engraving. Courtesy New-York Historical Society.*

Above: Calling card of the Hawthornes at the Wayside. Courtesy Essex Institute.

Below: The Wayside, with the Hawthornes standing at the left. Courtesy Concord Free Public Library.

Nathaniel Hawthorne, oil portrait by George P. A. Healy, 1852. Owned by the New Hampshire Historical Society.

Franklin Pierce, oil portrait by George P. A. Healy, 1852. Owned by the New Hampshire Historical Society.

Hawthorne's path on the hill behind the Wayside.
Courtesy Concord Free Public Library.

Annie Fields, a miniature executed by Lucia Fuller after her death, probably based on a Southworth and Hawes daguerreotype. Courtesy Boston Athenæum.

AND SHE IN WHOM SWEET CHARITIES VNI
THE OLD GREEK BEAVTIES SET IN HOLY
LIGH

Sophia Hawthorne, photograph, about 1855. Courtesy Essex Institute.

Gravestone of Dr. John Swinnerton, Charter Street Burying Point. Courtesy Essex Institute.

Letter from Nathaniel Hawthorne to Franklin Pierce (above), May 7, 1864, with a postscript by Sophia Hawthorne on the verso and a notation by Pierce. Courtesy Nathaniel Hawthorne Collection (6249-a), Clifton Waller Barrett Library, Manuscripts Division, Special Collections Department, University of Virginia Library.

Nath'l Hawthorne
64
May 7
This was the
was the last note
written by dear
Hawthorne —

Concord, Saturday May 7th 1864

My dear Pierce

I have received yours of Friday last, I believe, but have not it now by me to refer to. I am rejoiced to hear of your well-being, and shall do my best to join you at the Bromfield House on Wednesday next. My own health continues rather poor, but I shall hope to revive rapidly when once we are on the road. Excuse the brevity of my note, for I find some difficulty in writing.

Affectionately yours.
Nath'l Hawthorne

Gen'l Pierce.

My dear General Pierce

I am glad to find Mr Hawthorne could write you even such a short note, for he passed a very wretched night last night.

I am going to Boston also on Wednesday as I have a great many errands to do. It is clouding this morning and therefore I hope there will be a rain soon so as to leave Wednesday fair for your meeting and starting.

Most truly yours
S. Hawthorne.

The Pemigewasset House, Plymouth, New Hampshire. Courtesy Essex Institute.

Hawthorne's grave, Sleepy Hollow Cemetery, Concord. Photograph by the author.

Such attacks produced a visceral response. "I detest this town so much," Hawthorne exclaimed, "that I hate to go into the streets, or to have the people see me. Anywhere else, I shall at once be entirely another man." If he did not exaggerate, to which he was given in correspondence, he again wandered about apparently at night and like Dimmesdale shunned contact with townspeople. If he appeared to overreact we fail to comprehend the depth of the hurt he sustained in what he perceived as an attack upon his manhood.[6]

Years after Hawthorne's death when one could expect that the incident would have been buried among history's trivialities, a former resident of Salem recalled a friend's characterization of Hawthorne as a "hard-looking customer" when he stood outside the Custom-House wearing a cloak and seemingly "ashamed to look at any one." Henry B. Hill was "personally acquainted" with the employees: "They were old shipmasters, most of them, and in their day were the manliest of men. . . . No man displayed more meanness of character than Hawthorne did in his criticisms on those men. A fully developed man would have tried to help them in the discharge of their duties if they needed help (which they did not). . . . Hawthorne had no conception of men of that character—they were so far above him in all that constituted true manhood." In short, Hawthorne's manhood was once more, this time posthumously, questioned.[7]

A second edition of *The Scarlet Letter* of 2,500 copies included a preface by Hawthorne dated March 30, 1850, in which he observed that because of the "unprecedented excitement in the respectable community around him," he had reexamined "The Custom-House" and had decided to reprint it "without the change of a word." He threw down the gauntlet to Salem: "The only remarkable features of the sketch are its frank and genuine good-humor. . . . As to enmity, or ill-feeling of any kind, personal or political, he utterly disclaims such motives."[8]

The early reviews of *The Scarlet Letter* were on the whole favorable, although three of these notices were written by men on friendly terms with the author and his publishers. Evert Duyckinck reviewed the romance in the *Literary World*; George Ripley, formerly of Brook Farm, in the *New-York Tribune*; and Edwin P. Whipple, one of the lecturers at the Salem Lyceum during Hawthorne's tenure as secretary, in *Graham's Magazine*. The three reviewers approved the work without indicating adequately either its art or its subtlety or the fact that it was the most extraordinary work of the American imagination. Duyckinck preferred

the other Hawthorne of the Irving-like sketches. He and Ripley emphasized the historical setting of the romance. Whipple, who was Hawthorne's favorite critic, objected to "the morbid intensity" of the romance.
"There is a strange fascination to a man of contemplative genius in the
psychological details of a strange crime like that which forms the plot of
The Scarlet Letter, and he is therefore apt to become, like Hawthorne,
too painfully anatomical in his exhibition of them." [9]

The notices in religious journals, *Brownson's Quarterly* in October and
the *Church Review* in January 1851, examined the romance with a freely
admitted bias. Although their conclusions were predictable and inevitable, the reviews were in some respects more analytical than those in
secular journals. Orestes Brownson maintained that neither Hester nor
Dimmesdale suffers from "remorse" or "really repents of the criminal
deed." Brownson admitted that the "story is told with great naturalness,
ease, grace, and delicacy, but it is a story that should not have been told."
In the *Church Review*, Arthur Cleveland Coxe concurred with Brownson's judgment that the two main characters are not penitent and that
"the nauseous amour" is not appropriate subject matter in fiction. He
charged that in failing to call things "by their right names," Hawthorne
is like Mephistopheles, who "insinuates that the archfiend himself is a
very tolerable sort of person, if nobody would call him Mr. Devil. . . .
The 'Vicar of Wakefield' is sometimes coarsely virtuous, but 'The Scarlet
Letter' is delicately immoral." Coxe had a point: Hawthorne's unwillingness to mention adultery was not unlike Dimmesdale's evasiveness, but
in Hawthorne's love of Hester morality yielded to art. [10]

As was to be expected, Sophia took vigorous exception to almost every
critical response. To her sister Elizabeth's autobiographical construction
that Hawthorne had "purified himself by casting out a legion of devils,"
she replied that "it was a work of the imagination wholly & no personal
experience, as you know very well." She took a high but dubious line in
regard to the moral issue: "The questioning of its morality is of all criticisms the funniest—especially this notion some short sighted persons
have about the author's opinion of the crime! When the whole book is one
great tragic chorus of condemnation—when such horrible retribution follows, when even the retribution lives & breathes in Pearl from beginning
to end." [11]

About the middle of April the Hawthornes left Salem to live temporarily with the Peabodys in Boston. Hawthorne took the opportunity to visit Bridge at the Portsmouth navy yard. There, eight years after their marriage, at age forty-six, he wrote another of those tender love letters which, however, did not reveal fully his contradictory, moody nature. He had, he wrote playfully, "nothing to say to thee—save the unimportant fact that I love thee better than ever before, and that I cannot be at peace away from thee. . . . Thou didst much amiss, to marry a husband who cannot keep thee like a lady, as Bridge does his wife. . . . Thou hast a hard lot in life; and so have I that witness it, and can do little or nothing to help thee." [12]

When Hawthorne returned to Boston he did not stay with the Peabodys—"it seems a sin to add another human being to the multitudinous chaos of that house," he explained, no doubt with tongue in cheek—but took himself to a nearby boardinghouse where he could enjoy the gossip of the boarders and escape from the two Elizabeths, mother and daughter, as well as from his own family responsibilities and restrictions. He needed this fling to take stock and to accumulate experiences and observations, for his romances were grounded after their fashion in reality. His entries in his journals at this time were fuller and freer, perhaps because Sophia was not looking over his shoulder. [13]

The train ride from Portsmouth to Boston was preparation for the most memorable railroad ride in American literature, the hilarious but anxiety-ridden journey of those two dropouts from society, Hepzibah and Clifford Pyncheon in *The House of the Seven Gables*. At the boardinghouse Hawthorne resumed his role of Paul Pry, uninhibitedly enjoying the views as well as the speculations which brushed aside curtains. "Were I a solitary prisoner," he commented, "I should not doubt to find occupation of deep interest for my whole day, in watching only one of these houses." What he did not see fantasy supplied. He observed a light in one of the upper chambers "where perchance some lovely damsel is disrobing herself for bed." On another day he observed a young couple and speculated "that she began to look rather sleepy; for perhaps the time has not yet come when the new bride is allowed to have quiet rest from bedtime till sunrise. She may be much disturbed in the nighttime, though with pleasant and desirable awakenings." Some of these erotic daydreams reappeared in *The Blithedale Romance* in the narrative of the bachelor-voyeur Miles Coverdale, who, unlike Hawthorne in his notebooks, hints at doubts and fears when he finds himself "getting pretty well acquainted with that little portion of the backside of the universe which it presented to my view."[14]

During his brief stay in Boston, Hawthorne once again sat for a portrait, this time by Cephas G. Thompson, which was to be no more satisfactory than the earlier ones, at least in the judgment of Sophia. Hawthorne visited the Boston Athenaeum, the most famous private library and art gallery at the time in the country, and went to the apartment of George Ticknor, the distinguished professor at Harvard College and author of the three-volume *History of Spanish Literature*. He questioned Ticknor on his sister Elizabeth's behalf about translations of Cervantes. Hawthorne was respectful of Ticknor and other dignitaries whom he chanced to meet, but his journal bubbled when he described a pantomime at the National Theater entitled *Jack the Giant Killer*, which he attended on the evening of May 8.[15]

At the theater, Hawthorne did not sit in "the aristocratic part of the house." "I found myself," he wrote, "surrounded chiefly by young sailors, Hanover-street shopmen, mechanics, and other people of that kidney. It is wonderful the difference that exists in the personal aspect and dress, and no less in the manners, of people in this quarter of the city, compared with others." In the adjoining box were four people, an older man somewhat drunk and a younger one who tried to keep him quiet, as well as two young women whom Hawthorne described in detail, although they clearly were not members of Sophia's circle. The women seemed to share without fuss the care of a child who gradually became purple because of the heat in the theater. When it cried, the younger woman uncovered her bosom and without any self-consciousness fed the child. "There was nothing indecent in this; but a perfect naturalness," he commented, or perhaps reassured himself, although it is difficult to believe that Sophia would have concurred.[16]

While the pantomime itself was "somewhat heavy and tedious," Hawthorne delighted in the role of spectator of a seedy "May-pole of Merry Mount." "Throughout the evening, drunken young sailors kept stumbling into and out of the boxes, calling to one another from different parts of the house, shouting to the performers, and singing the burthens of songs. It was a scene of life in the rough." He recorded such scenes without condescension or middle-class morality, although he fastidiously shrank from dwelling except briefly or obliquely on such subject matter in his tales and romances. Hawthorne was of two or more minds on most subjects and despite his external grace limped internally with repressions and fears.[17]

Late in May the Hawthornes left for Lenox, a village in the heart of the Berkshires in western Massachusetts with a population at the time of slightly over 1,500. They moved about a mile and a half from the village into an old red farmhouse which they rented from their neighbors, the Tappans, for $150 annually. The house, which Hawthorne called the Scarlet Letter, was, in his words, "not very splendid in its outward aspects, but snug and comfortable." A year later, when he was once again restless and ready to uproot himself, his perception had changed: "This is certainly the most inconvenient and wretched little hovel that I ever put my head in."[18]

In the only extant picture, an engraving in a magazine, the house appears small and modest, without the usual charm of early New England dwellings. Yet in Melville's description in *Pierre* it is thoroughly charming, no doubt improved by the author's romantic heightening:

> . . . on the mild lake's hither shore . . . there the small and low red farm-house lay; its ancient roof a bed of brightest mosses; its north front (from the north the moss-wind blows), also moss-incrusted, like the north side of any vast-trunked maple in the groves. At one gabled end, a tangled arbor claimed support, and paid for it by generous gratuities of broad-flung verdure, one viny shaft of which pointed itself upright against the chimney-bricks, as if a waving lightning-rod. . . . In front, three straight gigantic lindens stood guardians of this verdant spot.[19]

In Sophia's eyes "La Rouge Maison" was a palace for her royal family. In a lengthy letter to her mother she provided a tour of the dwelling, supplying all the details that her mother wanted to hear. There were five rooms on the first floor and four on the second, all of which were quite small, and Sophia furnished them according to the dictates of her Victorian taste. In the sitting room were reproductions of *Madonna del Pesce* and Thomas Crawford's sculpture *Glory to God in the Highest*, and the carpet was purple and gold and the wallpaper buff. In the drawing room, on a "fairy tea-table—a Hawthorne heir-loom"—was the bust of Apollo, the gift of Caroline Sturgis Tappan, now their neighbor. The sculpture had suffered Hawthorne's fate during the move from Salem, decapitation.

What Sophia called a boudoir, evidently the smallest room on the first floor, was adorned with reproductions of Leonardo da Vinci and Salvator Rosa and a bust of Antinoüs, the favorite page of the emperor Hadrian. The view from this room she pronounced magnificent. On the second floor was Hawthorne's study, with a view even more magnificent. In "our golden chamber" was a "golden couch," too big for the room.[20]

The farmhouse overlooked one of the loveliest lakes in the Berkshires, Stockbridge Bowl, which mirrored, as it still does, the surrounding forests and "the summits of the more distant hills. It gleamed in perfect tranquillity, without the trace of a winged breeze on any part of its bosom." In the distance, about eight or more miles away, is Monument Mountain, celebrated by William Cullen Bryant in a poem that was shortly to be read during one of the most famous literary gatherings of the century.[21]

Hawthorne arrived in Lenox with a severe cold, and for a few days "the wounded bird of Jove remained caged up-stairs." "He took cold," Sophia explained to her mother, "because so harassed in spirit, & this cold, together with brain-work & disquiet, made a tolerable nervous fever—His eyes looked like two immense spheres of troubled light. . . . he is not so vigorous, yet as in former days, (it is a year now since he was expeled from the Custom-House). . . ." This was, she declared, "the trying year of his life, as well as of mine—I have not yet found again all my wings—neither is his tread yet again elastic." Sophia's world opened up when "our King descended from his study, to the great joy of all, & the air was so reviving & the earth looked so new, I proposed we shall go to the lake."[22]

The children played in the woods and on the shore of the lake, generally under Sophia's supervision, for, as in Salem, she kept them from contact with peers. She willingly paid the price of such exclusiveness. However, the adults had frequent visitors. Fanny Kemble, the actress, rode up on her white horse, as dramatic in life as on the stage. Catharine Sedgwick, the grand dame of the American domestic novel and the custodian of domestic virtues, lived not far away, and her family called soon after the arrival of the Hawthornes.

Not long after the Hawthornes settled into the red house Herman Melville came to Pittsfield with his wife and their eighteen-month-old son Malcolm. Melville was returning to the place where in his youth, after the death of his father, he had spent summer vacations with his uncle. This time he visited his cousin Robert Melvill, who retained the older spelling of the family name. Although Evert Duyckinck was the friend and literary advisor of the two men, Hawthorne and Melville had not yet met. By a remarkable coincidence, on July 18 Melville's aunt gave him a copy of *Mosses from an Old Manse,* a gift which had a profound impact on the lives of both men.[23]

Melville observed his thirty-first birthday on August 1, and on the following day two of his New York friends, Duyckinck and Cornelius Mathews, set out on the train for a holiday in the country. Mathews was a well-known author of novels, plays, and trivia, most of which have long been forgotten. In the eyes of the discriminating he was a bit of a fool addicted to a preciosity that strains one's patience. One contemporary critic attacked his "pretentious imbecility" when he assumed "the arduous duties of wet-nurse to that sturdy bentling, the National Literature." On the train Duyckinck and Mathews encountered David Dudley Field, a well-known New York lawyer who spent his summers in a village which he had known since he was fourteen. Apparently on the spur of the moment he decided to organize a pic-nic—to use the nineteenth-century form for an event which in those days deserved the impressive hyphen— for the following Monday.

On the morning of August 5, a cloudy day, Duyckinck, Mathews, and Melville were joined at the Pittsfield railroad station by Oliver Wendell Holmes, who had a summer place in the Berkshires. Holmes was at this time professor of anatomy at the Harvard Medical School and was known widely as a wit in prose and verse, although he had not yet emerged as "the autocrat of the breakfast table." The group had a merry ride on the train to Stockbridge, according to Mathews, who in reporting the day's happenings in the pages of the *Literary World* elevated that occasion into the realm of allegory, all the participants assuming appropriate epithets. Because the readers of the magazine consisted of literary people who knew the in-group, there was no need to supply the real names. Mathews appointed himself "Humble Self," Duyckinck "Silver Pen," Holmes "Mr. Town Wit," and Melville "New Neptune." The party was completed "with the addition of the charming sketcher of New England mystic life, Mr. Noble Melancholy, and . . . his publisher, Mr. Greenfield"—Nathaniel Hawthorne and James T. Fields.

Here Mathews's blithely undifferentiated prose failed its subject matter. This meeting of Mr. Noble Melancholy and New Neptune was one of those dramatic moments when genius meets genius or, more accurately, when genius collides with genius. Mathews failed to record either the greetings or the reactions when for the first time Nathaniel Hawthorne met Herman Melville.

There were three females in the party, Mrs. David Dudley Field and her twelve-year-old daughter Jeannie and Annie Fields, "the new wife, who is the violet of the season in Berkshires." According to Duyckinck, Annie Fields was attired in "delicate blue silk," which was a pictorially satisfying accompaniment to her husband's "curled whiskers" and his "patent leathers." Sophia remained at home with her mother—which is a distinct loss, since she had a fine eye for visual details and nuances of mood. There was one other male, who, as he noted years later, "enjoyed the distinction of being the only [male] of the party who had not written a book"—Henry Dwight Sedgwick, of a distinguished Stockbridge family and later a local historian.

In 1895 Sedgwick wrote, "I remember little more of their conversation than that they talked prose apparently as unconsciously as *M. Jourdain* himself." In the pages of the *Literary World* Mathews did not have Sedgwick's mellowed detachment. According to Humble Self, an almost maniacal exhilaration took possession of the participants. The party set out in three carriages, with Sedgwick on horseback, for the foot of the mountain about five miles away. Monument Mountain is distinguished by a summit of rocks that form a white chimney above pine and white birch trees. From below as one looks up at the cliff of rocks the ascent appears difficult, but, despite Mathews's heightened prose, it can be climbed, even by women in the inhibiting clothing of the nineteenth century or by men in patent leather shoes, in an hour or more by following a ridge that taxes neither breath nor skirts, until the last fifty or so feet.

"Higher, higher up we go," Mathews wrote, his participles keeping pace, "stealing glances through the trees at the country underneath; rambling, scrambling, climbing, rhyming—puns flying off in every direction, like sparks among the bushes." In a letter to his wife, Duyckinck reported that Hawthorne and he were "in advance, talking of the Scarlet

Letter." Mathews would have none of such matter-of-factness. He insisted that spirits mounted as the climbers reached the rocky top, "that watch-tower, so near up towards heaven." There Holmes ventured a pun "and is, righteously, near losing his foothold and tumbling straight down a thousand feet." Melville was "the boldest of all" and the wildest: "New Neptune is certainly fancying himself among the whalers of the Pacific, for he perches himself astride a jutting rock, like a bowsprit." As Melville "pulled and hauled imaginary ropes for our delectation," Holmes "peeped about the cliffs and protested it affected him like ipecac." Even Hawthorne, according to Duyckinck, "looked wildly about for the great carbuncle."

The day was not without ominous overtones. "A black thunder cloud from the south," Duyckinck wrote in his imagistic prose, "dragged its ragged edges toward us." Mathews was metaphorically more conventional: "The tempest . . . spreads his cloudy wings, which he presently shakes upon us, and compels us to a retreat, which, honored as the harbor of two lovely women, shall be henceforth known as the Fairy Shelter." There in the shelter, probably just below the pinnacle since heavily skirted women could not have scrambled about on the rocky cliffs, Holmes "cut three branches for an umbrella and uncorked the champagne which was drunk from a silver mug." As Holmes posed with his improvised umbrella, the frock coats, the manicured whiskers, the blue silk, the patent leather shoes, the silver goblets, and the sparkling foam should have ravished the eyes of a nineteenth-century genre painter.

Inspired by the iced champagne and accompanied by "the vast organbass of the rolling thunder," Mathews read Bryant's poem written after a visit to Monument Mountain, in which he relates the story of an Indian girl "With wealth of raven tresses, a light form, / And a gay heart." One summer day, accompanied by a friend, she climbed Monument Mountain, said farewell, and threw herself from the steep rocks.

After the storm, the champagne, and the poem, the picnickers got into their carriages and, "with a cool gallop along the road . . . returned to the Umbrage," to the Fields' home.

The dinner, Duyckinck wrote to his wife, was "a three hour's business from turkey to ice cream, well moistened by the way." At this point in his account Mathews became coy: "You would give the world to have an accurate account from so careful a pen as ours of what that picked company of wits and belles had to say to each other over the wine. But—we have sworn on oath—we have sealed a seal, never, never to divulge, no, never." Three of the participants recalled that Holmes discoursed on "the superiority of Englishmen." Duyckinck, writing on the following day, claimed that Melville attacked Holmes vigorously, Hawthorne looking on. In 1872, in *Yesterdays with Authors*, Fields recalled that at dinner "Hawthorne rayed out in sparkling and unwonted manner" and that in the bantering exchange with Holmes, it was "Hawthorne stoutly taking part in favor of Americans."

After three hours the participants, undaunted or perhaps stimulated by food, drink, and talk, were ready for one more excursion to complete the kind of day that appealed to that muscular century. The party, only the males this time, was guided by an after-dinner guest, John Tyler Headley, author of the popular biographies *Napoleon and His Generals* and *Washington and His Generals*. Headley, a former minister, had recently married and was spending the summer at an inn in Stockbridge. Poe considered Headley "the Autocrat of all the Quacks." "We readily forgive a man for being a fool," Poe added, "if he only be a *perfect* fool—and this is a particular in which we cannot put our hands upon our hearts and say that Mr. Headley is deficient. He acts upon the principle that if a thing is worth doing at all it is worth doing well:—and the thing that he 'does' especially well is the public."[24]

The destination in the late afternoon was Ice Glen, which, as Headley characterized it, seemed an ideal setting for one of Hawthorne's dreamlike processions. Boulders and trees have fallen in helter-skelter fashion into the gorge, and some of the rocks, topped with ferns and green mold, form tunnels that make voices resound with doomlike intensity. Hawthorne described Ice Glen "as looking as if the Devil had torn his way through a rock & left it all jagged behind him." When a few months later Melville was composing that extraordinary chapter in *Moby-Dick* entitled "A Bower in the Arsacides," he recalled "a wonderous sight. The wood was green as mosses of the Icy Glen; the trees stood high and haughty, feeling their living sap; the industrious earth beneath was as a weaver's loom, with a gorgeous carpet on it, whereof the ground-vine tendrils formed the warp and woof, and the living flowers the figures."[25]

According to Headley, the procession into Ice Glen was led by Hawthorne, "with his dreamy face and dark eyes, looking as if life itself were a glen filled with nought but strange shadows and weird scenes." He was followed by Duyckinck, Holmes, and Mathews, Fields bringing up "the rear of this remarkable *literary* column." For some reason Headley made no mention of Melville. After the passage of twenty-two years, Fields recalled that "Hawthorne was among the most enterprising of the merrymakers; and being in the dark much of the time, he ventured to call out lustily and pretend that certain destruction was inevitable to all of us."[26]

"The 5th of August was a happy day throughout, and I never saw Hawthorne in better spirits," Fields wrote in 1872. In his journal entry for August 5, 1850, Hawthorne kept to the facts:

Rode with Fields & wife to Stockbridge, being thereto invited by Mr. Field of S.—in order to ascend Monument mountain. Found at Mr. F's Dr. Holmes, Mr. Duyckinck of New-York, also Messrs. Cornelius Mathews & Herman Melville. Ascended the mountain—that is to say, Mrs. Fields and Miss Jenny Field—Messrs. Field & Fields— Dr. Holmes, Messrs. Duyckinck, Mathews, Melville, Mr. Henry Sedgwick, & I.—and were caught in a shower. Dined at Mr. F's. Afternoon, under guidance of J. T. Headley, the party scrambled through the Ice Glen.[27]

On Wednesday, August 7, "Messrs. Duyckinck, Mathews, Melville, & Melville, Jr., called in the forenoon." They met Sophia, Mrs. Peabody, and the Hawthorne children. Again Hawthorne recorded few details: "Gave them a couple of bottles of Mr. Mansfield's champagne, and walked down to the lake with them. At twilight, Mr. Edwin P. Whipple and wife called from Lenox." Sophia wrote about the morning guests with a good deal more animation than her husband permitted himself. "Mr. Typee is interesting in his aspect quite. I see Fayaway in his face—Mr Mathews . . . is a very chatty gossiping body—Mr. Duyckinck—a trim, dutch but very gentle, agreeable gentleman."[28]

On August 7 Hawthorne made a remarkable admission in a letter to Bridge: "I met Melville, the other day, and liked him so much that I have asked him to spend a few days with me before leaving these parts." For anybody else such a remark could hardly be considered effusive, but for Hawthorne, who generally kept strangers and sometimes even friends at a careful distance, it indicated that he was strongly, if perhaps ambiguously, attracted to Melville's assertive, seemingly outgoing personality. Duyckinck's characterization of Hawthorne at this social meeting, curiously, evokes Arthur Dimmesdale: "Hawthorne is a fine ghost in a case of iron—a man of genius and he looks it and lives it—He gave us some Heidsieck . . . popping the corks in his nervous way."[29]

So far as we know, Melville had nothing to say, directly, about the events that took place on August 5 or about this second meeting with Hawthorne. What he had to say in the *Literary World* on August 17 and 24, in what was intended as a review of Hawthorne's *Mosses from an Old Manse*, was more personal and impassioned than anything in Mathews's three installments. While Mathews and Duyckinck were still enjoying the sights about Pittsfield, Melville evidently found time to retreat to his study in "the *garret-way*, seated at that little embrasure of a window . . . which commands so noble a view of Saddleback," or Greylock, the tallest mountain in the Berkshires. There he wrote vigorously and rapidly, as though his life depended upon it—and indeed, in some sense, perhaps it did.

The review was unsigned. The subtitle read, "By a Virginian Spending July in Vermont." Melville had no southern ties, and he read Hawthorne's tales for the first time in Pittsfield. In the second installment he added to the fiction: "I never saw the man; and in the chances of a quiet plantation life, remote from his haunts, perhaps never shall." The disguise served its purpose at least for a while in deceiving the Hawthornes. Sophia urged her mother not to "wait an hour to procure the two last numbers of 'The Literary World,' and read a new criticism on Mr Hawthorne. . . . I know you will enjoy the words of this ardent Virginian as I do."[30]

The article opens conventionally—and prettily—enough, but before the conclusion of the first paragraph emotion breaks through.

> A papered chamber in a fine old farm-house, a mile from any other dwelling, and dipped to the eaves in foliage—surrounded by mountains, old woods, and Indian ponds,—this, surely, is the place to write of Hawthorne. . . . A man of a deep and noble nature has seized me in this seclusion. His wild, witch-voice rings through me; or, in softer cadences, I seem to hear it in the songs of the hill-side birds that sing in the larch trees at my windows.

The language at times is reminiscent of Mathews's precious pictorial sense in his articles in the *Literary World*, but Melville is not simply a passive recorder of literary and personal impressions. Hawthorne appears as a natural, even supernatural, force that enchants and hypnotizes, as Ahab overpowers physically and emotionally the crew of the *Pequod.*

After the opening paragraph, Melville playfully explains the appearance of his review four years after the publication of the book: "It may be . . . that all this while the book . . . was only improving in flavor and body." While a pleasant compliment, with the almost trite remark he inconspicuously introduces what will become a pattern of oral imagery.

> At breakfast the other day, a mountain girl, a cousin of mine, . . . this charming Cherry says to me—"I see you spend your mornings in the haymow; and yesterday I found their 'Dwight's Travels in New England.' Now I have something far better than that, something more congenial to our summer on these hills. Take these raspberries, and then I will give you some moss. . . ."
>
> With that she left me, and soon returned with a volume, verdantly bound, and garnished with a curious frontispiece in green: nothing less than a fragment of real moss, cunningly pressed to a fly-leaf. "Why this," said I, spilling my raspberries, "this is the 'Mosses from an Old Manse.'" "Yes," said cousin Cherry, "yes, it is that flowery Hawthorne." "Hawthorne and Mosses," said I, "no more: it is morning: it is July in the country: and I am off for the barn."

If truth may intrude for a moment upon Melville's somewhat romanticized account, the book was given to him not by Cousin Cherry but by his Aunt Mary, the wife of his favorite uncle, Thomas Melvill, at whose desk in the next fifteen months he was to rewrite *Moby-Dick*. Cherry's name is appropriate for her function as mistress of the breakfast banquet.

The constant references to food are neither accidental nor picturesque, as Melville himself will make clear before the end of the article. When he sees the little green book, he spills his raspberries. A playful detail perhaps, but in a significant scene in the last tale Melville wrote, Billy Budd spills his soup in a seemingly trivial episode tragic in its consequences and deep in its psychological relevancy.

Early in the day, then, in fertile July, Melville is off to the barn to absorb *Mosses from an Old Manse*. He stretches out on new-mown clover: "The soft ravishment of the man spun me round about in a web of dreams, and when the book was closed, when the spell was over, the wizard 'dismissed me with but misty reminiscences, as if I had been dreaming of him.'"

Gradually Hawthorne assumes a godlike role, combining male and female roles: he has "such a boundless sympathy with all forms of being,
such an omnipresent love," and "a great deep intellect, which drops down
into the universe like a plummet." Next Melville explores "this great
power of blackness in him" which "derives its force from its appeals to
that Calvinistic sense of Innate Depravity and Original Sin." "It is," he
admits, "that blackness in Hawthorne . . . that fixes and fascinates me,"
and this in turn leads to the assertion that Hawthorne is Shakespeare's
equal. "There are minds," he declares without naming them, "that have
gone as far as Shakespeare into the universe." Later he admits that in
praising Hawthorne "I have more served and honored myself, than him,"
which means, according to the logic of his associations, that he ranks
himself with Hawthorne and Shakespeare.

This admission leads him to acknowledge that art is often autobiography more or less veiled because of the cultural context and the artist's
inhibitions.

> And if you rightly look for it, you will almost always find that the
> author himself has somewhere furnished you with his own picture.
> For poets (whether in prose or verse), being painters of nature, are
> like their brethren of the pencil, the true portrait-painters, who, in
> the multitude of likenesses to be sketched, do not invariably omit
> their own. . . .

"Twenty-four hours," he informs us, "have elapsed since writing the
foregoing. I have just returned from the hay-mow, charged more and
more with love and admiration of Hawthorne." Now he arrives at his
climactic statement as he finds the right words to characterize the effect
upon him of *Mosses from an Old Manse*. "To what infinite height of loving wonder and admiration I shall have thoroughly *incorporated* their
whole stuff into my being,—that, I cannot tell." And the next sentence
makes Hawthorne the seedman, the penetrator: "Hawthorne has dropped
germinous seeds into my soul" and "expands and deepens down, the more
I contemplate him; and further and further, shoots his strong New England roots into the hot soil in my Southern soul."

"Hawthorne and His Mosses" is scarcely literary criticism in the ordinary sense. It is a love letter and a confession. Artistically it records an
epiphany of an artist whose search of thirty-one years culminated in an
erotic-aesthetic union.

Longfellow wrote to Hawthorne enthusiastically after reading the articles in the *Literary World*: "I have rarely seen a more appreciating and sympathizing critic; and though I do not endorse all he says about others, I do endorse all he says about you." Sophia could scarcely contain herself. "At last," she wrote to her mother, "some one dares to say what in my secret mind I have often thought—that he is only to be mentioned with the Swan of Avon; the great heart and grand intellect combined." Sophia had been of this opinion for a long time. In her diary on December 26, 1843, she had written: "What a miracle he is! He gives me a greater sense of universal power than any person I ever knew or heard of except Shakspere. He resembles him more than any one else."[31]

"I wish they could see each other," Sophia wrote. He "cannot be disappointed when he looks down into that vortex of suns, his eyes—with their shroud of silver mist. He must come here on his way home from Vermont to Virginia." To Duyckinck she exclaimed, with remarkable intuition since a Promethean fire was to burn in the pages of *Moby-Dick*: "The freshness of primeval nature is in that man, & the true Promethean fire is in him. Who can he be, so fearless, so rich in heart, of such fine intuition? Is his name altogether hidden?"[32]

Somewhat more tempered, although not much, Hawthorne confessed his "great pleasure" in the review. Recognizing the oral imagery and the magical or even mystical effect of his writings on Melville, Hawthorne commented: "The writer has a truly generous heart; nor do I think it necessary to appropriate the whole magnificence of his encomium, any more than to devour everything on the table, when a host of noble hospitality spreads a banquet before me. But he is no common man; and next to deserving his praise, it is good to have beguiled and bewitched such a man into praising me more than I deserve."[33]

Duyckinck did not reveal the identity of the Virginian when he sent illustrations of Washington Irving's work to Sophia and copies of three books by Melville to Hawthorne, *Mardi*, *Redburn*, and *White-Jacket*. According to Sophia, Hawthorne read the novels "on the new hay in the barn, which is a delightful place for the perusal of worthy books." Hawthorne summed up his reactions tersely: "I have read Melville's works with a progressive appreciation of the author. No writer ever put the reality before his reader more unflinchingly than he does in 'Redburn,' and 'White-Jacket.' 'Mardi' is a rich book, with depths here and there that compel a man to swim for his life. It is so good that one scarcely pardons the writer for not having brooded long over it, so as to make it a good deal better," which is a judicious evaluation of a deeply flawed and tediously extended romance.

Because of the shortage of bedrooms, Melville's stay with the Hawthornes had to be deferred until the departure of Mrs. Peabody. His authorship of the articles in the *Literary World* was known when in the forenoon on September 3 he arrived at the red farmhouse. On the next day the two men rode into Pittsfield to visit Melville's cousin and returned to Lenox "at about 8 P.M." On Saturday, September 7, "Herman Melville went away, after breakfast." Once again Hawthorne's entries in his journal kept to the facts. Fortunately Sophia did not emulate his reticence. After one day Sophia found Melville "a man with a true warm heart & a soul & an intellect—with life to his finger-tips." Always in search of eternal truths, she had not arrived at a definitive view of his stature: "I am not sure that he is not a very great man—but I have not quite decided upon my opinion—I should say, I am not quite sure that I *do not think* him a very great man—for my opinion is of course as far as possible from settling the matter."[34]

A few days later Sophia found Melville "a person of great ardor & simplicity—He is all on fire with the subject that interests him. It rings through his frame like a cathedral bell. His truth & honesty shine out at every point!" She intuited that the relationship was that of father and son, without knowing that Hawthorne was in the flesh an answer to Melville's fictional preoccupation with a son in search of either a father or an elder brother such as Whitman speaks of. The desire—actually a hunger, like Bartleby's—haunted him from his earliest published essay, a banal little piece in an Albany newspaper in 1839, to the story of Billy Budd which he left unfinished at his death in 1891.[35]

During the visit Hawthorne worked on the manuscript of *The House of the Seven Gables* in the mornings, and Melville took walks by himself or read Emerson's essays. Sophia confessed at the end of the four-day stay: "He was very agreeable; but as I had to spend every morning from breakfast to dinner in preparing dinners & overseeing all cooking, I was tired & glad to bid him farewell—I wish some way could be contrived to eat without cooking."[36]

While the Hawthornes resumed their usual patterns, Melville was negotiating for a house in Pittsfield. How much the presence of Hawthorne influenced his decision cannot be verified, but it may well have been overriding. About the middle of the month Melville's father-in-law, Judge Lemuel Shaw, advanced $3,000, and Melville drove up at the red farmhouse "one superb moonlight night," according to Sophia, to inform the Hawthornes that he had purchased "an estate six miles from us, where he is really going to build a real towered house—an actual tower." Perhaps Melville had spun fancies about a tower during his visit which had impressed Sophia, but he never got around to remodeling the former Brewster property in Pittsfield. Curiously—although there may be no association—Hawthorne added a tower to his second Concord house in 1860, long after the silence between the two men had become final.[37]

"I have had a glorious time here this summer," Hawthorne informed Zachariah Burchmore with more enthusiasm than usual, "but have been rather lazy, and am just taking hold of my work in earnest now." Actually, if his report to Fields can be trusted, he began work on *The House of the Seven Gables* about the middle of August, shortly after his meeting with Melville. Although, as he explained to his publisher, the summer was not his "natural season for work," he "religiously" secluded himself "every morning (much against my will)" until "dinner-time or thereabouts." He admitted freely that he preferred "gazing at Monument Mountain, broad before my eyes, instead of at the infernal sheet of paper under my hand."[38]

In September Ticknor and Fields ordered a third printing of *The Scarlet Letter*, making a total of six thousand copies in the first six months of publication. Hawthorne was paid a 15 percent royalty on a book costing seventy-five cents. When he received the royalties for the first three printings he had earned only $806.25. Excluding gifts at the beginning of the year from Boston and New York friends, he received in 1850 $25.00 from the *National Era* for "The Great Stone Face" and $50.00 from *International Miscellany* for "The Snow-Image." Clearly Hawthorne had no alternative but to keep his eyes on that "infernal sheet of paper under my hand."[39]

Her health now restored and a match for her unflagging enthusiasm, Sophia behaved that fall and winter as though she had no cares. "I never feel need of any variety of society," she explained to her sister Mary. "I never feel a want. All my needs are met & satisfied by my own little circle." She took her customary pleasure in her ardent involvement in the lives of Una, now six, and of Julian, now four. Mother and children were sometimes hard put for entertainment that winter. When Una was not too moody to be excused, the children acted out scenes from Bunyan, who dominated their imaginative lives as he had their parents'. With the aid of her mother and Julian, Una was rescued from the Giant Despair so that she could proceed to the Celestial City. Sophia's brother Nathaniel was much concerned: "How Sophia's children will turn out is problematical. I fear that they will not be able to live in a world which has so much to shock fine sensibilities. I should not like to have my children see only the beautiful colors of the rainbow." Nathaniel was perhaps unduly concerned, although the Hawthorne children were to experience many difficulties in adjustment and maturation. Sophia's noble phrasing and fluttering attempts to make over reality could not shield her children from the resonances of life experiences. One day that winter Julian carefully carved out a grave for Grandmother Hawthorne in the snow.[40]

As fall turned to what Hawthorne called "the Zeroic ages," the family continued the regimen Sophia had established in the Concord Eden. No one had colds for a simple, if icy, reason: "The children, in a cold room, recieve each a pail of fresh well water on their heads & bodies every morning, & then Papa & Moma each sit in a tub of the same pitiless water & splash & rub till warmth comes out of what Mr Hawthorne would call a 'hell of cold' for he thinks that the fabled depressed pit is not hot but cold. . . ." On another occasion she elaborated that the children's "skins are rubbed with the hand. Their father generally does it in a very animated manner."[41]

The Peabody sisters never let up in their criticism of Hawthorne, although it is easy to understand that Sophia's endless and lengthy praise could provoke a reaction. That winter when Mary Mann criticized Sophia's "Apollo with his lute," Sophia reaffirmed what her marriage meant to her.

> He never needed any one to defend him. As the years go on, I go deeper into the rich deep of his being, but I have by no means sounded it yet. . . . I am lost in wonder that I should be so blest & his love first awoke in me *consciousness*. I am conscious of the bliss of being now. *Before* I ignorantly lived. His society is the loftiest education. I feel myself rounding into a sphere. . . . And he is so childlike in unworldliness, in unsophisticatedness.

She was in fact "rounding" into pregnancy, but her husband was neither so childlike nor unworldly as she preferred to believe.[42]

Intercourse with the World

The House of the Seven Gables

One day in the summer of 1850 Hawthorne went upstairs to his study. It was a moment of excitement and tension: he was about to begin a new romance. Before he sat down at the desk which had belonged to Sophia's short-lived brother George, Hawthorne removed his everyday clothes and carefully put on the gown created by Sophia and Louisa to accommodate their vision of his kingship. Extant records make no reference to the presence of a mirror, but surely in his tremulous state he needed confirmation of his transformation.

The gown was created during the edenic honeymoon at the Manse when Nathaniel and Sophia became Adam and Eve. In his new romance Hawthorne was to depict in another embroidery the Eden that Hester Prynne was not permitted to enter. One of the characters, Clifford Pyncheon, an effete, world-weary lover of beauty, is to wear an "old-fashioned dressing-gown of faded damask" which is his threadbare tie to a vision that he is cheated of by the machinations of Judge Pyncheon, a man of iron on the order of William or John Hathorne. Clifford is the failed artist of Hawthorne's fears.

Putting on the gown facilitated, Hawthorne probably fancied, entry into the realm of romance and make-believe, the assumption of various roles which were part of his multifaceted personality, and the recovery of the inventive spirit he experienced for the first time in childhood when he began to translate his dreams and terrors into tales he told to his family. As pleased as he was with the gown and its evocations, he was not completely satisfied. He longed, according to Sophia, "to have a study with a soft, thick Turkey carpet upon the floor & hung round with full crimson curtains, so as to hide all rectangles," a setting that conjured up Aladdin and the *Arabian Nights' Entertainments*.[1]

When he looked out of the windows in his study, he could see in the distance Monument Mountain "in a recumbent position, stretching almost across the valley," which he compared to "a huge, headless Sphinx, wrapped in a Persian shawl." He summoned one of the recurrent images of nineteenth-century art and literature, the Greek sphinx, half-human, half-animal, a lion's body with a woman's breast, symbol of the castrating woman and guardian of the riddle which Oedipus unraveled.[2]

While Hawthorne shaped *The House of the Seven Gables*, Sophia kept the children out of sight. Even when he descended the stairs in the afternoon and reentered the world, she made the transition easier for him by keeping the children at a distance, for, as she explained to her sister Mary, "he still is mentally engaged when out of his study."[3]

In August 1850 Hawthorne was reasonably confident, at least when he wrote to his publisher, that his new romance would be finished by November. "If not," he commented, "it can't be helped. I must not pull up my cabbage by the roots, by way of hastening its growth." A few weeks later he expected that the book would be completed "by the end of the year." On October 1 he was so "deep" into his romance that he was unable to fulfill the editorial duties he had promised for the revision of Bridge's book. On the same day he informed Fields that the new story would not be ready in November, "for I am never good for anything in the literary way till after the first autumnal frost which has somewhat such an effect on my imagination that it does on the foliage here about me, multiplying and brightening its hues."[4]

In November Hawthorne offered Fields a candid explanation of the difficulties he was encountering:

> I find the book requires more care and thought than the "Scarlet Letter";—also, I have to wait oftener for a mood. The Scarlet Letter being all in one tone, I had only to get my pitch, and could then go on interminably. Many passages of this book ought to be finished

with the minuteness of a Dutch picture, in order to give them their proper effect. Sometimes, when tired of it, it strikes me that the whole is an absurdity, from beginning to end; but the fact is, in writing a romance, a man is always—or always ought to be—careening on the utmost verge of a precipitous absurdity, and the skill lies in coming as close as possible, without actually tumbling over. My prevailing idea is, that the book ought to succeed better than the Scarlet Letter, though I have no idea that it will.[5]

As the work progressed he had not unfamiliar reservations, doubts, even depressed moods. At the end of November he was "weary and my hand trembles with writing all day at it." The tone of the romance continued to concern him: "It darkens damnably towards the close, but I shall try hard to pour some setting sunshine over it." Ten days later he stopped writing completely: "I have been in a Slough of Despond, for some days past—having written so fiercely that I came to a stand still. There are points where a writer gets bewildered, and cannot form any judgment of what he has done, nor tell what to do next. In these cases, it is best to keep quiet." If Hawthorne invoked Bunyan frequently in depressed moods, the reason may have been that he began to read Bunyan for himself during depressed states in childhood.[6]

On January 12, 1851, The House of the Seven Gables was, "so to speak, finished; only I am hammering away a little on the roof, and doing up a few odd jobs that were left incomplete." The final step was the reading to Sophia, which took place on the evening of January 26. It "met with extraordinary success. . . . I likewise prefer it to the Scarlet Letter; but an author's opinion of his book, just after completing it, is worth little or nothing; he being then in the hot or cold fit of a fever, and certain to rate it too high or too low."[7]

Sophia was a great deal more positive and could hardly contain herself when she wrote to her mother:

Mr Hawthorne read me the close last evening. There is unspeakable grace & beauty in the conclusion, throwing back upon the sterner majesty of the commencement an ethereal light & a dear home-loveliness and satisfaction. How you will enjoy the book,—its depth of wisdom, its high tone, the flowers of Paradise scattered over all the dark places, the sweet wall-flower scent of Phoebe's character, the wonderful pathos & charms of old Uncle Venner. I only wish you could have heard the Poet sing his own song as I did. . . .[8]

Nearsighted, old, her fingers and her voice "tremulous," Hepzibah Pyncheon, the custodian of the House of the Seven Gables, looks one day at her fifty-year-old sampler with "some of the most recondite specimens of ornamental needlework." She sighs one of her endless sighs, almost the only sound ever heard inside the walls of the ancient house where for thirty years she has lived alone.

If *The Scarlet Letter* is a majestic, stately structured tapestry worthy of Hester's skills and vision, *The House of the Seven Gables* resembles that charming product of a domestic art, the sampler which glorified home, family, and simple virtues and their custodians, the American women, embroidered in a "peaceable kingdom" in which, as in Hawthorne's romance, there are robins in a pear tree, a chanticleer with two scrawny hens, roses, and a house with seven asymmetrical gables. It is customary to mention the Flemish or Dutch qualities of this domestic romance, as Hawthorne himself does, but *The House of the Seven Gables* has only a touch-and-run relationship with such realism or literalism, the atmosphere and the characters being suffused with romantic colorations that relate to but transcend reality to evoke an ideal, the lost Eden.

The House of the Seven Gables is a sampler far more sophisticated and artistic than those made by young women in the early years of the last century. Or, put another way, here Hawthorne emulates the delicacy of Owen Warland in his careful and loving attention to detail and simplicities. Nowhere else in his writings is so much care lavished, almost squandered, on exquisite trivia. Melville, who never was domesticated in life or in art, even in a domestic novel like *Pierre*, approved: "We think the book, for pleasantness of running interest, surpasses the other works of the author." Hawthorne appeared to concur but for other, somewhat questionable reasons. To Duyckinck he declared it "a more natural and healthy product of my mind" and to Bridge "a work more characteristic of my mind, and more proper and natural for me to write, than the Scarlet Letter."[9]

The romance centers around the descendants of two families of Puritan origins who have continued to feud and to be stained by their corruptness and wrath. The feud began when Colonel Pyncheon wanted land owned by a laborer named Matthew Maule and had him executed "for the crime of witchcraft." At his death Matthew placed a curse on the Pyncheons: "God will give him blood to drink!" Matthew's son, however, constructed the House of the Seven Gables for the Pyncheons over "an unquiet grave" of his father. On the day the house was to be dedicated the guests waited in vain in the parlors for the appearance of Colonel Pyncheon, who died of apoplexy beneath his portrait, the "print of a bloody hand on his plaited ruff." Matthew's curse haunts both families and exacts an awesome price.

The present-day Pyncheons include a distinguished judge, his two in-effectual cousins, Hepzibah and Clifford, who occupy the ancestral house in Salem, and a country cousin named Phoebe. The decline of the family is evidenced in Judge Pyncheon's imprisonment of Clifford for thirty years on a trumped-up charge. The Maules have also fallen on hard times, and apparently the only survivor is a young daguerreotypist and socialist who calls himself Holgrave. When the story opens he occupies the attic of the Pyncheon mansion, where he spies on his family's enemies and the town itself, not unlike the young Hawthorne in his attic study on Herbert Street.

Literary and biological logic decree only one conclusion to such a tale, which Hawthorne states with candor in his prefaces:

> . . . the Author has provided himself with a moral;—the truth, namely, that the wrong-doing of one generation lives into the succes-sive ones, and, divesting itself of every temporary advantage, be-comes a pure and uncontrollable mischief;—and he would feel it a singular gratification, if this Romance might effectually convince mankind (or, indeed, any one man) of the folly of tumbling down an avalanche of ill-gotten gold or real estate, on the heads of an unfor-tunate posterity, thereby to maim and crush them, until the accu-mulated mass shall be scattered abroad in its original atoms.

Modestly he doubts that his romance (or presumably any other literary work) can effect such transformations. "The author has considered it hardly worth his while, therefore, relentlessly to impale the story with its moral, as with an iron rod—or rather, as by sticking a pin through a butterfly—thus at once depriving it of life, and causing it to stiffen in an ungainly and unnatural attitude."

Hawthorne had no naive faith in the moral powers of literature, and he was perhaps an agnostic about the laws and logic of determinism which like most people he believed and simultaneously disbelieved depending upon situation and mood. Further, he claimed for himself as author a right denied to him by critics impaled on their theories: to transcend logic and even morality for his artistic and human purposes. And so the determinism of heredity—the curse of the Maules on the Pyncheons, the physical and emotional decadence and enervation of Clifford and Hepzibah Pyncheon, and the Maulean characteristics of Holgrave to invade the human personality, what Hawthorne later calls "cobwebby old hereditary nonsense"—is swept away in a new-old miracle of comic regeneration. [10]

The new House will be presided over by seventeen-year-old Phoebe, who is the fulfillment of Hester Prynne's vision of "the coming revelation . . . a woman . . . lofty, pure, and beautiful; and wise, moreover, not through dusky grief, but the ethereal medium of joy, and showing how sacred love should make us happy, by the truest test of a life successful to such an end!" [11]

In Hawthorne's version of an ancient family strife, reconciliation and reconstruction are to take place through the marriage of Phoebe and Holgrave. The fusion heralds the recovery of Eden, which, as some skeptical commentators have been quick to point out, is not recoverable, if (to go one step farther) it ever existed. Hawthorne, however, presents a greater, but not easily demonstrated, truth: Eden is recovered every time we fall in love, play house in love and marriage, and give birth to new Adams and Eves, who in turn will (regretfully perhaps) look like us and (happily) will also find their Edens (sometimes).

The first chapter of the romance provides the historical background, the decline of two families whose destructiveness is often turned against themselves. In the second chapter—"The Little Shop-Window"—we are in the present, witnesses of a great event in the life of Hepzibah Pyncheon, the occupant of the house. In the first version of the chapter Hawthorne—like Holgrave—was a detached commentator, and Hepzibah was the (in caps) "OLD MAID," an eccentric, unattractive, vain offspring or remnant of the Pyncheons. As he wrote, Hawthorne changed his attitude and fell in love with Hepzibah, as Henry James was to note, and at that moment—in an epiphany of love—*The House of the Seven Gables* was transformed into an American counterpart of Shakespeare's *Tempest*. What happened to Hawthorne in the fall of 1850 happened decades earlier to James Fenimore Cooper as he wrote *The Pioneers*, and suddenly, miraculously, Natty Bumppo was no longer an illiterate bumpkin but an American hero. Hepzibah does not rise to Natty's height; she is simply one of the lovable characters in one of America's lovable books.

Fearful, tremulous, Hepzibah squints nearsightedly and walks on tiptoe as though pursued by some villain or by her own shadow, sighing "gusty sighs" in the empty rooms. Nervously she examines herself in a mirror and then gazes at a miniature of a beautiful young man, "the only substance for her heart to feed on." After thirty years of self-imposed isolation she is readying herself, "full of little tremors and palpitations," to reenter the world as an "aristocratic hucksteress" of a cent-shop, although she is still perplexed as to "how to tempt little boys into her premises!" A relative as it were of Miss Havisham in *Great Expectations*, she will manage to be a good witch and fatten up a little boy named Ned Higgins.

Simulating Hepzibah's fearfulness, the narrator reluctantly intrudes: "All this time, . . . we are loitering faint-heartedly on the threshold of our story. In very truth, we have an invincible reluctance to disclose what Miss Hepzibah Pyncheon was about to do." The narrator is also on tiptoe as he plays with this world-shattering event—when Hepzibah ceases to be a lady and the House of the Seven Gables, like the House of Usher or the House of Atreus, begins to develop fissures—for we are to witness this sixty-year-old's loss of gentility. When Holgrave attempts to make the first purchase in the cent-shop and offers payment, she refuses, saying, "Let me be a lady a moment longer." Later she draws on her silk gloves to count her ill-gotten lucre.

Again Hawthorne intrudes into his narrative with affectionate mockery:

What tragic dignity, for example, can be wrought into a scene like this! How can we elevate our history of retribution for the sin of long ago, when, as one of our most prominent figures we are compelled to introduce—not a young and lovely woman, nor even the stately remains of beauty, storm-shattered by affliction—but a gaunt, sallow, rust-jointed maiden, in a long-waisted silk gown, and with the strange horror of a turban on her head!

Such intrusions undermine the inviolability of hereditary determinism, and we observe in the second chapter the quiet marriage of style and content. And why not? Hepzibah is in love with her brother Clifford, the young man of the miniature, and surely Hawthorne must have recognized—and hence the alteration from authorial detachment to love—that Hepzibah bears more than a few resemblances to the women, Sophia excepted, he knew best, his mother and his two sisters, all of whom were more than a little in love with him.

This exquisite chapter, one of the finest that Hawthorne ever wrote, quietly and comically establishes the resurrection theme or Lazarus motif which is hinted at in the previous chapter in unexplained references to a man (actually the imprisoned brother Clifford) "long-buried . . . to be summoned forth from his living tomb." Hepzibah's venture into the world—her resurrection—is an act of love for Clifford's sake as well as the only way she knows to support Clifford without assistance from Judge Pyncheon, who is to play the Bad Father or Witch in the story. Her venture is economically dubious, as the townspeople appear to agree in what will become a comic version of the Greek chorus: "This business of keeping cent-shops is overdone, like all other kinds of trade, handicraft, and bodily labor, . . . Poor business!"

Hepzibah is too old, too scowling, and too ineffectual to play the role to which she aspires. Suddenly Phoebe Pyncheon arrives from the country, and Hawthorne now has his beautiful young woman. With the advent of the sun goddess in Salem, there is a dramatic resurrection before the return of the imprisoned brother. Phoebe sweeps dust, shadows, and death out of the old house and, despite her youth, presides as the symbolic Good Mother, as Holden Caulfield's "kid sister" Phoebe is to do in *Catcher in the Rye*. That night there are mysterious sounds in the cavernous house—Clifford has returned—and the next morning Hepzibah is beside herself as she prepares to feed her beloved brother. She wants Clifford to see Phoebe first because he loves beautiful things, and her mirror has told her the truth about her scowls and grimaces. As Hepzibah steels herself, Clifford hesitates outside the door, afraid to enter the kitchen, to be reborn: "He took hold of the knob of the door; then loosened his grasp, without opening it. Hepzibah, her hands convulsively clasped, stood gazing at the entrance." Finally she has to lead Clifford in by hand. Then Phoebe sees the reality, the face in the miniature thirty years later: ". . . an elderly personage, in an old-fashioned dressing-gown of faded damask, and wearing his gray, or almost white hair, of an unusual length. It quite overshadowed his forehead, except when he thrust it back, and stared vaguely about the room." He moves "slowly, and with as indefinite an aim as a child's first journey across a floor." Here Hawthorne would appear to be evoking the rebirth of Rip Van Winkle and his return home after his twenty-year sleep.

With the appearance of Phoebe in the Pyncheon mansion the edenic motif emerges and fuses with the resurrection theme. A mildewed white rose planted decades earlier by Alice Pyncheon, who was bound over to a Maule in a hypnotic trance, looks "at a fair distance . . . as if it had been brought from Eden, that very summer, together with the mould in which it grew." When Clifford reenters the garden he has not seen for thirty years, the sunshine is "as fresh as that which peeped into Eve's bower, while she and Adam sat at breakfast there." (Here Adam and Eve get themselves domesticated into the American landscape as in a sampler.) On still another occasion in the Pyncheon garden, Clifford wants to prick himself with the rose's thorn in order to assure himself that he is alive. The narrator intrudes to explain, again his affection disclosing his feelings: "It was the Eden of a thunder-smitten Adam, who had fled for refuge thither out of the same dreary and perilous wilderness, into which the original Adam was expelled."

The garden is inhabited by the Pyncheon chickens, an almost impotent chanticleer and his weary, mangy hens. Phoebe, "to the poignant distress of her conscience," observes that the "distinguishing mark of the hens was a crest, of lamentably scanty growth, . . . but so oddly and wickedly analogous to Hepzibah's turban." If the chanticleer and the hens are unimpressive resurrection symbols, their very presence may posit the possibility of change, as does Hawthorne's language: "They were a species of tutelary sprite, or Banshee; although winged and feathered differently from most guardian-angels." In time they are to assert their mythic role.

When love enters Holgrave's life and he sees with the heart, not through the dead eye of a camera, he abandons Daguerre and Fourier for "a bower in Eden, blossoming with the earliest roses God ever made." Now charmed by the romance of moonlight, he realizes that his socialistic schemes are "moonshine," meaning that "Adam's grandchildren" cannot reform the world through ideology, only through self-reformation or self-reliance, Hawthorne at times being of Emerson's party.

Although these motifs support the comic resolution of the romance as two families are saved from destruction, external as well as internal, another motif or symbol hovers over the work, beautiful, ambiguous, and multifaceted, elaborating upon the other motifs but introducing reservations and doubts. *The House of the Seven Gables* is a romance of bubbles and a bubble itself. The dominant image is a recurrent one in Hawthorne's art and in his attitude toward life itself.

Like most children and most artists, many of whom recapture the landscape and edenic enthusiasms of childhood, Hawthorne was as fond of soap bubbles as is Clifford Pyncheon, who one day blows immortal bubbles from the balcony of the House of the Seven Gables. In discussing the manuscript of *The Scarlet Letter* which he has supposedly found in the attic of the Custom-House, Hawthorne notes the difficulties and the "folly" of attempting "to fling myself back into another age; or to insist on creating the semblance of a world out of airy matter, when, at every moment, the impalpable beauty of my soap-bubble was broken by the rude contact of some actual circumstance." Years later he delightedly characterized Robert Browning's "nonsense" in conversation as "the true bubble and effervescence of a bright and powerful mind, and he lets it play among his friends with the faith and simplicity of a child," which at the same time is a description of his own mind. On another occasion Hawthorne spoke of "lonely people," probably including himself, "glad to give utterance to their pent-up ideas, and often bubble over with them as freely as children with their new-found syllables."[12]

These bubbles with their rainbow hues have but a short life. No doubt Hawthorne knew the Renaissance proverb *Homo Bula*—the life of a human being is like a bubble. In *Our Old Home*, Hawthorne employs a bubble to symbolize "the momentary delights of short-lived human beings." As the utopian dream of communal life in *The Blithedale Romance* falls apart because individuals fail to subordinate ego to collective existence, Coverdale, the ironical narrator, comments: "Our great globe floated in the atmosphere of infinite space like an insubstantial bubble."[13]

The bubble, then, refers to the basic concern of fiction with baffling questions of illusion and reality and the nature of the creative act. It expresses but also qualifies Hawthorne's faith in the permanency and cathartic effects of art and reflects the skeptical cast of his mind. For Hawthorne, life like the bubble was bursting and collapsing, youth into age, beauty into ugliness, dreams into acceptance of what is. The bubble like the mirror confirmed the transiency of time, the reality of death.[14]

The Pyncheon dynasty rests upon a bubble that is physiological as well as personal. The founder and his descendants have a "gurgle" in their throats, which the superstitious attribute to the curse that they must drink "Maule's blood." Colonel Pyncheon dies following one of these gurgles, and Judge Pyncheon, the oppressor of Hepzibah and Clifford, dies in similar fashion centuries later: "At his decease, there is only a vacancy, and a momentary eddy—very small, as compared with the apparent magnitude of the ingurgitated object—and a bubble or two, ascending out of the black depth, and bursting at the surface."

The Pyncheons truly live out their lives in servitude to bubbles of greed, sexuality, and station in society. The descendants are dominated by a real-estate bubble in Maine, the claims to which are allegedly buried with the Colonel. In pursuit of this bubble one Pyncheon surrenders his daughter Alice to Thomas Maule, and the Judge, who believes that Clifford knows the whereabouts of the deed to this property, comes to the ancient seven-gabled house on what is to be the last day of his life to extract information from Clifford.

Like his ancestors, Judge Pyncheon, ignoring the physiological bubble that will take his life, believes that he is compelled to live according to the dictates of the clock, society, and a "rigid consistency," which is one way to characterize his obsessive-compulsive nature. His clothes, particularly the "gold-bowed spectacles" and "a gold-headed cane," reflect the accommodation of self-image to society's expectations. Even his ever-present "political" smile is "akin to the shine on his boots. . . . each must have cost him and his boot-black, respectively, a good deal of hard labor to bring out and preserve them." He considers himself a powerful sexual force, but his only conquest is apparently a wife who after three or four years of marriage decided that she could not make a cup of coffee and died, much to her and the Judge's relief. Pyncheon is never to know that his will-to-power is but another bubble.

The greed that holds the Pyncheons in bondage is counterpointed with other forms of greed. Clifford's appetite for food and for beauty hurts no one except himself and sometimes Hepzibah when he is insensitive to her never-ending love. After one of the hens lays a "diminutive" egg following an unusually extended period of sterility, Hepzibah sacrifices "the continuance, perhaps, of an ancient feathered race, with no better end than to supply her brother with a dainty that hardly filled the bowl of a teaspoon!" Clifford consumes it with his usual voracity, which he shares with his sister's best customer, Ned Higgins, who is a magnificent consumer. With unending appetite Ned eats a "little cannibal" (Jim Crow's head), an elephant, a camel, "two dromedaries and a locomotive," and "the great fish—reversing his experience with the prophet of Nineveh." (Here, perhaps, Hawthorne paid a playful compliment to his neighbor Herman Melville, who was at work on his extensive revisions of *Moby-Dick*.)

Holgrave exhibits greed for power both in his use of the daguerreotype to invade personality and in his desire to manipulate people through socialistic schemes for their supposed improvement. But perhaps he has changed his name from Maule to Holgrave for reasons more complicated than he supposes. Consciously he sets out to spy on the Pyncheons from the third-floor room he rents in the house, but unconsciously he may be ready for the transformation that Phoebe will effect as the Good Mother who lifts the curse of patriarchal hatred.

The story of Judge Pyncheon, the last of the line—the name will disappear with the marriage of Phoebe and Holgrave—may be subtitled, without injustice to the romance, "The Bubble Bursts in Three Acts," for the Judge is toppled in three steps from his seeming "topmost greatness," to borrow from Melville's description of Ahab at the end of his three-day pursuit of the whale. With his gold cane (a prop borrowed from the satanic apparition in "Young Goodman Brown"), the Judge appears at the House of the Seven Gables on the morning that Ned Higgins swallows the whale. When the Judge meets Phoebe for the first time and attempts to kiss her, "Phoebe, just at the critical moment, drew back; so that her highly respected kinsman . . . was betrayed into the rather absurd predicament of kissing the empty air. It was a modern parallel to the case of Ixion embracing a cloud."

The second confrontation involves fearful, timid Clifford: "He had not merely grown young; he was a child again." Even in dreams he assumes "the part of a child, or a very young man," and his mother appears to him in a chintz dress she once wore. One day, seated at an arched window which opens to the balcony of the second floor of the ancestral home, Clifford is "seized with an irresistible desire to blow soap-bubbles."

Behold him, scattering airy spheres abroad, from the window into the street! Little, impalpable worlds, were those soap-bubbles, with the big world depicted, in hues bright as imagination, on the nothing of their surfaces. It was curious to see how the passers-by regarded these brilliant fantasies, as they came floating down, and made the dull atmosphere imaginative, about them. Some stopt to gaze, and perhaps carried a pleasant recollection of the bubbles, onward, as far as the street-corner; some looked angrily upward, as if poor Clifford wronged them, by setting an image of beauty afloat so near their dusty pathway.

At length as a "very dignified" man passes below, a large bubble sails majestically down and bursts "right against his nose." The man looks up "with a stern, keen glance" and then smiles. "'Aha, Cousin Clifford!' cried Judge Pyncheon, 'What! Still blowing soap-bubbles!'"

What a delightful and subtle scene it is—even a comic variation on the opening scene in *The Scarlet Letter,* in which three town founders look down from the balcony on Hester Prynne and her child. Literally Clifford's bubble collides with Pyncheon's, or art and beauty assault materialism and ugliness. Psychologically—and this is the more telling point—Clifford's soap bubble turns out by accident (he is much too cowardly to take the offensive) to be his means of attacking his betrayer and emasculator, the man who has denied him maturity through false imprisonment. Once again the Judge's sexual power is attacked when the bubble bursts on that symbolic phallus, the nose. Symbolically, then, the child-man, or "son," has revenged himself on the Bad Father—by accident.

Judge Pyncheon has little reason to recognize that he has now been defeated twice. Unaware of the warnings, he returns to the house for the third time, determined to compel Clifford to reveal the location of the deed to the Maine properties, the lure of that bubble still exerting its attraction. Unannounced, he enters the house, and Hepzibah becomes aware of his presence when she hears "a kind of rumbling and reverberating spasm in somebody's capacious depth of chest." While she flees in search of Clifford, the Judge settles into the ancestral chair beneath the portrait of the founder. In his own eyes he is the greatest of all the Pyncheons, and that evening at a political banquet his candidacy for the governorship of the state is to be announced. When a few moments later Clifford peeks into the room, the Pyncheon bubble has burst—the Judge is dead, his watch in his hand. Clifford becomes manic and begins to laugh, perhaps for the first time in thirty years. "As for us, Hepzibah," he declares, "we can dance now!—we can sing, laugh, play, do what we will! The weight is gone, Hepzibah; it is gone off this weary old world. . . ."

It is not Clifford but Hawthorne who, in a chapter entitled with obvious irony "Governor Pyncheon," dances over the corpse in a virtuoso display of sadism unequaled in his writings. Hawthorne releases pent-up anger which some critics of delicate sensibility and with preconceptions about Hawthorne's gentility have found offensive. Hawthorne was not always a gentle man. With as it were a bow to Aristotle and his dramatic unities, Hawthorne records twenty-four unlived hours in the life of a man whose importance is confirmed by the watch he holds in his hand. He has imperative appointments and for Pyncheons time is money, but he has run out of time. He sits alone "in the old parlor, keeping house"—forever. His political associates will wait forever—"the Judge is a patriot: the fate of the country is staked on the November election"—but the country will somehow survive.

In the midst of this danse macabre Hawthorne intrudes to declare that "indulging our fancy in this freak, we have partly lost the power of restraint and guidance." This is, as Huck Finn is to say, a "stretcher." Hawthorne relates another when he asserts that the "fantastic scene" does not form "an actual portion of our story," for this is the greatest of his bubble scenes, as he well knew. "We were betrayed into this brief extravagance by the quiver of the moonbeams; they dance hand-in-hand with shadows, and are reflected in the looking-glass, which, you are aware, is always a kind of window or door-way into the spiritual world."

Despite disclaimers and excuses, Hawthorne is in rigid control of the scene—and of the Judge. Like one of the avenging Furies, he pursues Judge Pyncheon to the final confrontation of the man of iron with "one of your common house-flies," which "alights now on his forehead, now on his chin, and now, Heaven help us, is creeping over the bridge of his nose, towards the would-be chief-magistrate's wide-open eyes! Canst thou not brush the fly away? . . . Not brush away a fly! Nay, then, we give thee up!"

The use of the "thou" form is the culmination of the narrator's vindictive glee but also perhaps an admission of an association or relationship between pursuer and pursued. The Judge's death may be no cause for sorrow since in comedy the son must topple and succeed the father, and Judge Pyncheon has scarcely been an exemplar of fatherhood. Comedy has no time for "sentimentering." Here Hawthorne takes vengeance on iron-hearted fathers, including his two great ancestors, his father, and Robert Manning and Charles W. Upham, who unseated him in the Custom-House fracas. At the same time this brilliantly orchestrated revenge establishes him as their son.[15]

If Hawthorne is the artist of iron in the comeuppance he decrees for the Pyncheons, he is the artist of delicacy and empathy in his delineation of Clifford, although he does not hide his character's flaws. After discovering the Judge in the parlor, Clifford decides to flee with Hepzibah, arguing not very logically on the basis of his memory of *Pilgrim's Progress* that the Judge "will start up like Giant Despair in pursuit of Christian and Hopeful, and catch us yet!" In the chapter entitled "The Flight of Two Owls," which can be subtitled "The Virgins Meet the Dynamo," Hawthorne's irony is affectionate. At the beginning of Clifford's resurrection and brave venture from the house we learn that "the warmest tide of life is bubbling through his veins," which also forewarns us that the episode may be but another soap bubble.

The two sixty-year-old children make their way to the railroad station and board a train. Until this time Clifford has been almost paralyzed by the thunder of what he calls "the steam-devil," a fear which he shares with Owen Warland in "The Artist of the Beautiful." Now he is not overwhelmed by fear but awed by the speed of the train. With manic fervor he pours out words and ideas which match the speed of the train and the absurdities of one of his ancestors, Don Quixote. His crazy spiritualization of progress, the railroad, and electricity may be a parody of Emerson's ideas or anticipate Whitman's, but when he attacks the tyranny of the past and the evils of the family his comments are not cultural but personal, arising out of his experiences as a pawn of Judge Pyncheon. Hawthorne having still another end in view, Clifford burlesques Holgrave's socialistic theories, which allow no room for family structure and so-called bourgeois values, at the very time the young man is reevaluating his own life.

At last Clifford winds down, to the relief of bewildered passengers and perhaps of Hepzibah too, the "wild effervescence of his mood" sinking into exhaustion and his usual dependency after "giving vent to this bubbling up-gush of ideas." He surrenders himself to Hepzibah, "Do with me as you will!" She kneels, a mother with a boy-man: "Oh, God—our Father—are we not thy children?—Have mercy on us!"

Of all the characters, Holgrave is the most intellectual and therefore most resistant to the imperatives of the heart. Like Ethan Brand and other monomaniacs in Hawthorne's writings, he seeks "mental food; not heart-sustenance." His seeming strength, however, is his weakness: his theories, socialistic and other, are soap bubbles, and his intellectual

defenses cover up his vulnerabilities. He is a twenty-two-year-old orphan—"left early to his own guidance"—and he has drifted apparently
from one interest and profession to another. There is one constant: as
mesmerist, daguerreotypist, socialist, and finally artist, he is an observer, with a coolly detached eye. The world to him is "a theatre": he
thinks of himself as the stage director.

Holgrave's actions are frequently at odds with his cerebral and ideological verbalizations and indicate an underlying uncertainty. As he re-
counts to Phoebe the story of her ancestor, Alice Pyncheon, who was
betrayed by her father's greed to Matthew Maule, who through hypno-
tism reduced her to his will, Holgrave almost renders Phoebe powerless—the artist now brutalizing woman through his skill—until he wak-
ens her and prepares the way for the end of the Pyncheon-Maule feud.
The twilight, the appearance of the moon, and, above all, Phoebe's presence exert a power beyond words. On this night of nights he has what
appears to be a sudden vision (actually it has been repressed for twenty-
two years) of a "bower in Eden, blossoming with the earliest roses that
God ever made. Moonlight, and the sentiment in man's heart, responsive
to it, is the greatest of renovators and reformers. And all other reform
and renovation, I suppose, will prove to be no better than moonshine." [16]

With the transformation of Holgrave, everything is in place for the
greatest of all the processions in Hawthorne's writings. The sterility and
the depressing drabness of the House of the Seven Gables, stained for
two centuries by greed, lust, destructiveness, and pride, are to give way
to life-enhancement and emotional fulfillment, but not in the ancestral
home, Judge Pyncheon's mansion, houses themselves having no powers
for good or evil. Hester Prynne's vision of the future has come to pass as
patriarchy yields to matriarchy under the aegis of Phoebe, the sun goddess. Phoebe embodies the qualities that Margaret Fuller attributed to
her mother: "Of all persons whom I have known, she had in her most of
the angelic—of that spontaneous love for every living thing, for man and
beast and tree, which restores the golden age." If no such mother ever
existed, it is a small matter: it is a lovely dream or bubble. [17]

Small and dainty though Phoebe is, her embrace is large. Her love is
so inclusive it even includes the chanticleer, the two hens, and the chick
Speckle. As soon as the two hens arrive in their new home, they begin an
"indefatigable process of egg-laying, with an evident design, as a matter
of duty and conscience, to continue their illustrious breed under better

auspices than for a century past." The chanticleer struts again, a potent symbol of resurrection. As Edwin P. Whipple observed, the author "seems to indulge in a sort of parody on his own doctrine of the hereditary transmission of family qualities."[18]

Uncle Venner, the neighborhood handyman with a voice that to Clifford's ear sounds like fruit, and perhaps the most Dickensian character in Hawthorne's writings, is not to retire to the town poorhouse. Surrounded by "family," he will remain a "patched philosopher . . . as ready to give out his wisdom as a town-pump to give water." Hepzibah provides her best customer, Ned Higgins, "with silver enough to people the Domdaniel cavern of his interior with as various a procession of quadrupeds, as passed into the ark." What a delightful and playful touch, satisfying Ned's youthful appetite as it adds to the sampler, in the fashion perhaps of Edward Hicks's peaceable kingdoms, the mythic tales of human and animal salvation. Even the townspeople who, as a Salem chorus, have commented dourly on Hepzibah's foolish venturing into the cent-shop business change their minds and tune. Pragmatists, they know a good thing when they see it: "'Pretty good business!' quoth the sagacious Dixey. 'Pretty good business!'"

Shortly the miracle that is marriage will take place, and the new fertility of the chanticleer will presumably bless the house. Clifford and Hepzibah will have little cousins on whom to bestow the love once reserved for each other, and Uncle Venner will have a new generation to philosophize with. The lovers will have "transfigured the earth and made it Eden again, and themselves the two first dwellers in it." It is as though Hawthorne quoted from a letter he had written to Sophia a few months before their marriage in 1842: "But our hearts are new-created for one another, daily; and they enter upon existence with such up-springing rapture as if nothing had ever existed before—as if, at this very *now*, the physical and spiritual world were but just discovered, and by ourselves only."[19]

Hawthorne may not have recalled, at least not consciously, a letter he wrote in June 1821 before he went off to Bowdoin College. He urged his mother to remain in Raymond, Maine: "If you remain where you are, think how delightfully the time will pass, with all your children round you, shut out from the world, and nothing to disturb us. It will be a second Garden of Eden."[20]

All his life Hawthorne was to dream this dream. In one of his unfinished romances of his final years, the hero journeys to England because "he sought his ancient home . . . as if he had found his way into Paradise and were there endeavoring to trace out the signs of Eve's bridal bower, the birth-place of the human race and all its glorious possibilities of happiness and high performance."[21]

At the same time, Hawthorne understood that like Clifford he was in some sense blowing soap bubbles, that a modern Eden like the original will not last, humans being humans. But the conclusion of *The House of the Seven Gables* evokes the new-old dream of humanity which may vanish as it appears, but which love and imagination can summon to transcend the tragic principle and the discontents of civilization. Those discontents seem exaggerated in the presence of such lovable characters and in the ambience of the loveliest sampler this side of heaven or, if that claim is as excessive as some of Sophia's, at any rate in American literature.

Sophia thought it "funny" that some people "should think Holgrave Mr Hawthorne & Phoebe me! It is such a mistake." She neglected to comment on the coincidence that Holgrave, like Hawthorne, is five years older than his mate and that Phoebe bears the name bestowed on her in the love letters she received before her marriage. She also preferred not to recognize that Hawthorne's voyeurism and intellectual detachment influenced the characterization of Holgrave, that he feared the ravages of Clifford's narcissism and effeteness—they wore the same robe—and shared Clifford's suicidal despair, or that the Pyncheon ancestry—"Puritan soldier and magistrate" with "iron energy of purpose"—was his heritage.[22]

After Hawthorne completed *The House of the Seven Gables*, Sophia redecorated George Peabody's desk with black velvet and removed the ink stains. Hawthorne "is tired to death of the book," Sophia informed her sister Elizabeth. "It seems to him at present perfectly inane, but so it is, I think, every time." Hawthorne was convinced, or so he alleged, that his new romance, though superior to *The Scarlet Letter*, would "hardly make so much noise as that." But after his usual fashion he wavered. At one time he was categorical:

> The House of the Seven Gables, in my opinion, is better than the Scarlet Letter; but I should not wonder if I had refined upon the principal character a little too much for popular appreciation, nor if

the romance of the book should be found somewhat at odds with the humble and familiar scenery in which I invest it. But I feel that portions of it are as good as anything that I can hope to write; and the publisher speaks encouragingly of its success.

About a month later, in another mood, he had reservations: "I heartily pray Heaven the public may like the book a good deal better than I do—else we make a poor business of it. But I am in the cold fit now, and should not see its merits, if it had any." [23]

The critical reception was for the most part positive. Whipple declared *The House of the Seven Gables* Hawthorne's "greatest work" and was "equally sure of immediate popularity and permanent fame." In England, Henry F. Chorley announced on the basis of Hawthorne's two romances that "few will dispute his claim to rank amongst the most original and complete novelists that have appeared in modern times." [24]

24

Lenox, 1851

Intimations

In the middle of February 1851 Hawthorne sent the manuscript of *The House of the Seven Gables* to Ticknor and Fields. He was ready to relax and spend time with Sophia, who was due to give birth to their third child in May. During the long evenings in February and March Hawthorne resumed his readings, and for ten or eleven nights he read aloud Charles Dickens's latest and most autobiographical novel, *David Copperfield*. "How I enjoy it made vocal by him," Sophia exclaimed in her journal. Then he read Milton's *Paradise Regained*, *Samson Agonistes*, and *Comus*, as well as works by Thomas De Quincey and Alexander Pope.[1]

The Hawthorne children learned early that when their father was writing they were to stay out of his way, but they also knew that when he completed the daily stint or was relaxing between books, he was, as Julian reported in his biography, "their playmate." Sophia took care of their minds and morals, Hawthorne reentered childhood with their delighted assistance. Julian recalled an incident that took place in the Berkshires. Hawthorne had the children turn their backs and close their eyes. When at his shout they opened their eyes they saw him "swaying and soaring high aloft on the topmost branches, a delightful mystery and miracle." From that elevated perch he shook down ripe nuts. On another occasion the children, in the words of their mother, made their father "look like the mighty Pan by covering his chin and breast with long grass-blades, that looked like a verdant & venerable beard."[2]

Sophia Hawthorne's life continued to center about the children, sometimes to the annoyance of Elizabeth Peabody, who believed her sister should not neglect her painting and poetry. Elizabeth evidently expressed herself with her usual bluntness, and Sophia defended herself in a letter that ran to twelve pages:

> Painting & poetry are my life now. From my children I gain new ideas, new suggestions which enrich me every day—They are the best pictures I ever painted, the finest poetry I ever could write, better poetry than I ever can write. I sit at the feet of their innocence & learn to be wise—[3]

About the same time Elizabeth Peabody decided that Una should participate as a medium in the sessions of the rappers, the newest cultists in that century of occult crazes. Mrs. Peabody, who shared her oldest daughter's interest in spiritual quackery, opposed the idea because she wanted to spare Sophia "anxiety . . . till time has proved beyond all controversy the fact, that the Spirits of Departed Friends are always with us." Sophia, whose interest in such matters was checked by her husband's skepticism, informed her sister that he would "*never*" (underscored four times) allow Una to serve as a medium. In addition, "he says he cannot let you come here with Rappers in train—for he thinks it would injure Una physically & spiritually to be subjected to such influence." Elizabeth later claimed she agreed with Hawthorne but felt a "pure" medium could do Una no harm. No more was heard of the matter until Hawthorne perhaps commented obliquely in *The Blithedale Romance* through Zenobia's complicity in the use of their half-sister Priscilla by a hypnotist.[4]

After Melville's stay at the red farmhouse in Lenox in the fall of 1850, there was evidently a lull in the relationship while he moved his family into their Pittsfield home. It was a large household consisting of his wife and son, mother, and sisters. Elizabeth Melville was the daughter of Lemuel Shaw, chief justice of the Massachusetts Supreme Court and a friend and benefactor of Melville's father, whom he periodically rescued from debt as he did his son-in-law. Though a Bostonian, Elizabeth Melville did not move in the intellectual circles of the Peabodys, Emerson, Fuller, and other transcendentalists. She was to have no part in the Melville-Hawthorne friendship, which was scarcely surprising since Melville's universe, as his writings illustrate, had almost no space for women and children. He was intellectually and emotionally comfortable in male society—even in the sterility of the "paradise of bachelors"—and no one has perhaps depicted the birth process (what Emerson calls "the nine months' astonishment") in such a repellent fashion as Melville in "The Tartarus of Maids."

In the fall and winter Melville returned to his manuscript of the whale with inordinate energy. In monomaniacal fury, matched in Ahab's Shakespearian rhetoric and Ishmael's endless inventiveness, he transformed what had been until then another yarn of the sea with a tyrannical ship captain, no better or worse than the two recent self-styled potboilers, *White Jacket* and *Redburn*, into one of the most original and idiosyncratic works of the century.

Hawthorne and Melville apparently did not meet until the evening of January 22, 1851, "after a long procrastination," when Melville arrived in his sleigh at the red farmhouse which was "buried in snow . . . all wrapped up & tucked away under a blanket as it were." Melville invited all the Hawthornes to spend a day or so in Pittsfield. What Melville really looked forward to with "much pleasure," as he confessed to Duyckinck, was in having Hawthorne "in my snug room here, and discussing the Universe with a bottle of brandy & cigars."[5]

After accepting the invitation, Hawthorne presented Melville with a copy of the 1842 edition of *Twice-told Tales*, which apparently he had not read. Melville checked a passage in "A Gentle Boy"—"they call me Ilbrahim, and my home is here"—which he adopted ("Call me Ishmael") as the opening line of *Moby-Dick*. Although he believed the earlier collection superior to *Mosses from an Old Manse*, he noted "something lacking—a good deal lacking—to the plumb sphericity of the man. . . . He does'nt patronize the butcher—he needs roast-beef, done rare."[6]

A few days after Melville's visit, Sophia wrote to decline his invitation because of illness in the family. This "side-blow" Melville refused to accept. "I am not," he declared, "to be charmed out of my promised pleasure by any of that lady's syrenisms. *You*, Sir, I hold accountable, & the visit (in all its original integrity) must be made." Beds were ready, wood was cut for the fireplaces, and two fowls had their tail feathers "notched, as destined victims for the table." With gusto and delight Melville promised that Hawthorne could "spend the period of your visit *in bed*, if you like—every hour of our visit," but Melville looked forward to evenings when "we will have mulled wine with wisdom, & buttered toast with story-telling & crack jokes & bottles from morning till night." He threatened to send constables in pursuit of his prey, but Hawthorne remained in Lenox.[7]

Never discouraged, Melville arrived in Lenox on March 12 to invite the Hawthornes to spend the following day in Pittsfield. Sophia entertained him "with Champagne foam—manufactured of beaten eggs, loaf sugar, Champagne—bread & butter & cheese." On the following day Una accompanied her father to Melville's home where they were to spend two days. Because of the weather the two men had to spend most of their time in the barn "smoking and talking metaphysics," or so Melville recalled in old age. Hawthorne made no reference to the visit in his journal, probably because Sophia had inserted a nine-page account of her unhappiness during their separation. Julian had a tantrum, she retired early because she could not even sew while Hawthorne was away from home, and what she had to say about his absence from their bed she excised from the journal after his death. She concluded the account with the following: "How thou art adored, my husband. Was ever one so loved? I love thee 725 millions of times more than I ever did at this moment."[8]

On April 11 Melville delivered a bedstead and clock to the Hawthornes and received an inscribed copy of *The House of the Seven Gables*, dated in Sophia's hand. About five days later in a letter which was written in the form of a book review, Melville's response matched the "great exhilaration and exultation" which he experienced in reading the new romance. "We think," he wrote, "the book, for pleasantness of running interest, surpasses the other works of the author. The curtains are more drawn; the sun comes in more; genialities peep out more." At once, however, he singled out "deeper passages," Clifford's contemplating suicide from the balcony and Judge Pyncheon's death in the ancestral chair. "There is a certain tragic phase of humanity," he continued, "which, in our opinion, was never more powerfully embodied than by Hawthorne. We mean the tragicalness of human thought in its own unbiased, native, and profounder workings. We think that into no recorded mind has the intense feeling of the visible truth ever entered more deeply than into this man's."[9]

As Melville elaborated and attempted to define what he meant, he made over Hawthorne's romance in Ahab's (or his own) image. In the most famous paragraph of his letter he was no longer writing about *The House of the Seven Gables*, in which Hawthorne chooses amid the soap bubbles an Emersonian or Thoreauvian yes over Melville's no.

> There is the grand truth about Nathaniel Hawthorne. He says NO! in thunder; but the Devil himself cannot make him say *yes*. For all men who say *yes*, lie; and all men who say *no*,—why, they are in the happy condition of judicious unincumbered travellers in Europe; they cross the frontiers into Eternity with nothing but a carpet-bag—that is to say, the Ego. Whereas those *yes*-gentry, they travel with heaps of baggage, and, damn them! they will never get through the Custom House.[10]

About this time Sophia drew what on first reading may appear to be too idealized a portrait, but she perceived the bond between Melville and Hawthorne and the former's desire to please. Unlike many observers, she was apparently attuned to nonverbal communications. Melville, she explained,

> speaks his innermost about GOD, the Devil & life if he can get at the Truth—for he is a boy in opinion—having settled nothing as yet—informe—ingenes—. . . Nothing pleases me better than to sit & hear the growing man dash his tumultuous waves of thought up against Mr Hawthorne's great, genial, comprehending silences—out of the profound of which a wonderful smile, or one powerful word sends back the foam & fury into a peaceful, booming calm—or perchance, not into a calm—but a murmuring expostulation—for there is never a "mush of concession" in him—. . . it is astonishing how people make him their inmost Father confessor.[11]

Sophia perceived a father-son relationship in which Hawthorne was Apollo-Saturn to a youth of thirty-one, which was Melville's perception too. What she did not recognize, probably because of her idealistic rhetoric and her naive goodness, were the erotic undertones. As usual, it is not easy to determine Hawthorne's feelings. Perhaps he was flattered by

Melville's extravagances but also troubled by the burden confessions placed upon him. He maintained—here we can accept Sophia's word—his "great, genial comprehending silences," which, however, may have offered Melville more encouragement than Hawthorne intended, silences being subject to almost limitless misconstructions. Yet there is something strange, or perhaps ambivalent, about Hawthorne's response to Melville at this time. In letters written about ten days apart, to one correspondent he praised Melville as "an admirable fellow" and to another complained that in the mountains he felt "remote, and quite beyond companionship."[12]

In April and May Melville was so occupied with the writing of "The Whale" and taking care of spring planting that he did not rumble over to Lenox in his "chariot." Since Melville was uncomfortable with the birth process, the red farmhouse probably had little attraction: Sophia expected her third child in May, and his own wife was four months pregnant. Two months before its arrival Sophia knew that the new child was to be a girl and that her name was to be Rose.[13]

About the middle of May Dr. Peabody left his ill wife in Elizabeth's care and came to Lenox. Because Sophia went into labor earlier than expected, the midwife did not arrive in time to assist Dr. Peabody, who gave a full report to his wife:

> She was waked about 1 o'clock—with some premonitions—& Mr. Hawthorne called me 15 minutes before 2 o'clock. I went into her room about 5 minutes before 2. Slight pains had become regular & continued not severe till about 10 minutes before 3 o'clock; then she had a pain which continued about ten minutes when the child was born—a nice little girl. Nobody was in the room but myself & Mr Hawthorne came in at my call about 2 minutes before the birth. . . . she had a remarkably easy time—& is now comfortably in bed & the baby is nursing away as if she had been practicing a fortnight—& the after pains are not at all severe.[14]

Hawthorne claimed that Dr. Peabody's "imperturbalness" was heroic and, at the same time, "almost laughable." Sophia said that her father was "selfpossessed, gentle, firm & *patient*," but she had one regret: "I meant my husband should never be present at such a time."[15]

Sophia may have had an easy time in giving birth, but other problems soon surfaced. Julian had nothing to say about the new baby. In Sophia's ambiguous words, his emotions were "unspeakable." Six weeks after the event Una was still "sadly out of tune." Dr. Peabody, who was always helpful but always childlike, stayed on beyond his welcome and hampered Hawthorne's "artistic & domestic life." Sophia wrote that "the three months of my confinement were months of utter misery to him—it is complete separation—and when I was able to be down stairs, still he was separated this time." "You know," she explained to her sister, "he has but just stepped over the threshold of a hermitage—He is but just not a hermit still"—after, as she did not say, nine years of marriage.[16]

Rose, Hawthorne noted at age forty-seven, "is my last and latest, my autumnal flower, and will be still in her gayest bloom, when I shall be most decidedly an old man—the daughter of my age." According to Elizabeth Peabody, who was not always a reliable reporter, Sophia informed her that out of respect for her once delicate health Hawthorne had decided early in their marriage on three children, two and one-half years between the first and second, the third five years later. Sophia's explanation was, if Elizabeth reported correctly, that "Mr. Hawthorne's passions were under his feet," which may have been a figurative or Sophian way of saying that he was able to control his desire, or perhaps they used birth control devices as the middle and upper classes did at the time. However, in 1847, Hawthorne spoke of having "three or four more" children, and the spacing of the children was accidental since at least two miscarriages occurred. As it turned out, the family replicated Captain Hawthorne's: Elizabeth was two years older and Louisa four years younger than their brother. Hawthorne's life like his art had a way of falling into patterns.[17]

During the winter there was no evidence of Hawthorne's customary restlessness even though he never left the Berkshires after his arrival in May a year earlier. He informed his sister Elizabeth in March 1851 that the family had "spent a very pleasant winter; and upon the whole, I think winter the best time for living in the country," but, not uncharacteristically, this was not the whole story. Shortly before the birth of Rose he confessed to Longfellow that he wanted "to smell the sea-breeze and dock-mud, and to tread on pavements. I am comfortable here, and as happy as mortal can be; but sometimes my soul gets into a ferment, as it were, and becomes troublous and bubblous with too much peace and rest."[18]

On the day Rose was born he admitted to Louisa, "I am a little worn down with constant work (for I cannot afford any idle time now) but am pretty well, and expect to be greatly refreshed by my visit to the sea," a visit which was delayed until September. Up to this time he had no serious complaints, but the birth of Rose added to his economic problems and brought an end to the three-month respite from writing which began in February.[19]

Although his "baby books" of the early 1840s had not been successful, Hawthorne had over the years thought of reentering the field. In 1846 he outlined to Duyckinck a book consisting of stories "taken out of the cold moonshine of classical mythology, and modernized, or perhaps gothicized, so that they may be felt by children of these days." Two days after Rose's birth, which somehow he forgot to mention, Hawthorne proposed to Fields a collection of six tales drawn from myths along the lines of his 1846 proposal: "I shall aim at substituting a tone in some degree Gothic or romantic, or any such tone as may please myself, instead of the classic coldness, which is as repellent as the touch of marble . . . and, of course, I shall purge out all the old heathen wickedness, and put in a moral wherever practicable."[20]

He planned to do the book in six weeks. "It grieves me infinitely," he confessed to Fields, "to be compelled to write a book, at this season." He kept his schedule, the preface being dated July 15, 1851, and on the same day sent off the manuscript to Fields. "I am going to begin to enjoy the summer now," he wrote, "and to read foolish novels, if I can get any, and smoke cigars, and think of nothing at all—which is equivalent to thinking of all manner of things."[21]

Written with affection and warmth in a joyful, shimmering style, *A Wonder-Book* did not condescend to the youthful audience that it entertained for the next century, with the assistance of some of the best illustrators: Walter Crane in 1892, Maxfield Parrish in 1910, Arthur Rackham in 1922, and Valenti Angelo in 1927. *A Wonder-Book* delineates "this bright and beautiful world" when the weather is ideal. The children, who are out of the genre lithographs of Currier and Ives, watch the snow mounting about the "little red house" in which the tales were written. In fact, the characters know the "silent man, who lives in the old red house, near Tanglewood Avenue, and whom we sometimes meet, with two children at his side." "Not a word about that man, even on a hill-top!"

Eustace Bright warns. "He has but to fling a quire or two of paper into the stove; and [we] would all turn to smoke, and go whisking up the funnel!"

In *A Wonder-Book* Hawthorne took the opportunity to pay tribute to classical tales which he had learned to love as a child as well as to writings of some of his contemporaries. In the preface to the most beautifully realized adaptation, "The Chimaera," which relates the story of Bellerophon's friendship with Pegasus, Bright is reminded of the story of Rip Van Winkle, and at once Hawthorne renders homage to the "gentle father" of the American tale, Washington Irving, acknowledging "that the story had been told once already, and better than it ever could be told again, and that nobody would have a right to alter a word of it, until it should have grown as old as 'The Gorgon's Head,' and 'The Three Golden Apples,' and the rest of those miraculous legends." After receiving a copy of the book, Irving expressed his gratitude and delight to one "whose writings I have regarded with admiration as among the very best that have ever issued from the American press."[22]

Hawthorne also pays respects to his neighbor in the Berkshires: "On the hither side of Pittsfield sits Herman Melville, shaping out the gigantic conception of his 'White Whale,' while the gigantic shape of Graylock looks upon him from his study-window."

The charm and generosity of *A Wonder-Book* veiled Hawthorne's weariness. As he completed the book, he confessed to Louisa that he had come to "abominate the sight" of his pen. There were also other pressing realities. On July 24 he advised William B. Pike to be on the lookout for a house along the seashore: "I find that I do not feel at home among these hills, and should not like to consider myself permanently settled here. I do not get acclimated to the peculiar state of the atmosphere, . . . and am none so vigorous as I used to be on the seacoast."[23]

On July 29, the day after Sophia left him in the custody of Julian while she and the girls visited her mother, he poured out a blistering indictment in his notebook, which was often his way of communicating with his wife:

> This is a horrible, horrible, most hor-ri-ble climate; one knows not, for ten minutes together whether he is too cool or too warm; but he is always one or the other; and the constant result is a miserable disturbance of the system. I detest it! I detest it!! I de-test it!!! I hate

Berkshire with my whole soul, and would joyfully see its mountains laid flat. . . . here, where I hoped for perfect health, I have for the first time been made sensible that I cannot with impunity encounter Nature in all her moods.[24]

The overstatement, inaccurate to boot, probably originated in accumulated anger or depression after the birth of Rose, the pressures he was under to write without stop, the absence of Sophia, and the isolation of life in the Berkshires. But it was a strange way to communicate with his wife, who probably at times did not know what to believe about his reactions. As late as September 7 Sophia informed her mother, "We have extraordinary health in addition to more essential elements of happiness."[25]

About June 1 Melville wrote an unusually long letter to Hawthorne which seesawed almost in imitation of the rhythms of *Moby-Dick*. In his pursuit of the favor of an older, more reserved man, Melville accepted friendship on Hawthorne's terms and took on the role of a subordinate who managed everything. "Don't trouble yourself," Melville advised, "about writing; and don't trouble yourself about visiting; and when you *do* visit, don't trouble yourself about talking. I will do all the writing and visiting and talking myself."[26]

Worn out by his literary labors and his consuming desire for fame, Melville felt rejected by a public which preferred *Typee* and potboilers like *Redburn* and *White-Jacket* to *Mardi*. "I write a little bluely," he observed at one point just before his prose erupted in a grandiose fantasy of security, success, and companionship.

Would the Gin were here! If ever, my dear Hawthorne, in the eternal times that are to come, you and I shall sit down in Paradise, in some little shady corner by ourselves; and if we shall by any means be able to smuggle a basket of champagne there (I won't believe in a Temperance Heaven), and if we shall then cross our celestial legs in the celestial grass that is forever tropical, and strike our glasses and our heads together, till both musically ring in concert,—then, O my dear fellow-mortal, how shall we pleasantly discourse of all the things manifold which now so distress us,—when all the earth shall be but a reminiscence, yea, its final dissolution an antiquity.[27]

While Hawthorne was taking a holiday in *A Wonder-Book*, Melville wrestled with the white whale and the death of Ahab. "The tail is not yet cooked," he wrote on June 29, "though the hell-fire in which the whole book is broiled might not unreasonably have cooked it all ere this." Melville promised to visit Hawthorne shortly and commanded: "Have ready a bottle of brandy, because I always feel like drinking that heroic drink when we talk ontological heroics together." The remark led him to admit, "This is rather a crazy letter in some respects, I apprehend."[28]

Melville characterized Hawthorne's reply, later destroyed, as an "easy-flowing long letter . . . which flowed through me, and refreshed all my meadows, as the Housatonic—opposite me—does in reality." Once more Hawthorne's words penetrated Melville's being. Excited, Melville proposed to "roll down to you"—in a royal chariot no doubt—to arrange "some little bit of vagabondism, before Autumn comes." Melville wavered between subservience to Hawthorne and assertion of his equality. "But ere we start," he wrote, "we must dig a deep hole, and bury all the Blue Devils, there to abide till the Last Day." The letter was signed, "Goodbye, / his X mark." Hawthorne had no way of knowing that in *Moby-Dick*, Queequeg, the Prince of Wales in cannibal-land, signs documents with an X; nor did Hawthorne at this time have knowledge of the scenes depicting the erotic but farcical bonding of Ishmael and Queequeg in which Melville unveils once again his homosexual longings.[29]

On July 28, 1851, Sophia and her two daughters left Lenox for an extended stay with Mrs. Peabody, who, because of her health, had not been introduced to Rose. Julian remained behind with his father, who kept a record entitled "Thirty Days with Julian & Little Bunny / By Papa," which was intended to entertain Sophia on her return.

For the first time Julian had his father all to himself, and he took outrageous advantage of the situation. Hawthorne spared the rod and made his own life miserable. Julian made nasty comments about visitors, bellowed for more bread at the table, and hit his father when it was refused. Yet on August 10 Hawthorne duly extolled him, surely for the mother's benefit, as "a sweet and lovely little boy, and worthy of all the love that I am capable of giving him. Thank God! God bless him! God bless Phoebe for giving him to me! God bless her as the best wife and mother in the world! . . . Would I were worthier of her and them!" Two days later he admitted the truth. That evening after dinner "I sat down with a book in the boudoir; and, for the first time since his mother went away, he was absent in parts unknown, for the space of an hour." Hawthorne was truly a man of iron control.[30]

That control may have been more deeply challenged by Caroline Sturgis Tappan, who, it seems, began to visit her tenant the day after Sophia left Lenox. Sophia had known Caroline for some time, not intimately perhaps, and had admired her, and she, we recall, presented the Hawthornes with the plaster Apollo on their marriage and in Concord had stayed with them briefly, "an absolutely perfect guest," in Sophia's words.[31]

Sophia may not have been aware that Caroline had a difficult childhood. Like many women of her means with no clear public role in a male-oriented society, she suffered from ennui and depression. To relieve her boredom she formed intense relationships, purportedly platonic, with Emerson, Margaret Fuller, and Ellery Channing, among others, in which she shadowboxed seductively while invoking literary and classical precedents; it was a privilege of her position for which she had the sanction of Fuller and Emerson, who were infatuated with brother-sister friendships. Caroline's free-floating conduct apparently provided limited gratification, for while a houseguest of the Emersons in 1845 she dreamed of performing the tarantella and dancing herself to death. Perhaps her depressions led Emerson to arrange for her to meet William A. Tappan, one of his young disciples, "a lonely beautiful brooding youth who sits six hours of the day in some brokerage or other," the son of a wealthy silk merchant and well-known abolitionist. They were duly married in 1847, and their first child was born two years later.[32]

Sophia may have known little of Caroline Tappan's erotic involvements, but Hawthorne was not uninformed, for in a letter to George W. Curtis, who was another of Emerson's youths and later the editor of *Harper's Weekly*, he wrote with a kind of ugly suggestiveness of his neighbor: "(Is it not the strangest of ideas, that she should be a mother?)— . . . You would find it interesting to compare her present phase with what you have hitherto seen of her." The language suggests that Hawthorne placed her in the school of Mary Silsbee Sparks.[33]

On her first visit Caroline Tappan brought Hawthorne newspapers and the first volume of Thackeray's *Pendennis*. Two days later she delivered "two or three volumes of Fourier's works, which I wished to borrow, with a view to my next Romance." On another night he was at the Tappan house at her suggestion to see whether there was anything in the library he wanted to read. All of this Hawthorne reported to Sophia in the lengthy record he kept during her absence; whether the record is complete there is no way to determine. Caroline was pregnant and may have had no designs except to relieve the monotony of her existence, not necessarily to play the role of Salome. Since her husband spent a great deal of time in New York in the family business, she may have found little to occupy her in Lenox. On the other hand, she had few inhibitions and may have found Hawthorne an interesting challenge. Whatever the reasons or motivations, trouble was brewing.[34]

Melville too was more in evidence while Sophia was away, and as he completed the final chapters of *Moby-Dick*, he was understandably on a high much of the time: how could it be otherwise when he was wrestling with the stupendous life-and-death battle with the white whale and the Promethean outbursts of Ahab?

Late in the afternoon on August 1 Julian and his father were making their way home after going to the post office in Lenox. At Love Grove they climbed over the fence to rest, and "while thus engaged," Hawthorne recorded in his notebook, "a cavalier on horseback came along the road, and saluted me in Spanish; to which I replied by touching my hat, and went on with the newspaper." Only Hawthorne could have been nonchalant about the appearance of a Spanish cavalier in the outskirts of Lenox! "But the cavalier renewing his salutation, I regarded him more attentively, and saw that it was Herman Melville!" It was Melville's thirty-second birthday. The meeting in Love Grove was a coincidence, but Melville had assumed, perhaps unconsciously, the role and the Spanish attire of the middle-aged Apollo named Jack Chase, who is the idol of the handsome sailor hero of *White-Jacket*, which appeared shortly before he met Hawthorne. As depicted in the novel, Chase at times struts like a Don Juan in a flamboyant Spanish uniform among swooning women and is a seducer of youths, as well as addicted to affected literary allusions, perhaps as a disguise. Melville dedicated *Billy Budd* to Jack Chase; the story is another tale of a handsome sailor, this time in an Abraham-Isaac relationship with Captain Vere. At the end as at the beginning, Melville was emotionally engaged in the quest for an idealized father or brother, such as he found briefly in Chase and others and now in Hawthorne, another middle-aged Apollo.[35]

Melville accompanied father and son to the red farmhouse. After Julian went to bed, the two men settled down in Sophia's parlor, no doubt with some "heroic" drink, and "had a talk about time and eternity, things of this world and the next, and books, and publishers, and all possible and impossible matters." Hawthorne's prose revealed his pleasure. They smoked their cigars "within the sacred precincts of the sitting-room" in which smoking was forbidden. "Deep into the night," Melville saddled his horse and rode off to Pittsfield. "I hastened," Hawthorne wrote, "to make the most of what little sleeping-time remained for me."[36]

One week later, on August 8, Melville arrived before noon with Evert and George Duyckinck, who were again on holiday in the Berkshires. After drinking the last bottle of Mansfield's champagne, which Hawthorne served the year before when Melville came to his house for the first time, they set off for the Shaker village at Hancock and on the way had "a pic nic dinner . . . with sundry napkined parcels and a jolly black bottle." That evening, with the assistance of Mrs. Peters, the family domestic, and Caroline Tappan, Hawthorne served supper to his visitors. He retired before eleven. "It was a most beautiful night," he recorded in his notebook, "with full, rich, cloudless moonlight, so that I would rather have ridden the six miles to Pittsfield, than have gone to bed." Only rarely did Hawthorne permit himself to verbalize a desire to break out of the mold into which he had forced himself and which constricts the behavior of his fictional characters too.[37]

Hawthorne's account of the Shakers was nasty. He was elated that Julian had "to confer with himself" (to defecate) and "bestow such a mark of his consideration (being the one of which they were most worthy) on the system and establishment of these foolish Shakers." He was viscerally repelled. "The Shakers," he asserted, "are and must needs be a filthy sect. And then their utter and systematic lack of privacy; their close junction of man with man, and supervision of one man over another—it is hateful and disgusting to think of; and the sooner the sect is extinct the better." This reaction to the intimacy of two men occupying a narrow bed, couched in anal and sadistic imagery, appears to originate in unconscious fears perhaps exacerbated by Melville's exuberant, seductive behavior and erotic language.[38]

When Sophia returned to Lenox on August 16, "Apollo" was not at the railroad station in Pittsfield, although he had promised several times to meet her train. She, however, had postponed her return several times.

Sophia attempted to conceal her disappointment but mentioned the omission to her mother: in letters to her family she almost never made unflattering references to her husband.[39]

Shortly Sophia complained that Caroline Tappan's behavior was "strange and unaccountable." She was pleasant in Hawthorne's company but "silent, uncommunicative & solemn" in Sophia's. Then Caroline stopped a servant who was carrying a basket of fruit picked on the Hawthorne grounds, and in a note she rebuked Sophia for giving away the fruit. Hawthorne intervened in this teacup tempest with a whimsical comment to Caroline which probably helped not at all: "Sophia and I supposed ourselves to be in full possession of that part of the garden, and in having a right of property over its products more extensive than that of Adam and Eve in Eden, inasmuch as it excluded not a single tree."[40]

Some time later Sophia charged that Caroline had committed an overt act which "I could not have thought possible in a person of good taste, to say nothing of Christian sentiment (but I believe she despises Christ.)" Evidently Caroline, not unlike Elizabeth Hawthorne a few years earlier, tried to teach Una to "deceive and to be unhappy at home." The result was that, although William Tappan himself proved "of the true ideal of chivalry," the Hawthornes could no longer live in the red house "with Caroline at war."[41]

This was the first of the crises that would shortly send the Hawthornes on their way from Lenox.

"Big Hearts Strike Together"

About the middle of September 1851, Melville composed what was to become the most famous dedication in American literature:

IN TOKEN
of my admiration for his genius
This work is inscribed
to
NATHANIEL HAWTHORNE

In October, Melville was busy with the final details of publishing *Moby-Dick*, and his wife was expecting a second child, who was born on October 22. Hawthorne was arranging for the publication of *The Snow-Image* and was preparing, he informed Bridge, to leave Lenox "with much joy" on December 1. He concealed from Bridge that the new and last gathering of tales and sketches was to be prefaced with a lovely eulogy of his closest and oldest friend. He sent the preface to Ticknor and Fields on November 3 and four days later mailed to Melville's son Malcolm a copy of *A Wonder-Book*.[1]

About this time Melville must have presented a copy of *Moby-Dick* to Hawthorne, for on November 16 he received a "joy-giving" and "exultation-breeding letter" which at another point he characterized as "your plain, bluff letter." Perhaps Hawthorne mingled reservations with praise; there is no way of knowing since Melville evidently destroyed the letter. A few weeks later Hawthorne chided the Duyckincks for their qualified review of the book in the *Literary World*. "What a book Melville has written!" he exclaimed. "It gives me an idea of much greater power than his preceding ones. It hardly seemed to me that the review . . . did justice to its best points." Melville's response to the review was two-pronged: he immediately canceled his subscription to the *Literary World*, where he had praised Hawthorne extravagantly, and in *Pierre*, his next novel, he lashed out against the New York literary scene in which the Duyckincks, his guests of the previous two summers, played important roles among the Young Americans.[2]

Melville's letter to Hawthorne, written about November 17, was at times almost out of control in its gyrations between ecstasy and despair. Melville humbled himself before Hawthorne at one moment only to proclaim equality at another. Hawthorne was "my angel" and "archangel," and even the act of reading the letter and turning the pages was eroticized, as in Whitman's notoriously tactile lines, "Camerado, this is no book, / Who touches this touches a man. . . ."

> I say your appreciation is my glorious gratuity. In my proud, humble way,—a shepherd-king,—I was lord of a little vale in the solitary Crimea; but you have now given me the crown of India. But on trying it on my head, I found it fell down on my ears, notwithstanding their asinine length—for it's only such ears that sustain such crowns.
>
> Your letter was handed me last night on the road going to Mr. Morewood's, and I read it there. Had I been at home, I would have sat down at once and answered it. In me divine magnanimities are spontaneous and instantaneous—catch them while you can. The world goes round, and the other side comes up. So now I can't write what I felt. But I felt pantheistic then—your heart beat in my ribs and mine in yours, and both in God's. A sense of unspeakable security is in me this moment, on account of your having understood the book. I have written a wicked book, and feel spotless as the lamb. Ineffable socialities are in me. I would sit down and dine with you and all the gods in old Rome's Pantheon. It is a strange feeling—no hopefulness is in it, no despair. Content—that is it: and irresponsibility; but without licentious inclination. I speak now of my profoundest sense of being, not of an incidental feeling.
>
> Whence come you, Hawthorne? By what right do you drink from

my flagon of life? And when I put it to my lips—lo, they are yours and not mine. I feel that the Godhead is broken up like the bread at the Supper, and that we are the pieces. Hence this infinite fraternity of feeling. Now, sympathizing with the paper, my angel turns over another page. You did not care a penny for the book. But, now and then as you read, you understood the pervading thought that impelled the book—and that you praised. Was it not so? You were arch-angel enough to despise the imperfect body, and embrace the soul. Once you hugged the ugly Socrates because you saw the flame in the mouth, and heard the rushing of the demon,—the familiar,—and recognized the sound; for you have heard it in your own solitudes.

My dear Hawthorne, the atmospheric skepticisms steal into me now, and make me doubtful of my sanity in writing you thus. But, believe me, I am not mad, most noble Festus! But truth is ever in-coherent, and when the big hearts strike together, the concussion is a little stunning. Farewell. Don't write a word about the book. That would be robbing me of my miserly delight. I am heartily sorry I ever wrote anything about you—it was paltry. . . .

Melville could not stop until he had added two postscripts:

This is a long letter, but you are not at all bound to answer it. Possibly, if you do answer it and direct it to Herman Melville, you will missend it, for the very fingers that now guide this pen are not precisely the same that just took it up and put it on this paper. Lord, when shall we be done changing? Ah! it's a long stage, and no inn in sight, and night coming, and the body cold. But with you for a pas-senger, I am content and can be happy. I shall leave the world, I feel, with more satisfaction for having come to know you. Knowing you persuades me more than the Bible of our immortality.

What a pity, that, for your plain, bluff letter, you should get such gibberish! Mention me to Mrs. Hawthorne and to the children, and so, good-by to you, with my blessing.[3]

Melville signed the letter "Herman," adopting in a letter for the first and last time an intimate form that Hawthorne rarely permitted himself, even in his letters to Bridge. It confirmed his longing for a bond which his letter made impossible. How was Hawthorne with his accumulated repressions and fears, not unlike those of Arthur Dimmesdale, to respond to such an outpouring of emotion and hyperbole?

He had not shared Melville's exposure to the freewheeling licentiousness and uninhibited rites of both sexes in the South Seas or to the homosexual practices aboard ships on long, dreary, womanless voyages. Nor was he capable of the phallicism freely exhibited in wildly comic scenes in *Moby-Dick*. But he was not a naïf either. There was little that was subtle about Melville's suggestiveness. In denying "licentious inclination," he confirmed its presence. When Melville proposed that Hawthorne, evidently in the role of Alcibiades, hug "this ugly Socrates," meaning himself, he evoked Greek love, while at the same time indicating that consummation had not taken place. Melville was probably aware that the relationship was about to end and that he was to reexperience rejection after the seeming fulfillment of his life's longings, but the finale had to be phrased with all the brilliance he proved himself master of in the pages of *Moby-Dick*.

This was the last of perhaps the most extraordinary love letters in American literature, comparable in art, feeling, and despair to the love poetry of the century, Whitman's "Calamus."

Before sailing to England in 1853, Hawthorne "burned great heaps of old letters and other papers," including "hundreds of Sophia's maiden letters" written during their long courtship. "What a trustful guardian of secret matters fire is!" he wrote. "What should we do without Fire and Death?" The world was not to read Sophia's outpouring of love and idolatry, but, by accident or design, Hawthorne spared the letters of Melville. He never knew that presumably in anger and desolation Melville had destroyed his letters, only to re-create from painful but loving memories the unforgettable experience of his life.[4]

After Hawthorne's death in 1864 Melville, in one of his loveliest poems, "Monody," which he did not publish until shortly before his own death in 1891, confessed his love and the fulfillment Hawthorne satisfied temporarily in life but forever in memory:

> To have known him, to have loved him
>   After loneness long;
> And then to be estranged in life,
>   And neither in the wrong. . . .

His assessment relieves both of responsibility. Although Hawthorne apparently never recorded his evaluation, he may not have disagreed strongly, for appearances were maintained. Probably the wives knew nothing of any significance. Both men kept the secret except that inevitably they dealt with the relationship at length, protected by the veils of their art. As the thinly disguised narrator of *Pierre*, Melville admits as much: "It is impossible to talk or write without apparently throwing oneself helplessly open; the Invulnerable Knight wears his visor down." In the preface to *The Snow-Image*, which Hawthorne composed shortly before his departure from Lenox, he once more discusses autobiography in art, admitting his use of facts "which relate to myself" and which appear "in a slightly idealized and artistic guise," but at the same time informing readers in a candid revelation that they must "look through the whole range of his fictitious characters, good and evil, in order to detect any of his essential traits."[5]

In the absence of pertinent letters or other evidence from the two authors, their families, or their friends, what transpired in the Berkshires probably in September 1851 can be reconstructed only from indirect or explicit references to the episode in their writings—Hawthorne in *The Blithedale Romance* (1852) and Melville in *Pierre* (1852) and, most important of all, in *Clarel* (1876).

Late in 1851 Hawthorne and Melville began writing romances centering around unsuccessful poets, Miles Coverdale and Pierre Glendinning, both of whom become involved in male friendships which prove to be shattering experiences. This was a theme that Hawthorne had dealt with only peripherally, except perhaps in "The Artist of the Beautiful." Melville, on the other hand, from his first published work, "Fragments from a Writing Desk" (1838), depicts an unusually handsome youth or sailor in quest of an idyllic male friendship.

At the heart of *The Blithedale Romance* is the relationship of Miles Coverdale, the shy, voyeuristic poet-narrator, and Hollingsworth, a bearded and muscular blacksmith-reformer, overassertive in speech and physical presence. Coverdale is in main outlines a self-portrait of Hawthorne's seeming weaknesses and effeminacy as artist and chilled, detached observer, and Hollingsworth embodies Melville's aggression and need of a "brother" as well as the monomania and fanaticism, including the misogyny, of the two Hathornes with whom their descendant maintained a love-hate relationship.

Almost at once on their arrival at Blithedale, Coverdale and Hollingsworth, the artist and the ideologue, establish a problematical relationship based on their secret needs. When Coverdale becomes ill and takes to his bed, his disorder more emotional than physical in origin, Hollingsworth becomes his nurse, affectionately assuming a subordinate role at odds with his muscular appearance and his patriarchal ideology. After his recovery Coverdale sets out to develop a blacksmith's muscles through strenuous physical activity, as though compelled to prove his masculinity. Although he seeks approval, Coverdale does not hesitate to refute Hollingsworth's antifeminine views, partly because he cannot suffer "a bearded priest" to intrude upon his psychic space. There is, in other words, an ambivalent response on Coverdale's part, not unlike Hawthorne's reaction to Melville or to his ancestors.

In a chapter entitled "A Crisis," which could have been called "The Crisis," a discussion between Coverdale and Hollingsworth eventually becomes a painful, anxious confrontation between a man seemingly of "iron purpose" and a seemingly dilettantish poet. Although Hollingsworth assumes the prerogatives of the overman, untouched by morality or human compunctions, he needs the poet's "co-operation in this great scheme of good."

> "Be my brother in it: It offers you (what you have told me, over and over again, that you most need) a purpose in life, worthy of the extremest self-devotion. . . . Strike hands with me; and, from this moment, you shall never again feel the languor and vague wretchedness of an indolent or half-occupied man! . . . "
>
> It seemed his intention to say no more. But, after he had quite broken off, his deep eyes filled with tears, and he held out both his hand to me.
>
> "Coverdale," he murmured, "there is not the man in this wide world, whom I can love as I could you. Do not forsake me!"

Even in weakness Hollingsworth is an "almost irresistible force." "Had I but touched his extended hand," Coverdale admits twelve years after the event, "Hollingsworth's magnetism would perhaps have penetrated me with his own conception of all these matters." As the argument continues, the great man becomes angry and in the desperation of defeat offers Coverdale his only choice—"Be with me, . . . or be against me!" The answer is predestinated.

> "No!"
> I never said the word—and certainly can never have it to say,

hereafter—that cost me a thousandth part so hard an effort as did that one syllable. The heart-pang was not merely figurative, but an absolute torture of the breast. I was gazing steadfastly at Hollingsworth.[6]

In a later romance, *The Marble Faun*, Hawthorne defines the bounds and limitations of male friendship when Kenyon, often his spokesman, shuns the role of "guide and counseller": "Between man and man, there is always an insuperable gulf. They can never quite grasp each other's hands; and therefore man never derives any intimate help, any heart-sustenance, from his brother man, but from woman—his mother, his sister, or his wife." In life Hawthorne himself perhaps received something like "heart-sustenance" from Bridge, Pierce, and a few others but not from Ellery Channing and Melville, whose extravagant idolatry had a sexual resonance.[7]

After Melville began writing *Pierre* late in 1851, about the time Hawthorne left the Berkshires, neighbors, observing how almost in a frenzy he isolated himself day after day in his study, called him mad. They could not know that as he wrote he acted out the rage, the deviant desires, conflicts, losses, and self-destructiveness of his so-called hero. *Pierre* castigates and debases Pierre, or, put another way, Melville turns his rage against himself in almost unrelieved self-flagellation. Nowhere else in his writings does he lift the veils usually placed about his own life. The dissonant rhythm of the book, exhilaration followed by abysmal despair, becomes vomit as the narrator delineates Pierre's "charred landscape."

As Henry Murray pointed out years ago, there are many verbal parallels between the romance and Melville's letters to Hawthorne in 1851. Pierre's half-sister, Isabel, the abandoned offspring of his father's premarital philandering, stays at a red farmhouse which is an idealized replica of Hawthorne's Lenox home. The appearance of Isabel disrupts and alters Pierre's life negatively and positively, as the presence of Hawthorne disrupted Melville's, positively in bringing a simmering imagination to a boil in *Moby-Dick* but negatively in opening old wounds and replicating earlier rejections by idolized male figures. Falsgrave, Pierre's mother's sycophantic chaplain—his name conjures up Holgrave in *The House of the Seven Gables*—fails Pierre as Hawthorne did Melville. After *Moby-Dick* failed to excite the reading public, Melville proposed to his publisher that *Pierre* be issued anonymously, "By a Vermonter." Melville's praise of Hawthorne in the *Literary World* was signed "By a Virginian Spending July in Vermont."

At age twelve when Pierre seeks the blessing of his dying father, he is stunned when his father deliriously calls out for another child, who later is identified as the illegitimate Isabel. Pierre is deeply hurt by this rejection but in denial of his true feelings internalizes an ideal image of his father while at the same time he establishes a farcical brother-sister relationship with his mother. Seven years after his father's death Pierre meets his half-sister Isabel. In a quixotic attempt to defend the reputation of his father, the youth announces his marriage to Isabel, and his mother at once retaliates by disinheriting him.

On the way to New York with Isabel, Pierre discovers a strange pamphlet by Plotinus Plinlimmon. The first section, entitled "Chronometricals and Horologicals," evokes the "ontological heroics" in which Melville and Hawthorne indulged in their conversations. The following chapter, "The Cousins," suddenly introduces a retrospective account of "the preliminary love-friendship missives" of Pierre and his cousin Glendinning Stanly, who wrote gushingly adolescent letters to each other. If the logic of the transition escapes most readers, it is because they can scarcely be expected to be on Melville's associative wavelengths: the Plinlimmon-Pierre relationship is a fictionalization of the Hawthorne-Melville relationship, which had its beginnings in an infatuation in Melville's youth shortly after his father's death. When Glendinning refuses to admit Pierre and Isabel into his New York home, his rejection parallels Hawthorne's.

One day Pierre encounters Plinlimmon on the streets in the city. The elaborate portrait, actually an icon, evokes a middle-aged but beardless Hawthorne, who managed to retain his youthful beauty.

> . . . a very plain, composed, manly figure, with a countenance rather
> pale if any thing, but quite clear and without wrinkle. Though the
> brow and the beard, and the steadiness of the head and settledness
> of the step indicated mature age, yet the blue, bright, but still qui-
> escent eye offered a striking contrast. In that eye, the gay immortal
> youth Apollo, seemed enshrined; while on the ivory-throned brow,
> old Saturn cross-legged sat. . . . To crown all, a certain floating at-
> mosphere seemed to invest and go along with this man. That atmo-
> sphere seems only renderable in words by the term Inscrutableness.

Plinlimmon becomes in Pierre's fantasy a "spiritualized Paul Pry," which was Hawthorne's characterization of himself as man and artist. Plinlimmon discovers, Pierre convinces himself, that "Isabel is not my wife!" Or, translated autobiographically, perhaps Hawthorne had gained insight into Melville's sexual desires and knew his "secret." Toward the conclusion of the novel, when Pierre's world is in ruins, the narrator writes his hero's epitaph—"the toddler was toddling entirely alone and not without shrieks"—which sums up in one harrowing sentence Melville's feelings about his lot: though a man, he is still an abandoned child, without father, mother, or friend.

Finally, in a plot as senseless as his life, Pierre is charged with murder and in prison takes his own life, declaring, "Pierre is neuter now!" The final picture is of Isabel after swallowing a vial of poison: "Her long hair ran over him and arbored him in elm vines." Such is the logic of the associative process that in eulogizing Hawthorne in "Monody," Melville was to write, "Glazed now with ice the cloistral vine / That hid the shyest grape."[8]

In *Clarel* (1876), an immense poem of 150 cantos, Melville's subject is once more the bond he failed to establish with Hawthorne. Melville assumes the role of Clarel, a young theological student who goes to the Holy Land to recapture or reinvent his faith. On his arrival Clarel meets and believes himself in love with a woman named Ruth but soon finds himself magnetically attracted to an older man, Vine. He begins an active pursuit of Vine, not unlike Melville's pursuit of Hawthorne in 1850 and 1851.

The characterization of Vine originated in Melville's perceptions of Hawthorne.

> Vine's manner Shy
> A clog, a hindrance might imply;
> A lack of parlor-wont. But grace
> Which is in substance deep and grain
> May, peradventure, well pass by
> The polish of veneer. No trace
> Of passion's soil or lucre's stain,
> Though life was now half ferried o'er. . . .
> Apollo slave in Mammon's mine?
> Better Admetus' shepherd lie.

Some contemporaries found Hawthorne's shyness coy and seductive, but Clarel wonders whether Vine's "coyness" conceals his "fear" of attraction to a male.

> Like to the nunnery's denizen
> His virgin soul communed with men
> But through the wicket. Was it clear
> This coyness bordered not on fear—
> Fear of an apprehensive sense?
> Not wholly seemed it diffidence
> Recluse. Nor less did strangely wind
> Ambiguous elfishness behind
> All that: an Ariel unknown.

Driven by a longing beyond his control, Clarel makes "advances" and, even when they are ignored or turned aside, continues his pursuit.

> So pure, so virginal in shrine
> Of true unworldliness looked Vine.
> Ah, sweet clear ether of the soul
> (Mused Clarel), holding him in view
> Prior advances unreturned
> Not here he recked of, while he yearned—
> O, now but for communion true
> And close; let go each alien theme;
> Give me thyself!

In his musings Clarel detects, or convinces himself, that Vine like himself is a divided personality with masculine as well as feminine longings, a division which some of Hawthorne's friends also recognized.

> Divided man knew Clarel here;
> The heart's desire did interfere.
> Thought he, How pleasant in another
> Such sallies, or in thee, if said
> After confidings that should wed
> Our souls in one:—Ah, call me *brother*—
> So feminine his passionate mood
> Which, long as hungering unfed,
> All else rejected or withstood.

"Call me *brother*" evokes the passage in *The Blithedale Romance:* "Be my brother in it!" Melville may have misconstrued Hawthorne's silences and tremulousness or suspected an ambivalent response to his own hungry desire for an unequivocal bond. Clarel admits his "passionate mood" and hunger and then, like Hollingsworth, presses too insistently. Coverdale's "No!" resounds definitively, but Melville's depiction of Vine reflects more closely what actually happened in the Berkshires: Hawthorne's silence no doubt spoke more definitively, and painfully, than Coverdale's "No!"

Clarel accepts rejection but continues to allege that Vine harbors a secret to which Clarel never finds "the key." In his final recapitulation of the failed relationship Clarel admits his continuing hunger and compelling need for a male "bond."

> . . . and his glance
> Rested on Vine, his reveries flow
> Recalling that repulsed advance
> He knew by Jordan in the wood,
> And the enigma unsubdued—
> Possessing Ruth, nor less his heart
> Aye hungering still, in deeper part
> Unsatisfied. Can be a bond
> (Thought he) as David sings in strain
> That dirges beauteous Jonathan,
> Passing the love of woman fond?
> And may experience but dull
> The longings for it?[9]

On the basis of scenes in *The Blithedale Romance* and *Clarel*, then, Melville's "advances" were made as "summer was passing away" (*The Blithedale Romance*) in an outdoor setting ("by Jordan in the wood," *Clarel*). We may reasonably conclude that the meeting took place about the middle of September probably while the two men strolled in the woods near Stockbridge Bowl, with the sphinxlike Monument Mountain visible in the distance.

On the bleak morning of November 21, the Hawthornes loaded their trunks into a large wagon and set out for the railroad station in Pittsfield. Five abandoned cats scampered behind the wagon for a quarter of a mile. [10]

Only one document has surfaced to shed a little light on Hawthorne's situation, a letter from Ellery Channing to his wife on October 30, 1851, toward the conclusion of a ten-day stay evidently with the Tappans. Channing observed that Hawthorne "seems older, & I think he has suffered much living in this place. . . . I do not know that he is absolutely discontented but he seems rather dry & out of spirits." He attributed Hawthorne's discontent to his "strange way to live not attaching himself to a single new person year after year & having indeed scarcely any old acquaintances." But Channing, we recall, was not one of Hawthorne's intimates. Perhaps because he was staying with the Tappans, he dealt harshly with Sophia, who, he claimed, could not realize Hawthorne's "ideal at all. She is by no means prepossessing and has not added to her beauty by time. And she has none of the means whereby elegance & refinement may be shed over the humblest apartment." [11]

On December 29, from West Newton, Sophia wrote what Melville characterized as a "highly flattering letter" describing her response to *Moby-Dick*. In his reply Melville kept up the bantering tone characteristic of his letters to the Hawthornes, promising that his next book would be not "a bowl of salt water" but "a rural bowl of milk." Before he ended the letter the mood suddenly shifted; he quoted an unidentified poet, "we can't help ourselves," and acknowledged that neither he nor any one else could change. He concluded with a magnificent statement of despair:

> Life is a long Dardanelles, My Dear Madam, the shores whereof are bright with flowers, which we want to pluck, but the bank is too high; & so we float on & on, hoping to come to a landing-place at last—but swoop! we launch into the great sea! Yet the geographers say, even then we must not despair, because across the great sea, however desolate & vacant it may look, lie all Persia & delicious lands roundabout Damascus.

This passage more or less summarized his relationship with Hawthorne, modulated perhaps, in deference to Sophia, into a qualified statement of faith in the existence of "delicious" lands near Damascus, where Saul became Paul in one of the great epiphanies of the New Testament and where Melville as Clarel, a theological student, relived again the summer of 1851. [12]

On February 8, 1852, Melville responded to a note from Julian Hawthorne: "Remember me kindly to your good father, Master Julian, and Good Bye, and may Heaven always bless you, & may you be a good boy and become a great good man." Again Melville seemed to be saying farewell. In July 1852, however, Hawthorne sent him a copy of *The Blithedale Romance* along with an invitation to visit Concord, where the Hawthornes lived. Melville was grateful for the "note subscribed *Hawthorne* again,—Well, the Hawthorne is a sweet flower; may it flourish in every hedge," but he was unable to leave Pittsfield at that time. He praised the new romance briefly, although he had "not yet got far into the book." In August Melville forwarded an inscribed copy of *Pierre*—

> Mr: & Mrs: Hawthorne
> from Herman Melville
> August 13th 1852

—with a lengthy letter detailing the story of a woman named Agatha whose husband deserted her for seventeen years while he lived elsewhere with another wife. Melville considered it a Hawthorne story because of its similarity to "Wakefield," but, as Newton Arvin suggested years ago, perhaps he was relaying another message.[13]

In November 1852, shortly after the election of Franklin Pierce, Melville visited Hawthorne in Concord to discuss the tale of Agatha and a government appointment in the new administration. "I greatly enjoyed my visit to you," he wrote a few days later, "and hope that you reaped some corresponding pleasure." The tone was muted, a far cry from the outpouring in the letter written a year earlier.[14]

Intercourse with the World
The Blithedale Romance

After completing *A Wonder-Book* in the summer of 1851, Hawthorne began to search for a subject for another large-scale romance. Of one thing he was certain when he wrote to Bridge on July 22: "Should it be a romance, I mean to put an extra touch of the devil into it; for I doubt whether the public will stand two quiet books in succession, without my losing ground." Somehow two days later he knew in broad outlines the subject matter of his next work—"some of my experiences and observations at Brook Farm." About that time he borrowed some of Fourier's writings from Caroline Tappan's library and began apparently to do some background reading which had no influence at all upon the romance, Hawthorne evidencing here as elsewhere little interest in ideas or ideology: his subject as always was the family and human dysfunctioning. The narrator, Miles Coverdale, meditates on his life twelve years earlier at Blithedale, a utopian settlement on the order of Brook Farm.[1]

Blithedale provides a pastoral setting for the exploding emotions and destructive interactions of four characters—two half-sisters, Zenobia and Priscilla, one a feminist and the other a seamstress; Hollingsworth, a former blacksmith and now a monomaniacal believer in the reform of prisons; and Coverdale, a bachelor and author of mediocre poetry. All are in flight from the discontents of urban and industrial life—at least such is their rationalization—although actually they make "a voyage through chaos" because of turmoils traceable, as one would expect in Hawthorne's writings, more to familial than to social sources. They dream, vaguely, that they can transform Blithedale into a communal Eden, ridding themselves of their emotional and intellectual burdens. They are blowing philanthropic bubbles, feigning faith in a collective solution of individual problems. Not surprisingly, Blithedale quickly becomes a "broken bubble."

In the preface to the romance Hawthorne, anticipating objections, insists that he "has ventured to make free with his old, and affectionately remembered home at *Brook Farm*" and that the characters "are entirely fictitious." Such disclaimers are useless, people believing what they wish, and false, authors inevitably drawing more extensively upon personal experience than they usually care to acknowledge. Emerson, who knew Brook Farm at secondhand as an infrequent visitor and lecturer, objected to Hawthorne's "ghastly and untrue account of that community" and vowed, according to one contemporary commentator, "to give what I think the true account of it." Emerson could hardly have been expected to embrace Hawthorne's awareness that "truth" is often perception mislabeled or wish-fulfillment, nor was he perhaps responsive to Hawthorne's depiction of the communal experiment as a kind of masquerade or drama constructed upon illusion and self-deception.[2]

From the beginning *The Blithedale Romance* achieved notoriety because the characterization of Zenobia was construed as an unsympathetic portrait of Margaret Fuller. Emerson protested that no one "could recognize her rich and brilliant genius under the dismal mark . . . in that disagreeable story."[3]

Zenobia is not a literal portrait of Margaret Fuller, whose physical plainness is specifically attributed in the romance to Priscilla. Zenobia's erotic presence recalled Fuller as well as Mary Silsbee Sparks; her involvement in mesmerism is probably traceable to Elizabeth Peabody's attempt to have Una play medium; and her death reenacts an episode that took place on July 9, 1845, the third anniversary of the Hawthornes' marriage. The nineteen-year-old superintendent of a district school, Martha Hunt, "depressed and miserable for want of sympathy," Hawthorne wrote in his notebook, drowned herself in the Concord River not far from the Manse. Ellery Channing came to the Manse to borrow Hawthorne's boat and, joined by General Joshua Butterick and an unidentified "young man in a blue frock," set out to find the body. Hawthorne steered while the others dragged with long hooks and hay-rakes in the slow-moving water. Suddenly the young man in blue drew up the corpse and held the rigid body from the side of the boat while Hawthorne guided the boat toward shore. The pole had penetrated the heart, and the young woman's blood poured forth from her nose as she lay on the bank. The women who were summoned to lay out the body did not know how to arrange "that rigidly distorted figure into the decent quiet of the coffin." "I never saw nor imagined a spectacle of such perfect horror," Hawthorne commented.[4]

Because of Hawthorne's technical innovation, the new romance posed difficulties for some readers. Miles Coverdale is what we now describe as an unreliable narrator; that is, events and characters are refracted through his consciousness with inevitable distortions in perceptions which are not subject to correction since he is the sole source of information. To complicate matters, Coverdale indulges in self-mockery, only to confess, "I exaggerate my own defects." Although he at times appears passive and ineffectual, his aggressive nature is revealed usually during crises and, above all, in his control of his tale: the participants in the story underestimate his art, his insights, and his inner resources.

Like other great works produced in that extraordinary decade—*Moby-Dick*, "Song of Myself," and *Walden*—*The Blithedale Romance* cannot be confined in the usual literary rubric. Hence it has disappointed readers like Henry James, who found it flawed and inconsistent as satire, although Hawthorne had no intention of accepting such a limitation upon his authorial freedom. Because Hawthorne did not resolve mysteries and ambiguities, there will never be a consensus in the critical interpretation of the romance, which may be a strength or a weakness but which was clearly Hawthorne's design.

Responses to *The Blithedale Romance* are, then, divergent. Robert Browning admired it above Hawthorne's other romances. Hawthorne inquired in his notebook: "I wonder why. I hope I showed as much pleasure at his praise as he did at mine; for I was glad to see how pleasantly it moved him." Mark Van Doren, ordinarily a sympathetic commentator, was outraged. "Few poorer novels have been produced by a first-rate talent," he dogmatized. Zenobia's "tragedy is trash . . . Coverdale is an ass." Maybe so, although one could, and in modesty should, assume that Hawthorne knew what he was about.

The Blithedale Romance is perhaps the most complex of the four great romances. If it is not more "hell-fired" than *The Scarlet Letter*, it sounds in its desperateness and ennui more ominous chords of disintegration and futility. Everything is fluid, and values are in doubt. Things are not what they seem, for *The Blithedale Romance* is theater. The actors group and regroup in a carefully structured series of confrontations. They speak their minds but veil their meanings. Present behavior is predetermined by past hurts and deprivations. The characters journey to a utopian setting, mouthing great expectations, but, as it turns out, make a "voyage through chaos," which is little different from what they left behind. Hawthorne leads us to stereotype the characters and to misread the events. The seeming strong fall, and the seeming weak survive. Hollingsworth, a man of Michelangelesque proportions and a fierce advocate of prison reform in order to ameliorate the world's ills, and Zenobia, who at various times is likened to Pandora, Eve, and Eros, tower over the others, only to collapse in self-destructive combat. Priscilla and Coverdale endure, the one in the role of mother-wife and the other as author of the romance. They are not heroic: they are maimed and passive survivors content to hold the fragments together, resigned to human limitations.

The characters come to the communal farm not to give but to receive. They expect the collective to fill needs and voids, to free them of despair and depression. Hollingsworth is ready to exploit the naïveté of the Blithedalers and further his own social-engineering scheme by taking over their property. Zenobia, the exotic hothouse flower in her hair mocking the simplicity of the Blithedale agrarian life and the purity of its ideal, needs shelter from an existence in which all relationships, familial, social, and sexual, have failed to provide either gratification or security. Priscilla is in flight from Westervelt, who through hypnosis markets her as the veiled lady. She seeks to find in Zenobia a half-sister who will fulfill her fantasy of a fairy princess, restore the broken family, and salvage her damaged self-image. Coverdale, "a devoted epicure of my own emotions," leaves his "cosey-pair of bachelor rooms" to collect experiences for his novel. He does not want to involve himself in the group more than necessary. Like the others he is free but trapped. "I hopped and fluttered, like a bird with a string about its tail," he writes, "gyrating round a small circumference, and keeping up a restless activity to no purpose"— which accurately characterizes his emotional state but obscures his ability to cope.

The participants are Ilbrahims in maturity—unsheltered by a family structure, untouched by affection, unprotected by society. Theirs is a world without the authority or the love of parents. There is no center. The mothers of the half-sisters are dead. Zenobia is abandoned first by Moodie and later by a guardian uncle who dies when she is six years old. She is involved in an anomalous but exploitative relationship with Westervelt, who uses for his own ends her abilities as a pamphleteer, her overwhelming beauty, and, above all, her desperate emotional needs. Her "womanliness incarnated" overawes Coverdale, who, like a character out of Henry James, closes his eyes in order to protect himself from such potency; but she surrenders meekly to Hollingsworth despite his disdain of the emancipated woman, attracted perhaps by his physical and patriarchal authority. Her posturings as an actress and exponent of women's rights hide the inner emptiness and dependency. Priscilla loses her mother at an early age and as a seamstress supports an alcoholic father who fails to protect her from Westervelt. If she idealizes Zenobia, it is because she searches for a replacement for her mother, and she falls in love with Hollingsworth to fill the void in her life created by an ineffectual father.

In a rare moment of confession Hollingsworth admits to having had a mother whom he "loved," speaks of her as "the most admirable handiwork of God," but adds immediately according to his Old Testament code, "in her true place and character." For she is to be "the Sympathizer . . . lest man should utterly lose faith in himself."

> All the separate action of woman is, and ever has been, and always shall be, false, foolish, vain, destructive of her own best and holiest qualities, void of every good effect, and productive of intolerable mischiefs! Man is a wretch without woman; but woman is a monster—and, thank Heaven, an almost impossible and hitherto imaginary monster—without man, as her acknowledged principal!

For the "petticoated monstrosities" who have abandoned their ordained place, "I would call upon my own sex to use its physical force, that unmistakeable evidence of sovereignty, to scourge them back within their proper bounds! But it will not be needful. The heart of true womanhood knows where its own sphere is, and never seeks to stray beyond it!" Yet Hollingsworth during Coverdale's illness becomes an attentive nurse, and his climactic scene with the poet reveals that his dogma cloaks his dependency as well as his vulnerability. He is intellectually musclebound, emotionally in desperate need.

Coverdale is voluble on all subjects except his autobiography. Like Hawthorne himself he could have said, "So far as I am a man of really individual attitudes, I veil my face." At the same time the seemingly self-contained bachelor is in deep conflict. Supposedly a skeptic, he seeks out Blithedale and its dream, but on his arrival he uses illness to reestablish his privacy in "cosey" quarters where he gains the attention of Zenobia and Hollingsworth by establishing a child-parent relationship. From the sickbed he aggressively indulges in suggestive banter with Zenobia.

Because Hollingsworth is a monomaniac of the Ahab order, he underestimates Coverdale's character and resources and does not anticipate that after the poet repudiates his Old Testament views of women, he will also have the guts to reject the plea to be his "brother." After the fashion of Hester Prynne, Coverdale speaks with unusual intensity:

> . . . Heaven grant that the ministry of souls may be left in charge of women! . . . God meant it for her. He has endowed her with the religious sentiment in its utmost depth and purity, refined from that gross, intellectual alloy. . . . I have always envied the Catholics their faith in that sweet, sacred Virgin Mother, who stands between them and the Deity, intercepting somewhat of His awful splendor, but permitting His love to stream upon the worshipper, more intelligibly to human comprehension, through the medium of a woman's tenderness.

Perhaps the two women suspect his verbalizations since both are drawn to Hollingsworth: despite his muscular and patriarchal rhetoric he is capable of more affection than Coverdale and, at the same time, as disclosed in the chapter entitled "A Crisis," is more dependent than the poet.

Nobody changes at Blithedale. Each plays minor variations upon ingrained traits. As though imitating her biblical counterpart, Zenobia sets out to be queen of the simple farm, but exotic flowers, perhaps from a transcendental greenhouse, advertise her narcissism and her need for attention. Priscilla continues to embroider purses which provide her father with money for his "boozy kind of pleasure" and at the farm voluntarily subordinates herself to Zenobia and Hollingsworth instead of to Westervelt and Moodie. Hollingsworth, who has "immolated" himself on his quixotic philanthropic scheme, finds another platform in Eliot's Pulpit at the base of a granite rock formation twenty or thirty feet in height which like those in "Roger Malvin's Burial" and "Young Goodman Brown" evokes ambiguous associations of evil and death. Childlike and self-indulgent, always in search of cover, as his name and his regression to the sickbed suggest, Coverdale creates a "hermitage," a kind of womblike shelter in a tree. There he smokes his cigars, spies on the activities of the members of the community, and, most important, protects his privacy and celibacy. "At my height above the earth," he writes, "the whole matter looks ridiculous!"—but not ridiculous enough to send him on his way.

Through physical and intellectual forces, Hollingsworth assumes the role of the authoritarian parent and seeks to rule by fiat. Early in their relationship Hollingsworth pronounces judgment, "Miles Coverdale is not in earnest, either as poet or a laborer." Stung by this attack, Coverdale justifies himself feebly and soon retaliates by prying into and magnifying Hollingsworth's "peculiarities," which he realizes is "a great wrong." But he rationalizes: "I could not help it. Had I loved him less, I might have used him better." When the reformer commands the support of his "brother," the seemingly ineffectual poet's "No!" leads to his departure and later to the collapse of the commune.

Coverdale returns to Blithedale just as a second, even more devastating crisis is unfolding. In front of Eliot's Pulpit Zenobia has been tried and convicted by her accuser-judge-jury, Hollingsworth, in the presence of Priscilla. At last Zenobia has learned of her relationship to Priscilla, has suddenly been deprived of her inheritance, and has discovered that Hollingsworth's seeming love is tied to her wealth. In a rage of love and rejection Zenobia targets with keen insight Hollingsworth's greatest vulnerability, the intellectual defenses with which he has surrounded himself to create an illusion of authority and strength.

Zenobia shatters the illusion and his manhood. "Are you a man? No, but a monster! A cold, heartless, self-beginning and self-ending piece of mechanism!" "Aghast," Hollingsworth challenges, "show me one selfish end in all I ever aimed at, and you may cut it out of my bosom with a knife!" In her reply Zenobia wields the knife, an actress in the role of Salome or Judith.

"It is all self!" answered Zenobia, with still intenser bitterness. "Nothing else; nothing but self, self, self! . . . First, you aimed a

death-blow, and a treacherous one, at this scheme of a purer and
higher life, which so many noble spirits had wrought out. Then, because Coverdale could not quite be your slave, you threw him ruthlessly away. And you took me, too, into your plan, as long as there
was hope of my being available, and now fling me aside again, a broken tool! But foremost, and blackest of your sins, you stifled down
your inmost consciousness!—you did a deadly wrong to your own
heart!—you were ready to sacrifice this girl [Priscilla], whom, if God
ever visibly showed a purpose, He put into your charge, and through
whom He was striving to redeem you!"

His faith in himself "shaken," his forceful voice suddenly "tremulous"
like Arthur Dimmesdale's, Hollingsworth leaves the battle scene holding
the arm of Priscilla, the overman now a child with a "mother." Zenobia
has had, even perhaps enjoyed, her great dramatic moment—and illusion—for her victory, as she shortly realizes, is defeat, one more in an
endless list of rejections. She has shattered the man she loves.

A few hours later, in guilt and despair, Zenobia turns her rage against
herself and walks into one of the "blackest and most placid pools" of "the
dark, sluggish river, . . . with the barkless stump of a tree aslant-wise
over the water." When Coverdale discovers her handkerchief near the
edge of the pool, he awakens Hollingsworth and Silas Foster, the practical Yankee among the impractical Blithedalers. They set out in an "old
leaky punt." Hollingsworth sits "motionless, with the hooked-pole elevated in the air. But, by-and-by, with a nervous and jerky movement,
he began to plunge it into the blackness that upbore us, setting his
teeth, and making precisely such thrusts, methought, as if he were stabbing at a deadly enemy." Three times they row upstream and glide back.
Suddenly Hollingsworth's pole strikes an object at the bottom of the
river, and, "putting a fury of strength into the effort," he heaves up
Zenobia's body.

When the men examine the body, they discover that Hollingsworth's
pole "wounded the poor thing's breast. . . . Close by her heart, too."
They have witnessed, as only Coverdale recognizes, the pursuit of a
"deadly enemy" by the blacksmith-reformer, like Ahab in his love-hate
relationship with the erotic white monster of the deep. Hollingsworth
consummates the bond to Zenobia in what is a frightening parody of the
primal scene and another of Hawthorne's extraordinary displacements.

In his fall from "topmost greatness" Ahab achieves a tragic apotheosis, Melville transforming the terrifying destructiveness of self and others into a heroic act of defiance. Hollingsworth is denied such release: now truly emasculated, he is to be the dependent of Priscilla, who will substitute for the mother whom he has termed "the most admirable handiwork of God."

A few years after Zenobia's death, Coverdale, still haunted by his experiences at Blithedale, journeys to see Priscilla and Hollingsworth, whose face has "a depressed and melancholy look." Worse, "the powerfully built man showed a self-distrustful weakness, and a childlike, or childish, tendency to press close, and closer still, to the side of the slender woman whose arm was within his." Priscilla is "protective and watchful . . . as if she felt herself the guardian of her companion" and receives from Hollingsworth "a deep, submissive, unquestioning reverence." There is "a veiled happiness in her fair and quiet countenance."

Despite Priscilla's warning gestures, Coverdale makes himself known and then, "with a bitter and revengeful emotion, as if flinging a poisoned arrow at Hollingsworth's heart," which replicates the blacksmith's assault upon Zenobia, gloatingly asks how many criminals he has reformed.

> "Not one," said Hollingsworth, with his eyes still fixed on the ground. "Ever since we parted, I have been busy with a single murderer."
>
> Then the tears gushed into my eyes, and I forgave him. . . . I knew what murderer he meant, and whose vindictive shadow dogged the side where Priscilla was not.

Before the forgiveness, the intensity of Coverdale's feelings is not attributable to love of Zenobia but rests on Hawthorne's identification of Hollingsworth with Judge John Hathorne. "I saw in Hollingsworth," he writes, "all that an artist could desire for the grim portrait of a Puritan magistrate, holding inquest of life and death in a case of witchcraft." The body of the judge in the Charter Street Burying Point lies not far from the graves of William Hollingworth, age thirty-three (about Hollingsworth's age), and his mother Elianor.[5]

The last chapter is titled "Miles Coverdale's Confession." Now a middle-aged "bachelor, with no very decided purpose of ever being otherwise," no longer a poet or a believer in "human progress," Coverdale is not sure that "in this whole chaos of human struggle" there is anything worth dying for. He may "exaggerate" his defects, or he may be seeking sympathy. One thing is certain: nothing much has changed in his life. Yet he has "one secret" which, he avers, "will throw a gleam of light over my behavior throughout the foregoing incidents, and is, indeed, essential to the full understanding of my story." Like an adolescent he blushes and turns away his face as he declares with stumbling hesitations: "I—I my-self—was in love—with—*Priscilla!*"

Miles Coverdale may be in love with Priscilla because she is the wife of Hollingsworth, that "great, stern, yet tender soul" to whom he is ambivalently attracted. Or he may be in love with her because she has transcended sexuality and its anxiety for the role of the mother or nurturer whom he seeks. Or Coverdale may be heeding the direction of Zenobia "to fall in love with Priscilla." Or he may be in love with an artifact of his own creation. With the cold remoteness of the artist, Coverdale suggests early in his tale that he does not care "for her realities—poor little seamstress, as Zenobia rightly called her!—but for the fancy-work with which I have idly decked her out!" Is the statement, then, simply another instance of self-love, or is it possible that what he says he means, that he transcends self-love? Coverdale keeps his "secret"; he is never uncovered.

To the consternation of later commentators, Hawthorne insisted on a number of occasions, perhaps with a great deal of delight, that *The House of the Seven Gables* was more characteristic of his genius than the hell-firedness of *The Scarlet Letter*. The obvious fact is that both romances are characteristic of divisions in his being and constitute a diptych. *The Blithedale Romance* creates a triptych, for it too unfolds other facets of its conflicted, evasive creator. *The Blithedale Romance* qualifies the exuberant excesses of the edenic motif and conclusion of *The House of the Seven Gables*, and no one assumes the heroic stature of Hester, the refulgence of Phoebe, or the charm of Clifford and Hepzibah. Suicidal thoughts are translated into suicide. Depression and despair suffuse the atmosphere, and social schemes cannot lift despair. Survivors survive as best they can, but their freedoms are contracted by Hawthorne's seeming loss of faith or confidence.

One of the most perceptive contemporary comments on *The Blithedale Romance* appeared in a letter from Hawthorne's friend William Pike. "You probe deeply," Pike wrote; "you go down among the moody silences of the heart, and open those depths whence come motives that give complexion to actions, and make in men what are called states of mind." Other writers "go through only some of the strata; but you are the only one who breaks through the hard-pan."[6]

After he finished *The Blithedale Romance* early in May 1852, Hawthorne had his familiar doubts in the inevitable letdown that followed the birthing process. "Now that the book is off my mind," he explained to Edwin Whipple, "I feel as if it were out of the body; but (like a great many other translated spirits, I fear) the sense of it does not exactly increase my happiness." Not willing to trust Sophia's "too unreserved" judgment, he sought the counsel of Whipple, including advice as to the title which was at the time "Hollingsworth." On the basis of Whipple's opinion he stood ready, he emphasized, to "burn it or print it, just as he may decide." It was a gesture on the order of Coverdale.[7]

President Pierce's
"Prime Minister"

The stay at the Mann house in West Newton was a make-shift arrangement. The family was to return late in the spring from Washington, where Horace Mann served as a congressman, and the Hawthornes were provided with time to find a house within their means. It was not an easy period for the Hawthornes or the Peabodys. Mrs. Peabody, who was not expected to live through the winter, was ready to "submit without a murmur to God's will, while doing all we can to remedy existing evils." Sophia visited her mother almost daily, even during inclement weather. Elizabeth Peabody, who provided the principal support for her parents, was deeply in debt and was in the process of liquidating the bookstore on West Street. When Hawthorne was solicited for funds, he apparently reminded the Peabodys of his responsibility to his sisters, who to his embarrassment subsisted "on the charity of the Dikes." Although Hawthorne was generous and sometimes foolhardy, he was tightfisted in his dealings with members of the Peabody family.[1]

On the other hand his was a limited and uncertain income. In 1850 his royalties from Ticknor and Fields amounted to $806; in 1851, $2,282; and in 1852, $1,289, if the records of the firm are complete. Yet during the Berkshire period the Hawthornes managed by means of their frugality and the repayment of loans to accumulate between $1,500 and $2,000 in order to acquire a home. That winter of 1852, after learning that the Alcotts were moving to Boston, Hawthorne purchased Bronson Alcott's house in Concord for $1,500, as well as an additional eight acres across the road, for which he had no pressing need, from Emerson for $500. Alcott bought the frame house in 1845 on his return from his short-lived communal experiment at Fruitlands near Harvard, Massachusetts, and named it Hillside because it is at the base of a hill that rises about fifty or more feet above the generally flat landscape.[2]

Hawthorne "re-baptized" the house the Wayside because of its position at the side of the road from Lexington to Concord over which the English marched in 1775. Although the family had occupied eight houses in ten years of marriage, this was the first one he owned, and "for the first time in [his] life" he felt "at home," and here, he claimed, he was beginning "to take root" at the foot of "the sand-hill."[3]

Architecturally the old frame house was nondescript and, worse, too small for a family of five. Its appearance today bears little resemblance to what it was in 1852 when the paint was of "a rusty olive hue" and the house was without porches and a central entrance. Hawthorne learned from Thoreau that a generation or more ago it had been inherited by "a man who believed that he should never die. I believe, however, he is dead—at least, I hope so; else he may possibly appear, and disturb my title to his residence." The former resident reappeared not as a ghost but in the pages of "Septimius Felton," one of the romances Hawthorne was unable to complete in the last years of his life.[4]

During the summer of 1852 Hawthorne spent "delectable hours" on the hillside, "stretched out at my lazy length, with a book in my hand, or an un-written book in my thoughts." His pacing on the crown of the hill shortly created a well-worn path. There he commanded a view of the country-side, and there he was seen from the road, a tall figure dressed in black restlessly pacing and covertly spying, after the fashion of Coverdale. There was another reason why he was drawn to the hillside, "whither I can make my escape when the Philistines knock at the front-door."[5]

Sophia decorated the house in her usual way because, as she explained to her mother, "we intend to live in the presence of our most beautiful objects—for the sake of the children's cultivation as well as our own." In the study the patched bust of Apollo occupied its customary niche, a trib-ute to her husband's beauty and a moral guide to the children, since the myth of Apollo's slaying the Python corresponds to St. Michael's slaying the dragon. "The children know," Sophia declared, that "it invites them, with its superb beauty, to overcome all naughtiness & shine, like Apollo, with the light of suns." Perhaps Sophia had forgotten that the bust was the wedding gift of Caroline Tappan.[6]

July 9, 1852, was the tenth anniversary of the Hawthornes' marriage. There was probably no celebration because they were not given to such festivities and preferred not to be reminded of time's winged chariot. A few months later, however, Sophia expressed her contentment to her faithful confidant, her mother: "I know my husband ten years better, & I have not arrived at the end, for he is still an enchanting mystery, beyond the regions I have discovered & made my own."[7]

Early in June, on the forty-ninth ballot at the Democratic convention, a badly divided party decided on or resigned itself to a ticket consisting of Franklin Pierce for president and William R. King for vice-president. An old New Hampshire farmer was supposed to have commented: "Frank does well enough for Concord, [New Hampshire,] but he'll be monstrous thin, spread out over the United States." A story went about that after the nomination Hawthorne called on Pierce, sat on a sofa, heaved a deep sigh, and said, "Frank, *what* a pity! . . . But, after all, this world was not meant to be happy in—only to succeed in!" The story is too good to be true.[8]

Hawthorne did not hear of the nomination until June 8 because of the distance of the Wayside from the post office. On the following day he wrote to Pierce, "I hardly know whether to congratulate you; for it would be absurd to suppose that the great office to which you are destined will ever afford you one happy or comfortable moment—and yet it is an end worthy of all ambition, as the highest success that the whole world offers to a statesman." Probably both men had forgotten that twenty years earlier after Pierce's election to Congress, Hawthorne had hinted that one day his friend would be a candidate for the presidency and had concluded, "It is a pity that I am not in a situation to exercise my pen in your behalf; though you seem not to need the assistance of newspaper scribblers."[9]

It has been said, partly on the basis of Hawthorne's comments at one time or another, that he undertook the campaign biography at Pierce's insistence. But Hawthorne introduced the subject in his congratulatory letter: "It has occurred to me that you might have some thought of getting me to write the necessary biography. Whatever service I can do you, I need not say, would be at your command; but I do not believe that I should succeed in this matter so well as many other men." Clearly, if Pierce said the word, Hawthorne would write the biography, although with some reservations, he observed in a letter to Fields about a week later: "He wishes me to write his biography, and I have consented to do so—somewhat reluctantly, however."[10]

Sophia, whose loyalty to her husband and his friends had no bounds, informed her family that Hawthorne knew "that the lowest motives would be ascribed to him; but, provided his conscience is clear, he never cares a *sou* what people say. He knew he never should ask for an office; and not one word on the subject has ever passed between General Pierce and Mr. Hawthorne." Other people lacked Sophia's faith or naïveté. In Salem, Hawthorne's friend David Roberts gave Louisa "a catalogue of offices which would be at Nathaniel's disposal in the event of Pierce's election." " I told him," Louisa wrote, "I hoped he would have nothing to do with an office." The two women reflected Hawthorne's public position, but he disingenuously assured Fields, "I seek nothing from him, and therefore need not be ashamed to tell the truth of an old friend."[11]

Hawthorne may have made, as he later claimed, "an inward resolution" not to accept an office from Pierce (although the wording would indicate that he had given the matter consideration), but he was ready to change his mind: "I doubt whether it would not be rather folly than heroism to adhere to this purpose, in case he should offer me anything particularly good."[12]

From the beginning he knew that the decision to reenter politics as the official apologist would cost him friends, at least temporarily. Louisa, who learned of his decision through the newspaper, informed her sister that when Horace Conolly asked her "to tell Nathaniel that *he went for* Pierce, and to ask Nathaniel to meet him in Boston, I never saw such unblushing impudence in my life." If Louisa was ashamed, the Peabodys were irate on two counts: Pierce was a general and, worse, proslavery. As early as 1848 Mrs. Peabody had denounced Pierce as a man who enjoyed "the honors of Battle" and who had "sucked in" the martial spirit "with the mother's milk," his mother being the wife of a soldier in the Revolutionary War. Sophia answered her mother, with emphasis, that Pierce was "an angel of mercy & aid as well as brave as a lion."[13]

Mrs. Peabody deplored Hawthorne's decision but begged her daughters not to "poison our social intercourse by canvassing the question of Pierce's merits." As her life waned, she wanted peace among three dogmatic daughters whom she had encouraged to express their views, but she need not have worried, for their bonds to each other survived their ideological differences. That Thanksgiving, however, one person absented himself from a family festivity dominated by voluble and uncompromising women. Hawthorne spent the holiday in Concord with William Pike.[14]

Hawthorne arranged for Ticknor and Fields to publish the book, had Pierce sit for a daguerreotype which became the frontispiece, and began to collect from Pierce and his friends the materials he needed. By the time Hawthorne sat down to write on July 25, he had sorted out the central problems: Pierce's obscurity and unexciting personality, the military record in a war that had become unpopular, and the slavery question.

During his years in Congress, Franklin Pierce staunchly supported Andrew Jackson. According to Hawthorne, on his deathbed Jackson spoke "with energy" of Pierce, observing that "the interests of the country would be safe in such hands." The incident, whether true or not, fits almost too perfectly into the family romance Hawthorne renders. Hawthorne placed the best light on Pierce's undistinguished record as congressman and senator: "Instead of thrusting yourself forward on all good or bad occasions, it always required a case of necessity, to bring you out; and having done the needful with as little noise as possible, you withdrew into the back-ground." There were reports that during the Mexican War Pierce was considered by some a coward and that only the intervention of General Winfield Scott, now his opponent in the presidential race, had saved his reputation. In the climate of 1852 Hawthorne had to depict Pierce as "a man of peaceful pursuits." But the most "difficult and delicate part" of Hawthorne's tasks was the discussion of slavery. Because he realized the difficulties of appeasing abolitionists, he decided "to meet the question with perfect candor and frankness, . . . so as to put you on the broadest ground possible, as a man for the whole country."[15]

Horace Mann, who disliked Hawthorne's cigars and politics, was reported to have said with more wit than he was usually given to: "If he makes out Pierce to be a great man or a brave man, it will be the greatest work of fiction he ever wrote." For once Hawthorne agreed with Mann: "Though the story is true, yet it took a romancer to do it."[16]

The Life of Franklin Pierce is a tale of a "gentle boy" blessed with a father who was the very ideal of fatherhood. Neighbors described the young Franklin "as a beautiful boy, with blue eyes, light curling hair, and a serene expression of face." "The physical attributes," Hawthorne adds, "indicate moral symmetry, kindliness, and a delicate texture of sentiment, rather than marked prominences of character." Benjamin Pierce went off to war in 1775 at age seventeen and remained in the army for nine years. He was twice elected governor of New Hampshire. With warmth and affection and perhaps a little envy in view of what he had missed, Hawthorne dwelt upon the father-son relationship. In 1839, at eighty-one, Benjamin Pierce died "in perfect peace," and the mantle passed, as Hawthorne points up with care, to the son.

> Governor Pierce was a man of admirable qualities—brave, active, public-spirited, endowed with natural authority, courteous yet simple in his manners; and in his son we may perceive these same attributes, modified and softened by a finer texture of character, illuminated by higher intellectual culture, and polished by a larger intercourse with the world, but as substantial and sterling as in the good old patriot.[17]

The major part of the biography consists of more than forty pages of extracts from a journal Pierce kept during the Mexican War. This necessary padding to fill out a slender book also served to place the son in the tradition of the father—Pierce showing "paternal care for his men"—as well as to render a brief and undistinguished military career in the best light. Hawthorne reports that after a horse fell on him in battle, Pierce insisted on being tied to the saddle of a dead officer's mount. Despite his efforts, Hawthorne was unable to create an interesting narrative out of Pierce's prosaic account.

In the third part of the book Hawthorne presents Pierce as a conservative whose goal is to preserve the Union by accommodating the South and by appealing to those northerners, the majority, it would appear, who were not actively against slavery. Here Hawthorne takes risks. He refers to "the mistiness of a philanthropic system," meaning abolitionism, and then presents "another view" which was bound to outrage the activists of the age.

> It looks upon slavery as one of those evils which divine Providence does not leave to be remedied by human contrivances, but which, in

its own good time, by some means impossible to be anticipated, but of the simplest and easiest operation, when all its uses shall have been fulfilled, it causes to vanish like a dream. There is no instance, in all history, of the human will and intellect having perfected any great moral reform by methods which it adapted to that end; but the progress of the world, at every step, leaves some evil or wrong on the path behind it, which the wisest of mankind, of their own set purpose, could never have found the way to rectify.

Hawthorne later insisted that these "are my real sentiments, and I do not regret that they are on record," even though they "cost me hundreds of friends, here at the north."[18]

In the biography Hawthorne passed over two subjects, Pierce's drinking and his wife, Jane Appleton Pierce. Many years later Julian Hawthorne was to assert that his father extracted a promise from Pierce "to abstain entirely from drink during his Presidency." Such nonsense Julian got from his mother or aunt, or he concocted it. It was a hard-drinking age, and Pierce's propensity, like Daniel Webster's, was evidently widely known. Dutifully and ingenuously, Sophia came to Pierce's assistance by arguing that "it is a singular fact that this particular weakness of indulging in too much stimulants does not debase a noble mind as other vices do," an argument perhaps influenced by her morphine addiction in girlhood.[19]

For reasons now obscure Hawthorne had no fondness for Jane Pierce. When he records the death of the Pierces' four-year-old "boy of rare beauty and promise" in 1844, he terms it "the greatest affliction that his father has experienced." Then he adds: "His only surviving child is a son, now eleven years old." A month after the election the mother and father witnessed the death of this son in a railroad accident. According to Pierce's twentieth-century biographer, Jane Pierce was convinced that the presidency was purchased at the price of their son's life. Several years after the accident Bridge reported to Hawthorne some material about Pierce so derogatory that the letter had to be burned. Hawthorne obliged but not without a vicious comment: "I wish he had a better wife, or none at all. It is too bad that the nation should be compelled to see such a death's head in the pre-eminent place among American women; and I think a presidential candidate ought to be scrutinized as well in regard to his wife's social qualifications, as to his own political ones."[20]

Whatever Jane Pierce's flaws may have been, she deserved a great deal of sympathy—the loss of two children is a tragic burden for a mother—but deep-seated anger toward women, perhaps originating in his mother's real as well as imagined neglect in his youth, apparently drove Hawthorne at times to nasty outbursts. Of women authors he was to write, "I wish they were forbidden to write on pain of having their faces deeply scarified with an oyster-shell," a sentiment worthy of his ancestors. Sometimes ugly vituperation and extravagant idealization co-exist, uneasily, in his writings.[21]

Shortly after his family moved into the Wayside, Hawthorne wrote to his sister Louisa urging her "to come immediately," even though the "house is not yet in order." From past experiences he knew how she always dallied indecisively. Louisa delayed the journey for a month and then decided to go to Concord by way of Saratoga and New York City. Accompanied by John Dike, she went to Saratoga, where they boarded the *Henry Clay* bound for New York. As the vessel approached New York on July 27 and as Louisa was reading *Pilgrim's Progress*, a fire broke out in the center of the ship. In the confusion she apparently jumped into the Hudson River and drowned.[22]

The disaster was noted in New England newspapers, but Hawthorne did not learn until three days later that Louisa was aboard the *Henry Clay*. William Pike, who had been in Concord two days earlier, returned to inform the family. They were at breakfast. Hawthorne heard the news in silence, standing "with his hands behind him, in his customary attitude," and abruptly left the room for his study. Shortly Julian went there to console his father, but Hawthorne had climbed the hill behind the house to pace on his lonely path among the trees. It was July 30, and on the following day he would observe the third anniversary of his mother's death.[23]

Like Coverdale after the death of Zenobia in *The Blithedale Romance*, Hawthorne was paralyzed. Instead of going to Salem with Pike or traveling to New York while divers sought the body, he remained in Concord. Robert Manning, the twenty-five-year-old son of Hawthorne's Uncle Robert, and Dike, who survived the disaster, took charge. After the body was located, Pike wrote Hawthorne that the interment would have to take place immediately. Because of a delay in the mail Hawthorne did not arrive in Salem until the afternoon of August 3. Louisa had been buried in the morning in the Manning plot in the Howard Street Cemetery near her mother. Sophia was glad that Hawthorne had been spared the pain of listening to "the Calvinistic talk" at the funeral service. She was seemingly unaware of imperatives beyond Calvinistic doctrine which demanded that Hawthorne witness the conclusion of the life cycle.[24]

Consoling herself by recourse to the denials grounded in her optimistic credo, Sophia imagined Louisa "supremely happy with her mother in another world. For she was always inconsolable for her mother, & never could be really happy away from her." Elizabeth Hawthorne, she continued, "told my husband she could not realize her death at all, but felt as if she were still alive." Emerson, who left the ministry partly because of his inability to handle funeral rites, dealt with the death in his usual evasive way. After informing Sophia of local gossip, he finally referred to Louisa: "Who knows which is the shortest & most excellent way out of the calamities of the present world?"[25]

When Hawthorne returned to Concord after Louisa's funeral, he immediately resumed work on the biography. In a letter to Pierce he did not refer to Louisa directly: "I have been delayed by the necessity of going to Salem." Like his mother he could not share personal feelings or express them. Sophia understood and waited. She knew that it would be "an intrusion & impertinence to condole with him, & attempt suggesting ideas." When he was ready he confided in her without seeming to do so: "He has thrilled my heart strings by saying something to me, as if thinking aloud, in that tone of divine melody—so remote also, as if from another world—by which I found he was alleviating for himself the sorrow & loss."[26]

At the end of August Hawthorne delivered the final pages of the Pierce biography to Ticknor and Fields on his way to attend the fiftieth anniversary of the founding of Bowdoin College. Earlier he had declined to participate in the ceremonies but had promised to attend. Somehow he managed "by the grace of Divine Providence" to arrive late and to miss hearing himself "celebrated by orators and poets." Pierce attended as did eight of Hawthorne's classmates who were, he reported to Bridge, "a set of dismal old fellows, whose heads looked as if they had been out in a pretty shower of snow. . . . They flattered me with the assurance that time had touched me tenderly; but, alas, they were each a mirror, in which I beheld the reflection of my age." The portrait painted by G. P. A. Healy in the following year confirmed the view of his classmates, that externally he remained an Apollonian figure.[27]

Because there were no sleeping accommodations in Brunswick, Hawthorne spent the night in Bath, a port six miles away. At a tavern frequented by sailors he had what Sophia termed a "funny adventure." Some old sea captains, perhaps in their cups, insisted on calling him "Cap'n Hathorne." Forty-four years after the father's death sailors observed the son's resemblance, and such a boozy intimacy was established that Hawthorne was called "brother," the handsome, fastidious recluse being able to adapt readily to the jocular but short-lived intimacy of a rough-and-ready male society. Such scenes, however, never appeared in his fiction.[28]

He spent the following two weeks at an inn on the Isles of Shoals, those bleak, forsaken islands off Portsmouth, New Hampshire, where only rocks seem to thrive. Guests at the inn were few in September, and he wandered on the shore and went to the other desolate islands by boat. He had time to reflect and to work out his grief. When he informed Ticknor on September 7 that his health had improved, he probably meant that his reconciliation with death had begun—in a setting which in his mind's eye may have evoked Surinam, where his father died.[29]

This was Hawthorne's longest separation from his family. The children missed their father "miserably," and Sophia "could not bear the trial very well. I could not eat, sitting opposite his empty chair at table, and I lost several pounds of flesh." Sophia's understandable anxiety, however, made matters no easier for three fearful children who must have wondered during their father's extended time away from the family so soon after Louisa's death whether he would come back. On the evening of his return Una went to bed after confessing, "Oh, mamma, my head has tingled so, ever since I saw papa, that I could hardly bear the pain! Do not tell him, for it might trouble him!"[30]

That autumn Sophia wrote her customary letters to her mother, retelling at great length the acts of her children and extolling them and her husband with an extravagance which her mother understood and condoned. She frequently at this time signed her letters "Your child" or "Sophiechen," in silent recognition of the state of her mother's health and the separation that was shortly to occur. Sophia had convinced herself that she "bade farewell" to her mother while the Hawthornes lived in Lenox and had at that time gone "through the agony of parting with her." "Sophia is so hopeful," Mrs. Peabody confided to Mary Mann, "so trusting in providence that she inspires me with courage." The mother was grateful but not self-deceptive. She clung to life and duty. "I do not want to be separated from your Father," she wrote to Elizabeth. "Little as I am worth in my present feeble state, I serve to make a little variety in his life. It is absolutely better to have a troublesome object to occupy one than no object at all."[31]

Toward the end of her life Mrs. Peabody's faith sometimes stumbled. "But, the battle is not always to the strong," she wrote. "That is all for the best, and will eventuate in good to those who act from principle I have no doubt, but every day's history proves that to be honest, enterprising, industrious, wise, pious will not *ensure* enough of this world's geer to more than keep soul and body together."[32]

During the Pierce campaign Sophia wrote tenderly to her mother but doggedly supported Hawthorne's views. On the death of Daniel Webster that fall, she wrote with passionate pain to a family that scorned the noted statesman-orator because of his views on slavery, his alcoholic binges, and his mistresses of both races. Sophia filled more than eight pages in Webster's defense—"the archangel ruined"—but someone discovered that she had copied them verbatim from *Littel's Living Age.*[33]

Mrs. Peabody lingered. Toward the end she could barely speak. She died quietly on the evening of January 11, 1853, and entered, in Sophia's words, "the Celestial City." "Doubt not," Elizabeth Peabody wrote to Sophia, "that she is with you—more intimately than ever—for the spirit must be where the heart's affections are." Mary Mann wrote to her husband, "You are my mother now. I feel as happy in the event as I expected to, for I can suffer no longer for her sake." Elizabeth took charge of the funeral arrangements. Despite her commitment to causes and principles, she was, first of all, the loyal daughter and provider for her parents, but such was the poverty of the Peabodys and apparently of the two sons-in-law that interment had to wait until Elizabeth could raise the necessary funds.[34]

In the summer of 1852 Hawthorne planned a sequel to *A Wonder-Book*, but the campaign biography took precedence. In the fall he was exhausted and did little but watch the outcome of the Pierce-Scott race, although in October he informed Bridge that he planned in a day or two "to begin a new romance" that, "if possible," was to be "more genial than the last." Clearly he was giving no consideration to developing the story of Agatha, which Melville proposed he undertake. Probably in November he began the children's book and in January declined an invitation from James Russell Lowell because "I am trying hard to write something amidst innumerable interruptions and botherations." Despite his involvement in attending to the spoils following Pierce's election, he completed *Tanglewood Tales*, which consisted of six myths, as he explained with exuberant immodesty, "done up in excellent style, purified from all moral stains, re-created as good as new, or better—and fully equal, in their way, to Mother Goose." He had no self-doubts. "I never," he declared, "did anything else so well as these old baby stories," which returned him to the relatively untroubled world of little Annie and her ramble with a "father."

> . . . the stories . . . transform themselves, and re-assume the shapes which they might be supposed to possess in the pure childhood of the world. When the first poet or romancer told these marvellous legends . . . it was still the Golden Age. Evil had never yet existed; and sorrow, misfortune, crime, were mere shadows which the mind fancifully created for itself, as a shelter against too sunny realities—or, at most, but prophetic dreams, to which the dreamer himself did not yield a waking credence. Children are now the only representatives of the men and women of that happy era; and therefore it is that we must raise the intellect and fancy to the level of childhood, in order to re-create the original myths.

Here he wrote not for children, who had yet to learn of the loss of their paradise, but for adults like himself who could not reconcile themselves to the loss.[35]

Shortly after Pierce's election the jockeying began for the spoils: the politicians of that day, like their successors, flaunted their moralisms and took their loot. Because of his favored position as friend and biographer of the new president, Hawthorne was actively involved in securing posts for himself and others. Following the sudden death of the vice-president elect, Hawthorne claimed to have "as many office-seekers knocking at my door, for three months past, as if I were a prime minister."[36]

He had no interest in a prestigious post, only in "the cash." Everyone knew that Liverpool, one of the world's busiest shipping centers, provided consuls with large fees. Aware that there was a pecking order as well as trade-offs in the process, Hawthorne proposed at the appropriate time alternatives to Liverpool, but with little enthusiasm. He did not hound Pierce; he used Ticknor and others to keep his case conspicuous. He suggested that Ticknor "go to Washington. You ought to be seeing about the red tape and wrapping-paper. . . . The General means well; but it would be a great pity if he should be led into doing a wrong thing as regards that consulship."[37]

During these months Hawthorne got himself involved in the spoils in Salem and Boston. Although he professed that the Whigs did him a favor in ousting him from the Salem Custom-House, he took delight in unseating them when the Democrats were again the victors. He intervened actively on behalf of his old crony Zachariah Burchmore, even preparing letters for him to copy and sign. "I have strong hopes," Hawthorne said as an experienced Salem political hack, "of finding a soft spot in their gizzards, at all events, if not in their hearts. . . . Meanwhile, be quiet, and do not let them suspect you of founding your hopes upon any hostile section of the party. If you declare war against them, and try to fight your way in, I would not give a 'whore's cuss' (to borrow an elegant phrase from the old General) for your chance of being reinstated."[38]

Hawthorne also guided Richard H. Stoddard, the young poet and journalist who had recently published the first extended biographical sketch of Hawthorne. He advised Stoddard to settle for the Custom-House in New York or the post of librarian in some department in Washington. He was encouraged that Stoddard liked and held his brandy, "for most of these public people are inveterate guzzlers, and love a man that can stand up to them, in that particular. It would never do to let them see you corned, however." He counseled Stoddard to keep to himself all "moral, intellectual, or educational" deficiencies. Accept a job as a translator "without hinting that your acquaintance with foreign languages may not be the most familiar. If this unimportant fact be discussed afterwards, you can be transferred to some more suitable post." He drew a Machiavellian conclusion: "A subtle boldness, with a veil of modesty over it, is what is needed." Hawthorne was willing to do what he could for Stoddard except to take him to Liverpool: "I don't want to be bothered with a poet." The only person whom he was willing to consider as an assistant in Liverpool was Pike, who preferred to remain at the Custom-House in Salem.[39]

When Hawthorne decided that his presence in Washington would serve his interests, he persuaded Ticknor to accompany him, the "prime minister" needing a deputy or, more accurately, a trusted friend to look after him. In preparation for his first visit to Washington, he had Ticknor order him a new "black dress-coat and pantaloons." The two men left on April 14, 1853, and proceeded in leisurely stages to New York, then to Philadelphia and Baltimore, finally arriving in Washington on April 20. Ticknor kept his wife informed of their movements in detail and reported Hawthorne's pleasure in socializing, dining, and wining. Hawthorne, on the other hand, wrote during an absence of almost three weeks only three brief notes, unless Sophia destroyed part of the correspondence. He was too busy to write, he explained, because he had to attend obligatory affairs in which he was not interested. He was, he assured Sophia, "homesick for thee. My heart is weary with longing for thee. I want thee in my arms." After explaining that there would be still another delay he wrote, "How I long to be in thy arms is impossible to tell." While Hawthorne was in Washington, Dr. Peabody came and stayed briefly at the Wayside. "After you went away," Sophia wrote to her father, "I lost my enterprise & spirits in waiting for him, & during the long-expecting evenings when every breath of wind seemed his footsteps, I could no more have written a letter than have made a star or a flower."[40]

As an intimate of the president, Hawthorne wielded power, more imaginary than real perhaps, and was courted and lionized by men eager to advance their own interests. "Much attention is shown," Ticknor informed his wife, "and yet it annoys him very much." Ticknor was taken in. Despite what he may have said, Hawthorne delighted in his freedom from decorum—and perhaps from Sophia too. Ticknor deplored the "political intrigue and management" and concluded that "of all men these politicians are the most miserable here." Hawthorne refrained from moral judgments and enjoyed the spectacle, the power plays, the bargaining and horse trading (such as he had witnessed years before with Sam Manning), as well as the endless carousing at an American carnival.[41]

Hawthorne took up the cause of Donald Grant Mitchell (Ik Marvel), a minor essayist and novelist of the period, who was looking for a post in the Mediterranean area. Hawthorne arranged a "private interview" with Pierce and invited Mitchell to "a noisy supper" attended by politicians and office seekers. "I pity him!" Mitchell wrote in his diary. He could have, as Hawthorne would never have said, saved his pity. Another man who met Hawthorne for the first time in Washington, Edwin De Leon, later to be the American consul-general in Egypt, recorded his impression of a man "habitually cold and reserved in his manner, and very taciturn in most companies . . . especially when the company was not congenial to his taste. . . . But when he did unbend, and was in a good mood, no man could make his conversation more agreeable and instructive than he." Influenced no doubt by the convivial surroundings in which he saw Hawthorne, De Leon asserted: "There was nothing of the Puritan in him, . . . he believed in the enjoyment of the good things which the Creator has provided with so lavish a hand for the enjoyment of his creatures." [42]

Hawthorne's manipulations sometimes paid off, sometimes failed. After he had obtained the post at Liverpool, he managed to add the consulship at Manchester, a position which increased his annual income by $3,000. He promoted his old friend O'Sullivan, who eventually landed a post in Portugal, and Mitchell was appointed consul in Venice. He failed, however, to obtain "a consular appointment from General Pierce" for Herman Melville. Perhaps Hawthorne did not overexert himself, but Melville's almost defiant political naïveté and his unwillingness to play the game according to the rules of the spoils helped not at all. Ellery Channing also expected Hawthorne to intervene with the president to secure him an "appointment to any office" that presumably would get him away from Concord. It is doubtful that Hawthorne labored hard on Channing's behalf. He was, after all, no fool. [43]

Ticknor became increasingly impatient as the stay in Washington lengthened, but Hawthorne toured the town, visited Mount Vernon, drank and smoked nightly without fear of Sophia's pained eyes or words, and bantered with political hacks, their wives, and friends of both sexes in a fashion that no one in Concord was ever aware of. Early in May the holiday was over, and the "prime minister" returned to sleepy Concord. In retrospect the interlude was "a time of much enjoyment, especially of a liquid sort," but he was not, he confessed to Bridge, who experienced similar treatment, Pierce's intimate: "Frank was as free and kind, in our personal interviews, as ever he was in our college-days; but his public attentions to me were few and by no means distinguished—only inviting me once to tea, and once to go to a methodist meeting with him; while [other people] were invited to dinner and made much of."[44]

Hawthorne's nomination for the consul post in Liverpool was submitted to the Senate in March and approved on May 26. He received a letter from Pierce informing him that he would take office in Liverpool on August 1, when his predecessor completed his four-year stint. At once Hawthorne was on the alert. "The same favor," he wrote to Pike, "must be granted to me at the end of my term, or I shall be woefully out of pocket by Pierce's complaisance." Elizabeth Peabody had been told that the post was worth $30,000 to $40,000 annually and speculated that "Hawthorne could spend $50,000 in Europe & have a hundred thousand left." "Are you not pleased," she asked her father, "to think that *one* of your children is *rich?*" Sophia was delighted "to have the pinch & strain taken off his mind after such a long discipline of poverty & effort." "To be able to spend a dollar," she explained to her father, "without painful debate will be a great relief to me," but then in her incurable and wonderful optimism she noted that "we have all along been virtually richer than even old Midas was with his endless heaps of treasure."[45]

For the next two months the Wayside was the scene of frantic bustling. Sophia was too busy and anxious to write her usual quota of lengthy letters: there are no extant letters between May 10 and July 7. If she fluttered about more than ever, it was understandable, for she had the responsibility of providing for three children without much assistance from her husband. She was also breathless because a lifelong dream was soon to be fulfilled, four years in England to be followed by an extended stay in Italy during which she would see the artistic masterpieces that she had learned to love and live with through inadequate reproductions.

Hawthorne directed Ticknor to pay his sister Elizabeth $200 annually. On June 14 Longfellow gave a small farewell party, attended by Emerson, James Russell Lowell, Charles Eliot Norton, and Arthur Clough, who was visiting in America at the time. On the following day Longfellow made a gentle entry in his journal: "The memory of yesterday sweetens to-day. It was a delightful farewell to my old friend. He seems much cheered by the prospect before him; and is very lively and in good spirits." If before the beginning of the great adventure Hawthorne met in less decorous surroundings with his meaningful friends, the political hacks, no record has survived.[46]

On July 7, 1853, three days after his forty-ninth birthday and two days before their eleventh wedding anniversary, the Hawthornes sailed aboard the *Niagara* of the Cunard Company, under Captain John Leitch. The *Niagara*, a steamship of about 250 feet, carried approximately 150 passengers, with one cow to supply milk and a coop of chickens. There was a "cannonade" as the ship left the Boston harbor because of the presence of the United States consul and author, Nathaniel Hawthorne. He was returning to "our old home" of the Hathorne ancestors, for the first time sailing before the mast after the example of Captain Nathaniel Hathorne.[47]

During the period between 1849 and 1853 Hawthorne was bumped in disgrace from his post at the Salem Custom-House, entered his "major phase" in an amazing artistic renewal and crescendo which could not be sustained indefinitely and ended in feelings of depletion, and then set off for Liverpool to reap the rewards of an especially lucrative governmental sinecure. The period was preceded by four years in which his only significant literary achievement was "Ethan Brand" and followed by six years in which he filled notebooks with travel-book accounts of life in Europe.

After 1850 the world offered acclaim but not commensurate economic rewards. *The Scarlet Letter* and *The House of the Seven Gables* sold only in the thousands while a work like *Uncle Tom's Cabin* sold by the tens of thousands, as did the writings of other women writers whom Hawthorne denigrated and envied. No doubt the old fears of ending life in an almshouse again surfaced: they were never far below the surface. Ticknor was aboard the *Niagara* because of his firm's business interests in Europe, but Hawthorne may also have needed a companion on a journey perilous, to borrow from Bunyan. Ticknor in the last dozen years of Hawthorne's life assumed the role formerly played by Robert Manning and then Horatio Bridge. He managed Hawthorne's finances, paid his bills, sent money on demand; and Hawthorne asked no questions.

This four-year period was framed by the deaths of the mothers, Mrs. Hawthorne in 1849 and Mrs. Peabody in 1853. Perhaps fortified by her idealistic philosophy and unusual resiliency given her physical and psychosomatic disorders, Sophia handled these losses more satisfactorily than Hawthorne: she mourned appropriately, like Dorcas in "Roger Malvin's Burial," and went on with living; he was more on the order of Reuben Bourne, depressed and helpless, perhaps with unresolved feelings of guilt. In the closing days of Mrs. Hawthorne's life, old patterns had not changed: mother and son failed each other. Neither could reach out to touch or to verbalize; their silent love died in silence.

Sophia had lost a confidant to whom in over forty years she had written tens of thousands of words to confirm her love as well as her need of a parent who in the years before her marriage had unwittingly kept her favorite daughter in dependency. Now there was no one to whom she could unfold her feelings with complete trust. Such freedom she did not often experience with a husband whose reticences and veils kept all but the most intrepid, like Melville, at the distances he demanded for the sanctity and protection of his psyche. The death of her mother increased Sophia's dependency on him, but if, as seems likely, she could not discuss her feelings about this loss, she was denied the verbal and physical comfort which she had earned through her self-effacing devotion. Hawthorne quietly demanded great sacrifices, which Sophia quietly offered up. She probably never realized that she became one of the self-sacrificing women of his fiction.

During the long, isolated sojourn in the Berkshires Hawthorne made a few references to his health, but he was rarely frank, least of all to Sophia. Illness involved an admission of weakness, even of failure. To have aroused Sophia's anxieties would also have subjected him to more solicitude than he could have tolerated. Hence, admissions to friends were, he invariably warned, not to be relayed to Sophia. He rarely was willing to see doctors, who from his overly sensitive and fearful perspective invaded his person, which was literally and figuratively to remain untouchable, even at death.

Because of Hawthorne's secretiveness it is customary to assign the collapse of his health to the 1860s or at the earliest to his response to Una's brush with death from malaria in Rome in 1859, when he almost collapsed. Yet in a letter in 1853 he declared the Concord River, which was scarcely a mile from the Wayside, "quite out of my reach"—this from a man who two years earlier chopped logs, scrambled up trees for his children's amusement, and walked from the red farmhouse into Lenox two miles away. Ellery Channing, who was perhaps too idiosyncratic to be totally reliable, commented that Hawthorne walked, presumably figuratively, like a sea captain "because he was so stout—rolling and swaying about in walking. I have walked much with him; but he was not fond of that exercise." No one else, so far as we know, referred either to Hawthorne's obesity or the rolling motion. In view of Hawthorne's silences, Channing and others were unaware that Coverdale speaks for Hawthorne when he writes of the "ebb-tide of my energies" and likens his state to the "ache of a limb long ago cut off"—another image on the order of the "decapitated surveyor."[48]

In the absence of medical examinations it may be useless to speculate, but the slow decline in health would seem to be characteristic of a degenerative disorder of some kind. This is not, however, to overlook the swings of his moods—again because of the silences of most observers we know very little—which may have increased during this four-year period under the pressure and burdens of losses, overexertion, and depletion.

At the time of the flight to England—and in some senses it was a flight—Hawthorne was almost fifty. Aging and death were not subjects he handled with ease or detachment, as evidenced in the way he searched out cemeteries on the one hand and his fascination with elixirs of life from "Dr. Heidegger's Experiment" (1837) to "The Dolliver Romance," which he was writing at the time of his death. If he had little faith in such nonsense, he could not put the subject aside. He only half-believed, so he claimed, his Bowdoin classmates who insisted that he had not aged significantly, but in the ever-present mirror—he was preoccupied with the self-image in art and in life—he watched the wrinkles emerge and the hair recede. From infancy he had disdained, and dreaded perhaps, ugliness and the shadows of age. Sophia shared his views, and out of vanity in part but primarily in her desire to please an overly fastidious husband, who bore some similarities to Aylmer in "The Birth-mark," she made herself attractive and pleasing in his eyes. In a stern letter she reprimanded her sister Elizabeth, who evidently not for the first time had referred "to our age & coming infirmities." "My feeling is increased," Sophia said, "by observing that it is not agreeable to my husband to have you do this in his case—He wants to know nothing about the birth days you are so fond of. To him an infirmity, helpless old age, is not beautiful for himself, & I can see how he would not rejoice in any diminution of power & life."[49]

With the passage of years there were problems in the marriage—they were there potentially from the very beginning—but externally and publicly there were no dramatic changes. At no point, however, was there any reason to doubt that the marriage would survive since each satisfied the other's need in certain ways and each by life experience was conditioned to endure, like Priscilla and Hollingsworth at the conclusion of *The Blithedale Romance.* Very early in the marriage there were problems in communication which, being evaded instead of handled directly, increased. Husbands and wives usually talk to each other, they do not write notes in journals, as Hawthorne was inclined to do. But evasiveness was one of his most useful fictional strategies: he had learned the tactic early in life in a family that avoided displays of either joy or pain.

Hawthorne's demands led to inevitable concessions. He required the privacy of his study, which Sophia duly treated as inviolate from the first days of their marriage. Perhaps because tactility and affection made him uncomfortable—he was, after all, a Hawthorne—she lavished an excessive love upon her children, smothering them with affection but at the same time regulating their eating, health, and attire with the rigidity of a major general, isolating them from peers and supervising their education completely. There was no way for Hawthorne to alter arrangements without causing Sophia undue pain and himself inconvenience. His indecisiveness and her dogmatic idealism posed problems neither could resolve or for that matter face.

Understandably, as things got parceled out in the marriage, the home was under her complete control. The houses were excessively feminine in decoration, including his study, although apparently he approved, at least most of the time. Her taste was precious and conventional—she worshiped at the shrine of Art—while he was, not without ambivalence, attracted to rough-and-ready men and women and had to escape periodically from the rigidities of the genteel code which provided the security she needed. Like a naughty boy—and even with age he never lost his boyish qualities—Hawthorne recorded in his journal, perhaps with secret delight, that during Sophia's absence Melville and he had desecrated the pristine rooms of the red farmhouse by smoking and drinking during a session of "ontological heroics."

If in conversations Sophia voiced the quixotic idealism and the extravagant adoration characteristic of her letters—Ellery Channing observed, "She was foolish in her expression of admiration for Hawthorne"—she would have taxed anyone's patience and more than sated anyone's need of praise. One suspects that during Hawthorne's depressed moods she quickly learned to be silent. Under certain conditions her nonsensical but loving babble would have been unendurable.[50]

During the eighteen-month stay in the Berkshires Hawthorne was locked, as it were, in the red house and denied, except occasionally with Melville, his periodic freedom from Decorum and Duty, and he became depleted intellectually and artistically. This period was no doubt a time of crisis in the marriage which neither was to admit. There were the extreme isolation, the price he had to pay for Sophia's overindulgence of her children, the attraction-repulsion of the Melville relationship, and the birth of Rose which against Sophia's wishes Hawthorne was to witness. Her fears were probably justified. Overprotected by his own family and then by Sophia, a lover of beauty like Owen Warland and Clifford, Hawthorne could easily have been profoundly shaken by such an exposure, to the extent that apparently he pledged himself to chastity at forty-seven.

It is doubtful that Hawthorne and Sophia ever discussed his friendship with Melville. It must have been another secret he kept from her, like the publication of *Fanshawe*. In 1852 he began to take vacations alone, which eventually Sophia approved of and perhaps even welcomed. The stay in Washington in 1853 was, however, insensitively extended, given her fears, and his infrequent letters did not help matters or relieve her anxiety. Her loneliness and her denials, particularly to her sisters, were to increase and to exact a toll in the deterioration of her health, which had a physical basis but was markedly influenced by her repressions.

Whatever the reason or reasons for Hawthorne's burning all of Sophia's love letters—no doubt he could, if pressed, have advanced any number of rationalizations—the act served as an epitaph of the edenic relationship, which had in some ways proved but another bubble.

England

"I Do Not Take Root Anywhere"

The *Liverpool Chronicle* noted the arrival of the *Niagara* from Boston by way of Halifax "at an early hour" on Sunday morning, July 16, 1853: "Amongst the passengers by the *Niagara* was Mr. N. Hawthorne, the new United States Consul for this port."[1]

There was no consular residence, and the family had to seek its own quarters. For ten days they stayed at the Waterloo Hotel at $16 a day and for the following nine days lived with Mary Blodgett in Duke Street at about $7 a day. Within a week or so after arriving they decided to flee what Hawthorne termed "the most detestable place as a residence that ever my lot was cast in,— smoky, noisy, dirty, pestilential." They stayed briefly at the Royal Rock Hotel in Rock Ferry, which is on the Mersey River about two miles from Liverpool, and in September hired a furnished house at Rock Park for an annual rental of about $800.[2]

Ticknor remained only a few days in Liverpool, longer than he had intended because of Hawthorne's entreaty, and then went on to London. He had hardly left when Hawthorne complained: "I have had but little enjoyment in a solitary cigar, and seldom feel like visiting a beershop, without your countenance." As long as Ticknor was about, Hawthorne could escape from a family that was noisily homesick, annoyed at the confinement of temporary quarters and the frequent moves, and unwell with colds. Sophia suffered most, and in August Hawthorne expressed concern as to whether "she will be able to bear this abominable climate."[3]

Almost at once Hawthorne fretted about costs and expenditures that seemed out of control. He reported to Pike that in his first two months he had "already got rid of $2,000," which was, even if he overstated, a substantial sum and cause for concern for a man who had rarely earned that amount in a year either as a governmental employee or as an author. Although the Hawthornes were accustomed to living economically, they found life in Liverpool difficult to cope with, and Hawthorne concluded that they needed six thousand dollars annually for a simple existence that permitted some travel in England and Scotland. Sophia was a careful manager and worried when she discovered that a pound of fish cost twenty cents, a pound of meat fourteen cents, a peck of potatoes thirty cents, a pound of tea one dollar, and a peach twelve cents.[4]

On August 1 Hawthorne assumed his post in two gloomy rooms in the Washington Building near the Liverpool docks at the corner of Brunswick Street. From his window he had a Dickensian view "of a tall, dismal, smoke-blackened, ugly brick ware-house—uglier than any building I ever saw in America." He watched bags of salt "swinging and vibrating in the air" and adjusted himself to the "continued rumble of heavy wheels." Sophia informed her father that there was nothing worth looking at outside or inside the building "except Mr Hawthorne and that gentleman Mr Hawthorne cannot see." A young English poet, William Allingham, concluded after a visit to the consul's office that Hawthorne "looked oddly out of place in Liverpool."[5]

Liverpool was one of the world's busiest and grimiest ports, filled with human derelicts. In the first paragraph of a notebook which was to consist of over 300,000 words, Hawthorne wrote:

Every morning, I find the entry thronged with the most rascally set of sailors that ever were seen—dirty, desperate, and altogether pirate-like in aspect. What the devil they want here, is beyond my present knowledge; but probably they have been shipwrecked, or otherwise thrown at large on the world, and wish for assistance in some shape.[6]

Most Americans on their way to Europe landed in Liverpool and sailed home from there. As the ranking American official Hawthorne lived, it sometimes seemed to him, in a state of siege.

> The duties of the office carried me to prisons, police-courts, hospitals, lunatic asylums, coroner's inquests, death-beds, funerals, and brought me in contact with insane people, criminals, ruined speculators, wild adventurers, diplomatists, brother-consuls, and all manner of simpletons and unfortunates, in greater number and variety than I had ever dreamed of as pertaining to America; in addition to whom there was an equivalent multitide of English rogues, dexterously counterfeiting the genuine Yankee article.[7]

In the consular office Hawthorne was anything but the shy, retiring author from Concord. He listened to appeals for assistance but knew how to cut through the cant and the deceptions. He bent for some but firmly denied others. He acted in self-defense, as he explained: "All pennyless Americans, or pretenders to Americanism, look upon me as their banker; and I could ruin myself, any week, if I had not laid down a rule to consider every applicant for assistance an impostor, until he proves himself a true and responsible man."[8]

Since he had no comprehension of "the intricate and unintelligible machinery of Providence," he "hated to give advice, especially when there is a prospect of its being taken. It is only one-eyed people who love to advise, or have any spontaneous promptitude of action. When a man opens both his eyes, he generally sees about as many reasons for acting in one way as in any other, and quite as many for acting in neither."[9]

When Hawthorne could escape the demands of his post he again became the observer, life's voyeur, and, like Robin in "My Kinsman, Major Molineux," sought out "the darker and dingier streets, inhabited by the poorer classes. The scenes there are very picturesque in their way; at every two or three steps, a ginshop; also filthy in clothes and person, ragged, pale, often afflicted with humors; women, nursing their babies at dirty bosoms; men haggard, drunken, care-worn, hopeless, but with a kind of patience, as if all this were the rule of their life." Hawthorne was almost compulsively fastidious but also at times ashamed of himself. "I never walk through these streets," he commented, "without feeling as if I should catch some disease; but yet there is a strong interest in such walks; and moreover there is a bustle, a sense of being in the midst of life, and of having got hold of something real, which I do not find in the better streets of the city." [10]

Hawthorne took the post at Liverpool with two purposes in mind: to accumulate enough money in four years to make an extended stay on the Continent possible for the following year or two and, more important, to leave Europe with substantial savings that, combined with royalties from his books, would guarantee the family's security. He put it this way: "I shall have about as much money as will be good for me—enough to educate Julian, and portion off the girls in a moderate way. . . . And if I die, or am brain-stricken, my family will not be beggars;—the dread of which has often troubled me in times past." The object in 1853, then, was to begin the accumulation of more than the $25,000 his predecessor had "derived from his official savings." [11]

The position carried no fixed salary, the income being determined by the emoluments. The consul received $2 each time he signed a consul's certificate for goods on a ship. Some ships required such a large number of certificates that the consul could earn as much as $250 in a day. "The autograph of a living author," Hawthorne gloated, "has seldom been so much in request at so respectable a price." On his first day he established a ritual: "The pleasantest incident of the day, is when Mr. [James] Pearce (the vice-consul or head-clerk) makes his appearance with the account books, containing the receipts and expenditures of the preceding day, and deposits on my desk a little rouleau of the Queen's coin, wrapt up in a piece of paper. This morning, there were eight sovereigns, four half-crowns, and a shilling [about $43]—a pretty fair day's work, though not more than the average ought to be." [12]

Whether he felt elated or depressed was greatly influenced by the day's receipts, as was his attitude toward the United States, particularly when there were rumors of a change in policy. The consul's income from emoluments had become somewhat of a scandal in Congress, and in 1854 legislation was under consideration to eliminate the fees and establish a fixed annual salary. As Hawthorne confessed to Ticknor, "The truth is, it is a devilish good office;—if those Jackasses at Washington (of course, I do not include the President under this polite phrase) will but let it alone." [13]

Hawthorne was so preoccupied with the accumulation of money that he wrote of little else to Ticknor, who acted as his banker—"The gold begins to chink"—and even Sophia, who understood only what she was told and was not told much, got caught up in the quest. Despite high expenses during the early months of their stay in Liverpool, Hawthorne managed to send the publisher $1,500. He complained that he was "worn out with hard work, . . . but I think I shall live through it." By December 8 he was annoyed at the slow rate of accumulation: "I am sick of it, and long for my hillside; and—what I thought I never should long for—my pen! When once a man is thoroughly imbued with ink, he never can wash out the stain." When proceeds in the first two months of the new year grew to $3,400, he wrote with glee to Ticknor, "Invest—invest—invest! . . . I am in a hurry to be rich enough to get away from this dismal and forlorn hole. If I can once see $20,000 in a pile, I shan't care much for being turned out of office." [14]

In June 1854 he was confident that he would "bag" $10,000 in his first year in office, "and my expenses have been very heavy too." The affluence he was enjoying for the first time in his life increased expectations: "I do not see how it will be possible for me to live, hereafter, on less than the interest of $40,000. I can't imagine how I ever did live on much less than that. It takes at least $100,000 to make a man quite comfortable . . . and even then he would have to deny himself a great many very desirable things." Two months later he complained: "I am so sick and weary of this office, that I should hardly regret it if they were to abolish it altogether. . . . it is full of damnable annoyances," which he enumerated. "After all," he declared, "there are worse lives than that of an author." Soon he spoke vaguely of "a book calculated for schools" as well as to make money. Nothing came of these fancies, for Hawthorne could not alter a lifelong pattern: except for the voluminous notebooks there was no writing until he gave up his post. [15]

On March 1, 1855, Congress passed a law establishing fixed salaries for consuls and the payment of fees to the government. The effective date for the new system was postponed several times, and Hawthorne maintained his position. However, with customary caution Hawthorne decided in June to give up the house in Rock Ferry and to occupy lodgings at much lower rentals in Leamington, and he began commuting to Liverpool. Two of the three servants were dismissed in another economy move. [16]

Hawthorne had scarcely settled into his office when he was called upon to attend one of the public ceremonies which his post as the ranking American official in Liverpool made mandatory. As he explained, "I suppose some persons would console themselves with the dignity of the office, the public and private dinners, and the excellent opportunity of playing the great man on a small scale; but this is to me a greater bore than all the rest; so that you see I have nothing to comfort myself with but the emoluments." All his life he had refused invitations to lecture or to deliver afterdinner speeches. In the first week of office he "mumbled some d——d nonsense" on two occasions and found that he had nothing to fear in the way of competition from the English, "for the tongue of man never uttered worse speeches than theirs are." [17]

He had without any experimentation found a simple solution. "I charge myself pretty high with champagne and port before I get upon my legs; and whether the business is to make a speech or to be hanged, I come up to it like a man—and I had as lief it should be one as the other." Or as he put it on another occasion, he had come to the conclusion that "it is easy enough to speak, when a man is cornered and *corned*." [18]

The result was that Fields, who frequently performed on the lyceum circuit in the United States, listened with amazement to the performance of the "painfully shy" author: "I imagined his face a deep crimson, and his hands trembling with nervous horror; but judge of my surprise, when he rose to reply with so calm a voice and so composed a manner, that, in all of my experience of dinner-speaking, I never witnessed such a case of apparent ease." There was little humbug about Hawthorne: he could size up a situation quickly and knew how to play the con-artist when it suited his purposes not to be "painfully shy": "I flatter myself, however, that, by much practice, I attained considerable skill in this kind of intercourse, the art of which lies in passing off common-places for new and valuable truths, and talking trash and emptiness in such a way that a pretty acute auditor might mistake it for something solid." [19]

Hawthorne had more difficulty in coping with literary gatherings where he was honored as the foremost living American author. He found the lionizing "something between botheration and a satisfaction." At one dinner he did not know what to do with Samuel Carter Hall, who was "a little too demonstrative" and "besmeared me with a great deal more butter and treacle, before the dinner was over." At another affair a short time later Hawthorne asked for Hall's assistance because "if I had sought the whole world over, I could not have found a better artist in whip-syllabub and flummery." He grew "weary" of feminine admirers "who were rather superfluous in their oblations, quite stiffling me, indeed, with the incense that they burnt under my nose." His comment was nastier than warranted, as he recognized: "It is ungracious, even hoggish, not to be gratified with the interest they expressed in me, but then it is really a bore, and one does not know what to do or say."[20]

At a dinner in which he took second place only to Jenny Lind, who was at the height of her fame, he complained about admirers who unwittingly took advantage of his inability to indulge in small talk: "It is surely very wrong and ill-mannered in people to ask for an introduction, unless they are prepared to make talk; it throws too great an expense and trouble on the wretched lion, who is compelled, on the spur of the moment, to concoct a conversible substance out of thin air, perhaps for the twentieth time that evening." After the complaint he confessed that the evening was "agreeable." The lion was not really wretched.[21]

To one of the great entertainers of the age and the "literary ringmaster of London," who collected celebrities as well as pornography, Richard Monckton Milnes, first Baron Houghton, Hawthorne offered the following justification for refusing his invitation:

> . . . I am an absurdly shy sort of person, and have missed a vast deal of enjoyment, in the course of my life, by an inveterate habit (or more than habit, for I believe it was born with me) of keeping out of people's way. It is now too late to think of amendment. I never go anywhere (as a guest; I mean) except sometimes to a dinner, when there is no possibility of avoiding it.

Because of Milnes's persistence the two men eventually established a cordial relationship without becoming intimate.[22]

Charles Mackay, the editor of the *Illustrated London News* and author of one of the most popular songs of the decade, "Good Time Coming," recalled meeting Hawthorne at the Milton Club in London. "I endeavored to draw him into conversation," he noted, "but with such little success that I could not help thinking, as I looked at his massive head and full deep eyes, . . . that he must be an imposter, inasmuch as it was impossible for anybody to be as wise as he looked." Later at a small party

Hawthorne threw off some of his "constitutional reserve, and gambolled solemnly in his talk with the ponderosity of an elephant attempting to be playful."[23]

One day in 1857 at an art exhibition in Manchester, Hawthorne discovered that Tennyson was present. A friend guided him to the Salon of Old Masters, where the poet laureate was viewing the paintings. Hawthorne refused to introduce himself or to be introduced and was content like Miles Coverdale and all the other observers in his fiction to watch from a comfortable distance. He sketched a perceptive portrait:

> Tennyson is the most picturesque figure, without affectation, that I ever saw; of middle-size, rather slouching, dressed entirely in black, and with nothing white about him except the collar of his shirt, which methought might have been clean the day before. . . . His face was very dark, and not exactly a smooth face, but worn, and expressing great sensitiveness. . . . There was an entire absence of stiffness in his figure; no set-up in him at all; no nicety or trimness. . . . Gazing at him with all my eyes, I liked him well, and rejoiced more in him than in all the other wonders of the Exhibition.

He noted Tennyson's "shy and secluded habits" and was "indescribably sensible of a morbid painfulness in him, a something not to be meddled with." Perhaps inevitably it was as though Hawthorne looked at his own image. He refused to dog Tennyson's steps, but when Sophia heard of Tennyson's presence, she could scarcely restrain herself or her eager eyes, although she was too timid to intrude. When Tennyson left the room she grasped his youngest child in her arms and kissed him. "And I was well pleased," she declared, "to have had in my arms Tennyson's child." She probably never thought for a moment how frightened the little boy may have been to find himself in the arms of a palpitating, wide-eyed woman.[24]

Hawthorne had returned to the land of his paternal ancestors—he was to pay no attention to the Mannings—and when he published his impressions, the title was to be *Our Old Home*. One of the first things he did in Liverpool was to make his mandatory visit to a cemetery. There he examined inscriptions almost obliterated by the weather. He admitted his object: "Of all things I should like to find a grave-stone in one of these old church-yards, with my own name upon it."[25]

This quest for roots and the recovery of a past led him to search out the birthplace of his most distinguished ancestor, William Hathorne, who had come to be a kind of substitute father. "My ancestor," he wrote in his notebook, "left England in 1635. I return in 1853. I sometimes feel as if I myself had been absent these two hundred and eighteen years—leaving England just emerging from the feudal system, and finding it on the verge of Republicanism. It brings the two far separated points of time very closely together, to view the matter thus."[26]

As he roamed about the English countryside, sometimes he had visions: "I feel as if I might have lived here a long while ago, and had now come back because I retained pleasant recollections of it." "So powerful" were these illuminations that he wondered whether "any such airy remembrances might not be a sort of innate idea, the print of a recollection of some ancestral mind, transmitted with fainter and fainter impress through several descents, to my own." He fancied that after two hundred years he found again the village and "veiled sky" of his forebears, and "his own affinities for these things, a little obscured by disuse, were reviving at every step."[27]

Hawthorne lamented that the family papers were said "to have been burnt, about a hundred years ago, so that I have no records whatever." Yet he went to the British Museum "with a weary and heavy heart, wishing (Heaven forgive me!) that the Elgin marbles and the frieze of the Parthenon were all burnt into lime, and that the granite Egyptian statues were hewn and squared into building-stones, and that the mummies had all turned to dust two thousand years ago." By a curious association Hawthorne consigned the Elgin stones to Ethan Brand's limekiln, where that wanderer ends his life. "The present," Hawthorne's jeremiad continued, "is burthened too much with the past. We have not time, in our earthly existence, to appreciate what is warm with life, and immediately around us."[28]

During these years, then, Hawthorne was searching for roots like Ilbrahim, but two years after arrival his recurrent fear of impoverishment and life in an almshouse forced the family to become wanderers from lodging house to hotel to lodging house. "The moral effect of being without a settled abode is very wearisome," he declared, but he was unable to change his ways or to find rest. "I am a poor, wayside vagabond," he lamented on another occasion, "and only find shelter for a night or so, and then trudge onward again." If in a depressed mood he overstated, as he frequently did in his all-too-human self-dramatizations, he eloquently voiced the lostness of his fictional wanderers: "I feel quite homeless and astray, and as if I belonged nowhere."[29]

From a perspective of three thousand miles he saw America as fragmented and lacking a center. "We have so much country," he declared, "that we have really no country at all." Then, deeply moved, he added, "I feel the want of one, every day of my life." He praised Americans as "the best people in the world"—only to qualify, "but it is a poor world at that." In another mood he was sickened by the political in-fighting in America: "We are the most miserable people on earth." As tension mounted in the United States in the decade before the fratricide of the 1860s, the external divisions in the land reflected his internal divisions. He was angry because he knew that one day he would have to make the kind of commitment he preferred to avoid. "I sympathize with no party," he told Ticknor, "but hate them all—free-soilers, pro-slavery men, and whatever else—all alike." Such negatives constituted no position, as he recognized, and when the time "compelled" choice, he knew that he would "go for the North," as he did.[30]

In 1855, when there were rumors that the United States would go to war with England, Hawthorne was at once a fiery patriot hungering for battle. A strategist to boot, he favored an immediate attack on England and declared that there were no fortifications to "hinder an American fleet from sailing up the Mersey." "I should like well," he asserted, "to be superseded in my Consular duties by the arrival of a Yankee Commodore or General." Some time later he erupted: "We hold the fate of England in our hands, and it is time we crushed her—blind, ridiculous, old rump of beef, sodden in strong beer, that she is; not but what she has still vitality enough to do us a good deal of mischief, before we quite annihilate her." Three times he underscored the crucial word, "I *hate* England," before he qualified, "though I love some Englishmen, and like them generally, in fact." He was "not unconscious of a certain malevolence and hostility in my own breast, such as a man must necessarily feel, who lives in England without melting entirely into the mass of Englishmen." Unconsciously he assumed the viewpoint of the outsider, the Ilbrahim, the persecuted, which from the beginning was the viewpoint and posture of his fiction.[31]

After his fiftieth birthday in 1854, which as usual passed without celebration, he expressed admiration for English homogeneity and stability. "Every thing is so delightfully sluggish here!" he declared. "It is so pleasant to find people holding on to old ideas, and hardly now beginning to dream of matters that are already old with us! I have had enough of progress;—now I want to stand stock still; or rather, to go back twenty years or so;—and that is just what I seem to have done, in coming to England."[32]

The fear of death behind such utterances also emerged in a dream in which he saw Fields, who "had grown so old that I hardly knew him; and I myself looked so very old that he did not recognize me at all." He explained that the toils of office had given him "a long shove onward towards old age." When Hawthorne applied for a passport to Italy in 1857, at age fifty-three, he reported his age as "(I am sorry to say) fifty-one" and Sophia's as forty-two, when she was actually forty-six.[33]

On January 2, 1857, he declared himself "well content to spend the remainder of my days in England." On the last day of the same month, he admitted: "I do not take root anywhere, and never shall, unless I could establish myself in some old manor-house like those I see in England." In August, his nerves seemingly frayed, he began "to weary of England, and need another clime." At the end of the year he was "weary, weary" of London and England and sympathized with the Loyalists who had to live out their lives there after the Revolutionary War, but then the expected qualification: "And yet there is still a pleasure in being in this dingy, smoky, midmost haunt of men." He came to know the streets of London as well as "I ever knew Washington-street, in Boston, or even Essex-street in my stupid old native-town."[34]

In summing up these years in *Our Old Home* Hawthorne displayed acumen but also his tendency to see his life as the shadowy stuff of romance:

For myself, as soon as I was out of office, the retrospect began to look unreal. I could scarcely believe that it was I, that figure whom they called a Consul, but a sort of Double Ganger, who had been permitted to assume my aspect, under which he went through his shadowy duties with a tolerable show of efficiency, while my real self had lain, as regarded my proper mode of being and acting, in a state of suspended animation.[35]

      Hawthorne worried about his "real self" and released pent-up feelings in letters to his friends, while Sophia with her habitual self-effacement suffered silently, at a price. On two occasions, however, she confessed to her father that "Mr Hawthorne was for once very content with what he saw," which said much about his moods and depressions. Sophia's "sphere" had contracted with the death of her mother, and a dialog of gossip, love, and trivia, to which both had contributed, usually with delicacy and tact, had ended. On landing in Liverpool she found herself in a strange city and a strange land, without an official residence and servants, and she had to put up with the inconveniences of temporary quarters. She had no one in whom to confide, and after Hawthorne formally assumed his post, she had to adjust to his long hours and evening receptions which sometimes kept him in Liverpool overnight. She apparently never joined him because, even though there were servants now, the Hawthornes still could not separate themselves from their children. "He goes from us at nine," Sophia exclaimed to her father, "and we do not see him again till five!!!" Not knowing that he found time to explore the seamy underside of Liverpool life, she blamed "the tiresome old Consulate" which made her "infinitely desolate." There was no doubt that she was desolate and lonely, but when her sisters accused her husband of neglecting her, she refuted the charge at length.[36]

With or without her husband, Sophia continued to overengage herself in the education of her three children. Elizabeth Hawthorne asserted that Sophia "wished to keep her children in complete mental dependence upon herself." Elizabeth, however, was too unsympathetic to understand that Sophia had to shore up her life and give her unappropriated love to someone. Nor did she appreciate that Sophia's idealism and dogmatic advocacy of her views, which had been her mother's too, rested on a punishing insecurity which extended to a reluctance even to be photographed. She was by no means unattractive, but, she informed her father, "I never dreamed of putting myself into a picture, because I am not handsome enough." In 1856 she turned her back on the camera and later obliterated her head in a print.[37]

Every evening Sophia read two cantos of *The Faerie Queene* to Julian, "omitting certain passages," she explained. For the next few years Julian played knight with armor and helmet, and he recognized "that the first knight he is to do battle with & conquer is himself, & that the Dragon he is to slay is invisible to mortal eye. The effect of Spenser's divine creation upon him has been admirable." He was, in short, a worthy brother of the Spenserian heroine after whom his sister Una was named. Sophia's plan for Una's education was to interest her in history "so as to keep her mind from being dissipated & weakened by romance-reading in which she inclines to be absorbed." If the girl's sense of reality was at times confused, so was her mother's. "I should like to see you," Sophia wrote during an absence, "with your hair falling about your neck, and a ray of sun upon it, sitting at the foot of a tree, with a lion at your feet, my dearest Una." Eventually she took Una to dancing school in Liverpool, but the children were still educated at home by their mother.[38]

None of the children spoke later of their mother's educational schemes with any degree of enthusiasm, but Julian recalled his father's reading to them and his "tussling-bouts":

> . . . he would sit in his easy-chair, and bid me "come on!" I would fly at him like a little windmill, and we would grapple and wrestle heartily, he to get me across his knees, I to resist to the utmost: shouts of laughter, grunts, and outcries. When he got me in position, the conflict terminated in a redoubtable, old-fashioned spanking, and he laid on sincerely. . . . In the end I found a parry for the spanking—tickling him under the knee, which my prone position facilitated. He was very ticklish, and the rules of the game didn't forbid it, so the spankings were abbreviated.

Hawthorne provided the sense of play missing in the humorless, duty-driven regimen Sophia inherited from her mother, that is, when he was in the appropriate mood, but he was perhaps taking the easy way of winning the children's favor and undercutting Sophia's role.[39]

Dr. Peabody, now very feeble, lost strength, and once again Elizabeth took care of a dying parent. She ordered Sophia home to be with their father. Sophia in turn explained her "duty" to her family: "My life is really essential to him & the children; but *not* to dear father, whose heart & existence almost are already in another world." Sophia did not know until later that Hawthorne himself suggested to Elizabeth in his usual direct, but not necessarily unkind, manner that Sophia be spared "the vacillations of hope & fear." Hawthorne anticipated the effect that the death would have on Sophia, particularly as relayed through the agitated, rarely understated letters of Elizabeth.[40]

Dr. Peabody died early in January 1855 in Eagleswood, New Jersey, where he was buried. Elizabeth could not afford the expense of sending the body to Salem for interment next to her mother. Conforming to a mid-century custom, Elizabeth sent her sister a lock of their father's hair. "I could not believe it could be such a delight to me, but it shared his life," Sophia wrote, then added a small but meaningful detail, "& his hand had often passed over it, as was his habit."[41]

She confessed a few weeks later to her sister Mary that she had been "quite indisposed & anxious about father" and "much agitated & in grief for my own loss of him, & at the certainty I shall see him no more"—she withheld until the end of the sentence the main point—"& that I had no father on earth." She was an orphan, a stranger in a foreign land, and probably feared, as one often does in such situations, how vulnerable her own family was.[42]

After the Hawthornes gave up their house in Rock Ferry in 1855, Sophia, who dearly needed the security of a home, had to accept temporary accommodations which made planning for her family difficult. No doubt she feared to discuss her concerns with her husband, but her body eventually spoke. Soon she consulted a physician who concerned himself only with her persistent bronchial condition, probably because she hesitated to discuss her emotional state or because like most doctors he was interested only in the body. He recommended, as was to be expected, spending the cold, damp months in a southern climate. Apparently without much if any consultation, Hawthorne arranged to have Sophia and their two daughters spend the following winter in Lisbon, where John Louis O'Sullivan now held a diplomatic post, his reward for services in the election of Pierce. As Sophia perceived matters, she was being sent into exile. That summer she wrote to her husband what she probably could not say to him, "I want to be with you. . . . I am not fit to be without you. . . . I dread to go alone so far." It was truly the cry of a dependent child to a parent. Hawthorne did not heed the cry.[43]

To her sister Elizabeth, Sophia maintained with her customary firmness and fervor that Hawthorne took excellent care of her. She even insisted that she had inherited her mother's constitution, "or I should have been under the sod in part, & part above (I hope) very long ago." To her sister she fibbed, but to her husband, again like a child, she apologized in a letter which laid bare her agony and disclosed perhaps a trace of bitterness in the midst of her contrition.

> Since I must go away, I ought not to have said a word; but thou must ascribe what I said & say to infinite love of thee only—for it is only because thou art the soul of my life that I do not look forward with delight to a winter in Lisbon with the O'Sullivans. I could not be happy as you well know, if you made any sacrifice for me—& as our interests are indissoluble it would be my sacrifice too, & I will be good and not distress thee with any more regrets.

Again Hawthorne did not heed the cry, or perhaps he accepted the doctor's evaluation.[44]

On October 11, 1855, Sophia, Una, and Rose sailed for Lisbon, and father and son settled in at Blodgett's boardinghouse in Liverpool. The separation lasted until June of the following year. The relatively few surviving letters reveal beneath the suppressions that it was an exceedingly difficult period for Sophia and that Hawthorne was sometimes insensitive to his wife's feelings.

Shortly after her arrival in Lisbon Sophia advised Julian to "confide in him all your heart & life, so as not to become shut up & alone." She asked her son to do what she had been afraid to do during all the years of the marriage. It was also perhaps a plea to Hawthorne to ask questions that would unlock secrets. But he would ask no questions: he kept inviolate his own as well as others' privacy.[45]

In one of his letters to Sophia, Hawthorne swore that life with Julian made separation bearable: "We live together in great love and harmony, the best friends in the world." At the same time he used Sophia's absence to effect changes which could have been discussed when she was at hand. Mary Blodgett cut Julian's long hair, and, in the father's words, he "looked like a real boy now." In another letter he informed Sophia that the boy's "affections of the head" disappeared without medical diagnosis or prescription because Julian "had grown morbid for want of a wider sphere," meaning socialization with peers. One thing puzzled the father: at ten Julian still believed in "our first explanation" of his origin—"how I came down from Heaven; but I'm very glad I happened to tumble into so good a family!" Since Hawthorne never discussed sex with his son, then or later, and the family was conditioned to veiling emotions, perhaps Julian had secrets too. Years later Julian recalled with delight these months during which he had his father to himself and was able to do pretty much as he pleased, although they lived, he added condescendingly, among not very "cultivated persons." His father was, he remembered, on familiar terms with the sea captains who boarded at Blodgett's and excelled at card playing, particularly whist.[46]

In Lisbon Sophia made O'Sullivan her confidant. This relationship troubled Una, who observed O'Sullivan substituting for her father and also taking her mother away from her. "Uncle John," she informed her father, is now "next to you to her, she says. And I can be nothing but a trouble & a worry to her, I am afraid. For she cannot pour out her heart to me as she does to Uncle John. I am sorry, very sorry. I wish I were older & more experienced." Una's was still another cry to a father who, although he recognized that "life has never been light and joyous to her," never understood how to help her cope.[47]

Instead of supporting Sophia in this new but temporary relationship, Hawthorne perhaps in jealousy undercut it. He advised Sophia, quite gratuitously, not to sympathize "too much" with O'Sullivan following the death of his brother: "Thou art wholly mine, and must not overburthen thyself with anybody's grief—not even that of thy dearest friend next to me." In another letter he analyzed O'Sullivan at length, balancing in his usual fashion positives and negatives, only to conclude that O'Sullivan "is too much like a woman, without being a woman; and between the two characters [male and female], he misses the quintessential delicacy of both."[48]

His letters again assumed, almost too insistently, the erotic overtones and wordplay of those written during his four-year postponement of marriage earlier. He declared that her letters were "precisely" like those "my little Virgin Dove used to write to me," which lifted him "out of a state of half-torpor, half-misery." He had learned during their separation, he maintained, "the absolute necessity of expression. I must tell thee I love thee. I must be told that thou lovest me. It must be said in words and symbolized with caresses; or else, at last, imprisoned Love will go frantic, and tear all to pieces the heart that holds it." He felt it "a desperate thing that I cannot embrace thee this very instant," because "I need thee so insufferably."[49]

After Elizabeth Peabody sent a new remedy for afflictions of the lungs, a much certified medical miracle wrapped in flannel and oilcloth to be worn on the breast, Hawthorne spun at once an erotic cocoon. "Oh, mine ownest love," he wrote, "I shall clap this little flannel talisman upon thy dearest bosom, the moment thou dost touch English soil. Every instant when thy bosom is not pressed against mine, it shall be shielded by the flannel." This led to a passage almost out of John Donne: "Thou *never* again shalt go away anywhere without me. My two arms shall be thy tropics, and my breast thy equator; and from henceforth forever I will keep thee a great deal too warm, so that thou shalt cry out—'Do let me breathe the cool outward air for a moment!' But I will not!" Carried away by his ardor—and, perhaps more important, his verbal play—he eroticized his sentence structure and indulged in a pun which probably escaped Sophia. "Oh, dearest, dearest, interminably and infinitely dearest—I don't know how to end that ejaculation. The use of kisses and caresses is, that they supersede language, and express what there are no words for."[50]

He wrote of "my little Virgin Dove," only to add, "before I had brought all the troubles of womanhood upon her." A few months later he asked Sophia, "Art thou sure He made thee for me? . . . all through eternity, thou wouldst carry my stain upon thee; and how could thine own angel ever wed thee then!" But how was the exiled Sophia to construe these comments? If she was confused, it was no wonder. After fourteen years of marriage Hawthorne perceived the loss of virginity as violation, himself as a violator, and sexuality as an enduring "stain." He had not put to rest youthful anxieties and guilts, as well as misconceptions, and no more than Goodman Brown, Aylmer, Dimmesdale, or Coverdale, it seems, could he accept sexual union as part of the natural rhythm of life. In short, in these letters to Sophia he was secretly confirming what Henry James feared but rejected: that "Young Goodman Brown" is autobiography and that Brown's sexually distorted perception of the world as verbalized by the priest at the mass—"behold the whole earth one stain of guilt, one mighty blood-spot"—was Hawthorne's, at least in certain moods.[51]

About the time he made puzzling references to the loss of virginity, he revealed in the jottings in his notebooks a compulsive interest in a bloody footstep at the threshold of an English manor house occupied by a family stained by fratricide and incestuous desires. Coincidentally, Una was, as Sophia put it, "growing out of her childhood," and he was aware that "I shall not see her a child again," a passage which may resonate with a father's awareness—and jealous fear—that his daughter will soon lose her purity. Sophia was also moved by Una's gradual transformation, "budding into womanhood . . . with the loveliest forms you can imagine." As Sophia dreamed about her daughter's future, she described her own past: "I think if there is any thing in nature enchanting & touchingly beautiful, it is the gently budding bosom of a pure young girl. When one thinks how it may one day heave, with wifely love & maternal tenderness—how it may also swell with sorrow—it seems the chief scene of tender humanity—so quiet now and so innocent!"[52]

That winter of the separation Hawthorne complained of his heavy tread, loss of appetite, insomnia, and recurrent thoughts of death. "I have suffered woefully from low spirits for sometime past," he confided in his notebook, but then denied the by no means unusual gyrations of moods: "This has not often been the case, since I grew to be a man, even in the least auspicious periods of my life." Nothing, it seemed, gave him pleasure. "I have learned what the bitterness of exile is, in these days; and I never should have known it but for the absence of my wife," and then added what could have been a description of Ilbrahim: "I am like an uprooted plant, wilted and drooping. Life seems so purposeless as not to be worth the trouble of carrying it on any further."[53]

On the day after he made this entry in his notebook he complained to Ticknor, "I cannot express, nor can you conceive, the irksomeness of my position, and how I long to get free from it. I have no pleasure in anything—a cigar excepted. Even liquor does not enliven me; so I very seldom drink any, except at some of these stupid English dinners." A few weeks later he confessed, "Really, I am not well—I don't know what the matter is—but not well at all. This has seldom been the case with me through life." On the following day he said nothing about his health to his sister Elizabeth, and by the end of the month his health and spirits were "considerably better," as he looked forward to an excursion to London in March.[54]

When he arrived in London an English friend, Frances Bennoch, found him "utterly prostrated by depression. . . . I never saw a man more miserable." In a letter to Sophia, Hawthorne poured out his despair: "What a wretched world we live in! Not one little nook or corner where thou canst draw a wholesome breath! In all our separation, I have never once felt so utterly desperate as at this moment. I *cannot* bear it." Such an outburst

could only have exacerbated Sophia's anxiety. "Oh, my wife," he continued in a passage again reminiscent of the earlier love letters, "I do want
thee so intolerably. Nothing else is real, except the bond between thee
and me. The people around me are but shadows. I am myself but a
shadow, till thou takest me in thy arms, and convertest me into substance. Till thou comest back, I do but walk in a dream."[55]

Hawthorne found London "detestable" until Bennoch began to shepherd him about, "to lift him out of himself." Bennoch provided the kind of
support Hawthorne needed, and soon he attended receptions and parties,
where he in spite of his shyness basked in his great popularity. Occasionally he drank too much, which he blamed on his "Yankee Simplicity," although he found his drinking companion "the very ace of trumps." At the
end of his three-week stay he declared that he had enjoyed himself "gloriously—owing principally to Bennoch's kindness. I lived rather fast, to
be sure; but that was not amiss, after such a slow winter." A few weeks
later he toured Scotland for the first time, visiting Glasgow, the Highlands, and Edinburgh. As he informed Ticknor, "My health has grown
vastly better since I began to move about," but he could hardly have been
unaware of Sophia's disappointment that she was in exile when for the
first time since their arrival in England he began to tour.[56]

On June 11 Sophia returned to her husband. "Imagine some flower preserved in celestial ichor in immortal bloom & fragrance," she wrote to her
sister Elizabeth, "& that would be a faint emblem of my being in my
husband—As the years develop my soul & faculties, I am better conscious of the pure amber in which I find myself imbedded—of such a
golden purity that every thing is glorified as I look through it."[57]

In July, however, she was examined by a London physician who, like
Chillingworth, looked for nonphysical causes of seemingly physical disorders. "He saw through me as if I had been a glass bottle. . . . With his
soft, mellifluous eye he sees like an eagle pretending to veil himself." His
analysis was that for twelve years, since the birth of Una, she "had never
been wholly free from anxiety." As Sophia explained to Elizabeth, it was
now her "*duty* [underscored four times] to be self-indulgent,—I can be
so with a quiet conscience." Now she was to become "fat & jolly."[58]

For the first time in years, perhaps, Sophia talked freely about herself
to her husband, for the moment overcoming her fears of Apollo. She had
"not formerly made a clean breast to my husband of the extent of my
feebleness & illness, because while I did not concieve it *fatal*, I could not

bear to rouse wild alarms & anxieties. He knows *everything* now. He knows all I went through at Rock Ferry." She refused the assistance of Elizabeth, who was ready to come to England to take charge, and placed herself under the "guardianship" of a man equal to "any winged angel of the hosts."[59]

"To say I was broken up, divided, half alive, desolate cannot convey an adequate idea of the misery of separation," she informed Mary Mann. "It was not that I was hopeless or overanxious so much as I was, as it were annihilated."[60]

A governess was engaged, and Sophia was as free of responsibility for the children as she could permit herself to be. About this time she appeared for the first time at a London party. She was delighted with her attire:

I had on a sky blue glacé silk with three flounces embroidered with white floss—making a very silvery shine. It was low neck & short sleeves; but I wore a jacket of starred blonde with flowing sleeves— over the corsage—up to my throat—& had round me also a shawl of Madeira lace—. . . My head dress was pearl in the shape of bunches of grape leaves—mingled with blue ribbons—with a wreath of pearl traced leaves round my hair—which was rolled in coronet fashion.[61]

In the fall the family, still homeless, settled in lodgings in Southport, "a dull and dreary little watering-place," according to Hawthorne, and he commuted twenty-three miles to Liverpool. The air suited Sophia's lungs, and living was inexpensive after the summer tourists departed. They had hardly arrived when Hawthorne confessed, "I sigh for London, and consider it time mis-spent to live anywhere else." The family stayed on into May. Hawthorne bewailed time spent in "as stupid a place as ever I lived in" and concluded, "Our life here has been a blank."[62]

He had turned over no leaves. He was as difficult to please and as restless as ever, as anyone except Sophia would have anticipated.

On November 10, 1856, seated in a dingy office, Hawthorne looked up from his desk at an unexpected visitor, Herman Melville, "looking much as he used to do (a little paler, and perhaps a little sadder), in a rough outside coat, and with his characteristic gravity and reserve of manner." Hawthorne had probably not read the tale on its appearance in the last two issues of *Putnam's Monthly Magazine* in

1853, but he could have been describing the new employee of a New York lawyer—"pallidly neat, pitiably respectable, incurably forlorn! It was Bartleby."

The two novelists fumbled for words and poise until at last they found themselves, according to Hawthorne, "on pretty much our former terms of sociability and confidence." Then Hawthorne learned that *Moby-Dick* had not recaptured the audience Melville began to lose shortly after the appearance of his first book, *Typee. Pierre* was mocked and satirized; *Israel Potter* and the short stories and sketches printed in *Putnam's* produced neither livelihood nor popularity. Melville drove himself mercilessly, flagellating himself like Ahab or Pierre. At the conclusion of the last novel he was to write, *The Confidence-Man* (1857), he depicts a world in which the light has gone out and the cosmos is an outhouse. Worst of all, he had lost trust in life and himself. Deeply depressed, Melville was like his fictional characters at an abyss, and his family insisted on the nineteenth-century cure for all disorders: travel. And so Melville was on his way alone to the Holy Land, to the roots of Western culture and religion in which he no longer had faith.

The next day Hawthorne took Melville to Southport to meet his family. The two men, Hawthorne wrote,

> took a pretty long walk together, and sat down in a hollow among the sand hills (sheltering ourselves from the high, cool winds) and smoked a cigar. Melville, as he always does, began to reason of Providence and futurity, and of everything that lies beyond human ken, and informed me that he had "pretty much made up his mind to be annihilated"; but still he does not seem to rest in that anticipation; and, I think, will never rest until he gets hold of a definite belief. It is strange how he persists—and has persisted ever since I knew him, and probably long before—in wandering to-and-fro over these deserts, as dismal and monotonous as the sand hills amid which we were sitting. He can neither believe, nor be comfortable in his unbelief; and he is too honest and courageous not to try to do one or the other. If he were a religious man, he would be one of the most truly religious and reverential; he has a very high and noble nature, and better worth immortality than most of us.

Before Melville sailed, Hawthorne made this entry in his journal: "He said that he already felt much better than in America; but observed that he did not anticipate much pleasure in his rambles, for that the spirit of adventure is gone out of him. He certainly is much overshadowed since I saw him last; but I hope he will brighten as he goes onward." Melville wasted no words and disguised his feelings in this laconic entry: "Sailed about three o'clock. Fine sights going out of the harbor."

On May 4, 1857, Melville sailed from Liverpool for home. His entry in his journal consisted of two words, "Saw Hawthorne." Hawthorne made no record in journals or letters of what was to be their final meeting.

Hawthorne duly arranged for the English edition of *The Confidence-Man*, but if he read the work, his comments have not survived. In 1860 he did not send *The Marble Faun* to Melville, who purchased his own copy. A year before he died Hawthorne referred briefly in *Our Old Home* to Melville's *Israel Potter*, praising an often overlooked work. In the late 1880s, now almost forgotten, a cypher as it were like Pierre or Bartleby, almost a stranger in New York, the city in which he was born, Melville again turned to prose. In the manuscript of *Billy Budd*, which remained unpublished at his death, Melville referred for the last time to Hawthorne, not by name but by the title of one of his short stories, "The Birth-mark," which summed up the power Hawthorne exerted over his life after 1850.

When Julian Hawthorne was preparing a biography of his parents in 1884, he called on Melville, who appeared "pale, sombre, nervous, but little touched by age." Melville was convinced that an unrevealed "secret" in Hawthorne's life accounted for the "gloomy passages" in his writings. Julian commented: "It was characteristic in him to imagine so; there were many secrets untold in his own career."[63]

Hawthorne formed close friendships during the English years with two men to whom he "much grieved to bid farewell"—Henry A. Bright and, above all, Francis Bennoch. They were businessmen and literary enthusiasts of the kind the nineteenth century seemed to breed. Bright, a young man of twenty-two, came to Concord in 1852 with a letter of introduction from Longfellow. Emerson accompanied Bright to the Wayside, where Emerson talked too much and Hawthorne not at all, to the bewilderment of the English writer who had no way of knowing that both men behaved according to fixed patterns in their uncomfortable relationship. In Liverpool, Bright became acquainted with another Hawthorne, friendly, verbal, eager to enter sparring bouts. As Sophia observed, Bright "is one of Mr Hawthorne's enthusiastic lovers and they fight in all love and honor all the time." Such was Hawthorne's affection that he presented the manuscript of *The Marble Faun* to him. In *Our Old Home* Hawthorne recalled the association in an affectionate passage: "It would gratify my cherished remembrance of this dear friend, if I could manage, without offending him, or letting the public know it, to introduce his name upon my page. Bright was the illumination of my dusky little apartment, as often as he made his appearance there!" Bright reciprocated: "It is one of the best things in my life to have made a friend of you."[64]

Bennoch was one of the handsomest men in England, a genial host and friend of Fields's, as well as a self-made businessman. He journeyed from London to Liverpool shortly after Hawthorne's arrival, but because of the pressures of his position Hawthorne did not return the visit until March 22, 1856, when he went to London during Sophia's absence. He found Bennoch "a kindly, jolly, frank, off-hand, very good fellow." Later that spring Hawthorne praised him with unusual fervor and in deep gratitude: "If this man has not a heart, then no man ever had. I like him inexpressly, for his heart, and for his intellect, and for his flesh and blood; and if he has faults, I do not know them, nor care to know them, nor value him the less if I did know them." Bennoch in turn declared that "we were as brothers . . . and to me more than to any living man, was disclosed the inner workings of his marvellous genius. Retiring, modest, and silent in general society, he was ever joyous, outspoken, and cheerful with me. . . . how sacred I have held the privilege of such a friendship."[65]

After Sophia's return the Hawthornes stayed in the Bennoch house, where, Hawthorne recalled, "I, for my part, have spent some of the happiest hours that I have known since we left our American home." Bennoch came to Hawthorne's assistance whenever he got himself into difficulty, as in the publication of Delia Bacon's book, and Hawthorne tried to console Bennoch when he went through bankruptcy. After Hawthorne left England, Bennoch denied the charge of an unfriendly critic that Hawthorne was a heavy drinker and had disgraced himself at a formal dinner. In the trying years following Hawthorne's death, Sophia and the children went first to Dresden and then to England, where the Bennochs were constant companions and invaluable advisors. Mrs. Bennoch and her servant took care of Sophia in the last weeks of her life, and her husband was one of the pallbearers at her funeral.[66]

Hawthorne made no effort to meet English celebrities. He was satisfied to observe Tennyson at a distance and did not seek introductions to Carlyle, Dickens, Mill, or Thackeray. He met Charles Reade and Martin Tupper and had some unkind things to say about the latter. Only once was his heart engaged, in his brief call upon Leigh Hunt, the neglected poet and essayist, who was seventy-one, childlike, and totally lovable and may have had something of Clifford Pyncheon about him. Hunt, he observed, "must have suffered keenly in his life, and enjoyed keenly; keeping his feelings so much upon the surface as he does, and convenient for everybody to play upon. . . . A light, mildly joyous nature, gentle, graceful, yet perhaps without that deepest grace that results from strength."[67]

He showed similar insight into a brilliant but possibly paranoid woman, Delia Bacon, an American novelist and lecturer on history. Enthusiasts judged (or misjudged) her to be the successor of Margaret Fuller, and she occupied a place briefly in the literary sun. She dished up, in the words of a detractor, "*A Rasher of Bacon*," proving on the basis of her highly personal use of "evidence" that Francis Bacon wrote Shakespeare's plays. Elizabeth Peabody brought her to Hawthorne's attention, and Emerson provided her with a letter of introduction when she went to England in 1853. Carlyle considered her "quixotically tragic," but Emerson claimed, also somewhat quixotically, that America had two "producers" in the past decade: "Our wild Whitman, with real inspiration but checked by Titanic abdomen, & Delia Bacon, with genius, but mad & clinging like a tortoise to English soil."[68]

Bacon demanded complete acceptance of her theories and cut herself off from her family after she left America. In England she lived frugally but soon found herself in need of money and support. She wrote to Hawthorne. He met her only once, on July 29, 1856: "She is rather uncommonly tall, and has a striking and expressive face—dark hair, dark eyes, which shone as she spoke. . . . There was little or no embarrassment in her manner; and we immediately took a friendly and familiar tone together, and began to talk as if we had known one another a long while." Although he was not happy that Providence had employed him as an "instrument" to guide Bacon, he knew at once that he should not attempt to draw her out of her "delusions": "It is the condition on which she lives, in comfort and joy, . . . and it would be no business of mine to annihilate her, for this world, by showing her a miserable fact." He was not about to commit Zenobia's blunder.[69]

Although Hawthorne never managed to read Bacon's entire manuscript, he was convinced that it was "remarkable." With the assistance of Bennoch he sought a London publisher and at the same time tried to effect her reconciliation with her family. The attempt cost him her friendship, and he now had to correspond with her through Bennoch. Parker and Son agreed to publish the work with stipulations: Hawthorne was to assume the costs of printing and write a preface, and Ticknor was to take five hundred copies of an edition of one thousand for distribution in America. Whatever Hawthorne did on Bacon's behalf displeased her. "The woman is mad," he wrote, "but the book is a good one; and as she threw herself on me, I will stand by her in spite of her nonsense. . . . How funny, that I should come in front of the stage-curtain, escorting this Bedlamite!"[70]

Hawthorne turned over the reading of Bacon's manuscript to Sophia, who at once replaced his skepticism with an exuberance as uncontrollable as Bacon's. "I never read," Sophia wrote to her, "so profound & wonderful a criticism & I think there never was such a philosophic insight & apprehension since Lord Bacon himself." Now Hawthorne had to wrestle with Delia Bacon's monomania, Sophia's exuberance, and his own reluctance to write a preface for the book. "It is just as well," he rationalized, "that she should have somebody besides herself to wreak her mortification upon;—else she would tear herself to pieces." He procrastinated for months over the "wretched" preface which at last he "painfully screwed out of a pre-occupied and unwilling mind." Bacon, of course, was outraged. For the first time in months he wrote to her directly: "Dear Author of this Book, (For you forbid me to call you anything else)." Meanwhile the manuscript grew and grew because Bacon was unmanageable, and Hawthorne faced the prospect of a loss of one hundred pounds or more. As he observed to Ticknor, "She is the most impractical woman I ever had to do with—a crooked stick."[71]

When *The Philosophy of the Plays of Shakspere Unfolded* appeared in 1857, it received the critical roasting Hawthorne and almost everyone else anticipated. Bacon now lived in Stratford, friendless, penniless, and psychotic. Soon she was a public charge and had to be confined. She was later taken by a nephew to the United States and died on September 2, 1859. In *Our Old Home* Hawthorne drew a portrait of delicate sensitivity entitled "Recollections of a Gifted Woman." This middle-aged orphan had deeply touched him, imaginatively and personally. As he noted in the preface, "To have based such a system on fancy, and unconsciously elaborated it for herself, was almost as wonderful as really to have found it in the plays." He was fascinated by the monomaniac hovering at the edge of the abyss. She belonged, in short, with Ethan Brand, Alymer, Rappaccini, and Hollingsworth.[72]

While Hawthorne was invariably kind and courteous even when Delia Bacon was most exasperating, during the consular years he unleashed barbs and bolts with indiscriminate zest at English women and female authors. It was as though he assumed the misogynistic views of Hollingsworth and repudiated Coverdale's idolatry and idealization of women. More probably he revealed his own ambivalences in remarks gratuitously ugly and hostile. He had been in England only a few months when on the basis of inadequate observations he announced: "The women of England are capable of being more atrociously ugly than any other human beings; and I have not as yet seen one whom we should distinguish as beautiful in America." One exaggeration led to another, his diction almost trembling viscerally: "As a general rule, they are not very desirable objects in youth, and, in many instances, become perfectly grotesque after middle-age;—so massive, not seemingly with pure fat, but with solid beef, making an awful ponderosity of frame." A year later he termed the women of forty or fifty "gross, gross, gross." They wronged, he declaimed, "one's idea of womanhood. . . . Who would not shrink from such a mother! Who would not abhor such a wife? I really pitied the respectable elderly gentlemen whom I saw walking about with such atrocities hanging on their arms—the grim, red-faced monsters! Surely, a man would be justified in murdering them—in taking a sharp knife and cutting away their mountainous flesh, until he had brought them into reasonable shape. . . ." When such comments, somewhat toned down, appeared in *Our Old Home*, English admirers were shocked and offended.[73]

According to pattern, he was attracted to English women of the lower class who had "a grace of their own" not found in Americans of the same class. In a police court he observed the "graces" of a servant, "coarse, and her dress was none of the cleanest, and nowise smart. Her charm lay in all her manifestations, her tones, her gestures, her look, her way of speaking, and what she said, being so appropriate and natural." While Sophia languished in Lisbon, he observed in Liverpool the choreography of young women at corners and under archways, walking arm in arm, "hunting in couples," and separating "when they saw a gentleman approaching." He did not invite the streetwalkers to his lodging in order to save their endangered souls, but he felt "a curious and reprehensible sympathy for these poor nymphs; it seems such a pity that they should not each and all of them find what they seek!"—which is a rather marvelous transformation of prostitutes into nymphs from Spenser's allegorical land as well as an admission of sexual curiosity which he was no doubt too fastidious to gratify or to admit into his fiction.[74]

Charmed and amused, more attracted than he cared to acknowledge, he enjoyed street life, but "ink-stained women," he declared with a flourish, "are, without a single exception, detestable." But, as was to be anticipated, he made exceptions, for Julia Ward Howe, whose *Passion Flowers* (1854) he praised effusively, and for Fanny Fern, the pen name of Sara Payson Willis, N. P. Willis's sister. He deplored Howe's need "to let out a whole history of domestic unhappiness. What a strange propensity it is in these scribbling women to make a show of their hearts, as well as their heads, upon your counter, for anybody to pry into that chooses!" A few years later he still found the poems in *Passion Flowers* delightful, although "she ought to have been soundly whipt for publishing them." Hawthorne praised Sara Willis because she wrote in the only way a woman could be successful, "as if the devil was in her. . . . Generally, women write like emasculated men, and are only to be distinguished from male authors by greater feebleness and folly."[75]

As he watched the success of Stowe's *Uncle Tom's Cabin* or of Maria Cummins's *The Lamplighter* (1854), which sold more than 10,000 copies in the first year, he raged: "America is now wholly given over to a d——d mob of scribbling women, and I should have no chance of success while the public taste is occupied with their trash—and should be ashamed of myself if I did succeed." Although Grace Greenwood (Sara Jane Lippincott), a popular poet and essayist, was one of his admirers, Hawthorne was outraged that in *Little Pilgrim* there was "a description of her new baby!!! . . . I wonder she did not think it necessary to be brought to bed in public." To Sophia he erupted: "My dearest, I cannot enough thank God, that, with a higher and deeper intellect than any other woman, thou has never—forgive me the bare idea!—never prostituted thyself to the public, as that woman has, and as a thousand others do." It was craven to transform authoresses into prostitutes because, like men, they exposed themselves in their writings, but he had to rationalize the creative sterility of these years in England. His conclusion was nonsensical: "Women are too good for authorship, and that is the reason it spoils them so."[76]

Sophia, of course, agreed, as he expected. Although Hawthorne informed Ticknor that Sophia "altogether excels me as a writer of travels," he also reported that "neither she nor I would like to see her name on your list of female authors." Sophia's name appeared there only after his death when economic need compelled her to violate her husband's injunctions.[77]

Except for an excursion to Scotland during Sophia's absence and periodic trips to nearby places, Hawthorne during his first three years in England confined himself to his office and to the pursuit of a fortune for his family's protection. In the following years Sophia and he made extensive tours, and the notebooks which he began in 1853 grew by 1858 to six or seven volumes. Periodically Hawthorne suggested to Ticknor that the journals could be published if he deleted candid comments. He overstated his candor, except in the ill-tempered treatment of English women, and too often recorded with the drearily detailed fidelity of guidebooks of the era.

At other times his entries were refreshingly honest. When he was fed up with galleries, museums, or sightseeing, he confessed his boredom. Sophia, on the other hand, never ran out of enthusiasm: her whole body bubbled, her eyes sparkled, her voice quivered. Only her physical strength failed her, but she was capable of writing a seventy-two-page letter narrating the day's adventures. After a few days in the Lake Country, however, Hawthorne wrote: "To say the truth, I was weary of fine scenery; and it seemed to me that I had eaten a score of mountains, and quaffed down as many lakes, all in the space of two or three days." Unlike most visitors, he "felt no emotion whatever in Shakspeare's house—not the slightest—nor any quickening of the imagination. . . . I think I can form, now, a more sensible and vivid idea of him as a flesh-and-blood man; but I am not quite sure that this latter effect is altogether desirable."[78]

Despite periods of boredom, he remained visit after visit in awe of English cathedrals. He tried "in vain," as he freely recognized, to capture the artistic and spiritual essence of what "may be the greatest work man has yet achieved—a great stone poem." "I can only talk nonsense," he admitted, "by trying to give my sense" of cathedrals, but he succeeded better than most, even if he did not rise to the heights of John Ruskin or Henry Adams. He marveled at the gargoyles, "one of the Gothic quaint-nesses which pimple out over the grandeur and solemnity" of the cathe-dral. Three times he returned to York, drawn by the almost primeval attraction of the minster. It became his "present feeling" that this cathe-dral is "the most wonderful work that ever came from the hands of man." Indeed, it seems like a "house not made with hands, but rather to have come down from above, bringing an awful majesty and sweetness with it; and it is so light and aspiring, with all its vast columns and pointed arches, that one would hardly wonder if it should ascend back to heaven again, by its mere spirituality. . . . I thank God that I saw this Cathedral again, and thank Him that he inspired the builder to make it, and that mankind has so long enjoyed it." [79]

In 1857 at Manchester, while attending the greatest exhibition of paint-ings ever assembled in England, Hawthorne began "to receive some plea-sure from looking at pictures." He even toyed with the prospect that by the time he went home to Concord he would pass for "a man of taste." Immediately he voiced doubts traceable to his perception of his ancestors' hostility to art, which appeared also in the "The Artist of the Beautiful": "It is an acquired taste, like that for wines; and I question whether a man is really any truer, wiser, or better, for possessing it." He had similar reservations about the connoisseur who "is not usually, I think, a man of deep poetic feeling, and does not deal with the picture through his heart, nor set it in a poem, nor comprehend it morally." An artist himself, Haw-thorne understood the complex relationship of love and creativity. He was also perceptive in his comments as to the effect of art upon viewers. He speculated that depictions of the Holy Family and the Virgin and Child gratify the "natural longing" for earthly happiness of monks and nuns. "It was not Mary and her heavenly child that they really beheld, or wished for, but an earthly mother rejoicing over her baby, and displaying it proudly to the world." The first scene of *The Scarlet Letter* confirms that Hawthorne shared the same wish. [80]

Among the old masters, whom he frequently almost delighted in treat-ing disrespectfully, perhaps to shock Sophia, he was most attracted to Bartolomé Esteban Murillo, who was highly esteemed in the nineteenth century, one of his paintings fetching the highest price ever paid at auc-tion up to that time. Unlike most seventeenth-century painters, Murillo chose as subjects the youth of Jesus and idealized secular scenes of childhood not unlike the genre paintings of Hawthorne's age. Hawthorne concluded that Murillo was "about the noblest and purest painter that ever lived, and his 'Good Shepherd' the loveliest picture I ever saw." A few months later he decided that Murillo's *Saint John* "was the most beautiful picture I have ever seen; and that there never was a painter who has really made the world richer, except Murillo." He was particularly drawn to the "mischievous intelligence" in the face of the young androgynous John, who was to change from a "roguish" youth into a saint, a mysterious transformation which appealed deeply to the doubleness of his person and vision.[81]

One of the most memorable incidents recorded in *The English Notebooks* took place not in a museum but at the West Derby workhouse. Hawthorne arrived in a "handsome barouche" to see for himself the rejects of life whom the Victorian world, like the modern world, kept out of sight. In the first ward he observed elderly women in their uniforms, "homely blue-checked gowns," knitting away with agitated vigor their miserable lives, many having already crossed over into the land of nonsense and second childhood. The authorities would not even allow the poor souls to nod.

When Hawthorne entered the ward of the foundlings a child of about six took "the strangest fancy" to him. The child (he could not determine the sex) "was a wretched, pale, half-torpid little thing, with a humor [scurvy] in its eyes. . . . I never saw . . . a child that I should feel less inclined to fondle." Probably syphilitic, the child prowled about Hawthorne, clutching his clothes, following at his heels. At last it "held up its hands, smiled in my face, and standing directly before me, insisted on my taking it up! . . . its face expressed such perfect confidence that it was going to be taken up and made much of, that it was impossible not to do it." It was, Hawthorne observed, "as if God had promised the child this favor on my behalf, (but I wish He had not!) and that I must needs fulfil the contract." Hawthorne held the child and then put it down, only to have it follow him, "holding two of my fingers (luckily the glove was on) and playing with them, just as if (God save us!) it were a child of my own." Hawthorne and his guide went upstairs to another ward, and when they returned the child, "with sickly smile around its scabby mouth," was waiting with institutional patience.

As Hawthorne toured the other wards of the workhouse he saw infants—he drew upon Milton in characterizing them as "begotten by Sin upon Disease"—fleshless, misshapen, and malformed outcasts, moaning in the physical and emotional pain of rejection. In a classroom he observed diseased, pale girls and boys. "Uneasy within their skins—poor little wretches!—they scratched, they screwed themselves about within their clothes. It would be a blessing to the world—a blessing to the human race, which they will contribute to vitiate and enervate—a blessing to themselves, who inherit nothing but disease and vice—if every one of them could be drowned to-night, instead of being put to bed. If there be a spark of God's life in them, this seems the only chance of preserving it."

He inspected the entire establishment, ending with a visit to a shed, where cheap coffins were piled up. "I must say," he confessed, "that I should be at a loss how to suggest any improvement. But the world, that requires such an establishment, ought to be ashamed of itself and set about an immediate reformation." He left in the "handsome barouche" and rode to a beautiful English home, where he wondered whether those confined in the workhouse have no home "because other people have a great deal more home than enough!"

The foundling, pock-marked physically and intellectually, was about the same age as the beautiful Ilbrahim and also sought desperately for the laying on of hands. Rose Hawthorne after an unhappy marriage became a Catholic nun and devoted her long life to terminally ill cancer patients who were as abandoned as the children and the withered women in the workhouse. Her father's conduct in this scene was her model. "I wish," Hawthorne commented with customary ambivalence and honesty, "I had not touched the imp; and yet I never should have forgiven myself if I had repelled its advances." [82]

On July 4, 1855, his fifty-first birthday, Hawthorne journeyed alone to Lichfield and Uttoxeter to pay homage to Dr. Samuel Johnson, to whom he had been introduced "at a very early period" through Boswell's biography. In maturity he understood Johnson's weaknesses—"he meddled only with the surface of life, and never cared to penetrate farther than to plough-share depth; his very sense and sagacity were but a one-eyed clear-sightedness"—but he was powerfully attracted to the bas-relief in the marketplace at Uttoxeter which he had described in *Biographical Stories for Children*. It depicts Johnson "doing penance for an act of disobedience to his father committed fifty years before"—the "countenance extremely sad and woe-begone," suggesting "the gloom of his inward state." Among the people observing Dr. Johnson are "an aged man and woman, with clasped and uplifted hands," representing, Hawthorne believed, "the spirits of Johnson's father and mother, lending what aid they could to lighten his half-century burden of remorse." It was the type of picture of the family which Hawthorne creates again and again in his writings.[83]

Franklin Pierce sought renomination in 1856 with the ineffectiveness and ineptness that characterized his presidency. A compromise nominee of the party at the outset, he eventually compromised himself out of office, in the process losing the support of his native New Hampshire. Despite his long political career, Pierce failed to avail himself of the powers of his office in disciplining and coercing an unruly party. On February 13, 1857, Hawthorne submitted his resignation to the newly elected president, James Buchanan.

In a letter to Elizabeth Peabody, Hawthorne summed up his service at Liverpool with his usual absence of cant and with a clarity that no doubt bewildered a woman who almost daily, it seemed, produced a new scheme for restructuring the cosmos:

> I do not know what Sophia may have said about my conduct in the Consulate. I only know that I have done no good; none whatever. Vengeance and beneficence are things that God claims for Himself. His instruments have no consciousness of His purpose; if they imagine they have, it is a pretty sure token that they are *not* His instruments. The good of others, like our own happiness, is not to be attained by direct effort, but incidentally. All history and observation confirm this. I am really too humble to think of doing good! . . . God's ways are in nothing more mysterious than in this matter of trying to do good.[84]

On July 9, 1857, the Hawthornes celebrated their fifteenth anniversary—"our union has turned out to the utmost satisfaction of both parties"—and he presented Sophia with a "golden backed and blue bodied Cairn Gorme beetle." About this time he described Sophia in an application for a visé in a half-humorous fashion: "Hair brown, eyes grey, nose and forehead ordinary, chin round, complexion fair—no very striking points, though, as a whole, the face is exceedingly pleasant in my eyes."[85]

Before the Hawthornes left for the Continent they engaged as governess Ada Shepard, one of the brightest students in the first graduating class at Antioch College, of which Horace Mann was now president. "Tall, slender, and very fair with a shower of golden curls," Shepard was to receive no salary, only expenses, during a two-year stay. Because of her facility in language she served as their translator, although she believed that Hawthorne only pretended that he could not speak French. Shepard was greatly impressed with the Hawthornes. She was surprised "to see so *handsome* a man as he is. He has the most beautiful brow and eyes, and his voice is extremely musical. I do not wonder that Mrs. Hawthorne loved him any more than that her angelic loveliness attracted his poet-heart. Ah! What rare delight it is to see two rightly married!"[86]

Italy

"Dim Reflections
in My Inward Mirror"

The weather was frigid on January 6, 1858, when the Hawthornes began the long journey from London to Rome by boat and coach. Footwarmers did little against the cold, and the inns and hotels were often inadequately heated. Their stay in Paris was brief and not particularly pleasant, Hawthorne being cranky because of the cold he had picked up. On their departure for Marseilles the party—the five Hawthornes, Ada Shepard, another servant, one dozen trunks, and six carpetbags—was increased by the presence of Maria Mitchell, an American astronomer who in 1847 had discovered a comet and was later to become the first woman in the American Academy of Arts and Sciences. She asked to accompany the family, although Hawthorne wondered why "a person evidently so able to take care of herself should care about having an escort."[1]

Arriving in Rome on February 3 "at midnight, half-frozen, in the wintry rain," they shivered for two or three days in "a cold and cheerless hotel" while they sought lodgings "amongst the sunless, dreary alleys which are called streets in Rome." They were exhausted. Hawthorne, who could not shake his cold, was annoyed to find himself the only one ill and took out his anger by faulting the Eternal City and magnifying its defects. He complained about the streets and the statues "defiled with unutterable nastiness" and recommended for safety's sake keeping eyes fixed on the ground. Beneath the colonnade of St. Peter's one was "sensible of the evil smell—the bad odour of our fallen nature—which there is no escaping in any nook of Rome." Fleas, he alleged, came "home to everybody's business and bosom" and were "so common and inevitable" that no one felt any "delicacy" in "alluding to the sufferings they inflict."[2]

When Hawthorne wrote to Bennoch in March his wrath ran over. "I never in my life suffered," he asserted, "so much from severity of weather as here in Rome, where we expected to find a Paradise. . . . If my pen would but serve me as it has done of yore, I would send you such a description of this cold, rainy, filthy, stinking, rotten, rascally city, as would avenge me for all the incommodities I have suffered here. I hate it worse than any other place in the whole world." Despite his fulminations, in which he appeared to take a great deal of delight, Hawthorne enjoyed Rome more than he was willing to admit. A week after their arrival there was ice near a fountain at St. Peter's, and the shy man in the black cloak, now almost fifty-four, "took a slide, just for the sake of doing what I never thought to do in Rome." He attended the Carnival, and Caroline Tappan, who was in Rome at the time, pelted the Hawthornes every time they passed "with a handful of lime," an episode that reappeared in *The Marble Faun*.[3]

His cold gone, the weather moderating at the approach of spring, Hawthorne, like Owen Warland, underwent a metamorphosis. He now acknowledged to Ticknor that Rome "has a sort of fascination which will make me reluctant to take a final leave of it," and in his journal he wrote: "It may be because the intellect finds a home there, more than in any other spot in the world, and wins the heart to stay with it, in spite of a great many things strewn all about to disgust us." Nothing bothered Sophia, not the fleas, filth, weather, the responsibilities of her household with three children, or a restless husband. Almost at once her health improved and her spirits soared. She made herself acquainted, her husband declared, "with almost every temple and church in Rome." In her notebook her excitement bubbled: "How I like to write down the illustrious names of what I have all my life so much desired to see! I cluster them together like jewels, and exult over them." Her greed led to her customary superlatives, but she could no longer write at great length to her greatest admirer, her mother, whose replies would have matched her daughter's enthusiasm.[4]

In Rome and later in Florence, Hawthorne visited the studios of American artists, some of whom were to spend substantial parts of their lives in Italy. Sometimes he was seduced by the ambience of the studio, the personality of the artist, or even patriotism into ill-considered and dubious judgments. He renewed his friendship with Cephas G. Thompson, the painter of a not very successful portrait in 1850. Hawthorne declared Thompson one of the "better" living American painters and said that he preferred looking at Thompson's paintings more than "at any except the very finest of the Old Masters." Hawthorne took more pleasure in the landscapes of George Loring Brown, of Boston, than in those of Claude Lorrain. Again he was influenced by the man who on being complimented for the patient fidelity of his pictures said disarmingly, "Oh, it's not patience;—it's love!" Hawthorne concurred: "In fact, it was a patient and most successful wooing of a beloved object, which at last rewarded him by yielding herself wholly."[5]

Harriet Hosmer, whose widowed father brought her up as a boy, was one of the most colorful and lovable of the artists in the American colony. Hawthorne was charmed but also vaguely troubled by a woman whom he described after the first meeting as a "frank and pleasant little woman—if woman she be, as I honestly suppose, though the upper half is precisely that of a young man." On another occasion he described her unconventional mannish attire and then added, "I never should have imagined that she terminated in a petticoat, any more than a fish's tail." His wit revealed discomfort and embarrassment before a strong bisexual presence. Yet he praised Hosmer and admired her sculpture, particularly *Zenobia*, and in *The Marble Faun* paid his respects to "Harriet Hosmer's clasped hands of Browning and his wife, symbolizing the individuality and heroic union of two high, poetic lives!"[6]

Hawthorne established a more personal relationship with Hiram Powers, the most famous American sculptor in an age of mediocrity. The *Greek Slave* became an international sensation, its idealization reflecting the euphoria and idealism of the era and its nonphysicality troubling no one's sensibilities. Powers was a Swedenborgian and engaged, like Melville, in ontological discussions, which pleased Hawthorne's sense of fantasy, although he never wobbled into belief. When Hawthorne visited his studio he discovered that Powers had recently completed what was to become one of his most celebrated works, a bust of Jared Sparks, the man who in 1839 married the "Star of Salem," Mary Silsbee.

The sculptor Hawthorne most admired was William Wetmore Story, whom he had met in 1840 when Story, after graduating from Harvard Law School, joined the firm of George Hillard and Charles Sumner. Later Story gave up the law for sculpture, settled in Rome, and became in the judgment of his biographer, Henry James, the "precursor" of the cosmopolites who, with the exception of James himself, had the charm of amateurs without the imagination of geniuses. Story's *Cleopatra* became one of the sculptures fashioned by Kenyon in *The Marble Faun*. Unlike many of the American expatriates, Story, according to Hawthorne, was "sensible of something deeper in his art than merely to make beautiful nudities and baptize them by classical names."

Although Hawthorne sometimes impulsively overpraised, he was not unaware of the limitations of these expatriates. In *The Marble Faun* he notes the personal and even psychological support afforded by the "brotherhood" of the American colony, but the camaraderie cannot compensate for the loss of originality which "dies out of them, or is polished away as a barbarism." Although Hawthorne adapted Greek myths for children, he had little respect for those who spent a lifetime "making Venuses, Cupids, Bacchuses, and a vast deal of other marble progeny of dreamwork, or, rather, frost-work; it was all vapoury exhalation out of the Grecian mythology, crystallizing on the dull window-panes of to-day."[7]

Hawthorne continued his self-education and tirelessly, but not without complaints, visited museums, cathedrals, and catacombs. He was determined not to be bamboozled by received taste and critical opinion. He complained when he was exposed to the hundreds of paintings in a gallery, admitting that he was incapable of elephantine incorporation of the contents of museums. He recognized that a great artistic work deserved the personal involvement or engagement of the viewer, and for this reason he was caustic about the clutter he found in museums whose goal was, it seemed to him, to preserve the past uncritically. In his view only the best paintings, like the best poetry, were worth preserving: "One in a thousand, perhaps, ought to live in the applause of men from generation to generation, till his colors fade or blacken out of sight, and his canvas rots away; the rest should be put up garret, or painted over by newer artist, just as tolerable poets are shelved when their little day is over."[8]

He had almost no appreciation of Giotto, Cimabue, or the Sienese masters, who made his heart sink and his stomach sick. "All the early faces of the Madonna," he observed, "are especially stupid, and all of the same type; a sort of face such as one might carve on a pumpkin, representing a heavy, sulky, and phlegmatic woman, with a long and low arch of the nose." Although he continued to revere Murillo, he was now convinced that the "most beautiful picture in the world" was Raphael's *Madonna della Seggiola* in the Pitti Palace at Florence. Except for two paintings attributed to Guido Reni which were to play important roles in *The Marble Faun*, he preferred the subject matter and realism of the Dutch and Flemish painters, although Rubens's "plump nudities," especially "fat Graces ('greases,' rather)," repelled or shocked him because of their over-assertive nakedness and flabby ugliness. In this evaluation of Rubens even Sophia concurred: "Rubens must sometimes have taken beer-barrels for models, and touched them off with arms and heads and legs." [9]

At the Capitoline in Rome Hawthorne, like Henry James later, was deeply stirred when he saw for the first time the glories of the ancient world. He had the genius to place the sculptures—the Faun, the Dying Gladiator, Apollo, and Marcus Aurelius—in a modern romance which caught their psychological and universal appeal. After contemplating the imposing statue of Marcus Aurelius in the courtyard from every perspective, Hawthorne wrote, "I have a singular feeling of love and reverence for this old heathen Emperor, derived chiefly from his aspect and attitude of grand beneficence, as exhibited in this statue." The Faun in the gallery was to provide Hawthorne with a title and a character named Donatello as mysterious and evasive as the statue that veils its animalistic origins and evokes an Arcadia far removed from civilization and its discontents. [10]

During the four-month stay in Rome Hawthorne slumped into frequent periods of depression, but as he fell under the spell of history, mythology, religion, and dreams—the essence of Rome—he underwent a transformation and his spirits improved. By the time the family left Rome on May 24 or shortly thereafter, St. Peter's, which at first he had found disappointing, was "the grandest edifice ever built by man, painted against God's loveliest sky." [11]

The Hawthornes proceeded leisurely by way of Perugia to Florence, a ten-day journey which Hawthorne pronounced "one of the brightest and most uncareful interludes of my life." When he viewed the landscape of Florence for the first time on June 2, it emerged as in a dream from the mist, "its great dome and some of its towers out of a side-long valley, as it were between two great waves of the tumultuous sea of hills." Hawthorne also associated this arrival with another scene that had colored his imagination since childhood: "There being a haziness in the atmosphere, however, Florence was little more distinct to us than the Celestial City was to Christian and Hopeful, when they spied at it from the Delectable Mountain." [12]

For weeks the Hawthornes examined cathedrals, museums, galleries, and mansions and succumbed as every traveler must to the lovely reso-nances of Florence. Then one day, on July 14, Hawthorne stayed at home "principally employed sketching plot of a Romance." By July 27 he had established, or reestablished, the necessary rhythm for writing, although "whether it will ever come to anything, is a point yet to be decided." He had "little heart" for journalizing in his notebooks or sightseeing and de-clared that "six months of un-interrupted monotony would be more valu-able to me, just now, than the most brilliant succession of novelties." On August 1 the family moved into a "suburban villa," Villa Montauto, on a hill named Bellosguardo approximately a mile outside of Florence, which he rented for $28 a month. What fascinated Hawthorne was "a moss-grown tower, haunted by owls and by the ghost of a monk," alleged on flimsy evidence to be Savonarola. As he explained to Fields, he intended to take the eighty-five-foot tower "away bodily and clap it into a Ro-mance, which I have in my head ready to be written out . . . I have really a plethora of ideas, and should feel relieved by discharging some of them upon the public, What an unseemly simile is this!—but I am speaking of brains, not of bowels." [13]

In Florence Hawthorne renewed his acquaintance with the Brownings, whom he had met in 1856 at the home of Milnes. Hawthorne had been immediately attracted to Elizabeth Barrett Browning, this "small, deli-cate woman" with whom he had carried on an animated conversation: "She is of that quickly appreciative and responsive order of women, with whom I can talk more freely than with any men. . . . I like her very much—a great deal better than her poetry." He had found Robert Browning "very simple and agreeable in manner, gently impulsive, talk-ing as if his heart were uppermost." When Sophia met the Brownings for the first time, the event took on a charmed aura: "I stood in a purple dream, holding a pomegranate blossom in my hand which Mr Browning had just plucked for me from his tree on the balcony, when I heard a delicate sound like the whirr of a huming bird's wings, and turning, there she stood, so weird and fay-like, with a smile gleaming through a cloud of dark curls—summer lightning in shades of light." Hawthorne agreed that Elizabeth Barrett Browning was "a good and kind fairy" with the voice of a grasshopper. "I was never conscious," Sophia commented, "of so little unredeemed, perishable dust in any human being."[14]

On their second meeting Hawthorne still considered Robert Browning "an exceedingly likeable man" to whom he was strongly attracted but with his usual reticences and uncertainties. "I somewhat question," he observed in his notebook, "whether an intimate acquaintance with him would flow on quite smoothly and equally enough to be sure of lasting a great while." Within a few weeks Hawthorne praised his "nonsense" as "the true bubble and effervescence of a bright and powerful mind, and he lets it play among his friends with the faith and simplicity of a child." Then a one-sentence comment exposed a secretiveness as well as a calculated determination to pursue his own ends that conflicted with the appearance (and pose) of passivity and extreme modesty: "I should like him much (and should make him like me) if opportunities were favorable." Perhaps here he lifted a veil: this may be an admission that he was more aggressive in seeking out relationships than it sometimes appeared. Also by silence or other nonverbal communication he may have encouraged, or at least not checked, the intensities of a Melville or a Channing.[15]

Late in August the two women attended seances at which Ada Shepard, holding a pencil loosely between her fingers, recorded communications with spirits. "I kept aloof in mind," Sophia informed her sister Elizabeth, "because Mr Hawthorne has such a repugnance to the whole thing, and did not ask a question." At one of the sessions Mrs. Peabody began to communicate with her daughter: "My dear child, I am *near* you—I wish to speak to you. My dearest child, I am oftener with you than with any one. . . ." Sophia found the experience "curious and wonderful." After Hawthorne heard about the communications he attempted a rational explanation: "I cannot help thinking, that (Miss Shepard being unconsciously in a mesmeric state) all the responses are conveyed to her fingers from my wife's mind; for I discern in them much of her beautiful fancy and many of her preconceived ideas, although thinner and weaker than at first hand." Then he added with feeling insight, "They are echoes of her own voice returning out of the lonely chambers of her heart, mistaken by her for the tones of her mother." Sophia's continuing need five years after her mother's death to reassure herself that she was the favorite daughter and that her mother continued to be "near," to watch over her child, may have influenced the delineation of the motherless Hilda in *The Marble Faun*. [16]

The night before the family left Florence for Rome Hawthorne sat at the top of the tower in which part of *The Marble Faun* was written, smoking a cigar and watching the lights in the mists over Florence. As he listened to the "sweet bells" he was reluctant to descend to the earth, "knowing that I shall never again look heavenward from an old-tower-top, in such a soft, calm evening as this." Then reality and depression returned. "Yet I am not loath to go away;—impatient rather; for, taking no root, I soon weary of any soil that I may be temporarily deposited in. The same impatience I sometimes feel, or conceive of, as regards this earthly life; since it is to come to an end, I do not try to be contented, but weary of it while it lasts." Here his reveries foreshadow Donatello's despair and Kenyon's suicidal fantasy in the fictional tower of *The Marble Faun*. [17]

The family stayed about a week in Siena and arrived in Rome on the morning of October 16, 1858. Hawthorne "had a quiet, gentle, comfortable pleasure, as if, after many wanderings, I was drawing near home; for, now that I have known it once, Rome certainly does draw into itself my heart, as I think even London, or even little Concord itself, or old sleepy Salem, never did and never will." At 68, Piazza Poli, they established themselves in such "a comfortable, cosy little house, as I did not think existed in Rome." The house consisted of seven rooms and an antechamber, with carpeted stairs so narrow and steep that "I should not wonder if some of us broke our noses down them." His serenity was short-lived, for within a week he complained of a cold. "I do hate the Roman atmosphere," he declared; "indeed, all my pleasure at getting back—all my home-feeling—has already evaporated, and what now impresses me, as before, is the languor of Rome—its nastiness—its weary pavements—its little life pressed down by a weight of death." [18]

On Sunday, October 24, Ada Shepard and Una went to the Colosseum to sketch, and Una developed what at first appeared to be a severe cold but by October 28 turned into a raging fever. "It is not a severe attack," Hawthorne wrote in his notebook, "yet attended with fits of exceeding discomfort, occasional comatoseness, and even delirium to the extent of making the poor child talk in rhythmical measure, like a tragic heroine— as if the fever lifted her feet off the earth." His description, however, pointed to the diagnosis of malaria.[19]

Shortly after the beginning of Una's illness Hawthorne made no entries in his notebook from November 2, 1858, until February 27, 1859. He worked for a hour or two almost every day on his romance which, as he phrased it, "I have been trying to tear out of my mind." The phrasing, if not elegant, may have been accurate. Writing in his last years was increasingly painful but in this instance provided escape from the agony of watching his ill daughter. He considered it to his "credit" that he could "sternly" shut himself up in his room and write for an hour or two—it was what he had done all his life—but he perhaps forgot that Sophia had no such escape.[20]

He managed to scribble without serious interruption from November 25 to January 23, when he experienced some kind of writing blockage briefly. But on January 30 he finished "the rough draft of my Romance; intending to write it over after getting back to the Wayside." It was "in a very imperfect way" when he wrote to Fields on February 3. His brain was "tired of it just now." He was also tired of Rome, whose climate was responsible for Una's illness, and would "rejoice to bid it farewell forever; and I fully acquiesce in all the mischief and ruin that has happened to it, from Nero's conflagration downward. In fact, I wish the very site had been obliterated before I ever saw it." The young man who had enjoyed watching Salem's fires was often to play the role of the artist-destroyer, as in the toppling of Judge Pyncheon or Major Molineux. As he aged, annihilation also became an often-used word.[21]

In February when Una was much improved, Hawthorne took to his bed and for the first time since childhood saw a doctor. (It may have been the last time too.) As he explained to Ticknor, "This Roman climate is really terrible, and nobody can be sure of life or health from one day to another. . . . I never knew that I had either bowels or lungs, till I came to Rome, but I have found it out now at my cost."[22]

When Carnival time came, Una was well enough to attend. This time Hawthorne reacted positively to the "nonsensicalities" of the Roman version of "The May-pole of Merry Mount." Una wished that she was a boy like Julian so that she could plunge into the crowds, and her father wanted to bandy "confetti and nosegays as readily and as riotously as any urchin there," but he feared his black hat and "grave Talma" made him too good "a mark." Day after day he returned, stood on balconies, and threw confetti—in quest perhaps of the lost delights of youth as well as materials for his romance. "The spectacle," he commented, "is strangely like a dream, in respect to the difficulty of retaining it in the mind and solidifying it into a description," perhaps like the extraordinary procession in "My Kinsman, Major Molineux," evoking death and rebirth. [23]

On March 11 Franklin Pierce, who had been in Europe for some time but had delayed his trip to Rome because of his wife's illness, arrived—at a most opportune time, it turned out, for Hawthorne needed a companion. At first Hawthorne thought his friend whom he had not seen for six years seemed old and tired, but walks about the city, reminiscences, cigars, and a renewed friendship altered his perception. "He is singularly little changed; the more I see him, the more I get him back, just such as he was in our youth. This morning, his face, air, and smile, were so wonderfully like himself of old, that at least thirty years are annihilated." After two weeks of constant association Hawthorne summed up: "He is a most singular character, so frank, so true, so immediate, so subtle, so simple, so complicated." [24]

Late in March Una suffered a relapse and her condition deteriorated rapidly. On April 5 the doctor reported her lungs "terribly diseased"— galloping consumption—and three days later had "little hope." A doctor brought in for consultation diagnosed typhus. He too offered no hope. Americans in Rome, as well as the fragile Elizabeth Barrett Browning, visited or sent flowers. While Sophia, drawing without limit or self-pity upon all her resources, cared for the child and supervised the household, Hawthorne was as impotent as he had been in the period before his mother's death ten years earlier. [25]

He required, in fact, almost as much attention as the patient, but he was, in Sophia's still idolatrous eyes, "beautiful in endless woe—as if looking always on death." Every morning he expected, she said, "to find his hair turned to snow," his youth turned to age. Unable to endure alternations of hope and fear, "he sunk into fear alone." Pierce came to his assistance and in Sophia's exquisite phrase "wrapped him round with the most soothing cares." [26]

Pierce came to 68, Piazza Poli, as often as three times a day to accompany Hawthorne on walks about Rome, apparently neglecting his wife in favor of his old friend. Since both men were given to understatement or silence about personal matters, we shall know only through empathy the meaningfulness of their relationship at this critical juncture when it seemed that Hawthorne would lose yet another loved one. "Never having had any trouble, before, that pierced into my very vitals," Hawthorne observed, "I did not know what comfort there might be in the manly sympathy of a friend; but Pierce has undergone so great a sorrow of his own, and has so large and kindly a heart, and is so tender and strong, that he really did us good, and I shall always love him the better for the recollection of those dark days." He concluded in a loving passage that explains why, when others criticized his loyalty to Pierce, he kept his faith, friendship triumphing over ideology: "We have passed all the turning-off places, and may hope to go on together, still the same dear friends, as long as we live." And that was the way it turned out.[27]

While Pierce looked out for Hawthorne, delaying his departure until Una was out of danger, Sophia carried on alone. For thirty days she did not go to bed or sleep except for a brief period in the mornings when Ada Shepard relieved her. She had "no time," as she explained, "to give way to any natural expression of grief" and "no retreat," since she had to go from Una's room to her own chamber, where she soothed her husband's anxieties. "We could not dare to talk together," she said. "Words are hurricanes at such moments and would have driven us into deserts of dismay—to talk of contingencies."[28]

Una's recovery was slow, and she was never again robust. Later Sophia attributed the decline of Hawthorne's health in the last years of his life to the Roman experience. She herself after months of mothering daughter and husband finally experienced a long-postponed collapse following their return to England. When Una began slowly to improve, Hawthorne grew a mustache, perhaps to hide the lip that quivered tremulously during the crisis. According to Sophia, it made him look "like a bandit."[29]

In summing up their stay, Hawthorne professed to know Rome better than his birthplace and "though I have been very miserable there, and languid with the effects of the atmosphere, and disgusted with a thousand things in daily life, still I cannot say I hate it—perhaps might fairly own a love for it," only to conclude, "I desire never to set eyes on it again."[30]

On May 25, 1859, the Hawthornes began a leisurely journey to England designed not to tire Una unduly. They went from Rome to Leghorn, to Marseilles, to Geneva. In his Italian notebooks, which now amounted to almost 200,000 words, Hawthorne recorded his weariness with journalizing and traveling. He wished that "people were created with roots like trees, so that they could not befool themselves with wandering about." Traveling with a family he found "a bore beyond anything that can be pre-conceived." It was no doubt coincidental but appropriate that in Geneva he unveiled his despair. "Rest, rest, rest!" he wrote. "There is nothing else so desirable; and I sometimes fancy, but only half in earnest, how pleasant it would be to be six feet under ground, and let the grass grow over me." He lacked "energy . . . to seek objects of interest, curiosity even so much as to glance at them, heart to enjoy them, intellect to profit by them."[31]

He then attempted an explanation of his emotional state: "It may be disease; it may be age; it may be the effect of the lassitudinous Roman atmosphere; but such is the fact." The explanation, like so many of the others he offered, was not very informative, partly because moods influenced his judgments deeply. He had at various times in the past made similar statements as to the influence of Salem. Now, but only briefly, he idealized Concord. "I should be very reluctant," he observed, "to leave Concord, or to live anywhere else than by my own hill-side; that one spot . . . is the only locality that attaches me to my native land. I am tied to it by one of my heart-strings, all the rest of which have long ago broken loose." "I flag terribly," he wrote before the family left the Continent; "scenes and things make but dim reflections in my inward mirror." A few more lines followed, and then he closed his Italian notebooks, which were suffused with despondency.[32]

The family arrived at Southampton on June 23, 1859. A few days later Fields met Hawthorne in London to discuss his new romance. The publisher recalled years later that Hawthorne talked nervously about the book, "the muscles of his face twitching, and with lowered voice." Fields's observations confirmed Hawthorne's own admissions that at fifty-five he was no more confident than he had been at twenty-five, that he was experiencing "all the uncertainties of a new author," and that "if I were only rich enough, I do not believe I should ever publish another book, though I might continue to write them for my own occupation and amusement." At the same time he confessed that he had "another Romance ready to be written, as soon as this is off the stocks," an associative statement which anticipated the punishing ordeal of his final years.[33]

Fields was able to arrange for the publication of the Italian romance by

Smith, Elder and Company for $3,000, a sum which Hawthorne found, in the words of Pierce, "gratifying to his pride & agreeable enough to his purpose." Immediately Hawthorne changed his plans to sail for America with the Pierces and settled in at Redcar where, according to Sophia's unwittingly accurate phrasing, he would "bury himself to finish his book—away from the world."[34]

The English resort was chosen because of Sophia's health. There she was expected to regain her stamina after her vigil of many months. Fanny, a favorite domestic of the Hawthornes, was to devote herself exclusively to her mistress. Sophia, almost too weak to write, informed her sister Elizabeth that she needed to remain in England: "I am sure it would kill me to go home and go through all the hustle and excitement of arriving and seeing you all, and telling and hearing. . . . I need a suspension of all interest in every thing to recover."[35]

In August, on learning of the death of Horace Mann at sixty-three, Sophia wrote to Mary: "I thank you for withholding words which I could not have borne to read without frightful disorder which my present state would have ill supported." Mary, who idolized her husband as her sister did Hawthorne, was overwhelmed in grief. "He was too much my God," she wrote, "but like God he pervades all space to me." Hawthorne evidently made no comment on Mann's death. Lacking a fervid belief in immortality, which provided consolation to the Peabody sisters, he found death, despite its seductive attractiveness in certain moods, too much to bear.[36]

On July 24 and 25 Hawthorne examined the rough draft of his romance and on the following day began his revisions "in good earnest." He wrote from nine to two or three o'clock, had dinner, and walked along the seashore, usually accompanied by Julian. He sometimes resumed writing after tea and then walked again, this time alone. On August 6 he informed Fields that he was proceeding more slowly than he had expected "because it is so long since I touched the work that I now look at it critically, and therefore make many amendments." With his usual honesty and usual doubt he noted: "Whether I really do it any good is another question." Now, enjoying "perfect" health (temporarily, as it turned out), he expected to complete the manuscript by the end of September. On August 14, however, he was not able to write—"discouraged and depressed, & not very well." Early in October everything was completed except the final chapters. Sophia, not surprisingly, was rapturous, and he admitted that he admired the work "exceedingly, at intervals, but am liable to cold fits, during which I think it the most infernal nonsense. This happens to be the case just at the present moment. . . . the Romance has worn me down a little. It is not wholesome for me to write; but the bracing air of the German Ocean a little counteracted the bad effect, in the present instance." At five minutes before noon on November 8 he finished the manuscript.[37]

By the time Hawthorne completed his rewriting, the family was living at Leamington. Sophia had regained strength and was now "quite round and solid." Still following her old medical regimen, she bathed each morning in cold water in a cold room and took walks almost every day. But, she admitted, "I am easily tired, and still feel bruised when I wake." Shortly after the first of the year she had sharp attacks of her bronchial complaints and was confined to bed, where she remained for six weeks. Her sisters, fearing that Sophia had again resorted to her former secretiveness, wondered whether Hawthorne understood the seriousness of her illness. Sophia assured them that there were no "reserves" between her husband and herself and on no account would she "conceal from him any truth." No doubt she fibbed, while for the nth time she extolled Hawthorne's "delicately organized mortal mixture" as well as his "strength, courage and endurance . . . divine and unflinching, when needed."[38]

That winter the Hawthornes waited for warm weather to cross the Atlantic Ocean, and life was not easy for any member of the family. While Sophia sought to regain her health, Hawthorne underwent his usual emotional fluctuations. Alternately he longed to go home and dreaded it. He knew that as soon as he was in Concord he would be "tortured with life-long wishes to cross the sea again" but added candidly, "I fear I have lost the capacity of living contentedly in any one place." He did not enjoy the wait before sailing because "our roots are pulled up, and we cannot really live until we stick them into the ground again." At another time he thought of Concord as "a Paradise" but was afraid that he would change his mind "after a few months' trial. But I shall do my best to live contentedly at home." It was a promise that he should not have had to make as well as one he could not keep.[39]

In addition, there were the abiding concerns as to their financial lot, although, in the absence of Ticknor's records, there is no way of determining the actual situation. After he relinquished the consular post Hawthorne's only income was from royalties and the handsome sum paid by the English publishers of his most recent work. On the basis of perhaps incomplete entries in diaries during 1858 and 1859, the Hawthornes spent between $3,750 and $5,000 annually. However, when they traveled extensively, as during the journey from Rome to England between May 23 and June 20, 1859, expenses rose to about $1,100. There was cause for concern, if not for anxiety, neither of the Hawthornes knowing how to handle money.

The publication of *Transformation*, as *The Marble Faun* was called in England, made Hawthorne anxious. "With a cold and critical eye" he evaluated his own writings in a letter to Fields. He did not consider himself "a popular writer" and believed what popularity he had gained was "accidental, and owing to other causes than my own kind or degree of merit." He admitted he preferred works of "quite another class": "If I were to meet with such books as mine, by another writer, I don't believe I should be able to get through them." The novels of Anthony Trollope "precisely suit my taste," he declared, "solid and substantial, written on the strength of beef and through the inspiration of ale." Curiously, Melville had suggested to Duyckinck that *Twice-told Tales* needed "roast-beef, done rare."[40]

Meanwhile the family marked time and moved in May, for the third time, to Bath, a change which would supposedly prove beneficial to Sophia. She, however, entered a hospital briefly. Hawthorne journeyed to London to see his publisher and various friends. That he was leaving Sophia in a town where she knew no one perhaps never crossed his mind. Because of her timidity and her excessive dedication to her children, which despite the doctor's orders had not changed, she had formed no close relationships during the seven years abroad while he, unsociable as he could be under certain conditions, had Bennoch and Bright, as well as those admirers whom he continued to puzzle and to attract through a bashful modesty more characteristic of an adolescent than of a man in his late fifties. In London he accepted "a whole string of invitations" and performed "without a murmur," he informed Sophia, who must have been pleased but perhaps troubled. Hawthorne spent eleven days in London and then went to Cambridge and Canterbury. Taken out of himself for a while, Hawthorne reacted positively to the "stir": "I feel better than for months past."[41]

Hawthorne returned to Bath on May 31. The family sailed from Liverpool on June 16 aboard the *Europa*, commanded by the captain who had brought them to England seven years earlier.

Intercourse with the World

The Marble Faun

In the fiftieth and last chapter of *The Marble Faun*, his most elaborate embroidery and the culmination as it were of the artistry of Hester Prynne, Hawthorne addresses the "Gentle Reader" who

> is too wise to insist upon looking closely at the wrong side of the tapestry, after the right one has been sufficiently displayed to him, woven with the best of the artist's skill, and cunningly arranged with a view to the harmonious exhibition of its colours. If any brilliant or beautiful, or even tolerable, effect have been produced, this pattern of kindly Readers will accept it at its worth, without tearing the web apart, with the idle purpose of discovering how its threads have been knit together; for the sagacity, by which he is distinguished, will long ago have taught him that any narrative of human action and adventure— whether we call it history or romance—is certain to be a fragile handiwork, more easily rent than mended.

Hawthorne, perhaps deliberately, misled his readers in referring to his "fragile handiwork" and was no more accurate in a letter to Fields: "It is an audacious attempt to impose a tissue of absurdities upon the public by the mere art of style and narrative." *The Marble Faun* may be "a tissue of absurdities" in terms of plot contrivances and sometimes artificial coincidences, but what he dismisses as "fragile handiwork" and "the mere art of style and narrative" is in actuality a subtle and complex artifact that provides him with the necessarily ambivalent vehicle to unveil his loss of faith in art and in himself in the last romance he would be able to complete.[1]

Critics looking for neat formulations—and simplifications—have placed too much emphasis upon the fortunate fall which Hilda brushes aside in a sentence or two. Hawthorne is neither a theologian nor a moralist but a perhaps uneasy skeptic in matters of religion and art. Others have made too much of the fact that Hawthorne lifted passages from his Italian notebooks, as though he had lost his imaginative powers, but his romance has become for many readers the most charming guidebook to Rome, particularly after the publisher Christian Tauchnitz had the delightful idea of interleaving the book with photogravures of the churches, buildings, towers, and art referred to in its pages. Further, the visual delights of the romance are interwoven carefully with the needs, failures, and successes of the characters and are stamped upon our consciousness like Hester's scarlet letter, for Hawthorne is brilliant and persuasive in his depiction of nineteenth-century Rome in its timeless physicality.

Emerson pronounced *The Marble Faun* "mush," but his beautiful mind cringed uneasily when confronted with Hawthorne's illuminations of Dantean depths. Chaste, fearful Hilda, caught between puritanism and the Virgin Mary, has been endlessly disparaged—"a moral millionaire," "the true castrator," "nineteenth-century Marjorie Morningstar"—yet Henry James observes: "The character of Hilda has always struck me as an admirable invention—one of those things that mark a man of genius. It needed a man of genius and of Hawthorne's imaginative delicacy, to feel the propriety of such a figure as Hilda's, and to perceive the relief it would both give and borrow." Kenyon has been called "the most perceptive muttonhead in our literature," and Miriam has been censured because she is "oversexed" (whatever that may mean), although the veil about her sexual behavior is never lifted.[2]

The romance centers about five characters, three artists (a sculptor, Kenyon; a painter, Miriam; and a copyist, Hilda), an artifact (the Faun of Praxiteles, Donatello), and a Model (Antonio) who will in death assume another identity. These are orphaned children of the Ilbrahim order, in their maturity as desperate as the Quaker child to establish their identities and discover their places in a world in which they are adrift, foreigners, except Donatello, who temporarily reside in Rome. They are as beautiful and fragile as Ilbrahim, truly works of Hawthorne's art, and constitute a subtle, in-depth self-portrait of Hawthorne, artist and man. The artist theme is a recapitulation and summary of *Fanshawe*, "The Artist of the Beautiful," and other tales, but now elaborated in a dense tapestry such as we are accustomed to in the works of modern writers like Virginia Woolf, T. S. Eliot, and Thomas Mann.

In *The Marble Faun* Hawthorne had no need to invent forests and landscapes, to convert rock formations into gravestones and suggestive hieroglyphics, to call upon Puritan witches and sober pageantry. Rome has "grand hieroglyphics" on a scale unknown in the New World as well as pageantry more varied and ancient than that of Merry Mount.

Wherever he looked in Rome, Hawthorne found an exciting pattern of geometrical forms. Towers thrust into the sky, a more impressive sight than the vertical thrust of the steeples in the New England landscape but similarly masculine. The verticals are counterpoised to the circular configurations of the domes of two structures which epitomize their respective worlds, St. Peter's and the Pantheon, and the feminine principle. Structurally and thematically *The Marble Faun* moves in interlocking circles—setting, history, myths, and religions merging and separating; the past becoming the present momentarily in the endless repetition of human acts and fantasies; illusion and reality coalescing and then retreating into their artificial compartments.

Rome resonates with humanity's glories and inhumanities, ascents and falls. It is a city of precipices and parapets. The characters in Hawthorne's fiction climb to awesome heights, unleashing anxieties and fears, and descend into the "bowels" of Rome, where they encounter horrors out of the Inferno or its psychic equivalent, the unconscious. The rising-falling action is duplicated in the gyrations of moods, in the manic-depressive rhythms of people adrift, divorced from meaningful structures. The rocking motion unveils repressed sexual desires and a fascination with perversity, murder, and death. Amid the glorious structures are ruins and fragments of a world now dead, and the remnants sometimes resemble bodily parts from a dreamscape conjuring up emasculation and destruction. The lives of the five characters whose stories will be unveiled, but ambiguously, are similarly fragmented, in a city of fragments. Even one of the chapters is appropriately titled "Fragmentary Sentences."

Long-familiar paintings and sculpture, old companions as it were of Western culture, appear in the tapestry as motifs intricately tied to the delineation of the characters but lifting them out of specific time and place. Classical and biblical myths (Venus, Apollo, Jael, Judith, Salome), religious figures from the pagan and Christian worlds (Marcus Aurelius, the Virgin Mary, Saint Antony, Saint Michael, Pope Julian III), artists of both worlds (Praxiteles, Guido, ·Raphael), and historical figures (Cleopatra, the Cencis) all serve seemingly to decorate the canvas but actually universalize the lives and actions of the participants. Nowhere else in his writings is Hawthorne so literary as in *The Marble Faun*, anticipating symbolism and the twentieth-century allusive fusion of art, history, religion, and psyche.

As Harry Levin suggests, the romance takes on the aura of opera, with duets, trios, quartets, and quintets, although Hawthorne was according to his son almost deaf to the sensuous and dramatic resonances of music. Yet, with the flair and genius of Charles Ives, Hawthorne has the Americans in Rome sing "Hail, Columbia!" shortly before a tragic murder, perhaps reminding us that the hymn to America's glories rests upon the bloodstain of the nation's relationship with the Indians.[3]

Characters look down from parapets and balconies, while others on the ground look up, as Hawthorne presents seemingly various perspectives, but actually the characters are looking at mirror images of themselves: they watch as it were their murderous rages and perverse lusts being acted out supposedly by others, in a deeply troubled narcissistic fusion of Eros and Thanatos.

Two larger than life-size sculptures of Marcus Aurelius and Julius III, a pagan philosopher and a Catholic pope, are as conspicuous in the tapestry as the domes of St. Peter's and the Pantheon. These majestic paternal figures, idealizations of fantasy but embodiments of human needs, reach out their arms eternally to characters who seek as desperately as Ilbrahim for the solace of parental guidance and caresses. Not far from the Marcus Aurelius sculpture (on horseback, like Cotton Mather in "Alice Doane's Appeal") and over a parapet from which Romans threw betrayers of the state to their death, Donatello holds the body of the Model clasped in an embrace and drops it only after Miriam's eyes confirm *their* desire to kill her betrayer to whom only a few moments earlier she knelt in frightened, dreamlike reverence. "Was it horrour?—or ecstasy?—or both in one?" the narrator asks as the Model's shriek follows "quivering downward" until the body lands with a "dead thump," with hands "stretched out, as if they might have clutched, for a moment, at the small square stones." The action replicates the death of Butler in *Fanshawe*, and in the first moments the bond between Miriam and Donatello is "closer than a marriage-bond," the bloodstain of the murdered evoking loss of virginity.

In this romance, as in earlier tales, hands communicate love and hate more persuasively than words. Kenyon's "loving hands" can carve Hilda's hand in cold marble, but they cannot reach out to Miriam when she is in need of support. Art, we are to discover, does not often lead to empathic responses in life. The estrangement of Miriam and Donatello after the murder is dramatized tactilely: he cannot endure touching her until they are transformed beneath the outstretched arms of Julius in the "likeness of a Father." Such "heart-sustenance" there is no reason to articulate: it is felt.

The action of the romance is framed in that happy incongruity of the coexistence of carnival and Lent. The pagan celebration with its masked figures and often childlike antics sanctions culturally and personally the release of pent-up urges, while Lent is the season of fasting and inhibition preparatory to the celebration of renewal with the resurrection in the spring. Between the two carnivals depicted in the romance occurs a murder—an oedipal drama, as it turns out, but not without veiled parallels to Christ's death—which transforms the lives of the participants.

The fusion of these rites extends to the fusion of the characters. Miriam, a beautiful Jewish woman, appears to be the slave of a mysterious, elusive man variously called Model, Demon, Brother Antonio, and Father Antonio. From her childhood, when she apparently was sexually abused, they have fled each other, but there is also a bond "equally torturing to each," which neither her "slender fingers" nor his "masculine force" can sever. He looks at her fearfully, and she pities him. Yet her paintings depict the fury and rage of Judith, Jael, and Salome as they take revenge on male abusers. The Model is always in the shadows waiting for and spying on Miriam, and in her paintings there is a shadowy figure "with an expression of deep sadness," with "the face and form" of Miriam.

The Model's rival is Donatello, a faunlike character who is actually Count of Monte Beni, the last member of an ancient Italian family. The Model is "dark, bushy, bearded"; Donatello with his clustering curls has the "look of eternal youth," which derives from androgynous classical sculpture. Both the world-weary Model and the idyllic youth are descended from satyrs, "creatures, standing between man and animals." Miriam and her friends wonder whether Donatello's ears resemble the hidden ones of Praxiteles' Faun and what has happened to the caudal appendage of the statue. The thinly veiled sexual innuendos parallel the unexplained sexuality inherent in the Model's relationship with Miriam since childhood and foreshadow the fusion of sexuality and death in the murder scene. Donatello, who sometimes models for Miriam, assumes in life the part of the outraged women in Miriam's paintings who take revenge on males.

It turns out that the Model, who is probably Jewish like Miriam though a member of the Capuchin order, is called not by mistake Brother *and* Father Antonio. Perhaps he is Miriam's father or more probably her brother who revenges paternal incest, as suggested by the important role of the story of the Cencis in the action. When Donatello sits later for Kenyon, the clay in the sculptor's hands suddenly unveils a "look" as Donatello presumably relives the murder: "Cain never wore an uglier one!" Donatello is transformed into Antonio's brother, as the Eden tragedy is replayed.[4]

The fair Hilda, who bears the name of an English saint but has the Puritan's distrust of Catholicism, is contrasted in the familiar juxtaposition of literature with the dark, passionate Miriam. Despite cultural, religious, and temperamental differences, the two women become "sisters" in "the fervency of a girl's first friendship." Hilda's favorite painting is not Raphael's Madonna but Guido Reni's Beatrice Cenci, whose enigmatic, melancholic beauty, despite the horrors of her debasement, is replicated in Miriam, who has, it appears, a similar familial background. Though priggish and frightened of sexuality, Hilda is seemingly not troubled by or interested in Beatrice's story, although she may be unknowingly attracted to an abused daughter who like herself is motherless.[5]

After the murder, which she observes from the same shadows from which the Model Antonio emerged a few minutes earlier, Hilda returns to her tower, feeds the Virgin's doves, and resumes her work on a copy of Beatrice Cenci. Morally outraged by the deed, she spurns Miriam, who cries out for a confidant. A short time later a painter who surreptitiously depicts Hilda as she stands before a Leonardo painting finds that her appearance is "somewhat similar to poor Beatrice's forlorn gaze out of dreary isolation and remoteness, in which a terrible doom had involved a tender soul." His painting is called *Innocence, Dying of a Blood-stain*, but a gallery dealer changes the title to *The Signorina's Vengeance*: "She has stabbed her lover, over night, and is repenting it betimes, the next morning." And so the innocent Hilda is perceived as a courtesan acting out the subject matter of the Cenci portrait and Miriam's art.

Differences in appearance, creed, and even conduct, then, are superficial, and the stereotypical roles collapse when hidden internal conflicts surface following the murder. Hawthorne renders the lust, greed, envy, and murderous desires all humans share, as his analogies from the Garden of Eden to the Roman Empire to the Italian Renaissance to the modern age testify. The wastelands of Hawthorne and Eliot are the same.

Hilda appears to resemble the doves on her balcony, but the sunshine of her countenance is subject for no discernible reason to "recurring change." Only gradually do we realize that the seemingly strong inner resources cloak her compelling dependency upon her dead mother. The suicide motif which reverberates in the romance is introduced innocuously in one of Hilda's reveries: "The air so exhilarates my spirits, that sometimes I feel half-inclined to attempt a flight from the top of my tower, in the faith that I should float upward!" Miriam shudders as she looks over a parapet and imagines a body sprawled on the stones below. Donatello too seems "to feel that perilous fascination which haunts the brow of precipices, tempting the unwary one to fling himself over, for the very horrour of the thing." When Kenyon ascends Donatello's tower, he verbalizes the reverie Ethan Brand must have had on the night he hurled himself into the limekiln below. "If I were to do just as I like, at this moment," Kenyon informs Donatello, "I should fling myself down after that bit of lime. It is a very singular temptation, and all but irresistible." Kenyon wonders whether Donatello shares "this strange impulse of an Evil Spirit at your back, shoving you towards a precipice."

Longfellow called *The Marble Faun* "a wonderful book: but with the old, dull pain that runs through all Hawthorne's writings," which, as he did not add, runs through Hawthorne's life. The characters constitute a single portrait of Hawthorne, man and artist, the life inseparable from the art; the principal subject of this romance, as Millicent Bell observed years ago, is art and the artist.[6]

It is a commonplace of Hawthorne commentary to cite the parallels between Kenyon and the author, for particularly in sometimes lengthy, almost didactic passages, he voices Hawthorne's intellectualizations. Yet in many respects Miriam is closer to Hawthorne than the others, especially in the delineation of her inner life. When the narrator observes that Miriam acts "as if a melancholy maiden and a glad one were both bound within the girdle about her waist," he describes Hawthorne himself as well as the dualities of his romance: despite melancholic, even tragic undertones, the story concludes with lovely bubbles of optimistic affirmation which do not quite follow logically from the mixed tonalities and signals of the narrative.

Miriam's canvases, she acknowledges, delineate "ugly phantoms that stole out of my mind . . . , that haunt me." Hers are self-portraits originating in "the intimate results of her heart-knowledge," which leads her to depictions of "woman, acting the part of revengeful mischief toward man." Hawthorne, also burning beneath his placid demeanor with fierce hostility, assumes in his fiction at times the roles of men who abuse women, although he is both the abuser and the abused. Like Miriam, he too is frequently depressed and despondent, filled with "moody passion," and she, like Hawthorne, at times releases pressures in playful, manic outbursts and flights of imagination, particularly in her association with the childlike Donatello, who in turn resembles Hawthorne's self-portraits. She seeks a brother in Kenyon to whom she may divulge "a secret in my heart." Her expectations increase after he displays for the first time his plaster model of Cleopatra, disclosing not only unfamiliar subject matter but also interest in a fiercely passionate woman which his devotion to the chaste Hilda hides. But when she asks, "Were you not afraid to touch her, as she grew . . . beneath your hand?" the sexual innuendo does not escape him, and only after a pause does he say, "Speak freely, as to a brother." She hears "a certain reserve and alarm" and retreats, realizing, the narrator informs us, that she "would hate him, by-and-by, and herself still more, if he let her speak." She breaks the tension of their silence with an outburst, "You are as cold and pitiless as your own marble," ironically, just as "he was now ready to receive her trust." "Too nervous, too passionate," Miriam leaves his study, saying to herself, "My dark-red carbuncle—red as blood—is too rich a gem to put into a stranger's casket," which is an extraordinary confirmation of her desire to reverse gender roles and to satisfy pent-up sexual desire.

In this powerful scene Hawthorne lays bare articulated and unarticulated feelings with the clarity of his awareness of his own secret life: Miriam's role confusion is his own, as are Kenyon's hesitancies and simultaneous attraction to and fear of passion.

Kenyon is no "muttonhead," unless, that is, Hawthorne is a "muttonhead." Like Hawthorne, Kenyon takes "a slide in the Piazza of Saint Peter's" and creates a Cleopatra, who evokes such passionate women as Hester, Zenobia, and Miriam. He is aware that "all men must descend, if they would know anything beneath the surface and illusive pleasures of existence." He too becomes "sensible of a restless melancholy, to which the cultivators of the ideal arts are more liable than sturdier men." He is troubled that in his sculpture he is unable to depict the "inner man," although by accident, "entirely independent of his own will," he captures in clay the anguish and "animal fierceness" of Donatello. After Hilda's disappearance he "questioned, at that moment, whether Sculpture really ever softens and warms the material which it handles; whether carved marble is anything but limestone, after all; and whether the Apollo Belvedere itself possesses any merit above its physical beauty, or is beyond criticism even in that generally acknowledged excellence. In flitting glances, heretofore, he had seemed to behold this statue as something ethereal and godlike, but not now." The sculpture of Laocoön, not of Apollo, offers him clarification and awareness of "the Fate of interminable ages. Kenyon looked upon the group as the one triumph of Sculpture, creating the repose, which is essential to it, in the very acme of turbulent effort." The result is a "mood of unwonted despondency" and loss of faith in the ameliorative effects of art.[7]

Donatello is another of Hawthorne's familiar narcissistic images of a beautiful, androgynous youth more than a little in love with death. His antics and childish behavior evoke Hawthorne's climbing trees to shake down nuts to his delighted children and wife, who in turn decorate him as Pan. One day Donatello discovers a worm attacking an ancient plant and tosses the "ugly creature" over the wall, replicating the murder of Antonio and scenes from Hawthorne's youth when he threw a cat over the fence and refused the services of "ugly" servants. The beautiful youth in Hawthorne's writings, like Melville's handsome sailors, especially Billy Budd, and Tadzio in Thomas Mann's *Death in Venice*, reveals a homoerotic attraction which is encapsulated in a dazzling aura of mythic and literary allusions.

Contemporaries and later commentators have pointed to Sophia Hawthorne, despite her denials, as the model for Hilda, but Hilda's loss of faith in the efficacy of art is Hawthorne's. Sophia to the end held tenaciously to her idealizations. She could not have said: "There is something beyond all which pictorial genius has produced."

The murder of Antonio—symbolically the death of the father—shatters the fragile bonds of this little group adrift in Rome and exposes weaknesses concealed in their artistic pursuits. Although Kenyon is the only one not involved as participant or observer of the death, it takes place at the time he secretly gives birth to Cleopatra, the destroyer of Mark Antony. When Kenyon seeks out Donatello at his family estate, he perceives the young man's discontent but is powerless to help because of the inadequacies of males. Man, he declares, needs "woman—his mother, his sister, or his wife," and so once more we witness the search for the mother who will, presumably, free the son from the father and from the demands of art which unlocks the unconscious and hidden life.

Donatello finds comfort only before the shrines of the Madonna who will, he tries to persuade himself, "intercede, as a tender mother, betwixt the poor culprit and the awfulness of judgment." The narrator finds it "beautiful to observe, indeed, how tender was the soul of man and woman towards the Virgin Mother." Hilda also seeks "the sympathy of Divine Womanhood," which her Puritan heritage has denied her, and kneels as "a child, lifting its tear-stained face to seek comfort from a Mother!" She goes to St. Peter's in quest of "a Woman to listen to the prayers of women; a Mother in heaven for all motherless girls like me!" She settles for a priest with " the look of paternal benignity." On leaving the confessional booth, she seems released from depression and remorse and is transformed, evoking, however, the "image of a child, making its plaything of every object, but sporting in good faith, and with a kind of seriousness."

In the square at Perugia Miriam and Donatello are reunited under the right hand of Pope Julian, "raised and spread abroad as if in the act of shedding forth benediction": "the desolate heart, whatever be its religion, recognizes in that image the likeness of a Father!" (As we learn earlier, the sculptor of Marcus Aurelius knew "the heart of mankind, and how it craves a true ruler, . . . as a child its father!") The Faun is now "a man, revolving grave and deep thoughts in his breast. He still held Miriam's hand; and there they stood, the beautiful man, the beautiful woman, united forever."

After her apotheosis and return to America Hester Prynne assures the women of Boston that "a new truth would be revealed, in order to establish the whole relation between man and woman on a surer ground of mutual happiness, [and] the angel and apostle of the coming revelation must be a woman." And so after the papal blessing, the romance as it were rediscovers woman or mother when Kenyon finds among many fragments in an excavation of a suburban villa "a headless figure of marble" which is "either the prototype or a better repetition of the Venus of the Tribune. . . . It is one of the few works of antique sculpture in which we recognize Womanhood, and that, moreover, without prejudice to its divinity." Before this fragmented replica of womanhood, Kenyon experiences a kind of epiphany which, unlike Stephen Dedalus's, will lead him to seek reentry into the community. "He could hardly, we fear, be reckoned a consummate artist, because there was something dearer to him than his art; and, by the greater strength of human affection, the divine statue seemed to fall asunder again, and became only a heap of worthless fragments." Once again Hawthorne restates the position enunciated in *Fanshawe*, that art does not gratify one's affectional needs; Hawthorne's forebears would have concurred with his opinion, if for different reasons.

A year has passed since Kenyon's discovery, and it is time for the eternal rite of death and reintegration at the Carnival. While Kenyon observes the merrymaking with "troubled face"—Hilda has disappeared mysteriously—suddenly "a gigantic female figure, seven feet high," appears, and at once Hawthorne seizes the opportunity for a virtuoso performance of wonderful playfulness and sexual innuendo in which he recaptures the aura of "My Kinsman, Major Molineux" and "Young Goodman Brown." He presents a caricature of the fragmented Venus, a "Titaness" in hilarious confusion of gender who is hugely pregnant: the "preposterously swelling sphere of her crinoline skirts" takes up a third of the street. Completely uninhibited, she makes "a ponderous assault" upon Kenyon, but not after the fashion of the women in Miriam's paintings. She glances "at him out of her great goggle-eyes," establishing eye contact such as is not possible in viewing the Cenci portrait and anticipating the final scene beneath "the open Eye of the Pantheon." When her outrageously seductive tactics fail, "the rejected Titaness," a phallic earth-mother if there ever was one, draws out "a huge pistol": she has no simpering Cupid at her side posturing with a dart. She aims at Kenyon's breast and pulls the trigger, which goes off "like a boy's pop-gun" (a phallic byplay which Hawthorne seems to have borrowed from Melville's *Typee*), impregnating Kenyon "with a cloud of lime-dust," the powder of the destroyed marble sculpture of Venus or of Kenyon's own works, no doubt with an allusion to Ethan Brand's suicide in the kiln in the Berkshires.

At once Kenyon is surrounded by harlequins with enormous noses (commedia dell 'arte with reminiscences of the dwarfs Rip Van Winkle meets at the beginning of his twenty-year nap) who pretend to investigate the crime after the fashion of a "coroner's jury." A notary offers "to make the last will and testament of the assassinated man." But the notary is interrupted by the appearance of an awesomely farcical surgeon brandishing "a lancet, three feet long," and proposing "to let him blood," adding one more bloodstain to a recurrent motif of the romance in a wildly phallic scene that may owe a little to Melville's depiction of the "archbishoprick" in "The Cassock" chapter of *Moby-Dick*.

The "Titaness" has barely vanished when Kenyon meets Miriam and Donatello, both of whom have assumed the attire of Father Antonio. They extend their hands to Kenyon and in a tableau form "a linked circle of three, with many reminiscences and forebodings flashing through their hearts." In unison, they say "Farewell!" and at once "loosed their hands." Suddenly the "uproar" of the Carnival "swept like a tempestuous sea over the spot, which they had included with their small circle of isolated feeling." Once again at a crucial moment Hawthorne introduces the sea motif with its associations of fertility and birth, the cradle endlessly rocking and death, and the lost father.

On a balcony "richly hung with tapestry and damask" sits a group of English women who favor Kenyon "with a salvo of confetti." He is hit next by a cauliflower and then by "a single rosebud, so fresh it seemed that moment gathered." It gently smites his lips and falls into his hand. When he looks up he beholds "the face of his lost Hilda!" What a lovely touch it is! If the cauliflower recalls the pumpkin that terrifies Ichabod Crane into flight, in Hawthorne's version Kenyon becomes both Ichabod Crane and Brom Bones, the vanquished and the victor. In the endless fusions and allusions characteristic of this romance, the balcony scene evokes *Romeo and Juliet* as well as the opening of *The Scarlet Letter*, even to the rose. But Arthur Dimmesdale looks down at Hester Pyrnne with fear in his tremulous voice, while Kenyon looks up to Hilda, filled with loving hope.[8]

One more scene remains to complete the tapestry. It takes place in the Pantheon. The circular building fuses the pagan and Christian worlds, for inside "in the free space of that great circle" stand altars to Christians which were once dedicated to heathen gods. In the gray dome is an opening to the sky which Kenyon calls "that great Eye, gazing heavenward." In the ascending circles of the Pantheon, culminating in the "great central Eye," Hawthorne transforms the circular imagery that ends in deterministic disaster in "Ethan Brand" into a spiral or crescendo reflecting faith and renewal. The eye image may even be Hawthorne's adaptation of Emerson's "transparent eyeball" in "Nature," which was written in the Manse, or Thoreau's sun image at the conclusion of *Walden*.

On one of the altars a "very plump and comfortable tabby-cat" sleeps. Disturbed by the presence of Kenyon and Hilda, she wakes up, raises herself, and sits "blinking in the sun, yet with a certain dignity and self-possession, as if conscious of representing a Saint." Kenyon suggests that "this is the first of the feline race that has ever set herself up as an object of worship, in the Pantheon or elsewhere, since the days of ancient Egypt." A peasant is kneeling before the tabby-cat, and a veiled woman with her face upturned is kneeling "beneath the great central Eye," as Hilda and Kenyon begin to discuss the transformation of Donatello from faun to perpetrator of "a great crime." Kenyon speculates that sin has educated and elevated Donatello: "Did Adam fall, that we might ultimately rise to a far loftier paradise from his?" Hilda reacts in horror to this exposition of the doctrine of the fortunate fall. "Do not you perceive," she asks, "what a mockery your creed makes, not only of all religious sentiment, but of moral law, and how it annuls and obliterates whatever precepts of Heaven are written deepest within us? You have shocked me beyond words!"

Kenyon immediately abandons his metaphysical speculation, head surrendering to the imperatives of the heart and of womanhood. In his need for a "guide," "counsellor," and "inmost friend," he proposes to her: "Oh, Hilda, guide me home!" Hilda's eyes fill with tears as she admits her loneliness and confesses her weakness: "I am a poor, weak girl, and have no such wisdom as you fancy in me." At this miraculous moment they chance—through the happy machinations of their creator—to be standing before the tomb of Raphael that is adorned with a "marble Madonna," which evokes his most celebrated painting and Hester Prynne's appearances as a Puritan Madonna in the first and last scaffold scenes. As Kenyon and Hilda are about to abandon art for the gratification of marriage and domesticity, we are reminded that "Raphael's genius wore out that divinest painter before half his life was lived."

The veiled woman kneeling beneath "the open Eye of the Pantheon" rises:

> . . . she looked towards the pair, and extended her hands with a gesture of benediction. Then they knew that it was Miriam. They suffered her to glide out of the portal, however, without a greeting; for those extended hands, even while they blessed, seemed to repel, as if Miriam stood on the other side of a fathomless abyss and warned them from its verge.

Miriam's burden is not lifted, "the fathomless abyss" conjuring up the precipice scene and the inevitable punishment. At the edge of the tapestry she appears briefly in the role of "mother," which in life she will not be permitted to play, and blesses two who will unite and people the earth, in the tradition of Phoebe and Holgrave. As a wedding gift Miriam sends Hilda an Etruscan bracelet whose "entire circle" contains Miriam's mystery, which, however, remains forever a secret.

At that moment Hawthorne stretched out his hand and wrote, "But Hilda had a hopeful soul, and saw sunlight on the mountain-top." Then he wearily put down his quill pen. His tapestry was finished.

The pictures are lovely and memorable in their fusions, yet despite the loving touches and the exquisite detail the romance at times seems overcontrolled, as though he was straining for resolutions of personal conflicts which art cannot provide. He informed Ticknor, "I have never thought or felt more deeply, or taken more pains," and the characters, who constitute a self-portrait, renounce the pleasures and gratifications of art for the security and comforts of home and hearth. In his lifelong agon with his ancestors, he triumphed in establishing intercourse with the world and reaping the attendant fame, but he never silenced the doubts of his Puritan inheritance.[9]

Under the influence of John Bunyan, Hawthorne wanted to depict the circular journey from the City of Destruction to the Celestial City, as unfolded in the wonderfully imaginative pages of *Pilgrim's Progress*, but he was not sustained by Bunyan's faith. The Celestial City was only an artifact, like Owen Warland's butterfly or the Eden of *The House of the Seven Gables*. In life and art Hawthorne searched for the savior mother, but the doubts expressed in "The Birth-mark" could not be willed away through artistic contrivances. All seekers of the truth "sooner or later stumble" into awareness that "our great creative Mother, while she amuses us with apparently working in the broadest sunshine, is yet severely careful to keep her own secrets, and, in spite of her pretended openness, shows us nothing but results. She permits us, indeed, to mar, but seldom to mend, and, like a jealous patentee, on no account to make."[10]

Like Hilda and Kenyon, Sophia and Hawthorne were about to return home. "When I get home," he wrote to Fields, "I will try to write a more genial book; but the devil himself always seems to get into my inkstand, and I can only exorcise him by pensfull at a time." As he perhaps intuited, there was to be little "sunlight on the mountain-top" at the Wayside.[11]

Concord, 1860–1862

Aboard the *Europa* when it sailed from Liverpool on June 16, 1860, were, in addition to the Hawthornes, James T. Fields and his new wife, Annie, and Harriet Beecher Stowe. According to Fields, Hawthorne had a "passionate worship of the sea" and during the voyage repeated "in his quiet, earnest way, 'I should like to sail on and on forever, and never touch the shore again.'" Fields had no way of knowing that this was a variation of what he had said in his youth after the death of Captain Hathorne: "I want to go to sea and never return again." Late in the afternoons Hawthorne stood alone on the bow observing the sunsets and at midnight, still alone, walked the decks. "I used to watch," Fields recalled, "his dark, solitary figure under the stars, pacing up and down some unfrequented parts of the vessel, musing and half melancholy." Fields was seasick the whole time, and occasionally Hawthorne lay down beside him to "commiserate my unquiet condition." Annie Fields spent the evenings with Sophia, "the romancer in conversation," who wove "magic webs of her fancies, until we looked upon her as a second Scheherezade."[1]

The Hawthornes landed at Boston on June 28 and went directly to the Wayside. Mary Mann, who moved out of the house shortly before their return, pronounced the family "in the finest health." Sophia, she observed, "looks as fat & rosy as possible. They are enjoying the peace &

quiet of their little home very much. The children are very pleasant indeed." Her comments proved incorrect in almost every particular.[2]

Thoreau, who called almost at once, found Hawthorne unchanged: "He is as simple & child-like as ever." Louisa May Alcott, who lived next door at the Orchard, welcomed the return of the family because, as she informed a correspondent, she now had "something to talk about" besides the usual news, and she happily indulged herself in some acerbic comments. "Mr. H.," she wrote, "is as queer as ever and we catch glimpses of a dark mysterious looking man in a big hat and red slippers darting over the hills or skimming by as if he expected the house of Alcott were about to rush out and clutch him." She saved some of her nastier remarks for Sophia: "Mrs. H. is as sentimental and muffing as of old, wears crimson silk jackets, a rosary from Jerusalem, fire-flies in her hair and the dirty white skirts with sacred mud of London still extant thereon." Alcott next turned her sharp-eyed attention to the children. "Una is a stout English looking sixteen year old with the most ardent hair and eyebrows, Monte Bene airs and graces and no accomplishments but riding. . . . Julian is a worthy boy full of pictures, fishing rods and fun and Rose a little bud of a girl with scarlet hair and no particular raiment, which is cool and artistic but somewhat startling to the common herd."[3]

Emerson was cordial and invited Hawthorne to attend the Saturday Club in Boston, where he met Holmes, Longfellow, Lowell, Agassiz, and other intellectuals and artists from Boston and Cambridge. "It is an excellent institution," Hawthorne informed Bright, "with the privileges of first-rate society, and no duties but to eat one's dinner." Emerson "has become earthlier during these past seven years; for he puffs cigars like a true Yankee, and drinks wine like an Englishman." Moncure Daniel Conway, a clergyman and early biographer of Hawthorne who attended one of the Saturday Club dinners, found Hawthorne "improved by his heavy moustache, though this concealed the feminine sweetness of his mouth," and remarked on the "animation, and the fine candor of his expression" instead of the usual shyness.[4]

At another dinner the guest was Anthony Trollope, whom Lowell with American snobbery characterized as "a big, red-faced, rather underbred Englishman of the bald-with-spectacles type." Trollope and Holmes got into a good-natured, animated exchange, during which Trollope claimed that England was the only country where such a thing as a peach or grape was known. Lowell appealed to Hawthorne for his opinion. "His face

mantled and trembled for a moment with some droll fancy," Lowell remembered, "as one sees bubbles rise and send off rings in still water
when a turtle stirs at the bottom, and then he said, 'I asked an Englishman once who was praising their peaches to describe to me exactly
what he meant by a peach, and he described something very like a
cucumber.'"[5]

Shortly after their return strains among the Hawthornes emerged
abruptly and dramatically. Despite Mary Mann's optimistic report, Sophia had not regained her former health, and Una still suffered physically
as well as emotionally during a protracted recuperation, which was not
helped by the usual problems of adolescent adjustments. Hawthorne himself was the cause of the first crisis. The family had scarcely settled in
when he left to visit Pierce in Concord, New Hampshire. On July 14 Hawthorne informed Una, not Sophia, that he could not return until July 17.
Apparently Una was outraged because she was left alone with her
mother while her father enjoyed himself with his old friend. Una demanded to be allowed to leave home and would have nothing to do with
her mother. Of one thing she made certain: life in the Hawthorne household centered about her.[6]

While her father was still away, Una moved in with Aunt Mary Mann.
On his return Hawthorne began to send her placating notes. On July 19
her cousin, Richard Manning of Salem, perhaps at her demand, visited
her, and on the following day she wrote him an impassioned letter. She
was sorry that he had shed tears, although no doubt that had been her
intention, because "I felt as if I never could forgive myself for causing
you and everyone so much pain." She described an interview with the
doctor who "agreed with me in the most *unqualified* manner in everything I said, & he is going to talk to Papa and tell him his mind, and then
I shall be as free as air! Think how happy I must be!" She claimed, or
perhaps threatened, that she would have "a brain fever" if she remained
in Concord. She also could not decide whether to leave that day or the
next for Salem, because "I long to be there, out of this killing place."
Hearing of the plan, perhaps because she let her cousin Horace Mann in
on the secret, Hawthorne offered an alternative. As soon as arrangements could be made he himself would take her for a visit to Elizabeth
Hawthorne, and in the meantime Elizabeth Peabody would move to the
Wayside so that Una had a room to herself at Aunt Mary's.[7]

Una remained in Concord, her demands at least temporarily accommodated. She waited almost a week before she wrote to Richard Manning. "I was very unwell from many causes," she said, "and I knew my only safety was in keeping my mind off myself. From having followed that wise course until now & keeping away from home(!) I have greatly improved." She prided herself on being "a wilful & headstrong young woman," but surely she was acting out because of latent fears. Early in August Una was with Elizabeth Hawthorne at Montserrat, and her health was "already greatly improved by the change of air and scene." Apparently when Una came back to Concord, her mother went off to North Conway, New Hampshire, with Mary Mann's children. Almost pathetically Sophia reassured Una of her love in signing her letter, "Most entirely your own/Mamma." On Sophia's return Una and her father began a visit with the Bridges in Portsmouth, New Hampshire. Sophia wrote her daughter a tender letter in which she urged her not to be discouraged, "for it is a miracle that you are alive at all after the Roman death-struggle." Sophia promised not to be Sophia, the vulnerable, overanxious mother, a promise she could not keep. Concealing her pain, she concluded bravely, "We have every reason to be the happiest of family groups, and we will be happy and cheerful."[8]

As Sophia wrote, Una began to act strangely in Portsmouth, and when her father brought her to Mary Mann's house in Concord she was delirious and "insane." On the night of September 19 she had to be restrained, and her aunts sat up with her. Her parents were evidently not allowed in the house, at least not into the bedroom. The aunts, both of whom were addicted to medical quackery, summoned a Mrs. Rollins from Cambridge, and to Hawthorne's surprise and perhaps chagrin, after a week Una's symptoms yielded to what he called "the incantations of a certain electrical witch." He was reminded of a response made by a drunken sailor when he was asked how he felt, "'Pretty d——d miserable, thank God!' It very well expresses my thorough discomfort and forced acquiescence." The crisis passed—for a week Una had in the eyes of one romantic neighbor been "Ophelia"—and Mrs. Rollins assured the family that it should "have no apprehension of future mental disturbance."[9]

Sophia's humiliation was complete. She was banned from her daughter's sickroom, and her sisters—with whom she had for years quarreled as to how to bring up and educate children—were in charge. Una punished her mother, no doubt with the silent approval of a father who involved himself as little as possible in the family and instead of imposing controls upon his daughter allowed her to play off one parent against the other. Hawthorne's passivity was probably as great a problem for his children as the mother's overprotectiveness and her tendency to live her life through theirs.

Sophia's ordeal was not over. Early in September, while she was in the White Mountains, Julian, now fourteen, "for the first time in his life" went to school. Also attending this school, which was founded by Franklin B. Sanborn, an abolitionist and friend of John Brown, were sons of the Emersons and the Manns as well as two brothers of Henry James, Jr. At last Sophia's children were making a belated entrance into the world after being cut off from peers, schools, and even newspapers. Sophia informed Elizabeth Peabody that only "grown persons" should be exposed to the newspaper, "and even they must take care not to become demoralized by it."[10]

Before the family situation ameliorated—it is not known when Una returned home—Hawthorne undertook to remodel the Wayside partly because it was too small for his maturing family but also because he hoped "that the burthen of it upon my back will keep me from wishing to wander any more." He was too self-aware not to recognize that the wish was unrealizable. The renovation provided him with a tower and a panoramic view of the Concord countryside. There he recaptured the position and role of Paul Pry in the attic of 12 Herbert Street, site of the original "castle dismal," but in a structure modeled vaguely after the tower of the villa outside Florence, where he began to write *The Marble Faun*. The irony, however, was that the tower in Concord, a "pine-built structure of very humble pretensions," actually spoiled the lines of the old New England dwelling, although Hawthorne convinced himself, at least for a time, that it made "a pretty and rather picturesque abode at the foot of a terraced hill-side."[11]

In this tower Hawthorne, no longer faunlike but old and weary, would complete his autobiography. In whimsical moments of which there were a few, but now at longer intervals, he called the tower a "sky-parlour," drawing upon Bellerophon's reference to Pegasus as "my sky-skimmer" in that story of ideal friendship at the conclusion of *A Wonder-Book*. The tale is prefaced, it will be recalled, by a lovely tribute to Irving's genius in "Rip Van Winkle" and followed by a tribute to Herman Melville's "shaping out the gigantic conception of his 'White Whale.'" Memories and association are often mysterious, but it was Melville's intention in 1850 on moving to Pittsfield to construct "a real towered house—an actual tower," or so Sophia reported at the time to her mother.[12]

The tower became a subject of gossip among villagers and visitors. Hawthorne was supposed to have told Longfellow that he climbed into it through a trapdoor on which he placed his chair while he wrote. William Dean Howells had it that when Hawthorne spotted an unwelcome guest in the vicinity, he pulled up a rope ladder, not unlike Father Mapple after he climbs into his pulpit. Three years after he made over the Wayside he was of another mind about his "architectural projects" and admitted that he had "transformed a simple and small old farm-house into the absurdest anomaly you ever saw." Yet he blamed the village carpenter who "produced an unimaginable sort of thing instead of what I asked for. If it would only burn down! But I have no such luck."[13]

The renovations included the planting of 450 Norway spruces which Hawthorne had selected in England and of a woodbine which was "to climb," in Sophia's words, "to his study window." He "cut his cypher" in an aspen tree. On the hillside there was a large pine under which he reclined and listened "to the sea song in the branches while in May the grass was blue with large violets around him." By accident, so Sophia believed, he burned part of the tree when he tried to destroy the undergrowth around it.[14]

The time spent in supervising construction permitted delay in beginning a new romance, but the need to write was great since the renovation which was estimated to cost roughly $500 eventually exceeded $2,000. The family began to worry about its economic lot, and Ticknor probably did not help matters by advancing money on demand without sending an exact financial report.

Only Ticknor knew that shortly after his return Hawthorne once again took on the care of Zachariah Burchmore, the Salem political hack and heavy tippler who no longer could hold down a job. After Hawthorne failed to get Burchmore an appointment, he directed Ticknor to pay Burchmore $50 and ordered Burchmore not to acknowledge receipt and Ticknor not "to write to me about this; for I do not wish my wife to know how I throw away my money." Hawthorne also sought to renew his relationship with David Roberts, his friend from Salem. "We have reached the age, now," he noted, "when old friends ought to make the most of each other." Roberts paid a two-day visit in June, but Hawthorne avoided Salem and gradually isolated himself in Concord.[15]

The remodeling of the Wayside was not completed until spring, when the North and South were at war. The grounds about the house were scarcely cleaned up when Hawthorne commented to Ticknor, "I have never felt so earnest a desire to go back to England as now that I have irrevocably planted myself at home." He thought that he should have established himself at the seashore but a moment later considered it "folly for a mortal man to do anything more than pitch a tent." He sought to reconcile himself to his lot, that he could no longer drift about the world and had to make himself "at home in one dull spot." He admitted his inconsistency, "It is rather odd, that, with all my tendency to stick in one place, I yet find great delight in frequent change."[16]

Publicly, Hawthorne declared himself in better health than he had been for some time, although he doubted that he would "ever again be so well as I used to be in England." Without "sanction" Sophia wrote to Ticknor on May 15, 1861. It was a brave gesture on her part, for Hawthorne kept an eye on her correspondence, often reading her letters before they were sent. Sophia informed Ticknor that her husband needed wine but felt himself too poor "to indulge in the smallest luxury." She explained that he was "low in tone and spirits. . . . he has lost the zest for life." She asked Ticknor to send some wine and to "write him a cheerful letter."[17]

Sophia and the children lived with a man who sometimes regained his childlike exhilaration but who more frequently was despondent, in outlook and intonation recalling Goodman Brown or Tobias Pearson, the "father" of Ilbrahim. On holiday with Julian he engaged boyishly in battles with berries, which the son recalled with pleasure in his maturity, but of this vacation Hawthorne wrote to Una, "Indeed, Julian seems to like it exceedingly, and I am not much more discontented than with many other spots in this weary world." If he wanted to assuage Una's jealousy, that Julian had her father to himself, he should hardly have voiced his ennui to one as fragile and distraught as Una, but he never fully recognized his involvement in her problems.[18]

The mother, as fragile as her daughter, could not confide in her husband or her sisters who had answers even to unasked questions. Until she found Annie Fields, she had to fall back upon her overextended resources. She was increasingly troubled by Hawthorne's physical and emotional states, which she mirrored because she lived for and in many respects through him. "I have been weighed to the earth," she wrote to him during one of his absences, "by my sense of thy depressed energies and spirits in a way from which I tried in vain to rally." It became her truth that Rome was responsible for the undoing of the family. "Rome," she insisted, "has no sin for which to answer so unpardonable as this of wrenching off thy wings and hanging lead upon thy arrowy feet." Whenever he had a cold it was a "Roman cold." She claimed that he was convinced that he would "never recover" from the "melancholy days" in Rome, although she may have voiced only her own fears since she admitted that she had "never fully recovered from the shock to my heart and spirits encountered in that 'City of the Souls.'" [19]

She thought a change of scene would do immeasurable good for a man she characterized as "so apathetic, so indifferent, so hopeless, so unstrung," and would restore their long-lost paradise. When Hawthorne went off to the seashore in the summer of 1861 Sophia gave up her customary nap, "so restored am I by thy absence!" (Perhaps her language inadvertently revealed more than she realized.) Thereupon she looked at herself in the mirror and "was really attracted by the immense change in my own face." Una, who again was in residence, thought the change "miraculous." "So thou percievest," Sophia exalted, her spelling not keeping pace with her enthusiasm, "that the only way to restore *me* is for thee to remain at the sea, having thrown care into Walden Pond." [20]

On his return she was to discover, once again, that nothing much had changed, and she had to renew her faith as best she could. Rose and her mother went to Brattleboro, Vermont, to see Peabody cousins, while the older children remained at home with their father. Elizabeth Hawthorne chose to make one of her rare visits during her sister-in-law's absence. In Brattleboro Sophia had a recurrence of bronchitis. "I am homesick," she wrote to Una. "I have had to lie down every afternoon to loosen my bound up brain." Elizabeth Hawthorne, for unknown reasons, remained at the Wayside for several weeks following Sophia's return. She went her own way, staying in her room until dinner. In order not to annoy her, Sophia's sisters called in the morning. If Elizabeth Hawthorne unsettled Sophia, Una managed to annoy her aunt. She rowed her father and her aunt across Walden Pond and "when we were in the middle of it," Elizabeth reported, "told me that it was a most dangerous place."[21]

The only one of the children without problems may have been Julian, who seemingly with little difficulty adjusted himself to life at Sanborn's school. Even ten-year-old Rose had a bill of complaints. She informed Annie Fields that she had "a very pretty doll" and other amusements, "but it seems so desolate to play alone that I never play with my play things now." In a postscript Sophia added, "This is quite a melancholy cry for companionship," and she noted that Rose had "*one* playmate when she can come to see her." Sophia perhaps never thought of taking her daughter to the other child's home. Ironically, parents sensitive to loneliness in life as well as in art—Sophia had illustrated "The Gentle Boy"— had seemingly little awareness of the needs of their own children.[22]

In early 1862 Hawthorne had a "Roman cold" and was, as he admitted, "not very well, being mentally and physically languid." Horatio Bridge, who now served in the naval offices in Washington, suggested that Hawthorne spend time there in order to become acquainted with the war effort and to find diversion from life at Concord. Hawthorne was responsive, hoping, with some of Sophia's faith, that "the trip and change of scene might supply the energy which I lack." Unwilling or maybe afraid to travel unaccompanied, he persuaded Ticknor to join him, which meant to take charge of everything. As Ticknor informed his wife, "He has no care. He leaves the entire business part with me. If he wants a pair of gloves I pay for them. . . . He says this is the only way he can travel with comfort, and it is no trouble to me."[23]

The two men traveled leisurely with stops in New York and Philadelphia, and by the time they reached the latter city Hawthorne felt "perfectly well" and had "a great appetite." Soon he was caught up in the restless energy and exciting tensions of Washington. He went to Fort Monroe with Bridge, made two excursions to the headquarters of General McClellan and the battlefields in Virginia, attended sessions of Congress occasionally, and met President Lincoln. He was photographed by Mathew Brady and sat for a portrait by Emanuel Leutze, the celebrated painter of *Washington Crossing the Delaware*, who shortly after the appearance of *The Scarlet Letter* did a painting of Hester and Pearl. Hawthorne enjoyed Leutze's jolly approach to portraiture. At the beginning of the sitting Hawthorne received "a first-rate cigar," and when he got tired the artist brought out "a bottle of splendid champagne!" One day in April the sitting turned into "a blessed state of mutual good-will, for three hours and a half, during which the picture made a really miraculous progress." The conviviality did not result in a great portrait.[24]

Hawthorne stayed on in Washington even after Ticknor left to take care of business elsewhere, but he was sheltered and looked after by the Bridges, who understood the demands of his moods. After a month he informed Sophia, "It has done me a great deal of good, this constant activity of mind and body; but being perfectly well, I no longer need it as a medicine." When he returned to Concord improved in spirits and health, the family was, in Sophia's phrase, "in a state of full pœan." Rose burst out in an "original song" based on the tune of "John Brown's Body," much to the convulsive enjoyment of all the Hawthornes—"just so crazy with joy are we."[25]

The Hawthornes, it sometimes seemed, had returned to watch over the disintegration of the Union, which, as matters turned out, was a backdrop for but not a cause of Hawthorne's disintegration, although Sophia's sisters as usual held another opinion. Hawthorne tried to assume his customary role of the impassive observer of "the Union in its death-throes" and in December 1860 was "ashamed to say how little I care about the matter," a statement which was only partly true intellectually and almost completely false emotionally, for when hostilities broke out he seethed with excitement. He was of the opinion, which did not change, that the North and the South should be separate political entities. "We do not belong together," he declared; "the Union is unnatural, a scheme of man, not an ordinance of God." At the beginning of the war in April 1861 he rejoiced, or so he said, that "the old Union is smashed. We never were one people, and never really had a country since the Constitution was formed." He remained convinced that "amputation" was the better plan and that "all we ought to fight for is, the liberty of selecting the point where our diseased members should be lopt off. I would fight to the death for the Northern slave-states, and let the rest go." The emotionally charged diction was at odds with his supposed intellectual neutrality.[26]

"The war, strange to say," he confessed to Bridge, "has had a beneficial effect upon my spirits, which were flagging woefully before it broke out. But it was delightful to share in the heroic sentiment of the time, and to feel that I had a country—a consciousness which seemed to make me young again." He regretted that he was "too old to shoulder a musket" and rejoiced that Julian was too young. "But as the case stands," he wrote with reluctance, "I shall keep quiet till the enemy gets within a mile of my own house." The shadows of his moods shifting between letters, he was ready "to shoulder a musket" and lamented that the "invigorating" effect of the war had begun "to lose its influence. But it is rather unreasonable to wish my countrymen to kill one another for the sake of refreshing my pallid spirits; so I shall pray for peace." [27]

Two months later he had "little heart for anything." He claimed that people had "a very misty idea" of what they were fighting for, although the confusion may have been his own. At the same time he was "thoroughly aroused" by the "boundless" enthusiasm he observed among American youths. He wrote in the cadences of Whitman: "When I hear their drums beating, and see their banners flying, and witness their steady marching, I declare, were it not for certain silvery monitors hanging by my temples, suggesting prudence, I feel as if I could catch the infection, shoulder a musket, and be off to the war myself!" As he wrote, fantasy took over. "I truly regret," he informed Bright, "that my youth was not cast in these days, instead of in a quiet time." [28]

As he continued "meditating" on the strife, he concluded that "no man should go to war under fifty years of age, such men having already had their natural share of worldly pleasures, and life's enjoyments. And I don't see how they could make a more creditable or more honourable exit from the world's stage than by becoming food for powder, and gloriously dying in defense of their home and country." He claimed that Emerson was "breathing slaughter, like all the rest of us," and that "all sorts of theoretical nonsense" had vanished "in the strong atmosphere which we now inhale." Men were "more natural and sensible," walked "more erect," and cared less "about childish things. If the war only lasts long enough (and not too long) it will have done us infinite good." [29]

Following his stay in Washington in the spring of 1862, Hawthorne wrote an extended account of his reactions to the war at the suggestion of Fields, who was now editor of the *Atlantic Monthly*. In his article entitled "Chiefly about War Matters By a Peaceable Man," Hawthorne deliberately pursued a duplicitous course. He inserted what he called "very loyal" footnotes because in the text "I found it quite difficult not to lapse into treason continually; but I made manful resistance to the temptation." When the article was published, there was no indication that the "Peaceable Man" had indulged in a juggling act by means of notes which appeared to have been inserted by the editor. When one reader learned of this tactic, he was supposed to have commented, "Then I have no respect for a man who runs with the hare, and hunts with the hounds!"[30]

Before submitting the manuscript, Hawthorne informed Fields that he "half-spoilt it by leaving out a great deal of spicy description and remarks and whole pages of freely expressed opinions, which seemed to be as good as anything I every wrote, but which I doubted whether the public would bear." Then he added, "The remainder is tame enough in all conscience, and I don't think it will bear any more castration." When Fields insisted on alterations in the account of "Uncle Abe," itself a tasteless and hostile epithet, Hawthorne, finding it impossible to make changes, decided to "omit the only part of the article really worth publishing." Almost in self-pity Hawthorne commented, "What a terrible thing it is to try to let off a little bit of truth into this miserable humbug of a world!" Fields's fears about the reception of the article were confirmed when the *Atlantic Monthly* received "cruel and terrible notes."[31]

This piece by a self-styled "Peaceable Man" understandably confused readers. Burdened with his double vision, Hawthorne established neither a unifying purpose nor a consistent tone. He perceived the Manassas battlefield as "thickest thronged with ugly phantoms, ominous of mischief through ages beforehand." Sixty thousand men crossed the Potomac into "the Virginia mud," and "the phantasmagory of a countless host and impregnable ramparts . . . dissolved quite away." John Bunyan and other writers of romance colored Hawthorne's account of the Civil War, as in this passage: "It was as if General McClellan had thrust his sword into a gigantic enemy, and, beholding him suddenly collapse, had punctured an enormously swollen bladder."

When the "Peaceable Man" wrote about soldiers, Hawthorne reiterated statements in his letters in a strange mixture of idealism glorifying the brotherhood achieved in battle, about which he knew nothing from personal experience, and realistic awareness of how war satisfies destructive urges and how quickly men of peace, when armed, are ready to kill. "The enervating effects of centuries of civilization," he observed, "vanish at once, and leave these young men to enjoy a life of hardship, and the exhilarating sense of danger,—to kill men blamelessly, or to be killed gloriously,—and to be happy in following out their native instincts of destruction, precisely in the spirit of Homer's heroes." At the end of the passage Hawthorne's skepticism reasserted itself: "It is so odd, when we measure our advances from barbarism, and find ourselves just here." He added in the accompanying note: "We hardly expected this outbreak in favor of war from the Peaceable Man; but the justice of our cause makes us all soldiers at heart, however quiet in our outward life."

Hawthorne seized on his visit to the building at Harper's Ferry in which John Brown was imprisoned to comment on an act which provoked fierce disagreement. No admirer of Brown, he referred to a sage who maintained that Brown "made the Gallows as venerable as the Cross!" Then he stated without equivocation: "Nobody was ever more justly hanged. He won his martyrdom fairly, and took it firmly. . . . any common-sensible man, looking at the matter unsentimentally, must have felt a certain intellectual satisfaction in seeing him hanged, if it were only in requital of his preposterous miscalculations of possibilities." Hawthorne fully understood how his remarks would rankle, for in the note he asked: "Can it be a son of old Massachusetts who utters this abominable sentiment? For shame."

He was also needlessly provocative in his discussion of blacks. Although Hawthorne had almost no exposure to blacks, he concluded that southern blacks were "more agreeable" than northern ones, "so picturesquely natural in manners, and wearing such a crust of primeval simplicity (which is quite polished away from the northern black man), that they seemed a kind of creature by themselves, not altogether human, but perhaps quite as good, and akin to the fauns and rustic deities of olden times." After such sentiments he alleged that "whoever may be benefited by the results of this war, it will not be the present generation of negroes, the childhood of whose race is now gone forever, and who must henceforth fight a hard battle with the world, on very unequal terms." Although Hawthorne's prognostication proved true, he chose the wrong time and place to introduce such speculation.

The last word was placed in a note in which he averred that the war must end "in the complete triumph of Northern principles." Hawthorne was sorry "to cast a doubt on the Peaceable Man's loyalty" but suggested that he was "premature in his kindly feelings towards traitors and sympathizers with treason."

Fields was right: the passage on "Uncle Abe," giving and withholding praise in Hawthorne's characteristic pattern, was scarcely appropriate at a time when the Union was losing the war.

The whole physiognomy is as coarse a one as you would meet any-where in the length and breadth of the States; but, withal, it is re-deemed, illuminated, softened, and brightened by a kindly though serious look out of his eyes, and an expression of homely sagacity, that seems weighted with rich results of village experience. A great deal of native sense; no bookish cultivation, no refinement; honest at heart, and thoroughly so, and yet, in some sort, sly,—at least en-dowed with a sort of tact and wisdom that are akin to craft, and would impel him, I think, to take an antagonist in flank, rather than to make a bull-run at him right in front. But, on the whole, I like this sallow, queer, sagacious visage, with the homely human sympathies that warmed it; and, for my small share in the matter, would as lief have Uncle Abe for a ruler as any man whom it would have been practicable to put in his place.

"Chiefly about War Matters" confirmed the doubleness of Hawthorne's vision, but his familiar ambivalence afforded him a kind of cowardly pro-tection and freedom from commitment, his seesawing and evasiveness pleasing no one, probably not even himself. If at times his remarks bor-dered on the frivolous, an accusation Zenobia makes about Coverdale in *The Blithedale Romance*, he was personally as divided as the Union. He wanted for the Union and, above all, for himself "a quiet household."

Early in August 1862, Hawthorne admitted to a corre-spondent that since his return from England his health had "not been so good as formerly" but provided no details. On August 5 he went with Julian to Gouldsboro, Maine, much to the son's delight: "Papa and I carry on continual war with those peculiar green mulberry looking objects. . . . As far as I can see, peace will not be declared until the ammunition is consumed, and that time must be far distant." Hawthorne's playful spirit reappeared, and he bantered with his sixteen-year-old son, who was so elated that he wrote a sixteen-page letter to his mother.[32]

They returned to Concord early in September, and Sophia informed Una that Hawthorne's appetite was poor: he "eats no dinners except a little potato. But he is trying to write and locks himself into the library and pulls down the curtains." Sophia loyally refrained from comment on his behavior. In November she suffered an attack of her "old English bronchitis" and was "dumb and feverish" for about four weeks. Hawthorne was too ill in December to submit an article on England to the *Atlantic Monthly*, but by the end of the year he was in better spirits. "Lately," Sophia wrote to Annie Fields, "that exquisite frolic—which is natural to him—gleams out again at times—and no music is so sweet to my ear and no sunshine so golden to my eye." [33]

Despite Hawthorne's desire, the household at the Wayside was not "quiet." He himself was a cause of concern: his deteriorating health and his extended periods of depression aroused anxieties. He apparently retreated to the library or to the tower, where he struggled without success to regain the powers of the magician of romance. Sophia's lot was not easy, though it was in large part of her own making. She lived in her idealization of the family, in the role of model mother surrounded by model children. They, however, refused to remain children, preferring earthly to angelic status and peer relationships to an ambience of verbal superlatives and wide-eyed adoration. Sophia overloved, partly, it is true, to satisfy her own needs, and in the process exposed herself to hurts. She learned from one of the Alcott girls that Una was to be away for a month. "I felt mortified," she informed her daughter, but everything was quickly forgiven later in the month: "One more whole day now only before you return. Jubilate!" The children knew, as did the husband, that whatever they did would be forgiven. Such was Sophia's desperation to maintain her "sphere." [34]

Her illnesses seemed to increase, and psychosomatic disorders like those of her adolescence recurred. She tried, so she said, to keep her family ignorant of her physical state, although she may have used illness for her own ends. On one occasion Sophia informed Una, who was in Rockport, Massachusetts, with her father, that she had coughed until she thought all her "blood vessels would literally burst. . . . Oh I was thankful that Papa could not hear me! nor you." In an earlier letter she made no attempt to conceal her uneasiness while they were away and she was abandoned in Concord. "I sit here," she informed Una, "and listen to all kinds of strange noises. There seems to be somebody in the chimney, and I momentarily expect the rebels to break in and rob and slay. The furniture or something is all cracking and moving out in the dining room and kitchen." [35]

She needed an ideal female or maternal figure as well as a masculine or paternal one. She found shrines to worship, and supports for her dependency, in Annie Fields and General Ethan Allen Hitchcock.

Annie Fields was the cousin of James T. Fields's first wife, who accompanied Hawthorne and Melville to Monument Mountain on August 5, 1850, and died of tuberculosis in the following year. Annie was twenty when she married Fields, who was thirty-seven. A beautiful woman, a poet of sorts, and a friend of artists, she transformed her home at 148 Charles Street in Boston into a famous literary salon. Sophia met her for the first time on the voyage to America in 1860, and after their return to the Wayside the Hawthornes, particularly the daughters, stayed at times with Annie, who had no children of her own. Soon the two women established one of those passionate friendships characteristic of the nineteenth century. Fields, a poet himself and a kind of dandy, declared that his wife had fallen "in love with Mrs. Hawthorne and it does her a world of good to go to Concord." As he wrote, he recalled his own visit to the Wayside—"of our couch on the grass and the young voices singing to the river as we lay in the cool shadows. It was all very lovely, & I do not forget such happy thrills as you gave me and mine of real delight." He spoke of "Childe Hawthorne" and sent "our kindest love to all the dwellers in the Wayside Paradise."[36]

Sophia hardly needed Fields's encouragement or example to elevate husband and wife to royal status. She addressed him variously as "Prince James" or "Heart's Ease." He "must not be jealous" because she called Annie "my darling" in her salutation, for, she assured him with childish naïveté, "I do not intrude on his kingdom." Everybody, it would appear, was expected to enjoy verbal charades and platonic eroticism. She advised him that "it is pleasant to be able and desirous to behave like the gods. It is not every man who can sit down in a comfortable chair in a green library, wrapped in a velvet coat, folding inside his breast a royal heart, worthy of being the Lord's stewart." To imagine the obese Fields wrapped in velvet and overflowing in a chair was, depending upon point of view, impressive or ludicrous but wonderful Sophiana.[37]

Fields provided an ample royal backdrop for the beautiful Annie, who became to Sophia "my dear Moonlight" or the "naughty little invisible Peri." The Fields's house was now Sophia's "bower of Eden." On her visits she carefully stayed out of Annie's way: "You need not lose or defer any purpose for me, but go on just as if I were not in the world." The abasement as well as the extravagant language of the suitor apparently proved at times too much for Annie. Sophia accused "the naughty little Peri" of "taking care not to leave your address, so as to be sure not [to] be spoken to for a whole month." Annie was advised that she could "not escape, however, for I shall send this to Mr. Ticknor."[38]

Undeterred by Annie's attempts to curb her ardor, Sophia wrote in praise of "those deep dark stars of eyes, so absorbent of beauty & rich with poetry—crowned with the untameable coronet of shadowy brown gold hair."

> I *will* say just what I choose and you must hear it as you can. For how absurd for me to have these facts on the tip of my pen, and from a foolish conventional reticence, refrain from letting them crystallize on the paper, when I wish to do so. When folk are beautiful, why should the mirror alone have the satisfaction of telling folk? . . . You will therefore understand me when I refer to your beauty, and not feel personally attacked. I will endeavor never to speak of it in presence—but my pen shall have its own way, and enjoy itself as much as it can.

Toward the conclusion of this ten-page letter Sophia declared herself "so immensely meek that I can always put myself out of the question with ease," which referred to a moonlight walk taken by Hawthorne and Annie without her. She had Plato's *Phaedo* at her side as she wrote and anticipated reading it aloud with Annie.[39]

The friendship continued after the death of Hawthorne when more than ever Sophia needed Annie, but Sophia's passion proved an embarrassment. "Do not you know," she wrote in all innocence, "I like to see you dressed in your bravest, though I love to see you as well in undress." Sophia felt herself "united to immortal youth," meaning perhaps her three children or perhaps Annie. Eventually Fields intruded to check Sophia's ardor as kindly as he could, and Annie was not at home or too busy to see Sophia. It was more than Sophia could bear—"this endless separation." She poured out her love as well as her hurt:

> Annie, I love you.
> I wish to see you.
> I wish to hear you.
> Do you remember me at all, I wonder?
> Am I a tale that is told?[40]

Sophia accepted Fields's authority: she had no alternative. "No turtle dove," she lamented, "was more constant than I . . . Annie and I have drifted away from the lake of ink but we are united in a purple and gold lake of air and sun forever." And as always Sophia found compensation in that extraordinary verbal facility which might seem implausible and unreal in the pages of a romance but which provided her with a fragile defense against the pains and disappointments of existence. Sophia was not to know that after Fields's death in 1881 Annie and Sarah Orne Jewett were to live together for almost three decades in a so-called Boston marriage.[41]

In August 1862, while Hawthorne and Julian were vacationing in Maine, Sophia met General Ethan Allen Hitchcock and was overwhelmed when at parting the general said, "I am very sorry I could not see more of you," a remark which she characterized as "my plum cake of solace." A few weeks later, still during Hawthorne's absence, Hitchcock spent an hour at the Wayside in the drawing room decorated with roses, dahlias, and tiger lilies which, she declared, "looked lovelily." Here "I received my General. The most beautiful light of life beamed from his face at my recognition of his ideas, and at any expression of mine which showed a unity with his; or rather with truth." On Hitchcock's departure Una said, "Mama, you look perfectly transfigured!" The meeting was, it turned out, a kind of epiphany in Sophia's life. "We do love to be commanded when the Potentate has legitimate powers." For the next five years the general was her "Potentate." Transported by her words and fantasies, she troubled not at all for the moment about that other potentate, her husband, but consistency never crossed her affections: she could not abide disappointment.[42]

Hitchcock had in addition to great personal magnetism, at least in Sophia's adoring eyes, three significant attributes: he was a soldier of high rank who had returned to active duty during the Civil War; he espoused a mysticism based idiosyncratically upon Swedenborg, medieval alchemy, and other sources; and he interpreted Dante, Spenser, and Shakespeare according to his mystical illuminations. Above all, he supplied a need during a period in which her husband retreated into a world from which she was often excluded. She perhaps fulfilled Hitchcock's need for adulation, for it would have been a simple matter on his part not to reply to her letters. He, however, kept them. On the envelope of one he noted: "Preserves her enthusiasm. She is sincere—Of course I do not take to myself all Mrs. H seems disposed to attribute to me," although in his replies he did not reprove her adulation.[43]

In her first letter to Hitchcock, twelve pages in length, she wrote of the peace and understanding that had come over her. "I am sure that for all eternity I hold your hand, and that wherever you are I can never lose you." His writings provided "a glimpse of the Paradise of God. You are my St. Peter and hold the key. . . . You hold the magic wand that puts everything in its place and you offer it to all men to educe Eternal Order out of apparent confusion." Her "chalice" overflowed, as did her unknowingly erotic language. "I have not been able sufficiently to thank God for my felicity in my destiny as wife and mother, and now I have a friend whom I believe to be 'of the kingdom of God.'"[44]

Sophia's relationship with Hitchcock, which was primarily epistolary, permitted release of religious and mystical feelings pent up since her marriage. For years in conformity with Hawthorne's practice she had only rarely attended religious services, and at the Wayside she conducted a Sunday school for her own children and a few (selected) neighbor children. What she had bottled up she now poured forth in her letters, her nature being, as she declared, "very demonstrative and ardent." She did not mail many of the letters, the act of writing itself providing relief. A year after their first meeting General Hitchcock had become "diaphanous—such a crystal medium of Truth, that my enthusiasm for you, my great affection and reverence for you seem to me a love of Truth itself." Hitchcock had increased in stature in her eyes and was accordingly elevated transcendentally: "I can see the Sages who sit in the circles of the just look upon one another with immortal smiles as they recognize you as at last the man who can pierce through all their signs to the thing signified."[45]

After Hawthorne's death she clung to Hitchcock and occasionally had to retreat before her own excesses and tear up a letter because "it was so flaming I feared it would astonish you." Another time she commented, "If you received all the letters I write you in my mind, your cabinets could not contain them." After Sophia approved Hitchcock's explications of Shakespeare's sonnets—he too accepted the Bacon thesis—she wrote, "I place you and Lord Bacon at the top of the world. You as the most efficient Guide to the Life. Lord Bacon as the leader to the relief of man's estate here below." (Hitchcock commented on the envelope, "Her enthusiasm places me very high.") When she was considering residence in Germany after Hawthorne's death in order to conserve her dwindling resources, she planned to take along the writings of Plato, Shakespeare, and Hitchcock. She forgot to mention her husband. Again she reminded the general of her temperament. "Have you patience," she urged, "with my ardor, dear friend,—you must surely understand how I cannot be moderate in my joy and gratitude—and will you remember that I was born an enthusiast and cannot outgrow my nature. I would not tear a passion to tatters—but I must flame to the end."[46]

For many months in 1867 and 1868 Sophia was seriously ill and could not write. When she resumed her correspondence on June 7, 1868, she explained, "I was face to face with what we call Death so long that mortal life seems strange to me, and I come back with a calm surprise. I am glad to stay here longer for the sake of my children, though, for my own sake, the prospect of the other side was very sweet and peaceful." Early in 1868 Hitchcock at seventy married for the first time. Sophia offered her "sincere and joyful congratulations" to "the fortunate wife of the noblest, most refined, chivalrous and tender heart, as well as of the profound philosopher and original thinker."[47]

Apparently this was the last letter Sophia wrote to General Hitchcock. He or perhaps his wife, who may have had to protect her husband against the ardors he aroused in the hearts of women like Sophia, informed her that he could neither advise nor help her. "We have lost him," Sophia wrote. About the same time she lost faith in Fields: once a very prince and the husband of the woman who had helped her through trying years, he became in her pained eyes a conniving publisher who had, she thought, cheated her of royalties. It became difficult, impossible in fact, for Sophia to "flame to the end."

The Crack-up
The Unfinished Romances

If Hawthorne had been granted his wish, he would have undertaken no other romances after the enormous success of *The Marble Faun*. In his notebook he complained of the strain this work had imposed upon his physical and emotional resources, and he may have been prescient when he said, "It is not wholesome for me to write." What he meant perhaps was that as he aged and inevitably repeated himself, his repetitions would reveal what he had hidden for years behind the artfully constructed veils. The good Mr. Hooper does not allow the black veil which he assumes as punishment of an unspecified "secret sin" to be raised even on his deathbed. As a result his actions and sin are subject to multiple interpretations and misconstructions. Hawthorne himself spent a lifetime seducing readers into misreading his tales by means of veils while he almost compulsively made public confession, as Arthur Dimmesdale does Sunday after Sunday in his pulpit but so ambiguously—A may signify ambiguity—that his candor charms and even seduces parishioners. This was a game, even perhaps an art, in which the shy Hawthorne was most adept.[1]

Despite his denials, Hawthorne knew he was writing an autobiography which only a few readers would recognize. In *The Marble Faun* Miriam speaks for Hawthorne when she observes that in her drawings appear "ugly phantoms that stole out of my mind; not things I created, but things that haunt me." Kenyon also speaks for the author, and his precipitous retreat after the creation of a sensuous Cleopatra to the seeming security of the chaste, maternal Hilda, who will enfold him in the family circle, reflects Hawthorne's abiding distrust of art and his obeisance, though reluctant, to the dicta of the Hathorne ancestors. Although the possibilities of ful-fillment through family ties and bonds are broached in "The Artist of the Beautiful," *The House of the Seven Gables*, and *The Marble Faun*, he was acutely aware that such dreams are often bubbles and that the "ugly phantoms" cannot be banished by transforming an impotent rooster into a fertility symbol.[2]

At the Wayside he was never unaware of his own unsettled state and the foolishness of his belief that the physical transformation of the old Concord farmhouse would effect other changes. His own health and Una's were daily preoccupations, and there was turmoil, as we have seen, in the family. Sophia was losing control of her children. Because of her con-suming love and her own insecurity, she refused to allow the usual matu-ration process to proceed and imposed a code that was, despite her inten-tions, almost abusive. She had to summon to her assistance not only her two sisters, who never outgrew their sibling rivalry, but also outsiders like Annie Fields and General Hitchcock. Una's precarious health and emotional instability tried the family sorely, particularly Sophia, for daughter and mother were locked into a rivalry which was never to be resolved: they could live neither with nor without each other. Signifi-cantly, the Wayside was never characterized as a second Eden.

Despite Hawthorne's hesitancy and fears at the prospect of lifting veils and unleashing the ugly phantoms, he had no alternative but to retreat to the new "castle dismal," the study in a pseudo-Italianate tower, which was to become almost a torture chamber of self-flagellation. The profits realized during the Liverpool days and the success of his last romance notwithstanding, the Hawthornes were in need of funds to support their impractical life-style. For him there was also the prospect of the dreaded almshouse: Concord had its replica of the inadequate nineteenth-century welfare institution. Further, the economic crisis probably evoked the re-current sense of failure which Horatio Bridge tried to cope with while they were Bowdoin classmates and later in 1836 when Hawthorne melo-dramatically voiced suicidal despair, no doubt in exquisite prose.

Late in 1854 Hawthorne described what he labeled a "singular dream," not because he was experiencing it for the first time—he was well acquainted with it "these twenty or thirty years"—but because it recurred "when I may call myself famous, and prosperous!—and when I am happy too!" Of this rather commonplace anxiety dream he wrote, "I am still at college—or, sometimes, even at School—and there is a sense that I have been there unconscionably long, and have quite failed to make such progress in life as my contemporaries have; and I seem to meet some of them with a feeling of shame and depression that broods over me, when I think of it, even at this moment." He explained the dream as "one of the effects of that heavy seclusion in which I shut myself up, for twelve years, after leaving college, when everybody moved onward and left me behind." The same world-weariness and despair appeared in 1858 in his Italian journal: "The same impatience I sometimes feel, or conceive of, as regards this earthly life; since it is to come to an end, I do not try to be contented, but weary of it while it lasts."[3]

Over the Hawthorne landscape hovers what has been called "suicide of wish." Fanshawe, Ilbrahim, and Dimmesdale seek to escape from a world that does not not accommodate their needs. The effete Clifford toys with suicide from the balcony on which he blows his immortal soap bubbles. Hester in her isolation briefly contemplates suicide, but, unlike the others, she has inner resources, including a qualified faith in the future. Zenobia takes her life, defiant of humanity and God to the end. The four principal characters of *The Marble Faun* in their various dissatisfactions with their lives experience in fantasy Brother Antonio's fall from the parapet.[4]

The unfinished works of the last years were anticipated in "The Ancestral Footstep" and like it had to be abandoned after months of futile efforts. Hawthorne began the tale one day in Rome when he decided to restrict his sightseeing in order to compose a romance based on a haunting tale he heard after his arrival in England. A stone outside the entrance of an English manor was said to resemble in shape and color a bloody footstep, and occupants of the house were consumed by anomalous desires, lusts, and rivalries which led to at least one murder and the flight of a member of the family to America. The protagonist, Middleton, like Hawthorne, goes to England "to trace out the signs of Eve's bridal bower, the birth-place of the human race and all its glorious possibilities of happiness and high performance," only to find himself in a dreamlike state in which perspectives shift sometimes dizzily as if he is "recognizing the scenery and events of a former dream." He learns of a sordid feud between brothers and the theft of the older brother's wife. Accidentally (but perhaps inevitably, given the nature of the fantasies being unveiled), he kills an Englishman, we are told with startling and mysterious precision, at 5:21 P.M.[5]

Hawthorne fumbled for focus and purpose. "I have not yet struck," he wrote evasively, "the true key-note of this Romance, and until I do, I shall write nothing but tediousness and nonsense. I do not wish it to be a picture of life; but a Romance, grim, grotesque, quaint. . . . If I could but write one central scene in this vein, all the rest of the Romance would readily arrange itself around that nucleus. . . . It must be a humorous work, or nothing." After six weeks of frustration he became convinced that he could not find the "nucleus" or the "key." The last entries in the manuscript were dated May 19, 1858, which by one of those coincidences in Hawthorne's life was the anniversary of his father's birth and near the fiftieth anniversary of his death and may point to the oedipal material which John Lamont finds at the center of the work.[6]

When he began to write again in 1860 or early in the following year, instead of seeking new subject matter he took up "The Ancestral Footstep," although he wanted, as he confessed in one of his authorial intrusions, to avoid the circular journey back to his personal and artistic past and inevitable repetition:

> . . . it is very curious to see what turnings up there are in this world of old circumstances that seemed buried forever; how things come back, like echoes that have rolled away among the hills and been seemingly hushed forever. We cannot tell when a thing is really dead: it comes to life, perhaps in its old shape, perhaps in a new and unexpected one: so that nothing really vanishes out of the world. I wish it did.

His wish was not granted: he could not silence the echoes of "the irrevocable years" which he recorded for the first time in the pages of "Alice Doane's Appeal" when Leonard recalls the murder of his father.[7]

Like Reuben Bourne in "Roger Malvin's Burial" or Ethan Brand, Hawthorne made a circular journey when he decided to place the tale in Salem in the three-story frame house at the edge of the Charter Street Burying Point, which, the narrator comments, "might almost be called his natal spot." In two of the three romances which he was to attempt in his last years, it was Ilbrahim revisited. The children are orphans experiencing the anxieties associated with the loss of parental love and protection. The territory behind, not the territory ahead, loomed over Hawthorne threateningly. Still grieving, he continued to perceive himself as the abandoned son.

The familiar locale and story line instead of solving his artistic problems probably compounded them since the temptation to draw upon his own life experiences became almost irresistible. Hundreds and hundreds of pages followed with corrections, interpolations, exclamations of frustration, and unanswerable questions as to plot, characterization, and motivation. Names of characters changed, sometimes within a few pages. In the daytime he pronounced the material nonsensical. At nighttime the veil of seeming nonsense was raised and the truth laid bare: " . . . there seem to be things that I can almost get hold of, and think about; but when I am just on the point of seizing them, they start away, like slippery things."

"The Ancestral Footstep" became "Etherege" and at last "Grimshawe," the name of the guardian of two orphans, as Hawthorne toyed and speculated, following one false lead after another. "The story must not be founded at all on remorse or secret guilt—all that I've worn out. Alas me!" Hawthorne wondered whether one character should be "a friend of Swedenborg? A man with Medea's secret? There is a latent something lying hereabouts, which, could I grip it, 'twould be the making of the story." He continued asking himself questions, talking to himself: "It seems as if there were something almost within my grasp—not quite." The character, it turns out, "shall have come into possession of some terrible secret." Then he asked, "What shall it be that has made him and his ancestors anathema for so many ages?" and answered with the illogicality of *Alice's Adventures in Wonderland*: "Why don't you have oysters? Don't know, can't tell." One idea after another was rejected: "Twon't do. . . . I don't in the least see my way. . . . Nothing seems to do." If at times Hawthorne was witty about the blocks that he encountered in writing his romance, wit was the only defense he had left against the almost overwhelming sense of failure which confirmed the recurrent dream.[8]

In "Grimshawe" he unveiled a double self-portrait: Ned, the Ilbrahim of the tale, is the young Nat Hawthorne, and Grimshawe—the name it-self evokes Fanshawe as well as Hawthorne—is in broad outlines the artist in his last years, weary of life, darkly depressed, and almost mor-bidly concerned because of his inability to articulate or to demonstrate his deep feelings for human connections, particularly with his "children," his wards Ned and Elsie.

Nowhere in his writings is Hawthorne more narcissistic than in his depiction of Ned. He is a "beautiful, grave boy of brown cast, slender with his white brow, and dark, thoughtful eyes, so earnest upon some mysterious theme." He is an "intelligent, refined boy. With such a high bred air, handling common things with so refined a touch, yet grasping them so firmly; throwing a natural grace on all he did." He is "not demon-strative," not knowing in the absence of parental figures, particularly a substitute mother, "what to do to show his feelings." Ned's beautiful face changes color constantly, "always answering to the emotions of the mo-ment." At ten, we are told, he is "healthy, but pale; something there was . . . that made him look as if he was growing up in a shadow, with less sunshine than he needed for a robust and exuberant development. . . . He lived far too much an inward life for healthfulness, at his age." Like Hawthorne in his youth, Ned has no male playmates; his only companion is Elsie, the self-effacing half-sister fashioned probably after Elizabeth Hawthorne, who shares "the same dream-scenery."[9]

Inside the unpretentious house at the edge of the cemetery where Hawthorne wooed Sophia Peabody, Dr. Grimshawe sits in a cluttered, filthy study, comforted by his "black bottle" and surrounded by spiders. Hovering threateningly over his head is an extraordinarily large, awe-some spider filled with poison. The spider is "an emblem of the Doctor himself," the narrator informs us, and the boys in the neighborhood taunt him: "Doctor Grim, Doctor Grim! The devil wove a web for him."

In the popular imagination the spider has always been of the devil's party. Traditionally spiders have been perceived as spinners of silk, em-broiderers like Arachne, the great weaver of mythology whom Athena turned into a spider. Of this monster over his head, Grimshawe, speaking for Hawthorne, observes: "I have learned from his web how to weave a plot, and how to catch my victim and devour him!" Hawthorne perceived the association between the spider and the artist whose embroideries can have ambiguous or destructive effects through artistic entrapment and seductive decoration. "A great deal," he noted, "must be made out of the spiders, and their gloomy, dusky, flaunting tapestry," which, he could have added, resembles the ambience of this romance. But, as might be expected, he failed to amplify the motif.

Ned replicates Hawthorne's childhood ordeals, while Grimshawe is "a grown-up child, with the exceptions of lost simplicity and innocence, and refined evil," and is given to extreme swings of mood, to acting out without the usual controls of his years. "He would burst forth in wild diatribes and anathemas, having a strange, rough force of expression, and a depth of utterance, as if his words came from a bottomless pit within himself, where burned an everlasting fire, and where the furies had their home, and plans of dire revenge were welded into shape in the heat of a furnace." He seethes in rage, in "continual enmity against somebody," meaning no doubt himself. Hawthorne in life rarely vented his rage, although his son, in an unguarded moment in the pages of his hagiography, noted his father was "prone, upon occasion, to outbursts of appalling wrath." [10]

When Grimshawe decides to send Ned off to boarding school, the three members of the family are heartbroken. "Oh, how cold the world is!" Ned exclaims. "Would we three—the Doctor, and Elsie, and I—could have lain down in a row, in the old grave yard close under the eaves of the house—and let the grass grow over us." In fantasy Hawthorne was burying himself next to John Hathorne in that row of his ancestors. The passage also summons up "light-clad" Ilbrahim leaning "his face upon a hillock of fresh-turned and half-frozen earth," the grave of his father: "The autumn wind wandered among the branches, whirling away the leaves from all except the pine-trees, and moaning as if it lamented the desolation of which it was the instrument." When Ned repeats "the world is cold; and I am an almshouse child," Hawthorne recalled his visit to the English workhouse where he met and finally, after fastidious reluctance, picked up the scabby child, "the offspring of unspeakable sin and sorrow, whom it must have required several generations of guilty progenitors to render so pitiable an object." [11]

After Ned's departure, Grimshawe is overcome with loneliness and despair: "I will let myself die, therefore, before sunset." He wills his death and is buried in the Charter Street cemetery next to the grave of Dr. John Swinnerton, who was interred there in 1690 at the age of sixty-eight. Swinnerton's grave is near the rear entrance to the house at the edge of the cemetery and faces the row of Hathornes. It is two stones away from the grave of Nathaniel Mather, whose tombstone provided the epitaph for Fanshawe.[12]

At intervals the narrator intrudes upon the rambling, uncertain manuscript to discuss topics that troubled Hawthorne. The narrator observes that in the United States "no man dwells in his father's house" and "no man thinks of dying in his birth-place." At another time he insists: "Posterity! An American can have none." The narrator even raises the overwhelming question which evokes Cronos and Oedipus. "What is the crime?" he asks. "Each son murders his father at a certain age; or does each father try to accomplish the impossibility of murdering his successor?" Perhaps terrified, Hawthorne dropped the speculation—"This is not the right tack"—only to resume it in the next abortive romance.[13]

In one of his most moving passages, Hawthorne wrote with painful candor out of his own experiences and fantasies:

> We speak of the natural force of blood; we speak of the paternal relation as if it were productive of more earnest affection than can exist between two persons, one protective but unrelated; but there are wild, forcible, unrestricted characters, on whom the necessity and even duty of loving their own child is a sort of barrier of love. They perhaps do not love their own traits, which they recognize in their children; they shrink from their own features in the reflection presented by those little mirrors.

It would appear that Hawthorne himself, during the gyrations of his ambivalences, shrank from "those little mirrors" of his three children and, unknowingly, replayed Tobias Pearson's guilt-ridden relationship with Ilbrahim.[14]

Late in 1861 or early in the following year Hawthorne put aside the manuscript and confirmed his failure to weave the tale into a tapestry. Imprisoned in autobiography and circles of repetition, he found it too painful to continue. In a gracefully balanced passage—even in the gloom of failure his prose, as though it had a life of its own, rarely faltered—Hawthorne recognized that he stood at a threshold.

> Some strange, vast, sombre, mysterious truth, which he seemed to have searched for long, appeared to be on the point of being revealed to him; a sense of something to come; something to happen that had been waiting long, long to happen; an opening of doors, a drawing

away of veils, a lifting of heavy, magnificent curtains, whose dark folds hung before a spectacle of awe;—it was like the verge of the grave.[15]

One day he recalled a tale related to him by Thoreau after he moved into the Wayside. A former occupant of the house, Thoreau informed him, "in some long-past time . . . was resolved never to die. He, at all events, did not mean to make of his earthly abode a mere wayside rest, . . . he would sit there while oaks grew up and decayed; he would always be there." Nothing was known of the "character and history" of the former owner, but elixirs promising eternal life had fascinated Hawthorne despite inner skepticism for many years, as evidenced by an early tale, "Dr. Heidegger's Experiment." The locale now changed from Salem to Concord, but he was too depressed and weary to believe that anything mattered.

> . . . perhaps, however, in the course of lengthened time, we may find that the world is the same always, and mankind the same, and all possibilities of human fortune the same; so that, by and by, we shall discover that the same old scenery serves the world's stage in all ages, and that the story is always the same, yes, and the actors always the same, though none but we may be aware of it; and that the actor and spectators would grow weary of it, were they not bathed in forgetful sleep, and so think themselves new made in each successive lifetime. . . . As dramatists and novelists repeat their plots, so does man's life repeat itself and at length grows stale. This is what in my desponding moments I have sometimes suspected.[16]

As Hawthorne looked out the window of his study in the tower, he saw below him the famous road from Lexington to Concord over which English troops marched when the Revolutionary War began. From the rear of his study he looked up at the hilltop to which he fled when he sought to escape unwanted visitors and where daily he paced, in the words of his neighbor Bronson Alcott, "as if he feared his neighbor's eyes would catch him as he walked." In his journal the day after Hawthorne's funeral Emerson recalled that Hawthorne had said to him, *"this path is the only remembrance of me that will remain."*[17]

As "Septimius Felton" begins to unfold, stumblingly page after page, Septimius walks Hawthorne's path, fearfully and compulsively. At his desk Hawthorne observed and described himself "with his head bent down, brooding, brooding, with his eyes fixed on some chip, some stone, some common plant, any commonest thing, as if it were the clue and index to some mystery; and when, by chance startled out of these meditations, he lifted his eyes, there would be a kind of perplexity, a dissatisfied, wild look in them, as if, of his speculation, he found no end."[18]

Some critics have alleged that in "Septimius Felton" Hawthorne intended to comment on the fratricidal Civil War by means of a historical tale which opens in 1775 when English troops engaged untrained American farmers at the bridge over the Concord River near the Manse. "Our story," he declares, "has for its central object, to record the dreams, or realities, whichever they might be, of a young man who staked whatever prospects he had in life upon a strange pursuit." Hawthorne accepts the "necessity" of alluding to "historic events . . . only because it is unavoidable; not really caring much for anything that took place outside of Septimius's brains. . . . It is but incidentally, therefore, and with the above end in view, that we glance at a great historic incident."[19]

Septimius is a young seminary student undergoing a crisis of faith at the beginning of the Revolutionary War, but this conflict is never explored and has little effect upon the narrative, as Hawthorne, inescapably, depicted with evasions a youth experiencing his own lifelong conflicts. Septimius feels "a vague depression of the spirit, like a vapor settling down a landscape," and suffers the "black death of despair." After Septimius admits to knowledge of "weird ideas, notions, thoughts akin to madness," Hawthorne intrudes in the narrative with personal confirmation of Septimius's anguish:

> In short, it was a moment, such as I suppose all men feel (*at least I can answer for one*) when the real scene and picture of life swims, jars, shakes, seems about to be broken up and dispersed, like the picture in a smooth pond, when we disturb its smooth mirror by throwing in a stone; and though the scene soon settles itself, and looks as real as before, a haunting doubt keeps close at hand, as long as we live, asking—Is it stable? Am I sure of it? Am I certainly not dreaming? See; it trembles again, ready to dissolve.

Here we witness in another beautifully phrased passage Hawthorne's simultaneous terror and fascination in observing his own crack-up.[20]

Day after day Hawthorne, his eyes reflecting his body's weariness, trudged up the stairs to his study with so little enthusiasm and after such procrastination that even Sophia sometimes became impatient. Daily he had to convince himself that a few more paragraphs, a few more pages, would provide him with the "key" that would unlock the romance. Page followed page: there are almost 500 pages in the Centenary Edition of the two manuscripts, "Septimius Felton" and its retelling in "Septimius Norton."

As lifelong associations crossed back and forth across his consciousness, Hawthorne could faintly hear the sounds of his family in the distance, although the children had grown into adolescence adhering to the eleventh commandment, not to disturb "papa." While Sophia moved about stealthily, still frightened after twenty years of marriage, Hawthorne created for Septimius a familial context which like everything else about his romance, including the name of the principal character, remained in a state of flux, no more stable than the dreams the story often resembles.

Septimius is the last of the beautiful youths in Hawthorne's fiction, but his "dark beauty" is marred by "a dark, brooding brow, and eyes that usually seemed looking inward." There is a "perpendicular furrow between the eyebrows" which during the course of his emotional and intellectual disintegration deepens into a "fissure." His split personality is complicated by the introduction of the "monstrousness" of his "hybrid race," Septimius being half-Indian through the intermarriage of an ancestor. His mother died when he was about two, and his father after remarriage died when the boy was four, not long after the birth of a half-sister named Ruth. Here Hawthorne re-created the year 1808 when Louisa's birth preceded by a few months his father's death. Over fifty years later Hawthorne mourned with undiminished anger. Septimius had "no great intimacy" with his father who is termed a "clod," uncharitably but understandably in view of the youth's feeling of abandonment. At some later time Septimius comes to the house which Hawthorne renamed the Wayside, where he lives with his Aunt Keziah, who retains many vestiges of her Indian heritage, including a favorite tin pipe, but is a loving, devoted substitute mother. Septimius attributes his isolation and emotional coldness to the loss of his mother: "It is as if I had not been born of woman." Surely this is a veiled comment on Hawthorne's mother who loved him after her fashion but who could not coddle or touch her son because she was imprisoned in her own cold, inhibited world.

At the beginning of the story Septimius and two friends, Robert Hagburn and Rose Garfield, stand alongside the road before the English troops arrive in Concord. The young men are more or less in love with Rose, although neither has ventured a declaration. English troops appear, and an officer, "a petulant boy, extremely handsome, and of gay and buoyant deportment," Francis Norton, asks Rose, "my pretty," for a cup of water and pats her cheek. When Septimius rebukes him, Norton kisses her and in effect challenges the ministerial student to defend her. Before Septimius can act, the English are on their way.

Septimius is outraged by this assault upon his manhood but is so attracted to the officer, his beauty as well as his aggressiveness, that "somehow or other"—the text fumbling in imitation—he is angry at Rose "for having undergone the wrong," apparently wishing himself in her place.

After the incident Hagburn immediately takes up arms, identifying with his neighbors and his country without reservation or hesitation, but Septimius withdraws to his study to brood. "I am dissevered" from "the human race," he declares. "It is my doom to be only a spectator of life, to look on as one apart from it. . . . How cold I am now, while this whirlpool of public feeling is eddying around me," which also describes Hawthorne's response, at least at times, to the Civil War.

Later in the day Septimius goes stealthily to the hilltop behind the Wayside to observe the movements of the English troops. Suddenly the ministerial student experiences "this deep, wild passion that nature has planted in us, to be the death of our fellow-creatures, and which coexists at the same time with horror." Septimius spies an English officer, "a gray bearded, stalwart old warrior, on horseback," reminiscent of Cotton Mather in "Alice Doane's Appeal," the two-faced apparition in "My Kinsman, Major Molineux," and perhaps Marcus Aurelius in *The Marble Faun*. Septimius "thought of the strange fact, that it lay within his will to lift up his great-grandsire's ancient weapon, and in an instant, with hereditary Indian accuracy of aim, that the old man would lie wallowing in the dust, bleeding, gasping, breathing in bloody gulps, breathing no more—and he himself, instead of being hanged or driven forth with the mark of Cain, would receive great praise among the townspeople." He resists "the frightful temptation" and "the abhorred vision," although he gloats in the fantasy of the son standing over the father "wallowing in the dust," in which he, half-Indian, reenacts the killing of Father

Doane by an Indian warrior. With Septimius's "great-grandsire's ancient weapon" Hawthorne emulates the military prowess of the two Hathorne ancestors.[21]

After checking his parricidal lust and aggression, Septimius hides in the bushes, abruptly changing into a frightened voyeur like Goodman Brown or Miles Coverdale. Norton discovers him, mocks his cowardice, and haughtily proposes a duel—"our private affair on account of yonder pretty girl." Septimius, "often so morbid and sullen, never felt a greater kindness to a fellow-man, than at this moment, for this youth. . . . The young officer was so handsome, beautiful in budding youth; there was such a free, gay petulance in his manner, there seemed so little of real evil in him; he put himself on equal ground with the rustic Septimius so generously." Norton refuses Septimius's request to go "in peace" and threatens to take him prisoner. As fantasy and dream take over in a kind of tragic choreography, Septimius is aware that "the whole thing scarcely seemed real." Guns are raised and fired, and to his "horror" Septimius kills the officer, one beautiful youth killing another.

"With that playful, petulant smile flitting over his face again"—the text dwells narcissistically on Norton's Apollonian beauty—Norton, suddenly a little boy, another orphan like Septimius, reconstitutes the lost family: "Let me down as softly as you can on mother Earth—the mother of both you and me—so we are brothers; and this may be a brotherly act though it does not look so." Without hesitation Septimius accepts the familial bond—"I grieve for you like a brother"—and he has now performed "old Cain's work."[22]

Twice Norton instructs Septimius "not to uncover his body . . . , not to betray it to the hands of others." In a note to the manuscript Hawthorne pretended to advance an explanation: "Perhaps the young man had some personal defect that made him earnestly desirous that he should be buried without being undressed; and therefore he makes this request of Septimius. And perhaps, afterwards, in the story, it comes out what his defect was." The so-called explanation teases our curiosity, for Hawthorne delighted in secrets and in withholding information from readers to satisfy a personal "whim-wham." At the end of his life he refused to uncover his body even for medical examination, and he had instructed Sophia carefully as to the handling of his body at death.[23]

The "gay and beautiful young man" is secretly buried at the top of Hawthorne's hill, which he could see from his desk as he wrote. It became

Septimius's home and the center of Hawthorne's romance. Exotic flowers will grow there, beautiful but poisonous, as Hawthorne evokes Rappaccini's garden.

For a time Septimius keeps from Rose knowledge of the soldier's death and burial, but then suddenly he takes pride in his demonstration of manhood in the duel: "the recollection" of Norton's kiss "carried a thrill of vengeful joy," and unexpectedly he proposes to Rose, who to her own surprise accepts, at which moment both feel "a sort of reluctance and drawing back." They are "repelled" by the kiss (the touch) plighting their love, "and when they parted, they wondered at their strange states of mind, but would not acknowledge that they had done a thing that ought not to have been done." The biblical diction and the "ought not" may stem from Hawthorne's hardly unconscious concern about the engagement of an autobiographical character to a young woman who bears the name of his daughter Rose. It is surely no mistake that in the revision she is not his fiancée but a half-sister in love with Hagburn.

Not long after the engagement Rose comments: "No woman can help you much. You despise woman's thought, and have no need of her affection." Her analysis is confirmed when we learn that Septimius is "magnetized" by the misogynistic maxims or "moral dietetics" found on Norton's body: "a powerful intellect acted powerfully upon him."

> Kiss no woman if her lips be red; look not upon her, if she be very fair. Touch not her hand, if thy fingertips be found to thrill with hers ever so little. On the whole, shun women, for she is apt to be a disturbing influence. If thou love her, all is over, and thy whole past and remaining labor and pains will be in vain. . . . drink the breath of. . . . buxom maidens, if thou mayst without undue disturbance of the flesh, drink in as a morning draught or medicine; also, the breath of cows, as they return from rich pasture at eventide.

One wonders how much such nonsense reflects Hawthorne himself. He sometimes indulged in misogynistic brutalization, of English women, female writers, and Margaret Fuller, for example. Despite Coverdale's defense of women, Hawthorne seems at least in part to approve of Hollingsworth's fulminations. Brutalizers fascinate him in his fiction and notebook entries. Though Hawthorne depicted many beautiful males, Howells claimed that Hawthorne "said he had never seen a woman whom he thought quite beautiful." He may have hated his own feminine nature, secretly admiring his brutal ancestors, but his was a complex response: he was also capable of great sensitivity and love of women, in his fiction and even, though perhaps more limitedly, in life itself.[24]

One day Sibyl Dacy with a "malign and mysterious smile" appears on the hilltop and begins to attend the flowers on Norton's grave, and shortly Septimius discovers that she knows nothing about the elixir of life which he finds on Norton's body. For her ignorance she is to pay a price.

When Aunt Keziah, ill and dying, asks Septimius to brew her potion, for the missing ingredient he substitutes the essence of a flower growing on Norton's grave. While he is creating the mixture he is in "a state of infinite alarm and perplexity, expectation, hope, dread," and pale as though he has witnessed a murder or discovered the corpse of "someone whom he knew and loved." Like Aylmer he senses, unconsciously, what is about to happen but proceeds as though driven by an uncontrollable force, internal rather than external. Twice Keziah asks him to taste the potion, twice he refuses. After she drinks it, Septimius creeps three times to her door to listen at the keyhole. His aunt accepts the fact that she is dying but wonders whether Septimius loves her. His answer is an evasion and an admission: "Do not leave me, dear Auntie! . . . I shall be so lonely! We are the last of our race. The world is very desolate." Holding his hand, "the old herb-woman fell asleep quietly as ever did an infant on its mother's breast."

Hawthorne fumbled indecisively, timidly, in both versions of this death scene, for he was dealing with the disturbing, resonating emotions of a "son" killing a tender mother substitute. Through a lapse of memory not unusual in a woman of her years, Keziah cannot recall the name of the most important ingredient of the Indian elixir of life and so denies Septimius the immortality promised by her concoction. Like a hurt child he retaliates. We recall that at his mother's death Hawthorne experienced what Sophia described as "brain fever," and the portrait of Hester Prynne can be construed at least in part as a criticism of his mother and retaliation for her denials of affection.

In the second version of Septimius's tale, Hawthorne suddenly began to substitute the name of Hilliard Veren, the court clerk who recorded the charges over a century earlier against Captain Nicholas Manning of "whorish carriage" with two sisters. Through Veren, Hawthorne had learned probably years earlier of Manning's brutalization of his wife Elizabeth, who knew of the incestuous ménage à trois as well as his repeated sexual assaults upon servants. Perhaps the incestuous aura surrounding Rose evoked the misdeeds of Captain Manning.

In this sprawling, sometimes incoherent manuscript by an author wrestling like Jacob with an elusive demon to tell and at the same time not to tell his life story, it is difficult to know what restrictions to place upon interpretations. Adultery and incest are not central in the Septimius story, but Hawthorne was magnetically attracted to destructive males in his fiction—Chillingworth, Hollingsworth, Rappaccini, Ethan Brand—and in the family history. In his shyness and androgynous beauty Hawthorne seemingly bore little resemblance to them, but the sadomasochistic fantasies recorded in his notebooks and the artistic sadism of a teller of tales toppling Judge Pyncheon or of an artist savaging English women and female writers expose the surging angers and fears of a man not always gentle, although the prose dilutes the turbulence. Because he understood and even shared perverse desires and the enchantment of destructiveness, but remained ambivalent, readers too have shared his ambivalence.[25]

At the wedding of Rose and Hagburn, Hawthorne once again unfolds a perversion of the marriage at Cana. The good Mr. Hooper spills the wine when he sees in the goblet a reflection of his veiled, frightening face. While the guests at Rose's wedding are enjoying themselves, Septimius offers Sibyl a goblet of the potion that has killed Keziah and agrees to drink from it after her. Looking "mockingly in his eyes," she drinks and drops the goblet to the floor. She fulfills the desire of the Cumaean sibyl whom her name evokes—"I wish to die."

In fantasy Septimius commits parricide before he assumes the role of Cain and slays his "brother," whom he falls in love with. Then he destroys his "mother" with a concoction poisoned evidently by a flower growing on Norton's grave, and later he poisons his brother's mistress, his rival for Norton's affection.

Finally—and there is no preparation except perhaps in the hostility directed toward women who disappoint him—we learn that Septimius is repelled by Rose, "by that pure atmosphere of truth, reason, and right feeling, which was not the medium in which his sick spirit could find fitting breath." Here Hawthorne lifts the veil which often successfully conceals the confessional nature of his writing. Like Septimius, Hawthorne wanted release from the Wayside, a "forlorn and wretched place," from his children (those "mirrors"), from his destructive desires, and from the "pure atmosphere" of Sophia. He too recognized his sickness of spirit. From the study window Hawthorne searched the hillside behind the house for a tree "on which to hang himself" or a grave to share with Norton.

Septimius's monomaniacal and destructive quest for an elixir of life parallels many authors' exclusive and inhuman dedication to their fiction. Romance writers, Hawthorne comments,

> make themselves at home among their characters and society, and know them better than they know anything actual, and feel a blessed warmth that the air of this world does not supply, and discern a fitness of events that the course of human life has not elsewhere; so that all seems a truer world than they were born in; but sometimes, if they step beyond the limits of the spell, ah! the sad destruction, disturbance, incongruity, that meets the eye; distortion, impossibility, everything that seemed so true and beautiful in its proper atmosphere, and nicely adjusted relations, now a hideous absurdity.

At the conclusion of the passage Hawthorne emphasizes the personal applicability: "Thus he that writes the strange story of [Septimius] may well sympathize with the emotion of that moment."[26]

The "cold despair" which suffuses the final paragraph of his "dusky tapestry" is indeed Hawthorne's. His character is given three alternatives in the revisions: death by hanging like Ilbrahim's father, departure from Concord for Boston and the sea, where he would follow in the steps of Hawthorne's father, or engagement in the battlefields of the War for Independence, where he would prove to Major William Hathorne, Colonel John Hathorne, and Captain Nathaniel Hathorne that he was worthy to be their "gentle boy."

After the death of her mother, Una Hawthorne in 1872 published a bowdlerized version of the two manuscripts entitled *Septimius Felton; or, The Elixir of Life*. She had the assistance of Robert Browning. On its appearance Elizabeth Hawthorne found "some things absolutely shocking," without being specific, and declared with finality, "The author never would have published them, and it is a shame that somebody could not have done for him what death deprived him of the power of doing." As always the sister, attuned to her brother's consciousness, saw deeply and darkly, but she failed to consider that if Hawthorne had wanted to add his manuscripts to the "earth's holocaust," he had had many opportunities before his death.[27]

On August 1, 1872, Elizabeth Melville presented her husband with a copy of the book on his fifty-third birthday. There is no record as to Melville's reaction to the romance. We do not even know that he read it, but about this time Melville was composing his lengthy poem of 150 cantos, *Clarel*, which is the tale of a young theological student adrift in doubt like Septimius. Clarel is in love with Ruth, as Septimius thinks he is with Rose, but passionately seeks a brotherly bond with Vine (or Hawthorne), not unlike that established between Septimius and Norton. Melville may even have found the "secret" he mentioned to Julian in the pages of Hawthorne's romance.[28]

"The Great, Generous, Brave Heart Beat No More"

At one point in "Septimius Felton," the narrator, speaking for Hawthorne, observes: "I think old age is something like the feeling, as if you had a cold for the rest of your life." Yet almost to the very end Hawthorne remained a presence, but now of a different order. After seeing him on February 28, 1863, Longfellow wrote in his journal: "He looks gray and grand, with something very pathetic about him." It is doubtful that Hawthorne perceived his reflection in the mirror as "gray and grand." He observed to Annie Fields late in 1863, "How sad middle life looks to people of erratic temperaments. Everything is beautiful in youth—all things are allowed to it." For the moment he forgot the hurts gentle boys had to suffer, but she found him "as courteous and as grand as ever, and as true," although she noted that "he does not lose that all-saddening smile either."[1]

Hawthorne lost his physical elasticity and remained indoors much of the times. He now walked slowly or stood, as Julian recalled, "with his hands in the side-pockets of his coat,—a wistful, grave look." Day after day he worked on his romances, but he was experiencing what he had described years earlier in "The Artist of the Beautiful," artistic paralysis and enervation. Unlike Owen Warland, however, he was not fated except in one extraordinary chapter of "The Dolliver Romance" to emerge and translate dream into artistic reality. And so he watched, with those large sad eyes, the physical deterioration and the collapse of his genius. He understood himself too well for his own comfort.[2]

Depending upon mood or the need to rationalize, he could either claim he had "been beaten into insensibility" by the war or, to another correspondent, his English friend Henry Bright, deny that "I make myself very miserable about the war. The play (be it tragedy or comedy) is too long drawn out, and my chief feeling about it now is a sense of infinite weariness." He waited for "the end to come, and the curtain to drop, and then to go to sleep. . . . I sympathize with nobody and approve of nothing." At the Saturday Club Emerson was "as merciless as a steel bayonet" in his attitude toward the South and was eager to establish a weekly journal to advocate a militant policy. Hawthorne expressed his "distrust, and declined having anything to do with it."[3]

Increasingly he withdrew from the larger world. Sometimes he struck melodramatic poses, not unlike Fanshawe's, and gave way to self-pity as at the time he asked for sympathy. In January 1863 he wrote to Ticknor, "I don't know whether I shall ever see you again; for I have now staid here so long that I find myself rusted into my hole, and could not get out even if I wished." In the following month he declared that he had become such a "hermit" that the thought of leaving the Wayside for a visit to Boston affected him "somewhat as it would to invite a lobster or a crab to step out of his shell." The analogy was apt. Yet about this time Sophia declared him "decidedly better" and hoped to "persuade him to go to Boston." No doubt he was restless but also, like one of his characters, afraid to venture into the world. He managed to get to Boston on February 28 when Longfellow saw him. Despite Sophia's expectations, change of scene had no effect.[4]

On his return to Concord he continued to edit selections from the English notebooks which were appearing at intervals in the *Atlantic Monthly*, a project he had begun in 1860. The strain of meeting deadlines and of producing income was too much for his weakened body. By autumn he was more feeble. Sophia managed a nine-day visit with her sister early in October, a rest she no doubt needed, but when she returned she found her husband in such a "negative state" that he was unable to resist "damp and the world's jar."

She took Annie Fields into what she called "sacred confidence." He required "city-life" rather than Concord as long as there was "a secure retreat in its midst," a hermitage such as his fictional characters create. But when Sophia proposed moving to Cambridge he seemed "suddenly to find the Wayside very pleasant." Hawthorne took cold, Sophia said, every day and often had "slight feverishness." In describing his state she likened him obliquely to his fragile creations, Ilbrahim, Owen Warland, and Arthur Dimmesdale. "Mr. Hawthorne," she wrote, "is made of too fine porcelain. . . . It seems to me that more and more delicate melodies are struck out from his mind at every revolution of the earth-ball, so that it gets to be a swan-song almost." Two months later she noted that "he is very nervous and delicate. He cannot bear any thing, and he must be handled like the airiest venetian glass." Not once did Sophia complain of his moods or of her difficulties in ministering to a man almost impossible to please.[5]

In the last years of his life Hawthorne dwelled obsessively on the poorhouse, much to the distress of his vulnerable wife. He informed Ticknor that he expected to "die in the alms-house." In the summer of 1863 Hawthorne was "so tremendously economical," according to Sophia, that he would not hire a man to do chores about the house and grounds. Apparently it cost the Hawthornes more than $2,500 annually to live at the Wayside, although they seemed, he said, "to spend little or nothing." He was especially irked at that moment because his taxes rose to $170, "more than twice as much as last year." Expenses were increasing. Julian entered Harvard in 1863, Una drifted capriciously from one household to another, and prices rose during the war.[6]

His economic lot was not desperate, although it was by no means secure in view of his inability to complete a new romance. Royalties from *The Marble Faun* amounted to $2,175 in 1860 and 1861, but in the latter year there had been only one printing. He published only one article in the *Atlantic Monthly* in 1860 and 1861, but the three in 1862 were followed by five in 1863. Until December 1862 he received $100 for each essay; after that date reimbursement was $100 for articles of ten pages or less and $10 for each additional page. Such insubstantial sums promised little in the way of security. However, the articles were collected and published as *Our Old Home*, and in June 1863 Smith and Elder paid an advance of approximately $750 for the English rights. The London firm was ready to publish Hawthorne's next romance as well, and Fields promised $200 for each installment printed in the *Atlantic Monthly*.[7]

The typesetting of *Our Old Home* proceeded satisfactorily until July 4, 1863, Hawthorne's fifty-ninth birthday, when he informed Fields that the book was to be dedicated to Pierce and include a laudatory letter to the former president. Fields, a committed abolitionist, was upset, but before a decision could be reached Hawthorne left for Concord, New Hampshire. At a Fourth of July celebration Pierce delivered a fiery speech in which he maintained that the war could have been avoided through compromise and accused Lincoln of unconstitutional assumption of powers in issuing the Emancipation Proclamation. In the judgment of his modern biographer, Pierce in this speech lost whatever credibility he may have had.[8]

On July 15 Fields informed Hawthorne that "it is the opinion of wiser men than I am in the 'Trade' that the Dedn. & Letter to F. P. will ruin the sale of yr. book. . . . A large dealer told me he shd. not order any copies, much as his customers admired yr. writings, and a very knowing literary friend of yours says it will be, in these days, the most damaging move you could possibly do."[9]

Hawthorne pondered "deeply" on Fields's advice, smoked some "cigars over it," and, probably not to his publisher's surprise, failed to change his mind.

> My long and intimate personal relations with Pierce render the dedication altogether proper, especially as regards this book, which would have had no existence without his kindness; and if he is so exceedingly unpopular that his name is enough to sink the volume, there is so much the more need that an old friend should stand by him. I cannot, merely on account of pecuniary profit or literary reputation, go back from what I have deliberately felt and thought it right to do; and if I were to tear out the dedication, I should never look at the volume again without remorse and shame. As for the literary public, it must accept my book precisely as I think fit to give it, or let it alone.

However, since he had no "fancy" for making himself "a martyr"—"I always measure out my heroism very accurately according to the exigencies of the occasion"—he made a few changes in phraseology in order to placate Fields.[10]

When Elizabeth Peabody learned of the dedication, she informed Hawthorne at once and with vigor of "the momentous political consequences" of his act. With good humor but firmness he defended Pierce against charges of treason: "The Dedication can hurt nobody but my book and myself. I know that it will do that, but am content to take the consequences, rather than go back from what I deliberately judge it right to do." He reminded Elizabeth that because he had rejected the same kind "of advice as when I was going to write the Life of Cilley, and the Life of Pierce, and which availed nothing, then as now, because I trusted to my own instinct to guide me into my own right way. . . . The older I grow, the more I hate to write notes, and I trust I have here written nothing now that may make it necessary for me to write another." Apparently she respected his graceful but also barbed request, for the rest was silence between these two strong-willed people who for over twenty-five years had maintained not without difficulties an ambivalent relationship. Following his death she was, as could be anticipated, an ardent defender: he graduated into one of her causes.[11]

After *Our Old Home* appeared, Emerson and others may have carried out their threats to cut out the dedication and the letter, although such copies are not known. Harriet Beecher Stowe regretted that she had called on Hawthorne in the summer of 1862. While notices of the book were mixed, sales demonstrated that Fields, Elizabeth Peabody, and the others, mostly abolitionists, did not reflect public taste. In 1863 there were two printings of 5,500 copies of *Our Old Home* and a third printing of 1,000 copies in the following year. The royalties amounted to about $975. In England readers were surprised, and sometimes annoyed, to discover Hawthorne's harsh, humorless criticism of English women. Some English readers proved thin-skinned, like many Americans years earlier when they came upon Frances Trollope's hilariously unfair account of manners in the United States.[12]

Hawthorne himself summed up the book with honesty: "It is not a good nor a weighty book, nor does it deserve any great amount either of praise or censure."[13]

As soon as Fields observed the sales of *Our Old Home*, business took precedence over ideology, and he proposed that Hawthorne issue another collection of essays drawn from his English notebooks. Fields also pressed Hawthorne for a romance which he intended to publish serially in the *Atlantic Monthly*. After his abortive attempts over a period of three years with the other romances, Hawthorne had little confidence that he would succeed this time. "There is something preternatural," he explained to Fields on October 18, 1863, "in my reluctance to begin. I linger at the threshold, and have a perception of very disagreeable phantasms to be encountered if I enter." [14]

A week later, on October 24, he knew that the subject of the new work would be a variation on the life of a deathless man, which was the subject of "Septimius Felton." He planned to precede the romance with a short sketch of Thoreau: "It seems the duty of a live literary man to perpetuate the memory of a dead one, . . . but how Thoreau would scorn me for thinking that *I* could perpetuate *him*!" He confessed that he had done no writing because he was "not yet robust enough to begin, & I feel as if I should never carry it through." He found, he told Fields, Longfellow's poem "Weariness" "profoundly touching. I too am weary, and begin to look ahead for the Wayside Inn," at once a graceful tribute to Longfellow's popular poem in which Hawthorne is praised with the delicacy of which these sometimes friends were masters and another admission of his desire, perhaps even need, for rest. [15]

Jane Appleton Pierce, Franklin Pierce's wife, died on December 2, 1863, and in spite of his physical condition and his mixed feelings toward her, Hawthorne attended her burial in Concord, New Hampshire. At the cemetery he shivered in the bitter December cold, and Pierce in the midst of his own grief drew up the collar of Hawthorne's coat. Years later Pierce recalled that Hawthorne uttered "very few words, but expressing in his glorious face and wonderful eyes a depth of unutterable sympathy and sorrow." It was another tender moment in their friendship. [16]

About this time Hawthorne began his tale of Dr. Dolliver but made the mistake of promising Fields copy for the January issue of the *Atlantic Monthly*. Unable to meet the deadline, he complained about the condition of his pens and then said, "I am glad that my labor with the abominable little tool is drawing to a close." [17]

By the end of 1863 Hawthorne had uncomfortable gastrointestinal disorders. Sophia was "amazed that such a fortress as his stomach should give way." There were occasional fainting spells as well as excessive nosebleeding. More and more Hawthorne confined himself to the couch in the parlor. Sophia kept her faith that "the splendor and pride of strength" could be restored, although she recognized—she could hardly deceive herself—that his weakness grew more marked each day. [18]

At the beginning of the new year he told Longfellow that he had the "notion" that "this last book would be my best; and full of wisdom about matters of life and death." Immediately he muted this expression of confidence—"and yet it will be no deadly disappointment if I am compelled to drop it." A few days later, on January 7, 1864, Hawthorne informed Ticknor that he felt "considerably better of late, and begin to be conscious of an inclination to resume the pen." By January 16 he had "fallen into a quagmire of disgust and despondency with respect to literary matters." After this Bunyanesque remark he made a painful confession: "I am tired of my own thoughts and fancies, and my own mode of expressing them." He denied himself any gratification, including pleasure in his exquisite prose.[19]

On the following day he advised Fields of "a further state of decay." Half in jest or perhaps in relief, he linked himself with "other broken-down authors." Then he continued: "Seriously, my mind has, for the present, lost its temper and its fine edge, and I have an instinct that I had better keep quiet. Perhaps I shall have a new spurt of vigor, if I wait quietly for it—perhaps not."[20]

He waited and then returned to the romance. He struggled with it evidently until February 25 when he sent Fields a letter intended only "for your own eye": there was to be "no echo of it . . . in your notes to me." Sophia was not to be informed by Fields—or himself. "It is not quite pleasant," he admitted, "for an author to announce himself, or to be announced, as finally broken down as to his literary faculty." He regretted that he had allowed the work to be advertised, "for I had always a presentiment that it would fail us at the pinch." Then despite melancholy and lassitude he let loose in a wildly comitragic fantasy. Though about to put aside his pen forever, he was still a virtuoso.

Say to the Public what you think best, and as little as possible;—for example—. . . "Mr. Hawthorne's brain is addled at last, and, much to our satisfaction, he tells us that he cannot possibly go on with the Romance announced on the cover of the Jan.y Magazine. We consider him finally shelved, and shall take early occasion to bury him under a heavy article, carefully summing up his merits (such as they were) and his demerits, what few of them can be touched upon in our limited space."

His last manic flight in prose finally collapsed—like Clifford's verbal bubble during the train ride in *The House of the Seven Gables*. Or perhaps the analogy should be to Coverdale's confession at the conclusion of

The Blithedale Romance in which he acknowledges his failure in life and art.

> Say anything you like, in short though I really don't believe that
> the Public will care what you say, or whether you say anything. . . .
> I cannot finish it, unless a great change comes over me; and if I make
> too great an effort to do so, it will be my death; not that I should
> care much for that, if I could fight the battle through and win it, thus
> ending a life of much smoulder and scanty fire in a blaze of glory. But
> I should smother myself in mud of my own making.

At the conclusion of his letter to Fields, Hawthorne wrote with full awareness: "I am not low-spirited, nor fanciful, nor freakish, but look what seem to be realities in the face, and am ready to take whatever may come." And so it was to be.[21]

Before his imagination and energy failed him, a kind of miracle had taken place at the Wayside for a few weeks in December or January when Hawthorne began his last embroidery, "The Dolliver Romance." The tired magician once more bubbled over creatively, his touches certain and his sympathies deeply engaged.

The setting of the last romance is again the house at the corner of the Charter Street Burying Point in Salem. The cantankerous Dr. Grimshawe is now Dr. Dolliver, a gentle, "tremulous" man of uncertain age on the order of Rip Van Winkle and an apothecary, trained by Dr. Swinnerton, next to whom Grimshawe is buried. Ned and Elsie become Pansie, the three-year-old great-great-granddaughter of Dr. Dolliver, "as apprehensive and quick of motion as a fawn." Her father, also an apothecary, was the victim of his own potions, perhaps a suicide, and her mother promptly died and followed her husband to the cemetery outside the house. In tone and tact "The Dolliver Romance" evokes the lighter side of Hawthorne's genius in "Little Annie's Ramble," for he wanted once more to write "a sunshiny book" despite the cemetery setting. His goal confirms a lifelong ambition which, despite successes like *The House of the Seven Gables*, he could not sustain. Yet he succeeded magnificently in the first chapter in his re-creation of a day in the life of Dr. Dolliver, which perhaps he intended to juxtapose with the unlived day in the life of Judge Pyncheon in *The House of the Seven Gables*.[22]

As in the "Grimshawe" tale, Hawthorne is the aged apothecary and the abandoned, parentless child. As the former he creates an ideal father, loving, indulgent, tender, such as he had never known from personal experience as well as an old man who fearfully faces the inevitabilities of his years. As Pansie, Hawthorne reexperiences for the last time the hurts of his earliest years.

The romance opens with a loving, affectionate, but mock-heroic description of an old man rising in the morning after he hears his great-great-granddaughter clamoring for the assistance of the housekeeper.

> The old gentleman woke with more than his customary alacrity, and, after taking a moment to gather his wits about him, pulled aside the faded moreen curtains of his ancient bed, and thrust his head into a beam of sunshine that caused him to wink and withdraw it again. This transitory glimpse of good Dr. Dolliver showed a flannel night-cap, fringed round with stray locks of silvery white hair, and surmounting a meagre and duskily yellow visage, which was crossed and criss-crossed with a record of his long life in wrinkles, faithfully written, no doubt, but with such cramped chirography of Father Time that the purport was illegible.

For a moment reality intrudes: "It seemed hardly worth while for the patriarch to get out of bed any more, and bring his forlorn shadow into the summer day that was made for younger folk." The "patriarch," it turns out, manages "the toil of living twenty-four hours longer" with the assistance of an elixir that killed his grandson, Pansie's father.

Tentatively Dr. Dolliver places one foot on the floor and experiences twinges of his familiar rheumatism, but "a little less poignant than those of yesterday." As the discomfort passes quickly, he, or the narrator, concludes: "Pain is but pleasure too strongly emphasized." Steadying himself on the bedpost, he slowly surveys the room which he has occupied since the death of his wife, Bessie, fifty years earlier and rediscovers, as though for the first time, "an enormous serpent twining round a wooden post, and reaching quite from the floor of the chamber to its ceiling," which was the apothecary sign of his predecessor, Dr. Swinnerton. Hawthorne quickly and affectionately capitalizes on this "mysterious symbol . . . snatched bodily out of his dreams." It is a phallic totem reminiscent of Satan's staff in "Young Goodman Brown" and of the maypole at Merry Mount, suggesting at the same time sexual desires and fears of nighttime as well as the phallic origins of comedy. Hawthorne may even have recalled Ishmael, the Presbyterian, worshipping Queequeg's phallic idol, Yojo.

> It looked like a kind of manichean idol, which might have been elevated on a pedestal for a century or so, enjoying the worship of its votaries in the open air, until the impious sect perished from among men—all save old Dr. Dolliver, who had set up the monster in his bed-chamber for the convenience of private devotion. But we are unpardonable in suggesting such a fantasy to the prejudice of our venerable friend, knowing him to have been as pious and upright a Christian, and with as little of the serpent in his character, as ever came of Puritan lineage.

Dr. Dolliver dresses himself "in the parallelogram of bright sunshine" on the uncarpeted floor, which is a lovely, magical effect. Then he looks out at the burial ground where his family, including Bessie, lies. He clears his throat "of the dregs of a ten-years' cough," shakes "his silvery head at his own image in the looking-glass, as if to impress the apothegm on that shadowy representative of himself," and determines to live as long as possible for Pansie's sake.

He puts on an ancient "patchwork morning-gown" (or mourning-gown) originally made from "the embroidered front of his own wedding waist-coat and the silken skirt of his wife's bridal attire," the gown reflecting his age and his dual parental role in relation to Pansie. Another of Haw-thorne's elaborate embroideries, the robe also serves as an ever-present calendar of the Dolliver family.

> Throughout many of the intervening years, as the garment got rag-ged, the spinsters of the old man's family had quilted their duty and affection into it in the shape of patches upon patches, rose-color, crimson, blue, violet, and green, and then (as their hopes faded, and their life kept growing shadier, and their attire took a somber hue) sober gray and great fragments of funereal black; until the doctor could revive the memory of most things that had befallen him by looking at his patchwork-gown as it hung upon a chair.

The gown made for Hawthorne twenty years earlier by Sophia and Louisa is in effect worn by Clifford Pyncheon, then by Uncle Venner (his clothing "patched together, too of different epochs; an epitome of times and fashions") and in its final appearance becomes a New England version of Joseph's coat or Achilles' shield. Even in this exquisite scene the narrator has to bow to reality: Dolliver resembles "a mummy," which is a pun upon his dual role as parent and his slender hold on life.[23]

Dr. Dolliver descends the stairs with the aid of a staff but in his unaccustomed haste almost stumbles. In the dining room he finds Pansie, "a rather pale and large-eyed little thing, quaint in her aspect, as might well be the case with a motherless child." She lives in a house with no playmates except a cat (like those of Hawthorne's youth). Her home is next to the burial ground "where all her relatives, from her great-grandmother downward, lay calling to her—'Pansie, Pansie, it is bedtime!'—even in the prime of the summer-morning." She is the last of the Dollivers. The doctor is devoted to Pansie—she renews his life—but he is not spared age's confusions of past and present: "So mistily did his dead progeny come and go in the patriarch's decayed recollection, that this solitary child represented for him the successive babyhoods of the many that had gone before. The emotions of his early paternity came back to him. She seemed the baby of a past age oftener than she seemed Pansie. . . . "

As the oldest inhabitant of Salem village, Dr. Dolliver is the honored "Grandsir," as well known in his outdated garb as "the meeting-house steeple or the town-pump," which is perhaps Hawthorne's bittersweet reminder of the witty self-disparagement at the conclusion of "The Custom-House" in *The Scarlet Letter*: "It may be, however,—O, transporting and triumphant thought!—that the great-grandchildren of the present race may sometimes think kindly of the scribbler of bygone days, when the antiquary of days to come, among the sites memorable in the town's history, shall point out the locality of THE TOWN-PUMP!"

Although the townspeople honor him, Dr. Dolliver seeks to escape observation, for he has "that nightmare feeling which we sometimes have in dreams, when we seem to find ourselves wandering through a crowded afternoon, with the noonday-sun upon us, in some wild extravagance of dress or nudity." Dolliver is still the deathless man, haunted by the anxieties of Hawthorne's youth when he sought to cross the bridge to sexual maturity. In one of his truest but saddest passages, the dying author clings to a vision of eternal youth.

Youth, however eclipsed for a season, is undoubtedly the proper, permanent, and genuine condition of man; and if we look closely into this dreary delusion of growing old, we shall find that it never absolutely succeeds in laying hold of our innermost convictions. A sombre garment, woven of life's unrealities, has muffled us from our true self, but within it smiles the young man whom we knew; the ashes of many perishable things have fallen upon our youthful fire, but beneath them lurk the inextinguishable flame.

That evening after Pansie goes to bed another miracle takes place in the flickering light from the fireplace. Dolliver and Pansie fuse in a fantasy of age and youth and of "perfect trust," which neither the young nor the old often achieve.

Over our friend's face, in the rosy flicker of the fire-gleam, stole an expression of repose and perfect trust that made him as beautiful to look at, in his high-backed chair, as the child Pansie on her pillow; and sometimes the spirits that were watching him beheld a calm surprise dawn slowly over his features and brighten into joy, yet not so vividly as to break his evening quietude.

In the twilight of his tale and his life Hawthorne is still the boy-man Clifford Pyncheon blowing soap bubbles whose lovely life spans are measured in seconds.

The fusion of great-great-grandfather and great-great-granddaughter consummates two of Hawthorne's lifelong dreams. One is of a great-great-grandson living in perfect harmony with his great-great-grandfather, Judge John Hathorne, who in the metamorphosis of dream is no longer the stern, unyielding patriarch but the very model of a loving paternal figure. The other summons up the wish expressed in a letter to his mother in 1820: "Why was I not a girl that I might have been pinned all my life to my Mother's apron?" Once more, in short, Hawthorne is Annie, cared for in this reincarnation not by a stranger-father but by an ancient and distinguished member of the family, the harmony extending far into the past as fantasy inevitably molds over history in its own mirror image—or mirage. [24]

This first chapter of "The Dolliver Romance" is one of Hawthorne's loveliest achievements. As a fragment or a sketch this chapter could have been a final statement worthy of a master, but no one sets out to write a fragment. There were, however, the imperatives of Duty—his promise to Fields and his family's need. And so he continued. It was an obligatory mistake.

The major plot deals with the machinations of a Colonel Dabigny, who on learning that Dolliver possesses an elixir of life proceeds to blackmail the gentle apothecary. A monster of greed, Dabigny gulps down the contents of a vial of the elixir and dies with "a loud, unearthly screech . . . as if some unseen hand were throttling him," struggling like Zenobia against an unseen and unknown violator. At this point Hawthorne intrudes, evidencing a desire to evade the symbolism of this anxiety dream surfacing from the dreams of childhood: "I would fair quit this scene, and be done with the old Colonel, who I am glad has happened to die and take himself off my hands at so early a period of the narrative."

At another point in the manuscript Hawthorne found himself with a subject which he could not get off his hands so easily. We suddenly learn that Dolliver's wife shortly before her death began to wear on her bosom exotic flowers from a tropical plant that Dr. Swinnerton had bequeathed to his successor: "One glowed like a gem, and deepened her somewhat pallid beauty with a richness never before seen in it." Suddenly Bessie is molded into the pattern of Beatrice Rappaccini, Hester Prynne, and Zenobia and is renamed Phoebe. Annually when Swinnerton's plant blooms, Dolliver recalls his wife "radiant with this glow that did not really belong to her naturally passive beauty, quickly interchanging with another image of her form with the snow of death on cheek and forehead."

What appears to be fumbling and uncertainty on Hawthorne's part as a narrator may yield to an explanation, or at least to a speculation, based upon his associations. Dolliver's wife could have had any one of many names, but she is baptized Bessie. As Hawthorne developed his tale and identified more and more with Dolliver, consciously or unconsciously, he recognized that he had married himself to his mother, whom her family called "Betsy" as did his father in a poem recorded in the ship's log which came into the son's possession apparently in the 1820s. And so Bessie-Betsy was renamed Phoebe, after his wife and the heroine of *The House of the Seven Gables*. But the exotic flower she wears on her bosom evokes Hester Prynne's embroidered A and confirms once again Hawthorne's longing for the breast of the Madonna mother. Pansie, like Pearl, is a perceptive observer when she calls the flower a "big naughty weed," or deed, before she uproots the plant on the great-great-grandmother's grave. By this act Hawthorne perhaps censures his incestuous longing.

One day as Dr. Dolliver and Pansie walk in the cemetery outside their house—repeating Hawthorne's youthful experiences in the Charter Street cemetery—they stand in front of "his own peculiar row of grave-stones, consisting of eight or nine slabs of slate, adorned with carved borders, rather rudely done." In the tale Dolliver's wife occupies the grave of Judge Hathorne. Dolliver, the narrator informs us, "felt a strange repugnance, stronger than he had ever felt before, to linger by these graves, and felt none of the tender sorrow, mingled with high and tender hopes, that had sometimes made him feel it good to be there. Such moods perhaps often come to the aged, as hardened earth-crust over their souls shuts them out from spiritual influences." But Hawthorne was perhaps no longer describing Dolliver's reaction so much as his own inability to feel or to relate to anyone.

Dr. Dolliver "carefully closed the gate." It was Hawthorne's last visit to the Charter Street Burying Point.

In the course of writing the romance Hawthorne made a jotting that appears to have little to do with the story of Dolliver and Pansie, as he speculated about the meeting of a man at fifty-five with a young man at twenty-five. The older man by means of an elixir is growing young, the youth is aging naturally. At forty they are the same age. When the young man is seventy, the old man is eleven. "At last," Hawthorne wrote, "the young man should die old, and an infant be found on his door-step." And, as he did not say, it would be the same story continued—the tale of "a gentle boy" named Ilbrahim or Ned or Nathaniel Hawthorne.[25]

After Hawthorne put aside "The Dolliver Romance" his physical decline was rapid, and he was more difficult than ever to live with: weary, depressed, and irritable. As he closed up like a clam and shut her out, Sophia took her fears elsewhere. She was so afraid to upset him that she asked Ticknor to write to "tell him he must take his *shawl*. He has such a horror of luggage that I fear he will not listen to me about it." Apparently silence more and more characterized the lives of the Hawthornes.[26]

Early in March 1864 he was, according to Sophia, "very indisposed," and Mary Mann noted that "he looks altered." She offered her diagnosis: "He is a victim of dyspepsia. I cannot help thinking that his malady origi-nates in mental trouble. I suspect that he feels that he has been duped, & is beginning to open his eyes to the truth." Despite his physical condition, everyone apparently agreed that Hawthorne should take another excursion to Washington in the company of Ticknor. He was strong enough in the middle of March to go into Boston despite his self-styled "desperate condition" and enjoyed beefsteak and oysters. It was a test to see whether he could undertake the projected trip.[27]

On March 28, accompanied by Sophia, Hawthorne again journeyed to Boston to the Fields's home on Charles Street, where he stayed until he left for New York with Ticknor. Years later Fields recalled that he was "shocked at his invalid appearance" and noted that he seemed "quite deaf. The light in his eye was beautiful as ever, but his limbs seemed shrunken and his usual stalwart vigor utterly gone." Hawthorne complained, as Fields remembered, "Why does Nature treat us like children! I think we could bear it all if we knew our fate; at least it would not make much difference to me now what became of me."[28]

Because of the children, apparently Sophia could not spend the night in Boston, even though Una was over twenty, Julian eighteen, and Rose thirteen. When she left the Fields's house and no longer had to keep up appearances, she was so overcome that she "could have lain down upon the sidewalk." A few days later in a letter marked "Private," she poured out her misgivings to Horatio Bridge. Hawthorne, she wrote, had been very ill all winter, not confined to bed "but miserable on a lounge or sofa—and quite unable to write a word—even a letter—and lately unable to read. I have felt the wildest anxiety about him because he is a person who has been immaculately well all his life, and this illness has seemed to me an awful dream which could not be true. But he has wasted away very much and the suns in his eyes are collapsed, and he has no spirits, no appetite, and very little sleep." She said that Hawthorne planned to go to the Isles of Shoals and remain there, presumably alone, until the tourist season began. She had decided that he needed "the damp sea air for health, comfort and enjoyment," and she hoped the Wayside could be sold "for his sake," so that he "could wander on sea beaches all the rest of his days," still looking for what could not be recovered. Faithful, self-sacrificing according to her custom, Sophia never uttered a word of criticism. She became a lonely spectator as he went off either alone or with the "boys": she was once again in exile.[29]

Hawthorne was exhausted when he arrived in New York, and Richard Stoddard, who had not seen him for twelve years, was "pained . . . even to look at him." Ticknor contracted a cold at the beginning of the journey, and when the two men arrived in Philadelphia, where they were to spend some time on their leisurely trip to Washington, Ticknor took to his bed on the very day Hawthorne felt better. A physician evidently diagnosed the illness as "bilious colic" and "proceeded to cup, and poultice, and blister, according to the ancient rule of that tribe of savages." Ticknor's condition rapidly worsened. No nursing help was available, and Hawthorne, who shrank tremulously from such situations, became, in Sophia's words, "nurse and watcher," as roles got reversed. On one occasion Hawthorne "sat on the side of the bed holding Mr. Ticknor's hand for *three hours*! in one position, and began to feel they should die together." Ticknor died on April 10 of congestion of the lungs. When George W. Childs, the owner of the *Philadelphia Public Ledger*, arrived at the Continental Hotel, he found Hawthorne "apparently dazed" and immediately took charge. A few days later a Bishop Howe accompanied Hawthorne to Boston, where he passed the night at the home of the Fieldses, "very excited and nervous."[30]

The next day, apparently unaccompanied and without advance notice, he arrived in Concord. There was no carriage at the station, and he walked to the Wayside, his brow "steaming with a perfect rain—so great had been the effort to walk so far." When Sophia heard his step on the piazza she was lying on the couch "feeling quite indisposed." She was "frightened out of all knowledge of myself—so haggard, so white, so deeply scored with pain and fatigue was the face—so much more ill he looked than I ever saw him before." He needed to be home, Sophia wrote, to relieve feelings "pent up and kept back for so long. . . . It relieved him somewhat to break down as he spoke of that scene." He was wearied unto death as he lay restlessly on the couch, and he did not want to be read to because he was "not able to attend or fix his thoughts at all." Weaker than ever, he had to lie down every morning after getting "through his toilette."[31]

Una confirmed her mother's report. "He is bilious," she wrote to her cousin, and "daily loses his flesh, strength and spirits, in a way that is indeed melancholy to see." To the family's annoyance he refused medical attention: "The idea of consulting a physician disturbs him so much that we cannot insist upon it, and poor Mamma feels the burden of responsibility as almost too great to bear, as I think it really is. It is such an aggravation to think that all is not being done that might be, and that he might be getting daily better instead of the contrary."[32]

Hawthorne rambled in his conversations but fixated on his future in an almshouse. Sophia wrote to Pierce "without his knowledge" and begged him to persuade her husband that "there is no fear of his entering the Alms' House, to which he philosophically looks forward—considering himself entirely useless in the world henceforth. He declares no one shall prevent him—but his wife and children can joyfully work for him." Perhaps Sophia preferred not to recognize what Hawthorne seemed to say beneath the surface, that he longed for release from life and family. About this time Mary Mann said that Sophia considered his malady "partly mental" and attributed it to the fact that "he *agonizes* about the country . . ." Hawthorne, Mary added, "has that sort of imagination which realizes things just as they are, and all the uncertainty and the suffering are daguerrotyped in him. . . . We shall have it all bye and bye in books; for he always puts himself into his books; he cannot help it."[33]

As the days passed Hawthorne seemed to make a slight recovery, although after each relapse body and spirits weakened. He was restless, impatient, and taxing to himself and others. He moved about little and rarely left the house. Early in May, Bronson Alcott saw Hawthorne at his gate: "He seemed unequal to meeting anyone, and I had but a word with him, he asking me if I was well only."[34]

Every weekend Julian walked from Cambridge to Concord. On May 7 or 8 father and son sat alone in the study where they chatted, although they never had "any serious man-and-boy talks together." Once again, and for the last time, Hawthorne failed his son. Before he left his father that day, Julian picked up *Evangeline* and read aloud the final scene in which the heroine finds the long-missing Gabriel on his deathbed, where he dies in her arms. Perhaps Julian read the scene at the suggestion of his father, who may have used this tactic to deliver a message to his son. Or perhaps Julian chose the passage in order to express his desire for the tactile bond that his father had denied him, except at intervals which became rarer as Julian matured and Hawthorne retreated into his own world. His behavior as a father was foreshadowed in the characterization of Pearson, who fears to display the deep affection he feels for Ilbrahim.[35]

Despite his feeble condition, Sophia wanted Hawthorne to go off on a trip through New Hampshire with Franklin Pierce. "The boy-associations with the General," she declared, "will refresh him. They will fish and muse and rest, and saunter upon horses' feet and be in the air all the time in the fine weather." "Without leave"—to the end there was a childlike fear of her husband—she informed Pierce of Hawthorne's physical condition: he required assistance getting into carriages, his eyes were affected by his "weakness," and his step was "uncertain." She also confided that he got "very weary of people in a few minutes here," a confidence which probably concealed her own exclusion. She had faith that once again, as he had during Una's illness in Rome, Pierce would assume the role of "the guard angellic." How wonderfully, but sadly, Sophia protected herself from reality.[36]

Hawthorne agreed to meet Pierce in Boston on May 11. In the last letter he was to send, he confessed to Pierce that he wrote with "some difficulty," but he feigned confidence. "My own health continues rather poor," he admitted, "but I shall hope to revive rapidly when once we are on the road."[37]

On the same day Sophia sent Fields a letter marked *"Private* (except from Annie)," informing them that she would accompany her husband to Boston and admitting increased "anxiety" because "he absolutely refuses to see a physician officially." She asked Fields to arrange to have Oliver Wendell Holmes see Hawthorne "in some ingenious way" and offer a medical evaluation of his condition. "It almost deprives me of my wits," she wrote, "to see him growing weaker with no aid. He seems quite bilious—and has a restlessness that is infinite—His look is more distressed and harassed than before—and he has so little rest, that he is getting worn out." According to Una, her father was "visibly" weaker early in May. She now alleged that he objected only to the homeopathic doctors by whom (as she did not say) her mother swore.[38]

On May 10 Hawthorne left the Wayside on his final journey. How he felt that morning is not known, but the conclusion of the second version of "Septimius Felton" may have foreshadowed his farewell: " . . . his home seemed a more forlorn and wretched place than he could endure; a dismal dungeon, and his hillside, a growth of gloomy pines, among which he would gaze around seeking one on which to hang himself. . . ."[39]

Assisted by Sophia, he arrived in Boston "looking very ill," according to Annie Fields. Holmes came to the hotel where Hawthorne was staying and from the lobby watched Hawthorne walk toward the building: "He seemed to have shrunken in all his dimensions, and faltered along with an uncertain, feeble step, as if every movement were an effort." Holmes walked with him for about half an hour during which he asked questions without raising anxieties and offered suggestions that might be useful during his journey. According to Annie Fields's entry in her notebook, Holmes admitted that "the shark's tooth is upon him, but would not have this known."[40]

Pierce and Hawthorne boarded the train for Concord, New Hampshire, but stopped at Andover, Massachusetts, to call on Jane Pierce's sister, Mary Appleton Aiken, in whose house Mrs. Pierce had died five months earlier. The two men then proceeded to Concord, where they remained almost a week because of bad weather. At last they set out by carriage for the White Mountains, their destination Dixville Notch, the most northerly of the passes, close to the Canadian border. On May 18 they reached Center Harbor. Hawthorne "was weary and very restless during the night." He ate a "slight breakfast" and from the piazza enjoyed the splendid scenery. Although Pierce suggested that they remain at Center Harbor a day or two, Hawthorne insisted that they continue.

He felt comfortable in the carriage, its rocking motion suggestive of a cradle or a ship. "We conversed but little during that afternoon's drive," Pierce wrote. "But his eye was quick to catch every object striking or beautiful." At one point during the ride Hawthorne spoke of Thackeray's death and "remarked in a low, soliloquizing tone—what a boon it would be, if when life draws to its close one could pass away without a struggle."

As the sun was setting on May 18, 1864, they arrived in Plymouth, New Hampshire, which is at the foot of the White Mountains and near the junction of the Pemigewasset and Baker rivers. They stayed at the Pemigewasset House, a large frame building accommodating over 150 guests, which had been rebuilt after a disastrous fire in the preceding year. They were thirty miles south of the site of one of the last of his tales, which concluded: "At a distance, but distinctly to be seen, high up in the golden light of the setting sun, appeared the Great Stone Face, with hoary mists around it, like the white hairs around the brow of Ernest. Its look of grand beneficence seemed to embrace the world."

Hawthorne took only a cup of tea and a little food and dropped into a slumber on the sofa. About ten o'clock he awoke and retired for the night. Pierce left the door between their rooms open after placing a lamp so that, while its rays were not in Hawthorne's face, he could see his friend from his bed. Just before midnight Pierce awoke and observed that Hawthorne was lying "in a perfectly natural position, like a child with his right hand under his cheek. The noble brow and face struck me as more grand and serenely calm then than ever before." Probably Pierce did not recall the description of the beautiful youth Cyrus in "Roger Malvin's Burial": "His cheek rested upon his arm, his curled locks were thrown back from his brow, his limbs were slightly relaxed."[41]

At three A.M. Pierce found Hawthorne in the same position. "Hastening softly to his bed side," Pierce wrote four years later, reenacting the scene empathically:

> I could not perceive that he breathed, altho no change had come over his features. I seized his wrist but found no pulse—run my hand down upon his bare side, but the great, generous, brave heart beat no more—The boon of which he spoke in the afternoon had before morning's dawn been graciously granted to him. He had passed from natural sleep to that from which there is no earthly waking—without the slightest struggle—evidently without moving a muscle.[42]

"The wanderer" came home on May 19, 1864. It was the anniversary of the birth of Captain Nathaniel Hathorne.[43]

The circle was closed.

Instead of notifying Sophia directly, Pierce sent a telegram to Elizabeth Peabody, who was to deliver the news in person. Sophia had received only one message from Hawthorne, "a little letter," now apparently lost. At noon Elizabeth Peabody and Mary Mann arrived at the Wayside. Sophia sat at dinner and was about to go to Boston with Rose, who planned to spend a few days with Annie Fields. The aunts intended to talk privately to Una, who in turn would inform her mother. As soon as Una saw the faces of her aunts she screamed, "Oh what is the matter! What has happened?" Forgetting the plan, Mary Mann said abruptly, "Papa is gone." Sophia overhead Una's shriek and had to be informed immediately without preparation.[44]

Sophia told her sisters and daughter to go away. She retired to another room to "weep & groan." Soon she permitted Una to be with her and later entered the parlor to talk to her sisters. She recognized, she said, the hand of God, for Hawthorne had not wanted to live if he required anybody's attention. "He dreaded illness & infirmity & old age more than death," Sophia told her sisters in an admission she refused to make while he lived, "& made himself miserable all the time with these dreads."[45]

Sophia was too bereft to handle the funeral arrangements. These she left to Una and Julian and to Judge Rockwood Hoar of Concord. At first it was her plan to attend the service in the church but not to go to the cemetery. She decided to wear black but objected when Una proposed to appear in black because Hawthorne would not have liked it. Una acceded but regretted that her mother's wish denied her "a sort of shield."[46]

Sophia sent a note marked "Private" to Fields in which she begged him not to say a word to her sisters about Hawthorne's mental state. She feared they "would *talk* of it to others and inevitably exaggerate. . . . Why not leave him intact as he is—oh do try to shield him, dear Mr Fields." Her fears proved justified, for Elizabeth Peabody, who had a deep conviction that insanity ran in the Hawthorne family (she troubled herself little as to evidence), alleged with her customary certainty that Hawthorne was insane before his death. Elizabeth's opinions were subject to revision, and she later declared that in the final months of his life he feared "a living death of unutterable horror" from paralysis and on another occasion that he "died despairing" of the fate of the Union.[47]

Pierce accompanied the body to Boston, where Julian met him on May 20. The body was embalmed without Sophia's knowledge. "She can not bear the idea," Julian informed Fields, "of his being touched in any way, and it is a great comfort to her to think that he has not been."[48]

On the morning after the news of his death reached Concord, Louisa May Alcott climbed the hill behind the Wayside to Hawthorne's favorite path and picked some violets which she sent to Sophia. She and others decorated the lovely Congregational Church for the afternoon service on May 23 when Concord, as Holmes observed, "was luminous with the whitest blossoms of the luxuriant spring." At Sophia's request the coffin was taken to the church, not to the Wayside, and it was not to be open before the service. It was covered with lilies and two wreaths, one of apple blossoms from the orchard at the Manse and the other of hothouse flowers, the gift of the Fieldses. "Unwillingly," the family bowed to the wishes of friends to see the body. The corpse, Emerson wrote, "was noble and serene in its aspect—nothing amiss—a calm and powerful head." Holmes also spoke of "the noble forehead and still, placid features" which "never looked fuller of power than in this last aspect with which they met the eyes that were turned upon them."[49]

As Sophia sat in the church, the service was transformed into a "Festival of Light" at which the "lily-bells" rang in "for him the Eternal Year of Peace." The "tropical gorgeousness" of the Fields's wreath "steeped me in Paradise. We were the new Adam and new Eve again and walked in the garden in the cool of the day. . . . indeed it seems to me that now again there is no Death. His life has swallowed it up."[50]

Despite what the abolitionists may have thought, Pierce sat with members of the family. The pallbearers came from the intellectual elite of Concord and Boston—Emerson, Longfellow, Lowell, Holmes, Alcott, Agassiz, Fields, Hillard, Hoar, Whipple, and Norton. Nobody seemingly remembered, not even Sophia, that some of his Salem friends should have served in that capacity; Hawthorne would have preferred that.

The service began at three o'clock with the choir chanting "Thy will be done." James Freeman Clarke, the clergyman who had married the Hawthornes, conducted the service. Clarke said, according to Emerson, that "Hawthorne had done more justice than any other to the shades of life, shown a sympathy with the crime in our nature, &, like Jesus, was the friend of sinners."[51]

After the church service the body was taken to the newly established Sleepy Hollow Cemetery. "It was a lovely day," Longfellow wrote in his journal, "the village all sunshine and blossoms and the song of birds. You cannot imagine anything at once more sad and beautiful." Sophia watched the pallbearers carry the coffin. Longfellow, "his long white hair blowing in the fresh air," was an impressive sight. Fields, "so true a lover," carried the manuscript of "The Dolliver Romance." "I was soothed," Sophia wrote, "as with the music of the spheres of their motion—I wish they could ever know how they comforted me." Hawthorne was buried on a hilltop under the pines along what was to become a well-worn path, like the one behind the Wayside. The ridge was to be the resting place of Thoreau, Emerson, the Alcotts, Elizabeth Peabody, and Ellery Channing.[52]

Following the graveside rites Sophia and her family rode in their carriage to the gates of the cemetery. Sophia was surprised that all the friends and dignitaries stood on either side of the gate, the men with their heads uncovered. Self-effacing as ever, she did not realize at once that they were honoring the widow.[53]

She then returned to the Wayside. "Upon entering the house door— the GREAT ABSENCE opened a mighty void from which human endurance nearly shrank." But the duties of hospitality "bridged over the awful chasm for the hour—as the benign Father willed it. For He would give me a little time; He is so tender and merciful." As always God was the ideal parent.[54]

Elizabeth Hawthorne, who had not attended the Hawthornes' wedding in 1842, was too shocked and "ill" to come to Concord. She grieved for her brother—and herself. "When I look forward," she wrote to Una, "I can anticipate nothing but sorrow; few people are so completely left alone as I am,—all have gone before me." Elizabeth, who never forgave Sophia for depriving her of the only meaningful male in her life, was convinced, forever, that Sophia's insistence upon staying in Rome was responsible for her brother's death.[55]

In view of Hawthorne's prohibitions an autopsy was not performed, and much of what we know about his physical state in the last years of his life is colored by the emotional involvement or lack of medical sophistication of the commentators. Holmes, the only professional who saw Hawthorne in the closing days, was also professional in his careful avoidance of a definitive statement, probably because he had to diagnose while he strolled the Boston streets with his patient. Two months after Hawthorne's death Holmes observed in the *Atlantic Monthly*:

> His aspect, medically considered, was very unfavorable. There were persistent local symptoms, referred especially to the stomach,—"boring pain," distension, difficult digestion, with great wasting of flesh and strength. He was very gentle, very willing to answer questions, very docile to such counsel as I offered him, but evidently had no hope of recovering his health. He spoke as if his work were done, and he should write no more.

Holmes speculated that Hawthorne "died by the gentlest of all modes of release, fainting, without the trouble and the confusion of coming back to life,—a way of ending liable to happen in any disease attended with much debility." Years later Holmes wrote to Rose Hawthorne's husband, George P. Lathrop, "I feared that there was some internal organic—perhaps malignant—disease; for he looked wasted and as if stricken with a mortal disease."[56]

Mary Mann shared her sister Elizabeth's view that Hawthorne feared paralysis, although she characterized it "the dread of infirmity" which he brooded over. "It is better for them all," she declared, "that he died just as he did, for he could have been an incubus upon their souls if an invalid, for he had no power to bear cheerfully." Others—Emerson, Una, and even Sophia—toyed with the idea that he in effect willed his death, like Fanshawe, Ilbrahim, and Dimmesdale. Recent biographers have suggested a brain tumor and, more plausibly, gastrointestinal cancer.[57]

On the day following the funeral Emerson noted in his journal that Clarke had overemphasized Hawthorne's concern with sin and slighted "a tragic element in the event, that might be more fully rendered—in the painful solitude of the man—which, I suppose, could no longer be endured, & he died of it." Emerson went on to sum up his own response to Hawthorne's life. "I have found," he wrote, "in his death a surprise & disappointment. I thought him a greater man than any of his works betray, that there was still a great deal of work in him, & that he might one day show a pure power." Emerson had waited patiently for Hawthorne to transcend "his unwillingness & caprice" so that one day he might "conquer a friendship. It would have been a happiness, doubtless to both of us, to have come into habits of unreserved intercourse." He could not refrain from voicing his "indignation," or perhaps envy, that Hawthorne had maintained a lifelong friendship with "that paltry Franklin Pierce." Emerson was not always a generous man and in death as in life could understand neither the man nor his genius.[58]

In contrast with Emerson's chilled summation were the eulogies of Ellery Channing and Herman Melville. A few weeks after the funeral, Channing, unlike Emerson, wrote from the heart: "My poor Hawthorne! the dearest, sweetest, kindest of all human creatures to me. I loved him as one loves a pet. He was all love and sweetness and dearness to me. Where is he now?" In 1891, the year of his own death, Melville at last published his tenderest and most deeply felt poem, "Monody":

> To have known him, to have loved him
>   After loneness long;
> And then to be estranged in life,
>   And neither in the wrong;
> And now for death to set his seal—
>   Ease me, a little ease, my song!
>
> By wintry hills his hermit-mound
>   The sheeted snow-drifts drape,
> And houseless there the snow-bird flits
>   Beneath the fir-trees' crape:
> Glazed now with ice the cloistral vine
>   That hid the shyest grape.[59]

Epilog
"The Great Absence"

In September 1864 Sophia Hawthorne was at last ready to venture beyond the confines of the Wayside and Concord. She planned to return to Salem to visit relatives and no doubt the grave of her mother. It was an awesome event, like Hepzibah's opening of the cent-shop in *The House of the Seven Gables*. "I tremble," Sophia wrote, "at the prospect of plunging into the world again."[1]

Alone in her "sphere," without her "lord," Sophia had reason to tremble. She had the responsibility of three unruly, essentially troubled children, although this would not have been her evaluation. In the folly of her love— love, as Bruno Bettelheim observes, is not enough—she never realized how she had hurt her children by denying them peer relationships and the socialization schools provide and by imposing upon them an all-inclusive but quixotic and inconsistent regimen. They had suffered from but also had taken shameless advantage of their mother's desire to live her life through theirs. She was willing, even eager, it seemed, to subordinate herself to them, but for a lifetime she had bowed before her mother and then before her husband.

Although the almshouse was not an imminent prospect, despite Hawthorne's obsessive fears, Sophia had to deal with a diminished income, declining royalties from his books, and rising costs after the Civil War. She was no manager, and with the unexpected death of Ticknor, she no longer had a faithful advisor.

Out of respect for her husband's injunctions, she at first resisted the suggestions of Fields to publish excerpts from the notebooks in the *Atlantic Monthly* but eventually yielded and in 1866 became what her husband scorned, a female writer. So anxious was she to have the public accept her idealization of her husband that she struck out and rephrased passages, his vigor and occasional unconventionality yielding to her timidity and gentility. His life was still hers, her beacon and comfort in a lonely world which was closing in more rapidly than she realized. In her diary Annie Fields characterized Sophia as a "poor rudderless craft," with children who were "most fatiguing and ungrateful."[2]

Fields persuaded Sophia to publish the American notebooks in book form, but by the time they appeared in 1868 the publisher and Sophia had a dispute because she believed that he was cheating her of royalties. It turned out that she was mistaken, but she had "proved disloyal," in the words of Annie Fields. There was no reconciliation, and she lost the Fieldses and shortly thereafter the moral support of General Hitchcock's letters. She found herself without friends, with only her sisters whose advice she usually resisted with the dogmatism characteristic of the Peabody women.

In 1867 Una became engaged to Storrow Higginson, an army chaplain during the Civil War and a nephew of Thomas Wentworth Higginson. It is not clear what happened, whether Storrow had second thoughts and declared himself unworthy to spare Una's feelings or, abetted by her mother, Una decided that a man who talked vaguely of wandering in South America would prove an unworthy husband. Whatever the explanation, Una was deeply hurt: nothing was to turn out well for her.[3]

In the following year, Una and Rose still drifted in and out of schools and art classes, and Julian was again performing poorly at Harvard. His failure was a disappointment to Pierce, who had assumed responsibility for the youth's education out of dedication to Hawthorne and probably in memory of his own dead sons. (Not much succeeded for Pierce, who was to live only another year.) Julian evidently convinced his mother that he would be able to complete his education if they moved to Dresden, Germany, where he would enter an engineering school. Sophia had learned that the cost of living there was less than it was in Concord. It was a venture as ill conceived and pathetic as Clifford's train ride in *The House of the Seven Gables*.

In Dresden Julian was soon more interested in a young American girl, May Albertina Amelung, than in engineering. Shortly they were engaged and were married in 1870. The couple returned to the United States, leaving his mother and two sisters in Germany. About this time Una and Rose met George P. Lathrop, the son of a distinguished New York physician, and, report had it, both fell in love, although it became clear to most observers that Lathrop's interest was Rose. After Lathrop returned to study law at Columbia University, the Hawthornes went to England, where they had the assistance and care of Hawthorne's old friends, the Bennochs.

Sophia's health began to fail, and she did not survive the winter, dying of typhoid pneumonia at 12:25 P.M. on February 26, 1871, according to Rose. "Sophia, Wife of Nathaniel Hawthorne," was buried at Kensal Green, not far from the grave of Leigh Hunt but thousands of miles from the Charter Street Burying Point or the Sleepy Hollow Cemetery in Concord.

Shortly after the funeral Lathrop, who had quickly abandoned law school for a literary career, arrived in London. Almost at once Rose and he were engaged, and, if Una had not known earlier, she now learned that her twenty-year-old sister was the chosen one. Una had to accept Lathrop's rejection, and so at twenty-seven found herself with a younger sister eager to marry immediately and a brother whose wife gave birth to the first of nine children on September 1. Alone and abandoned, she apparently had a psychotic episode which led Rose to marry on September 10 and accept Lathrop as "a protector" against a wrathful sister. According to her uncle, Nathaniel Peabody, Una "became dangerously insane, spent great sums of money, [and] nearly took the lives of three people" before being "confined in an asylum." Elizabeth Peabody, as was her custom, came to the rescue.[4]

When in 1872 Julian, now the father of two children, lost his job in New York, he decided to return to Dresden and undertake a literary career. Julian idealized his father—"I saw and knew him simply as the handsomest, strongest, greatest, and best of mankind, who could do anything and was everything; not the author of *The Scarlet Letter*, but Papa"—but he was to live out his life in the paternal shadow.[5]

Una gradually recovered from her depression and took refuge in an
orphanage under the supervision of the Church of England, where she
performed social services in an institution not unlike the one in which her
father met the insistent little child. Then, with the assistance of Robert
Browning, she pieced together a text from the two manuscripts of "Septimius Felton"—a dubious undertaking for a woman whose ties to reality
were fragile. In her anguish she may have been attracted to the story of
the suicidal theological student and of the tormented, perhaps demented
Sibyl Dacy, who wants to die. Worst of all, she was reactivating her father's crack-up which she had observed with fear and trembling only a few
years earlier. Una seemed destined to make one unfortunate decision after another. Driven but headstrong as ever and without inner peace, she
returned to the United States and lived with Rose and her husband, only
to discover that the Lathrops had entered not into matrimonial bliss but
rather into conflicts and reconciliations, although Rose was now pregnant. At this time Julian and Lathrop were feuding—soon they took to
the newspapers—both desirous of advancing their careers by exploiting
Nathaniel Hawthorne in biographical studies.

While Una stayed with the Lathrops she met and became engaged to a
young poet, Albert Webster, Jr. Apparently everybody except Una knew
he was dying of tuberculosis. When Webster set off for the Sandwich
Islands in search of a favorable climate, Una returned to England to wait
for him. She lived with Julian, who had now settled in England to further
his career. Webster died at sea. It was the final rejection Una had to bear.
She retreated to an Anglican convent, took ill one day, and died at age
thirty-three. She was buried next to her mother in Kensal Green.

For a time Lathrop seemed to be establishing a career for himself with
the *Atlantic Monthly*, where he was associated with Howells. The death
of the Lathrops' child in 1881 was a crushing blow in a relationship
strained by incompatibility and Lathrop's alcoholism. He purchased the
Wayside, but when he lost his post at the *Atlantic Monthly*, they lived
there like paupers.

Julian wrote novels which enjoyed some brief popularity. Although
deeply influenced by his father's example, he lacked his father's genius.
His marriage evidently failed sometime after the death at birth of their
last child, Perdita. When writing provided inadequate returns, he drifted
into other activities. He speculated in gold shares in a Canadian mine and
was convicted of embezzlement. He served a jail term, continued to write

about his father, and married his companion of twenty-five years one month after his wife's death in 1925. Julian died in San Francisco in 1934.

The only Hawthorne child who achieved happiness and contentment was Rose, who entered a Catholic order in 1895. Two years later she published *Memories of Hawthorne*, in which she maintained that her father was her guide: "My own convictions about human duties . . . towards human suffering were clearly formed in youth by countless passages" in his writings, particularly the account of his visit to the English workhouse. In Hawthorne, New York, as Mother Alphonsa she devoted herself to the care of cancer patients who at the beginning of the century were treated like lepers.[6] On July 9, 1926, the anniversary of the marriage of her parents, she died peacefully in her sleep at the Rosary Hill Home in Hawthorne.

Perhaps she fulfilled Hester Prynne's dream: "The angel and apostle of the coming revelation must be a woman, indeed, but lofty, pure, and beautiful; and wise, moreover, not through dusky grief, but the ethereal medium of joy; and showing how sacred love should make us happy, by the truest test of a life successful to such an end!"

Notes

ABBREVIATIONS

Antioch	Antioch College, typed transcriptions by Robert L. Straker
Bancroft	The Bancroft Library, the University of California, Berkeley
Berg	Henry W. and Albert A. Berg Collection, New York Public Library
BPL	Boston Public Library
Bowdoin	Bowdoin College, the Hawthorne-Longfellow Library
C.	*The Centenary Edition of the Works of Nathaniel Hawthorne*
EIHC	*Essex Institute Historical Collections*
Essex	Essex Institute, Salem, Massachusetts
EN	*The English Notebooks of Nathaniel Hawthorne*
AF	Annie Fields
JTF	James T. Fields
Folger	Folger Shakespeare Library
Harvard	Harvard University, the Houghton Library
EH	Elizabeth Hawthorne
JH	Julian Hawthorne
MLH	Maria Louisa Hawthorne
NH	Nathaniel Hawthorne
SH	Sophia Hawthorne
UH	Una Hawthorne
Huntington	Henry E. Huntington Library and Art Museum
NHJ	*Nathaniel Hawthorne Journal*
RHL	Rose Hawthorne Lathrop
LC	Library of Congress
MPM	Mary Peabody Mann
MHS	Massachusetts Historical Society
NHHS	New Hampshire Historical Society
NYPL	New York Public Library

EP	Elizabeth Peabody
FP	Franklin Pierce
Smith	Sophia Smith Collection, Smith College
Virginia	Clifton Waller Barrett Library, University of Virginia

PREFACE

1. The youths appear in the following works: Ilbrahim in "The Gentle Boy," Robin Molineux in "My Kinsman, Major Molineux," Cyrus Bourne in "Roger Malvin's Burial," Owen Warland in "The Artist of the Beautiful," Giovanni in "Rappaccini's Daughter," Donatello in *The Marble Faun,* and Ned in "Grimshawe."
2. C.13: 15–16; C.11: 4; C.13: 391.
3. Donald Hall, *Remembering Poets* (New York: Harper and Row, 1978), 102.
4. 1866-[3-1?], SH to JTF, BPL; 1870-12-3, EH to Richard Manning, Essex; [1876]-4-12 and 5-7, EH to Cousin Maria, Bowdoin.
5. Reynolds Price, *A Common Room—Essays 1954–1987* (New York: Atheneum, 1989), 39.

PROLOG. *The Contemporary Portrait*

1. Holden, 262; Ellis, 149.
2. Cleve Gray, ed., *John Marin by John Marin* (New York: Holt, Rinehart, and Winston, [1977?]), 51.
3. Stewart (1945), 320; 1865-11-25, SH to Horatio Bridge, Bowdoin; Trollope, in Austin, 215; Channing (1967), 273; Curtis, in Cameron (1968), 35; Conway, ed., *The Blithedale Romance* (London: James Nisbet, 1901), xxxvi.
4. G. P. Lathrop, 12: 451; 1842-8-30, SH to her mother, Berg; Bremer, 2: 597; Headley, in C.8: 631n; Stoddard (1971), 122; Fields, in E. W. Emerson, 208; Howe, in Higginson, 39; Conway (1904), 1: 135.
5. Hillard, in Cameron, 130; Sedgwick, 397; "hawk-eye," C.8: 92; Bright, 397; Bremer, in R. Lathrop, 200.
6. Sedgwick, 397; Bowdoin professor, in Arvin (1929), 22; North Adams citizen, in Bliss Perry, *The Amateur Spirit* (Boston: Houghton Mifflin, 1904), 128; Holmes, 359.
7. Bremer, 2: 597; English admirer (Bright), in Hull (1980), 25; contemporary, in Goodrich, 2: 270; Loring, in Conway (1890), 106n.
8. M. Hawthorne (1937), 265; Howells, 51; Sanborn (1908-1), 55–56; Fields, in Austin, 209; Channing (1967), 266.
9. J. Hawthorne (1938), 50, and (1932), 505; "low musical voice," in Dicey, 241–246, and see G. P. Loring, in Cameron, 213–218; Mitchell, 2: 247; Conolly, in M. Hawthorne (1937), 265.

10. Alcott (1938), 336, 335; Duyckinck, in Leyda, 422; Bowdoin professor, in Arvin (1929), 22; Emerson, in Bright, 397, but according to Wagenknecht, Longfellow made a similar comment, 17; 1885, G. P. A. Healy to unidentified correspondent, Essex; Fields, in Austin, 209; Hillard, in Cameron, 130; Holmes, 359; Lowell (1897), 136.

11. Hillard, in Cameron, 130; Newcomb, 57; 1885, G. P. A. Healy to unidentified correspondent, Essex; Henry James, Sr., in Higginson, 193–194.

12. Longfellow, in Cohen (1969), 10; Fuller, *Letters*, 2: 66; Duyckinck (1845), 377.

13. Hillard, in G. P. Lathrop, 562; Alcott, in Matthiessen, 230; Duyckinck, in Leyda, 385–386.

14. C.10: 33; *North American Review* 76 (1853): 229; C.16: 325.

15. MPM to her son Horace, Antioch; Holmes, 359. According to Howells, Holmes warned him in 1860: "I don't know that you will ever feel you have really met him. He is like a dim room with a little taper of personality burning on the corner of the mantel" (38).

16. [1864?], SH to unidentified correspondent, Berg; C.1: 66, 113, 67.

O N E. *"Salem Is My Dwelling Place"*

1. Northend, 106.
2. See Phillips (1947), 9.
3. Osgood and Batchelder, 205; see Spofford, 314.
4. Matthiessen, 197.
5. James, 9.
6. C.9: 123–124.
7. C.2: 161–162.
8. Mouffe, 67–68.
9. C.15: 518, 521, 596.
10. See Coolidge and Moore, 155; C.1: 8.
11. C. H. King, 43.
12. C.9: 451–455, 459–460.
13. C.11: 267.
14. C.12: 91, 343.
15. C.12: 182.
16. C.12: 347.
17. In this account of the Salem almshouse I have drawn on the following sources: Osgood and Batchelder, Tolles, Webber and Nevins, and *Visitor's Guide to Salem* (1892). The almshouse was partly torn down in 1954 and completely demolished in 1985. I am indebted to Eugenia A. Fountain of the Essex Institute Library for additional information.

T W O. *The Heritage: The Hathornes and the Mannings*

1. C.11: 68.
2. See Perley, 3: 137, and Loggins, 63, 61, 42.
3. C.11: 70.
4. See Loggins, 83, and Phillips (1933), 140, 189, 250.
5. C.12: 368.
6. C.1: 10.
7. Loggins, 160–167.
8. Ibid., 176–179; Hoeltje (1953), 331; and see Perley, 3: 193–194.
9. Hoeltje (1953), 333–334, 338–342; Matlack, 295, 297. The ship's logs are in the Essex Institute. See also M. Hawthorne (1940-1), 1–13.
10. Certificate of citizenship, 1803-12-13, Bowdoin; J. Hawthorne (1884), 1: 182.
11. Baym (1982), 8–9.
12. Brooks, 288–291; probate of wills, 1808-4-19, Bowdoin; Hoeltje (1953), 351–354; Goodspeed, 268–269. The modern spelling is Suriname.
13. J. Hawthorne (1884), 1: 98–99.
14. [1870]-12-13, EH to JTF, Essex; printed in J. T. Fields, 44. Baym (1982) suggests that NH "probably never missed his dead father consciously," his response being intellectual rather than emotional, and that the Manning uncles became substitute fathers (11–12).
15. C.11: 314; C.12: 327.
16. C.17: 497; C.5: 63; C.10: 64.
17. Probate of wills, 1808-4-19, Bowdoin; EH, "Some Facts about Hawthorne," [25], Essex.
18. C.12: 481, 455, 453. Orphans are present in *Fanshawe*, "The Gentle Boy," "Alice Doane's Appeal," "Young Goodman Brown," "Rappaccini's Daughter," *The Scarlet Letter*, *The House of the Seven Gables*, *The Blithedale Romance*, *The Marble Faun*, "Grimshawe," "Septimius Felton," and "The Dolliver Romance."
19. Erlich (1984), 99; and see W. A. Jones (1977), 18. Drawing upon undeveloped suggestions of Randall Stewart and Norman Holmes Pearson, Gloria C. Erlich (1984) has presented, with the assistance of Erik Erikson's theories and a great deal of original research, the most elaborate argument for the importance of the Mannings, particularly Robert, in the development of NH. By emphasizing the family romance in any discussion of NH's life and writings, she has also corrected the distortions of Frederick C. Crews's application of Freudian principles to the writings.

    According to Erlich's construction, Robert Manning is the subject of much of NH's fiction, beginning as early as "Roger Malvin's Burial," in which the "father" has the same initials. She finds veiled allusions to Manning's interest in botany in such characters as Rappaccini and Chillingsworth; and blacksmiths like Robert Danforth in "The Artist of the Beautiful" and Hollingsworth in *The Blithedale Romance* reflect earlier Mannings who were blacksmiths. Although she finds "an erotic attachment" (118), she rejects James R. Mellows's speculation that there was a "homosexual assault" (610) during the years in which Robert Manning and his nephew slept in the same bed. It is unnecessary to detail my objections to her thesis since my emphasis upon the Hathorne inheritance is in effect my answer.

20. Erlich (1984), 101.
21. 1853-1-1, *National Magazine*, in Cameron, 39. NH may have been referring to the Mannings in the following: "And the child feels a confidence both in the wisdom and affection of his parents, which he cannot transfer to any delegate of their duties, however conscientious" (C.10: 406).
22. EH, "Some Facts about Hawthorne," [27, 6, 2–3], Essex.
23. J. Hawthorne (1884), 1: 99; Stewart (1945), 319, 325.
24. EH, "Some Facts about Hawthorne," [6], Essex.
25. Ibid., [16].
26. See Baym (1982) for the most perceptive treatment of the mother in recent decades. She rightly attacks the received portrait of the recluse, although she may neglect the effect of what must have appeared in the eyes of the children as excessive passivity and withdrawal. The suggestion that "representation of the mother as absent actually marks an oppressive sense of her presence in his psychic world" (7) is a brilliant speculation, but it is not supported satisfactorily by the writings.
27. For psychoanalytic evaluations, see Oberndorf and especially Zangwill, who, though too schematic and clinical, offers penetrating insights. See also Crews, Morris, and Normand.
28. EH, "Some Facts about Hawthorne," [28], Essex.
29. C.18: 456; J. Hawthorne (1884), 1: 5.
30. R. H. Lathrop, 12: 476.
31. Ibid., 473–475; letters of EH, 35, 46, Bowdoin.
32. See Young, 126ff.

T H R E E. *"The Gentle Boy"*

1. C.18: 521.
2. C.12: 95–96, 108, and see also 355, 377–378, 257–258.
3. C.12: 353.
4. On the first appearance of this tale in the *Token* in 1832, the incident is described as follows: "The poor child's arms had been raised to guard his head from the storm of blows; but now he dropped them at once, for he was stricken in a tender part." In *Twice-told Tales* the final clause was omitted; see J. Donald Crowley's commentary in C.9: 503–504. NH may have removed this reference to an injury to the groin on the grounds of its "prurient" suggestiveness, as Crowley proposes, but one wonders why he included it in the first place, particularly in view of the recurrent emasculation imagery in his

writings. If, as I suggest, the characterization of Ilbrahim is in large part autobiographical, perhaps NH was describing that mysterious injury he sustained in his youth which incapacitated him for a number of years and led him to withdraw from his peers.

5. Longfellow, in Cohen (1969), 10.
6. 1862-1-1, SH to JTF, BPL. See also Miller (1978), 47–54.
7. C. 17: 406; C.18: 13–14, 95.

F O U R. *"Living upon Uncle Robert"*

1. J. Hawthorne (1884), 1: 99.
2. Bentley, 3: 331; "War of 1812," *EN*, 64; see Loggins and "A List of the Occupants of the Tomb of Richard Manning in the Howard Street Cemetery of Salem," Essex.
3. 1814-1-12, EH to Robert Manning, Essex.
4. "Grievous disinclination," J. Hawthorne (1884), 1: 95; C.16: 30–31.
5. Stewart (1945), 326.
6. 1815-1-20, NH's mother to Richard Manning, Bowdoin.
7. C.5: 122; Alcott, in Bedell, 11.
8. C.17: 510.
9. See Stewart (1945); Bassan (1964), 276–277; and Erlich (1984), 102.
10. 1813-8-14, Richard Manning to NH, Bowdoin.
11. 1816-8-9, Robert Manning to NH's mother, Bowdoin.
12. See 1818-8-11 and 11-[ca. 4], letters of EH, Bowdoin.
13. Fields, in Howe (1922), 59; 1841-6-11, MLH to NH, Berg; 1818-12-15, EH to Priscilla M. Dike, Bowdoin; Stewart (1945), 322.
14. Jacob Dingley and Robert Manning, in M. Hawthorne (1939-1), 107, 109; NH to Robert Manning, C.15: 109, 111. I have not drawn on the material in Pickard (1897), whose attempts to explain the sources of his book are unconvincing. I completely concur in the judgment of Erlich (1984).
15. 1819-6-6, Mary Manning to NH's mother, Bowdoin.
16. C.15: 112.
17. 1819-8-3, Mary Manning to NH's mother, Bowdoin; NH to MLH, C.15: 114; 1820-1-25, NH's mother to Robert Manning, Bowdoin; 1820-2-8, Robert Manning to MLH, Bowdoin.
18. 1820-2-20, Mary Manning to NH's mother, Bowdoin.
19. C.15: 117–118.
20. C.15: 119.
21. "Oratorio," see Ryan, 243–255; C.15: 120, 122; 1820-5-11, Robert Manning to NH, Bowdoin; 1820-6-6, Mary Manning to NH's mother, Bowdoin; 1820-7-4, MLH to her mother, Bowdoin; 1820-11-7, MLH to her mother, Bowdoin.
22. C.15: 124, 126–127; 1820-5-11, Robert Manning to NH, Bowdoin; C.15: 137.
23. C.15: 132.

24. C.15: 136, 131.
25. Bassan (1964), 277–278.
26. C.15: 114–115.
27. C.15: 114, 132, 134.
28. C.15: 252; Hillard, 258. See also Kesselring, Holsberry, and Turner (1972).
29. Chandler (1931) has transcribed the entire run of the publication.
30. C.15: 132.
31. C.15: 137, 153, 138, 150. See also chapter 2, note 19.
32. C.15: 138–139.
33. C.15: 150.

F I V E. *Bowdoin College: Venturing into the World*

1. Bridge (1968), 25. See also Burnham, 131–138; Hoeltje (1958), 205–228; G. T. Little (1894) and (1904), 179–186; Slattery, 449–469; and L. Thompson, 23–29, 349.
2. C.15: 159.
3. Slattery, 457; C.16: 579.
4. See Cleaveland and Packard, 130–131, 303; Slattery, 458–459; Bridge (1968), 53; and Turner (1980), 36–40.
5. Clark (1975), 16.
6. Ibid., 16–17.
7. G. T. Little (1894), lxviii, and see Bridge (1968), 39.
8. G. T. Little (1894), lxviii, and see Bridge (1968), 39.
9. Nichols, 17.
10. G. T. Little (1894), xlii–xliii.
11. Bridge (1968), 45.
12. 1821-10-15, Robert Manning to Miriam Manning, Bowdoin; Bridge (1968), 3.
13. C.15: 155.
14. 1821-10-15, Robert Manning to Miriam Manning, Bowdoin; and see C.15: 155.
15. 1821-10-15, Robert Manning to Miriam Manning, Bowdoin; C.15: 155, 159.
16. See C.16: 616.
17. N. Hawthorne (1852), 14.
18. C.15: 223; N. Hawthorne (1852), 17.
19. C.11: 4–5.
20. C.11: 4; [1866 after 1-16], SH to Horatio Bridge, Bowdoin.
21. Bridge (1968), 6, 40, 14, 5.
22. *Merchant of Venice*, V. i. 1–24; Bridge (1968), 35–36.
23. Bridge (1968), 47; J. Hawthorne (1884), 1: 44.
24. C.11: 4–5.
25. C.15: 168, 171, 173.
26. 1822-5-29, William Allen to NH's mother, Essex.
27. C.15: 174.

28. Harwell, 14–15.
29. See 1822-5-22, MLH to EH, Bowdoin; and C.15: 168.
30. C.15: 184.
31. "Constitution of Pot-8-O Club," Bowdoin. The signers of the document were Jonathan Cilley, Alfred Mason, Jeremiah Dummery, George W. Pierce, David Shepley, and NH.
32. Cilley and "another student" (James Ware Bradbury), in Slattery, 461–462; and see Burnham, 136–137. Bradbury also reported that NH ogled Professor Cleaveland's beautiful maid.
33. C.15: 194.
34. Ibid.
35. M. Hawthorne (1940-2), 278.
36. Bridge, 57.
37. C.16: 523; J. Hawthorne (1884), 1: 96; Stoddard (1853), 18.

S I X. *Intercourse with the World:* Fanshawe

1. See J. Hawthorne (1884), 1: 123–125; W. A. Jones (1977), and Clark (1978), 5–6.
2. See Hedges, 22–26.
3. Cantwell suggests that Walcott is "modeled" after Pierce (122).
4. Burnham, 135; Kesselring, #372; Robbins, 22–23, a copy of which is in the Harvard library.
5. Silverman, 77; and see Loggins, 107.
6. Colacurcio terms the youths "fictive versions of the young Hawthorne-self" (50); and see Levy.
7. Harwell, 18–20.
8. Hale, in C.3: 304.

S E V E N. *"Castle Dismal"*

1. J. Hawthorne (1884), 1: 96; EH, "Some Facts about Hawthorne," [29], Essex; C.15: 209.
2. [1870]-12-13/16, EH to JTF, BPL; C.7: 149.
3. *EN*, 256; C.15: 494.
4. C.8: 24; C.9: 192.
5. C.15: 251–253.
6. 1870-12-26, EH to JTF, BPL; C.8: 12.
7. C.15: 659; M. Hawthorne (1937), 267, 278.
8. 1843-9-15, SH to MLH, Berg; 1843-8-13/15, SH to her mother, Berg. See also Osgood and Batchelder, 59.
9. C.8: 89.
10. 1870-12-26, EH to JTF, BPL; C.14: 367.

11. Tucker, 25; C.15: 211, 213.
12. C.15: 198, 211, 213–214.
13. C.15: 212, 213.
14. Mouffe, 10–11.
15. C.15: 220.
16. C.9: 312. See also "The Susan 'Affair,'" in *NHJ 1971*, 12.
17. Mouffe, 8, 11.
18. C.8: 11, 13; Mouffe, 40, 26, 36; C.8: 29–30.
19. Mouffe, 37; C.8: 15, 22–23, 10–11.
20. Adkins, 122.
21. J. Hawthorne (1884), 1: 131–132; Adkins, 122.
22. W. A. Jones (1975), 91–140.
23. J. Hawthorne (1884), 1: 134.
24. C.15: 230, 234, 236–237.
25. C.15: 236.
26. C.15: 247.
27. J. Hawthorne (1884), 1: 138, 146.
28. C.15: 230, and see Chorley, in Crowley, 49.
29. Bridge (1968), 49. Bridge denied Elizabeth Peabody's report that NH was called "Oberon" by his Bowdoin classmates.
30. C.11: 170, 171, 173, 177.
31. C.11: 314.
32. C.11: 314, 316, 318.
33. C.15: 38; Bridge (1968), 68; Charles Fenno Hoffman in the *American Monthly Magazine* (March 1838), in Crowley, 62.
34. Bridge (1968), 74, 70; J. Hawthorne (1884), 1: 138.
35. Bridge (1968), 79, 72
36. Ibid., 73.
37. C.9: 532; Bridge (1968), 74.
38. Bridge (1968), 75.
39. C.8: 33, 46.
40. C.8: 33, 44, 64, 46, 65–66. For Eliza Gibbs, see Stewart (1948), 43–44, and C.8: 576.
41. C.8: 33, 64.

E I G H T. *Intercourse with the World: The Early Tales*

1. C.15: 252.
2. Colacurcio argues brilliantly what seems to me a dubious thesis, that NH in his historical tales is a kind of predecessor of Perry Miller.
3. Melville (1850), 126; James, 46–47.
4. "Concord, May 23, 1864"; see Kesselring, 70, 90, 91, 94, 285, 335, 353, 356, 379, 385.

5. C.9: 4–5; C.11: 315; C.10: 172; C.1: 103; C.7: 36. The subject is thoroughly discussed in Luther S. Luedtke's *Nathaniel Hawthorne and the Romance of the Orient* (Bloomington: Indiana University Press, 1989), which appeared after the completion of this biography.
6. C.12: 115.
7. C.9: 175, 180.
8. C.11: 279.
9. C.11: 227.
10. Mayo, in Crowley, 222.
11. At the beginning and end of the tale, the landscape in which Roger Malvin, the father, lies unburied is, although a forest, described in sea images—"the summit of one of the gentle swells" (338) and "the base summit of a swell of land" (356)—the imagery like the tale coming full circle, repeating itself.

    In this reading of "Roger Malvin's Burial" I have drawn, among others, upon R. P. Adams, Crews, Donohue, and Waggoner (1963). Above all, I am indebted to a study by a former student, Dr. George Satran.
12. C.11: 269.
13. C.11: 273.
14. Melville (1850), 124, 147, 126; James, 81; Van Doren, 76.
15. *EN*, 64.
16. C.15: 249, 252.
17. C.15: 255; Longfellow, in Crowley, 57–58.

N I N E. *The Peabodys*

1. C.8: 173.
2. Pearson (1958-2), 263–264.
3. 1800-2-17, Mrs. Peabody to her future husband, MHS.
4. 1834-8-26/30, EP to her sister Mary, Berg.
5. See 1822-6-?, Mrs. Peabody to EP, Antioch; 1829-6-?, journal of Mrs. Peabody, Antioch.
6. 1830-8-22, journal of Mrs. Peabody; undated letter, probably 1827, Mrs. Peabody to her daughters Elizabeth and Mary, Antioch.
7. 1851-1-21, Mrs. Peabody to EP, Antioch.
8. Emerson, in Fuller, *Memoirs*, 1: 321.
9. Saxton, 224; Alcott, in Saxton, 60–61.
10. Matthiessen, 321n.
11. 1869-7-29, W. L. Garrison to his wife, BPL; C. Dall, 419; 1826-9-?, EP to Mrs. Richard Sullivan, Antioch.
12. [1850-9-?], SH to her mother, Berg; [ca. 1870], JH to Minnie Amelung, Essex.
13. 1838-8-1, EP to Horace Mann, Antioch; 1830-7-6 and 1828-4-21, EP to Mrs. Richard Sullivan, Antioch.

14. Tharp (1950), 40; EP, in Roberts, 173; "the pleasures," in Baylor, 149; S. Clarke, 131.
15. 1834-8-26/30, EP to her sister Mary, Berg.
16. [1844]-1-30, SH to her sister Mary, Berg; 1851-2-3, SH to her sister Mary, Berg; 1828-2-7, Mrs. Peabody to her daughters, Antioch.
17. 1859-9-17 and 1859-10-5?, MPM to SH, MHS; 1849-2-21, MPM to Horace Mann, Antioch.
18. Mann, 1: vi.
19. 1834-2-3 and 1834-4-9, Cuba journals, Berg, transcription of Claire Badaracco, 23, 81.
20. 1851-8-3, Mrs. Peabody to SH, Berg; 1851-4-3, SH to EP, Berg; 1851-4-24, Margaret Corlies to EP, Virginia.
21. [1845-1-?], MPM to SH, Berg; [1837?]-8-8, SH to EP, Ohio State.
22. 1835-3-27, SH to her mother, Virginia; Cuba journals, 1834-6-6/8, Berg, 114.
23. [1838], SH to EP, Berg; 1827-10-8/10, SH to Maria Chase, Smith; 1834-8-18, EP to her sister Mary, Antioch; 1834-8-31, Elizabeth Williams to SH, Huntington.
24. 1827-10-8/10, SH to Maria Chase, Smith; 1834-3-11, Cuba journals, Berg, 49; [1853?]-12-26, SH to EP, Berg; [1859? after 10-20], SH to EP, Berg.
25. 1845-3-13, SH to MLH, Berg; 1842-8-[5], SH to her mother, Berg; 1846-12-20, SH to Horatio Bridge, in Bridge (1968), 189; 1851-2-3, SH to her sister Mary, Berg.
26. 1868-12-4, SH to EP, Ohio State.
27. 1851-2-3, SH to MPM, Berg; 1834-3-9/22 and 6-12/18, Cuba journals, Berg.
28. 1846-10-8, Mrs. Peabody to SH, Huntington.
29. 1850-7-29, N. C. Peabody to EP, Antioch.

T E N. *Two Sisters in Love*

1. Pearson (1958-2), 265.
2. 1837-11-16, MPM to her brother George, Berg.
3. Ibid.
4. J. Hawthorne (1884), 1: 165–166.
5. [1838-11-10?], EP to MLH, Berg; J. Hawthorne (1884), 1: 166; [1839-1-19], EP to EH, Berg; Loggins, 287, and see J. Hawthorne (1938), 44.
6. Pearson (1958-2), 266–267.
7. [1837 or 1838], EP to EH, Berg.
8. 1838-3-3, MPM to Horace Mann, MHS.
9. Burley, in Pearson (1963), 10; Fuller, *Memoirs*, 1: 320; and see Tharp (1950), 119.
10. Very, in Gittelman, 161; Lidian Emerson, in McAleer, 284, 282; Emerson's detractors, in Gittelman, 227–228.
11. E. Peabody (1984), 409.

12. Ibid., 406.
13. Ibid., 208, 221; Gittelman, 282.
14. 1839-1-5, MPM to SH, Berg; Gittelman, 282.
15. C.15: 262, 269, 270.
16. Dorfer, 199, 197–198.
17. Dall, in Pearson (1958-1), 283n. Dall concludes: "It was a very unhappy thing for Nathaniel Hawthorne that he married Sophia. It would have been worse had he married Elizabeth[;] she was old enough to have been his mother." EP was exactly NH's age. Dall's review of *Twice-told Tales* is reprinted in *NHJ 1974*, 75–84.
18. See Pearson (1958-2), 267; [1838?-6-17/18?], EP to SH, Berg.
19. 1838-4-26, SH to EP, Berg.
20. 1838-4-27, SH to EP, Bancroft.
21. 1838-5-14 and 6-1, SH to EP, Bancroft.
22. 1838-5-2, journal, SH to EP, Berg.
23. E. Peabody (1984), 432.

E L E V E N. *Mary Silsbee: "Star of Salem"*

1. Pearson (1964), 304; Tharp (1950), 347. For an account of the Silsbee house, see Tolles, 29–30.
2. C.15: 278.
3. J. Hawthorne (1884), 1: 173.
4. Ibid., 167–169, 173.
5. 1828-5-1, Ann Storrow to Jared Sparks, in Blanshard, 230–231.
6. Roberts, 164–165; [1833?], Mrs. Peabody to EP, Antioch; Tharp (1950), 61, 347.
7. C.15: 54; Harris, 375; H. W. Longfellow, *Letters*, 2: 162–163.
8. J. Hawthorne (1884), 1: 159.
9. C.17: 437–438.
10. J. Hawthorne (1884), 1: 170.
11. E. Peabody (1984), 420.
12. C.15: 58.
13. Sparks, 294. See also her letter after her husband's death, 1870-2-14, Harvard.
14. C.15: 279.
15. Ibid.
16. Pearson (1964), 304.
17. J. Hawthorne (1884), 1: 171.
18. C.15: 262; and see his letter in 1853 to O'Sullivan, C.16: 663.
19. H. King, 400.
20. J. Hawthorne (1884), 1: 173–174; Bridge (1968), 21–22. See also Turner (1980), 97–98.

21. *Democratic Review* 3 (September 1838): 73; C.8: 62.
22. H. King, 404; *Democratic Review* 10 (May 1842): 484; 1843-11-24, John L. O'Sullivan to Henry A. Weiss, in *NHJ 1971*, 121.
23. [1838-9-24/25?], EP to EH, Berg.
24. C.8: 167–170.
25. Mouffe, 68, 69.
26. 1838-7-23, SH to EP, Berg.
27. C.8: 85; C.15: 274.
28. C.8: 105, 126, 127, 106, 89, 105, 96, 92.
29. C.15: 276.

T W E L V E. *The Comedy of Manners Ends Happily*

1. C.15: 278–279.
2. H. B. Adams, 2: 541–542; C.15: 288; [1838?-11-17], S. J. Goodrich to MPM, Antioch. By one of those strange coincidences of life, Una Hawthorne was briefly engaged to the son of Ann Storrow's brother-in-law.
3. C.15: 312.
4. C.15: 312, 448. Mary Sparks apparently still suffered from poor health a year later; see 1841-8-3, MLH to NH, Berg.
5. E. Peabody (1984), 431–432.
6. 1866-1-4 and [1864-5-20], SH to AF, BPL; 1865-2-20, SH to FP, NHHS.
7. [1864?], SH to unidentified correspondent, Berg.
8. C.15: 494; 1846-3-6, SH to her mother, Berg; [1854-9-24], SH to her father, Berg.
9. [1838-10]-29, SH to EP, Virginia; *Twice-told Tales* (1837), Berg; Clark (1978), 14–15. The model for Ilbrahim, the son of Dr. E. A. Holyoke, rested his head on a bolster from the "best bedroom" in the Peabody house; see 1901-11-10, George O. Holyoke to G. M. Wilson, in Turner (1980), 411n.
10. 1838-12-6/8, SH to NH, Virginia.
11. Ibid.
12. Mouffe, 80.
13. Turner (1980), 121, dates the engagement about the middle of 1839.
14. See E. Peabody (1984), 217.

T H I R T E E N. *Port-Admiral at the Boston Custom-House*

1. 1837-4-19, O'Sullivan and editors of the *Democratic Review* to NH, in J. Hawthorne (1884), 1: 159. According to Bufford Jones, between 1837 and 1842 "no fewer than 128 items appeared on Hawthorne and his works"; see the *Nathaniel Hawthorne Review*, 14 (Spring 1988): 3.
2. C.15: 266.

3. S. Longfellow, 1: 281; C.15: 276, 288.

4. S. Longfellow, 1: 281; C.15: 276, 288.

5. C.15: 489, 287.

6. 1837-3-26, Horatio Bridge to NH, in J. Hawthorne (1884), 1: 152; 1837-3-28, FP to NH, in J. Hawthorne (1884), 1: 154.

7. 1837-4-14 and 4-7, Horatio Bridge to NH, in J. Hawthorne (1884), 1: 158, 156.

8. Tharp (1950), 45; [1838-10-19], EP to EH, in *EIHC* 100 (1964): 303–304.

9. 1838-11-6, EP to Mrs. George Bancroft, in Mellow, 155; C.15: 279.

10. Facsimile of pay voucher in Cameron, 516; 1839-1-5, MPM to SH, Berg; 1839-1-17, George Bancroft to Levi Woodbury, in Cameron, 515.

11. C.16: 124; [1845-4-6], MPM to SH, Berg; C.15: 313. To illustrate the purchasing power of the dollar, in 1845 Sophia Hawthorne hired a domestic at $1.25 a week, and her sister Mary rented a house in Hingham, Massachusetts, for $75.00 annually.

12. C.15: 700. Hillard had a brilliant undergraduate career at Harvard. In 1835 he married the daughter of a judge, but the marriage was apparently not successful. More interested in literature than in law, Hillard edited the poetry of Edmund Spenser and wrote a popular travel book as well as the campaign biography of General George McClellan in 1864. A Boston newspaper described him as "midway between the sexes" with "the right of exercising the privileges of the softer portion of humanity." See Palfrey, 339, 48; and Donald, 76, 127.

13. C.15: 430, 464; C.8: 194.

14. C.15: 422, 410–411, 419.

15. C.15: 418, 313, 447.

16. C.15: 497, 508.

17. C.15: 388, 310.

18. C.15: 456; Clark (1978), 63–64. For an account of EP's financial involvement in the publication of these little books, see 1850-7-26, Nathaniel Peabody to EP, and [1850]-12-25, Mrs. Peabody to EP, Antioch.

19. Clark (1978), 69, 74.

20. C.6: 85, 52.

21. C.15: 547, 609–610n.

22. C.15: 563; for Munroe, see *NHJ 1972*, 138.

23. C.15: 281, 310–311, and notes; [1840?], EH to EP, in *NHJ 1972*, 95.

24. C.15: 569–571, 573; and see Fredson Bowers, in C.6: 313–336. For more detailed accounts of NH's somewhat confused publishing career at this time, see *NHJ 1972*, 91–139, C.8: 485–533, C.6: 287–311, and *NHJ 1971*, 3–11.

FOURTEEN. *"Thou Art My Type of Womanly Perfection"*

1. C.15: 398.

2. C.15: 290.

3. C.15: 362–363.
4. C.15: 369, 439.
5. C.15: 620.
6. C.15: 449–450, 523; C.2: 308; C.15: 435.
7. C.15: 329, 334.
8. C.15: 338, 339.
9. C.15: 513, 326.
10. C.15: 342, 357, 358.
11. C.15: 406, 400.
12. C.15: 75.
13. C.15: 471 (emphasis added), 323.
14. C.15: 316.
15. C.15: 524, 542.
16. C.15: 494, 398, 444.
17. C.15: 299, 442, 465.
18. C.15: 374, 330.
19. C.15: 495.
20. C.15: 606, 396, 596.
21. C.15: 368, 511, 382, 428, 431, 335. SH's brother George died of "consumption of the spinal marrow," according to Sophia's journal of 1838–1839, Berg. He had fled to New Orleans in search of a new start, only to become fatally ill.
22. 1841-5-30/31, SH to NH, Berg.
23. C.15: 305.
24. C.15: 317–318.
25. C.15: 427–428.
26. C.15: 521.
27. C.15: 517, 305.
28. C.15: 469.
29. C.15: 611, 612.
30. C.15: 620.
31. C.15: 565.

FIFTEEN. *Brook Farm: "That Abominable Gold-Mine"*

1. C.15: 526.
2. Codman, 11.
3. EP published "A Glimpse of Christ's Idea of Society" in the October issue of the *Dial* and "A Plan of the Roxbury Community" in January 1842; for Fuller and Emerson, see Frothingham, 315, and Crowe, 139.
4. For Ripley and Carlyle, see Swift, 15–16, 143.
5. See Metzdorf, 235–241.
6. R. W. Emerson, *Complete Works*, 10: 364, 366–367; and see Rusk, 291.
7. Crowe, 160.

8. C.15: 527.

9. C.15: 527, 528, 531.

10. C.15: 528. Frank Farley was the handyman at the farm.

11. C.15: 543, 545.

12. 1841-5-30/31, SH to NH, Berg.

13. 1841-5-10 and 6-11, MLH to NH, Berg.

14. 1841-5-6, Mrs. Ripley to Dwight, in Haraszti, 18; Kirby, in Codman, 21.

15. Sedgwick, 397.

16. Emerson, *Complete Works*, 10: 362; 4: 174.

17. Rusk, 285–286; Newcomb, 29; R. W. Emerson, *Journals*, 8: 378; 9: 222.

18. Newcomb, 18.

19. Newcomb, 138, 139; Emerson, *Complete Works*, 10: 362–363.

20. *Dial* 3 (July 1842): 122, 123.

21. Emerson, *Journals*, 8: 179; C.10: 636.

22. 1843-1-16, Margaret Fuller to NH, Berg; C.8: 371.

23. Newcomb, 149, 151.

24. R. W. Emerson, *Letters*, 4: 516.

25. C.15: 553, 557–558.

26. C.15: 563–564.

27. C.15: 565, 566.

28. C.15: 575, 576, 582.

29. C.15: 586; C.8: 209, 210.

30. C.15: 592; C.8: 216–217, 220, 221.

31. C.15: 588, 590.

32. C.15: 624.

33. C.15: 655; C.10: 637. NH made his first attempt to recover his investment in Brook Farm in October 1842; see C.15: 655n. Although Hawthorne was roundly condemned for his depiction of Brook Farm in his romance, his comments are mild next to those of the man who succeeded him as "president" of the "cow-stable," John Van Der Zee Sears: "There was a constant succession coming to the Farm; reformers of everything under the sun; fanatics demanding the instant adoption of their nebulous theories; mental aliens not quite crazy but pretty near it; egoists, wild to be noticed, freaks and fakirs and humbugs of every description, and, worst of all, wrecks of humanity seeking refuge from the slings and arrows of outrageous fortune" (132–133).

SIXTEEN. *"I Take This Dove in Bed and Board"*

1. [1841]-11-13, Lucretia Hale to Sarah J. Hale, Smith.

2. [1842]-4-23, Mary Wilder Foote to SH, in Tileston, 90; 1842-6-19, SH to Mary Wilder Foote, Berg; C.15: 617n. O'Sullivan at this time was a member of the New York legislature.

3. See Tileston, 71–73; R. W. Emerson, *Letters*, 3: 50; [1842]-5-11, SH to Margaret Fuller, Harvard.
4. C.15: 626.
5. 1842-5-23, EH to SH, Berg.
6. C.15: 628–629.
7. 1842-6-15, EH to SH, Berg.
8. [1869]-1-15, EH to Maria, Essex; M. Hawthorne (1947-1), 231.
9. Fuller, *Letters*, 2: 66.
10. C.15: 630.
11. 1842-8-[5], SH to her mother, Berg.
12. Ibid.
13. J. Hawthorne (1884), 1: 264–265.
14. 1853-10-9/16, SH to MPM, Berg.
15. C.15: 637.
16. Turner (1980), 142.
17. 1842-7-10, SH to her mother, Berg.
18. C.15: 639.
19. Emerson, *Letters*, 3: 68; 1842-7-17, MPM to SH, Berg.
20. *NHJ 1973*, 132.

SEVENTEEN. *Eden in Concord*

1. R. W. Emerson, *Complete Works*, 10: 589n.
2. Ibid., 389.
3. C.8: 325–326, 316; C.10: 3, 4.
4. C.8: 320, 321, 345.
5. C.8: 319.
6. C.8: 328.
7. Higginson, 38; C.10: 5; [1845]-1-26, SH to her mother, Berg; [1842]-7-28, Caroline Sturgis to SH, Saint Lawrence University; 1842-8-30-[9-4], SH to her mother, Berg.
8. C.10: 5; Ticknor (1926), 66; C.8: 324.
9. C.10: 9–10.
10. C.8: 322, 334.
11. C.10: 17–18; C.14: 419; 1844-8-27, MLH to her mother, Bowdoin.
12. 1842-7-15, SH to her mother, Berg; C.8: 331; C.15: 671.
13. 1842-8-11, 8-[5], 8-22, 8-30, SH to her mother, Berg.
14. 1842-12-29/30, SH to her mother, Berg.
15. 1842-8-30, SH to her mother, Berg; [1844]-2-6, SH to MPM, Berg.
16. Fuller (1973), 325; C.16: 11.
17. Emerson, *Complete Works*, 11: 84–85; see Yanella, 1–24.
18. R. W. Emerson, *Journals*, 8: 385.
19. Ibid., 172–173, 261.

20. 1842-9-29, SH to her mother, Berg; C.8: 362; [1843]-9-3, SH to her mother, Berg.

21. J. Hawthorne (1884), 1: 394; and see Merton M. Sealts, "Melville and Emerson's Rainbow," *Emerson Society Quarterly* 26 (1980): 77.

22. Emerson, *Journals*, 7: 21; C.8: 336, 357; C.10: 31. See also C.8: 371: "Mr. Emerson came, with a sunbeam in his face; and we had as good a talk as I ever remember experiencing with him."

23. [1843]-9-3, SH to her mother, Berg.

24. C.8: 356, 357; 1842-9-20, SH to MLH, Berg; Curtis, in Cameron, 350.

25. C.15: 656; C.8: 353–354; C.16: 106.

26. Thoreau, *Correspondence*, 124; Henry David Thoreau, *A Week on the Concord and Merrimack Rivers*, Sentry Edition (Boston: Houghton Mifflin, 1961), 16.

27. R. H. Lathrop, 53.

28. Thoreau, *Journal*, 3: 99.

29. Channing (1972), xxxix–xl.

30. Fuller (1973), 324; McGill, vii; Thoreau, *Journal*, 3: 108.

31. Emerson, in McGill, 45; Thoreau, *Journal*, 3: 118; Poe, 113.

32. "Emersonianism," in McGill, 62; see Fuller's letters in R. W. Emerson, *Letters*, 2: 446, 449–450.

33. See C.15: 646–647; C.8: 316, 357.

34. C.10: 21; and see Sanborn (1908-1), 36–37, and Sanborn (1909), 2: 528; C.16: 47.

35. Bridge, in J. Hawthorne (1884), 1: 282; SH to Horatio Bridge, in C.16: 78.

36. C.16: 201; Sanborn (1909), 2: 526; C.16: 199; J. Hawthorne (1884), 1: 324.

37. Channing (1967), 267, 268, 270.

38. Ibid., 273, 270.

39. 1843-4-6, SH to Mary Wilder Foote, in R. H. Lathrop, 55–56.

40. 1843-4-13/14 and 4-20, SH to her mother, Berg.

41. [1843-7-ca. 23/24], SH to her mother, Berg; 1843-11-9, SH and NH to MLH, Berg, reprinted in C.16: 5, 7–8. The most detailed description of the robe appears in J. Hawthorne (1903): "The groundwork was purple, covered all over with conventional palm-leaf in old-gold color; the lining was red. This lining, under the left-hand skirt of the gown, was blackened with ink over a space as large as your hand; for the author was in the habit of wiping his pen thereon; but my mother finally parried this attack by sewing in the centre of the place a pen-wiper in the shape of a butterfly" (15).

42. 1843-12-[3], SH journal, Berg.

43. 1843-1-4, SH to MLH, Berg. See also 1843-1-12, SH to her mother, Berg; and 1843–1844, SH journal, Berg. Although some found NH's voice musical, his son wrote of "his insensibility to music—he was wont to declare that he never could distinguish between 'Yankee Doodle' and 'Hail Columbia' . . ."; J. Hawthorne (1884), 1: 103.

44. Higginson, 37. In one of her letters Flannery O'Connor reported an anecdote (too good to be true) related by a friend: ". . . Hawthorne couldn't stand Emerson or any of that crowd. When one of them came in the front door, Hawthorne went out the back. He met one of them one morning and snarled, 'Good Morning Mr. G., how is your Oversoul this morning?'"; Flannery O'Connor, *The Habit of Being*, ed. Sally Fitzgerald (New York: Farrar, Straus, Giroux, 1979), 145.
45. C.15: 696, 691.
46. [1843]-9-3, SH to her mother, Berg.

E I G H T E E N. *Margaret Fuller in Concord*

1. 1843-1-4, SH to MLH, Berg.
2. 1843-2-23/24, SH to her mother, Berg.
3. Ibid.
4. C.8: 366; C.15: 682.
5. [1843]-3-[28], SH to MPM, Berg; [1843]-5-1, MPM to her mother, MHS; C.15: 686.
6. C.8: 368, 378.
7. C.8: 387, and 649n; 1843-[7]-6/7, SH to her mother, Berg.
8. C.8: 390.
9. [1843]-8-9, SH to MPM, Berg; 1843-12-24, SH journal, Berg; 1844-2-4, SH to MLH, Berg; see [1844]-2-6, SH to MPM, Berg; [1843]-12-23, SH journal, Berg.
10. 1844-2-4, SH to MLH, Berg; 1844-2-4, SH to her mother, Berg; and see 1844-2-11, SH to Mary Wilder Foote, Berg.
11. C.16: 15.
12. C.16: 22.
13. 1843-1-29, SH to MLH, Berg; Thoreau, *Correspondence*, 77; R. W. Emerson, *Letters*, 3: 146–147; 1844-5-4, SH to Mary Wilder Foote, Berg.
14. C.16: 22–23, 25.
15. [1844-4-17/18], SH to her mother, Berg; 1844-4-?, SH (writing for Una) to MLH, Berg; 1844-8-4/6, SH to MLH, Berg; 1844-11-25, MPM to SH, Berg.
16. C.16: 24; "Arethusa," [1844]-5-[21?], SH to her mother, Berg; 1844-8-4/6, SH to MLH, Berg.
17. 1844-9-16, SH to MPM, Berg; 1844-7-2, SH to MLH, Berg.
18. [1845]-2-16, SH to her mother, Berg; 1845-3-13, SH to MLH, Berg; 1845-3-6, SH to her mother, Berg.
19. Fuller, *Memoirs*, 1: 65; C.8: 371; Alcott (1938), 410; Blanchard, 166.
20. Carlyle, in Anthony, 11; Fuller, *Memoirs*, 1: 90; "childlike self," Chevigny, 76–77.

21. Fuller, *Memoirs*, 1: 15, 24; Chevigny, 51. Perhaps the portrait of Beatrice in "Rappaccini's Daughter," which appeared in the *Democratic Review* in December 1844, was influenced by Fuller's involvement with flowers.
22. Chevigny, 61–62.
23. Fuller, 1844 journal, 48–49, 62, MHS.
24. Fuller (1973), 340; 1844 journal, 62–63, 55, MHS.
25. Fuller, 1844 journal, 50–51, 101–102, MHS.
26. Ibid., 61, 74, and see Fuller, *Letters*, 3: 217.
27. Fuller, 1844 journal, 97, MHS; Fuller (1973), 336.
28. Fuller, 1844 journal, 98, 103, MHS.
29. Ibid., 129.
30. 1845-3-6, SH to her mother, Berg.
31. See C.16: 158; Chevigny, 196.
32. C.14: 156–157.
33. Foote, see C.15: 224; rent, see 1843-6-2, SH to her mother, Berg; C.15: 658.
34. C.15: 678, 681, 682.
35. C.8: 367; C.16: 9–10, 23, 21.
36. C.16: 41. See also C.9: 520–527, and Crowley, 74.
37. C.16: 1; 1845-10-2, E. A. Duyckinck to NH, in Bridge (1968), 106; C.16: 126.
38. C.16: 105; C.15: 686–687; SH to Bridge, in C.16: 108.
39. Osgood and Batchelder, 261; C.16: 65, 102–103.
40. 1845-3-21, J. L. O'Sullivan to NH, in J. Hawthorne (1884), 1: 285.
41. C.15: 688; 1845-5-[18 or 25], SH to her mother, Berg. See 1845-5-11, FP to George Bancroft, MHS; C.16: 102–103; 1845-4-19, Seth J. Thomas to George Bancroft, MHS.
42. 1845-5-31 and 8-4, J. L. O'Sullivan to George Bancroft, MHS.
43. 1845-5-27, SH to Mary Wilder Foote, Berg; C.16: 119.
44. 1845-8-24, SH to MLH, Berg; 1845-9-3, MLH to SH, Berg; [1845]-9-22, SH to MLH, Berg; 1845-9-7, SH to her mother, in J. Hawthorne (1884), 1: 286, 287.
45. C.16: 120; 1845-9-28, Horatio Bridge to NH, Bowdoin; C.16: 122.
46. 1845-10-25, John Fairfield to George Bancroft, MHS; C.16: 130; 1845-12-22, J. L. O'Sullivan to John Fairfield, MHS.
47. C.16: 142.
48. See 1846-2-23, George Bancroft to Benjamin F. Browne, and 1846-3-5, Bancroft to James Knox Polk, MHS; Stewart (1948), 79.
49. C.16: 148, 150–151.

N I N E T E E N. *Intercourse with the World:* Mosses from an Old Manse

1. C.15: 462.
2. 1843-12-8, SH journal, Berg, McDonald, 8; 1851-9-30, SH to MPM, Berg.
3. C.8: 240, 235–236, 254.

4. C.8: 249, 253, 242–243, 239.
5. C.8: 244.
6. C.8: 379–380; Holden, 260–267.
7. 1844-1-9, SH to her mother, Berg.
8. C.15: 550, and see 600.
9. C.8: 388.
10. C.16: 105.
11. C.16: 94, 105, 122, 126.
12. C.16: 136.
13. C.10: 32–33.
14. C.17: 201.
15. Melville (1850), 126.
16. Melville (1850), 147; C.10: 64.
17. Lesser, 87–90; Bachelard, 53.
18. J. Hawthorne (1884), 1: 360.
19. In this discussion of "The Artist of the Beautiful" I have drawn upon Bell and Stein. See Idol, 455–460.
20. C.16: 52.
21. C.16: 140, 105.

T W E N T Y. *Salem, Hail and Farewell*

1. C.10: 33–34.
2. C.16: 154n; C.1: 5.
3. C.1: 35; 1846-3-22/23, SH to her mother, in J. Hawthorne (1884), 1: 309; C.16: 156.
4. 1846-11-12/13, SH to her mother, Berg; C.16: 188, 194.
5. 1846-3-6, SH to her mother, Berg; 1846-5-3, SH to MLH, Berg.
6. 1846-3-6, SH to her mother, Berg; C.16: 173–174.
7. [1846?-7?-?] and 1846-10-8, Mrs. Peabody to SH, Huntington; 1847-2-5, SH to her mother, Berg; 1846-12-24, SH to Horatio Bridge, in Bridge (1968), 187; [1847-2-2?], SH to MLH, Berg; C.16: 206.
8. 1846-11-12/13, 9-19, [1847]-9-9, 11-22, SH to her mother, Berg.
9. 1846-5-3 and 6-12, SH to MLH, Berg.
10. [1847]-9-9/10, SH to her mother, Berg.
11. 1847-7-?, SH to NH, Berg; 1848-11-5/6, 1846-3-22/23, [1846]-8-8/9, SH to her mother, Berg; Milton, see [1847]-1-8, Mrs. Peabody to SH, Berg; [1849]-11-30, SH to EP, Berg; 1849-3-18, SH to MPM, Berg.
12. [1848]-7-16, SH to MPM, Berg; J. Hawthorne (1884), 1: 328.
13. C.8: 414, 404.
14. C.16: 229.
15. C.8: 281; C.16: 233–234, 240.

16. C.1: 24. See also C.16: 256–257.
17. C.16: 409, 457; Turner (1980), 257.
18. C.16: 466.
19. C.8: 191; 1853-2-24, W. B. Pike to NH, Berg; C.16: 466; C.17: 421. In this account of Pike I have drawn on Osgood and Batchelder, Holden, D. M. Little, and *EIHC* 72 (1936): 76–77.
20. C.1: 7.
21. C.1: 12, 6–7, 8, 10.
22. C.16: 177, 158, 153, 207.
23. C.16: 302; C.17: 198; C.16: 319, 320, 325. See Blodgett, 173–184.
24. See Oliver, 48–51; *Salem Observer*, in Meltzer and Harding, 125; 1849-2-20, Thoreau to NH, in *EIHC* 94 (1958): 191. NH received an inscribed copy of Thoreau's book; see Hull (1963), 26. See also R. H. Lathrop, 92–93.
25. C.16: 215.
26. C.16: 251. See also Vanderbilt's interpretation of this tale.
27. C.16: 263.
28. C.16: 283.
29. C.16: 263; and see Nevins, 101, 105, 106.
30. C.16: 264.
31. C.16: 269–270.
32. C.16: 273; J. Hawthorne (1884), 1: 340.
33. 1849-6-[9?], SH to her father, Berg.
34. C.16: 271; 1849-6-17/21, SH to her mother, Berg.
35. 1849-6-10, SH to her father, Berg; C.16: 280; 1849-6-12, Dr. Peabody to SH, in J. Hawthorne (1884), 1: 337; see C. A. Wilson, 1: 154, and Turner (1980), 198.
36. 1849-7-4, SH to her father, Berg; and see Oliver, 48–50.
37. 1849-6-9, Rufus Choate to William Meredith, in Nevins, 128; 1849-6-30, W. H. Prescott to Daniel Webster, in Nevins, 128; and see Webster to Meredith, in Cameron, 4. See also Cohen (1955), 246–247.
38. See C.16: 287; Nevins, 118.
39. Cameron, 3.
40. C.16: 225.
41. This account is based on C.8: 423–432 and 1849-8-1, SH to her mother, Berg. In "Some Facts about Hawthorne," EH years later insisted that Louisa and she were in "constant attendance": "They loved their mother too devotedly to be willing to leave her to her daughter in law" (7–8, Essex).
42. C.16: 293.
43. C.16: 293, 296.
44. 1849-9-27, SH to her mother, Berg; 1849-9-2, SH to her mother, in J. Hawthorne (1884), 1: 353.
45. Lowell, *Letters*, 1: 283–284; 1850-1-17, George Hillard to NH, in J. Hawthorne (1884), 1: 355.

46. C.16: 309.
47. C.17: 154–155.
48. C.16: 329, 344–345.
49. C.16: 329; C.1: 8, 9.

T W E N T Y - O N E. *Intercourse with the World:* The Scarlet Letter

1. See Loggins, 278–279, and Young, 15.
2. 1849-9-27, SH to her mother, Berg; 1849-11-4, SH to MPM, Berg.
3. See C.16: 304–306, 307.
4. For discussion of Fields as publisher consult Tryon, Tryon and Charvat, Austin, and Oliver.
5. C.18: 365.
6. C.16: 311.
7. Normand, 264.
8. See also C.14: 305.
9. See R. P. Warren, 75–111.
10. [1850-2-3?], SH to EP, Berg; C.16: 311; *EN*, 225.
11. See Baym (1982), 21–22; Greenacre, in *The Psychoanalytic Study of the Child* 13 (1958): 560. See also Cuddy; Mellow, 305–307; Nissenbaum, 86; and Herbert, 285–297. In support of his thesis that the romance deals with incest, which is Hawthorne's "secret," rather than adultery, Young proposes that "Dimmesdale is Hawthorne, Hester stands for his sister [Elizabeth], and Pearl is his daughter [Una]. Chillingworth represents the controlling force of 'witchcraft'" (141).

T W E N T Y - T W O. *The Berkshires, 1850: Enter Herman Melville*

1. C.16: 311–312.
2. C.16: 312.
3. C.16: 340, 325; C.15: 140.
4. [1850-3?-?], Mrs. Peabody to her daughter Mary, Antioch. Appended to the transcription is a note that, according to Manning Hawthorne, Sophia "had 'several' miscarriages." In a letter to me dated June 4, 1981, Manning Hawthorne had not "the slightest memory of making that statement." See also C.16: 324.
5. C.16: 322; "Salem Register," in *New England Quarterly* 44 (1971): 113–117.
6. C.16: 312–313.
7. Hill, 30–31.
8. C.1: 1.
9. Crowley, 161.

10. Ibid., 176, 180, 182, 183.
11. 1850-6-21, SH to EP, Berg.
12. C.16: 333–334.
13. C.16: 334.
14. C.8: 487–488, 506, 508, 492; C.3: 148.
15. C.8: 497–498, 499. Thompson's portrait is now in the Grolier Club, New York.
16. C.8: 501–502, 504.
17. C.8: 501, 504.
18. C.16: 340, 454.
19. Melville, *Pierre*, 110.
20. 1850-6-23/25, SH to her mother, Berg. See also 1850-6-8, SH to EP, Berg.
21. C.7: 35–36.
22. 1850-6-9/[10] and 8-1, SH to her mother, Berg.
23. For the account that follows see Leyda, 378–386; C.8: 295–296; Miller (1975), 19–26; [1850-8-4], Mrs. Peabody to her husband, Antioch.
24. E. Wilson, 1: 184.
25. Headley, 145; 1850-8-8, SH to EP, Berg; Melville, *Moby-Dick*, ch. 102; Miller (1975), 27.
26. Headley, 145; Miller (1975), 27.
27. J. T. Fields, 53; C.8: 295. In addition to my biography of Melville, I have drawn upon Leyda and Matthews.
28. C.8: 295; 1850-8-8, SH to EP, Berg.
29. C.16: 355; Leyda, 385–386; and see Miller (1975), 30–36.
30. [1850-8-?], SH to her mother, in R. H. Lathrop, 173.
31. H. W. Longfellow, *Letters*, 3: 266; [1850-8-?], SH to her mother, in R. H. Lathrop, 173; SH diary, in *NHJ 1974*, 16.
32. 1850-8-22, SH to EP, Berg; C.16: 361. Melville's sister Augusta admired SH's "beautiful tribute"; see Leyda, 396.
33. C.16: 362.
34. C.8: 297; 1850-9-4, SH to her mother, in Leyda, 393.
35. [1850-9-9], SH to MPM, Berg. See also Miller (1975), 42–43.
36. 1850-9-?, SH to MPM, Berg.
37. Leyda, 395; [1859-9-9?], SH to EP, Berg.
38. C.16: 365, 359.
39. Tryon and Charvot, 156, 163, 170; see Pickard (1895), 1: 343, and Bayless, 208. What NH received from the *Boston Weekly Museum* for "Ethan Brand," published January 1, 1850, is not known. I have assumed that income from *True Stories*, published in December 1850, was received in the following year.
40. 1851-2-3/4, SH to MPM, Berg; 1851-1-27, SH to her mother, Berg; 1850-7-29, Nathaniel Peabody, Jr., to EP, Antioch; 1850-12-25, SH to her mother, Berg.
41. 1850-12-25, SH to her mother, Berg; 1850-11-22? and 1851-2-3, SH to MPM, Berg.
42. 1850-10-24, SH to EP, Berg; 1851-2-3, SH to MPM, Berg.

TWENTY-THREE. *Intercourse with the World:* The House of the Seven Gables

1. 1850-9-29, SH to her mother, Berg.
2. C.7: 36. See the discussion of the sphinx by Gay, 204–206.
3. 1850-9-9, SH to MPM, Berg.
4. C.16: 359, 365, 368, 369.
5. C.16: 371.
6. C.16: 376, 378.
7. C.16: 382, 386.
8. 1851-1-27, SH to her mother, Berg.
9. Melville, *Letters* 124; C.16: 421, 461.
10. C.12: 127.
11. C.1: 263.
12. C.1: 37; C.14: 339; C.5: 106.
13. C.5: 117; C.3: 140. See also C.11: 172; C.16: 407; Bewley, 181; and Dryden, 140.
14. Virginia Woolf draws this analogy: "Blowing bubbles out of a pipe gives the feeling of the rapid crowd of ideas and scenes which blew out of my mind, so that my lips seemed syllabling of their own accord as I walked. What blew the bubbles? Why then? I have no notion. But I wrote the book very quickly; and when it was written, I ceased to be obsessed by my mother." See *Moments of Being*, ed. Jeannie Schulkind (New York: Harcourt Brace Jovanovich, 1976), 81.
15. C.15: 15.
16. Baym (1976) discusses the "Alice Pyncheon" chapter perceptively: the reading of the manuscript "re-creates Alice's erotic response in Phoebe," demonstrating the "sexual power of art and its near relation to witchcraft" (161).
17. Wade, 4–5.
18. *Atlantic Monthly* (May 1860), in Cohen (1969), 86.
19. C.15: 620.
20. C.15: 150.
21. C.12: 3.
22. 1851-5-7, SH to EP, Berg.
23. 1851-2-16, SH to EP, Berg; C.16: 402, 406, 417.
24. Whipple and Chorley, in Crowley, 198, 201.

TWENTY-FOUR. *Lenox, 1851: Intimations*

1. 1851-1-30/2-9, SH journal, Berg.
2. J. Hawthorne (1884), 1: 397; 1851-9-7, SH to her mother, Berg.
3. 1851-2-16, SH to EP, Berg.

4. 1851-1-12, Mrs. Peabody to EP, Antioch; 1851-2-3, SH to EP, Berg; 1851-3-23, EP to SH, Berg.

5. Melville, *Letters*, 121.

6. Ibid.

7. Ibid., 118, 119.

8. Leyda, 407; Wolfe, 191; 1851-3-13/14, SH journal, Berg.

9. Leyda, 409; Melville, *Letters*, 123, 124.

10. Melville, *Letters*, 125.

11. 1851-5-7/10, SH to EP, Berg.

12. C.16: 425, 431.

13. 1851-3-13, SH journal, Berg.

14. [1851-5-20], Dr. Peabody to his wife, Antioch.

15. C.16: 442; [1851]-6-22, SH to MPM, Berg.

16. [1851]-6-22 and 7-4, SH to MPM, Berg; 1851-7-10, SH to EP, Berg.

17. C.16: 441; EP, in Pearson (1958-2), 276; C.16: 212.

18. C.16: 402–403, 431.

19. C.16: 434.

20. C.16: 153, 417, 436–437.

21. C.16: 443, 460. In *My Friends at Brook Farm*, Sears claims that Charles Hosmer "gave us modern versions of the Greek myths and hero legends," and he was "surprised and indignant to find the author had actually taken our Brook Farm stories, told us by Charles Hosmer and printed them, and that, too, without a word of credit" (88).

22. See also C.16: 570–571; J. Hawthorne (1884), 1: 440.

23. C.16: 453, 454, 465.

24. C.8: 439–440.

25. 1851-9-7/8, SH to her mother, Berg.

26. Melville, *Letters*, 129.

27. Ibid., 128.

28. Ibid., 133.

29. Ibid., 135.

30. C.8: 454, 472–473, 477.

31. 1845-5-[18 or 25], SH to her mother, Berg.

32. See R. W. Emerson, *Letters*, 2: 332; Allen, 449; Rusk, 309–310, 297; and McGill, 84.

33. C.16: 425.

34. C.8: 446, 442, 451, 460, 467, 477–478.

35. C.8: 447–448.

36. C.8: 448.

37. 1851-8-9, George Duyckinck to Joann Miller, NYPL; C.8: 468.

38. C.8: 465, 466.

39. 1851-8-19, SH to her mother, Berg.

40. [1851]-9-4, SH to EP, Berg; C.16: 481–482.

41. 1851-10-2, SH to EP, Berg; Mellow, 639n.

TWENTY-FIVE. *"Big Hearts Strike Together"*

1. C.16: 495.
2. Melville, *Letters*, 149; C.16: 508. There is always the danger of overinterpreting in order to understand the workings of the artist's mind, particularly in the case of a work as baffling and autobiographical as *Pierre*. But surely the choice of the name Pierre Glendinning takes on significance: Gansevoort was Melville's mother's maiden name and his older brother's first name, and her brother to whom by her own admission she was more attached than to her husband was named Peter. There is still another possible association: Pierre may be a hidden reference to Pierce, Hawthorne's close friend, whose campaign biography he was preparing when *Pierre* was entered for publication.
3. Melville, *Letters*, 142–143.
4. C.8: 552.
5. Melville, *Pierre*, 259; C.11: 4.
6. C.3: 121, 133, 134, 135. Curiously, the effect of Hollingsworth upon Coverdale, even in choice of language, closely resembles that of Hawthorne on Melville.
7. C.4: 285.
8. Melville, *Pierre*, 86, 210ff, 217, 289–290, 296, 362.
9. Melville, *Clarel*, 94, 95, 237, 238, 395–396. One of Melville's friends in the Berkshires, J. E. Smith, commented on the "brotherly friendship" of the two men (318). See also Melville, *Letters*, 161.
10. Leyda, 436–437; J. Hawthorne (1884), 1: 429–430.
11. 1851-10-30, William Ellery Channing to Ellen Channing, MHS. This letter was brought to my attention by Francis B. Dedmond, who is about to publish *The Selected Letters of William Ellery Channing the Younger*.
12. 1851-11-5, Maria Gansevoort Melville to her daughter Augusta, NYPL; Leyda, 441; Melville, *Letters*, 146, 147.
13. Melville, *Letters*, 148, 152, 153–161; Arvin, *Melville* (New York: William Sloane, 1950), 206. The inscribed copy of *Pierre* is in the Rosenbach Museum and Library in Philadelphia.
14. Melville, *Letters*, 163; Leyda, 468–469. In this discussion of the relationship of NH and Melville, I have drawn upon the following, in addition to my own biography of Melville: Murray in his edition of *Pierre*, Bezanson in his edition of *Clarel*, Lueders, Seelye, and Watson.

TWENTY-SIX. *Intercourse with the World:* The Blithedale Romance

1. C.16: 462 (referring to *The House of the Seven Gables* and *A Wonder-Book*), 465.
2. C.3: 2; A. Fields, 72.
3. R. W. Emerson, *Complete Works*, 10: 363–364.

4. C.8: 261–267; Moncure Conway, Introduction to *The Blithedale Romance* (1901), xxvi–viii. Apparently this was not Martha Hunt's first attempt at suicide in the Concord River; see Mellow, 251–253.

5. Robert S. Rantoul was told by Edwin Whipple that Hollingworth was "the name of an ancestor and land-holder from whom the Hathorne Farm on Salem Neck descended"; see *EIHC* 41 (1905): 4.

6. 1852-7-18, W. B. Pike to NH, in J. Hawthorne (1884), 1: 444.

7. C.16: 537, 539.

TWENTY-SEVEN. *President Pierce's "Prime Minister"*

1. 1852-1-4, Mrs. Peabody to EP, Antioch.

2. C.16: 465; Curtis, in Cameron (1968), 36; see H. A. Clarke, Lothrop, Sanborn (1908-2), and *Concord Town* 2(1) (June 1966).

3. C.16: 548, 602.

4. C.16: 568.

5. C.16: 567–568, 636. Emerson's son Edward compared NH to "the wood chuck, with his second hole for safety," which was the back door that "gave him secure flight to the birch and pitch-pine grove of the hill" (E. W. Emerson, 207).

6. 1852-6-6 and [1852?], SH to her mother, Berg.

7. 1852-10-3, SH to her mother, Berg.

8. Conway (1890), 146; Lowell, *Letters*, 1: 303.

9. C.16: 545; C.15: 224.

10. C.16: 545, 551.

11. J. Hawthorne (1884), 1: 484; 1852-7-16, MLH to EH, Berg; C.16: 551.

12. C.16: 605.

13. 1852-7-16, MLH to EH, Berg; [1848]-3-20, Mrs. Peabody to SH, Berg; 1848-3-26, SH to her mother, Berg.

14. 1852-8-?, Mrs. Peabody to EP, Antioch; and see 1852-9-10, Mrs. Peabody to EP, Antioch; and C.16: 619.

15. C.16: 560, 561; and see Warner, 213–220.

16. Tharp (1950), 221; C.16: 605.

17. See Richard C. Robey's introduction to the facsimile edition (N. Hawthorne, 1970). All quotations are from this edition.

18. C.16: 605. See also his letter to Burchmore, C.16: 456.

19. J. Hawthorne (1938), 161; (1884) 1: 483.

20. N. Hawthorne (1852), 65; Nichols, 225; C.17: 298. Jane Appleton Pierce was the daughter of the president of Bowdoin College and the sister-in-law of Packard, one of the college's most distinguished professors; see Nichols, 75.

21. C.16: 624.

22. C.16: 555; 1852-8-5, SH to her mother, Berg.

23. J. Hawthorne (1884) 1: 455–457.

24. 1852-8-5, SH to her mother, Berg.
25. 1852-7-30 and 8-5, SH to her mother, Berg; R. W. Emerson, *Letters*, 4: 301.
26. C.16: 585; 1852-8-5, SH to her mother, Berg.
27. C.16: 593, 607.
28. 1852-9-19, SH to her mother, in R. H. Lathrop, 203.
29. C.16: 595.
30. [1852]-9-19, SH to her mother, in R. H. Lathrop, 204, 205.
31. 1853-2-13, SH to her father, Berg; [1852]-2-29, Mrs. Peabody to MPM, Antioch; 1852-2-29, Mrs. Peabody to EP, Antioch.
32. [1852]-4-13, Mrs. Peabody to MPM, Antioch.
33. See 1852-10-31, SH to her mother, Berg; 1852-12-4, Mrs. Peabody to EP, Antioch. In the letter Mrs. Peabody writes: "Did you find out that Sophia's long tirade about the wicked-great man, was a copy from Littlle's living age? By her transcribing it, we had a right to infer that she thought the thoughts expressed, yet I felt glad to find they did not originate in her mind. There is no harm in discussing these men [Webster and Pierce], if we do not let the seeds of bitterness be cast over the soil of domestic love."
34. 1853-2-3, SH to her father, Berg; [1853-1-11], EP to SH, Berg; 1853-1-11 and 1-23, MPM to Horace Mann, Antioch.
35. C.16: 604, 627, 649; C.7: 179.
36. C.16: 649.
37. C.16: 642.
38. C.16: 645, 687–688.
39. C.16: 648, 649, 663.
40. C.16: 658, 675, 678, 679; 1853-5-8, SH to her father, Berg.
41. [1853]-4-22, W. D. Ticknor to his wife, in Ticknor (1913), 44, 45.
42. Diary of D. G. Mitchell, in Dunn, 257, 259, and see Mitchell, 2: 246–247; De Leon, 2: 106–107, 110.
43. Ticknor (1913), 46; C.16: 639–640n.
44. C.18: 54; C.17: 775.
45. C.16: 659; [1853-3?-?], EP to her father, Antioch; 1853-3-20, SH to her father, Berg.
46. C.8: 552; 1853-6-14/15, Longfellow journal, in S. Longfellow, 2: 234.
47. Ticknor (1913), 48–53.
48. C.16: 637; Channing, in Sanborn (1905), 78–79; C.3: 148, 154.
49. [Undated, between 1853 and 1859], SH to EP, Berg.
50. Sanborn (1905), 79.

TWENTY-EIGHT. *England: "I Do Not Take Root Anywhere"*

1. Hull (1980), 13. In this discussion of the English years I am indebted to Hull's comprehensive examination of the period.
2. 1853-8-9, SH to her father, Berg; C.17: 119.

3. C.17: 101, 106.

4. C.17: 119; 1853-10-4/5, SH to her father, Berg.

5. *EN*, 3; 1853-9-14; SH to her father, Berg; *EN*, 628.

6. *EN*, 3.

7. C.5: 31.

8. *EN*, 33.

9. C.5: 30.

10. *EN*, 13.

11. C.17: 327, 204.

12. *EN*, 11, 3.

13. C.17: 210.

14. C.17: 113, 146, 152, 186.

15. C.17: 226, 247–248, 307.

16. C.14: 727; Hull (1980), 59, 49; C.17: 357.

17. *EN*, 12; C.17: 105.

18. C.17: 106; C.18: 14.

19. J. T. Fields, 78–79; C.5: 11.

20. C.17: 463; *EN*, 311, 322, 416.

21. *EN*, 377.

22. C.17: 272.

23. Mackay, 2: 272.

24. *EN*, 553, 554; 1857-8-1, SH to EP, Berg.

25. C.17: 124; and see *EN*, 10.

26. *EN*, 92.

27. *EN*, 160, and 124n; C.5: 63–64.

28. C.17: 319.

29. *EN*, 186, 424; C.18: 95; C.17: 406.

30. C.17: 266–267, 188, 559; and see the almost identical statement in 1851 in C.16: 456.

31. C.17: 394, 397, 401, 540.

32. C.17: 250.

33. C.18: 77, 97.

34. C.18: 4, 14; *EN*, 562, 618.

35. C.5: 38.

36. SH to her father, in R. H. Lathrop, 275, 269, 273. See also 1855-8-17, SH to EP, Berg.

37. 1876-2-18, EH to a cousin, Essex; [1854]-4-14, SH to her father, in R. H. Lathrop, 271; and see Hull (1980), 95.

38. [1853-ca. 10-25] and 1855-3-24, SH to EP, Berg, Historical Society of Pennsylvania; [1857]-8-21, SH to UH, Berg.

39. J. Hawthorne (1932), 503. Julian published these reminiscences at age eighty-six.

40. 1854-11-14 and 1855-1-25/26, SH to EP, Berg.

41. C.17: 302; and see E. Peabody (1984), 276; 1855-2-8, SH to EP, Berg.

42. 1855-3-17/24, SH to MPM, Berg.

43. See Harris, 346–354, 362; *EN*, 59–60, 77–82; [1855]-7-31, SH to NH, Berg.

44. 1855-8-17, SH to EP, Virginia; [1855]-9-19/20, SH to NH, Berg.

45. 1855-10-27, SH to JH, Berg.

46. C.17: 396, 411, 417; J. Hawthorne (1884), 2: 74–75.

47. 1856-2-3, UH to NH, Berg; C.17: 418–419.

48. C.17: 410, 438.

49. C.17: 410, 436–437.

50. C.17: 455–459.

51. C.17: 410, 436; C.10: 87.

52. C.17: 418; [1856]-4-13/22, SH to MPM, Berg.

53. *EN*, 271–272.

54. C.17: 429, 434, 446, 448.

55. Hull (1974), 55; C.17: 464–465.

56. Hull (1974), 55; C.17: 467, 471, 485.

57. [1856-7-?], SH to EP, Berg.

58. 1856-7-22, SH to NH, Berg; [1856-7-?], SH to EP, Berg.

59. [1856]-8-[6]/7, SH to EP, Berg.

60. 1856-8-12, SH to MPM, Berg.

61. [1856?], SH to EP, Berg.

62. C.17: 558; *EN*, 461.

63. J. Hawthorne (1903), 33. This account of Melville and Hawthorne is based on *EN*, 432–437, and Leyda, 527–531.

64. C.14: 570; H. W. Longfellow, *Letters*, 3: 355–356; Hull (1980), 25; 1857-8-7/12, SH to EP, Berg; C.18: 208; C.5: 39; 1863-10-20, H. A. Bright to NH, in Bright (1978), 17.

65. *EN*, 350; Bennoch, x–xi.

66. *EN*, 424; Ticknor (1913), 64. For this account of Bennoch, I have drawn extensively on Hull (1974, 1980). As for Hawthorne's drinking, Hillard, who as friend and lawyer knew NH for about thirty years, twice denied in an article published in 1870 that NH was given to excessive drinking, but Hillard never knew his friend to be gloomy and depressed (261, 262). Melville, facetiously perhaps, referred to NH as "up to the lips in the *Universe* again" (*Letters*, 121). Bridge omitted, without ellipses, NH's account of himself in a letter written April 17, 1854: ". . . had got myself into that state of pot-valor which (as you and [Pierce] know) is best adapted to bring out my heroic qualities" and on May 10, 1856, NH informed Ticknor that "I was about half-seas over when I got up to speak" (C.17: 205, 485). On December 27, 1882, Julian Hawthorne wrote to Bridge to inquire about "a belief prevalent in some quarters that [NH] died in consequence of a debauch in which he and Pierce had indulged; and that he was at all times prone to excessive drinking" (Bowdoin).

67. *EN*, 255–256.

68. Hopkins, 179; Emerson, *Letters*, 5: 87.

69. *EN*, 387, 388.

70. C.17: 570.
71. [1856]-8-3 and [1856]-9-7, SH to Delia Bacon, Folger; C.17: 583; C.18: 17, 24, 37.
72. Hopkins, 217.
73. *EN*, 27–28, 88.
74. *EN*, 116, 232.
75. C.17: 161, 177, and see 277–278, 307–308; C.18: 53; C.17: 308.
76. C.17: 304, 456–457.
77. C.18: 63–64.
78. *EN*, 182, 132, and see 540.
79. *EN*, 149, 468, 450, 544–545. For a more detailed study, see Gollin (1979).
80. *EN*, 554, 556, 559.
81. *EN*, 558, 596, 619. See *Bartolomé Esteban Murillo* (New York: Aldine Fine Arts, 1984), 26, 27. George Peabody, the great Salem philanthropist, owned what SH characterized as a "magnificent Murillo picture" of the Madonna; see [1848?-?-?], SH to EP, Berg.
82. *EN*, 275–278; and see Goldman, "Hawthorne's Old Home," in Lee, 165.
83. C.5: 121, 122, 132.
84. C.18: 116.
85. *EN*, 537; C.18: 97–98, 110.
86. Tharp (1953), 343; C.18: 83–84; C.14: 719–720; Hull (1980), 133.

TWENTY-NINE. *Italy: "Dim Reflections in My Inward Mirror"*

1. C.14: 17.
2. C.14: 53, 87, 135, 225.
3. C.18: 138–139; C.14: 60, 581, 68–69.
4. C.18: 140; C.14: 232–233; C.18: 138; S. Hawthorne, 198.
5. C.14: 128, 177.
6. C.14: 159, 229, and see 772; C.4: 120.
7. For Story, see C.14: 73; C.4: 132, 134.
8. See C.14: 350, 126, and see 414n.
9. C.14: 344, 451, 305, 297; S. Hawthorne, 452.
10. C.14: 184, and see 101.
11. C.4: 107.
12. C.14: 279, 278.
13. C.14: 603, 604, 375; C.18: 150–151.
14. *EN*, 381, 382; 1861-8-4, SH to JTF, Berg; C.14: 301; S. Hawthorne, 345.
15. C.14: 299, 339. Nowhere else, so far as I know, does Hawthorne suggest that he was the aggressor in male relationships. If this was not a chance remark such as he was given to, depending upon circumstances and mood, the depiction of Melville as the aggressor may have to be qualified.

16. 1858-8-25/27, SH to EP, Berg; 1858-8-24, SH journals 4: 99–100, Berg; C.14: 399.
17. C.14: 436
18. C.14: 488, 491, 494.
19. C.14: 495; 1859-7-3, SH to EP, Berg.
20. C.18: 160.
21. C.14: 638, 640; C.18: 161, 160.
22. C.18: 163.
23. C.14: 501.
24. C.14: 510, 514.
25. C.14: 656, 657.
26. 1859-7-3, SH to EP, Essex.
27. C.14: 518, 519.
28. 1859-7-3/4, SH to EP, Essex.
29. C.14: 659; C.19: 178.
30. C.14: 524.
31. C.14: 474–475, 548–549, 551.
32. C.14: 551–552; C.19: 164; C.14: 571.
33. Fields, in C.14: 889; C.19: 164.
34. C.14: 679, 891; [1859]-7-15, SH to EP, Berg.
35. 1859-8-5, SH to EP, Berg.
36. [1859]-8-24, SH to MPM, Berg; 1859-9-17, MPM to SH, MHS.
37. C.14: 638–684, and see 1859-9-9, UH to Richard Manning, Essex; C.18: 189; C.14: 687; C.18: 196–197; C.14: 700.
38. [1859]-10-28/31 and 1860-3-14, SH to MPM, Berg.
39. C.18: 217, 248, 267.
40. C.18: 229; Melville, *Letters*, 121.
41. C.18: 284; and see 1860-5-27, SH to MPM, Berg.

T H I R T Y. *Intercourse with the World:* The Marble Faun

1. C.18: 271.
2. Baym (1971), 371; Fossum, 169; James, 133; Pearce, 183; Crews, 215.
3. Levin (1966), 206.
4. Before the murder Kenyon refers to the blood of the "thirty wounds of Caesar's breast" and the "pure little rivulet" from the bosom of Virginia, who was slain by her father to save her from the lust of Appius Claudius in 449 B.C., a story which is retold in Chaucer's "The Doctor's Tale" and in John Webster's *Appius and Virginia* (1654).
5. The relationship of Miriam and Hilda may reflect that of Pierre and his cousin in Melville's novel which, as noted earlier, comments on his relationship with Hawthorne: "The eventual love for the other sex forever dismiss[es] the preliminary love-friendship of boys" (217).

6. S. Longfellow, 2: 351; Bell, 90–91.
7. The word "repose" appears frequently in this romance, as in the description of Cleopatra in "the repose of despair" (126), and is tied to the aura of resignation suggested by the presence of Marcus Aurelius and Kenyon's eagerness to find in Hilda a substitute mother figure.
8. The romance fuses East and West in the allusions to Aladdin (219, 366) and to fairy tales such as Bluebeard, as retold in translation by Charles Perrault and Ludwig Tieck, and in music by André Grétry and Jacques Offenbach.
9. C.18: 262.
10. C.10: 42.
11. C.18: 272. One of the most penetrating discussions of this romance appears in Baym (1971). See also Crews and Strout.

THIRTY-ONE. *Concord, 1860–1862*

1. J. T. Fields, 92; Annie Fields, ed., *Life and Letters of Harriet Beecher Stowe* (Boston: Houghton Mifflin, 1898), 282.
2. 1860-7-1, MPM to her son Horace, Antioch.
3. Thoreau, *Correspondence*, 582; L. M. Alcott, in Worthington, 109–110.
4. C.18: 355–356; Conway (1904), 1: 316.
5. Scudder, 2: 82, 84.
6. C.18: 306.
7. 1860-7-20. UH to Richard Manning, Essex; C.18: 309.
8. 1860-7-25 and [1860]-8-2, UH to Richard Manning, Essex; 1860-8-28 and [1860]-9-9, SH to UH, Berg.
9. C.18: 323, 319, 327.
10. C.18: 317; Sanborn (1909), 2: 516; [1860?], SH to EP, Berg. According to a poem Rose wrote about 1861, all was not well with the children, at least from her perspective when she was left alone with her parents:

> Una & Julian don't like me
> And if they do, it you will see.
> Unas a tirant
> And Julians a bore
> And thats the way forever more.

See Maynard, 116.
11. C.18: 352.
12. C.7: 159, 169; [1850-9-?], SH to EP, Berg.
13. Stewart (1948), 215; C.18: 631.
14. 1868-4-5, SH to F. G. Tuckerman, Harvard.
15. C.18: 326, 339, 340, 359, 384.
16. C.18: 379, 382, 380.

17. C.18: 382; [1861]-5-15, SH to W. D. Ticknor, Berg.
18. C.18: 396.
19. [1861?]-7-25, SH to NH, Berg; 1862-12-14 and [1862?-3-18], SH to AF, BPL.
20. [1861?]-7-25, 7-28, [7-30], SH to NH, Berg.
21. 1861-9-25, SH to UH, Berg; [1861?-10-?], Wednesday, SH to EP, Berg; [1861?]-12-31, EH to Rebecca, Bowdoin.
22. 1861-?-?, Rose Hawthorne to AF, BPL.
23. C.18: 427; Ticknor (1913), 262.
24. C.18: 443; see Bridge, in Cameron, 244; 1851-10-10, JTF to NH, Berg; C.18: 445.
25. C.18: 443; 1862-4-11, SH to AF, BPL.
26. C.18: 355, 381, 412.
27. C.18: 380, 379, 382.
28. C.18: 388, 421.
29. C.18: 388, 421.
30. C.18: 455; J. Hawthorne (1884), 2: 312.
31. C.18: 456, 461.
32. C.18: 468; 1862-8-10/13 and 8-21/24, JH to his mother, Berg.
33. [1862]-9-7, SH to UH, Berg; 1862-11-3, SH to JTF, BPL; 1862-11-28, SH to AF, BPL; C.18: 508; 1862-12-31, SH to AF, BPL.
34. 1863-1-1/2 and 1-22, SH to UH, Berg.
35. 1863-10-10 and [1863-9]-5/6, SH to UH, Berg.
36. [1861], in Austin, 214.
37. [1864]-2-28, SH to AF, BPL; 1863-9-20, SH to JTF, BPL.
38. [1862-7-?], [1863]-4-11, and 6-14, SH to AF, BPL. Sophia and Annie Fields often drew upon *The Arabian Nights' Entertainments*, as in the reference to the Peri, a female or male supernatural being. See also Dodge, 1: 350–351.
39. [1863]-6-14 and 8-2, SH to AF, BPL.
40. 1865-3-16 and 1866-11-24, SH to AF, BPL.
41. 1867-6-16, SH to JTF, BPL. See Faderman, 197–201, and Strouse, 200.
42. 1862-8-18, SH to JH, Berg; [1862]-9-7, SH to NH, in R. H. Lathrop, 427 (misdated 1869); 1862-11-30, SH to E. A. Hitchcock, LC; [1863]-6-14, SH to AF, BPL.
43. 1867-7-14, SH to E. A. Hitchcock, LC.
44. 1862-11-30, SH to E. A. Hitchcock, LC.
45. 1863-8-9, SH to E. A. Hitchcock, LC.
46. 1866-2-20, 12-30, 1867-2-6, 6-2, SH to E. A. Hitchcock, LC.
47. 1868-6-7, SH to E. A. Hitchcock, LC.

THIRTY-TWO. *The Crack-up: The Unfinished Romances*

1. C.18: 197.
2. C.4: 45.

3. *EN*, 98; C.14: 436. If Sophia still read his journals, such entries must have shocked her idealistic faith, which, it must be admitted in view of his indirect communications with his wife, may have been his somewhat cowardly, even cruel, intention.

4. Robert Lowell's death was characterized as a "suicide of wish" by one of his friends. Another "felt 'angry' with Cal, as if Lowell had voluntarily elected to walk out on his old friend"; see Ian Hamilton, *Robert Lowell—A Biography* (New York: Random House, 1982), 473.

5. *EN*, 193–199.

6. C.12: 58; Lamont, 17.

7. C.12: 284.

8. C.12: 198–203.

9. Here and elsewhere I have conflated the various versions of these unfinished romances because my concern is not with the genesis of the works but with the veiled, fumbling delineation of character, meaning as here the portrait of NH as recollected and perceived in age.

10. J. Hawthorne (1884), 1: 32.

11. C.12: 431; C.9: 71, 70; C.5: 300; C.12: 149.

12. There was still another reason for introducing Swinnerton: he was a witness to a deed of Hathorne property in the seventeenth century and thus associated with the awesome ancestors.

13. C.12: 327.

14. C.12: 377.

15. C.12: 307.

16. C.13: 499, 175–176.

17. Alcott (1938), 335; Emerson, *Journals*, 15: 60.

18. C.13: 6, 209–210, and see 15–16.

19. C.13: 209–210, and see 15–16.

20. C.13: 48, 147, 101 (emphasis added).

21. C.13: 230.

22. C.13: 27–28.

23. C.13: 34, 511–512; and see 1862-1-1, SH to JTF, BPL.

24. C.13: 65, 103–106; Howells, 53.

25. See Young as well as Phillips (1933), 131, 248, 252. A contemporary of Veren and Manning was named Benjamin Felton; see Phillips (1933), 173. The name of Keziah may be traceable to Keziah Dingley, the sister of the wife of NH's uncle Richard Manning, with whom he had a falling-out about the time of his graduation from Bowdoin; see M. Hawthorne (1939-1), 120.

26. C.13: 446, 447.

27. [1872?]-5-8, EH to Rebecca, Bowdoin.

28. Leyda, 727. In my readings of these manuscripts I have been influenced by the oedipal constructions of Lamont, which Waggoner anticipated many years earlier; by Crews's sometimes overemphasis on sexual anxiety and

obsession with incest; and by Erlich's (1982) discussion of autobiographical materials.

THIRTY-THREE. *"The Great, Generous, Brave Heart Beat No More"*

1. C.13: 297; S. Longfellow, 2: 391; 1863-12-4, Annie Fields's diary, in Howe (1922), 59, 57.
2. J. Hawthorne (1884), 2: 329.
3. C.18: 526, 543–545.
4. C.18: 517, 537; 1863-2-21, SH to AF, BPL.
5. 1863-10-11 and [1863-10-?], SH to AF, BPL; [1863-12]-19, SH to UH, Berg.
6. C.18: 597; [1863-7-?], SH to AF, BPL; C.18: 606.
7. Clark (1978), 250–251; 1862-12-14, 1863-6-30, and 8-31, JTF to NH, in Austin, 222, 229, 232.
8. Nichols, 522–523.
9. 1863-7-15, JTF to NH, in Austin, 230.
10. C.18: 586.
11. C.18: 590–592.
12. Howe (1922), 15n; Austin, 231; C.5: xxx–xxxvi; Clark (1978), 262. About this time a young Englishman commented in his diary: "[Hawthorne] is a copperhead of copperheads, Mr. Hawthorne has all the prejudices about the negroes—'they smell, their intellects are inferior!' etc., etc."; see H. Y. Thompson, 46 (entry dated July 19, 1863). According to Horace Traubel, Walt Whitman held a similar opinion about Hawthorne: "What a devil of a Copperhead he was! I always more or less despise the Copperheads, irrespective of who they are, . . . but aside from that, all my tendencies about Hawthorne are towards him—even affectionate, I may say—for his work, what he represented"; see *With Walt Whitman in Camden* (Carbondale: Southern Illinois University Press, 1982), 6: 123.
13. C.18: 603.
14. C.18: 604.
15. C.18: 605–606.
16. Howe (1922), 58, and see Nichols, 524; 1868-3-16, FP to Sarah Webster, Virginia.
17. C.18: 609.
18. [1863-12]-19, SH to UH, Berg.
19. C.18: 626, 629, 632.
20. C.18: 634.
21. C.18: 640–641.
22. C.13: 476.
23. C.2: 62.
24. C.15: 117.

25. Davidson and Van Doren propose an autobiographical reading of the romance in which Dolliver is NH, Bessie is Sophia, and Pansie is Una at age five.
26. [1864-3-13], SH to W. D. Ticknor, Berg.
27. [1864]-3-31, SH to AF, BPL; 1864-3-6, MPM to her son Horace, Antioch; C.18: 649.
28. J. T. Fields, 117.
29. [1864]-3-31, SH to AF, BPL; 1864-4-5, SH to Horatio Bridge, Bowdoin.
30. Stoddard (1971), 131; [1864-4-?], SH to MPM, Berg; C.18: 651; and see 1864-4-11, MPM to her son Horace, Antioch; Childs, 19–21.
31. [1864-4-18], SH to AF, BPL.
32. 1864-4-25, UH to Horace Mann, Jr., in Turner (1973), 124.
33. 1864-4-20, SH to FP, NHHS; [1864-4-24], MPM to her son Horace, Antioch.
34. Alcott (1938), 364.
35. J. Hawthorne (1932), 506, and (1938), 156.
36. [1864-4-29], SH to AF, BPL; 1864-5-6, SH to FP, NHHS.
37. C.18: 655.
38. [1864-5-7], SH to JTF, BPL; [1864-5-?], UH to JTF, in Austin, 236.
39. C.13: 447.
40. 1864-5-11, Annie Fields's diary, in Howe (1922), 27; Holmes, in the *Atlantic Monthly* 14 (July 1864): 98–101.
41. C.10: 359–360.
42. 1868-3-18, FP to Sarah Webster, Virginia. For Pierce's account an hour or so after finding NH dead, see J. T. Fields, 123.
43. C.8: 421, and see Van Doren, 263; Bassan (1970), 3.
44. Nichols, 525; 1864-5-22, MPM to her son Horace, Antioch.
45. Nichols, 525; 1864-5-22, MPM to her son Horace, Antioch.
46. [1864-5-19], UH to AF, BPL.
47. [1864-5-21], SH to JTF, BPL; E. Peabody (1984), 455, 334.
48. J. Hawthorne (1884), 2: 347; [1864-5-22], JH to JTF, BPL.
49. Wagner, 41; Holmes, in Cameron, 98; Emerson, in Morris, 361; and see J. T. Fields, 123.
50. [1864-5-30], SH to AF, BPL.
51. Emerson, *Journals*, 15: 59.
52. S. Longfellow, 2: 407; [1864]-5-25, SH to EP, Berg.
53. Bassan (1956), 565n.
54. [1864]-5-25, SH to EP, Berg.
55. 1864-5-?, EH to UH, in J. Hawthorne (1884), 2: 348.
56. Holmes, in the *Atlantic Monthly* 14 (July 1864): 98–101.
57. 1864-7-10, MPM to her son Horace, Antioch; see Turner (1980), 391, and Baym (1976), 251n.
58. 1864-5-24, Emerson, *Journals*, 10: 39–40. In *The Lost Childhood* Graham Greene observes: ". . . surely we choose our death much as we choose our job. It grows out of our acts and our evasions, out of our fears, and out of our moments of courage" (13).

59. Channing, in Sanborn (1909), 2: 533; Melville, *Timoleon* (New York: Caxton Press, 1891), 34.

EPILOG

1. 1864-9-14, SH to JTF, BPL.
2. Gollin (1989): 120n.
3. 1871-2-27, RHL to EP, Bowdoin. See also Hull (1976): 87–119.
4. See Gollin (1981): 398; and Loggins, 303ff.
5. J. Hawthorne (1932): 502. See also Bassan (1970).
6. Maynard, 258.

Selected Bibliography

Adams, Herbert B. *The Life and Writings of Jared Sparks*. 2 vols. Boston: Houghton Mifflin, 1893.

Adams, Richard P. "Hawthorne's Provincial Tales." *New England Quarterly* 30 (1957): 39–57.

Adkins, Nelson F. "The Early Projected Works of Nathaniel Hawthorne." *Papers of the Bibliographical Society of America* 39 (1945): 119–155.

Alcott, A. Bronson. *The Journals*. Ed. Odell Shepard. Boston: Little, Brown, 1938.

———. *The Letters*. Ed. Richard L. Herrnstadt. Ames: Iowa State University Press, 1969.

Allen, Gay Wilson. *Waldo Emerson*. New York: Viking, 1981.

Anthony, Katharine. *Margaret Fuller: A Psychological Biography*. 1920. Reprint. Folcroft, Pa.: Folcroft Press, 1969.

Arvin, Newton. *Hawthorne*. Boston: Little, Brown, 1929.

———. *Longfellow: His Life and Work*. Boston: Little, Brown, 1963.

Austin, James C. *Fields of the Atlantic Monthly: Letters to an Editor, 1861–1870*. San Marino, Calif.: Huntington Library, 1953.

Bachelard, Gaston. *The Psychoanalysis of Fire*. Boston: Beacon, 1964.

Bacon, Theodore. *Delia Bacon: A Biographical Sketch*. Boston: Houghton Mifflin, 1888.

Badaracco, Claire. "The Night-blooming Cereus: A Letter from the 'Cuba Journal' 1833–35 of Sophia Peabody Hawthorne, with a Check List of Her Autograph Materials in American Institutions." *Bulletin of Research in the Humanities* 81 (1978): 56–73.

Bancroft, George. *Life and Letters*. Ed. M. A. De Wolfe Howe. New York: Scribner's, 1908.

Bartlett, William Irving. *Jones Very: Emerson's "Brave Saint."* 1942. Reprint. New York: Greenwood, 1968.

Bassan, Maurice. *Hawthorne's Son: The Life and Literary Career of Julian Hawthorne*. Columbus: Ohio State University Press, 1970.

————. "Julian Hawthorne Edits Aunt Ebe." *Essex Institute Historical Collections* 100 (1964): 274–278.

————. "A New Account of Hawthorne's Last Days, Death, and Funeral." *American Literature* 27 (1956): 561–565.

Bayless, Joy. *Rufus Wilmot Griswold: Poe's Literary Executor.* Nashville: Vanderbilt University Press, 1943.

Baylor, Ruth M. *Elizabeth Palmer Peabody: Kindergarten Pioneer.* Philadelphia: University of Pennsylvania Press, [1965].

Baym, Nina. "*The Marble Faun*: Hawthorne's Elegy for Art." *New England Quarterly* 44 (1971): 355–376.

————. "Nathaniel Hawthorne and His Mother: A Biographical Speculation." *American Literature* 54 (1982): 1–27.

————. *The Shape of Hawthorne's Career.* Ithaca: Cornell University Press, 1976.

Bedell, Madelon. *The Alcotts: Biography of a Family.* New York: Potter, 1980.

Bell, Millicent. *Hawthorne's View of the Artist.* New York: State University of New York Press, 1962.

Bennoch, Francis. *Poems, Lyrics, Songs, and Sonnets.* London: Hardwick and Bogue, 1877.

Bentley, William. *The Diary.* 4 vols. Salem: Essex Institute, 1905–1914.

Bewley, Marius. *The Eccentric Design: Form in the Classic American Novel.* New York: Columbia University Press, 1963.

Birdsall, Richard D. *Berkshire County: A Cultural History.* New Haven: Yale University Press, 1959.

Blanchard, Paula. *Margaret Fuller: From Transcendentalism to Revolution.* New York: Delacorte, 1978.

Blandshard, Frances Bradshaw, ed. *Letters of Ann Gilliam Storrow to Jared Sparks. Smith College Studies in History* 6 (April 1921).

Blodgett, Harold. "Hawthorne as Poetry Critic: Six Unpublished Letters to Lewis Manfield." *American Literature* 12 (1940): 173–184.

Bode, Carl. *The American Lyceum: Town Meeting of the Mind.* 1956. Reprint. Carbondale: Southern Illinois University Press, 1968.

"Books Read by Nathaniel Hawthorne, 1828–1850. From the 'Charge Books' of the Salem Athenaeum." *Essex Institute Historical Collections* 68 (1932): 65–87.

Brancaccio, Patrick. "'The Black Man's Paradise': Hawthorne's Editing of *An African Cruiser.*" *New England Quarterly* 53 (1980): 23–41.

Bremer, Fredrika. *The Homes of the New World; Impressions of America.* 2 vols. New York: Harper and Brothers, 1853.

Bridge, Horatio. *Journal of an African Cruiser.* 1853. Reprint. Detroit: Negro History Press, n.d.

————. *Personal Recollections of Nathaniel Hawthorne.* 1893. Reprint. New York: Haskell House, 1968.

Bright, Henry Arthur. *Happy Country This America: The Travel Diary of Henry Arthur Bright*. Ed. Anne Henry Ehrenpreis. Columbus: Ohio State University Press, 1978.

Brooks, Alfred Mansfield. "Gloucester and the Surinam Trade." *Essex Institute Historical Collections* 89 (1953): 288–291.

Burnham, Philip E. "Hawthorne's *Fanshawe* and Bowdoin College." *Essex Institute Historical Collections* 80 (1944): 131–138.

Byers, John R., Jr. "Selections from the Official Consular Dispatches of Nathaniel Hawthorne." *Essex Institute Historical Collections* 113 (1977): 239–344.

Cameron, Kenneth Walter, ed. *Hawthorne among His Contemporaries*. Hartford: Transcendental Books, 1968.

Cantwell, Robert. *Nathaniel Hawthorne: The American Years*. New York: Rinehart, 1948.

Chandler, Elizabeth L., ed. "Hawthorne's *Spectator*." *New England Quarterly* 4 (1931): 289–330.

———. "A Study of the Sources of the Tales and Romances by Nathaniel Hawthorne before 1853." *Smith College Studies in Modern Languages* 7 (July 1926).

Channing, William Ellery. *The Collected Poems*. Ed. Walter Harding. Gainesville: Scholars' Facsimiles and Reprints, 1967.

———. *Poems of Sixty-Five Years*. Ed. F. B. Sanborn. [1902(?)]. Reprint. New York: Arno Press, 1972.

Charvat, William. *Literary Publishing in America, 1790–1850*. Philadelphia: University of Pennsylvania Press, 1959.

Chevigny, Bell Gale. *The Woman and the Myth: Margaret Fuller's Life and Writings*. Old Westbury, N.Y.: Feminist Press, [1976].

Childs, George W. *Recollections*. Philadelphia: Lippincott, 1890.

Clark, C. E. Frazer, Jr. "Nathaniel Hawthorne . . . The College Experience." *Among Friends (The Friends of the Detroit Public Library)*, 68 (Winter 1975): 10–23.

———. *Nathaniel Hawthorne: A Descriptive Bibliography*. Pittsburgh: University of Pittsburgh Press, 1978.

Clarke, Helen A. *Hawthorne's Country*. New York: Baker and Taylor, 1910.

Clarke, Sarah. "Sarah Clarke's Reminiscences of the Peabodys and Hawthorne." Ed. Joel Myerson. *Nathaniel Hawthorne Journal 1973*: 130–133.

Cleaveland, Nehemiah, and Alpheus Spring Packard. *History of Bowdoin College*. Boston: Osgood, 1882.

Codman, John Thomas. *Brook Farm: Historic and Personal Memoirs*. Boston: Arena, 1894.

Cohen, B. Bernard. "Edward Everett and Hawthorne's Removal from the Salem Custom House." *American Literature* 27 (1955): 245–249.

———, ed. *The Recognition of Nathaniel Hawthorne*. Ann Arbor: University of Michigan Press, [1969].

Colacurcio, Michael J. *The Province of Piety: Moral History in Hawthorne's Early Tales.* Cambridge: Harvard University Press, 1984.

Conway, Moncure Daniel. *Autobiography, Memories and Experiences.* 2 vols. Boston: Houghton Mifflin, 1904.

——. *Life of Nathaniel Hawthorne.* London: Walter Scott, [1890].

Coolidge, George, and Darrel and Moore. *The Boston Almanac for the Year 1851.* Boston: Mussey, [1851].

Cott, Nancy F., and Elizabeth H. Pleck, eds. *A Heritage of Her Own: Toward a New Social History of American Women.* New York: Simon and Schuster, 1979.

Crews, Frederick C. *The Sins of the Fathers: Hawthorne's Psychological Themes.* New York: Oxford University Press, 1966.

Crowe, Charles. *George Ripley: Transcendentalist and Utopian Socialist.* Athens: University of Georgia Press, 1967.

Crowley, J. Donald, ed. *Hawthorne: The Critical Heritage.* New York: Barnes and Noble, 1970.

Cuddy, Lois A. "Mother-Daughter Identification in *The Scarlet Letter.*" *Mosaic* 19 (1986): 101–115.

Dall, Caroline W. *Margaret and Her Friends, or Ten Conversations with Margaret Fuller.* Boston: Robert Brothers, 1895.

Dall, Constance. "Constance Dall's Reminiscences of Margaret Fuller." Ed. Joel Myerson. *Harvard Library Bulletin* 22 (1974): 414–428.

Davidson, Edward H. *Hawthorne's Last Phase.* New Haven: Yale University Press, 1949.

Dedmond, Francis B. "The Letters of Caroline Sturgis to Margaret Fuller." *Studies in the American Renaissance 1988* (University of Virginia): 201–251.

Deiss, Joseph Jay. *The Roman Years of Margaret Fuller: A Biography.* New York: Crowell, 1969.

De Leon, Edwin. *Thirty Years of My Life on Three Continents.* 2 vols. London: Ward and Downex, 1890.

Dicey, Edward. "Nathaniel Hawthorne." *Macmillan's Magazine* 10 (July 1864): 241–246.

Dodge, Mary Abigail. *Gail Hamilton's Life in Letters.* 2 vols. Ed. H. Augusta Dodge. Boston: Lee and Shepard, 1901.

Donald, David. *Charles Sumner and the Coming of the Civil War.* New York: Knopf, 1968.

Donohue, Agnes McNeill. "'From Whose Bourn No Traveller Returns': A Reading of 'Roger Malvin's Burial.'" *Nineteenth-Century Fiction* 18 (1963): 1–19.

Dorfer, Margaret Neussen. "Elizabeth Palmer Peabody to William Wordsworth: Eight Letters, 1825–1845." *Studies in the American Renaissance 1984* (Boston): 197–204.

Dryden, Edgar A. *Nathaniel Hawthorne: The Poetics of Enchantment.* Ithaca: Cornell University Press, 1977.

Dunn, Waldo H. *The Life of Donald G. Mitchell: (Ik Marvel).* New York: Scribner's, 1922.

Duyckinck, Evert A. "Diary: May 29–November 8, 1847." Ed. Donald and Kathleen Malone Yanella. *Studies in the American Renaissance 1978* (Boston): 207–258.

———. "Nathaniel Hawthorne." *Democratic Review* 16 (1845): 376–384.

Dwight, Marianne. *Letters from Brook Farm, 1844–1847*. Ed. Amy L. Reed. Poughkeepsie: Vassar University Press, 1928.

Ellis, Stewart March. *The Solitary Horseman or The Life and Adventures of G. P. R. James*. Kensington: Cayme Press, 1927.

Emerson, Edward Waldo. *The Early Years of the Saturday Club*. Boston: Houghton Mifflin, 1918.

Emerson, Ralph Waldo. *The Complete Works*. 12 vols. Wayside Edition. Boston: Houghton Mifflin, 1904.

———. *The Journals and Miscellaneous Notebooks*. 16 vols. Ed. William H. Gilman, Alfred R. Ferguson, et al. Cambridge: Harvard University Press, 1960–1982.

———. *The Letters*. 6 vols. Ed. Ralph L. Rusk. New York: Columbia University Press, 1939.

Emmerton, James A. "Henry Silsbee and Some of His Descendants." *Essex Institute Historical Collections* 17 (1880): 257–310.

Erlich, Gloria C. "Doctor Grimshawe and Other Secrets." *Essex Institute Historical Collections* 118 (1982): 49–58.

———. *Family Themes and Hawthorne's Fiction: The Tenacious Web*. New Brunswick: Rutgers University Press, 1984.

Faderman, Lillian. *Surpassing the Love of Men*. New York: Morrow, 1981.

Fields, Annie. *Authors and Friends*. Boston: Houghton Mifflin, 1897.

Fields, James T. *Yesterdays with Authors*. 1900. Reprint. New York: AMS Press, 1970.

Fossum, Robert H. *Hawthorne's Inviolable Circle: The Problem of Time*. Deland, Fla.: Everett/Edwards, [1972].

Foster, Edward Halsey. *Catharine Maria Sedgwick*. New York: Twayne, 1974.

Frothingham, Octavius Brooks. *George Ripley*. 1883. Reprint. New York: AMS Press, 1970.

Fuller, Margaret. *The Letters*. 5 vols. Ed. Robert N. Hudspeth. Ithaca: Cornell University Press, 1983–1988.

———. "Margaret Fuller's 1842 Journal: At Concord with the Emersons." Ed. Joel Myerson. *Harvard Library Bulletin* 21 (1973): 320–340.

———. *Memoirs of Margaret Fuller Ossoli*. 2 vols. Ed. Ralph Waldo Emerson and J. F. Clarke. Boston: Phillips, Sampson, 1852.

Fussell, Edwin. *Frontier: American Literature and the American West*. Princeton: Princeton University Press, 1965.

Gay, Peter. *The Bourgeois Experience: Victoria to Freud*. Vol. 1, *Education of the Senses*. New York: Oxford University Press, 1984.

Gittleman, Edwin. *Jones Very: The Effective Years, 1833–1840*. New York: Columbia University Press, 1967.

Golemba, Henry L. *George Ripley*. Boston: Twayne, 1977.

Gollin, Rita K. "The Hawthornes' 'Golden Dora.'" *Studies in the American Renaissance 1981* (Boston): 393–401.

———. *Nathaniel Hawthorne and the Truth of Dreams*. Baton Rouge: Louisiana State University Press, 1979.

———. "'Pegasus in the Pound': The Editor, the Author, Their Wives, and *The Atlantic Monthly*." *Essex Institute Historical Collections* 125 (1989): 104–122.

———. *Portraits of Nathaniel Hawthorne*. DeKalb: Northern Illinois University Press, 1983.

Goodrich, S. G. *Recollections of A Lifetime, or Men and Things I Have Seen*. 2 vols. New York: Miller, Orton and Mulligan, 1857.

Goodspeed, Charles E. "Nathaniel Hawthorne and the Museum of the East India Marine Society." *The American Neptune* 5 (1945): 266–285.

Haraszti, Zoltan. *The Idyll of Brook Farm As Revealed by Unpublished Letters*. Boston: Boston Public Library, 1937.

Harding, Walter. *The Days of Henry Thoreau*. New York: Knopf, 1965.

Harris, Sheldon Howard. "The Public Career of John Louis O'Sullivan." Ph.D. diss., Columbia University, 1958.

Harwell, Richard. *Hawthorne and Longfellow: A Guide to an Exhibit*. Brunswick: Bowdoin, 1966.

Hawthorne, Julian. *Hawthorne and His Circle*. New York: Harder, 1903.

———. *The Memoirs*. Ed. Edith Garriges Hawthorne. New York: Macmillan, 1938.

———. *Nathaniel Hawthorne and His Wife*. 2 vols. Boston: Osgood, 1884.

———. "Nathaniel Hawthorne's Blue Cloak: A Son's Reminiscences." *Bookman* 75 (1932): 501–506.

Hawthorne, Manning. "Aunt Ebe: Some Letters of Elizabeth M. Hawthorne." *New England Quarterly* 20 (1947-1): 209–231.

———. "A Glimpse of Hawthorne's Boyhood." *Essex Institute Historical Collections* 83 (1947-2): 178–184.

———. "Hawthorne and 'The Man of God.'" *Colophon*, n.s., 2 (Winter 1937): 262–282.

———. "Hawthorne's Early Years." *Essex Institute Historical Collections* 74 (1938): 1–21.

———. "Maria Louisa Hawthorne." *Essex Institute Historical Collections* 75 (1939-1): 103–134.

———. "Nathaniel and Elizabeth Hawthorne, Editors." *Colophon*, n.s., 3 (1939-2): 251–262.

———. "Nathaniel Hawthorne at Bowdoin." *New England Quarterly* 13 (1940-2): 246–279.

———. "Nathaniel Hawthorne Prepares for College." *New England Quarterly* 11 (1938): 66–88.

————. "Parental and Family Influences on Hawthorne." *Essex Institute Historical Collections* 76 (1940-1): 1–13.

Hawthorne, Nathaniel. *The Centenary Edition of the Works of Nathaniel Hawthorne.* 20 vols. Ed. William Charvat, Roy Harvey Pearce, Claude M. Simpson, et al. Columbus: Ohio State University Press, 1962–1988.

————. *The English Notebooks.* Ed. Randall Stewart. 1941. Reprint. New York: Russell and Russell, 1962.

————. *The Life of Franklin Pierce.* 1852. Reprint. New York: MSS Information Corp., 1970.

Hawthorne, Sophia. *Notes in England and Italy.* Italy: Putnam and Sons, 1869.

Headley, Joel T. "Berkshire Scenery." *New-York Observer* 28 (September 14, 1850): 145.

Hedges, William L. "Irving, Hawthorne, and the Image of the Wife." *American Transcendental Quarterly* 5 (1970): 22–26.

Higginson, Thomas Wentworth, ed. *The Hawthorne Centenary Celebration . . . July 4–7, 1904.* Boston: Houghton Mifflin, 1905.

Hill, Henry B. *Jottings from Memory, from 1823 to 1901.* N.p., [1910?].

Hillard, George B. "The English Note-books of Nathaniel Hawthorne." *Atlantic Monthly* 26 (1870): 257–272.

Hitchcock, Ethan Allen. *Forty Years in Camp and Field.* Ed. W. A. Croffut. New York: Putnam's, 1909.

Hoeltje, Hubert H. "Captain Nathaniel Hathorne: Father of the Famous Salem Novelist." *Essex Institute Historical Collections* 89 (1953): 329–356.

————. "Hawthorne as Senior at Bowdoin." *Essex Institute Historical Collections* 94 (1958): 205–228.

————. *Inward Sky—The Mind and Heart of Nathaniel Hawthorne.* Durham: Duke University Press, 1962.

Holden, George Henry. "Hawthorne among His Friends." *Harper's Monthly* 63 (1881): 260–262.

Holmes, Oliver Wendell. *The Poetical Works.* Boston: Houghton Mifflin, 1895.

Holsberry, John E. "Hawthorne's 'The Haunted Mind,' The Psychology of Dreams, Coleridge, and Keats." *Texas Studies in Language and Literature* 2 (1979): 307–331.

Hopkins, Vivian C. *Prodigal Puritan: A Life of Delia Bacon.* Cambridge: Harvard University Press, 1959.

Howe, M. A. De Wolfe. *The Life and Letters of George Bancroft.* 2 vols. New York: Scribner's, 1908.

————. *Memories of a Hostess: A Chronicle of Eminent Friendships Drawn Chiefly from the Diaries of Mrs. James T. Fields.* Boston: Atlantic Monthly Press, 1922.

Howells, William Dean. *Literary Friends and Acquaintances.* New York: Harper and Brothers, 1900.

Hudspeth, Robert N. *Ellery Channing.* New York: Twayne, 1973.

Hull, Raymona A. "Bennoch and Hawthorne." *Nathaniel Hawthorne Journal 1974*: 48–74.

———. "Hawthorne's Efforts to Help Thoreau." *Emerson Society Quarterly* 33 (4th Quarter, 1963): 24–28.

———. *Nathaniel Hawthorne: The English Experience, 1853–1864.* Pittsburgh: University of Pittsburgh Press, 1980.

———. "Una Hawthorne: A Biographical Sketch." *Nathaniel Hawthorne Journal 1976*: 87–119.

Idol, John L., Jr. "A Show of Hands in 'The Artist of the Beautiful.'" *Studies in Short Fiction* 22 (1985): 455–460.

James, Henry. *Hawthorne.* 1879. Reprint. Ithaca: Cornell University Press, 1956.

Jones, Bufford. "Some 'Mosses' from *The Literary World*: Critical and Biographical Survey of the Hawthorne-Melville Relationship." In *Ruined Eden of the Present.* Ed. G. R. Thompson and Virgil L. Lokke. West Lafayette: Purdue University Press, 1981.

Jones, Wayne Allen. "The Hawthorne-Goodrich Relationship and a New Estimate of Hawthorne's Income from *The Token.*" *Nathaniel Hawthorne Journal 1975*: 91–140.

———. "Hawthorne's 'Slender Means.'" *Nathaniel Hawthorne Journal 1977*: 1–34.

Kesselring, Marion L. "Hawthorne's Reading, 1828–1850: A Transcription and Identification of Titles Recorded in the Charge-Books of the Salem Athenaeum." *Bulletin of the New York Public Library* 53 (1949): 55–71, 121–138, 173–194.

King, Caroline Howard. *When I Lived in Salem, 1822–1866.* Brattleboro: Stephen Daye Press, 1937.

King, Horatio. "History of the Duel between Jonathan Cilley and William J. Graves." *Collections and Proceedings of the Maine Historical Society*, 2d series, 3 (1892): 127–148, 393–409.

Lamont, John. "Hawthorne's Unfinished Works." *Harvard Medical Alumni Bulletin* (1962): 13–20.

Lathrop, George P. *Biographical Sketch of Nathaniel Hawthorne.* Wayside Edition. Boston: Houghton Mifflin, 1888.

Lathrop, Rose Hawthorne. *Memories of Hawthorne.* Boston: Houghton Mifflin, 1897.

Lawrence, D. H. *Studies in Classic American Literature.* New York: Anchor, 1953.

Lee, A. Robert, ed. *Nathaniel Hawthorne: New Critical Essays.* [London]: Vision, 1982.

Lesser, Simon O. *Fiction and the Unconscious.* 1957. Reprint. New York: Vintage, 1962.

Levin, Harry. *The Power of Blackness: Hawthorne, Poe, Melville.* New York: Vintage, 1960.

———. *Refractions: Essays in Comparative Literature*. New York: Oxford University Press, 1966.

Levy, Leo B. "*Fanshawe*: Hawthorne's World of Images." *Studies in the Novel* (North Texas State University) 2 (1970): 440–448.

Leyda, Jay. *The Melville Log: A Documentary Life of Herman Melville, 1819–1891*. 2 vols. New York: Harcourt, Brace, 1951.

Little, David Mason. "Documentary History of the Salem Custom House." *Essex Institute Historical Collections* 67 (1931): 265–280.

Little, George Thomas. *General Catalogue of Bowdoin College . . . 1794–1844*. Brunswick: Bowdoin College, 1894.

———. "Hawthorne's 'Fanshawe,' and Bowdoin's Past." *Bowdoin Quill* 8 (June 1904): 179–186.

Loggins, Vernon. *The Hawthornes: The Story of Seven Generations of an American Family*. New York: Columbia University Press, 1951.

Longfellow, Henry Wadsworth. *The Letters*. 6 vols. Ed. Andrew Hilen. Cambridge: Harvard University Press, 1966–1982.

Longfellow, Samuel. *Life of Henry Wadsworth Longfellow*. 2 vols. Boston: Ticknor, 1886.

Lothrop, Margaret M. *The Wayside: Home of Authors*. New York: American Book Company, 1940.

Lowell, James Russell. *The Letters*. 2 vols. Ed. Charles Eliot Norton. New York: Harper and Brothers, 1894.

———. *The Poetical Works*. Boston: Houghton Mifflin, 1897.

Leuders, Edward G. "The Melville-Hawthorne Relationship in *Pierre* and *The Blithedale Romance*." *Western Humanities Review* 4 (1950): 323–334.

McAleer, John. *Ralph Waldo Emerson: Days of Encounter*. Boston: Little, Brown, 1984.

McDonald, John J., ed. "A Sophia Hawthorne Journal, 1843–1844." *Nathaniel Hawthorne Journal 1974*: 1–30.

McGill, Frederick T., Jr. *Channing of Concord: A Life of William Ellery Channing II*. New Brunswick: Rutgers University Press, 1967.

Mackay, Charles. *Forty Years' Recollections of Life, Literature, and Public Affairs, from 1830 to 1870*. 2 vols. London: Chapman and Hall, 1877.

Mann, Mary Peabody. *Life of Horace Mann*. 1865. Reprint. Washington, D.C.: National Education Association of the United States, 1937.

Manning, William H. *Genealogical and Bibliographical History of the Manning Families of New England*. Salem: Salem Press Company, 1902.

Matlack, James H. "Hawthorne and Elizabeth Bastow Stoddard." *New England Quarterly* 50 (1977): 278–302.

Matthews, Cornelius. "Several Days in Berkshire." *Literary World* 7 (August 24, 31 and September 7, 1850): 145–147, 166, 185–186.

Matthiessen, F. O. *American Renaissance: Art and Expression in the Age of Emerson and Whitman*. New York: Oxford University Press, 1941.

Maynard, Theodore. *A Fire Was Lighted: The Life of Rose Hawthorne Lathrop*. Milwaukee: Bruce, 1948.

Mellow, James R. *Nathaniel Hawthorne in His Times*. Boston: Houghton Mifflin, 1980.

Meltzer, Milton, and Walter Harding. *A Thoreau Profile*. Concord: Thoreau Foundation, 1962.

Melville, Herman. *Clarel*. Ed. Walter E. Bezanson. New York: Hendricks House, 1960.

———. "Hawthorne and His Mosses." *The Literary World* 7 (August 17–24, 1850): 125–127, 145–147.

———. *The Letters*. Ed. Merrell R. Davis and William H. Gilman. New Haven: Yale University Press, 1960.

———. *Moby-Dick*. Ed. Harrison Hayford, Hershel Parker, and G. Thomas Tanselle. Evanston: Northwestern University Press, 1988.

———. *Pierre*. Ed. Harrison Hayford, Hershel Parker, and G. Thomas Tanselle. Evanston: Northwestern University Press, 1971.

———. *Pierre*. Ed. Henry A. Murray. New York: Hendricks House, 1962.

Messerli, Jonathan. *Horace Mann: A Biography*. New York: Knopf, 1972.

Metzdorf, Robert F. "Hawthorne's Suit against Ripley and Dana." *American Literature* 12 (1940): 235–241.

Miller, Edwin Haviland. "A Calendar of the Letters of Sophia Peabody Hawthorne." *Studies in the American Renaissance 1986* (University of Virginia): 199–281.

———. *Melville*. New York: Braziller, 1975.

———. "'Wounded Love': Nathaniel Hawthorne's 'The Gentle Boy.'" *Nathaniel Hawthorne Journal 1978*: 47–54.

Milne, Gordon. *George William Curtis and the Genteel Tradition*. Bloomington: Indiana University Press, 1956.

Mitchell, Donald Grant. *American Land and Letters*. 2 vols. New York: Scribner's, 1901–1904.

Moore, Margaret B. "Hawthorne's Uncle John Dike." *Studies in the American Renaissance 1984* (University of Virginia): 325–330.

Morris, Lloyd. *The Rebellious Puritan: Portrait of Mr. Hawthorne*. New York: Harcourt, Brace, 1927.

Mouffe, Barbara S., ed. *Hawthorne's Lost Notebook, 1835–1841*. University Park: Pennsylvania State University Press, 1978.

Neussendorfer, Margaret. "Elizabeth Palmer Peabody to William Wordsworth: Eight Letters, 1825–1845." *Studies in the American Renaissance 1984* (University of Virginia): 197–204.

Nevins, Winifield S. "Nathaniel Hawthorne's Removal from the Salem Custom House." *Essex Institute Historical Collections* 53 (1917): 97–132.

Newcomb, Charles King. *The Journals*. Ed. Judith Kennedy Johnson. Providence: Brown University Press, 1946.

Nichols, Roy Franklin. *Franklin Pierce*. Philadelphia: University of Pennsylvania Press, 1958.

Nissenbaum, Stephen. "The Firing of Nathaniel Hawthorne." *Essex Institute Historical Collections* 114 (1978): 57–86.

Normand, Jean. *Nathaniel Hawthorne: An Approach to an Analysis of Artistic Creation*. Cleveland: Case Western Reserve, 1970.

Northend, Mary Harrod. *Memories of Old Salem: Drawn from the Letters of a Great-Grandmother*. New York: Moffatt, Yard, 1917.

Oberndorf, C. P. "The Psychoanalytic Insight of Nathaniel Hawthorne." *Psychoanalytic Review* 29 (1942): 373–385.

Oldham, Ellen M. "Letters of Mrs. Hawthorne to Mrs. Fields." *Boston Public Library Quarterly* 9 (July 1957): 143–154.

Oliver, Henry K. *Historical Sketch of the Salem Lyceum*. Salem: Salem Gazette, 1879.

Osgood, Charles S., and H. M. Batchelder. *Historical Sketch of Salem, 1626–1879*. Salem: Essex Institute, 1879.

Palfrey, Francis W. "Memoir of the Hon. George Stillman Hillard, LL.D." *Proceedings of Massachusetts Historical Society* 19 (1881–1882): 339–348.

Peabody, Elizabeth. *Aesthetic Papers*. Gainesville, Fla.: Scholars' Facsimiles and Reprints, 1957.

———. *Letters*. Ed. Bruce A. Ronda. Middletown, Conn.: Wesleyan University Press, 1984.

Peabody, Selim Hubart. *Peabody Genealogy*. Ed. Charles Henry Pope. Boston: Charles H. Pope, 1909.

Pearce, Roy Harvey. *Historicism Once More*. Princeton: Princeton University Press, 1969.

Pearson, Norman Holmes. "Elizabeth Peabody on Hawthorne." *Essex Institute Historical Collections* 94 (1958-2): 256–276.

———. "A 'Good Thing' for Hawthorne." *Essex Institute Historical Collections* 100 (1964): 300–305.

———. "Hawthorne's Duel." *Essex Institute Historical Collections* 94 (1958-1): 229–242.

———. *Hawthorne's Two Engagements*. Northampton: Smith College, 1963.

Perley, Sidney. *The History of Salem, Massachusetts*. 3 vols. Salem: Sidney Perley, 1928.

Phillips, James Duncan. *Salem and the Indies: The Story of the Great Commercial Era of the City*. Boston: Houghton Mifflin, 1947.

———. *Salem in the Eighteenth Century*. Salem: Essex Institute, 1969.

———. *Salem in the Seventeenth Century*. Boston: Houghton Mifflin, 1933.

Pickard, Samuel T. *Hawthorne's First Diary*. Boston: Houghton Mifflin, 1897.

———. *Life and Letters of John Greenleaf Whittier*. 2 vols. London: Sampson Low, Marston, 1895.

Poe, Edgar Allan. "Our Amateur Poets. . . . William Ellery Channing." *Graham's Magazine* 23 (August 1843): 113–117.

Robbins, Chandler. *Remarks on the Disorders of Literary Men, or, An Inquiry into the Means of Preventing the Evils Usually Incident to Sedentary and Studious Habits.* Boston: n.p., 1825.

Roberts, Josephine E. "Horace Mann and the Peabody Sisters." *New England Quarterly* 18 (1945): 164–180.

Rusk, Ralph L. *The Life of Ralph Waldo Emerson.* New York: Scribner's, 1949.

Ryan, Pat M., Jr. "Young Hawthorne at the Salem Theater." *Essex Institute Historical Collections* 94 (1958): 243–255.

Sanborn, F. B. *Bronson Alcott at Alcott House.* Cedar Rapids: Torch Press, 1908-2.

———. "A Concord Note-Book: Ellery Channing and His Table-Talk." *The Critic* 47 (July 1905): 76–81.

———. *Hawthorne and His Friends: Reminiscences and Tribute.* Cedar Rapids: Torch Press, 1908-1.

———. *Recollections of Seventy Years.* 2 vols. Boston: R. G. Badger, 1909.

Saxton, Martha. *Louisa May: A Modern Biography of Louisa May Alcott.* Boston: Houghton Mifflin, 1977.

Scudder, Horace Elisha. *James Russell Lowell: A Biography.* 2 vols. Boston: Houghton Mifflin, 1901.

Sears, John Van Der Zee. *My Friends at Brook Farm.* New York: Desmond FitzGerald, 1912.

Sedgwick, Ora Gannett. "A Girl of Sixteen at Brook Farm." *Essex Institute Historical Collections* 85 (1949): 394–404.

Seelye, John D. "'Ungraspable Phantom': Reflections of Hawthorne in *Pierre* and *The Confidence-Man.*" *Studies in the Novel* 1 (1969): 436–443.

Shattuck, Lemuel. *A History of the Town of Concord.* Boston: Russell, Osborne, 1835.

Shaw, Peter. "Fathers, Sons, and the Ambiguities of Revolution in 'My Kinsman, Major Molineux.'" *New England Quarterly* 99 (1976): 559–576.

Shepard, Odell. *Pedlar's Progress: The Life of Bronson Alcott.* Boston: Little, Brown, 1937.

Silsbee, Nathaniel. "Biographical Notes." *Essex Institute Historical Collections* 35 (1899): 1–79.

Silverman, Kenneth. *The Life and Times of Cotton Mather.* New York: Harper and Row, 1984.

Slattery, Charles Lewis. "Brunswick and Bowdoin College." *New England Magazine* 5 (1891): 449–469.

[Smith, J. E.] *Taghonic; The Romance and Beauty of the Hills.* Boston: Lee and Shepard, 1879.

S[parks], M[ary] C[rowninshield]. *Hymns, Home, Harvard.* Boston: A. Williams, 1883.

Spofford, Jeremiah. *A Historical and Statistical Gazetteer of Massachusetts.* Haverhill: E. G. Frothingham, 1860.

Stein, William Bysshe. "'The Artist of the Beautiful': Narcissus and Thimble." *American Imago* 18 (1961): 35–44.

Stewart, Randall. *Nathaniel Hawthorne: A Biography.* 1948. Reprint. Hamden, Conn.: Archon, 1970.

———. "Recollections of Hawthorne by His Sister Elizabeth." *American Literature* 16 (1945): 316–331.

Stoddard, Richard Henry. "Nathaniel Hawthorne." *National Magazine* 2 (1853): 17–24.

———. *Recollections Personal and Literary.* 1903. Reprint. New York: A. S. Barnes, 1971.

Strouse, Jean. *Alice James.* Boston: Houghton Mifflin, 1980.

Strout, Cushing. "Hawthorne's International Novel." *Nineteenth-Century Fiction* 24 (1969): 169–181.

Swayne, Josephine Lathrop, ed. *The Story of Concord: Told by Concord Writers.* Boston: E. F. Worcester, 1906.

Swift, Lindsay. *Brook Farm: Its Members, Scholars, and Visitors.* 1900. Reprint. New York: Corinth, 1961.

Tharp, Louise Hall. *The Peabody Sisters of Salem.* Boston: Little, Brown, 1950.

———. *Three Saints and a Sinner: Julia Ward Howe, Louisa, Annie and Sam Ward.* Boston: Little, Brown, 1956.

———. *Until Victory: Horace Mann and Mary Peabody.* Boston: Little, Brown, 1953.

Thompson, Henry Yates. *An Englishman in the American Civil War: The Diaries of Henry Yates Thompson.* Ed. Christopher Chancellor. New York: New York University Press, 1971.

Thompson, Lawrance. *Young Longfellow (1807–1843).* New York: Octagon, 1969.

Thoreau, Henry David. *The Correspondence.* Ed. Walter Harding and Carl Bode. New York: New York University Press, 1958.

———. *The Journal.* 2 vols. Ed. Bradford Torrey and Francis H. Allen. 1906. Reprint. New York: Dover, 1962.

Ticknor, Caroline, ed. *Classic Concord.* Boston: Houghton Mifflin, 1926.

———. *Hawthorne and His Publisher.* 1913. Reprint. Port Washington, N.Y.: Kennikat, 1969.

Tileston, Mary Wilder, ed. *Caleb and Mary Wilder Foote: Reminiscences and Letters.* Boston: Houghton Mifflin, 1918.

Tolles, Bryant F., Jr. *Architecture in Salem: An Illustrated Guide.* Salem: Essex Institute, 1983.

Tryon, Warren S. *Parnassus Corner: A Life of James T. Fields.* Boston: Houghton Mifflin, 1963.

———, and William Charvat, eds. *The Cost Books of Ticknor and Fields and Their Predecessors, 1832–1858.* New York: Bibliographical Society of America, 1949.

Tucker, T. W. *Waifs from the Way-Bills of an Old Expressman.* Boston: Lee and Shepard, 1872.

Turner, Arlin. *Hawthorne as Editor: Selections from His Writings in the American Magazine of Useful and Entertaining Knowledge.* 1941. Reprint. Port Washington, N.Y.: Kennikat, 1972.

———. "Hawthorne's Final Illness and Death. Additional Reports." *Emerson Society Quarterly* 19 (2d Quarter, 1973): 124–127.

———. *Nathaniel Hawthorne: A Biography.* New York: Oxford University Press, 1980.

Vanderbilt, Kermit. "The Unity of Hawthorne's 'Ethan Brand.'" *College English* 24 (1963): 453–456.

Van Doren, Mark. *Nathaniel Hawthorne: A Critical Biography.* 1949. Reprint. New York: Viking, 1966.

Visitor's Guide to Salem. Salem: Eben Putnam, 1892.

Wade, Mason. *Margaret Fuller: Whetstone of Genius.* New York: Viking, 1940.

Wagenknecht, Edward. *Nathaniel Hawthorne: Man and Writer.* New York: Oxford University Press, 1961.

Waggoner, Hyatt H. *Hawthorne: A Critical Study.* Rev. ed. Cambridge: Harvard University Press, 1963.

———. *The Presence of Hawthorne.* Baton Rouge: Louisiana State University Press, 1979.

Wagner, Frederick. "All Pine and Apple Orchard: Hawthorne and the Alcotts." *Essex Institute Historical Collections* 118 (1982): 31–41.

Warner, Lee H. "With Pierce, and Hawthorne, in Mexico." *Essex Institute Historical Collections* 111 (1975): 213–220.

Warren, Robert Penn. "Hawthorne Revisited: Some Remarks on Hellfiredness." *Sewanee Review* 81 (1973): 75–111.

Watson, Charles N., Jr. "The Estrangement of Hawthorne and Melville." *New England Quarterly* 46 (1973): 380–402.

Webber, C. H., and W. S. Nevins. *Old Naumkeag: A Historical Sketch of the City of Salem.* Salem: A. A. Smith, 1877.

Whipple, Edwin Percy. *Character and Characteristic Men.* Boston: Houghton Mifflin, 1866.

Wilson, Carroll A. *Thirteen Author Collections of the Nineteenth Century.* 2 vols. Ed. Jean C. S. Wilson and David A. Randell. New York: Scribner's, 1950.

Wilson, Edmund, ed. *The Shock of Recognition.* 2 vols. 1943. Reprint. New York: Grosset and Dunlap, 1955.

Wolfe, Thomas F. *Literary Shrines: The Haunts of Some Famous American Authors.* Philadelphia: Lippincott, [1895].

Woodson, Thomas, James A. Rubino, and Jamie Barlowe Kayes. "With Hawthorne in Wartime Concord: Sophia Hawthorne's 1862 Diary." *Studies in the American Renaissance 1988* (University of Virginia): 281–359.

Worthington, Marjorie. *Miss Alcott of Concord.* Garden City: Doubleday, 1958.

Yanella, Philip R. "Socio-Economic Disarray and Literary Response: Concord and Walden." *Mosaic* 14 (Winter 1981): 1–24.

Young, Philip. *Hawthorne's Secret: An Un-told Tale.* Boston: David A. Godine, 1984.

Zangwill, O. L. "A Case of Paramesia in Nathaniel Hawthorne." *Character and Personality* 13 (1945): 246–260.

Index